Lecture Notes in Computer Scien

Commenced Publication in 1973
Founding and Former Series Editors:
Gerhard Goos, Juris Hartmanis, and Jan van Leeuwen

Advanced Research in Computing and Software Science

Subline of Lectures Notes in Computer Science

Stefania Gnesi   Arend Rensink (Eds.)

Fundamental Approaches to Software Engineering

17th International Conference, FASE 2014
Held as Part of the European Joint Conferences
on Theory and Practice of Software, ETAPS 2014
Grenoble, France, April 5-13, 2014
Proceedings

 Springer

Volume Editors

Stefania Gnesi
Istituto di Scienza e Tecnologie dell'Informazione "A. Faedo"
Consiglio Nazionale delle Ricerche, Pisa, Italy
E-mail: stefania.gnesi@isti.cnr.it

Arend Rensink
University of Twente, Enschede, The Netherlands
E-mail: arend.rensink@utwente.nl

ISSN 0302-9743   e-ISSN 1611-3349
ISBN 978-3-642-54803-1   e-ISBN 978-3-642-54804-8
DOI 10.1007/978-3-642-54804-8
Springer Heidelberg New York Dordrecht London

Library of Congress Control Number: 2014933951

LNCS Sublibrary: SL 1 – Theoretical Computer Science and General Issues

Typesetting: Camera-ready by author, data conversion by Scientific Publishing Services, Chennai, India

Printed on acid-free paper

Springer is part of Springer Science+Business Media (www.springer.com)

Foreword

ETAPS 2014 was the 17th instance of the European Joint Conferences on Theory and Practice of Software. ETAPS is an annual federated conference that was established in 1998, and this year consisted of six constituting conferences (CC, ESOP, FASE, FoSSaCS, TACAS, and POST) including eight invited speakers and two tutorial speakers. Before and after the main conference, numerous satellite workshops took place and attracted many researchers from all over the globe.

ETAPS is a confederation of several conferences, each with its own Program Committee (PC) and its own Steering Committee (if any). The conferences cover various aspects of software systems, ranging from theoretical foundations to programming language developments, compiler advancements, analysis tools, formal approaches to software engineering, and security. Organizing these conferences in a coherent, highly synchronized conference program, enables the participation in an exciting event, having the possibility to meet many researchers working in different directions in the field, and to easily attend the talks of different conferences.

The six main conferences together received 606 submissions this year, 155 of which were accepted (including 12 tool demonstration papers), yielding an overall acceptance rate of 25.6%. I thank all authors for their interest in ETAPS, all reviewers for the peer reviewing process, the PC members for their involvement, and in particular the PC co-chairs for running this entire intensive process. Last but not least, my congratulations to all authors of the accepted papers!

ETAPS 2014 was greatly enriched by the invited talks of Geoffrey Smith (Florida International University, USA) and John Launchbury (Galois, USA), both unifying speakers, and the conference-specific invited speakers (CC) Benoît Dupont de Dinechin (Kalray, France), (ESOP) Maurice Herlihy (Brown University, USA), (FASE) Christel Baier (Technical University of Dresden, Germany), (FoSSaCS) Petr Jančar (Technical University of Ostrava, Czech Republic), (POST) David Mazières (Stanford University, USA), and finally (TACAS) Orna Kupferman (Hebrew University Jerusalem, Israel). Invited tutorials were provided by Bernd Finkbeiner (Saarland University, Germany) and Andy Gordon (Microsoft Research, Cambridge, UK). My sincere thanks to all these speakers for their great contributions.

For the first time in its history, ETAPS returned to a city where it had been organized before: Grenoble, France. ETAPS 2014 was organized by the Université Joseph Fourier in cooperation with the following associations and societies: ETAPS e.V., EATCS (European Association for Theoretical Computer Science), EAPLS (European Association for Programming Languages and Systems), and EASST (European Association of Software Science and Technology). It had

support from the following sponsors: CNRS, Inria, Grenoble INP, PERSYVAL-Lab and Université Joseph Fourier, and Springer-Verlag.

The organization team comprised:

General Chair: Saddek Bensalem
Conferences Chair: Alain Girault and Yassine Lakhnech
Workshops Chair: Axel Legay
Publicity Chair: Yliès Falcone
Treasurer: Nicolas Halbwachs
Webmaster: Marius Bozga

The overall planning for ETAPS is the responsibility of the Steering Committee (SC). The ETAPS SC consists of an executive board (EB) and representatives of the individual ETAPS conferences, as well as representatives of EATCS, EAPLS, and EASST. The Executive Board comprises Gilles Barthe (satellite events, Madrid), Holger Hermanns (Saarbrücken), Joost-Pieter Katoen (chair, Aachen and Twente), Gerald Lüttgen (treasurer, Bamberg), and Tarmo Uustalu (publicity, Tallinn). Other current SC members are: Martín Abadi (Santa Cruz and Mountain View), Erika Ábráham (Aachen), Roberto Amadio (Paris), Christel Baier (Dresden), Saddek Bensalem (Grenoble), Giuseppe Castagna (Paris), Albert Cohen (Paris), Alexander Egyed (Linz), Riccardo Focardi (Venice), Björn Franke (Edinburgh), Stefania Gnesi (Pisa), Klaus Havelund (Pasadena), Reiko Heckel (Leicester), Paul Klint (Amsterdam), Jens Knoop (Vienna), Steve Kremer (Nancy), Pasquale Malacaria (London), Tiziana Margaria (Potsdam), Fabio Martinelli (Pisa), Andrew Myers (Boston), Anca Muscholl (Bordeaux), Catuscia Palamidessi (Palaiseau), Andrew Pitts (Cambridge), Arend Rensink (Twente), Don Sanella (Edinburgh), Vladimiro Sassone (Southampton), Ina Schäfer (Braunschweig), Zhong Shao (New Haven), Gabriele Taentzer (Marburg), Cesare Tinelli (Iowa), Jan Vitek (West Lafayette), and Lenore Zuck (Chicago).

  I sincerely thank all ETAPS SC members for all their hard work in making the 17th ETAPS a success. Moreover, thanks to all speakers, attendants, organizers of the satellite workshops, and Springer for their support. Finally, many thanks to Saddek Bensalem and his local organization team for all their efforts enabling ETAPS to return to the French Alps in Grenoble!

January 2014   Joost-Pieter Katoen

Foreword

ETAPS 2014 was the 17th instance of the European Joint Conferences on Theory and Practice of Software. ETAPS is an annual federated conference that was established in 1998, and this year consisted of six constituting conferences (CC, ESOP, FASE, FoSSaCS, TACAS, and POST) including eight invited speakers and two tutorial speakers. Before and after the main conference, numerous satellite workshops took place and attracted many researchers from all over the globe.

ETAPS is a confederation of several conferences, each with its own Program Committee (PC) and its own Steering Committee (if any). The conferences cover various aspects of software systems, ranging from theoretical foundations to programming language developments, compiler advancements, analysis tools, formal approaches to software engineering, and security. Organizing these conferences in a coherent, highly synchronized conference program, enables the participation in an exciting event, having the possibility to meet many researchers working in different directions in the field, and to easily attend the talks of different conferences.

The six main conferences together received 606 submissions this year, 155 of which were accepted (including 12 tool demonstration papers), yielding an overall acceptance rate of 25.6%. I thank all authors for their interest in ETAPS, all reviewers for the peer reviewing process, the PC members for their involvement, and in particular the PC co-chairs for running this entire intensive process. Last but not least, my congratulations to all authors of the accepted papers!

ETAPS 2014 was greatly enriched by the invited talks of Geoffrey Smith (Florida International University, USA) and John Launchbury (Galois, USA), both unifying speakers, and the conference-specific invited speakers (CC) Benoît Dupont de Dinechin (Kalray, France), (ESOP) Maurice Herlihy (Brown University, USA), (FASE) Christel Baier (Technical University of Dresden, Germany), (FoSSaCS) Petr Jančar (Technical University of Ostrava, Czech Republic), (POST) David Mazières (Stanford University, USA), and finally (TACAS) Orna Kupferman (Hebrew University Jerusalem, Israel). Invited tutorials were provided by Bernd Finkbeiner (Saarland University, Germany) and Andy Gordon (Microsoft Research, Cambridge, UK). My sincere thanks to all these speakers for their great contributions.

For the first time in its history, ETAPS returned to a city where it had been organized before: Grenoble, France. ETAPS 2014 was organized by the Université Joseph Fourier in cooperation with the following associations and societies: ETAPS e.V., EATCS (European Association for Theoretical Computer Science), EAPLS (European Association for Programming Languages and Systems), and EASST (European Association of Software Science and Technology). It had

support from the following sponsors: CNRS, Inria, Grenoble INP, PERSYVAL-Lab and Université Joseph Fourier, and Springer-Verlag.

The organization team comprised:

General Chair: Saddek Bensalem
Conferences Chair: Alain Girault and Yassine Lakhnech
Workshops Chair: Axel Legay
Publicity Chair: Yliès Falcone
Treasurer: Nicolas Halbwachs
Webmaster: Marius Bozga

The overall planning for ETAPS is the responsibility of the Steering Committee (SC). The ETAPS SC consists of an executive board (EB) and representatives of the individual ETAPS conferences, as well as representatives of EATCS, EAPLS, and EASST. The Executive Board comprises Gilles Barthe (satellite events, Madrid), Holger Hermanns (Saarbrücken), Joost-Pieter Katoen (chair, Aachen and Twente), Gerald Lüttgen (treasurer, Bamberg), and Tarmo Uustalu (publicity, Tallinn). Other current SC members are: Martín Abadi (Santa Cruz and Mountain View), Erika Ábrahám (Aachen), Roberto Amadio (Paris), Christel Baier (Dresden), Saddek Bensalem (Grenoble), Giuseppe Castagna (Paris), Albert Cohen (Paris), Alexander Egyed (Linz), Riccardo Focardi (Venice), Björn Franke (Edinburgh), Stefania Gnesi (Pisa), Klaus Havelund (Pasadena), Reiko Heckel (Leicester), Paul Klint (Amsterdam), Jens Knoop (Vienna), Steve Kremer (Nancy), Pasquale Malacaria (London), Tiziana Margaria (Potsdam), Fabio Martinelli (Pisa), Andrew Myers (Boston), Anca Muscholl (Bordeaux), Catuscia Palamidessi (Palaiseau), Andrew Pitts (Cambridge), Arend Rensink (Twente), Don Sanella (Edinburgh), Vladimiro Sassone (Southampton), Ina Schäfer (Braunschweig), Zhong Shao (New Haven), Gabriele Taentzer (Marburg), Cesare Tinelli (Iowa), Jan Vitek (West Lafayette), and Lenore Zuck (Chicago).

I sincerely thank all ETAPS SC members for all their hard work in making the 17th ETAPS a success. Moreover, thanks to all speakers, attendants, organizers of the satellite workshops, and Springer for their support. Finally, many thanks to Saddek Bensalem and his local organization team for all their efforts enabling ETAPS to return to the French Alps in Grenoble!

January 2014   Joost-Pieter Katoen

Foreword

ETAPS 2014 was the 17th instance of the European Joint Conferences on Theory and Practice of Software. ETAPS is an annual federated conference that was established in 1998, and this year consisted of six constituting conferences (CC, ESOP, FASE, FoSSaCS, TACAS, and POST) including eight invited speakers and two tutorial speakers. Before and after the main conference, numerous satellite workshops took place and attracted many researchers from all over the globe.

ETAPS is a confederation of several conferences, each with its own Program Committee (PC) and its own Steering Committee (if any). The conferences cover various aspects of software systems, ranging from theoretical foundations to programming language developments, compiler advancements, analysis tools, formal approaches to software engineering, and security. Organizing these conferences in a coherent, highly synchronized conference program, enables the participation in an exciting event, having the possibility to meet many researchers working in different directions in the field, and to easily attend the talks of different conferences.

The six main conferences together received 606 submissions this year, 155 of which were accepted (including 12 tool demonstration papers), yielding an overall acceptance rate of 25.6%. I thank all authors for their interest in ETAPS, all reviewers for the peer reviewing process, the PC members for their involvement, and in particular the PC co-chairs for running this entire intensive process. Last but not least, my congratulations to all authors of the accepted papers!

ETAPS 2014 was greatly enriched by the invited talks of Geoffrey Smith (Florida International University, USA) and John Launchbury (Galois, USA), both unifying speakers, and the conference-specific invited speakers (CC) Benoît Dupont de Dinechin (Kalray, France), (ESOP) Maurice Herlihy (Brown University, USA), (FASE) Christel Baier (Technical University of Dresden, Germany), (FoSSaCS) Petr Jančar (Technical University of Ostrava, Czech Republic), (POST) David Mazières (Stanford University, USA), and finally (TACAS) Orna Kupferman (Hebrew University Jerusalem, Israel). Invited tutorials were provided by Bernd Finkbeiner (Saarland University, Germany) and Andy Gordon (Microsoft Research, Cambridge, UK). My sincere thanks to all these speakers for their great contributions.

For the first time in its history, ETAPS returned to a city where it had been organized before: Grenoble, France. ETAPS 2014 was organized by the Université Joseph Fourier in cooperation with the following associations and societies: ETAPS e.V., EATCS (European Association for Theoretical Computer Science), EAPLS (European Association for Programming Languages and Systems), and EASST (European Association of Software Science and Technology). It had

support from the following sponsors: CNRS, Inria, Grenoble INP, PERSYVAL-Lab and Université Joseph Fourier, and Springer-Verlag.

The organization team comprised:

General Chair: Saddek Bensalem
Conferences Chair: Alain Girault and Yassine Lakhnech
Workshops Chair: Axel Legay
Publicity Chair: Yliès Falcone
Treasurer: Nicolas Halbwachs
Webmaster: Marius Bozga

The overall planning for ETAPS is the responsibility of the Steering Committee (SC). The ETAPS SC consists of an executive board (EB) and representatives of the individual ETAPS conferences, as well as representatives of EATCS, EAPLS, and EASST. The Executive Board comprises Gilles Barthe (satellite events, Madrid), Holger Hermanns (Saarbrücken), Joost-Pieter Katoen (chair, Aachen and Twente), Gerald Lüttgen (treasurer, Bamberg), and Tarmo Uustalu (publicity, Tallinn). Other current SC members are: Martín Abadi (Santa Cruz and Mountain View), Erika Ábráham (Aachen), Roberto Amadio (Paris), Christel Baier (Dresden), Saddek Bensalem (Grenoble), Giuseppe Castagna (Paris), Albert Cohen (Paris), Alexander Egyed (Linz), Riccardo Focardi (Venice), Björn Franke (Edinburgh), Stefania Gnesi (Pisa), Klaus Havelund (Pasadena), Reiko Heckel (Leicester), Paul Klint (Amsterdam), Jens Knoop (Vienna), Steve Kremer (Nancy), Pasquale Malacaria (London), Tiziana Margaria (Potsdam), Fabio Martinelli (Pisa), Andrew Myers (Boston), Anca Muscholl (Bordeaux), Catuscia Palamidessi (Palaiseau), Andrew Pitts (Cambridge), Arend Rensink (Twente), Don Sanella (Edinburgh), Vladimiro Sassone (Southampton), Ina Schäfer (Braunschweig), Zhong Shao (New Haven), Gabriele Taentzer (Marburg), Cesare Tinelli (Iowa), Jan Vitek (West Lafayette), and Lenore Zuck (Chicago).

I sincerely thank all ETAPS SC members for all their hard work in making the 17th ETAPS a success. Moreover, thanks to all speakers, attendants, organizers of the satellite workshops, and Springer for their support. Finally, many thanks to Saddek Bensalem and his local organization team for all their efforts enabling ETAPS to return to the French Alps in Grenoble!

January 2014   Joost-Pieter Katoen

Preface

This volume contains the proceedings of FASE 2014, the 17th International Conferences on Fundamental Approaches to Software Engineering, which was held in Grenoble, Italy, in April 2014 as part of the annual European Joint Conferences on Theory and Practice of Software (ETAPS).

As with previous editions of FASE, this year's papers presented foundational contributions to a broad range of topics in software engineering, including software verification and validation, model-driven engineering, debugging, and testing. This year we received 125 submissions from 35 countries, of which 28 were accepted by the Program Committee for presentation at the conference, constituting an acceptance rate of approximately 22%. Each paper received a minimum of three reviews; acceptance decisions were reached through online discussions among the members of the Program Committee.

We were honored to host Christel Baier from the Technische Universität Dresden (Germany) as the FASE keynote speaker at ETAPS 2014. She gave a talk entitled "Probabilistic Model Checking and Non-standard Multi-objective Reasoning" (the paper is included in these proceedings). Christel is an internationally recognized researcher who has made major contributions to the field of quantitative analysis of stochastic systems and probabilistic model checking.

Many persons contributed to the success of FASE 2014. Authors of all submitted papers represent the core of such a conference, and we believe that the accepted papers make significant advances in the foundations of software engineering. However, the program could not have been assembled without the great effort of the Program Committee members and their sub-reviewers in critically assessing and discussing the papers: thanks a lot for your active participation! We also express our full gratitude to the additional reviewers coming to our aid at the last minute to provide additional insights for papers under dispute, for producing high-quality reviews in a very short time. Finally, we thank Gabriele Taentzer, the FASE Steering Committee Chair, for her timely and accurate responses to our queries about the whole process management, and the ETAPS Steering and Organizing Committees for their coordination work.

We sincerely hope you enjoy these proceedings!

January 2014

Stefania Gnesi
Arend Rensink

Organization

Program Committee

Marsha Chechik	University of Toronto, Canada
Myra Cohen	University of Nebraska-Lincoln, USA
Vittorio Cortellessa	Università dell'Aquila, Italy
Krzysztof Czarnecki	University of Waterloo, Canada
Nancy Day	University of Waterloo, Canada
Juan De Lara	Universidad Autonoma de Madrid, Spain
Ewen Denney	SGT/NASA Ames, USA
Juergen Dingel	Queen's University, Canada
José Luiz Fiadeiro	Royal Holloway, University of London, UK
Dimitra Giannakopoulou	NASA Ames, USA
Holger Giese	University of Potsdam, Germany
Stefania Gnesi	CNR-ISTI, Pisa, Italy
Reiko Heckel	University of Leicester, UK
John Hosking	Australian National University, Australia
Jochen Kuester	IBM Research, Switzerland
Ralf Laemmel	Universität Koblenz-Landau, Germany
Yves Le Traon	University of Luxembourg, Luxembourg
Antónia Lopes	University of Lisbon, Portugal
Mieke Massink	CNR-ISTI, Pisa, Italy
Richard Paige	University of York, UK
Rosario Pugliese	Università degli Studi di Firenze, Italy
Arend Rensink	University of Twente, The Netharlands
Bernhard Rumpe	RWTH Aachen University, Germany
Alessandra Russo	Imperial College London, UK
Ina Schaefer	Technische Universität Braunschweig, Germany
Andy Schürr	TU Darmstadt, Germany
Gabriele Taentzer	Philipps-Universität Marburg, Germany
Daniel Varro	Budapest University of Technology and Economics, Hungary
Eelco Visser	Delft University of Technology, The Netherlands
Martin Wirsing	Ludwig-Maximilians-Universität München, Germany

Additional Reviewers

Abreu, Rui
Ahn, Ki Yung
Albarghouthi, Aws
Almeida Castelo Branco, Moises
Alrajeh, Dalal
Anjorin, Anthony
Arcelli, Davide
Arendt, Thorsten
Baldan, Paolo
Bartel, Alexandre
Berardinelli, Luca
Berger, Thorsten
Bergmann, Gábor
Beyhl, Thomas
Binder, Walter
Bodden, Eric
Boreale, Michele
Bracciali, Andrea
Bruni, Roberto
Bürdek, Johannes
Cesari, Luca
Ciancia, Vincenzo
Clarisó, Robert
Cohen, David
Deckwerth, Frederik
Di Ciccio, Claudio
Diskin, Zinovy
Dyck, Johannes
Fantechi, Alessandro
Faria, Joao Pascoal
Fazal-Baqaie, Masud
Fischer, Bernd
Garbajosa, Juan
Gerth, Christian
Greenyer, Joel
Groenewegen, Danny
Guimaraes, Mario
Guo, Jianmei
Gutin, Gregory
Gönczy, László
Haber, Arne
Hebig, Regina
Hegedüs, Ábel

Heindel, Tobias
Hermans, Felienne
Hermerschmidt, Lars
Holthusen, Sönke
Horváth, Ákos
Howar, Falk
Hénard, Christopher
Hölldobler, Katrin
Izsó, Benedek
Khan, Tamim
Kiss, Akos
Klein, Jacques
Kolassa, Carsten
Konat, Gabriël D.P.
Lachmann, Remo
Lambers, Leen
Lamo, Yngve
Latella, Diego
Lavygina, Anna
Leblebici, Erhan
Legay, Axel
Lindt, Achim
Lluch Lafuente, Alberto
Lochau, Malte
Loreti, Michele
Ma, Jiefei
Maoz, Shahar
Margheri, Andrea
Martinez, Jabier
Martins, Francisco
Matos, Carlos
Mazzanti, Franco
Mottu, Jean-Marie
Mouelhi, Tejeddine
Mueller, Klaus
Navarro Pérez, Antonio
Neron, Pierre
Neumann, Stefan
Nunes, Isabel
Nyman, Ulrik
Orejas, Fernando
Paci, Federica
Pai, Ganesh

Papadakis, Mike
Patzina, Lars
Patzina, Sven
Polini, Andrea
Puviani, Mariachiara
Raco, Deni
Ravn, Anders
Roveri, Marco
Rozier, Kristin Yvonne
Rubin, Julia
Rungta, Neha
Ráth, István
Salay, Rick
Saller, Karsten
Santos, André L.
Schulze, Christoph
Schulze, Sandro
Schumann, Johann
Senni, Valerio
Sunye, Gerson
Sánchez Cuadrado, Jesús
T. Vasconcelos, Vasco
Tegawendé, Bissyandé
Ter Beek, Maurice H.

Tiezzi, Francesco
Torres Vieira, Hugo
Traonouez, Louis-Marie
Tribastone, Mirco
Trubiani, Catia
Turliuc, Calin-Rares
Ulidowski, Irek
Varanovich, Andrei
Varro, Gergely
Varró-Gyapay, Szilvia
Vaupel, Steffen
Venet, Arnaud
Vergu, Vlad
Vidács, László
Vogel, Thomas
von Wenckstern, Michael
Vörös, András
Wachsmuth, Guido
Weber, Michael
Wieber, Martin
Winkelmann, Tim
Wortmann, Andreas
Wtzoldt, Sebastian

Table of Contents

Graph Transformation

Debugging and Testing

Probabilistic Model Checking and Non-standard Multi-objective Reasoning*

Christel Baier, Clemens Dubslaff, Sascha Klüppelholz, Marcus Daum,
Joachim Klein, Steffen Märcker, and Sascha Wunderlich

Institute for Theoretical Computer Science
Technische Universität Dresden, Germany

Abstract. Probabilistic model checking is a well-established method
for the automated quantitative system analysis. It has been used in various application areas such as coordination algorithms for distributed
systems, communication and multimedia protocols, biological systems,
resilient systems or security. In this paper, we report on the experiences
we made in inter-disciplinary research projects where we contribute with
formal methods for the analysis of hardware and software systems. Many
performance measures that have been identified as highly relevant by the
respective domain experts refer to multiple objectives and require a good
balance between two or more cost or reward functions, such as energy and
utility. The formalization of these performance measures requires several
concepts like quantiles, conditional probabilities and expectations and
ratios of cost or reward functions that are not supported by state-of-
the-art probabilistic model checkers. We report on our current work in
this direction, including applications in the field of software product line
verification.

1 Introduction

Probabilistic phenomena occur rather naturally for many types of hardware-
and software systems. Typical examples are randomized algorithms for the coordination of distributed systems, such as mutual exclusion, leader election
or consensus protocols where coin-tossing actions are used to break symmetry,
or systems with unreliable or only partially known components where stochastic
distributions can be used to model the system load or the frequency of failures
(e.g. message losses, bit flips in hardware components). Various models and formal methods for the analysis of probabilistic systems have been proposed in the
literature. We focus here on *probabilistic model-checking* (PMC) on Markovian
models, which can be seen as automata annotated with probabilistic distributions and cost or reward functions modeling resource requirements. The Markovian property that the future system behavior only depends on the current state

* The authors are supported by the DFG through the collaborative research centre
HAEC (SFB 912), the cluster of excellence cfAED, Deutsche Telekom Stiftung, the
ESF young researcher group IMData (100098198), the Graduiertenkolleg QuantLA
(1763) the DFG/NWO-project ROCKS, and the EU-FP-7 grant MEALS (295261).

but not on the history makes these models best-suited for algorithmic quantitative analysis. Whereas Markov chains (MCs) are purely probabilistic and can be seen as transition systems where the probabilities are attached to the outgoing transitions of each state, Markov decision processes (MDPs) support both nondeterministic and probabilistic choices. This is useful for modeling randomized distributed protocols where the nondeterminism models the interleaving of independent (possibly randomized) actions executed in parallel. The nondeterminism in MDPs can be resolved by schedulers, allowing to reason about extremal probabilities. The typical task of PMC on a given MDP is to compute the maximal or minimal probabilities of path properties specified by some formula of linear temporal logic (LTL) [37,18], the path-formula fragment of probabilistic computation tree logic (PCTL) or its variant PRCTL with reward-bounded temporal modalities [27,9,19,2]. Algorithms for Markovian models and LTL- or PRCTL-specifications were implemented in various model checkers, such as PRISM [29] and MRMC [31]. They provide several engines with sophisticated techniques to tackle the state-explosion problem and have been continuously extended by new features and were successfully applied in various areas, such as randomized distributed systems, multimedia, security protocols and systems biology.

In current inter-disciplinary research projects, where we apply (among others) PMC for the analysis of low-level resource-management algorithms, we made a series of interesting observations concerning the strengths and limitations of state-of-the-art PMC-techniques. Within these projects, the PMC-based approach is complementary to the measurement- and simulation-based analysis conducted by project partners to provide insights in the energy-utility, reliability and other performance characteristics from a global and long-run perspective. The evaluation results obtained by a probabilistic model checker guide the optimization of resource-management algorithms. They can be useful to predict the performance of management algorithms on future hardware or low-level protocols that have not been implemented yet, making measurements are impossible. We successfully applied PMC, e.g., for the analysis of a spinlock protocol [5], a lock-free synchronization protocol for read-write problems [6], a bonding network device [22] and an energy-aware job scheduling scenario [4].

The application of PMC was, however, not straightforward. Besides the expected state-explosion problem, difficulties arose to find appropriate probabilistic distributions to model cache-effects and other hardware details. These problems have been addressed in [5] by means of a simple spinlock example. To our surprise, our case studies revealed the lack of performance measures that have been identified as most significant by our cooperation partners, but were not supported by existing probabilistic model checkers. This mainly concerns the calculation of measures that provide insights in the tradeoff between multiple cost and reward functions, such as energy and utility. Usually, the gained utility increases (within certain bounds) with the price to be payed. For example, the performance of a CPU (measured, e.g., in the maximum number of instructions per second) crucially depends on its frequency, but so does its energy consumption. The tradeoff is now to maximize the performance, while at the same time minimizing the energy consumption. In the described setting, one has the freedom to select the frequency the CPU is operating with. The maximal number of instructions per second then appears as a consequence of the choice for the frequency. The goal is now to find "optimal" solutions for the above tradeoff. In requirement specification it is very natural to introduce lower bounds for the gained utility and upper bounds for the costs. One could either ask for the minimal amount of energy to be spend given a lower bound on the performance, or for the maximal performance given a certain upper bound on the energy consumption. Other examples for low-cost objectives and high quality-of-service objectives are constraints on the maximal time to recover from failures in a resilient system or the penalty to be paid for missed deadlines, the average amount of time that a process has to wait for a requested resource, or the frame rate of a video platform. Assuming such a given cost function for the energy consumption and a reward function for the achieved degree of utility, we consider the design of algorithms answering multi-objective problems for MDPs exemplified by the following tasks:

(M) Given an energy budget e and a utility threshold u, find a scheduler for completing a task such that the expected achieved utility is at least u and there is a 80% chance that the energy consumption is at most e.

(Q) Given an energy budget e, maximize the utility value that can be guaranteed for the completion of a task when consuming e or less energy with probability 0.8.

(Qe) Find a scheduler requiring a minimal energy budget to ensure the expected utility for completing a task to be larger than a given utility threshold u.

(C) Suppose the total energy consumption for completing a task is at most e. Find a scheduler maximizing the probability for the property stating that the utility value achieved by completing a task is at least u.

(Cq) Find a scheduler maximizing utility in terms of completed tasks, such that the probability for utility being at least u under the assumption that the energy consumed does not exceed a given threshold e is greater than 0.8.

(R) Find a scheduler for completing infinitely many tasks such that almost surely the ratio between the achieved utility and the consumed energy is always greater than a given quality threshold.

(Rc) Under the assumption that the consumed energy is always smaller than a given threshold e, find a scheduler which guarantees almost surely the energy-utility ratio being greater than a quality threshold.

The first task **(M)** can be seen as a standard multi-objective query [14,23], where the task is to check the existence of a scheduler satisfying a probability condition and an expectation condition. This type of multi-objectives is not in the scope of this paper, which addresses non-standard multi-objectives exemplified by all the other tasks. **(Q)** and **(Qe)** can be formalized as *quantiles*, where the latter stands for an *expectation quantile*. **(C)** is an instance of *conditional probabilities* and **(Cq)** describes a *conditional quantile*. Although quantiles and conditional probabilities and expectations are standard concepts in mathematics and statistics, they have drawn very few attention in the context of PMC. Our recent work [36,4] shows how quantiles can be derived from computation schemes for the probabilities or expectations of reward-bounded path properties. A brief summary will be provided in Section 3. Explanations on the computation of conditional probabilities are provided in Section 4, based on our recent work [8]. Tasks **(R)** and **(Rc)** refer to the quotient of two cost or reward functions in an MDP (e.g., one for the energy and one for the utility). There has been some work on such ratios, e.g., by [1,38] for expected ratios or [20] for long-run ratios when the denominator has the purpose of a counter. This work does not seem to be adequate for solving the tasks stated above. Instead, we show in Section 5 that instances of **(R)** are reducible to problems that have been studied for probabilistic energy games [12] or probabilistic push-down systems [11]. Combining these results with methods presented in Section 4 for conditional probabilities, yields solutions for **(Rc)**. We illustrate how the exemplified tasks stated above can be used in the field of software product line verification. Based on our recent work [22], we detail its application to the energy-aware server system EBOND+.

2   Theoretical Foundations

The reader is supposed to be familiar with ω-automata and temporal logics. See, e.g., [15,25,7]. At several places, we will use notations of linear temporal logics (LTL) and computation tree logic (CTL) where $\Diamond$, $\Box$, $\bigcirc$, U and R stand for the temporal modalities "eventually", "always", "next", "until" and "release", while $\exists$ and $\forall$ are used as CTL-like path quantifiers. The notion *path property* will be used for any language consisting of infinite words over 2^{AP}, where AP is the underlying set of atomic propositions. LTL-formulas are often identified with such path properties that are models for the formulas. Having in mind temporal logical specifications, we use the logical operators $\vee$, $\wedge$, $\neg$ for union, intersection and complementation of path properties.

In the remainder of this section, we provide a brief summary of our notations for Markov decision processes and related concepts. For further details we refer to textbooks on model checking [15,7] and on probability theory and Markovian models [33,32,28]. Let S be a nonempty, countable set. A distribution on S is a function $\mu : S \to [0,1]$ with $\sum_{s \in S} \mu(s) = 1$.

Markov Decision Processes (MDPs). MDPs can be seen as a generalization of transition systems where the operational behavior in a state s consists of a nondeterministic selection of an enabled action α, followed by a probabilistic choice of the successor state, given s and α. Formally, an MDP is a tuple $\mathcal{M} = (S, Act, P, AP, L)$ where S is a finite set of states, Act a finite set of actions, AP a finite set of atomic propositions and $L : S \to 2^{AP}$ a labeling function. The enabled actions and transition probabilities are specified by a function $P : S \times Act \times S \to [0,1] \cap \mathbb{Q}$ with $\sum_{s' \in S} P(s, \alpha, s') \in \{0,1\}$ for all $s \in S$ and $\alpha \in Act$.

The triples (s, α, s') where $P(s, \alpha, s') > 0$ are called transitions. We write $Act(s)$ for the set of actions that are enabled in s, i.e., $P(s, \alpha, s') > 0$ for some $s' \in S$. For technical reasons, we require that $Act(s) \neq \varnothing$ for all states s. If the sets $Act(s)$ are singletons for all states s, $\mathcal{M}$ is called a Markov chain.

Paths in $\mathcal{M}$ are finite or infinite alternating sequences $\zeta = s_0 \, \alpha_0 \, s_1 \, \alpha_1 \, s_2 \, \alpha_2 \ldots$ of states and actions built by consecutive transitions, i.e., $P(s_{i-1}, \alpha_{i-1}, s_i) > 0$ for all $i \geqslant 1$. The length $|\zeta|$ denotes the number of transitions in π. If $k \leqslant |\zeta|$ then $\zeta[k] = s_k$ denotes the $(k{+}1)$-st state in ζ. *FinPaths*(s) and *InfPaths*(s) stand for the sets of all finite resp. infinite paths starting in s. If $\zeta = s_0 \, \alpha_0 \, s_1 \, \alpha_1 \, s_2 \, \alpha_2 \ldots$ is an infinite path then its trace $trace(\zeta) = L(s_0) \, L(s_1) \, L(s_2) \ldots \in (2^{AP})^\omega$ is obtained by the projection to the state labels.

Schedulers and Probability Measure. Reasoning about probabilities for path properties in an MDP $\mathcal{M}$ requires t selection of an initial state and the resolution of the nondeterministic choices between the possible transitions. This is formalized via *schedulers*, which take as input a finite path and select an action to be executed. For the purposes of this paper, we define schedulers as functions $\mathfrak{S} : FinPaths \to Act$ such that $\mathfrak{S}(\pi) \in Act(last(\pi))$ for all finite paths π, where $last(\pi)$ denotes the last state of π. For a pointed MDP $(\mathcal{M}, s)$, i.e., an MDP as before with some distinguished initial state $s = s_{init} \in S$, the behavior of $(\mathcal{M}, s)$ under $\mathfrak{S}$ is purely probabilistic. The probability measure $\mathrm{Pr}_s^{\mathfrak{S}}$ for measurable sets of the infinite $\mathfrak{S}$-paths starting in s is defined in the standard way (see, e.g, [7]) and yields the probability for a path property φ under $\mathfrak{S}$ starting in s:

$$\mathrm{Pr}_s^{\mathfrak{S}}(\varphi) \stackrel{\mathrm{def}}{=} \mathrm{Pr}_s^{\mathfrak{S}}\{\, \zeta \in InfPaths(s) : \zeta \models \varphi \,\}$$

For a worst-case analysis of a system modeled by a pointed MDP $(\mathcal{M}, s)$, one ranges over all schedulers (i.e., all possible resolutions of the nondeterminism) and considers the maximal or minimal probabilities for φ:

$$\mathrm{Pr}_s^{\min}(\varphi) \stackrel{\mathrm{def}}{=} \min_{\mathfrak{S}} \mathrm{Pr}_s^{\mathfrak{S}}(\varphi) \qquad\qquad \mathrm{Pr}_s^{\max}(\varphi) \stackrel{\mathrm{def}}{=} \max_{\mathfrak{S}} \mathrm{Pr}_s^{\mathfrak{S}}(\varphi)$$

Automata-Based PMC for LTL-Specifications. Figure 1 sketches the main steps of the automata-based PMC-approach for MDP against LTL-specifications. Maxima and minima are taken over all potential resolutions of the nondeterminism, formalized by schedulers. We suppose here that the formula φ describes the undesired behaviors where the requirement does not hold, in which case the maximal probability for φ and a corresponding scheduler that maximizes the probabilities for φ provides insights in the worst-case scenarios.

The idea is to apply at first known algorithms that transform the given LTL-formula into a deterministic automaton $\mathcal{A}$ over infinite words (see [25]) and then to compute the maximimal probabilities for the paths satisfying $\mathcal{A}$'s acceptance condition in the product-MDP $\mathcal{M} \otimes \mathcal{A}$. The latter reduces to a probabilistic reachability problem and is solvable by linear-programming techniques [9,7].

A worst-case analysis as in Fig. 1 is adequate if the choices between the nondeterministic alternatives in the given MDP are uncontrollable (e.g. if they represent the possible interactions with an unknown or unpredictable environment). Likewise, if the given LTL-formula φ formalizes the desired behaviors, the computation of the maximal probability for φ can be seen as a best-case analysis. Then, a scheduler maximizing the probability for φ serves as an optimal controller for the objective φ.

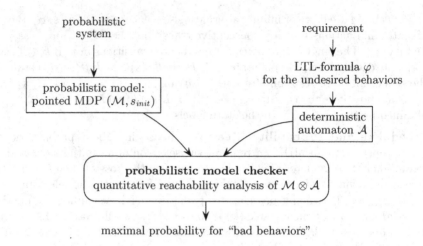

Fig. 1. Automata-based PMC-approach for MDP and LTL-specifications

Weight and Reward Functions. A weight function for $\mathcal{M}$ is a function of the form $wgt : S \times Act \to \mathbb{Z}$ that assigns an integer for all state-action pairs where $wgt(s, \alpha) = 0$ if $\alpha \notin Act(s)$. If wgt is non-negative, i.e., $wgt(s, s') \geqslant 0$ for all states s, s', then we refer to wgt as a *reward function*. We say wgt is positive if $wgt(s, \alpha) > 0$ for all state-action pairs (s, α) where α is enabled in s. Occasionally, we also consider weight functions with rational values and refer to them as *rational-valued* weight functions. The *accumulated weight* of finite paths is defined as $wgt(s_0 \, \alpha_0 \, s_1 \, \alpha_1 \ldots \alpha_{n-1} \, s_n) = \sum_{0 \leqslant i < n} wgt(s_i, \alpha_i)$.

Expected Accumulated Reward. Let χ be a predicate for finite paths and rew a reward function. The random variable $rew_\chi : InfPaths \to \mathbb{Z} \cup \{\infty\}$ assigns to each infinite path ζ the accumulated reward of the longest prefix of ζ where χ does not hold. That is:

$$rew_\chi(\zeta) \overset{\text{def}}{=} \sup\{\, rew(\zeta[0 \ldots k]) : k \in \mathbb{N}, \, \zeta[0 \ldots k]) \not\models \chi \,\}$$

We will use two types of predicates for finite paths: reachability constraints $\chi = \text{Reach}(goal)$ where $goal$ is a state predicate (i.e., Boolean combination of atomic propositions) and predicates χ of the form $rew > r$ or $rew \geqslant r$ imposing a lower bound on the accumulated reward (where $r \in \mathbb{N}$). If π is a finite path of length n then $\pi \models \text{Reach}(goal)$ if $\pi[k] \models goal$ for some $k \in \{0, 1, \ldots, n\}$ and $\pi \models rew > r$ if $rew(\pi) > r$. For these types of predicates, the set of finite paths π with $\pi \models \chi$ is prefix-closed and the set $\Diamond\chi$ of infinite paths ζ with $\zeta[0 \ldots k] \models \chi$ for some position $k \in \mathbb{N}$ is measurable. Obviously, reachability predicates $\text{Reach}(goal)$ can be mimicked by the predicate $rew \geqslant 1$ where rew is a fresh reward function with $rew(s, \alpha) = 1$ if $s \models goal$ and $\alpha \in Act(s)$ and $rew(s, \alpha) = 0$ in all other cases.

Given state s of $\mathcal{M}$ and a scheduler $\mathfrak{S}$ such that $\text{Pr}_s^{\mathfrak{S}}(\Diamond\chi) = 1$, the *expected accumulated reward* until χ, denoted $\mathbb{E}[rew]_s^{\mathfrak{S}}(\Diamond\chi) = \sum_\pi \text{prob}^{\mathfrak{S}}(\pi)$ is the expectation of the random variable rew_χ. Here, π ranges over all finite $\mathfrak{S}$-paths with $\pi \not\models \chi$. If $\Pr_s^{\min}(\Diamond\chi) = 1$, then

$$\mathbb{E}[rew]_s^{\max}(\Diamond\chi) = \max_{\mathfrak{S}} \mathbb{E}[rew]_s^{\mathfrak{S}}(\Diamond\chi), \quad \mathbb{E}[rew]_s^{\min}(\Diamond\chi) = \min_{\mathfrak{S}} \mathbb{E}[rew]_s^{\mathfrak{S}}(\Diamond\chi)$$

are computable using linear-programming techniques [33,21].

3 Quantiles

Quantiles are well-established in statistics (see, e.g., [34]), where they are used to reason about the cumulative distribution function of a random variable R. If $p \in {]}0, 1{[}$, then the p-quantile is the maximal value r such that the probability for the event $R > r$ is at least p. Although quantiles can provide very useful insights in the interplay of various cost functions and other system properties, they have barely obtained attention in the model-checking community. We provide here a brief summary of the concepts presented in [36,4]. The formula

$$\phi_{e,u} = \Diamond\big(\, goal \wedge (energy \leqslant e) \wedge (utility \geqslant u) \, \big)$$

states that eventually a goal state will be reached along some finite path where the accumulated energy is at most e and the accumulated utility value is at least u. Path properties $\varphi[e]$ (and $\psi[u]$) parametrizing only over the energy costs (utility reward, respectively) are obtained from $\phi_{e,u}$ by fixing the maximal energy costs e (minimal utility u, respectively). Whereas $\varphi[e]$ is *increasing* with the available energy budged e, $\psi[u]$ is *decreasing* with the requested utility u.

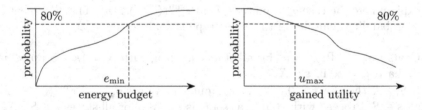

Fig. 2. Quantiles for increasing (left) and decreasing (right) properties

Quantiles now ask for the minimal e (maximal u) such that the probability of all paths starting in a designated state and fulfilling $\varphi[e]$ ($\psi[u]$, respectively) exceed a given probability bound p. The arising quantile values are illustrated in Figure 2 for $p = 0.8$. In order to formally define the quantiles used throughout this paper, let us fix an MDP $\mathcal{M}$ and a reward function $rew : S \times Act \to \mathbb{N}$ as in Section 2. Given an increasing path property $\varphi[r]$, where parameter $r \in \mathbb{N}$ stands for some bound on the accumulated reward, we can define the following types of *existential quantiles*, where $\psi[r] = \neg\varphi[r]$, $\unrhd \in \{\geqslant, >\}$ and $p \in [0, 1] \cap \mathbb{Q}$:

$$\min\{ r \in \mathbb{N} : \Pr_s^{\max}(\varphi[r]) \unrhd p \} \quad \text{and} \quad \max\{ r \in \mathbb{N} : \Pr_s^{\max}(\psi[r]) \unrhd p \}$$

Analogously, *universal quantiles* are defined by considering the probability of a path property which can be guaranteed under every scheduler, i.e., replacing $\mathrm{Pr}_s^{\max}$ above by $\mathrm{Pr}_s^{\min}$. If the extrema are taken over the empty set, they are defined to be ∞ in the case of minima and as undefined in the case of maxima. One example is reward-bounded path properties. For instance, $\varphi[r] = \Diamond^{\leqslant r} a$ and $\varphi[r] = \Box^{\geqslant r} a$ are increasing, while their duals $\psi[r] = \Diamond^{\geqslant r} a$ and $\psi[r] = \Box^{\leqslant r} a$ are decreasing. Here, a is an atomic proposition or a Boolean combination thereof.[1] Within these notations, the formula $\phi_{e,u}$ above can be reformulated as $\Diamond^{\leqslant e}(goal \wedge (utility \geqslant u))$ when the consumed energy is modeled by a reward function and the accumulated utility is assumed to be encoded in the states, or as $\Diamond^{\geqslant u}(goal \wedge (energy \leqslant e))$ when utility is represented by a reward function and the consumed energy is augmented to states. Thus, query **(Q)** of the introduction corresponds to the task of computing an optimal scheduler $\mathfrak{S}$ for the quantile:

$$\max \left\{ u \in \mathbb{N} : \mathrm{Pr}_{s_{init}}^{\max}(\Diamond^{\geqslant u}(goal \wedge (energy \leqslant e))) \geqslant 0.8 \right\}$$

Similar to the already mentioned quantiles, we can define expectation quantiles, where the probability bound is replaced by a bound on an expected accumulated reward. For example, given two reward functions *energy* and *utility*, we may ask for $\min \left\{ e \in \mathbb{N} : \mathbb{E}[utility]_{s_{init}}^{\max}(\Diamond(energy > e)) > u \right\}$ given a fixed utility threshold u, which corresponds to task **(Qe)** from the introduction.

Computation of Quantiles. For qualitative quantiles with upper-bounded eventually properties, i.e., quantiles with the probability bounds $= 1$, < 1, $= 0$ or > 0, the quantile values can be computed in polynomial time using a greedy method that shares some ideas of Dijkstra's shortest-path algorithm [36]. For other probability bounds, the schema for computing the quantile is as follows. We explain here the case $q_s = \min\{r \in \mathbb{N} : \mathrm{Pr}_s^{\min}(\Diamond^{\leqslant r} a) > p\}$. The treatment of other probability quantiles of the above type is analogous.

1. Compute $p_s = \mathrm{Pr}_s^{\min}(\Diamond a)$ for all states s. Then, with $X = \{s \in S : p_s \leqslant p\}$ we have $q_s = \infty$ iff $s \in X$.
2. If $S \neq X$ then for $r = 0, 1, 2, \ldots$, compute the values $p_{s,r} = \mathrm{Pr}_s^{\min}(\Diamond^{\leqslant r} a)$ for all $s \in S$. Proceed with step 3, as soon as $p_{s,r} > p$ for all states $s \in S \setminus X$.
3. For each $s \in S \setminus X$, return $q_s = \min\{r \in \mathbb{N} : p_{s,r} > p\}$.

The computation of the values $p_{s,r}$ in step 2 can be carried out using linear-programming techniques and reusing the values $p_{t,i}$ for $i < r$ computed in previous iterations. The computation of expectation quantiles can follow an analogous approach as for probability quantiles. The idea is first to identify the states where the expectation quantile is infinite. We then iteratively compute the values $u_{s,e} = \mathbb{E}[utility]_s^{\max}(\Diamond(energy > e))$ for $e = 0, 1, \ldots$ solving linear programs until $u_{s,e} > u$. Detailed explanations for computing quantiles can be found in [4].

---

[1] The semantics of the reward-bounded eventually and always operator is as follows. If ζ is an infinite path, then $\zeta \models \Diamond^{\bowtie r} a$ where $\bowtie \in \{\leqslant, \geqslant\}$ if there exists a position $k \in \mathbb{N}$ with $rew(pref(\zeta, k)) \bowtie r$ and $\zeta[k] \models a$. Similarly, $\Box^{\bowtie r} a \equiv \neg(\neg\Diamond^{\bowtie r}\neg a)$.

4 Conditional Probabilities and Expectations

Probabilities and expectations under the assumption that some additional temporal condition holds are often needed within the quantitative analysis of protocols. Constraints in conditional probabilities or expectations can be seen as a non-standard type of multi-objective properties. For example, in the context of energy-utility analysis, conditional probabilities or expectations are useful to analyze the energy-efficiency, while assuming that a certain condition on the achieved utility is guaranteed. Vice versa, one might ask, e.g., for the expected utility, while not exceeding a given energy budget.

Conditional probabilities in Markov chains can be computed simply by the definition of conditional probabilities as the quotient of ordinary probabilities:

$$\mathrm{Pr}_s^{\mathcal{M}}(\varphi \mid \psi) = \frac{\mathrm{Pr}_s^{\mathcal{M}}(\varphi \wedge \psi)}{\mathrm{Pr}_s^{\mathcal{M}}(\psi)}$$

where $\mathrm{Pr}_s^{\mathcal{M}}(\psi) > 0$. In what follows we refer to φ as the *objective* and to ψ as the *condition*. This approach has been taken in [3], where the condition and the objective are specified as PCTL path properties. The quotient method has been extended recently [24,30] for discrete and continuous-time Markov chains and patterns of path properties with multiple time- and cost-bounds. An alternative approach relies on a transformation $\mathcal{M} \rightsquigarrow \mathcal{M}_\psi$ such that for all measurable path properties φ the conditional probability for φ of $\mathcal{M}$ under condition ψ agrees with the standard (unconditional) probability for φ in $\mathcal{M}_\psi$ [8].

More challenging is the task to reason about conditional probabilities in MDPs. The crux is that for the computation of, e.g.,

$$\mathrm{Pr}_s^{\max}(\varphi \mid \psi) = \max_{\mathfrak{S}} \mathrm{Pr}_s^{\mathfrak{S}}(\varphi \mid \psi) = \max_{\mathfrak{S}} \frac{\mathrm{Pr}_s^{\mathfrak{S}}(\varphi \wedge \psi)}{\mathrm{Pr}_s^{\mathfrak{S}}(\psi)}$$

we cannot simply maximize the nominator and denominator independently. This problem has been addressed first in [3], where an extension of PCTL over MDPs [9] by a conditional probability operator has been introduced. The presented model-checking algorithm relies on an exhaustive search (with heuristic bounding techniques) in some finite, but potentially exponentially large class of finite-memory schedulers. In [8] we improved this result by presenting a polynomial transformation $\mathcal{M} \rightsquigarrow \mathcal{M}_{\varphi|\psi}$ for reachability objectives and conditions, which has been shown to be the core problem for reasoning about ω-regular objectives and conditions by using automata representations of the objective and the condition. In this approach, we fix an initial state s_{init} of $\mathcal{M}$. The idea for the construction of the transformed MDP $\mathcal{M}_{\varphi|\psi}$ is to redistribute the probabilities of paths where the condition ψ does not hold by adding reset-transitions to s_{init}. In the case of prefix-independent conditions (e.g. a reachability or a fairness condition) reset-transition $t \longrightarrow s_{init}$ are introduced for all states t where $\mathrm{Pr}_t^{\max}(\psi) = 0$.

The transformation explained in [8] relies on a preprocessing depending on both the condition ψ and the objective φ and generates a normal form for conditional probabilities. This preprocessing can, however, be dropped resulting in a transformation $\mathcal{M} \rightsquigarrow \mathcal{M}_\psi$ that only depends on the condition such that $\Pr^{\max}_{\mathcal{M},s_{init}}(\varphi \,|\, \psi)$ equals $\Pr^{\max}_{\mathcal{M}_\psi,s_{init}}(\varphi \wedge \psi)$ for all objectives φ, e.g., formalized as LTL or PRCTL path formulas. With this approach we can, for instance, compute *conditional quantiles* as in **(Cq)**, which are of the form

$$\min\{r \in \mathbb{N} : \Pr^{\max}_{\mathcal{M},s_{init}}(\varphi[r] \,|\, \psi) \geqslant p\} = \min\{r \in \mathbb{N} : \Pr^{\max}_{\mathcal{M}_\psi,s_{init}}(\varphi[r] \wedge \psi) \geqslant p\}$$

where $\varphi[r]$ is an increasing path property such as $\Diamond^{\leqslant r} a$ (see also Section 3).

5   Reasoning about the Energy-Utility Ratio

As a third type of non-standard multi-objective reasoning in MDPs we consider conditions on the quotient of two reward functions. The problem to compute expected ratios of accumulated rewards in MDPs was already addressed, e.g., in [1,38]. Probabilistic constraints on special types of long-run limits of accumulated rewards were studied in [20]. The results by [10,35] indicate that reasoning about long-run limits of (ratios of) accumulated values is algorithmically simpler than reasoning about the accumulated values along the prefixes of infinite paths. Indeed, [10] proves the undecidability of the model-checking problem for temporal logics extended by assertions on the accumulated values along the prefixes of infinite paths. Nevertheless, as the work on energy games [12,13] shows, there are several interesting patterns of formulas with prefix-accumulation assertions.

We consider here a pointed MDP $(\mathcal{M}, s_{init})$ with two weight functions, say *energy* and *utility* where the energy reward function is supposed to be positive. Let $ratio = \frac{utility}{energy} : FinPaths \to \mathbb{Q}$ given by $ratio(\pi) = utility(\pi)/energy(\pi)$ if $|\pi| \geqslant 1$ and ϑ a rational number specifying a *quality threshold*. Using an LTL-like syntax, we define the path property $\psi_\vartheta = \Box(ratio > \vartheta)$ where $\zeta \models \psi_\vartheta$ iff $ratio(\,pref(\zeta,k)\,) > \vartheta$ for all positions $k \in \mathbb{N}$ with $k \geqslant 1$. We now discuss the following questions assuming a given LTL-formula φ:

(E1) $\Pr^{\max}_{s_{init}}(\psi_\vartheta \wedge \varphi) = 1$ **(A1)** $\Pr^{\min}_{s_{init}}(\psi_\vartheta \wedge \varphi) = 1$

(E0) $\Pr^{\max}_{s_{init}}(\psi_\vartheta \wedge \varphi) > 0$ **(A0)** $\Pr^{\min}_{s_{init}}(\psi_\vartheta \wedge \varphi) > 0$

Problems (A1) and (E1). Obviously, the almost-sure problems **(A1)** and **(E1)** relate to the problems of deciding whether $\Pr^{\mathfrak{S}}_{s_{init}}(\psi_\vartheta \wedge \varphi) = 1$ for all schedulers $\mathfrak{S}$ (problem **(A1)**) respectively some scheduler $\mathfrak{S}$ (problem **(E1)**). We can rely on a simple transformation $(energy, utility) \mapsto wgt$ that permits to replace the ratio-constraint ψ_ϑ with a constraint $\Box(wgt > 0)$ for a single rational-valued weight function $wgt : S \times Act \to \mathbb{Q}$ defined by $wgt(s,\alpha) = utility(s,\alpha) - \vartheta \cdot energy(s,\alpha)$. It is clear that for all finite paths π we have $ratio(\pi) > \vartheta$ iff $wgt(\pi) > 0$, such that for all infinite paths ζ it holds that $\zeta \models \psi_\vartheta \wedge \varphi$ iff $\zeta \models \Box(wgt > 0) \wedge \varphi$. Since the weight functions for the energy and the utility are supposed to be integer-valued, we multiply wgt with the denominator of ϑ to obtain an integer-valued weight function. This permits to assume that $wgt(s,\alpha) \in \mathbb{Z}$ for all states s, $s' \in S$.

We now address **(A1)**. Clearly, $\mathrm{Pr}^{\min}_{s_{init}}(\Box(wgt>0)\wedge\varphi)=1$ iff $\mathrm{Pr}^{\min}_{s_{init}}(\Box(wgt>0))=1$ and $\mathrm{Pr}^{\min}_{s_{init}}(\varphi)=1$. The condition $\mathrm{Pr}^{\min}_{s_{init}}(\varphi)=1$ can be checked in time polynomial in the size of $\mathcal{M}$ using standard techniques. The condition $\mathrm{Pr}^{\min}_{s_{init}}(\Box(wgt>0))=1$ is equivalent to $s\not\models\exists\Diamond(wgt<0)$ and can be checked in polynomial time using standard shortest-path algorithms.

By the results established in [12] for energy games with an MDP game arena, problem **(E1)** is in NP∩coNP, when φ is a reachability, Büchi or parity condition. If φ is an LTL formula, we can rely on standard techniques to generate a deterministic parity automaton $\mathcal{A}$ for φ and then switch from $(\mathcal{M},\varphi)$ to $(\mathcal{M}\otimes\mathcal{A},\varphi_{\mathcal{A}})$, where $\varphi_{\mathcal{A}}$ is the acceptance (parity) condition of $\mathcal{A}$.

Problems (A0) and (E0). Let us now turn to **(A0)** and **(E0)**, where the task is to check whether $\mathrm{Pr}^{\mathfrak{S}}_{s_{init}}(\psi_\theta\wedge\varphi)>0$ for all schedulers $\mathfrak{S}$ (problem **(A0)**) or for some scheduler $\mathfrak{S}$ (problem **(E0)**). The challenge in providing algorithms for these two problems becomes clear as they depend on the concrete transition probabilities of $\mathcal{M}$. This even holds for the case of $\mathcal{M}$ being a Markov chain. Consider the Markov chain $\mathcal{M} = \mathcal{M}_p$ in the following picture where $p \in\,]0,1[$ is a probability parameter.

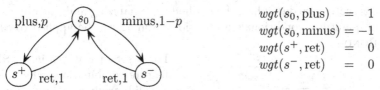

$$wgt(s_0,\text{plus}) = 1$$
$$wgt(s_0,\text{minus}) = -1$$
$$wgt(s^+,\text{ret}) = 0$$
$$wgt(s^-,\text{ret}) = 0$$

Finite paths in $\mathcal{M}$ starting and ending in s_0 constitute a biased random walk, for which it is well-known that for $p > \frac{1}{2}$, the random walk drifts to the right and never reaches position -1 with positive probability, whereas for $0 < p \leqslant \frac{1}{2}$, position -1 will be visited almost surely. Thus, $\mathrm{Pr}^{\mathcal{M}}_{s_0}\big(\Box(wgt\geqslant 0)\big) > 0$ iff $p > \frac{1}{2}$. As a consequence, the answers for questions **(A0)** and **(E0)** may depend on the concrete transition probabilities. This observation rules out simple algorithms relying on shortest-path arguments as for **(A1)**. Nevertheless, problems **(A0)** and **(E0)** and even the task to check whether $\mathrm{Pr}^{\mathcal{M}}_{s_{init}}(\psi_\vartheta\wedge\varphi)\bowtie p$ for some given $p\in[0,1]\cap\mathbb{Q}$ and $\bowtie\in\{\leqslant,<,\geqslant,>\}$ is decidable when $\mathcal{M}$ is a Markov chain. For this, we can rely on a reduction to the probabilistic model-checking problem for probabilistic push-down automata (pPDA) and apply the techniques presented, e.g., in [11]. The idea is simply to consider the states of $\mathcal{M}$ as control states of a pPDA and to mimic each transition $s \to s'$ in $\mathcal{M}$ of weight $k > 0$ by k push operations and each transition $s \to s'$ with weight $-k$ by k pop operations. This reduction is exponential, but shows the decidability of the problems mentioned above for Markov chains. To the best of our knowledge, the decidability of problems **(E0)** and **(A0)** for MDPs is an open problem.

6   Multi-objective Analysis of Software Product Lines

The previously presented methods are also suitable for feature-oriented software engineering areas such as *software product line (SPL)* engineering. An SPL specifies a collection of software products by their commonalities in terms of features rather than specifying all software products separately [17]. Formal analysis of SPLs has to tackle the combinatorial blow-up in the number of features arising from composing features and their dynamical changes during runtime of the system (e.g., by software updates or in-app purchases). Family-based analysis approaches [39], where all possible software products are checked at once instead of checking each feature combination one-by-one, turned out to be very successful [16]. Recently, we proposed a compositional framework for probabilistic SPLs which supports dynamic feature changes and has an MDP-based semantics, allowing for quantitative analysis using standard PMC-methods [22]. We demonstrated feasibility of our approach by analyzing an extended version of the energy-aware bonding network device EBOND [26]. The so-called EBOND+ describes how energy can be saved by switching to various network-card combinations in a server depending on the requested traffic load. Already the analysis of single objectives in terms of performance measures, energy consumption and monetary costs revealed interesting insights of the influence of feature combinations. In this section we detail how the methods for analyzing multiple objectives in terms of quantiles, conditionals and ratio reasoning can be applied to SPLs such as EBOND+.

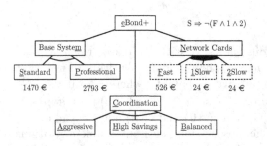

Fig. 3. Feature diagram of EBOND+ SPL

For a set of features in an SPL, feature combinations which yield a valid product are usually defined through a *feature diagram*, providing a hierarchical structure of features. As shown in Figure 3, the EBOND+ SPL consists of a base feature containing one base standard or professional system, one coordination feature which defines how network traffic is distributed on the network cards (aggressive, high or balanced energy savings) and one fast or two slow network cards which can be plugged into the system in several combinations. The latter is illustrated in the feature diagram by dashed *optional features* that can be activated or deactivated during runtime of the system. Feature diagrams may be further annotated with propositional formulas over features, e.g., $S \Rightarrow \neg(F \wedge 1 \wedge 2)$ states that within a standard version of the base system, at most two network cards can be plugged simultaneously.

Various measures in terms of cost and rewards can now be investigated. We considered the different measures within a fixed time horizon of t minutes the system is observed. The amount of time a service-level agreement (SLA) is fulfilled, i.e., the number of minutes within this time horizon the requested bandwidth is served, can be used as a measure for utility that is decreasing over time. The opposite, an SLA violation, occurs, e.g., due to a probabilistically modeled system failure or due to aggressively putting network cards into sleeping mode by the energy savings coordination feature. Costs for keeping SLA violations as rare as possible may be formalized as increasing measures in terms of energy (the fast network card consumes more energy than the slower ones) or money (monetary costs as annotated in Figure 3 are higher for better equipped EBOND+ product).

The EBOND+ model is an MDP encoding all the cost and utility measures described above, allowing for PMC-based analysis. In order to minimize SLA violations, money investments or energy consumption we are thus able to construct optimal schedulers for activating and deactivating network cards during runtime according to rules fixed by an operational model called *feature controller* (solving the *strategy synthesis problem*). All of the exemplified tasks described in the introduction and formalized in the last sections are also useful in the EBOND+ setting, employing the utility and energy measures described above and choosing the goal set T of states representing the states where the time horizon t is reached. For instance, the expectation quantile task **(Qe)** with $u = 0.99 \cdot t$ amounts to minimizing the energy required to ensure that at least 99% of the time no SLA violation can be expected. A similar task can also be stated minimizing the money which needs to be invested for expecting a quality of service of at least 99%, replacing *energy* by *money* in the formula stated in Section 3.

To reason about feature combinations, conditional probabilities turned out to be very useful: The rules for feature changes defined by the feature controller can be further restricted according to assumed behavior of the environment, e.g., by fairness assumptions. For instance, the maximal probability that no SLA violation occurs under the condition that infinitely often a slow network card (1 or 2) is plugged in can be expressed by $\mathrm{Pr}_{s_{init}}^{\max}(\,\Diamond NoSla \mid \Box\Diamond(1 \lor 2)\,)$, where $NoSla \subseteq T$ denotes the set of states where $utility \geqslant t$, i.e., the time horizon has been reached without an SLA violation in the past. Conditional expectations also play an important role when expected costs and rewards do not yield proper values, e.g., if $\mathrm{Pr}_{s_{init}}^{\min}(\Diamond\chi) < 1$ and hence the expectation $\mathbb{E}[energy]_{s_{init}}^{\min}(\Diamond\chi)$ is infinite. While $\Diamond NoSla$ does not hold almost surely without any further assumptions, this can be guaranteed for a plugged fast network card (F) and assuming that no failures occur. When the set of states *Fail* represents that a failure of network cards occurred, $\mathbb{E}[energy]_{s_{init}}^{\min}(\Diamond NoSla \mid \Box(\neg Fail \land F))$ thus yields a proper energy expectation. Hence, this expectation can be used for best-case analysis which may help to schedule further development steps of the EBOND+ SPL or estimate overall system quality.

Departing from the finite time horizon perspective and having in mind that the fast network card consumes most energy, one could also ask for a scheduler which guarantees the ratio between energy and utility to be almost surely above a certain threshold and infinitely often switches from the fast network card to a slower one. This task corresponds to **(R)**, which can be furthermore combined with requiring the total accumulated energy to be always below a given energy threshold e if the system intents to use the fast network card **(Rc)**.

That extension, which requires the energy consumption to be encoded into the states of the model, can be formalized by asking whether

$$\mathrm{Pr}^{\mathfrak{S}}_{s_{init}}\left(\ \Box(ratio > \vartheta)\ \wedge\ \neg\Diamond\Box F\ |\ \Box(F \Rightarrow (energy \leqslant e))\ \right)\ =\ 1.$$

It is obvious that the approaches of computing quantiles, conditionals and ratios can be further combined, which enables to provide even more insights on feature-oriented quantitative properties of EBOND+ than already demonstrated in [22] within single objectives.

Detailed case studies for multi-objective reasoning and theoretical considerations of nesting such objectives are subject of our current work.

References

1. Aggarwal, V., Chandrasekaran, R., Nair, K.: Markov ratio decision processes. Journal of Optimization Theory and Application 21(1) (1977)
2. Andova, S., Hermanns, H., Katoen, J.-P.: Discrete-time rewards model-checked. In: Larsen, K.G., Niebert, P. (eds.) FORMATS 2003. LNCS, vol. 2791, pp. 88–104. Springer, Heidelberg (2004)
3. Andrés, M., van Rossum, P.: Conditional probabilities over probabilistic and nondeterministic systems. In: Ramakrishnan, C.R., Rehof, J. (eds.) TACAS 2008. LNCS, vol. 4963, pp. 157–172. Springer, Heidelberg (2008)
4. Baier, C., Daum, M., Dubslaff, C., Klein, J., Klüppelholz, S.: Energy-utility quantiles. In: NFM 2014. LNCS (to appear, 2014)
5. Baier, C., Daum, M., Engel, B., Härtig, H., Klein, J., Klüppelholz, S., Märcker, S., Tews, H., Völp, M.: Locks: Picking key methods for a scalable quantitative analysis. Journal of Computer and System Sciences (to appear, 2014)
6. Baier, C., Engel, B., Klüppelholz, S., Märcker, S., Tews, H., Völp, M.: A probabilistic quantitative analysis of probabilistic-write/copy-select. In: Brat, G., Rungta, N., Venet, A. (eds.) NFM 2013. LNCS, vol. 7871, pp. 307–321. Springer, Heidelberg (2013)
7. Baier, C., Katoen, J.-P.: Principles of Model Checking. MIT Press (2008)
8. Baier, C., Klein, J., Klüppelholz, S., Märcker, S.: Computing conditional probabilities in Markovian models efficiently. In: TACAS 2014. LNCS (to appear, 2014)
9. Bianco, A., de Alfaro, L.: Model checking of probabilistic and non-deterministic systems. In: Thiagarajan, P.S. (ed.) FSTTCS 1995. LNCS, vol. 1026, pp. 499–513. Springer, Heidelberg (1995)
10. Boker, U., Chatterjee, K., Henzinger, T.A., Kupferman, O.: Temporal specifications with accumulative values. In: LICS 2011, pp. 43–52. IEEE Computer Society (2011)
11. Brázdil, T., Kučera, A., Stražovský, O.: On the decidability of temporal properties of probabilistic pushdown automata. In: Diekert, V., Durand, B. (eds.) STACS 2005. LNCS, vol. 3404, pp. 145–157. Springer, Heidelberg (2005)
12. Chatterjee, K., Doyen, L.: Energy and mean-payoff parity Markov decision processes. In: Murlak, F., Sankowski, P. (eds.) MFCS 2011. LNCS, vol. 6907, pp. 206–218. Springer, Heidelberg (2011)

13. Chatterjee, K., Doyen, L.: Energy parity games. Theoretical Computer Science 458, 49–60 (2012)
14. Chatterjee, K., Majumdar, R., Henzinger, T.: Markov decision processes with multiple objectives. In: Durand, B., Thomas, W. (eds.) STACS 2006. LNCS, vol. 3884, pp. 325–336. Springer, Heidelberg (2006)
15. Clarke, E., Grumberg, O., Peled, D.: Model Checking. MIT Press (2000)
16. Classen, A., Cordy, M., Schobbens, P.-Y., Heymans, P., Legay, A., Raskin, J.-F.: Featured transition systems: Foundations for verifying variability-intensive systems and their application to ltl model checking. In: IEEE TSE (2012)
17. Clements, P., Northrop, L.: Software Product Lines: Practices and Patterns. Addison-Wesley Professional (2001)
18. Courcoubetis, C., Yannakakis, M.: The complexity of probabilistic verification. Journal of the ACM 42(4), 857–907 (1995)
19. de Alfaro, L.: Formal Verification of Probabilistic Systems. PhD thesis, Stanford University, Department of Computer Science (1997)
20. de Alfaro, L.: How to specify and verify the long-run average behavior of probabilistic systems. In: LICS 1998, pp. 454–465. IEEE Computer Society (1998)
21. de Alfaro, L.: Computing minimum and maximum reachability times in probabilistic systems. In: Baeten, J.C.M., Mauw, S. (eds.) CONCUR 1999. LNCS, vol. 1664, pp. 66–81. Springer, Heidelberg (1999)
22. Dubslaff, C., Klüppelholz, S., Baier, C.: Probabilistic model checking for energy analysis in software product lines. In: MODULARITY 2014 (to appear, 2014)
23. Etessami, K., Kwiatkowska, M., Vardi, M., Yannakakis, M.: Multi-objective model checking of Markov decision processes. Logical Methods in Computer Science 4(4) (2008)
24. Gao, Y., Xu, M., Zhan, N., Zhang, L.: Model checking conditional CSL for continuous-time Markov chains. IPL 113(1-2), 44–50 (2013)
25. Grädel, E., Thomas, W., Wilke, T. (eds.): Automata, Logics, and Infinite Games. LNCS, vol. 2500. Springer, Heidelberg (2002)
26. Hähnel, M., Döbel, B., Völp, M., Härtig, H.: ebond: Energy saving in heterogeneous R.A.I.N. In: Proc. of the Fourth International Conference on Future Energy Systems, e-Energy 2013, pp. 193–202. ACM (2013)
27. Hansson, H., Jonsson, B.: A logic for reasoning about time and reliability. Formal Aspects of Computing 6, 512–535 (1994)
28. Haverkort, B.: Performance of Computer Communication Systems: A Model-Based Approach. Wiley (1998)
29. Hinton, A., Kwiatkowska, M., Norman, G., Parker, D.: PRISM: A tool for automatic verification of probabilistic systems. In: Hermanns, H., Palsberg, J. (eds.) TACAS 2006. LNCS, vol. 3920, pp. 441–444. Springer, Heidelberg (2006)
30. Ji, M., Wu, D., Chen, Z.: Verification method of conditional probability based on automaton. Journal of Networks 8(6), 1329–1335 (2013)
31. Katoen, J.-P., Zapreev, I., Hahn, E., Hermanns, H., Jansen, D.: The ins and outs of the probabilistic model checker MRMC. Performance Evaluation 68(2) (2011)
32. Kulkarni, V.: Modeling and Analysis of Stochastic Systems. Chapman & Hall (1995)
33. Puterman, M.: Markov Decision Processes: Discrete Stochastic Dynamic Programming. Wiley (1994)
34. Serfling, R.J.: Approximation Theorems of Mathematical Statistics. Wiley (1980)

35. Tomita, T., Hiura, S., Hagihara, S., Yonezaki, N.: A temporal logic with mean-payoff constraints. In: Aoki, T., Taguchi, K. (eds.) ICFEM 2012. LNCS, vol. 7635, pp. 249–265. Springer, Heidelberg (2012)
36. Ummels, M., Baier, C.: Computing quantiles in Markov reward models. In: Pfenning, F. (ed.) FOSSACS 2013. LNCS, vol. 7794, pp. 353–368. Springer, Heidelberg (2013)
37. Vardi, M.: Automatic verification of probabilistic concurrent finite-state programs. In: FOCS 1985, pp. 327–338. IEEE Computer Society (1985)
38. von Essen, C., Jobstmann, B.: Synthesizing systems with optimal average-case behavior for ratio objectives. In: iWIGP 2011. EPTCS, vol. 50, pp. 17–32 (2011)
39. von Rhein, A., Apel, S., Kästner, C., Thüm, T., Schaefer, I.: The PLA model: On the combination of product-line analyses. In: Proc. of VaMoS 2013. ACM (2013)

Target Oriented Relational Model Finding

Alcino Cunha, Nuno Macedo, and Tiago Guimarães

HASLab — High Assurance Software Laboratory
INESC TEC & Universidade do Minho, Braga, Portugal
{alcino,nfmmacedo,tguimaraes}@di.uminho.pt

Abstract. Model finders are becoming useful in many software engineering problems. Kodkod [19] is one of the most popular, due to its support for relational logic (a combination of first order logic with relational algebra operators and transitive closure), allowing a simpler specification of constraints, and support for partial instances, allowing the specification of *a priori* (exact, but potentially partial) knowledge about a problem's solution. However, in some software engineering problems, such as model repair or bidirectional model transformation, knowledge about the solution is not exact, but instead there is a known target that the solution should approximate. In this paper we extend Kodkod's partial instances to allow the specification of such targets, and show how its model finding procedure can be adapted to support them (using both PMax-SAT solvers or SAT solvers with cardinality constraints). Two case studies are also presented, including a careful performance evaluation to assess the effectiveness of the proposed extension.

1 Introduction

In the last decades SAT solvers have shown great potential in many areas. However, their applicability to software engineering problems is somehow hampered by the low-level nature of SAT problems and the low expressiveness of propositional logic. Specifying high-level constraints in such solvers can be quite cumbersome, and using them to solve software engineering problems usually requires a complex embedding. Recently, some higher-level solvers have been proposed that are more suitable for such problems. Among those, Kodkod [19] is one of the most popular, mainly due to its support for relational logic, an extension of first-order logic with relational operators and transitive closure. The former gives an object-oriented feeling to Kodkod specifications, making it accessible to software engineering practitioners, and the latter allows the specification of (many times essential) reachability properties.

The most well-known application of Kodkod is the automated analysis of specifications written in Alloy [6], a lightweight formal specification language also based on relational logic. The Alloy Analyzer supports model finding via an embedding to Kodkod. Alloy has a type system that supports overloading and sub-typing, and allows the detection of many erroneous expressions that could render the specification trivially unsatisfiable [4]. This makes it more suitable

S. Gnesi and A. Rensink (Eds.): FASE 2014, LNCS 8411, pp. 17–31, 2014.
© Springer-Verlag Berlin Heidelberg 2014

for the interactive development of specifications, while Kodkod is more suitable as an engine for automated analysis. This is particularly true because, unlike Alloy, Kodkod allows the specification of *partial instances* – *a priori* partial (but exact) knowledge about a problem's solution. This enables, for example, the specification of expected examples to validate the problem constraints, to bound (and speed-up) model finding within a particular class of instances, or to use Kodkod as a configuration solver, in which the goal is no longer to check the consistency of the constraints but to find an extension of a partial configuration to a full and valid instance of the problem.

Albeit extremely useful, such partial instances are not expressive enough to specify an interesting class of software engineering problems in which the *a priori* knowledge is not exact, but just a description of an idealized (in the sense that it may be unsatisfiable) instance one wishes to approximate. One such application is *model repair*. While interactively developing models, users often introduce inconsistencies. Manually repairing them to meet meta-model constraints is tedious and many times unfeasible due to model size or the complexity of the constraints. As such, tools for automatic model repair abound, and they all attempt to produce minimal repairs that yield valid models that are as close as possible to the original. Closely related is *data repair*. Programs typically assume the consistency of their data, but it can sometimes be corrupted by bugs or erroneous/malicious inputs, leading to unpredictable behavior. A conservative approach to tackle this problem is to regularly check data integrity and gracefully terminate execution when problems are found. An alternative is to repair data on the fly and allow the program to resume execution. Some data repair tools resort to model finders to accommodate complex integrity constraints, needing *ad hoc* procedures to achieve repair minimality. While model repair is concerned with intra-model consistency, a *bidirectional model transformation* [3] tries to solve the problem of inter-model consistency. Given a consistency relation between two meta-models, the goal is to derive forward and backward transformations to propagate updates between conforming models. Ideally they should satisfy the *principle of least change*, meaning that the inconsistent target model must be kept as intact as possible.

Model finders are excellent for *scenario exploration*, namely finding concrete instances of a specification to help users understand and validate it. Any interesting specification is likely to have many (or an infinite number of) possible scenarios, and tools have been proposed to help users parameterize and guide the search to yield interesting (namely, minimal) scenarios [12]. Even so, sometimes it takes considerable manual work to produce an interesting and revealing scenario, and it would be quite useful if such interesting scenarios could be reused and automatically adjusted every time the specification is changed, to highlight the consequences of such modifications. To do so, the model finder must have the ability to specify a previous instance as a target to be approximated by the next solving iteration.

The potential for such optimization extensions to solvers has long been recognized in the SAT solving community, with a plethora of solvers now supporting some sort of *maximum satisfiability* problem (Max-SAT). However, as argued above, SAT solvers are not the ideal target for the described applications. The contribution of this paper is precisely to show how such optimization features can be seamlessly integrated in a higher-level model finder. In particular, we will show how Kodkod partial instances can be extended to support the specification of target instances, and how the analysis of Kodkod problems can be adapted to effectively yield instances that are as close as possible to the specified targets. With this extension, Kodkod can be used to directly implement the above applications, without having to resort to *ad hoc* procedures to constrain the desirable optimal solutions.

In the next section, we present a brief overview of Kodkod. In Sect. 3 we show how it can be extended to support targets in partial instances. Section 4 evaluates the effectiveness of the proposed extension, by resorting to two case studies illustrative of the above applications. Section 5 presents some related work and Sect. 6 points some conclusions and ideas for future work.

2   An Overview of Kodkod

A Kodkod problem $\mathcal{P}$ consists of:

- A universe declaration $\mathcal{U}$, which consists of a set of atoms.
- A set of relation declarations: given a relation r, its declaration $r :_k [r_L, r_U]$ consists of its arity k and two relational constants r_L and r_U, denoting its lower- and upper-bounds, respectively. A relational constant of arity k is just a set of tuples of size k, that is, sequences of atoms of length k drawn from $\mathcal{U}$.
- A relational logic formula whose free relational variables are part of the above declarations. Relational logic is essentially first order logic with transitive closure, extended with relational algebra operators (such as composition, converse or union), allowing us to build complex relational expressions out of simpler ones. These operators enable a navigational (OO-like) style that simplifies property specification for non-logic experts, and transitive closure is key to specify common reachability properties.

A solution to a problem is a model, or instance, of its formula – a binding to the declared relations that makes the formula true. The lower-bounds specify tuples that must be present in every solution, and thus can be used to express *a priori* knowledge about the problem (with the positive side-effect of speeding up model finding). The union of the lower-bounds is known as a *partial instance*.

Figure 1 presents a Kodkod problem, that will later be adapted to a simple case study illustrative of data repair. Suppose we are given a directed graph with nodes A, B, C, and D and edges A $\rightarrow$ B, B $\rightarrow$ C, and C $\rightarrow$ B. Imagine that this is a dependency graph between software services, and we wish to color the different *strongly connected components* (SCCs) with different colors (Red, Green, Blue, and Yellow), denoting for example the nodes in a distributed network on which to deploy the services – the idea would be to map services in the same SCC to

{A, B, C, D, Red, Green, Blue, Yellow}

Node :₁ [{A, B, C, D}, {A, B, C, D}]
adj   :₂ [{⟨A, B⟩, ⟨B, C⟩, ⟨C, B⟩}, {⟨A, B⟩, ⟨B, C⟩, ⟨C, B⟩}]
color :₂ [∅, {⟨A, Red⟩, ⟨A, Green⟩, ⟨A, Blue⟩, ⟨A, Yellow⟩, ⟨B, Red⟩, . . .}]

all n : Node | one n.color
all n, m : Node | (n in m.*adj and m in n.*adj) iff (n.color = m.color)

Fig. 1. A Kodkod problem to color SCCs

the same node in order to minimize the communication overload between them. Of course, we could run Tarjan's algorithm [17] to find such components in linear time, but here we'll resort to Kodkod instead, as this is a simple example that illustrates well the need for partial instances and the usefulness of transitive closure.

In the universe of the problem we declare atoms to represent each of the nodes and the available colors. We then declare three relations: the set Node (in Kodkod sets are just relations with arity 1) containing all the nodes of the graph, the binary relation adj describing its vertices, and a binary relation color whose value is unknown but is restricted by the upper bound to be a valid assignment from nodes to colors. The value of Node and adj is known *a priori* (as signaled by the equal lower- and upper-bounds). The problem does not declare a relation for the available colors since there is no need to mention that set in the constraints. The model finder will in this case act as a configuration solver, that is, extend this partial instance to a complete one satisfying the problem constraints:

- The first states that every node must be assigned a color. Notice how relational composition is used to navigate the model structure: n.color is a set containing all colors associated with node n. Kodkod syntax also provides handy keywords to check the cardinality of sets. Here we use one to force the set of colors associated with each node to be a singleton.
- The second states that nodes share the same color iff they are accessible from each other (that is, they are in the same SCC). To compute the set of all nodes accessible from n we compose it with the transitive and reflexive closure of the relation adj, determined with the unary operator *.

Expressing this problem directly at the SAT level would be very cumbersome, and it exposes very well the elegance and compactness provided by relational algebra operators and transitive closure.

Kodkod problems are analyzed by translation to off-the-shelf SAT solvers. Each relation r of arity k is represented by a k-dimensional matrix with capacity for $|\mathcal{U}|^k$ propositional variables. Given the relation declaration each entry of the matrix is filled as follows:

$$r[i_1, \ldots, i_k] = \begin{cases} \top & \text{if } \langle A_{i_1}, \ldots, A_{i_k} \rangle \in r_L \\ r_{i_1, \ldots, i_k} & \text{if } \langle A_{i_1}, \ldots, A_{i_k} \rangle \in r_U \setminus r_L \\ \bot & \text{otherwise} \end{cases}$$

Entries corresponding to tuples in the lower-bound are set to true; a propositional variable is created for each entry denoting a tuple whose membership to the relation is still unknown; the others are just set to false. Relational formulas are translated to propositional formulas by interpreting relational operators as matrix operations. For example, composition is the product, union is the sum, and intersection is the Hadamard product. Existential quantifiers are skolemized to yield witnesses to the quantified variables, and universal quantifiers are expanded (note that every relational expression is bounded). Kodkod performs several optimizations to decrease SAT complexity. The most significant is symmetry breaking – since atoms are uninterpreted, many instances are isomorphic, and it is very unlikely that the user wants to retrieve them all. For example, in the above problem a possible solution is to assign $\{\langle A, Red\rangle, \langle B, Green\rangle, \langle C, Green\rangle, \langle D, Blue\rangle\}$ to color, and any permutation of the colors will yield another solution that is essentially the same.

3   Extending Partial Instances with Targets

We propose to extend Kodkod partial instances by allowing targets in the declaration of relations. More specifically, a declaration can also take the form $r :_k [r_L, r_U, r_T]$, where r_T is a constant stating an *a priori* known goal for the value of r. Obviously, such declarations must satisfy the constraint $r_L \subseteq r_T \subseteq r_U$. Besides making the respective formula true, a model of a problem with targets is a binding that must also be as close as possible to the specified targets, that is, that requires the fewest mutations (tuple deletions or insertions) to make the target a satisfying binding. When seeing instances as graphs, a valid instance should then minimize the *graph edit distance* (GED) to the target. Formally, a binding B is an instance of a problem $\mathcal{P}$ with targets (denoted by $B \models \mathcal{P}$) if it satisfies the declared lower- and upper-bounds, makes its formula true, and, for all possible bindings B' that also satisfy the bounds and the formula, we have

$$\sum_{r\in\mathcal{T}} |B(r) \ominus r_T| \leq \sum_{r\in\mathcal{T}} |B'(r) \ominus r_T|$$

Here $\mathcal{T}$ denotes the set of relations that have targets declared, and $B(r) \ominus r_T$ denotes the symmetric difference between sets $B(r)$ (the value of relation r according to B) and r_T, i.e., $(B(r) - r_T) \cup (r_T - B(r))$. This summation just counts the number of mutations in all relations.

Going back to the example of the previous section, suppose that services A, B, C and D were previously assigned to nodes Red, Green, Blue and Yellow, respectively, and that we wish to reassign services to nodes taking into account the problem constraints and minimizing node transfers. Such (re-)configuration can be done using Kodkod with targets, by changing the declaration of color to[1]

color $:_2$ $[\emptyset, \{\langle A, Red\rangle, \langle A, Green\rangle, \langle A, Blue\rangle, \langle A, Yellow\rangle, \langle B, Red\rangle, \ldots\},$
$\{\langle \mathbf{A, Red}\rangle, \langle \mathbf{B, Green}\rangle, \langle \mathbf{C, Blue}\rangle, \langle \mathbf{D, Yellow}\rangle\}]$

---

[1] Bold type will be used to highlight targets in relation declarations.

According to the above semantics, the only two valid instances of this problem bind color to either $\{\langle A, Red\rangle, \langle B, Green\rangle, \langle C, Green\rangle, \langle D, Yellow\rangle\}$ or $\{\langle A, Red\rangle, \langle B, Blue\rangle, \langle C, Blue\rangle, \langle D, Yellow\rangle\}$. Both these instances are at distance 2 from the specified target, requiring one tuple deletion and one tuple insertion (to change the color of either B or C, respectively). The next sections present two different approaches to the analysis of a Kodkod problem with targets.

3.1   Analysis via Cardinality Constraints

Some SAT solvers allow the specification of *cardinality constraints*, a bound on the number of literals within a given set that can be assigned true. Given a set of literals $\{l_1, \ldots, l_n\}$ a cardinality constraint takes the form $l_1 + \ldots + l_n \gtrless k$, where $\gtrless$ is any of the comparisons in $\{\leq, =, \geq\}$, to specify *atmost*, *exactly*, and *atleast* bounds, respectively.

Cardinality constraints can be encoded with standard CNF boolean formulas and thus handled by standard SAT solvers. The best known encoding for *atmost* constraints requires $n \log^2 k$ extra clauses [1]. They can also be handled natively by the solver by tweaking the standard unit propagation and conflict analysis procedures [9]: the former is updated to keep track of how many literals in the set have been assigned true and propagates the negation of the remaining when the limit is reached; when a conflict is detected, the latter adds a conflict clause with the literals that were assigned true and rewinds those assignments.

The analysis of a Kodkod problem with targets can be done by creating an *atleast* constraint describing the structure of the ideal instance (i.e., containing a positive literal for each tuple in the targets and a negative one for each allowed tuple not in the targets), and then solving with decreasing bounds starting from the total size of the targets until SAT or reaching 0 (or dually using *atmost* constraints, negating all literals, and starting from 0). Formally, the CNF formula generated by Kodkod is repeatedly extended with the cardinality constraint

$$\sum_{r \in \mathcal{T}, \langle A_{i_1}, \ldots, A_{i_k}\rangle \in r_T} r_{i_1, \ldots, i_k} + \sum_{r \in \mathcal{T}, \langle A_{i_1}, \ldots, A_{i_k}\rangle \in r_U \setminus r_L \setminus r_T} \neg r_{i_1, \ldots, i_k} \geq n$$

with n starting with value $\sum_{r \in T} |r_U - r_L|$ (the number of propositional variables created by Kodkod for the relations with targets), and iteratively decreased until SAT or reaching 0. If the result is UNSAT for $n = 0$ then the Kodkod problem has no valid instance. Notice that this iterative process is performed after all Kodkod simplifications are done, and thus they can be reused in every incremental call of the SAT solver. As detailed in Sect. 4, one of the consequences of this approach is that the performance of the analysis will decrease as the number of mutations required to make the target a valid instance increases.

3.2   Analysis via PMax-SAT Solvers

Max-SAT is an optimization extension to SAT where, instead of finding an assignment that satisfies all the clauses, one tries to find an assignment that maximizes the number of clauses that can be satisfied. Unfortunately, in real world optimization-like problems, there are constraints that are mandatory and whose unsatisfaction deems the solution meaningless. The *partial maximum satisfiability problem* (PMax-SAT) was introduced [11,2] precisely to address such scenarios: clauses can either be *soft* or *hard*, and the goal is to find an assignment that satisfies all *hard* clauses and that maximizes the number of satisfied *soft* clauses. A typical approach to this problem takes advantage of the UNSAT core extraction feature already present in many SAT solvers [5]: an UNSAT core is a subset of the original clauses whose conjunction is still unsatisfiable, and with an iterative procedure it is possible, by introducing extra variables and clauses, to relax one soft clause in the UNSAT core at a time until a satisfying assignment is found.

To analyze an extended Kodkod problem with targets using PMAX-SAT solvers it suffices to generate, besides the normal hard clauses originating from the problem formula, a set of soft clauses containing:

- One soft clause for each $\langle A_{i_1}, \ldots, A_{i_k} \rangle \in r_T$ and $r \in \mathcal{T}$, containing a single literal $r_{i_1, \ldots, i_k}$.
- One soft clause for each $\langle A_{i_1}, \ldots, A_{i_k} \rangle \in r_U \setminus r_L \setminus r_T$ and $r \in \mathcal{T}$, containing a single literal $\neg r_{i_1, \ldots, i_k}$.

Likewise to the implementation with cardinality constraints, these soft clauses describe the ideal solution specified in the targets. If the hard clauses are satisfiable, maximization of the satisfied soft clauses will yield a binding that is as close as possible to the target.

3.3   Symmetry Breaking

One of the optimizations performed by Kodkod is symmetry breaking. A permutation l of the atoms in $\mathcal{U}$ is a *symmetry* of the problem iff, for all bindings B, we have $B \models \mathcal{P} \iff l(B) \models \mathcal{P}$. Here $l(B)$ is the binding that results from applying l to all atoms in B. A symmetry induces an equivalence relation in the bindings, and the goal of symmetry breaking is to restrict model finding to yield only one witness of each equivalence class. One of the main results in [19] states that l is a symmetry iff it fixes all relational constants in the lower- and upperbounds of the problem (i.e., maps each constant to itself). Based on this result, an efficient algorithm is proposed to compute such permutations: this algorithm is not complete, in the sense that it does not always generates all permutations that fix all constants in the bounds, but in practice succeeds in doing so for most problems.

The above result is no longer true when considering targets: namely, there are symmetries that may not fix the constants in the targets. Consider for example our running example: the permutation {Red → Red, Green → Blue, Blue → Green, Yellow → Yellow} is a symmetry of the problem (note that the two instances of the problem are not truly different – the essence of the solution is that both B and C should have the same color and it should be one of their original colors) but it does not fix the target of the relation color. However, it can be shown that any permutation that fixes the lower- and upper-bounds and the targets is still a symmetry of the problem[2], and as such we can still reuse Kodkod algorithm for symmetry breaking, provided it is adapted to take targets into account. In practice, when targets are present, the algorithm will be less complete, in the sense that it will miss more symmetries than when no targets are specified. For example, the above symmetry will not be detected. As an example of a symmetry that would be detected, consider the case of adding to the problem a new (unconnected) node and two new colors: in this case only one instance will be produced, assigning one of the new colors to the new node.

4   Evaluation

We have implemented the proposed extension in Kodkod 2.0, and added support for the following solvers: Sat4J 2.3.5 (http://www.sat4j.org), a pure Java SAT solver that handles both native cardinality constraints and PMax-SAT problems, and Yices 1.0.39 (http://yices.csl.sri.com), a SMT solver claimed to be competitive as a standard SAT and PMax-SAT solver.

4.1   Case-Study 1: Data Repair

To evaluate our approach we developed two case studies. The first illustrates the usage of targets in data (and model) repair, and builds on our running example of coloring the SCCs of a graph. To assess the scalability of the proposed analysis techniques, we will resort to a parametrized version of this problem. Suppose we have a directed graph of size n (n nodes named N_1 to N_n) organized as a chain, i.e., with $n - 1$ arcs connecting node N_i with node N_{i+1} for every $i < n$. Obviously, in this graph there are n SCCs, each containing exactly 1 node. These SCCs are currently colored with colors C_1 to C_n. Suppose now that the graph is updated and a new arc is added, between node N_n and node $N_{n-\Delta}$, where $\Delta < n$. The updated graph is depicted in Fig. 2. This change puts the last $\Delta + 1$ nodes together in the same SCC, and will (at least) require the color of Δ nodes to also change, in order for the problem constraints to be satisfied (requiring 2Δ mutations to the original color). Figure 3 shows how this problem can be specified in Kodkod with targets. Note how the adj relation is set to the updated graph configuration, and the target of color is set to the previous color assignment.

---

[2] In addition to Lemmas 1 and 2 in [18], that prove that a permutation l that fixes all constants in declarations preserves the validity of bounds and formulas, respectively, it suffices to show that it also preserves the distance to the targets: for all $r \in \mathcal{T}$, since $l(r_T) = r_T$, then, by applying standard equational laws relating permutations with set operations, we have $|l(B(r)) \ominus r_T| = |l(B(r)) \ominus l(r_T)| = |l(B(r) \ominus r_T)| = |B(r) \ominus r_T|$.

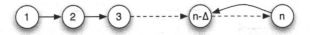

Fig. 2. Adding a backlink to a chain with n nodes

$\{N_1, \ldots, N_n, C_1, \ldots, C_n\}$

Node $:_1$ $[\{N_1, \ldots, N_n\}]$
adj $\quad :_2$ $[\{\langle N_1, N_2\rangle, \langle N_2, N_3\rangle, \ldots, \langle N_n, N_{n-\Delta}\rangle\}, \{\langle N_1, N_2\rangle, \langle N_2, N_3\rangle, \ldots, \langle N_n, N_{n-\Delta}\rangle\}]$
color $:_2$ $[\emptyset, \{\langle N_1, C_1\rangle, \langle N_1, C_2\rangle, \langle N_1, C_3\rangle \ldots\}, \{\langle N_1, C_1\rangle, \langle N_2, C_2\rangle, \ldots\}]$

all n : Node | one n.color
all n, m : Node | (n in m.*adj and m in n.*adj) iff (n.color = m.color)

Fig. 3. Kodkod problem to update the color of SCCs

4.2   Case-Study 2: Bidirectional Transformation

The second case study illustrates the potential of targets in bidirectional model transformation. This case study is a very simplified version of the mapping between class diagrams and relational database schemas [3]. The basic idea of the forward transformation is to map a class marked as persistent to a table with the same name, mapping also its attributes (including inherited ones) to columns. If the schema is updated, the backwards transformation can be used to propagate the changes back to the class diagram. Since the forward transformation loses information (namely about non-persistent classes) the backward transformation must consider not only the updated schema but also the original class diagram.

Figure 4 depicts a (parametrized) example of a simplified class diagram with n persistent classes. There are $2n$ classes in total, denoted $C_1, \ldots, C_{2n}$. Class C_i is named N_i, class C_{i+1} extends class C_i for $i < n$, and C_{i+n} extend class C_i for $i \leq n$. Classes $C_1, \ldots, C_n$ are marked as persistent (grey shade) and each of these has an attribute with the same name as the class (whose type will be ignored in this example). Applying the forward transformation to this class diagram produces a schema with n tables $T_1, \ldots, T_n$, named $N_1, \ldots, N_n$ respectively, with each T_i, for $i \leq n$, containing i columns named $N_1, \ldots, N_i$. Suppose that the name of the first Δ tables is changed from N_i to N_{i+n} and we would like to propagate this update back to the source model. A backwards transformation that follows the principle of least change should simply move the persistent flag from class C_i to class C_{i+n} for every $i \leq \Delta$ (requiring 2Δ mutations).

Using Kodkod extended with targets such least change backwards transformation can be easily implemented, as shown in Fig. 5. First we declare relations to represent both models. Sets Class, Table and Name capture the model elements. Relations name$_C$ and name$_T$ capture the association between classes and tables and their names, respectively. Similarly, attributes and columns map classes to their attributes and tables to columns, respectively. Finally, persistent denotes the set of persistent classes and parent the inheritance relationship. The values of

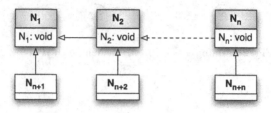

Fig. 4. Simple class diagram example

$\{C_1, \ldots, C_{2n}, N_1, \ldots, N_{2n}, T_1, \ldots, T_n\}$

Class	$:_1$	$[\emptyset, \{C_1, \ldots, C_{2n}\}, \{\mathbf{C_1}, \ldots, \mathbf{C_{2n}}\}]$
Table	$:_1$	$[\{T_1, \ldots, T_n\}, \{T_1, \ldots, T_n\}]$
Name	$:_1$	$[\emptyset, \{N_1, \ldots, N_{2n}\}, \{\mathbf{N_1}, \ldots, \mathbf{N_{2n}}\}]$
$name_C$	$:_2$	$[\emptyset, \{\langle C_1, N_1 \rangle, \langle C_1, N_2 \rangle, \ldots\}, \{\langle \mathbf{C_1}, \mathbf{N_1} \rangle, \langle \mathbf{C_2}, \mathbf{N_2} \rangle, \ldots\}]$
$name_T$	$:_2$	$[\{\langle T_1, N_{n+1} \rangle, \ldots, \langle T_{\Delta+1}, N_{\Delta+1} \rangle \ldots\}, \{\langle T_1, N_{n+1} \rangle, \ldots, \langle T_{\Delta+1}, N_{\Delta+1} \rangle \ldots\}]$
attributes	$:_2$	$[\emptyset, \{\langle C_1, N_1 \rangle, \langle C_1, N_2 \rangle, \ldots\}, \{\langle \mathbf{C_1}, \mathbf{N_1} \rangle, \langle \mathbf{C_2}, \mathbf{N_2} \rangle, \ldots\}]$
columns	$:_2$	$[\{\langle T_1, N_1 \rangle, \langle T_2, N_1 \rangle, \langle T_2, N_2 \rangle, \ldots\}, \{\langle T_1, N_1 \rangle, \langle T_2, N_1 \rangle, \langle T_2, N_2 \rangle, \ldots\}]$
persistent	$:_1$	$[\emptyset, \{C_1, \ldots, C_{2n}\}, \{\mathbf{C_1}, \ldots, \mathbf{C_n}\}]$
parent	$:_2$	$[\emptyset, \{\langle C_1, C_1 \rangle, \langle C_1, C_2 \rangle, \ldots, \}, \{\langle \mathbf{C_2}, \mathbf{C_1} \rangle, \langle \mathbf{C_3}, \mathbf{C_2} \rangle, \ldots \langle \mathbf{C_{n+1}}, \mathbf{C_1} \rangle, \ldots\}]$

persistent in Class	all c : Class | one $c.name_C$
attributes in Class $\rightarrow$ Name	all n : Name | lone $name_C.n$
$name_C$ in Class $\rightarrow$ Name	all c : Class | lone c.parent
parent in Class $\rightarrow$ Class	all c : Class | c not in c.^parent

all c : persistent \| some t : Table \| $c.name_C = t.name_T$ and c.*parent.attributes$=$t.columns
all t : Table \| some c : persistent \| $c.name_C = t.name_T$ and c.*parent.attributes$=$t.columns

Fig. 5. Kodkod problem specifying a bidirectional object to relational mapping

the relations that represent the updated schema are fixed in the partial instance (by setting the lower- and upper-bounds equal). To ensure the principle of least change, targets are used to capture the original class diagram, whose update is to be determined by model finding. The first set of constraints specifies the class diagram meta-model constraints, such as, uniqueness of class names (note how relational composition is used in $name_C.n$ to determine all classes that have name n), or non circularity of the inheritance relationship (expression c.^parent uses the transitive closure of relation parent to determine all ancestors of c). The last two constraints specify the desired consistency relation, in a style similar to the bidirectional model transformation language QVT-R standardized by OMG [13]. Using the *forall-there-exists* pattern, every persistent class is required to have a matching table and vice-versa. By matching we mean a table with the same name and columns for every declared and inherited attribute of the class. Again (reflexive) transitive closure is key to specify this constraint.

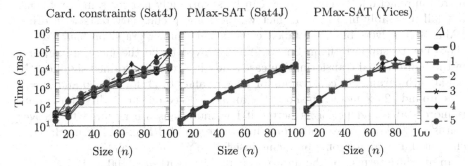

Fig. 6. Results for the graph SCC coloring problem

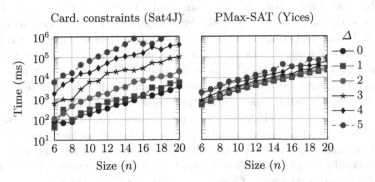

Fig. 7. Results for the bidirectional object to relational mapping problem

4.3   Discussion

The first case study was tested with size $10 \leq n \leq 100$ (with increments of 10), and for $0 \leq \Delta \leq 5$. The results can be seen in Fig. 6. The vertical axis shows solving time in milliseconds and log-scale; the horizontal axis shows the problem size; and in different line styles we have the timings for different values of Δ. The second case study was tested with sizes $6 \leq n \leq 20$, and for $0 \leq \Delta \leq 5$. The results can be seen in Fig. 7. The tests were conducted on an Intel CORE i7 3517U with 4Gb of memory and the Ubuntu 13.4 operating system.

In both problems the total time to find a solution grows exponentially with the size of the problem. For the first one, the analysis using PMax-SAT clearly outperforms the one with cardinality constraints for values of $\Delta > 3$, and is only slightly worst in the remaining cases. For example, using Sat4J, for $n = 100$ and $\Delta = 5$ the former is around 5.8× faster than the latter. This is due to the iterative nature of the analysis with cardinality constraints, that requires as many calls to the solver as the number of mutations required to recover consistency. The analysis with PMax-SAT is more insensitive to Δ, as confirmed also in the bidirectional transformation example. In Fig. 7 we present no results for Sat4J with PMax-SAT because this solver failed to handle the problem in question for most values of $\Delta > 0$. In fact, PMax-SAT solvers tend to exhibit a more unpredictable behavior: they can be surprisingly fast for some problems, but fail miserably in others. In fact we did some preliminary tests with other PMax-SAT solvers but they failed even in our simpler graph problem, so we chose not to support them. So far, Yices proved to be the more stable, and in the bidirectional transformation case study it also outperformed significantly Sat4J with cardinality constraints for bigger values of Δ: for $n = 20$ and $\Delta = 5$ it is around 12.6× faster. In short, the analysis based on cardinality constraints is more stable and performs better if few mutations are required to recover consistency. When more mutations may be required, PMax-SAT is much more efficient, but may for some problems just fail to produce a solution.

In absolute terms, for the data repair problem with $n = 100$ and $\Delta = 5$ the best solver was Sat4J with PMax-SAT, taking around 17s to yield a solution. In this problem we have a total of 200 atoms and 100 edges in the targets. In the bidirectional transformation case study, for $n = 20$ and $\Delta = 5$ the best solver was Yices with PMax-SAT, taking 93s to yield a solution. Here we have a total of 100 atoms and 200 edges in the targets. For applications like scenario exploration, where instances are typical small, this performance suffices. For model repair and bidirectional transformation, the proposed approach will only be able to tackle realistic models of medium size, within the hundreds of model elements. Finally, we also checked if the specification of targets induced performance gains, when compared to normal solving without targets. Obviously, in the latter case the returned instance can differ substantially from the target. In the first case study the analysis with targets using Yices is roughly 3.8× faster in average for $n = 100$, being 6.7× faster for the case of Sat4J with PMax-SAT. In the other case study, for $n = 20$ it is in average 1.8× slower using Yices and 12× slower using Sat4J with cardinality constraints. Although inconclusive, this suggests that targets may sometimes considerably speed-up solving, and using PMax-SAT does not impose a big penalty, besides, of course, yielding optimum solutions.

5   Related Work

This research was mainly motivated by our previous work on Echo [7,8], a tool for bidirectional model transformation obeying the principle of least change. Echo works by embedding both QVT-R transformations and the meta-models they relate into Alloy [6]. One of the least change criteria supported by Echo is precisely to minimize GED. To do so, Echo uses an analysis technique similar to cardinality constraints, but encodes them directly in Alloy (using a relational logic formula) using the size of the symmetric difference of relations. To avoid problems with overflows this encoding requires the usage of the Forbid Overflow option, that is currently supported by a modified Kodkod version [10]. Moreover, for each iteration of the search algorithm (starting at GED 0 and with successive increments until SAT) a new Kodkod problem must be generated, preventing incremental solving, namely the reuse of simplifications performed in previous iterations. We implemented our first case study with this *ad hoc* approach and compared the results to the ones presented in Sect. 4. The implementation with targets and analysis via native cardinality constraints outperformed the previous technique by 4.3× in average for $n = 100$. The gains with PMax-SAT would be even higher. Given these promising results, we are currently reimplementing Echo on top of the extended Kodkod proposed in this paper.

Most of the existing model repair tools are not fully automatic, in the sense that the suggested fixes consist of sequences of abstract edit operations (which the user must manually instantiate to actually repair the models). The work of Egyed et al. is a prime example of this approach [14]. Fully automatic model repair tools usually rely on solvers and use *ad hoc* non-optimal procedures to minimize repairs. Some of them already target Kodkod (or Alloy) due to the effectiveness of relational logic in specifying rich constraints. For example, Van Der Straeten et al. [16] assessed the viability of using Kodkod to perform model repair. To minimize repairs, they first use an external (non specified) procedure to identify tuples suspect of causing the inconsistency, which are then removed from the lower-bound of the respective relations. The upper-bound of those relations is also relaxed to allow tuple insertions. This technique does not ensure minimality of the repairs, only handles one inconsistency at a time, and is still not fully automatized (e.g., the relaxation of upper-bounds is performed manually). This study concluded that, performance wise, Kodkod is not viable for model repair of large size models. Our evaluation does not invalidate this conclusion, but as shown in Sect. 4, by resorting to specialized SAT solving procedures (namely PMax-SAT) substantial performance gains can be obtained, somehow alleviating this problem, without having to resort to approximate solutions.

Zaeem and Khurshid proposed an Alloy/Kodkod based data repair framework that attempts to keep the perturbation to the faulty data structure to a minimum [21]. To do so, they try to find a minimal subset of relations that needs to be relaxed (that is, allowed to contain any possible tuple) in order to recover consistency. Several algorithms are proposed to find such minimal subset, for example exhaustive search (first relax one relation at a time, then two relations, and so on). Likewise to [16] this heuristic method is not guaranteed to yield a minimal repair, and its implementation using the standard version of Kodkod is far from trivial, unlike with targets.

Xiong el at. [20] propose a technique for generating minimal fixes for software configuration, based on Reiter's theory of diagnosis [15]. This theory is quite similar to PMax-SAT, in that it tries to find a minimal subset of soft clauses that can be removed to restore satisfiability (and to do so also resorts to the UNSAT core extraction). To be able to handle constraints over integers and strings, this fix generation technique is implemented using a SMT solver. Although the support for primitive types is very convenient, the logic supported by this tool is quite limited, namely lacking the expressiveness afforded by the relational logic (and closures), that makes Kodkod so useful for many software engineering applications. The ideal would be to combine both, namely analyze relational specifications using SMT solvers, a technique we intend to explore in the future.

Minimality is also key in scenario exploration. Aluminum [12] is a modification of the Alloy Analyzer that allows the visualization of minimal scenarios, i.e, instances from which no tuple can be removed without becoming UNSAT. The algorithm proposed to find such minimal instances can be adapted to handle targets, provided the closest instance can be found just by resorting to tuple insertions (or dually just deletions). For example it could not handle any of our case studies, which required both insertions and deletions to recover satisfiability.

6   Conclusion

In this paper we have shown how the Kodkod model finder can be extended with targets, allowing the specification of *a priori* knowledge about the ideal solution for a problem. We have also shown how the analysis of such extended Kodkod problems can be performed (to yield instances that are as close as possible to the specified targets), by resorting to two different techniques: SAT solvers with native cardinality constraints and PMax-SAT solvers. As illustrated by our case studies, this extension simplifies considerably the implementation of many software engineering applications where such targets were needed: Kodkod's relational logic allows a very direct encoding of constraints, and the native support for targets renders obsolete *ad hoc* techniques previously implemented in tools that used model finders (in particular Kodkod) to implement such applications. The proposed analysis techniques deem the approach viable for problems of medium size. Native cardinality constraints are more stable and efficient when the optimum solution is very close to the target, but PMax-SAT solvers can largely outperform them when reaching the optimum requires several mutations.

In the future we intend to implement some optimizations to our analysis procedure, namely trying to apply some of the techniques described in [21] to infer which relations can be given exact bounds instead of targets. For example, in our bidirectional transformation case study, if we could somehow infer that only the persistent relation needs to be changed, solving would be substantially faster. We also intend to implement a larger set of case studies and real applications in order to validate our conclusions. In particular, we are currently reimplementing our Echo [8] bidirectional model transformation tool using the proposed Kodkod extension. We also intend to implement a scenario exploration feature in the Alloy Analyzer, to allow the automatic readjustment of a previously calculated instance in order to accommodate changes in the specification.

Acknowledgments. This work is funded by ERDF - European Regional Development Fund through the COMPETE Programme (operational programme for competitiveness) and by national funds through the FCT - Fundação para a Ciência e a Tecnologia (Portuguese Foundation for Science and Technology) within project FATBIT with reference FCOMP-01-0124-FEDER-020532. The second author is also sponsored by FCT grant SFRH/BD/69585/2010.

References

1. Asín, R., Nieuwenhuis, R., Oliveras, A., Rodríguez-Carbonell, E.: Cardinality networks: a theoretical and empirical study. Constraints 16(2), 195–221 (2011)
2. Cha, B., Iwama, K., Kambayashi, Y., Miyazaki, S.: Local search algorithms for partial MAXSAT. In: AAAI 1997, pp. 263–268. AAAI (1997)
3. Czarnecki, K., Foster, J., Hu, Z., Lämmel, R., Schürr, A., Terwilliger, J.: Bidirectional transformations: A cross-discipline perspective. In: Paige, R.F. (ed.) ICMT 2009. LNCS, vol. 5563, pp. 260–283. Springer, Heidelberg (2009)
4. Edwards, J., Jackson, D., Torlak, E.: A type system for object models. In: FSE 2004, pp. 189–199. ACM (2004)
5. Fu, Z., Malik, S.: On solving the partial MAX-SAT problem. In: Biere, A., Gomes, C.P. (eds.) SAT 2006. LNCS, vol. 4121, pp. 252–265. Springer, Heidelberg (2006)
6. Jackson, D.: Software Abstractions: Logic, Language, and Analysis, revised edn. MIT Press (2012)
7. Macedo, N., Cunha, A.: Implementing QVT-R bidirectional model transformations using Alloy. In: Cortellessa, V., Varró, D. (eds.) FASE 2013. LNCS, vol. 7793, pp. 297–311. Springer, Heidelberg (2013)
8. Macedo, N., Guimarães, T., Cunha, A.: Model repair and transformation with Echo. In: ASE 2013, pp. 694–697. IEEE (2013)
9. Maglalang, J.C.: Native cardinality constraints: More expressive, more efficient constraints. Honors Projects, Paper 19. Illinois Wesleyan University (2012)
10. Milicevic, A., Jackson, D.: Preventing arithmetic overflows in Alloy. In: Derrick, J., Fitzgerald, J., Gnesi, S., Khurshid, S., Leuschel, M., Reeves, S., Riccobene, E. (eds.) ABZ 2012. LNCS, vol. 7316, pp. 108–121. Springer, Heidelberg (2012)
11. Miyazaki, S., Iwama, K., Kambayashi, Y.: Database queries as combinatorial optimization problems. In: CODAS 1996, pp. 448–454 (1996)
12. Nelson, T., Saghafi, S., Dougherty, D.J., Fisler, K., Krishnamurthi, S.: Aluminum: principled scenario exploration through minimality. In: ICSE 2013, pp. 232–241. IEEE (2013)
13. OMG: MOF 2.0 Query/View/Transformation specification (QVT), version 1.1 (January 2011), http://www.omg.org/spec/QVT/1.1/
14. Reder, A., Egyed, A.: Computing repair trees for resolving inconsistencies in design models. In: ASE 2012, pp. 220–229. ACM (2012)
15. Reiter, R.: A theory of diagnosis from first principles. Artificial Intelligence 32(1), 57–95 (1987)
16. Van Der Straeten, R., Pinna Puissant, J., Mens, T.: Assessing the Kodkod Model Finder for Resolving Model Inconsistencies. In: France, R.B., Kuester, J.M., Bordbar, B., Paige, R.F. (eds.) ECMFA 2011. LNCS, vol. 6698, pp. 69–84. Springer, Heidelberg (2011)
17. Tarjan, R.: Depth-first search and linear graph algorithms. SIAM Journal on Computing 1(2), 146–160 (1972)
18. Torlak, E., Jackson, D.: The design of a relational engine. Tech. Rep. MIT-CSAIL-TR-2006-068, MIT (2006)
19. Torlak, E., Jackson, D.: Kodkod: A relational model finder. In: Grumberg, O., Huth, M. (eds.) TACAS 2007. LNCS, vol. 4424, pp. 632–647. Springer, Heidelberg (2007)
20. Xiong, Y., Hubaux, A., She, S., Czarnecki, K.: Generating range fixes for software configuration. In: ICSE 2012, pp. 58–68. IEEE (2012)
21. Nokhbeh Zaeem, R., Khurshid, S.: Contract-based data structure repair using Alloy. In: D'Hondt, T. (ed.) ECOOP 2010. LNCS, vol. 6183, pp. 577–598. Springer, Heidelberg (2010)

Bidirectionally Tolerating Inconsistency: Partial Transformations

Perdita Stevens

School of Informatics
University of Edinburgh

Abstract. A foundational property of bidirectional transformations is that they should be correct: that is, the transformation should succeed in restoring consistency between any models it is given. In practice, however, transformation engines sometimes fail to restore consistency, e.g. because there is no consistent model to return, or because the tool is unable to select a best model to return from among equally good candidates. In this paper, we formalise properties that may nevertheless hold in such circumstances and discuss relationships and implications.

1 Introduction

In software engineering, it has long been understood that data involved in the development of a software system will, at least at certain points, be inconsistent, and that it can be unproductive – or even counterproductive – to try to maintain consistency at all times. Rather, mechanisms are needed to tolerate, manage and understand inconsistency so that it does not threaten the overall aim of the project [3,13,12]. Although consistency is a central notion for bidirectional transformations, tolerating inconsistency has so far not been studied in this context. This paper aims to rectify the situation.

In model-driven development, a bidirectional transformation (abbreviated bx) has two jobs. First, it has to be able to say when two models (or more: but in this paper, for clarity of exposition, we will treat only the case of two) are consistent according to the definition embodied in the transformation. Second, it has to be able to take a pair of models and modify a specified one of them so as to restore consistency. The question of what properties are desirable in such a transformation is an interesting one on which there is a growing literature. Most of it, however, does not allow the bx ever to fail, or to put it more positively, to succeed only partially. Consistency is all-or-nothing, and consistency restoration must always succeed for the bx to be considered *correct*.

Practical model transformation engines, by contrast, frequently fail to restore consistency between models when asked to do so. Although it is useful to try to develop languages and tools that will allow this to happen seldom, we suggest that there is also a need for a formal framework which recognises the inevitability of such failure. Without one, we cannot discuss and reason about the good properties that such "imperfect" bx may still have. Since a bx is usually assumed/required to restore perfect consistency, we could think of a bx that does

S. Gnesi and A. Rensink (Eds.): FASE 2014, LNCS 8411, pp. 32–46, 2014.

not as *partial*, its domain being the pairs of models on which it succeeds in restoring consistency. We shall, in fact, set up a more informative framework than this idea suggests, but, to motivate it, let us first consider three reasons why a bx engine may fail to restore consistency.

Let us assume that we are trying to check and, if necessary, restore consistency between a model m in a model space M and a model n in a model space N (for present purposes a model space may be thought of as just a set of models). In this paper we will consider *state-based* bx that modify just one of the two models, regarding the other as authoritative, so the bx has access to the two models, but not to information about what edits have been performed, traceability links, etc. (But see Section 6 for comment about ongoing work.)

First, it may be that the consistency relation itself is partial. For example, perhaps m and n are not fully consistent, we are asked to modify n to restore consistency, but there is no model $n' \in N$ that is fully consistent with m. This may happen for a number of reasons. For example, it may be that the notion of consistency being used imposes a condition on m which is currently not satisfied (say, "m and n are consistent if they both satisfy all their metamodel constraints, and ..." where m fails a metamodel constraint). In this case, since the bx has been asked to modify only n, regarding m as authoritative, it will not be able to succeed. What, then, should the tool do? Should it simply make no changes and report failure? This may be the only reasonable course (corresponding to a simple admission that (m, n) is not in the domain of this partial bx). On the other hand, perhaps there are certain changes that, even though they cannot completely restore consistency, bring the models closer to being consistent. We might prefer that the tool make these changes, leaving a "smaller" (in an appropriate sense) inconsistency that must be tolerated.

Second, it may be that there is a fully consistent model n', but the transformation engine, for some reason, may fail to return it. Perhaps we know as a matter of theory that a fully consistent model always exists, but finding it may require an infeasible amount of exploration and backtracking, so that a "quick and dirty" tool that achieves some improvement, leaving human intelligence to do the rest, is preferable. Another reason might be a desire to limit the kind of changes that the bx engine is allowed to make to a model. We see such a case in practice where the "models" are file systems and the "bx engine" is a file synchroniser. Typically, users are quite happy for the file synchroniser to propagate "non-conflicting" changes. However, where "conflicting" changes have been made to files on each side, users typically prefer to resolve conflicts manually. In this case, the consistency restoration that does not restore perfect consistency is actually preferred to one that did, because it is considered more trustworthy. A bx that does not have to resolve every problem and restore consistency perfectly may be faster, more understandable, easier to verify and generally safer than one that restores perfect consistency at all costs.

Third, it may be that there is more than one consistent model that the bx tool could return, but the transformation does not provide information that would allow the tool to choose between them, either through oversight or because the best choice depends on factors that are not formalisable. There are then three options, any of which may be preferred depending on the circumstances. The first two are variants of non-deterministic (but total) transformations. The tool might make an arbitrary (or heuristically guided) choice of consistent model, e.g., by returning the first one that is found by some search algorithm. This may be fine if the differences between the different consistent models are really arbitrary, i.e. of no interest to users of either model. The tool may find all consistent models, and return them, or a concise description of them, to the user for the user to pick one, with the transformation not being considered complete until the choice has been made. This is difficult to make practical, tending to be expensive both in computational and human effort terms. In this paper we wish to consider a third option: that the tool returns a model n' which is not fully consistent with m, but which is, in a sense to be formalised, more consistent with m than n was, incorporating only "uncontroversial" modifications. For example, n' may add model elements that are common to all fully consistent models, but not those that are present in only some fully consistent models. The user may modify n' further to make it fully consistent at a later date, but need not do so immediately. (Perhaps, even, a later change to m and a later application of a bx may obviate the need to edit the model on the N side manually at all.)

In each case, it is desirable to have a framework in which we can unambiguously state the properties that a bx has or should have, so that ultimately these properties can be verified and guaranteed, granting the developer greater confidence about what applying the bx will do.

Such a framework also facilitates modular development of, and reasoning about, total bx, which can now be built by chaining partial bx. This lets us separate concerns, e.g., let different partial bxes fix different parts of a model, if these are sufficiently independent. Or we may let one partial bx delete elements, and another add. We say more about this in Section 4. To talk about the properties of the parts and about their composition, we need to make explicit the existence of situations that are in-between perfect consistency and "all bets are off" inconsistency.

The remainder of this paper is structured as follows. In Section 2 we discuss related work. In Section 3 we introduce some fundamental definitions. In Section 4 we illustrate these with examples. Section 5 discusses how different partial bidirectional transformations, involving the same or different model spaces, may be related. In Section 6 we conclude and briefly discuss further work to be done.

2   Related Work

Much of the work on bx is done with the special kind of bidirectional transformations that are lenses[4], in which one model space (the *view*) is a strict abstraction of the other (the *source*). In this case[1] $\overrightarrow{R}$ is replaced by get, a one-argument function from concrete source to abstract view, and $\overleftarrow{R}$ by put, a

---

[1] Forward reference to notation defined in Sect 3.

two-argument function which, given an updated view and a source, produces an updated source.

Diskin's seminal paper [7], which is not limited to the lens case, already briefly considered partial bidirectional transformations. He points out that in the lens setting, partiality of put follows from the lens laws if get is allowed to be non-surjective. This paper did not, however, model different levels of consistency; as far as the author is aware, that is being done for the first time here.

Indeed, the lens approach to bidirectionality described in e.g. [9,4] arose, historically, from earlier work relating to file synchronisation [2]. This gave a precise semantics to a file synchroniser, in the process discussing properties that a synchroniser should have. It made a clean separation between update detection and conflict resolution, formalising the slogan "non-conflicting updates are propagated". Propagating non-conflicting updates, while leaving conflicts for a user to resolve manually, is an example of the kind of scenario we deal with here.

Another, more recently active, strand of related work is that in bidirectionalization [17]. This, too, applies in the lens special case of bidirectional transformations. Its premise is that a get function is given, and a put function must be inferred from it. Of course, sometimes it is not possible to determine a reasonable put function, while sometimes many different put functions are possible; part of the interest of this problem area is to investigate the situation. The work aims to determine under what circumstances it is possible – and then how – either to determine the "best" put function in an appropriate sense, or to give a choice of good put functions to the transformation developer in a reasonable way.

The connection between bidirectionalization and the present work is as follows. In the lens scenario, giving a get function is equivalent to giving a consistency relation; m is consistent with n iff $n = get(m)$. Key to [17] is a distinction between shape-preserving and shape-changing updates to a model. In the list case considered, the shape of a model is its length, while its content is the actual list elements. The bx is assumed to respect the division into shape and content in that, for example, the results of applying get to two lists having the same shape will be two lists that also have the same shape (as one another, not necessarily as the inputs). This enables syntactic bidirectionalization to be used as a plug-in for semantic bidirectionalization: the bidirectionalization problem is factored into how to deal with shape and how to deal with content. One can, for example, produce a put function that works only in the case that the shapes of its arguments are appropriately related. This has the same flavour as our concerns here: we wish to support bx tools that can do the right thing in straightforward cases, with a clear specification of what that means, even if they cannot succeed in all cases. More formally, we may model the bidirectionalization case using a consistency structure with three possible values: inconsistent < shape-consistent < perfectly consistent. Then we may separate two actions: first, the process of making an update that increases consistency to shape-consistent; second, the process of making an update that achieves perfect consistency, provided that shape-consistency is given to begin with. This separation of concerns may make it easier to identify the design choices. It may also allow us to build a bx out of components, each able to do one of these two actions. Even if this is not possible, there may be value in automating one of the actions.

In the database literature, consideration of one aspect of partial bidirectional transformation goes back at least to [10,11]. This is the issue of how the user of a view may limit updates on the view to the admissible ones, that is, may stay within the domain of an automatically definable put function. More recently, study of related problems has been driven by the need to query, update and repair databases that contain errors or omissions, leading them to violate integrity constraints. A seminal paper in this area was [1], which discusses how to produce, in response to a query, all the tuples that would have to be present in a response to its being made against any repair of the actual database to one that satisfied its integrity constraints. One may normally see a query answer as a model which is consistent with a database, with respect to a particular query, when it is the answer to that query on the database. In this case, however, the ideally desired query answer is actually what would be returned from the ideal repaired database (which does not, in fact, exist). Because it does not exist, the best that can be done is an approximation; the answer set here can be seen as one that is partially consistent, having made (to the empty model) only the uncontroversial changes (adding the tuples that will definitely be present).

We note in passing that the promisingly named [8] is not about partial (model transformations) but about (partial model) transformations and though interesting is not closely related.

3   Basic Definitions

We begin by presenting a framework in which we generalise the possible results of a consistency check from true/false to a more nuanced judgement.

Let $(\Lambda, \leq_\Lambda)$ (which we will normally refer to just as Λ) be a partially ordered set, the *consistency structure*, having a top element $\top$ ("perfectly consistent"; all $\lambda \leq_\Lambda \top$). This will often be a lattice.

Let a partial bidirectional transformation $R : M \leftrightarrow N$ over Λ be defined by specifying

- a consistency indicator $R : M \times N \to \Lambda$ that says how consistent a given pair of models is
- consistency restoration functions $\overrightarrow{R} : M \times N \to N$ and $\overleftarrow{R} : M \times N \to M$.

From now on this is what we shall mean by a bidirectional transformation (bx) – when we want to use the usual definition in which the consistency indicator is a relation, we shall talk about *total bx*. A total bx may be represented as a special case of a partial bx, over the two element lattice with elements $\top$ (consistent) and $\bot < \top$ (inconsistent).

Note that the restoration functions of a partial bx are still total, but, as we shall see, they may not succeed in restoring consistency. In the worst case (corresponding intuitively to a partial bx being invoked outside its domain) it is always open to the function to return the argument with appropriate type, i.e. to propose no change. Thus making these total functions is no restriction. Of course, those definitions of properties of bxs that refer only to the consistency restoration functions do not need to be altered in this setting, though they may need reinvestigation. An example (following the terminology of [7]) is

Definition 1. *A bx* $R : M \leftrightarrow N$ *is* history ignorant *if for all* $m, m' \in M$ *and* $n \in N$, *we have* $\overrightarrow{R}(m, \overrightarrow{R}(m', n)) = \overrightarrow{R}(m, n)$ *and dually.*

Other standard definitions need minor adjustments to their notation, to make them apply to partial bx:

Definition 2. *A bx* R *is* consistency-total *if for any* m *there is some* n *such that* $R(m, n) = \top$, *and dually.*

Definition 3. *A bx* R *is* correct *if for all* $m \in M$ *and* $n \in N$ *we have* $R(m, \overrightarrow{R}(m, n)) = \top$, *and dually.*

Definition 4. *A bx* R *is* hippocratic *if for all* $m \in M$ *and* $n \in N$ *we have* $R(m, n) = \top \Rightarrow \overrightarrow{R}(m, n) = n$, *and dually.*

We can now define

Definition 5. *A bx* R *is* improving *if it always returns a model that is at least as consistent as its argument was. That is,* $R(m, \overrightarrow{R}(m, n)) \geq_\Lambda R(m, n)$, *and dually.*

An improving bx is allowed to return something that is no more consistent than its argument, but yet is not identical to it. Whether it is desirable to permit this depends on circumstance. If a model is an XML file, not intended for human reading, then changing things that are not important to consistency may be perfectly acceptable. Modelling tools often silently change the identifiers of model elements, for example. On the other hand, at times it is essential that users can be confident their models are not changed unnecessarily. For example, the layout of a diagram is typically irrelevant to consistency and indeed semantics, yet users of diagrams intensely dislike their layouts being changed. So that we can talk about this, we define

Definition 6. *A bx* R *is* as hippocratic as possible *(AHAP) if its consistency restoration functions return exactly their argument of appropriate type, unless returning something strictly more consistent. That is,*

$$\overrightarrow{R}(m, n) = n \lor R(m, \overrightarrow{R}(m, n)) > R(m, n)$$

and dually.

Note the need for this definition to make use of *strict* increase in Λ. Intuitively, properties that do this tend to be harder to work with than those that can be expressed just with the partial order's $\leq$.

This begins to let us specify what damage a partial bx satisfying certain properties may *not* do; next we turn to how to ensure that it *does* achieve what it should.

Definition 7. *Given $m \in M$, the set of $\overrightarrow{R}$ candidates with respect to m is $\{n' \in N : R(m, n')$ is maximal$\}$. That is, n' is a candidate iff $R(m, n') = \lambda \in \Lambda$ such that there does not exist any $n'' \in N$ with $R(m, n'') >_\Lambda \lambda$. If a candidate n' further satisfies $\forall n'' \in N.R(m, n') \geq_\Lambda R(m, n'')$ then it is dominant. Dually for $\overleftarrow{R}$.*

We normally abbreviate and say n is a (dominant) candidate wrt m. Notice that n being a candidate wrt m does not in general imply that m is a candidate wrt n. It turns out to be theoretically convenient if it does, though:

Definition 8. *A bx is* balanced *if for all $m \in M$ and $n \in N$, m is a candidate wrt n iff n is a candidate wrt m.*

In particular this will be the case if the bx is consistency-total. Otherwise, we obviously cannot expect a bx to be correct, but the next best thing is:

Definition 9. *A bx R is* as correct as possible *(ACAP) if it always returns a candidate.*

An ACAP bx must not return something if there is something strictly better it could have returned instead. In particular if, for given $m \in M$, a dominant $\overrightarrow{R}$ candidate exists, an ACAP bx must return one. If the consistency structure is a total order, all candidates are dominant. Then the consistency *level* λ achieved when $\overrightarrow{R}$ or $\overleftarrow{R}$ is applied to (m, n) is determined by (m, n) and the consistency indicator R, even though R does not determine $\overrightarrow{R}, \overleftarrow{R}$.

Let us collect some immediate consequences of the definitions.

Proposition 1. *1. If R is correct, then it is consistency-total and ACAP.*
2. If R is AHAP, then it is hippocratic.
3. If R is correct, then it is hippocratic if and only if it is AHAP.
4. If R is consistency-total, then it is correct if and only if it is ACAP.
5. If R is consistency-total then R is balanced; the candidates and the dominant candidates (wrt m) are both just the set of perfectly-consistent elements (wrt m).
6. If R is either AHAP or ACAP, then it is improving.

3.1   Subspaces and Subspace Pairs

A natural partner of the idea that some model pairs are more consistent than others is the idea that some regions of a pair of model spaces are more compatible than others. It turns out that the connection is more than just intuitive.

Definition 10. *Let $M' \subseteq M$ and $N' \subseteq N$ and let $R : M \leftrightarrow N$ be a bx (partial or total). We say (M', N') is a* subspace pair *if $\forall m \in M'.\forall n \in N'.\overrightarrow{R}(m, n) \in N' \wedge \overleftarrow{R}(m, n) \in M'$. We say M' is a* subspace, *and write $M' \trianglelefteq M$, if (M', N) is a subspace pair. (We define $N' \trianglelefteq N$ dually.)*

A subspace pair is a place where two teams of developers, each modifying a model that may be synchronised by a bx, may agree to stay. If (M', N') is a subspace pair with respect to R, then provided neither team moves their model outside M', N' respectively, the transformation will never move them outside. A subspace is a place where one team may unilaterally decide to stay.

It often happens, in MDD, that there are properties of a model that are ultimately desirable, but not enforced by the tool in which the model is developed – maybe not even desired at some stages of development. Strict compliance with metamodel constraints is an example. During development we may need the bx to propagate changes even though the models are not metamodel-compliant, say; the most helpful bx may also guarantee that, provided the human developers do not break compliance, the transformation will not. The tool may do what it can on non-compliant models, but it is natural to think that models that are also compliant are more consistent than those that are not. That is, the metamodel-compliant model pairs form a subspace pair within which a higher consistency value is obtainable than outside. In Section 5 we shall see how to relate bx on a subspace pair to bx on the whole model spaces. For now:

Lemma 1. *Let $R : M \leftrightarrow N$ be a partial bx over Λ.*

1. *M, N are subspaces. Unions and intersections of subspaces are subspaces.*
2. *If M_1 and N_1 are subspaces, then (M_1, N_1) is a subspace pair. For example, (M, N) is a subspace pair.*
3. *If (M_i, N_i) is a subspace pair for each $i \in I$ an index set (of any cardinality), then*
   $(\bigcap_{i \in I} M_i, \bigcap_{i \in I} N_i)$ is a subspace pair.
4. *If R is AHAP, then for any $m \in M$ and $n \in N$ such that each is a candidate with respect to the other (e.g., $R(m, n) = \top$), $(\{m\}, \{n\})$ is a subspace pair.*
5. *Let $M_\top = \{m \in M : \exists n \in N s.t. R(m, n) = \top\}$ and define $N_\top$ similarly. If R is ACAP, then $(M_\top, N_\top)$ is a subspace pair.*
6. *If R is ACAP and the consistency structure Λ is a total order, then for each $\lambda \in \Lambda$ we define $M_\lambda = \{m \in M : \exists n \in N s.t. R(m, n) \geq_\Lambda \lambda\}$ and N_λ similarly. Then (M_λ, N_λ) is a subspace pair.*

Of course, in general the component-wise union of two subspace pairs is not one.

4   Examples

In this section we set up a collection of examples, briefly described, to illustrate the definitions already given and what follows.

4.1   Families of Trivial Examples to Illustrate Definitions

1. Let Λ be the one-point lattice whose only point is $\top$. Then any bx over Λ is consistency-total, balanced, correct, ACAP and improving, but generally not AHAP or hippocratic.

2. Let M and N be any sets, let Λ be any partial order, and let $R : M \times N \to \Lambda$ be any function, serving as consistency indicator.

   (a) Let $\overrightarrow{R}$ be the second projection, that is, $\overrightarrow{R}(m, n) = n$ for any m and n, and let $\overleftarrow{R}$ be first projection. Then this bx – which makes no attempt ever to restore consistency – is hippocratic, AHAP and improving. In general it will not, of course, be correct or ACAP.

   (b) Alternatively, let $\overrightarrow{R}$ be defined by $\overrightarrow{R}(m, n) = n$ if $R(m, n) = \top$, otherwise $\overrightarrow{R}(m, n) = \Omega_N$, the special "no information" or empty model, which is perfectly consistent with the corresponding empty model in M, Ω_M, only. That is, suppose that $\overrightarrow{R}$ deletes everything if it finds anything other than perfect consistency. Then R is hippocratic, but does not in general have any of our other properties.

4.2   Composer Examples

For ease of presentation, our remaining examples of partial bx will be variants on the (total) COMPOSERS example [16,6], illustrated in Fig. 1. Until we introduce a slight variation later, our bxes will use the same pair of model spaces as COMPOSER. A model $m \in M$ comprises a set of (unrelated) Composer objects, each with a name, dates and nationality. A model $n \in N$ is an ordered list of pairs each giving a name and a nationality.

Now we consider different ways to define consistency and consistency restoration. We will refer to the consistency partial orders shown in Fig. 2.

Consistency as a Conjunction. To be perfectly consistent, models may have to satisfy several conditions, which need not be ranked. In QVT-R [14], for example, consistency is specified as a conjunction of two directional checks. That is, to check whether m is consistent with n, we must check whether m is acceptable from the point of view of n, and vice versa; m and n are considered consistent iff both of these checks succeed. The most faithful QVT-R tool, TATA's Model-Morf, actually requires the two directions to be checked separately by the user, even though the QVT-R standard's notion of consistency is the conjunction of the two results.

We may model such a situation using the consistency structure Λ_{LR} from Fig. 2. Following COMPOSERS [16], our composer models (say (m, n)) are deemed to be perfectly consistent ($R(m, n) = \top$) iff both: for every composer in m, there is at least one entry in the table comprising n with the same name and nationality; and, for every composer in n, there is at least one entry in m with the same name and nationality. If only the first condition holds, let $R(m, n) = \lambda_L$, if only the second, let $R(m, n) = \lambda_R$, if neither holds, let $R(m, n) = \bot$.

Given this notion of consistency as part of a partial bx over Λ_{LR}, we still have a choice about the consistency restoration functions. One user might be happy with automatically deleting composers, but dislike the "kludge" of making dates "????-????" and prefer manually inserting new composers to making the bx, in effect, choose among consistent models (the dates being irrelevant

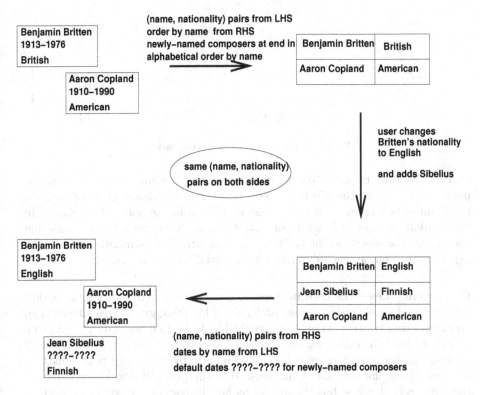

Fig. 1. Two kinds of composer model, illustrating a total bx

to consistency). Another user might be happier about elements being automatically added than about them being deleted. Then a suitable option is to make $\overrightarrow{R}$ add to n any missing composers – thus ensuring that consistency reaches at least λ_L – but not to make it delete any composers who do not occur in m. Together with the dual behaviour for $\overleftarrow{R}$, this gives a partial bx that improves consistency, and will not make any change except to do so, but does not guarantee to make the models completely consistent. That is, it is improving, indeed AHAP, but not correct or ACAP. (The same can be made true of the first user's preferred partial bx.)

The discipline for using such a bx manually must be considered carefully. Suppose the $\overrightarrow{R}$ just discussed is applied, and does not restore perfect consistency because there is a composer in n but not m. Now if $\overleftarrow{R}$ is immediately applied – without the extra composer being manually deleted – this composer will be re-added to m.

A different scenario is where such a bx is used as a phase within a total bx; then this discipline is in effect provided automatically. In QVT-R, which does not discuss partial consistency, ensuring that both checks succeed while modifying only one of the models motivates the two-phase enforce process. When n must be modified so that it is consistent with fixed m, the first phase adds model

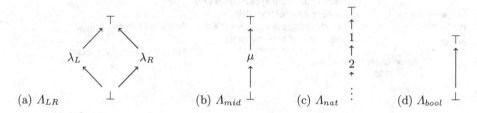

Fig. 2. A few consistency partial orders

elements that are required to exist in order for n to become acceptable from the point of view of m; the second, delete, phase removes model elements from n that cannot be present if m is to be acceptable from the point of view of n. In fact, making this work is far from trivial and is the source of some confusion concerning the semantics of QVT-R [5]. Separating the semantics of such bx explicitly into phases each described by a partial bx may be useful.

Consistency Levels as Diagnostics. Even if we have an ordinary total bx that is correct and hippocratic, we may prefer something that gives more information, for engineering reasons. That is, we might like to be told not only that a given pair of models is inconsistent, but something about why they are inconsistent. If we want our framework to model this, it can do so by means of a partial bx that corresponds to the original in the sense that the perfectly-consistent pairs are the same in both cases, but the partial bx has, instead of a single judgement ⊥, "inconsistent", a collection of possible consistency levels. Both bx may have the same consistency restoration functions, so the partial bx will, like the original it is based on, be correct and hippocratic (hence ACAP, AHAP and improving).

To give a simple example, we might use the natural numbers as consistency levels to indicate the number of errors counted in some way. In our example, this could be the number of composers who occur on one side but not the other. We could define a bx whose consistency restoration was just like the total bx illustrated in Fig. 1, but over the consistency structure Λ_{nat} from Fig. 2.

Separation of Consistency Concerns. An example somewhat reminiscent of those used in the bidirectionalization work discussed in Section 2 is the following.

Consider bx between M and N over consistency structure Λ_{mid} from Fig. 2. Let the middle consistency element, μ, indicate that the same names occur in each model. Let perfect consistency, ⊤, as before indicate that the same (name,nationality) pairs occur on both sides. This allows us to separate the task of designing consistency restoration functions, if we like, into the two parts of making sure the right names are present, and making sure the right nationality/ies also occur with each name.

A Non-consistency-Total Example. So far all our examples have been consistency-total. Now suppose we have the usual "same (name, nationality) pairs" requirement for consistency, but we also have a constraint (not enforced, but desirable) that composer names in a table in $n \in N$ must be no more than 16 characters long (while those in m are still unrestricted). We may model this using a bx over Λ_{LR} from Fig. 2. Suppose λ_L means both models comply with their constraints, λ_R means the same (name, nationality) pairs occur in both models, $\bot$ means neither holds and $\top$ means both hold.

The models illustrated in Fig. 1 are unaffected, but now consider $m \in M$ that includes a composer with name Pyotr Ilyich Tchaikovsky (and no other composers, for simplicity). Now there is no model $n \in N$ which is perfectly consistent with m. A bx that is asked to modify n must choose: either it can include this name, which will allow it to achieve consistency level λ_R, or it can comply with its constraints, achieving λ_L, but it cannot do both.

Suppose the bx writer settles on preferring metamodel compliance, and writes a bx that we shall call T as we shall refer to it again in Section 5.

Note that T is not balanced. Say we have m as above and a model n whose single row reads PI Tchaikovsky. Because n cannot be modified so that its composer name matches m's without violating the constraint, n is a candidate with respect to m. (It is not a dominant candidate, because the alternative choice of making the names the same but violating the constraint would have given an incomparable consistency value.) On the other hand, m could if we wish be modified so that its composer name matched n's, which would restore perfect consistency, so m is not a candidate with respect to n.

5   Relating Partial Bx

A major motivation for studying bx that tolerate inconsistency is to support the use of bx during development. At some stages we may have a well-developed notion of perfect consistency, yet not be in a position to enforce it immediately (e.g. because a model is currently incomplete, awaiting more information; it might even be syntactically incorrect). We do not want the inability to enforce perfect consistency to stop us synchronising models at all; we would like to be able to run bx and get some guarantees about what a bx will do. We also want to be able to give more information about the nature of the inconsistency discovered by a check. Later in development, a total bx may be usable, and we would like to know it is compatible in an appropriate sense with the partial bx used earlier.

This motivates the study of relationships between different partial bx. Many interesting examples relate bx that relate the same sets of models (perhaps restricting to a subset) but we start with a more general notion:

Proposition 2. *Let $R_1 : M_1 \leftrightarrow N_1$ be a partial bx on Λ_1. Let $f_\Lambda : \Lambda_1 \to \Lambda_2$ be a total function preserving the partial order, that is, satisfying $x \leq y \Rightarrow f_\Lambda x \leq f_\Lambda y$. Let $f_M : M_1 \to M_2$ and $f_N : N_1 \to N_2$ be surjective partial functions satisfying the following coherence condition: if $f_M m = f_M m'$ and $f_N n = f_N n'$ (in particular, m, m', n, n' are in the appropriate domains) then*

- $f_\Lambda R_1(m,n) = f_\Lambda R_1(m',n')$;
- f_N is defined on $\overrightarrow{R_1}(m,n)$, and dually;
- $f_N\overrightarrow{R_1}(m,n) = f_N\overrightarrow{R_1}(m',n')$, and dually.

Then the following gives a well-defined partial bx $R_2 : M_2 \leftrightarrow N_2$ on Λ_2, which by slight abuse of notation we will denote $f(R_1)$:

- $R_2(f_M m, f_N n) = f_\Lambda R_1(m,n)$
- $\overrightarrow{R_2}(f_M m, f_N n) = f_N\overrightarrow{R_1}(m,n)$ and dually.

In particular, notice that if $M_1 = M_2$ and $N_1 = N_2$, with f_M and f_N being total identity functions, the coherence conditions become trivial. That is, given a bx $R : M \leftrightarrow N$ over Λ_1, and a partial order preserving function $f_\Lambda : \Lambda_1 \to \Lambda_2$, we can always build a bx $f(R) : M \leftrightarrow N$ over Λ_2.

Of course the proof of Prop. 2 is easy: the coherence conditions are exactly what is needed. More interesting is to see what happens to properties of R_1.

Proposition 3. *If R_1 is improving then so is $f(R_1)$.*

To go further we need to impose further conditions on f_Λ, involving when one consistency value is *strictly* greater than another:

Proposition 4. *If R_1 is ACAP and, in addition to the conditions of Prop. 2, f_Λ satisfies $f_\Lambda x > f_\Lambda y \Rightarrow x > y$, then $f(R_1)$ is ACAP.*

The condition is necessary in order to handle situations like the composer example T on Λ_{LR}, in which consistency means the conjunction of two properties that are considered incomparable and cannot always both be achieved. Now suppose that f_Λ privileges one property over the other, so that ensuring that one is "better". In our example, suppose we consider $f_\Lambda : \Lambda_{LR} \to \Lambda_{mid}$ sending λ_L to $\bot$ and λ_R to μ; that is, f_Λ models that we now consider having the same (name, nationality) pairs to be better than obeying the constraints, in cases where it's not possible to do both. Our bx T over Λ_{LR} was ACAP, but $f(T)$ over Λ_{mid} is not. The condition captures the idea that turning incomparability into dominance in the consistency structure may break ACAP.

The next result might be considered dual:

Proposition 5. *If R_1 is AHAP and, in addition to the conditions of Prop. 2, f_Λ satisfies $x > y \Rightarrow f_\Lambda x > f_\Lambda y$, then $f(R_1)$ is AHAP.*

The condition is necessary because without it, R_1 may make a consistency improvement that is "erased" by f_Λ. That is, we may have $R_1(m, \overrightarrow{R_1}(m,n)) > R_1(m,n)$, but $f_\Lambda(R_1(m, \overrightarrow{R_1}(m,n))) = f_\Lambda(R_1(m,n))$. Unless the difference between n and $\overrightarrow{R_1}(m,n)$ is likewise erased by f_N, $f(R_1)$ will fail AHAP.

5.1   Example: Restricting to a Subspace Pair

Let (M_2, N_2) be a subspace pair in (M_1, N_1) and let f_M, f_N be the identity on M_2, N_2, undefined elsewhere. Then as these are also injective where defined, the coherence conditions in Prop. 2 hold for any f_Λ preserving the partial order. If we take f_Λ to be the identity, what we get is just the restriction of a bx to a subspace pair. The conditions of Prop. 4 and Prop. 5 both hold, so we see that the restriction will be ACAP and AHAP if the original was.

Next, let us use Prop. 1 to consider the subspace pair $(M_\top, N_\top)$ in (M_1, N_1), and consider $f_\Lambda : \Lambda_1 \to \{\top, \bot\}$ given by $f_\Lambda(\lambda) = \top$ if $\lambda = \top$, otherwise $\bot$. We see that we can construct a total bx from any ACAP partial bx by, intuitively, throwing out all the elements on which consistency cannot be restored. The Prop. 4 condition holds, and since the consistency relation is, by construction, total on $(M_\top, N_\top)$ our restricted bx is correct. The Prop. 5 condition fails, but in this particular case we have thrown out all potential counterexamples, so:

Proposition 6. *Let $R : M \leftrightarrow N$ be a partial bx which is ACAP and AHAP. Define $R_\top : M_\top \leftrightarrow N_\top$ by:*

- *$M_\top = \{m \in M : \exists n \in N.R(m, n) = \top\}$, and $N_\top$ dually;*
- *$\overrightarrow{R_\top}(m, n)$ holds iff $R(m, n) = \top$;*
- *$\overrightarrow{R_\top}(m, n) = \overrightarrow{R}(m, n)$ and dually.*

Then $R_\top$ is a correct and hippocratic total bx.

6 Conclusions and Future Work

In this paper we have begun a study of partial bidirectional transformations, being a generalisation of bidirectional transformations in which the consistency definition, rather than being a relation, is a function taking values in a partially ordered structure. We have given examples to show the practical potential of such bx, and have established a framework in which to discuss their properties and to understand the relationships between them and their properties.

Beyond this paper, we have begun a study of the implication, for this framework, of considering the edit monoid on each model space. This is promising from the point of view of least change: intuitively, difficulties arise when the edit path towards a candidate must involve going via a model that is less consistent than the original. It is good if edit paths in the model spaces project onto paths in the consistency structure.

More generally, we are studying the many ways in which bx formalisms go beyond the state-based approach we work with here, to include extra information e.g. edits, traces or an archive [9]. We are also studying the properties of bidirectional transformations that are related for total bidirectional transformations in [15], to see what happens when we transfer them to the partial setting. Do the same relationships hold between the notions? Are other special properties more important in this setting? Balanced bx are much more tractable than others, as they allow foundational results about the equivalences used in [15] to carry over.

Acknowledgements. I thank James McKinna for very helpful conversations. I thank the referees for their constructive suggestions, including some that could not be implemented in this version for space reasons. The work is partly supported by EPSRC grant EP/K020218/1.

References

1. Arenas, M., Bertossi, L.E., Chomicki, J.: Consistent query answers in inconsistent databases. In: Proc. PODS, pp. 68–79. ACM Press (1999)
2. Balasubramaniam, S., Pierce, B.C.: What is a file synchronizer? In: Proceedings of MobiCom 1998 (October 1998)
3. Balzer, R.: Tolerating inconsistency. In: Proceedings of ICSE 1991, pp. 158–165. IEEE Computer Society/ACM Press (1991)
4. Bohannon, A., Nathan Foster, J., Pierce, B.C., Pilkiewicz, A., Schmitt, A.: Boomerang: Resourceful lenses for string data. In: Proceedings of POPL 2008 (January 2008)
5. Bradfield, J., Stevens, P.: Enforcing QVT-R with mu-calculus and games. In: Cortellessa, V., Varró, D. (eds.) FASE 2013. LNCS, vol. 7793, pp. 282–296. Springer, Heidelberg (2013)
6. Cheney, J., Gibbons, J., McKinna, J., Stevens, P.: Towards a repository of bx examples. In: Proceedings of Bx 2014 (2014)
7. Diskin, Z.: Algebraic models for bidirectional model synchronization. In: Czarnecki, K., Ober, I., Bruel, J.-M., Uhl, A., Völter, M. (eds.) MODELS 2008. LNCS, vol. 5301, pp. 21–36. Springer, Heidelberg (2008)
8. Famelis, M., Salay, R., Chechik, M.: The semantics of partial model transformations. In: Proceedings of ICSE Workshop on Modeling in Software Engineering, pp. 64–69 (June 2012)
9. Nathan Foster, J., Greenwald, M.B., Kirkegaard, C., Pierce, B.C., Schmitt, A.: Schema-directed data synchronization. Technical Report MS-CIS-05-02, University of Pennsylvania (March 2005)
10. Gottlob, G., Paolini, P., Zicari, R.: Properties and update semantics of consistent views. ACM Trans. Database Syst. 13(4), 486–524 (1988)
11. Hegner, S.J.: Foundations of canonical update support for closed database views. In: Kanellakis, P.C., Abiteboul, S. (eds.) ICDT 1990. LNCS, vol. 470, pp. 422–436. Springer, Heidelberg (1990)
12. Nöhrer, A., Biere, A., Egyed, A.: A comparison of strategies for tolerating inconsistencies during decision-making. In: 16th International Software Product Line Conference, SPLC 2012, pp. 11–20. ACM (2012)
13. Nuseibeh, B., Easterbrook, S.M., Russo, A.: Leveraging inconsistency in software development. IEEE Computer 33(4), 24–29 (2000)
14. OMG. MOF2.0 query/view/transformation (QVT) version 1.1. OMG document formal/2009-12-05 (2009), www.omg.org
15. Stevens, P.: Observations relating to the equivalences induced on model sets by bidirectional transformations. In: EC-EASST, vol. 49 (2012)
16. Stevens, P., McKinna, J., Cheney, J.: COMPOSERS v0.1 in Bx Examples Repository, http://bx-community.wikidot.com/examples:home (retrieved January 16, 2014)
17. Voigtländer, J., Hu, Z., Matsuda, K., Wang, M.: Combining syntactic and semantic bidirectionalization. In: Proc. ICFP, pp. 181–192. ACM (2010)

Splitting Models Using Information Retrieval and Model Crawling Techniques

Daniel Strüber[1], Julia Rubin[2,3], Gabriele Taentzer[1], and Marsha Chechik[3]

[1] Philipps-Universität Marburg, Germany
[2] IBM Research – Haifa, Israel
[3] University of Toronto, Canada
{strueber,taentzer}@mathematik.uni-marburg.de,
mjulia@il.ibm.com,chechik@cs.toronto.edu

Abstract. In team environments, models are often shared and edited by multiple developers. To allow modularity and facilitate developer independence, we consider the problem of splitting a large monolithic model into sub-models. We propose an approach that assists users in incrementally discovering the set of desired sub-models. Our approach is supported by an automated tool that performs model splitting using information retrieval and model crawling techniques. We demonstrate the effectiveness of our approach on a set of real-life case studies, involving UML class models and EMF meta-models.

Keywords: model management, model splitting, feature location.

1 Introduction

Model-based engineering – the use of models as the core artifacts of the development process – has gained increased popularity across various engineering disciplines, and already became an industrially accepted best practice in many application domains. For example, models are used in automotive and aerospace domains to capture the structure and behavior of complex systems, and, in several cases, to generate fully functional implementations. Modeling frameworks themselves, such as UML and EMF, are defined using models – an approach known as *meta-modeling*.

Together with the increased popularity of modeling, models of practical use grow in size and complexity to the point where large monolithic models are difficult to comprehend and maintain. There is a need to *split* such large models into a set of dependent modules (a.k.a. *sub-models*), increasing the overall comprehensibility and allowing multiple distributed teams to focus on each sub-model separately.

Most existing works, e.g., [3], suggest approaches for splitting models based on an analysis of strongly connected components, largely ignoring the semantics of the split and the user intention for performing it. In our work, we propose an alternative, heuristic approach that allows splitting a model into *functional* modules that are explicitly specified by the user using *natural-language descriptions*. It is inspired by code-level feature location techniques [2,10], which discover implementation artifacts corresponding to a particular, user-defined, functionality.

S. Gnesi and A. Rensink (Eds.): FASE 2014, LNCS 8411, pp. 47–62, 2014.
© Springer-Verlag Berlin Heidelberg 2014

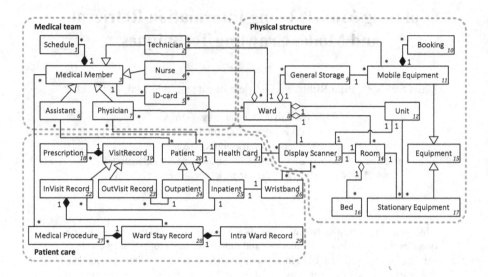

Fig. 1. A UML Class Model of a Hospital System

In the core of our approach is an automated technique that employs *information retrieval (IR)* and *model crawling*. Given an input model and a set of its sub-model descriptions, the technique assigns each element to one of the specified sub-models, effectively producing a partitioning. The technique is applicable to any model for which a split results in sub-models that satisfy the well-formedness constraints of the original one, e.g., UML Class models, EMF models and MOF-based meta-models.

Motivating Example. Consider the UML Class Model of a Hospital System (HSM) [7, p. 125] shown in Fig. 1. It describes the organization of the hospital in terms of its medical team (elements #1-7), physical structure (elements #8-17), and patient care (elements #18-29). Each of these concepts corresponds to a desired sub-model, visually encircled by a dashed line for presentation purposes. The goal of our work is to assist the user in determining elements that comprise each sub-model. The user describes the desired sub-models using natural-language text, e.g., using parts of the system documentation. For example, the medical team sub-model in Fig. 1 is described in [7]. A fragment of the description is: *"Nurses are affiliated with a single ward, while physicians and technicians can be affiliated with several different wards. All personnel have access to a calendar detailing the hours that they need to be present at the various wards. Nurses record physicians' decisions. These are written on paper and handed to an administrative assistant to enter. The administrative assistant needs to figure out who needs to be at a particular procedure before they enter it in the system."* The technique uses such descriptions in order to map model elements to desired sub-models. The labels for the sub-models, e.g., "Medical Team", are assigned manually.

The user can decide whether the list of sub-models describes a *complete* or a *partial* split of the input model. In the former case, each input model element is assigned to exactly one sub-model, like in the example in Fig. 1, where the three sub-models "cover" the entire input model. In the latter case, when the complete set of the desired

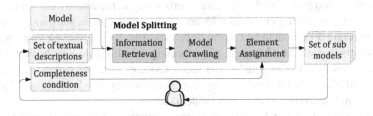

Fig. 2. An overview of the approach

sub-models is unknown upfront, the technique produces assignments to known sub-models only. The remaining elements are placed in a sub-model called "rest". The user can inspect the "rest" sub-model in order to discover remaining sub-models in an incremental and iterative fashion, until the desired level of completeness is achieved.

Contributions and Organization. This paper makes the following contributions: (1) we describe an automated model splitting technique which combines information retrieval and model crawling; (2) we propose a computer-supported iterative process for model splitting; (3) we evaluate our approach on a set of benchmark case studies, including real-life UML and EMF models. Our results demonstrate that the proposed approach achieves high accuracy compared to the manually produced results and is able to assist the user in the iterative discovery of the desired sub-models.

The rest of the paper is structured as follows. Sec. 2 gives the high-level overview of our approach. We describe the necessary preliminaries in Sec. 3 and present the automated splitting algorithm in Sec. 4. We report on the results of evaluating our approach in Sec. 5-6. In Sec. 7, we put our contribution in the context of related work, and conclude in Sec. 8 with the summary and an outline of future research directions.

2 Overview of the Approach

The high-level overview of our approach is given in Fig. 2. The user provides as input a model that requires splitting, a set of textual descriptions of the desired sub-models, and the completeness configuration parameter that declares whether this set of sub-models is complete or partial. For the example in Fig. 1, the complete set would contain descriptions of all three sub-models – medical team, physical structure, and patient care, while a partial set would contain only some of these descriptions.

Automated Technique. In the core of our approach is an automated technique that *scores* the model elements w.r.t. their relevance to each of the desired sub-models. The scoring is done in two phases. The first one is based on *Information Retrieval (IR)* and uses sub-model descriptions: it builds a textual query for each model element, e.g., based on its name, measures its relevance to each of the descriptions and identifies those elements that are deemed to be most relevant for each of the descriptions.

The identified elements are used as *seeds* for the second phase, *Model Crawling*. In this phase, structural relationships between model elements are explored in order to identify additional relevant elements that were missed by the IR phase. The additional elements are scored based on their structural proximity to the already scored elements. In HSM, when identifying elements relevant to the medical team sub-model using the description fragment shown in Sec. 1, the IR phase correctly identifies elements #2,4,6,7 as seeds. It misses element #3 though, which is assigned a high score in the first iteration of crawling as it is closely related to the seeds. Once element #3 is scored, it impacts the scoring of elements identified during later iterations of crawling. Eventually, each model element's relevance to each sub-model is scored.

The third phase, *Element Assignment*, assigns elements to sub-models based on their score. If a complete set of sub-models is given, each element is assigned to a sub-model for which it has the highest score[1]. In this case, the assignment results in a model partition. If a partial set of sub-models in given as an input, some model elements might not belong to any of these sub-models. Hence, we apply a threshold-based approach and assign elements to sub-models only if their scores are above a certain threshold.

Iterative Process. A partial set of sub-model descriptions can be further refined in an *iterative* manner, by focusing user attention on the set of remaining elements – those that were not assigned to any of the input sub-models. Additional sub-models identified by the user, as well as the completeness parameter assessing the user's satisfaction with the set of known sub-models are used as input to the next iteration of the algorithm, until the desired level of completeness is achieved.

Clearly, as additional sub-models are identified, element assignments might change. For example, when only the description of the medical team sub-model is used during a split, element #8 is assigned to that sub-model due to the high similarity between its name and the description: the term ward is used in the description multiple times. Yet, when the same input model is split w.r.t. the sub-model descriptions of both the medical team and the physical structure, this element is placed in the latter sub-model: Both its IR score and its structural relevance to that sub-model are higher. In fact, the more detailed information about sub-models and their description is given, the more accurate the results produced by our technique become, as we demonstrate in Sec. 6.

3   Preliminaries

In this section, we describe our representation of models and model elements and capture the notion of model splitting. We also introduce IR concepts used in the remainder of the paper and briefly describe the feature-location techniques that we used as an inspiration for our splitting approach.

3.1   Models and Model Splitting

Definition 1. *A model* $M = (E, R, T, src, tgt, type)$ *is a tuple consisting of a set E of model elements, a set R of relationships, a set T of relationship types, functions src and tgt : $R \to E$ assigning source and target elements to relationships, and a function type : $R \to T$ assigning types to relationships. Model elements $x, y \in E$ are related, written*

---

[1] An element that has the highest score for two or more sub-models is assigned to one of them randomly.

related(x, y), *iff* $\exists r \in R$ *s.t. either* $src(r) = x \wedge trg(r) = y$, *or* $src(r) = y \wedge trg(r) = x$. *If* *type(r)* $= t$, *we further say that* x *and* y *are* related *through* t, *written* $related_t(x, y)$.

For example, the HSM in Fig. 1 has three relationship types: an association, a composition, and an inheritance. Further, element #7 is related to elements #3, #8 and #20.

Definition 2. *Let a model* $M = (E, R, T, src, tgt, type)$ *be given.* $S = (E_S, R_S, T, src_S, tgt_S, type_S)$ *is a sub-model of* M, *written* $S \subseteq M$, *iff* $E_S \subseteq E$, $R_S \subseteq R$, $src_S = src_{|R_S}$ *with* $src_S(R_S) \subseteq E_S$, $tgt_S = tgt_{|R_S}$, *and* $type_S = type_{|R_S}$[^2].

That is, while sources of all of a sub-model's relationship are elements within the model, it does not have to be true about the targets. For example, each dashed frame in the example in Fig. 1 denotes a valid sub-model of HSM. All elements inside each frame form the element set of the corresponding sub-model. There are two types of relationships between these elements: those with the source and the target within the sub-model, e.g., all inheritance relations within the medical team sub-model, and those spanning two different sub-models (often, these are association relationships).

Definition 3. *Given a model* M, *a* model split $Split(M) = \{S | S \subseteq M\}$ *is a set of sub-models s.t.* $\forall S_1, S_2 \in Split(M) : (S_1 \neq S_2) \Rightarrow (E_{S_1} \cap E_{S_2} = \emptyset)$.

By Def. 2, if $\bigcup_{S \in Split(M)} E_S = E$, then $\bigcup_{S \in Split(M)} R_S = R$. The split of HSM, consisting of three sub-models, is shown in Fig. 1.

Definition 4. *A model* M *satisfying a constraint* φ *is* splittable *iff every sub-model of* M *satisfies* φ.

All UML class models (without packages) are splittable since we can take any set of classes with their relationships and obtain a class model. Models with packages have a constraint "every class belongs to some package". To make them splittable, we either relax the constraint or remove the packages first and then reintroduce them after the splitting is performed, in a new form.

3.2 Relevant Information Retrieval Techniques

Below, we introduce the basic IR techniques used by our approach.
Term Frequency - Inverse Document Frequency Metric (*TF-IDF*) [8]. *Tf-idf* is a statistical measure often used by IR techniques to evaluate how important a term is to a specific document in the context of a set of documents (*corpus*). It is calculated by combining two metrics: *term frequency* and *inverse document frequency*. The first one measures the relevance of a specific document d to a term t ($tf(t, d)$) by calculating the number of occurrences of t in d. Intuitively, the more frequently a term occurs in the document, the more relevant the document is. For the HSM example where documents are descriptions of the desired sub-models, the term nurse appears in the description d of the medical team sub-model in Sec. 1 twice, so $tf(\text{nurse}, d) = 2$.

[^2]: For a function $f : M \to M'$ with $S \subseteq M$, $f_{|S} : S \to M'$ denotes the restriction of f to S.

The drawback of term frequency is that uninformative terms appearing throughout the set D of all documents can distract from less frequent, but relevant, terms. Intuitively, the more documents include a term, the less this term discriminates between documents. The *inverse document frequency, idf(t)*, is calculated as follows: $idf(t) = \log(\frac{|D|}{|\{d \in D \mid t \in d\}|})$. This metric is higher for terms that are included in a smaller number of documents.

The total *tf-idf* score for a term t and a document d is calculated by multiplying its *tf* and *idf* scores: $tf\text{-}idf(t, d) = tf(t, d) \times idf(t)$. In our example, since the term nurse appears neither in the description of the physical structure nor in patient care, $idf(\text{nurse}) = \log(\frac{3}{1}) = 0.47$ and $tf\text{-}idf(\text{nurse}, d) = 2 \times 0.47 = 0.94$.

Given a query which contains multiple terms, the *tf-idf* score of a document w.r.t. the query is commonly calculated by adding the *tf-idf* scores of all query terms. For example, the *tf-idf* score of the query *"medical member"* w.r.t. the description of the medical team sub-model is $0 + 0 = 0$ as none of the terms appear in the description and thus their *tf* score is 0. The latent semantic analysis (LSA) technique described below is used to "normalize" scores produced by *tf-idf*.

Latent Semantic Analysis (LSA) [4]. LSA is an automatic mathematical/statistical technique that analyzes the relationships between queries and passages in large bodies of text. It constructs vector representations of both a user query and a corpus of text documents by encoding them as a *term-by-document co-occurrence matrix*. It is a sparse matrix whose rows correspond to terms and whose columns correspond to documents and the query. The weighing of the elements of the matrix is typically done using the *tf-idf* metric.

Vector representations of the documents and the query are obtained by normalizing and decomposing the term-by-document co-occurrence matrix using a matrix factorization technique called *singular value decomposition* [4]. The similarity between a document and a query is then measured by calculating the cosine between their corresponding vectors, yielding a value between 0 and 1. The similarity increases as the vectors point "in the same general direction", i.e., as more terms are shared between the documents. For example, the queries *"assistant"*, *"nurse"* and *"physician"* result in the highest score w.r.t. the description of the medical team sub-model. Intuitively, this happens because all these queries only have a single term, and each of the terms has the highest *tf-idf* score w.r.t. the description. The query *"medical member"* results in the lowest score: none of the terms comprising that query appear in the description.

3.3 Feature Location Techniques

Feature location techniques aim at locating pieces of code that implement a specific program functionality, a.k.a. a *feature*. A number of feature location techniques for code have been proposed and extensively studied in the literature [2,10]. The techniques are based on static or dynamic program analysis, IR, change set analysis, or some combination of the above.

While the IR phase of our technique is fairly standard and is used by several existing feature location techniques, e.g., SNIAFL [17], our model crawling phase is heavily inspired by a code crawling approach proposed by Suade [9]. Suade leverages static program analysis to find elements that are related to an initial *set of interest* provided by

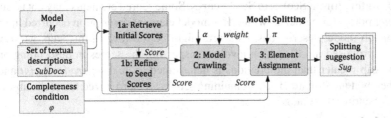

Fig. 3. An outline of the algorithm for creating a splitting suggestion

the user – a set of functions and data fields that the user considers relevant to the feature of interest. Given that set, the system explores the *program dependance graph* whose nodes are functions or data fields and edges are function calls or data access links, to find all neighbors of the elements in the set of interest. The discovered neighbors are scored based on their *specificity* – an element is specific if it relates to few other elements, and *reinforcement* – an element is reinforced if it is related to other elements of interest. The set of all elements related to those in the initial set of interest is scored and returned to the user as a sorted *suggestion set*. The user browses the result, adds additional elements to the set of interest and reiterates.

Our modifications to this algorithm, including those that allow it to operate on models rather than code and automatically perform multiple iterations until a certain "fixed point" is achieved, are described in Sec. 4.

4   Splitting Algorithm

Fig. 3 shows a refined outline of the algorithm introduced in Fig. 2. The algorithm receives a model M to be split, a set of textual descriptions of desired sub-models *Sub-Docs*, and a completeness condition ϕ which is *true* if the set of descriptions represents a desired partitioning of M and *false* if this set is partial. The algorithm is based on scoring the relevance of model elements for each target sub-model (steps 1-2), and then assigning each element to the most relevant sub-model (step 3). The relevance scoring is done by first applying the IR technique and then using the scored sets of elements as seeds for model crawling. The latter scores the relevance of all model elements w.r.t. specificity, reinforcement, and cohesiveness of their relations. The algorithm also uses parameters w, α and π which can be user adjusted for the models being analyzed. Our experience adjusting them for class model splitting is given in Sec. 5.

Step 1a: Retrieve Initial Scores Using LSA. The user provides the input model M and natural-language sub-model descriptions *SubDocs* as unrelated artifacts. They need to be preprocessed before LSA can establish connections between them. *SubDocs* are textual and can be used as input documents directly. Textual queries are retrieved from elements of M by extracting a description – in class models, the element's name. LSA then scores the relevance of each sub-model description to each model element description. The resulting scores are stored in *Score*, a data structure that maintains a map from *(sub-model number, element)* pairs to scores between 0 and 1.

Step 1b: Refine Initial Scores to Seed Scores. Some scored elements may not be suited as starting points for model crawling. If a model element description occurred in many different sub-model descriptions, its score might be too low. In this step, we use the technique proposed in [17] which involves inspecting the scores in descending order. The first gap greater than the previous is determined to be a *separation point* and all scores below it are discarded. The remaining scores are normalized for each sub-model to take the entire (0, 1] range.

Step 2: Model Crawling. The aim of model crawling is to score the relevance of each model element for each target sub-model. Intuitively, model crawling is a breadth-first search: beginning with a set of seeds, it scores the neighbors of the seeds, then the neighbors' neighbors, et cetera.

This step is outlined in Fig. 4: An exhaustive crawl is performed for each target sub-model. While there exists a scored element with unscored neighbors, we determine for each of these elements x and each relationship type t the set of directly related elements, calling it *OneHop* (lines 5-7). To score each unscored element in *OneHop*, the *TwoHop* set comprising *their* related elements is obtained (lines 8-9). The score is computed at line 10 as a product of x's score, a fraction quantifying specificity and reinforcement, and a weighting factor. A constant exponent α is applied to fine-tune the scoring distribution. Finally, we use a special operator, proposed by [9], to account for elements related to already scored elements through multiple relations. The operator, denoted by the underlined *put* command, merges the scores obtained for each relationship. It assigns a value higher than the maximum of these scores, but lower than 1.

This procedure adjusts the feature location algorithm proposed in [9] in three respects: (A1) We perceive neighborhood as being undirected; relations are navigated in both directions. Not considering directionality is powerful: It allows to eventually access and score *all* model elements, provided the model is connected. (A2) The weighting factor embodies the intuition that some relations imply a stronger coherence than others. An example is *composition* in UML, which binds the life cycles of elements together. (A3) We modified the scoring formula to reflect our intuition of reinforcement and specificity. The enumerator rewards a large overlap of the set of scored elements and those related to the element being scored, promoting high specificity and high reinforcement. The denominator punishes high connectivity of elements being analyzed, i.e., low specificity, and elements being scored, i.e., low reinforcement.

Step 3: Element Assignment. A splitting suggestion *Sug* is constructed by assigning suggested model elements to sub-models. When the complete split is desired, i.e., $\phi = true$, each element is put into the sub-model for which it has the highest score. Ties are broken by selecting one at random. This guarantees that each element is assigned to exactly one sub-model. For a partial split, i.e., $\phi = false$, an element is assigned to a sub-model only if its score exceeds the user-provided threshold value π. As a result, each element is assigned to zero or one sub-models.

Proposition 1. *For a splittable model M, the algorithm described in this section computes a model split Split(M) as defined in Def. 3.*

Input: $M = (E, R, T, src, trg, type)$: Model
Input: *SubDocs*: A set of i target sub-model descriptions
Input: *Score* : $((1..i) \times E) \rightarrow [0, 1]$: Map of (*sub-model number, element*) pairs to scores
Constant: $w : T \rightarrow (0, 1]$: Weighting parameters for relationship types
Constant: $\alpha \in (0, 1]$: Calibration parameter
Output: *Score* : $((1..i) \times E) \rightarrow [0, 1]$

```
 1  function CRAWLMODEL(M, SubDocs, Score)
 2      for each 1 ≤ j ≤ i do
 3          while ∃x, y ∈ E s.t. related(x, y) ∧ (Score(j, x) > 0) ∧ (Score(j, y) = 0) do
 4              for each t ∈ T do
 5                  Var Scored ← {x ∈ E | Score(j, x) > 0}
 6                  for each x ∈ Scored do
 7                      Var OneHop ← {y ∈ E | relatedₜ(x, y)}
 8                      for y ∈ OneHop \ Scored do
 9                          Var TwoHop ← {z ∈ E | relatedₜ(z, y)}
10                          Score.put((j, y),(Score(j,x) * |TwoHop ∩ Scored| / (|OneHop| * |TwoHop|) * w(t))^α)
11      return Score
```

Fig. 4. Algorithm 1: Crawl model

Table 1. Subject models

Example	Decomposition Type	Sub-Models	Classes, Interfaces	Assoc.	Comp.	Aggr.	Gener.	Interf. Real.
HSM	Diagram split	3	28	10	5	4	16	0
GMF	Sub-model decomposition	4	156	62	101	0	70	65
UML	Package decomposition	14	242	283	213	0	205	0
WASL	Package decomposition	4	30	18	13	0	14	0
WebML	Package decomposition	2	23	11	13	0	12	0
R2ML	Package decomposition	6	104	96	27	0	76	0

Proof sketch: In step 3, each model element is assigned to at most one sub-model. Thus, all pairs of sub-models eventually have disjoint sets of model elements, as required by Def. 3. The resulting sub-models satisfy all constraints satisfied by M because M is splittable (Def. 4).

5 Experimental Settings

Our goal is to study the applicability and the accuracy of model splitting techniques when applied to real-life models. In this section, we describe our experimental setting. We focus the evaluation on two research questions: **RQ1:** How useful is the incremental approach for model splitting? and **RQ2:** How accurate is the automatic splitting?

5.1 Subjects

We chose subject models for our evaluation based on the following criteria: (1) the models should be splittable, as per Def. 4, modulo trivial pre- and post-processing; (2)

we have access to an existing, hand-made splitting of the model which can be used for assessing our results; and (3) the splitting is documented, so that we can extract descriptions of the desired sub-models without introducing evaluator bias.

We selected six models that satisfy these criteria. The first four of these were known to the authors (convenience sampling); the last two were obtained by scanning the At-lanMod Zoo on-line collection of meta-models[3]. All models were either initially captured in UML or transformed from EMF to UML. The subjects are shown in Table 1 along with their particular decomposition types and metrics: The number of sub-models, classes and interfaces, associations, compositions, aggregations, generalizations, and interface realizations.

The first model, HSM [7], comprises three different diagrams and was already described in Sec. 1. Textual descriptions of the sub-models were extracted from [7]. The second, GMF[4], is a meta-model for the specification of graphical editors, consisting of four viewpoint-specific sub-models. Three out of four textual descriptions of the sub-models were obtained from the user documentation on the GMF website. One missing description was taken from a tutorial web site for Eclipse developers[5]. The UML meta-model[6] is organized into 14 packages. The descriptions of these packages were extracted from the overview sections in the UML specification. The description of the four WASL packages was extracted from [16]. The description of the two WebML packages was obtained from the online documentation. Finally, R2ML is a markup language designed for rule interchange between systems and tools. It comprises six packages, each documented in [15].

The second and the third columns in Table 1 list the decomposition type and the number of target sub-models for each of the subjects. The last four columns present the size of the subject models in terms of the number of classes and relationships.

5.2   Methodology and Measurement

To investigate **RQ1**, we performed a qualitative analysis using a case study (Sec. 6.1) while for **RQ2**, we performed a set of quantitative experiments (Sec. 6.2). To evaluate the accuracy of our splitting technique, we used the following metrics:

1. *Expected*: the number of elements in the predetermined result, i.e., sub-model.
2. *Reported*: the number of elements assigned to the sub-model.
3. *Correct*: the number of elements correctly assigned to the sub-model.
4. *Precision*: the fraction of relevant elements among those reported, calculated as $\frac{Correct}{Reported}$.
5. *Recall*: the fraction of all relevant elements reported, calculated as $\frac{Correct}{Expected}$.
6. *F-measure*: a harmonized measure combining precision and recall, whose value is high if both precision and recall are high, calculated as $\frac{2 \times Precision \times Recall}{Precision + Recall}$. This measure is usually used to evaluate the accuracy of a technique as it does not allow trading-off precision for recall and vice versa.

---

[3] http://www.emn.fr/z-info/atlanmod/index.php/Zoos

[4] http://www.eclipse.org/modeling/gmp/

[5] http://www.vogella.com/articles/EclipseEMF/article.html

[6] http://www.omg.org/spec/UML/2.5/Beta1/

Table 2. Parameter assignment for class models

Association	Aggregation	Composition	Generalization	Interface Realization	α
0.04	0.13	0.26	0.44	0.13	0.86

5.3 Implementation

We implemented the proposed splitting algorithm for UML class models, considering the relationship kinds shown in table 1. Our prototype implementation is written in Java. As input, it receives an input model and text files providing the sub-model descriptions and configuration parameters.

For the IR phase, we used the LSA implementation from the open-source Semantic Vectors library[7], treating class and interface names as queries, and sub-model descriptions as documents. The crawling phase is performed using a model-type agnostic graph-based representation allowing us to analyze models of different types. We thus transformed the input UML models into that internal representation, focusing only on the elements of interest described above. We disregarded existing package structures in order to compare our results against them. The output sub-models were then transformed back to UML by creating a designated package for each.

Our technique relies on a number of configuration parameters described in Sec. 4: the calibration parameter α shaping the distribution of scores and the *weight* map w balancing weights of specific relationship types. We fine-tuned these parameters using the hill climbing optimization technique [6]. Our goal was to find a *single* combination of parameter values yielding the best average accuracy for all cases. The motivation for doing so was the premise that a configuration that achieved good results on most members of a set of unrelated class models might produce good results on other class models, too. The results are summarized in Table 2.

6 Results

In this section, we discuss our evaluation results, individually addressing each of the research questions.

6.1 RQ1: How Useful is the Incremental Approach for Model Splitting?

We evaluate this research question on a case study based on the Graphical Modeling Framework (GMF). GMF comprises four sub-models: *Domain*, *Graphical*, *Tooling*, and *Mapping*. While the sub-models of GMF are already known, they may not necessarily be explicitly present in historically grown meta-models comparable to GMF. We assume that the person in charge of splitting the model is aware of two major viewpoints, *Domain* and *Graphical*, and wants to discover the remaining ones. She provides the meta-model and describes the sub-models as follows: "**Sub-model Domain** *contains*

---

[7] http://code.google.com/p/semanticvectors/

the information about the defined classes. It shows a root object representing the whole model. This model has children which represent the packages, whose children represent the classes, while the children of the classes represent the attributes of these classes. **Sub-model Graphical** is used to describe composition of figures forming diagram elements: node, connection, compartment and label."

The user decides to begin with an incomplete splitting, since her goal is discovery of potential candidates for new sub-models. An incomplete splitting creates suggestions for sub-models *Domain, Graphical* as well as a *"Rest"* – for elements that were not assigned to either of the first two because they did not score above a predefined threshold value. The user can control the size of the *Rest* part by adjusting the threshold value according to her understanding of the model. After a suitable splitting is obtained, the *Rest* part contains the following elements: *ContributionItem, AuditedMetricTarget, DomainElementTarget, Image, Palette, BundleImage, DefaultImage, ToolGroup, MenuAction, MetricRule, NotationElementTarget, ToolRegistry.* From the inspection of these, the user concludes that a portion of the monolithic model seems to be concerned with tooling aspects of graphical editors comprising different kinds of toolbars, menu items, and palettes aligned around the graphical canvas. She describes this intuition: *"**Sub-model Tooling** includes the definitions of a Palette, MenuActions, and other UI actions. The palette consists of basic tools being organized in ToolGroups and assigned to a ToolRegistry."*

A next iteration of splitting is performed. This time, the *Rest* comprises only four items: *MetricRule, DomainElementTarget, NotationElementTarget, AuditedMetricTarget.* Three out of these four elements signify a notion of defining relationships between elements of already known sub-models. She concludes that a separate sub-model is required for defining the integration and interrelation of individual sub-models. She performs a third and last splitting after providing a final sub-model description: *"**Sub-model Mapping** binds the aspects of editor specification together. To define a mapping, the user creates elements such as NotationElementTarget and DomainElementTarget establishing an assignment between domain and notational elements."*

To investigate **RQ1** we further split it into two research questions: **RQ1.1:** Does the accuracy of splitting improve with each iteration? and **RQ1.2:** Does the approach assist the user in identifying missing sub-models?

RQ1.1: This question can be explored by considering the delta of each sub-model's F-measure during multiple incremental splitting steps. As shown in Table 3, the increase of accuracy is monotonic in all sub-models! The same threshold value was used for all splits. The discovery process not only helped the user to discover the desired sub-models but also to create short sub-model descriptions which can later be used for documentation.

RQ1.2: In the first query, the *Rest* part has 12 elements, whereas in the original model, its size was 139. All 12 elements actually belong to the yet undiscovered sub-models, *Tooling* and *Mapping*. Thus, we are able to conclude that the user was successfully guided to concentrate on discovering these sub-models without being distracted by contents of those sub-models she knew about upfront.

Table 3. F-Measure during three runs of incremental splitting

Run	Domain	Graphical	Tooling	Mapping
1	80%	77%	–	–
2	80%	84%	90%	–
3	86%	94%	90%	68%

Table 4. Accuracy of model splitting

	1: IR Only			2: IR + Plain			3: IR + Undirected			4: Overall		
	Prec.	Recall	F-M.	Prec.	Recall	F-M.	Prec.	Recall	F-M.	Prec.	Recall	F-M.
HSM	93%	42%	56%	93%	53%	67%	78%	78%	75%	90%	92%	89%
GMF	100%	9%	17%	99%	30%	38%	68%	72%	68%	86%	87%	86%
UML	57%	21%	24%	37%	20%	22%	34%	38%	30%	50%	58%	48%
WASL	88%	48%	61%	72%	29%	38%	68%	64%	63%	92%	91%	89%
WebML	100%	37%	52%	100%	40%	56%	88%	94%	90%	93%	97%	95%
R2ML	81%	22%	32%	74%	30%	30%	46%	49%	42%	75%	77%	74%
UML_{funct}	67%	22%	30%	76%	24%	33%	64%	66%	61%	84%	80%	80%

6.2   RQ2: How Accurate is the Automatic Splitting?

We investigate **RQ2** by answering two research questions: **RQ2.1:** What is the overall accuracy of the splitting approach? and **RQ2.2:** What is the relative contribution of individual aspects of the splitting algorithm on the overall quality of the results?

RQ2.1: Column 4 in Table 4 presents average precision, recall and F-measure of our automated technique for each of the subject models. For five out of the six models, the achieved level of accuracy in terms of F-measure was good to excellent (74%-95%). However, the result for UML was not as good (48%). Detailed inspection of this model revealed that package organization of UML has a special, centralized structure: it is based on a set of global hub packages such as *CommonStructure* or *CommonBehavior* that provide basic elements to packages with more specific functionality such as *Use-Case* or *StateMachine*. Hub packages are *strongly coupled* with most other packages, i.e., they have a low ratio of inter- to intra-relations. For example, the class *Element* is a transitive superclass for all model elements. This violation of the software engineering principle of *low coupling* hinders our topology-based approach for splitting.

To evaluate whether our algorithm produces meaningful results *except for hubs*, we derived a sub-model of UML which is restricted only to the functional packages. This sub-model, uml_{funct}, comprises 10 out of 14 packages and 188 out of 242 model elements of UML. As shown in Table 4, the accuracy results of uml_{funct} were similar to the five successful case studies (80%).

RQ2.2: Columns 1, 2 and 3 of Table 4 list contributions of individual steps of the algorithm and of the adjustments (A1-3) described in Sec. 4. The results after the IR phase are shown in column 1. Compared to the overall quality of the algorithm (column 4), the results are constantly worse in terms of the F-measure, due to low recall values. That is, IR alone is unable to find a sufficient number of relevant elements.

In column 2, we present the results of IR augmented with basic crawling which respects directionality, i.e., does not navigate relations from their inverse end. This version is similar to the crawling technique proposed by Suade but adjusted to operate on models rather than on code-level artifacts. The results are again worse than those of the overall technique due to low recall values. Interestingly, in some cases, e.g., WASL, the results are also worse than those of the plain IR technique in terms of both precision and recall, making the scoring schema related to this crawling strategy really inefficient.

Column 3 shows the results when crawling discards directionality, i.e., applies A1. This strategy results in a significant improvement in recall and the overall F-measure compared to the previous approach, but comes together with some decrease in precision.

Column 4 shows the results when the previous approach is extended with scoring modifications (A2-A3). This approach is clearly superior to the previous ones in terms of both precision and recall, and, as a consequence, of the overall F-measure.

We conclude that the basic crawling technique that worked well for code in case of Suade is not directly applicable to models, while our improvements allowed the algorithm to reach high accuracy in terms of both precision and recall.

6.3   Threats to Validity

Threats to external validity are most significant for our work: the results of our study might not generalize to other cases. Moreover, because we used a limited number of subjects, the configuration parameters might not generalize without an appropriate tuning. We attempted to mitigate this threat by using real-life case studies of considerable size from various application domains. The ability to select appropriate sub-model descriptions also influences the general applicability of our results. We attempted to mitigate this threat by using descriptions publicly available in online documentation.

7   Related Work

In this section, we compare our approach with related work.

Formal Approaches to Model Decomposition. A formally founded approach to model splitting was investigated in [3]. This approach uses strongly connected components (SCCs) to calculate the space of possible decompositions. The user of the technique may either examine the set of all SCCs or try to find reasonable unions of SCCs according to her needs. In a recent publication [5], the same authors rule out invalid decompositions by providing precise conditions for the splitting of models conforming to arbitrary meta-models. This work is orthogonal to ours: Our technique requires a basic notion of a model being splittable, mostly motivated by the need to split class models and meta-models.

Another formal approach to model splitting is discussed in [13]: The authors show that a split of a monolithic meta-model into a set of model components with export and import interfaces can be propagated for the automatic split of instances of the meta-model. However, this technique does not automate the meta-model splitting; the user has to assign model elements to target components by hand.

Graph Clustering for Meta-models and Architecture Models. *Graph clustering* is the activity of finding a partition of a given graph into a set of sub-graphs based on a given objective. Voigt [14] uses graph clustering to provide a divide-and-conquer approach for the matching of meta-models of 1 million elements. Of the different graph clustering algorithms, the author chose Planar Edge Separator (PES) for its run-time performance, and then adapted it to meta-model matching. Like us, he provides weighting constants for specific relationships kinds; yet [14] only presents the values of these constants and does not evaluate their impact on the quality of the match. From a software engineering perspective, the main drawback of this approach is that the user cannot influence the decomposition in terms of the concepts represented in the resulting sub-models. The same objection may be raised for the meta-model splitting tool proposed in [12]. Our approach bases the decomposition on user description of the desired sub-models, thus avoiding the need for the user to comprehend and classify the resulting components.

The architecture restructuring technique by Streekmann [11] is most similar to our approach. This technique assumes a legacy architecture that is to be replaced by an improved one. Similar to our technique, the starting point for the new organization is a set of target components together with a set of seeds ([11] calls them *initial mappings*) from which the content is derived. Yet, unlike in our approach, these seeds are specified manually by the developer. The clustering is performed by applying a traditional hierarchical clustering algorithm assigning model elements to components. The algorithm supports the weighting of different types of relationships; tuning these strongly impacts the quality of the decomposition. For the scenarios given in [11], the weighting differs from case to case significantly. In this work, in turn, we were able to find a specific setting of values that produced good results for an (albeit small) selection of unrelated class models. Streekmann also discusses algorithm stability w.r.t. arbitrary decisions made by it. During hierarchical clustering, once two elements are assigned to the same cluster (which, in the case of multiple assignment options, may be an arbitrary choice), this decision is not reversible. Arbitrary decisions in this style do not occur in our approach since we calculate relevance scorings for each sub-model individually.

Model Slicing. *Model slicing* is a technique that computes a fragment of the model specified by a property. In the approach in [1], slicing of a UML class model results in a sub-model which is either *strict*, i.e., it satisfies all structural constraints imposed by the meta-model, or *soft*, if conformity constraints are relaxed in exchange of additional features. For example, slicing a class model can select a class and all of its subclasses, or a class and its supertypes within radius 1, etc. Compared to model splitting, model slicing concentrates on computing a sub-model of interest, ignoring the remainder of the model. In contrast, we use textual descriptions as input to IR to identify sub-models. The techniques are orthogonal and can be combined, as we plan to do in the future.

8   Conclusions and Future Work

Splitting large monolithic models into disjoint sub-models can improve comprehensibility and facilitate distributed development. In this paper, we proposed an incremental approach for model splitting, supported by an automated technique that relies on information retrieval and model crawling. Our technique was inspired by code-level feature location approaches which we extended and adapted to operate on model-level artifacts. We demonstrated the feasibility of our approach and a high accuracy of the automated model splitting technique on a number of real-life case studies.

As part of future work, we intend to enhance our technique with additional types of analysis, e.g., considering cohesion and coupling metrics when building sub-models. We also plan to extend our approach to consider information obtained by analyzing additional model elements such as class attributes, methods and their behavior.

In addition, we are interested in further investigating the impact of sub-model descriptions on the overall accuracy of our approach and in suggesting strategies both for identifying good descriptions and for improving existing ones. Further involving the user in the splitting process, e.g., allowing her to provide partial lists of elements to be present (absent) in particular sub-models, might improve the results of the automated analysis significantly. We aim to explore this direction in the future.

Acknowledgements. We wish to thank Martin Robillard for making the source code of Suade available to us and the anonymous reviewers for their valuable comments.

References

1. Blouin, A., Combemale, B., Baudry, B., Beaudoux, O.: Modeling Model Slicers. In: Whittle, J., Clark, T., Kühne, T. (eds.) MODELS 2011. LNCS, vol. 6981, pp. 62–76. Springer, Heidelberg (2011)
2. Dit, B., Revelle, M., Gethers, M., Poshyvanyk, D.: Feature Location in Source Code: A Taxonomy and Survey. Journal of Software: Evolution and Process 25(1), 53–95 (2013)
3. Kelsen, P., Ma, Q., Glodt, C.: Models Within Models: Taming Model Complexity Using the Sub-Model Lattice. In: Giannakopoulou, D., Orejas, F. (eds.) FASE 2011. LNCS, vol. 6603, pp. 171–185. Springer, Heidelberg (2011)
4. Landauer, T.K., Foltz, P.W., Laham, D.: An Introduction to Latent Semantic Analysis. Discourse Processes (25), 259–284 (1998)
5. Ma, Q., Kelsen, P., Glodt, C.: A Generic Model Decomposition Technique and Its Application to the Eclipse Modeling Framework. J. Soft. & Sys. Modeling, 1–32 (2013)
6. Pitsoulis, L., Resende, M.: Handbook of Applied Optimization. Oxford Univ. Press (2002)
7. Rad, Y.T., Jabbari, R.: Use of Global Consistency Checking for Exploring and Refining Relationships between Distributed Models: A Case Study. Master's thesis, Blekinge Institute of Technology, School of Computing (January 2012)
8. Rajaraman, A., Ullman, J.D.: Mining of Massive Datasets. Cambridge Univ. Press (2011)
9. Robillard, M.P.: Automatic Generation of Suggestions for Program Investigation. In: Proc. of ESEC/FSE 2013, pp. 11–20 (2005)
10. Rubin, J., Chechik, M.: A Survey of Feature Location Techniques. In: Reinhartz-Berger, I., et al. (eds.) Domain Engineering: Product Lines, Conceptual Models, and Languages. Springer (2013)
11. Streekmann, N.: Clustering-Based Support for Software Architecture Restructuring. Springer (2011)
12. Strüber, D., Selter, M., Taentzer, G.: Tool Support for Clustering Large Meta-models. In: Proc. of BigMDE 2013 (2013)
13. Strüber, D., Taentzer, G., Jurack, S., Schäfer, T.: Towards a Distributed Modeling Process Based on Composite Models. In: Cortellessa, V., Varró, D. (eds.) FASE 2013 (ETAPS 2013). LNCS, vol. 7793, pp. 6–20. Springer, Heidelberg (2013)
14. Voigt, K.: Structural Graph-based Metamodel Matching. PhD thesis, Univ. of Dresden (2011)
15. Wagner, G., Giurca, A., Lukichev, S.: A Usable Interchange Format for Rich Syntax Rules Integrating OCL, RuleML and SWRL. In: Proc. of WSh. Reasoning on the Web (2006)
16. Wolffgang, U.: Multi-platform Model-driven Software Development of Web Applications. In: ICSOFT 2011, vol. 2, pp. 162–171 (2011)
17. Zhao, W., Zhang, L., Liu, Y., Sun, J., Yang, F.: SNIAFL: Towards a Static Noninteractive Approach to Feature Location. ACM TOSEM 15, 195–226 (2006)

Sound Merging and Differencing
for Class Diagrams

Uli Fahrenberg[1], Mathieu Acher[1,2], Axel Legay[1], and Andrzej Wąsowski[3,*]

[1] IRISA / Inria Rennes, France
[2] University of Rennes 1, France
[3] IT University of Copenhagen, Denmark

Abstract. Class diagrams are among the most popular modeling languages in industrial use. In a model-driven development process, class diagrams evolve, so it is important to be able to assess differences between revisions, as well as to propagate differences using suitable merge operations. Existing differencing and merging methods are mainly syntactic, concentrating on edit operations applied to model elements, or they are based on sampling: enumerating some examples of instances which characterize the difference between two diagrams. This paper presents the first known (to the best of our knowledge) automatic model merging and differencing operators supported by a formal semantic theory guaranteeing that they are semantically sound. All instances of the merge of a model and its difference with another model are automatically instances of the second model. The differences we synthesize are represented using class diagram notation (not edits, or instances), which allows creation of a simple yet flexible algebra for diffing and merging. It also allows presenting changes comprehensively, in a notation already known to users.

1 Introduction

Model management is an essential activity in a model-driven development process. Numerous tools exist to visualize, validate, transform, refactor, compute differences, or merge models and structured data. The basic management operations can be combined to realize complex maintenance and design tasks. In this paper, we consider merging and differencing of models—two crucial management operations—for class diagrams, the most popular modeling language used in the industry [12]. Class diagrams are used to create domain models, structural system models, and lower level design models. Class diagrams also serve as meta-models, or abstract syntax types, in implementation of domain specific languages (DSLs).

Merging. When a single model is not sufficient to capture all the aspects of a problem or a system, engineers have to merge several models to produce a single integrated model [11, 13, 19, 20, 23, 25]. Model merging also arises when factoring out commonalities of different variant models, e.g., following a product line approach (e.g., see [1, 21, 22]).

---

* Supported by The Danish Council for Independent Research under *Sapere Aude* project VARIETE.

S. Gnesi and A. Rensink (Eds.): FASE 2014, LNCS 8411, pp. 63–78, 2014.

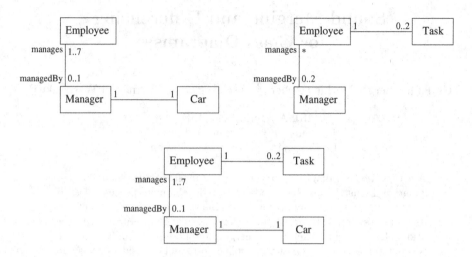

Fig. 1. Two simple class diagrams (above) and their merge (below). Note that the object models of the merge are precisely the ones which model both individual aspects: here, the merge is both sound and complete.

Differencing. Models naturally evolve through editing operations (e.g., adding an inheritance relationship in a class diagram) for refactoring or extending a system. Computing differences of two revised models has applications in comprehension of an evolution, identification of instances not supported by the two models [6, 14], etc. Merging and differencing operations can be combined when engineers have to propagate differences from one version of the model to another, as in the case of revision control systems.

Key requirements. We highlight two requirements that arise when merging or differencing models. In many engineering scenarios, the result of a merge or difference is subject to *analysis*: automated tools can ensure that certain instances are still present in the composed diagram; engineers (humans) can visualize the result and therefore understand the evolution of the system. Another important requirement is that the result of a merge (resp. difference) *advances the design of a system*, so it produces a new model that can later be used in construction. Again, both automated tools and manual activities can operate over this model. For instance, code can be generated from a class diagram; engineers can relate the class diagram to other modeling artefacts or specify a transformation.

The two requirements impact the design of merging and differencing operations. First, it is beneficial that a merge (resp. difference) of two class diagrams should be a class diagram—in line with the vision exposed in [10] that a difference between models should be a model. This allows engineers to visualize the difference and to manipulate it using the usual tools for working with models. Second, merge (resp. difference) operations should be ideally both sound and complete, to enable further precise analysis by automated tools. In particular, an *unsound* merge operator can authorize objects (instances) actually not conformant to the merged diagrams. Figure 1 introduces a simple example of a merge between two class diagrams. The result (below) *is* a class diagram, and the merge is both sound and complete. (Note that we assume an open-world semantics, which is consistent with the view semantics used by most modeling tools, i.e. it attempts to compute a minimal model such that the two original models can be derived as its views.)

As further discussed in Sect. 2, existing merging or differencing methods, though extremely useful in practice, do not meet the two requirements. First, syntactic methods suffer from possible lack of soundness, since they do not take the semantics into account. Second, enumerative semantic methods (e.g., [15–17]) only synthesize a finite set of instance and are thus not complete. In both methods, the result is no longer a class diagram, precluding an algebraic combination of operations or a direct manipulation by tools and engineers.

We follow the methodology presented by us in an earlier work [10]—we develop the difference operator systematically, via a number of well-defined formal definition steps. We believe that these steps yield a substantial understanding of what the differences between diagrams can be (unlike methods that simply encode a lot of knowledge in a large constraint system solved by an external solver). This knowledge can later be used to advance language design for structural modeling.

The contributions of the paper include:

- A *concise formal semantics* for the core language of class diagrams (concise and mathematically mature definitions of such are surprising hard to find). The semantics relies purely on set theory, which is crucial for avoiding dependencies on description logics, reasoners and proof systems.
- A formalisation of the standard (conjunctive) *merge* operator used to compute the conjunction of class diagrams (by "putting them on the same page"). To the best of our knowledge, no previous such formalisations exist; using our formalization, we can show that merge is always, automatically, *sound*.
- An intuitive notion of *subtyping* which is closely related to the merge operator (which is the greatest lower bound for subtyping), and a corresponding notion of a *disjunctive merge*, which computes disjunctions of class diagrams (and is the lowest upper bound for subtyping). Using our formalization, we show that disjunctive merge is semantically *complete*.
- A *compositional algebra* for class diagrams: We can show that using only (conjunctive) merge, all class diagrams can be constructed from a few *elementary* class diagrams. Together with subtyping, this gives an algebra which allows for high-level computations with class diagrams.
- A *difference* operator which computes, in a precise sense, the best possible approximation to an inverse to conjunctive merge. Our difference operator is semantically sound, computable entirely automatically, and produces finite syntactic descriptions of infinite (semantic) differences.

The intended audience are researchers interested in semantics of structural modeling, evolution of meta-models and builders of differencing or merging tools.

We proceed by discussing related work in Sect. 2. Section 3 introduces a simple abstract syntax for class diagrams, along with subtyping and compositions.

Sect. 4 defines differencing. Both sections work at syntactic level. In Sect. 5, we justify these constructions by showing that they are semantically sound. We introduce a concise, set-based semantics for class diagrams and show that our operators respect it. We conclude in Sect. 6, indicating possible variants and extensions.

2 Related Work

Our objective is to represent merges and differences of two class diagrams *as a class diagram*, overcoming limitations of enumerative and syntactical methods in terms of soundness, completeness, and further exploitation by engineers. We achieve this by developing syntactic methods (with sound theoretical basis), which guarantee representation of difference in one description as a diagram.

Limitations of existing syntactic approaches. A syntactic approach to differencing operates purely by manipulating syntactic elements of diagrams, mostly without paying attention whether these manipulations are sound with respect to semantics of the language (for example that they do not ignore some instances).

   Syntactic differencing methods are extremely useful in practice, for example, users can visualize a set of syntactic edit operations (e.g., create, modify, delete [3]) and easily understand the evolution of two models. Most of the studies in the field of model differencing (see, e.g., [6]) present syntactic differencing at either the concrete or the abstract syntax level. However, syntactic methods are inherently incomplete and unsound. They may not be able to expose and represent the semantic (meaningful) differences between two versions of a class diagram. They can also report false positives by operating at the syntactical level. The incompleteness and unsoundness can both disturb automated analysis and a further exploitation by an engineer.

Limitations of enumerative approaches. As argued in some papers and illustrated for some formalisms [2, 7, 10, 15–17], models that are syntactically very similar may induce very different semantics, and a list of differences should be best addressed *semantically*. Recently, semantic approaches have been proposed which enumerate some examples of *instances* of one model that are not instances of the other [17]. For instance, Maoz *et al.* tackle the problem of semantic model differencing, specifically for class and activity diagrams [15, 16]. The *cddiff* operator for class diagrams [16] computes diff witnesses using the Alloy Analyzer, a solver for relational logic with transitive closure. For the *addiff* operator for activity diagrams, they present algorithms that take as input activity diagrams [15]. The advantage of enumerative methods is that they operate at the semantic level and are sound by construction: no false positives can be reported. However they are clearly incomplete since only a small, finite number of examples can be synthesized. In fact, the set of instances in the difference might well be infinite. A related problem is that engineers cannot visualize and manipulate the (infinite) set of witnesses—a concrete and compact representation is missing. It also precludes an algebraic combination of merging and differencing operations, as in the case of versioning control systems (see Fig. 3, page 72 for more details).

Other approaches and existing tools. Model *matching* is another important related problem [6, 7, 9]. Numerous algorithms and techniques are already integrated in model-based tools (e.g., see [14, 19, 23]). For simplicity the theoretical framework we develop assume a basic matching strategy (based on names, see next section). Numerous "diff" or merging tools (e.g., EMF Diff[1], Kompose [11, 20], Epsilon [13], UMLDiff [25], TReMer+ [19, 23], etc.) offer the means to specify user directives (using a specific language or an API). Users can override (customize) the default behaviour of the merging or differencing algorithm and thus handle the semantics of the models. However, the manual specification, if not properly defined, does not guarantee semantic properties and can lead to unsound or incomplete merging (resp. differencing). The objective of the paper is precisely to study the soundness and completeness of operations that can be incorporated into modeling tools. Our approach is both algebraically and semantically justified: to the best of our knowledge, no previous effort guarantees such properties of merging and differencing of class diagrams. Any matching strategy that defines an equivalence on the space of class names could be naturally incorporated in our framework.

3 Compositional Algebra of Class Diagrams

We start by introducing an abstract syntax for class diagrams. We remark that the operators defined in this section are entirely syntactical; no reference to the semantics of class diagrams is made. The same holds for the properties we expose: they are proven at the syntactic level. In Sect. 5 we will introduce a semantics for class diagrams and show that our operators are semantically sound, but their properties as shown in the present section are completely independent of any semantics one wishes to give to class diagrams.

Let $\mathcal{N}$ be the set of all finite unions of finite or unbounded intervals of natural numbers (including the empty set of intervals). $\mathcal{N}$ is closed under union, intersection and complementation; let $\neg A = \mathbb{N} \backslash A$ be the complement of $A \in \mathcal{N}$.

3.1 Abstract Syntax

Let Σ_c, Σ_a and Σ_e be disjoint infinite sets of names, for classes, associations and association ends, respectively.

Definition 1. *A* class diagram *is a tuple* $\mathcal{C} = (\mathsf{cla}, \mathsf{asc}, \mathsf{gen}, \mathsf{disj}, \mathsf{ccard}, \mathsf{aends}, \mathsf{acards})$ *consisting of*

(i) A finite set $\mathsf{cla} \subseteq \Sigma_c$ *of classes,*
(ii) A finite set $\mathsf{asc} \subseteq \Sigma_a$ *of associations,*
(iii) A reflexive transitive relation $\mathsf{gen} \subseteq \mathsf{cla} \times \mathsf{cla} \cup \mathsf{asc} \times \mathsf{asc}$ *capturing generalizations between classes and between associations,*
(iv) An irreflexive symmetric relation $\mathsf{disj} \subseteq \mathsf{cla} \times \mathsf{cla}$ *representing class disjointness constraints,*

---

[1] http://eclipse.org/diffmerge/

(v) A mapping ccard : cla → $\mathcal{N}$ encoding class cardinality *constraints,*

(vi) A partial function aends : asc → Σ_e ⇀ cla *mapping each association to its endpoints, and*

(vii) A partial function acards : asc → Σ_e ⇀ $\mathcal{N}$ *mapping each association to its endpoint cardinality constraints.*

Also $|\text{dom}(\text{aends}(a))| = 2$ *and* $\text{dom}(\text{acards}(a)) = \text{dom}(\text{aends}(a))$ *for all* $a \in \text{asc}$.

Note that we handle generalizations of both classes and associations; this is common in modern modeling approaches. In the usual concrete syntax of class diagrams, the generalization relation is essentially transitively reduced, but in (iii) we require it to be transitively closed, in order to simplify presentation. Given that the sets of classes and associations are finite, switching between both viewpoints is just a technicality. Another common assumption in class modeling is that two classes which do not share a common subclass are disjoint. This default assumption does not work well with the open-world semantics that we will build up in this paper. It would make the semantics non-monotonic—adding a shared subclass would relax constraints on instances. To prevent this, we prefer to add, in (iv), an explicit representation of binary disjointness constraints in the abstract syntax. Again, switching between explicit and implicit disjointness constraints is just a technicality, but it will allow us to simplify presentation later on. The last condition means that we only consider binary associations. With this in mind, the function aends (vi) maps the two association ends (or, more precisely, their names) of each association to their classes. Similarly, the function acards (vii) associates cardinality constraints to association ends.

As mentioned we will use an open-world semantics, which can be summarized by the slogan that *anything which is not forbidden is allowed.* So, intuitively, there will be no semantic difference between a class c that does not appear in a given class diagram, and one which does, but has unrestricted cardinality. Formally, we call a class $c \in$ cla in some class diagram $\mathcal{C}$ *restricted* if ccard$(c) \neq \mathbb{N}$, and let rcla $\subseteq$ cla denote the subset of restricted classes.

3.2 Merge

Ultimately, we want to create class diagrams by composing smaller chunks of them. This reflects the practice of modeling with views, as supported by many modeling tools (for example Eclipse Modeling Framework, Papyrus, or IBM Rational Modeler). Users of such tools work with projections of one large single model represented implicitly in a unified syntax tree. From the users' perspective it may often appear that they work with a number of diagrams that are unified (composed) as if they were *put together on the same page*, merging entities (e.g., classes) that have the same name. In the following, we propose a conjunctive *merge* operator, written ⊗, that composes two diagrams, as if they were put on the same page, interpreted as views of the same underlying model.

Due to syntactic restrictions, it is not possible for us to merge diagrams that have the same association with different association ends. Since we only allow one name per endpoint in abstract syntax, there is no way to merge different names. This is consistent with the behavior of common modeling tools, where different views of the same association always maintain the same end points.

Definition 2. *Two class diagrams* C_1, C_2 *are said to be* composable *if it holds for all* $a \in \mathsf{asc}_1 \cap \mathsf{asc}_2$ *that* $\mathsf{aends}_1(a) = \mathsf{aends}_2(a)$.

Definition 3. *The* (conjunctive) merge *of two composable class diagrams* C_1, C_2 *is* $C_\otimes = C_1 \otimes C_2$ *defined as follows:*

- $\mathsf{cla}_\otimes = \mathsf{cla}_1 \cup \mathsf{cla}_2$, $\mathsf{asc}_\otimes = \mathsf{asc}_1 \cup \mathsf{asc}_2$, $\mathsf{gen}_\otimes = (\mathsf{gen}_1 \cup \mathsf{gen}_2)^*$, $\mathsf{disj}_\otimes = \mathsf{disj}_1 \cup \mathsf{disj}_2$,
- $\mathsf{aends}_\otimes = \mathsf{aends}_1 \cup \mathsf{aends}_2$, *and*

$$\mathsf{ccard}_\otimes(c) = \begin{cases} \mathsf{ccard}_1(c) & \textit{if } c \in \mathsf{cla}_1 \setminus \mathsf{cla}_2, \\ \mathsf{ccard}_2(c) & \textit{if } c \in \mathsf{cla}_2 \setminus \mathsf{cla}_1, \\ \mathsf{ccard}_1(c) \cap \mathsf{ccard}_2(c) & \textit{if } c \in \mathsf{cla}_1 \cap \mathsf{cla}_2, \end{cases}$$

$$\mathsf{acards}_\otimes(a)(e) = \begin{cases} \mathsf{acards}_1(a)(e) & \textit{if } a \in \mathsf{asc}_1 \setminus \mathsf{asc}_2, \\ \mathsf{acards}_2(a)(e) & \textit{if } a \in \mathsf{asc}_2 \setminus \mathsf{asc}_1, \\ \mathsf{acards}_1(a)(e) \cap \mathsf{acards}_2(a)(e) & \textit{if } a \in \mathsf{asc}_1 \cap \mathsf{asc}_2 \end{cases}$$

for all $c \in \mathsf{cla}_\otimes$, $a \in \mathsf{asc}_\otimes$, *and* $e \in \mathsf{dom}(\mathsf{aends}(a))$.

Intuitively, the above merging attempts to approximate *conjunction* of class diagrams. Due to our open-world semantics ("anything which is not mentioned is unrestricted"), we have to apply a *disjunction* to the syntactic elements (classes, associations, etc.) to get a conjunctive merge. The merge in Fig. 1 in the introduction gives a simple example of the operation.

3.3 Subtyping

With the above definitions we have gathered enough structure to propose a definition of *subtyping* between two class diagrams:

Definition 4. *For class diagrams* C_1, C_2, *we say that* C_1 (syntactically) refines C_2, *denoted* $C_1 \leq C_2$, *if all the following conditions hold:*

(i) $\mathsf{cla}_1 \supseteq \mathsf{rcla}_2$, $\mathsf{asc}_1 \supseteq \mathsf{asc}_2$

(C_1 *is an extension of* C_2)

(ii) $\mathsf{gen}_1 \supseteq \mathsf{gen}_2$, $\mathsf{disj}_1 \supseteq \mathsf{disj}_2$

(*generalization and disjointness constraints are inherited*)

(iii) $\mathsf{ccard}_1(c) \subseteq \mathsf{ccard}_2(c)$ *for all* $c \in \mathsf{rcla}_2$

(*class cardinalities are restricted*)

(iv) $\mathsf{aends}_1(a) = \mathsf{aends}_2(a)$ *for all* $a \in \mathsf{asc}_2$

(*association ends are preserved*)

(v) $\mathsf{acards}_1(a)(e) \subseteq \mathsf{acards}_2(a)(e)$ *for all* $a \in \mathsf{asc}_2$ *and all* $e \in \mathsf{dom}(\mathsf{acards}_2(a))$

(*association cardinalities are restricted*)

Due to the open-world semantics, subtyping on syntactic elements becomes reversed subset inclusion. Also, we have to use *restricted* classes in the inclusion $cla_1 \supseteq rcla_2$ above; otherwise one could easily find subtypings which were *not sound*, i.e., where the subtype admits models which the supertype does not.

Our selections of subtyping and merging are strongly related, in the sense that $\oslash$ is the *greatest lower bound* for $\leq$. In practice, this means that the merge does indeed "behave like a conjunction".

Theorem 1. *For all class diagrams C_1, C_2, D with C_1 and C_2 composable, $D \leq C_1 \oslash C_2$ iff $D \leq C_1$ and $D \leq C_2$.*

We believe that this compatibility of subtyping and merging is of fundamental importance. Subtyping captures the intuitive notion of constraining the set of instances during modeling. A merge operator considered without subtyping can create merges that admit far fewer, or many more, instances than the user would expect. Introducing the above subtyping preorder on diagrams will later allow us to follow the method presented in [10] for defining differences. Intuitively, we need an order because notions of difference, distance and order are intimately related. It is surprising that so few works on merging and differencing structural models consider subtypes or other orderings (unlike for behavioral models, e.g. [8]).

Theorem 1 immediately entails that the merge operator has the core properties expected of composition, viz. commutativity and associativity. Also, merge is monotonic with respect to the subtyping order, or, in other words, *subtyping is compositional*. This is a highly desirable property that introduces some regularity in the framework.

Theorem 2. *The $\oslash$ operator is commutative and associative, and for all class diagrams C_1, C_2, D_2, D_2 with C_1 and D_1 composable and C_2 and D_2 composable, $C_1 \leq C_2$ and $D_1 \leq D_2$ imply $C_1 \oslash D_1 \leq C_2 \oslash D_2$.*

3.4 Class Diagram Algebra

Compositionality allows us to develop an algebra for class diagrams, using a few elementary diagrams and the composition operator $\oslash$. What we obtain is a small structural modeling calculus that is of interest by itself — class diagrams can be written concisely, in a manner that is friendly to a linear mathematically oriented text, unlike the concrete syntax representation of class diagrams, and unlike the rather unwieldy abstract syntax presented in Def. 1.

The calculus is built around a set of elementary class diagrams which are merged to obtain bigger structures. The elementary diagrams are as follows:

- $\top = (\emptyset, \emptyset, \emptyset, \emptyset, \emptyset, \emptyset, \emptyset)$: the empty class diagram that admits all object models;
- $\langle c^n \rangle$, for $c \in \Sigma_c$ and $n \in \mathcal{N}$: the class diagram with $cla = \{c\}$, $asc = \emptyset$, $gen = \{(c,c)\}$, $disj = \emptyset$, $ccard(c) = n$, and $aends = acards = \emptyset$;
- $\langle c_1 \; \frac{e_1}{n_1} a \frac{e_2}{n_2} \; c_2 \rangle$, for $c_1, c_2 \in \Sigma_c$, $e_1, e_2 \in \Sigma_e$ and $n_1, n_2 \in \mathcal{N}$: the class diagram with $cla = \{c_1, c_2\}$, $asc = \{a\}$, $gen = \{(c_1, c_1), (c_2, c_2)\}$, $disj = \emptyset$, $ccard(c_1) = ccard(c_2) = \mathbb{N}$, $dom(aends(a)) = \{e_1, e_2\}$, $aends(a)(e_1) = c_1$, $aends(a)(e_2) = c_2$, $acards(a)(e_1) = n_1$, and $acards(a)(e_2) = n_2$;

$$\top \qquad \langle c^n \rangle \qquad \langle c_1 \; \frac{e_1}{n_1} \text{-}a\text{-} \frac{e_2}{n_2} \; c_2 \rangle \qquad \langle c_1 \longrightarrow c_2 \rangle \qquad \langle c_1 \text{---} /\!/ \text{---} c_2 \rangle$$

$$\langle E^N \rangle \oslash \langle T^N \rangle \oslash \langle M^N \rangle \oslash$$
$$\langle E \; \frac{}{\{1\} \quad \{0,1,2\}} \; T \rangle \oslash \langle E \; \frac{ms \quad mB}{N \quad \{0,1\}} \; M \rangle$$
$$\oslash \langle M \longrightarrow E \rangle$$
$$\oslash \langle E \text{---} /\!/ \text{---} T \rangle \oslash \langle M \text{---} /\!/ \text{---} T \rangle$$

Fig. 2. The five types of elementary class diagrams (above), a simple class diagram in concrete syntax (below left), and its decomposition into elementary class diagrams (below right, where we have abbreviated names)

- $\langle c_1 \longrightarrow c_2 \rangle$, for $c_1, c_2 \in \Sigma_c$: the class diagram with $\mathsf{cla} = \{c_1, c_2\}$, $\mathsf{asc} = \emptyset$, $\mathsf{gen} = \{(c_1, c_1), (c_2, c_2), (c_1, c_2)\}$, $\mathsf{disj} = \emptyset$, $\mathsf{ccard}(c_1) = \mathsf{ccard}(c_2) = \mathbb{N}$, and $\mathsf{aends} = \mathsf{acards} = \emptyset$;
- $\langle c_1 \text{---} /\!/ \text{---} c_2 \rangle$, for $c_1, c_2 \in \Sigma_c$: the class diagram with $\mathsf{cla} = \{c_1, c_2\}$, $\mathsf{asc} = \emptyset$, $\mathsf{gen} = \{(c_1, c_1), (c_2, c_2)\}$, $\mathsf{disj} = \{(c_1, c_2), (c_2, c_1)\}$, $\mathsf{ccard}(c_1) = \mathsf{ccard}(c_2) = \mathbb{N}$, and $\mathsf{aends} = \mathsf{acards} = \emptyset$.

However simple, the above language of class diagrams is quite powerful—it is fully expressive in the sense that it can express every finite diagram as a finite composition; see also Fig. 2 for an example:

Theorem 3. *Every class diagram can be written as a finite conjunctive merge of elementary class diagrams.*

4 Difference and Disjunctive Merge

We enrich our algebra with two more operators, difference and disjunctive merge. The difference operator, which is a formal adjoint to the conjunctive merge, will have the property that merging a class diagram $\mathcal{C}_1$ with a difference $\mathcal{C}_2 \oslash \mathcal{C}_1$ is semantically *sound*, i.e., the composition $\mathcal{C}_1 \oslash (\mathcal{C}_2 \oslash \mathcal{C}_1)$ is a subtyping of $\mathcal{C}_2$. Later this will translate to a perhaps more intuitive semantic property that the difference does not admit too many instances; adding them to instances of diagram $\mathcal{C}_1$ still obeys the constraints of $\mathcal{C}_2$.

Definition 5. *The difference of two composable class diagrams $\mathcal{C}_1$, $\mathcal{C}_2$ is $\mathcal{C}_\oslash = \mathcal{C}_2 \oslash \mathcal{C}_1$ defined as follows:*

- $\mathsf{cla}_\oslash = \mathsf{cla}_2$, $\mathsf{asc}_\oslash = \mathsf{asc}_2 \setminus \mathsf{asc}_1$, $\mathsf{disj}_\oslash = \mathsf{disj}_2 \setminus \mathsf{disj}_1$, *and*

$$\mathsf{gen}_\oslash = \left(\bigcap \{ r \subseteq \mathsf{cla}_2 \times \mathsf{cla}_2 \mid (\mathsf{gen}_1 \cup r)^* \supseteq \mathsf{gen}_2 \} \right)^*,$$

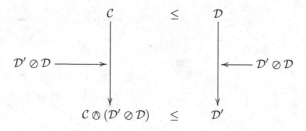

Fig. 3. Use of difference for automatic evolving of subtypes: If $\mathcal{C}$ is a subtype of $\mathcal{D}$, then $\mathcal{C}$ merged with the difference $\mathcal{D}' \oslash \mathcal{D}$ is a subtype of $\mathcal{D}'$

– $\mathsf{aends}_\oslash = \mathsf{aends}_2 \setminus \mathsf{aends}_1$, and

$$\mathsf{ccard}_\oslash(c) = \begin{cases} \mathsf{ccard}_2(c) & \textit{if } c \notin \mathsf{cla}_1, \\ \mathsf{ccard}_2(c) \cup \neg\mathsf{ccard}_1(c) & \textit{otherwise,} \end{cases}$$

$$\mathsf{acards}_\oslash(a)(e) = \begin{cases} \mathsf{acards}_2(a)(e) & \textit{if } a \notin \mathsf{asc}_1, \\ \mathsf{acards}_2(a)(e) \cup \neg\mathsf{acards}_1(a)(e) & \textit{otherwise} \end{cases}$$

$for\ all\ c \in \mathsf{cla}_\oslash,\ a \in \mathsf{asc}_\oslash,\ and\ e \in \mathsf{dom}(\mathsf{aends}(a)).$

Let us give some intuition about the rather complicated formula for $\mathsf{gen}_\oslash$: Like ordinary set difference, e.g. in $\mathsf{asc}_\oslash = \mathsf{asc}_2 \setminus \mathsf{asc}_1$, is an adjoint to set union, what is on the right-hand side of the $\mathsf{gen}_\oslash$ formula is an adjoint to *transitive union of transitive relations*. That is, $\mathsf{gen}_\oslash$ is the *smallest* transitive relation for which $(\mathsf{gen}_\oslash \cup \mathsf{gen}_1)^* \supseteq \mathsf{gen}_2$. The next theorem states the fundamental property of the difference operator.

Theorem 4. *For all class diagrams* $\mathcal{C}_1, \mathcal{C}_2, \mathcal{C}_3, \mathcal{C}_1 \otimes \mathcal{C}_2 \le \mathcal{C}_3$ *iff* $\mathcal{C}_1 \le \mathcal{C}_3 \oslash \mathcal{C}_2$.

This means that $\mathcal{C}_3 \oslash \mathcal{C}_2$ is the *most permissive* class diagram for which $(\mathcal{C}_3 \oslash \mathcal{C}_2) \otimes \mathcal{C}_2 \le \mathcal{C}_3$ still holds; in that sense, $\oslash$ is the *natural diff operator* induced by $\otimes$. In this sense, $\oslash$ is the most precise difference operator which can be soundly represented using the class diagram syntax defined in this paper. Since the language elements that we omit do not deal with restricting those that we include, there is no hope that using a richer selection of language elements from the standard set can lead to a better operator. One could, instead, resort to using Object Constraint Language to obtain more precise differencing.

Example 1. Consider a situation as presented in Fig. 3. We have a class diagram $\mathcal{C}$ which is a subtype of another, $\mathcal{D}$. Now the diagram $\mathcal{D}$ is evolved, e.g. by adding more classes or streamlining its associations, into a new class diagram, $\mathcal{D}'$. Our abstract properties of composition and difference now ensure that $\mathcal{C}$ can be evolved to a subtyping of $\mathcal{D}'$, *automatically*, by merging it with $\mathcal{D}' \oslash \mathcal{D}$:

$$\mathcal{C} \otimes (\mathcal{D}' \oslash \mathcal{D}) \le \mathcal{D} \otimes (\mathcal{D}' \oslash \mathcal{D}) \le \mathcal{D}' \qquad \qquad \square$$

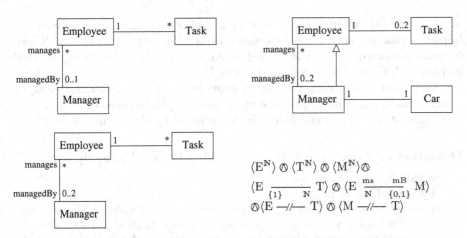

Fig. 4. A disjunctive merge of two diagrams (top) presented in concrete syntax (bottom left) and as a composition of elementary diagrams (bottom right). The overlap between "Manager" and "Employee" seen in the abstract syntax to the right (no disjointness constraint) is not visible in the concrete syntax on the left. The classes can overlap due to the generalization in the rightmost input diagram.

We turn now to another kind of merge operator that can also be induced by subtyping: a "merge in union mode", the *least upper bound* for subtyping:

Definition 6. *The* disjunctive merge *of two composable class diagrams* C_1, C_2 *is* $C_{\otimes} = C_1 \otimes C_2$ *defined as follows:*

$$\mathsf{cla}_{\otimes} = \mathsf{cla}_1 \cap \mathsf{cla}_2, \qquad \mathsf{asc}_{\otimes} = \mathsf{asc}_1 \cap \mathsf{asc}_2, \qquad \mathsf{gen}_{\otimes} = \mathsf{gen}_1 \cap \mathsf{gen}_2$$
$$\mathsf{disj}_{\otimes} = \mathsf{disj}_1 \cap \mathsf{disj}_2, \qquad \mathsf{ccard}_{\otimes}(c) = \mathsf{ccard}_1(c) \cup \mathsf{ccard}_2(c)$$
$$\mathsf{aends}_{\otimes} = \mathsf{aends}_1 \cap \mathsf{aends}_2, \qquad \mathsf{acards}_{\otimes}(a)(e) = \mathsf{acards}_1(a)(e) \cup \mathsf{acards}_2(a)(e)$$

for all $c \in \mathsf{cla}_{\otimes}$, $a \in \mathsf{asc}_{\otimes}$, *and* $e \in \mathsf{dom}(\mathsf{aends}(a))$.

Note the "contravariance" again: disjunctive merge becomes a conjunction of syntactic elements. As expected, $\otimes$ is least upper bound for $\leq$:

Theorem 5. *For all class diagrams* C_1, C_2, D *with* C_1 *and* C_2 *composable,* $C_1 \otimes C_2 \leq D$ *iff* $C_1 \leq D$ *and* $C_2 \leq D$.

Example 2. Figure 4 shows two variants of the simple class diagram from Fig. 2 together with their disjunctive merge. We see that $\otimes$ extracts precisely the *common features* of the two diagrams. Hence disjunctive merge can be used for factoring out common features in diagrams. □

5   Semantic Soundness

In this section we give a precise semantics to class diagrams and use this to show that our constructions of subtyping $\leq$, composition $\otimes$, and difference $\ominus$

are semantically sound. That is, subtypings of a class diagram $\mathcal{C}$ have fewer implementations than $\mathcal{C}$, the implementations of a merge $\mathcal{C} \oslash \mathcal{D}$ are all also implementations of both $\mathcal{C}$ and $\mathcal{D}$, and the implementations of a difference $\mathcal{D} \oslash \mathcal{C}$ merged with $\mathcal{C}$ are also implementations of $\mathcal{D}$.

The semantics of a class diagram is given by a set of *instance diagrams*, or *object models*, which implement the class diagram. An instance diagram essentially consists of objects and links which are typed by classes and associations:

Definition 7. *An* instance diagram *is a tuple* $\mathcal{M} = (\mathsf{obj}, \mathsf{lnk}, \mathsf{oty}, \mathsf{lty}, \mathsf{lends})$ *of*

- *A finite set* obj *of objects,*
- *A finite set* lnk *of links,*
- *A total relation* oty $\subseteq$ obj $\times \Sigma_c$ *associating objects with their object types,*
- *A total relation* lty $\subseteq$ lnk $\times \Sigma_a$ *associating links with their link types,*
- *A partial function* lends : lnk $\rightarrow \Sigma_e \rightharpoonup$ obj *mapping each link to its endpoints.*

We require that $|\mathrm{dom}(\mathsf{lends}(\ell))| = 2$ *for each* $\ell \in$ lnk.

We use the common notation "$a : A$" for object and link typing, instead of the more cumbersome "(a, A)". An object type relation specifying one object a of type A and another, b, of type B, will thus be denoted by oty $= \{a : A, b : B\}$.

Definition 8. *An instance model* $\mathcal{M}$ *is said to* implement *a class diagram* $\mathcal{C}$, *denoted* $\mathcal{M} \models \mathcal{C}$, *if there exist extended typing relations* Oty $\supseteq$ oty, Lty $\supseteq$ lty *such that the following hold:*

1. $|\{o \in \mathsf{obj} \mid \mathsf{Oty}(o, c)\}| \in \mathsf{ccard}(c)$ *for all* $c \in$ cla
   (class cardinalities are respected)
2. *For all* $o \in$ obj *and all* $c, c' \in$ cla *with* $\mathsf{Oty}(o, c)$ *and* $\mathsf{gen}(c, c')$, *also* $\mathsf{Oty}(o, c')$
   (object types are consistent with generalizations)
3. *For all* $\ell \in$ lnk *and all* $a, a' \in$ asc *with* $\mathsf{Lty}(\ell, a)$ *and* $\mathsf{gen}(a, a')$, *also* $\mathsf{Lty}(\ell, a')$
   (link types are consistent with generalizations)
4. *For all* $\ell \in$ lnk *and all* $a \in$ asc *with* $\mathsf{Oty}(\ell, a)$, $\mathrm{dom}(\mathsf{lends}(\ell)) = \mathrm{dom}(\mathsf{aends}(a))$
   (link endpoints inherit their names from their type)
5. *For all* $\ell \in$ lnk *and all* $a \in$ asc *with* $\mathsf{Lty}(\ell, a)$, *it holds for all* $e \in \mathrm{dom}(\mathsf{lends}(\ell))$ *that* $\mathsf{Oty}(\mathsf{lends}(\ell)(e), \mathsf{aends}(a)(e))$
   (link endpoints are well-typed)
6. *For all* $o \in$ obj, $a \in$ asc *and* $e \in \mathrm{dom}(\mathsf{aends}(a))$ *with* $\mathsf{Oty}(o, \mathsf{aends}(a)(e))$, *we have* $|\{\ell \in \mathsf{lnk} \mid \mathsf{Lty}(\ell, a) \ \& \ \mathsf{lends}(\ell)(e) = o\}| \in \mathsf{acards}(a)(e)$
   (association end cardinalities are respected)
7. *There are no* $o \in$ obj, $c, c' \in$ cla *for which* $\mathsf{disj}(c, c')$, $\mathsf{Oty}(o, c)$ *and* $\mathsf{Oty}(o, c')$
   (disjointness constraints are respected)

The set of implementations *of* $\mathcal{C}$ *is* $[\![\mathcal{C}]\!] = \{\mathcal{M} \mid \mathcal{M} \models \mathcal{C}\}$.

The first, and most important, theorem in this section shows that subtyping is semantically sound. The proof is basically a careful inspection of the conditions for subtyping and implementation.

Theorem 6. *For all class diagrams* $\mathcal{C}_1, \mathcal{C}_2, \mathcal{C}_1 \le \mathcal{C}_2$ *implies* $[\![\mathcal{C}_1]\!] \subseteq [\![\mathcal{C}_2]\!]$.

We sum up the semantic properties of our operators; all follow easily from their syntactic properties and Theorem 6. Note that $\oslash$ and $\oslash$ are semantically *sound*, i.e., under-approximations, whereas $\oslash$ is semantically *complete*.

Theorem 7. *For all pairs of class diagrams* C_1, C_2: $[\![C_1 \oslash C_2]\!] \subseteq [\![C_1]\!] \cap [\![C_2]\!]$, $[\![C_1 \oslash (C_2 \oslash C_1)]\!] \subseteq [\![C_2]\!]$, *and* $[\![C_1 \oslash C_2]\!] \supseteq [\![C_1]\!] \cup [\![C_2]\!]$

Intuitively, Thm. 7 states that our operators behave as expected *not only* with respect to the syntactic subtyping, as shown in Sections 3–4, but also with respect to the semantics (our ultimate goal). Crucially, Thm. 7 follows almost directly from the theorems of those sections, once we have Thm. 6. So the main work required to transfer the results of this paper to another semantic variation for class diagrams, is to obtain the equivalent of Thm. 6 for the new semantics.

Using simple examples, we can show that subtyping and composition are not semantically complete. For subtyping, we use inconsistency: Let $C_1 = \langle A^\emptyset \rangle$ and $C_2 = \langle B^\emptyset \rangle$. Then $[\![C_1]\!] = [\![C_2]\!] = \emptyset$, but $C_1 \nleq C_2$, because C_2 contains a restricted class which is not in C_1; for the same reason, $C_2 \nleq C_1$.

This also exposes the fact that $\leq$ does not have a unique bottom element; there is no class diagram B such that $B \leq C$ for all class diagrams C.

For incompleteness of composition, we observe that generalizations can implicitly force object typing in one diagram which is forbidden in another: Let

$$C_1 = \langle A \longrightarrow B \rangle, \qquad C_2 = \langle B^1 \rangle,$$

then $C_1 \oslash C_2 = \langle A \longrightarrow B^1 \rangle$. Now let $\mathcal{M} = \{a : A, b : B\}$, the instance model with one object a of type A and another, b, of type B. Then $\mathcal{M} \models C_1$, as witnessed by the extended object typing $\mathsf{Oty}_1 = \{a : A, a : B, b : B\}$, and $\mathcal{M} \models C_2$, witness by $\mathsf{Oty}_2 = \mathsf{oty}_{\mathcal{M}} = \{a : A, b : B\}$. However, $\mathcal{M} \nvDash C_1 \oslash C_2$, as any witness to this would have to include the typing $\{a : A, a : B, b : B\}$ with *two* objects of type B.

6 Conclusion and Final Remarks

We have presented a compositional algebra of class diagrams with subtyping, conjunctive and disjunctive merge and difference. All operators are described by means of manipulations of minimal syntactic elements of the diagrams, which are also basic terms of our class diagram algebra. To the best of our knowledge, this is the first attempt to define these syntactic operations in a provably sound manner. The operations are all efficiently computable and thus can be automated. The results of operations are represented in the syntax of the input language (they are class diagrams themselves), so that they can later be further processed using regular tooling for class diagrams.

We have worked with a simple core part of the class diagram language, which has allowed us to include all the technical constructions in the paper. Some extensions to other language elements are straightforward, some others require more extensive work. From the point of view of differencing, treating attributes is relatively simple, e.g. by boxing these as classes and treat them in the same way as classes. This is somewhat unsatisfactory though, as treating attributes specially would allow presenting the differences in a more concise and clear manner. Operations would require also computing differences between their signatures—we have decided not to discuss this, as it is not specific to structural modeling, but can be done using techniques for textual programming languages. To handle n-ary associations, one could introduce association classes and treat them in the same way as we treat regular classes. Allowing association classes to be evolved into regular classes (and vice-versa) would require more extensive changes though. Handling abstract classes is not much different from handling concrete ones, and the same goes for directed associations (vs. undirected ones). However, computing differences between diagrams where classes are changed from concrete to abstract, or associations from directed to undirected, or where association endpoints are moved, seems more challenging. Finally, note that we have used element identities to match them for the purpose of merging and differencing. Clearly, in a real application one should use an externally computed mapping, using for instance existing matching heuristics.

We have chosen to work with sound approximations for simplicity and clarity. Experience with building theories for behavioral models shows that a search for precise (i.e., both sound and complete) refinements and compositions leads to complex constructions with high computational complexity [4, 5], so it should only be done once the overall structure and properties of the design space are well understood on simpler cases. We speculate that more precise operators could be expressed in our algebra if we had a *complementation* for class diagrams. Unfortunately, in our current framework, complements of class diagrams will need infinitely many classes, hence are outside the syntax. Alternatively, to overcome the limitations of the class diagram notation, one can consider using Object Constraint Language to specify more precise differences and merges. We intend to investigate these possibilities in future work.

We remark that the semantics we give to class diagrams in this paper is only one out of a plethora of different existing class diagram semantics which are being used, c.f. [18]. We have shown that our constructions are semantically sound for our particular semantics, but this soundness may break if other semantics are used. However, to check that the constructions are sound, one only needs to see that subtyping is semantically sound, i.e. that the semantics is monotonic with respect to subtyping; if this is in place, then all other semantic properties follow. Hence our work lends itself easily to different semantics configurations [18], a point we intend to elaborate in the future. The work reported here is part of a larger project on model management. Our long term objective is to develop semantically sound (and reasonably complete) model management operations for other formalisms, beyond class diagrams and feature models [1, 2, 10].

References

1. Acher, M., Combemale, B., Collet, P., Barais, O., Lahire, P., France, R.B.: Composing your compositions of variability models. In: Moreira, A., Schätz, B., Gray, J., Vallecillo, A., Clarke, P. (eds.) MODELS 2013. LNCS, vol. 8107, pp. 352–369. Springer, Heidelberg (2013)

2. Acher, M., Heymans, P., Collet, P., Quinton, C., Lahire, P., Merle, P.: Feature model differences. In: Ralyté, J., Franch, X., Brinkkemper, S., Wrycza, S. (eds.) CAiSE 2012. LNCS, vol. 7328, pp. 629–645. Springer, Heidelberg (2012)
3. Alanen, M., Porres, I.: Difference and union of models. In: Stevens, P., Whittle, J., Booch, G. (eds.) UML 2003. LNCS, vol. 2863, pp. 2–17. Springer, Heidelberg (2003)
4. Antonik, A., Huth, M., Larsen, K.G., Nyman, U., Wąsowski, A.: EXPTIME-complete decision problems for modal and mixed specifications. Electr. Notes Theor. Comput. Sci. 242(1), 19–33 (2009)
5. Beneš, N., Křetínský, J., Larsen, K.G., Srba, J.: EXPTIME-completeness of thorough refinement on modal transition systems. Inf. Comput. 218, 54–68 (2012)
6. Bibliography on comparison and versioning of software models, http://pi.informatik.uni-siegen.de/CVSM
7. Brunet, G., Chechik, M., Easterbrook, S., Nejati, S., Niu, N., Sabetzadeh, M.: A manifesto for model merging. In: GaMMa 2006, pp. 5–12. ACM (2006)
8. Brunet, G., Chechik, M., Uchitel, S.: Properties of behavioural model merging. In: Misra, J., Nipkow, T., Sekerinski, E. (eds.) FM 2006. LNCS, vol. 4085, pp. 98–114. Springer, Heidelberg (2006)
9. Euzenat, J., Shvaiko, P.: Ontology matching. Springer (2007)
10. Fahrenberg, U., Legay, A., Wąsowski, A.: Vision paper: Make a difference (semantically). In: Whittle, et al. (eds.) [24], pp. 490–500
11. France, R.B., Fleurey, F., Reddy, R., Baudry, B., Ghosh, S.: Providing support for model composition in metamodels. In: EDOC, pp. 253–266. IEEE (2007)
12. Hutchinson, J., Whittle, J., Rouncefield, M., Kristoffersen, S.: Empirical assessment of MDE in industry. In: ICSE 2011. ACM (2011)
13. Kolovos, D.S., Paige, R.F., Polack, F.A.C.: Merging models with the epsilon merging language (EML). In: Wang, J., Whittle, J., Harel, D., Reggio, G. (eds.) MoD-ELS 2006. LNCS, vol. 4199, pp. 215–229. Springer, Heidelberg (2006)
14. Kolovos, D.S., Di Ruscio, D., Pierantonio, A., Paige, R.F.: Different models for model matching: An analysis of approaches to support model differencing. In: CVSM/ICSE, pp. 1–6. IEEE (2009)
15. Maoz, S., Ringert, J.O., Rumpe, B.: ADDiff: semantic differencing for activity diagrams. In: ESEC/FSE, pp. 179–189. ACM (2011)
16. Maoz, S., Ringert, J.O., Rumpe, B.: CDDiff: Semantic differencing for class diagrams. In: Mezini, M. (ed.) ECOOP 2011. LNCS, vol. 6813, pp. 230–254. Springer, Heidelberg (2011)
17. Maoz, S., Ringert, J.O., Rumpe, B.: A manifesto for semantic model differencing. In: Dingel, J., Solberg, A. (eds.) MODELS 2010. LNCS, vol. 6627, pp. 194–203. Springer, Heidelberg (2011)
18. Maoz, S., Ringert, J.O., Rumpe, B.: Semantically configurable consistency analysis for class and object diagrams. In: Whittle, et al. (eds.) [24], pp. 153–167
19. Nejati, S., Sabetzadeh, M., Chechik, M., Easterbrook, S., Zave, P.: Matching and merging of statecharts specifications. In: ICSE, pp. 54–64. IEEE (2007)
20. Reddy, Y.R., Ghosh, S., France, R.B., Straw, G., Bieman, J.M., McEachen, N., Song, E., Georg, G.: Directives for composing aspect-oriented design class models. In: Rashid, A., Akşit, M. (eds.) Transactions on AOSD I. LNCS, vol. 3880, pp. 75–105. Springer, Heidelberg (2006)

21. Rubin, J., Chechik, M.: Combining related products into product lines. In: de Lara, J., Zisman, A. (eds.) FASE 2012. LNCS, vol. 7212, pp. 285–300. Springer, Heidelberg (2012)
22. Rubin, J., Chechik, M.: Quality of merge-refactorings for product lines. In: Cortellessa, V., Varró, D. (eds.) FASE 2013. LNCS, vol. 7793, pp. 83–98. Springer, Heidelberg (2013)
23. Sabetzadeh, M., Nejati, S., Easterbrook, S.M., Chechik, M.: Global consistency checking of distributed models with TReMer+. In: ICSE, pp. 815–818 (2008)
24. Whittle, J., Clark, T., Kühne, T. (eds.): MODELS 2011. LNCS, vol. 6981. Springer, Heidelberg (2011)
25. Xing, Z., Stroulia, E.: UMLDiff: an algorithm for object-oriented design differencing. In: ASE, pp. 54–65. ACM (2005)

Heterogeneous and Asynchronous Networks of Timed Systems

José Luis Fiadeiro[1] and Antónia Lopes[2]

[1] Dep. of Computer Science, Royal Holloway University of London, UK
jose.fiadeiro@rhul.ac.uk
[2] Dep. of Informatics, Faculty of Sciences, University of Lisbon, Portugal
mal@di.fc.ul.pt

Abstract. We present a component algebra and an associated logic for heterogeneous timed systems. The components of the algebra are asynchronous networks of processes that abstract the behaviour of machines that execute according to the clock granularity of the network node in which they are placed and communicate asynchronously with machines at other nodes. The main novelty of our theory is that not all network nodes need to have the same clock granularity: we investigate conditions under which we can guarantee, a priori, that any interconnections generated at run time through dynamic binding of machines with different clock granularities leads to a consistent orchestration of the whole system. Finally, we investigate which logics can support specifications for this component algebra.

1 Introduction

The software systems that are now operating in cyberspace are best modelled as networks of machines, where each machine performs local computations and can be interconnected dynamically (at run time) to other machines to achieve some goal. Because of the distributed nature of such networks, it does not make sense to assume that all nodes of the network, where machines execute, have the same clock granularity. This means that interconnections can only be established asynchronously and through communication channels (other machines) that can orchestrate the interactions between machines according to the clock granularities of the nodes in which they execute.

In this paper, we put forward a component algebra for such heterogeneous and asynchronous networks of timed systems. Our algebra abstracts the behaviour of timed machines as processes whose traces are generated according to the clock granularity of the network node in which they execute. We define a composition operator through which networks can be interconnected and investigate properties of such networks, namely conditions that guarantee consistency, i.e., that the interconnected processes collectively generate a non-empty behaviour. Finally, we discuss how specifications for this component algebra can be supported through a continuous-semantics metric temporal logic.

Contributions. In [6] we put forward a component and interface algebra for service-oriented computing that is based on asynchronous networks of processes interconnected through communication channels. A first extension of this model for timed systems was presented in [4] based on a homogeneous notion of time – all processes execute according to the same time granularity. The present extension to a heterogeneous setting is not

S. Gnesi and A. Rensink (Eds.): FASE 2014, LNCS 8411, pp. 79–93, 2014.

trivial (which justifies this paper) because, where the algebraic properties of composition in an homogenous-time domain generalise those of the un-timed domain presented in [6], interconnection in a heterogeneous setting is much more involved – indeed, not even always admissible. The main challenges come from (a) the fact that the topological properties of timed traces are more intricate than those of un-timed ones, which requires the definition of a new time-related refinement relation and a new time-related closure operator that does not reduce to the Cantor topology of trace-based domains; and (b) the fact that, in a heterogeneous timed domain, different clock granularities interfere with the way processes need to be coordinated in order to ensure that they can cooperate.

We have also generalised the notion of asynchronous relational network (ARN) proposed in [6] so as to capture a larger class of systems where coordination of interactions takes place among groups of processes, not just between pairs of processes. This extension requires a different algebraic structure for the networks, which is why we moved from graphs to hypergraphs. From a software engineering point of view, this shift enables us to provide a much richer mathematical model where, essential properties of run-time interconnections (such as consistency) can still be formulated and analysed, i.e., the ability for systems to work effectively when interconnected. We provide compositionality results for consistency through criteria that can be checked on processes at design time that guarantee the consistency of interconnections when performed at run time across different clock granularities.

In terms of logics through which the behaviour of machines can be specified or analysed, we abandoned the implicit-time model used in [6], which is not realistic for the class of applications that need to run across heterogeneous time domains, in favour of a metric temporal logic [10]. The challenges here concern the requirements of the component model for topological notions of closure that go beyond the traditional safety-related ones, which led us to adopt a continuous semantics with a new operator that captures the required notion of closure.

Related Work. Several researchers have recently addressed discrete timed systems with heterogeneous clock granularities but the focus has not been on the the development of theories of composability for these systems as we do in this paper. An exception is [11], which studies when the composition of heterogeneous tag machines [2] is sound and complete. However, the notion of composition considered therein is more relaxed than ours (allowing for the delay between events to be modified) and, as a consequence, not appropriate for addressing global properties of systems interconnected at run time as actually implemented, which we do by adopting instead a trace-based model in which composition corresponds to intersection. A trace-based model has also the advantage of abstracting from the specificities of the different classes of automata that can be chosen as models of implementations. Because un-timed networks were investigated in [6] over traces, adopting a similar model for timed ones also allows us to better appreciate the differences between un-timed and timed domains.

Formal clock calculi have also been developed that address heterogeneity, for example [7] in which a synchronous data-flow language is proposed that supports the modelling of multi-periodic systems and the refinement of clock granularities in a way that is similar to what we propose this paper. However, the main focus of such calculi has been on modelling and simulation, not so much on the challenges that heterogeneity raises on run-time interconnection of systems and, therefore, they are too specific on aspects that do not directly impact on system properties such as consistency. In fact, to the best of our knowledge, ours is the first model that adopts networks as components of systems and, therefore, addresses (run-time) compositionality at the network level.

Several frameworks have also been proposed for component/service-based software systems that exhibit timed properties, although not in a heterogeneous-time context. Algebraic frameworks such as [5,8,9,13] address global properties similar to consistency, such as compatibility – whether the conversation protocols (modelled as timed automata) followed by the peers in a choreography lead to deadlocks or time conflicts that prevent them from completing (e.g., reaching final states). However, the focus in this context is on the modelling of the (timed) conversation protocols that characterise the global behaviour of a (fixed) number of peers. What we investigate in this paper is, instead, conditions through which we can guarantee that the orchestrations of components, whose interconnection is performed at run time, can work together. This has implications on the properties that are required of networks in order to guarantee consistency. An example is the way time is managed: in choreography, this is done globally for the (fixed) set of peers; in our approach, this needs to be done locally at the level of each process because composition is dynamic through run-time binding to machines that may be executing in platforms where the clock granularity is different.

2 Preliminaries

We start by recalling a few concepts related to traces and their Cantor topology. Given a set A, a *trace* λ over A is an element of A^ω. We denote by $\lambda(i)$ the $(i+1)$-th element of λ. A *segment* π is an element of A^*, the length of which we denote by $|\pi|$. We use $\pi < \lambda$ to mean that the segment π is a prefix of λ. Given $a \in A$, we denote by $\pi \cdot a$ the segment obtained by extending π with a. A *property* Λ over A is a set of traces. For every property Λ, we define $\Lambda^f = \{\pi : \exists \lambda \in \Lambda(\pi < \lambda)\}$ — the segments that are prefixes of traces in Λ, also called the *downward closure* of Λ — and $\bar{\Lambda} = \{\lambda : \forall \pi < \lambda(\pi \in \Lambda^f)\}$ — the traces whose prefixes are in Λ^f, also called the *closure* of Λ. A property Λ is said to be *closed* iff $\Lambda \supseteq \bar{\Lambda}$ (and, hence, $\Lambda = \bar{\Lambda}$).

In our model, traces consist of an infinite sequence of pairs of an instant of time and a set of actions — the actions that are observed at that instant. In order to model networks of systems, we allow sets of actions to be empty: on the one hand, this allows us to model finite behaviours, i.e., systems that stop executing actions after a certain point in time while still part of a network; on the other hand, it allows us to model observations that are triggered by actions performed by components outside the system.

Definition 1 (Timed traces). *Let A be a set (of actions).*

- *A* time sequence τ *is a trace over* $\mathbb{R}_{\geq 0}$ *such that:* $\tau(0) = 0$; $\tau(i) < \tau(i+1)$ *for every* $i \in \mathbb{N}$; *the set* $\{\tau(i) : i \in \mathbb{N}\}$ *is unbounded, i.e., time progresses (the 'non-Zeno' condition). An* action sequence σ *is a trace over* 2^A *such that* $\sigma(0) = \emptyset$.
- *A* timed trace *over* A *is a pair* $\lambda = \langle \sigma, \tau \rangle$ *of an action and a time sequence. We denote the sets of timed traces and segments over* A *by* $\Lambda(A)$ *and* $\Pi(A)$, *respectively.*

- *Given a timed property* $\Lambda \subseteq \Lambda(A)$ *we define, for every time sequence* τ, $\Lambda_\tau = \{\sigma \in (2^A)^\omega : \langle \sigma, \tau \rangle \in \Lambda\}$ — *the action property defined by* Λ *and* τ, *and* $\Lambda_{time} = \{\tau : \exists \sigma \in (2^A)^\omega (\langle \sigma, \tau \rangle \in \Lambda)\}$ — *the time sequences of traces in* Λ.
- *Given* $\delta \in \mathbb{R}_{>0}$, *the* δ-*time sequence* τ_δ *is defined by* $\tau_\delta(i) = i \cdot \delta$ *for every* $i \in \mathbb{N}$. *A* δ-*timed trace over* A *is a timed trace* $\langle \sigma, \tau_\delta \rangle$, *the set of which is denoted by* $\Lambda^\delta(A)$. *A* δ-*timed property is a timed property that consists of* δ-*timed traces.*

Definition 2 (Time refinement). *Let* $\rho : \mathbb{N} \to \mathbb{N}$ *be a monotonically increasing function that satisfies* $\rho(0) = 0$.

- *Let* τ, τ' *be two time sequences. We say that* τ' *refines* τ *through* ρ, *which we denote by* $\tau' \preceq_\rho \tau$, *iff, for every* $i \in \mathbb{N}$, $\tau(i) = \tau'(\rho(i))$. *We say that* τ' *refines* τ, *which we denote by* $\tau' \preceq \tau$, *iff* $\tau' \preceq_\rho \tau$ *for some* ρ.
- *Let* $\lambda = \langle \sigma, \tau \rangle$, $\lambda' = \langle \sigma', \tau' \rangle$ *be two timed traces. We say that* λ' *refines* λ *through* ρ — *which we denote by* $\lambda' \preceq_\rho \lambda$ — *iff* $\tau' \preceq_\rho \tau$ *and, for every* $i \in \mathbb{N}$ *and* $\rho(i) < j < \rho(i+1)$, $\sigma(i) = \sigma'(\rho(i))$ *and* $\sigma'(j) = \emptyset$. *We also say that* λ' *refines* λ — *which we denote by* $\lambda' \preceq \lambda$ — *iff* $\lambda' \preceq_\rho \lambda$ *for some* ρ.
- *The r-closure of a timed property* Λ *is* $\Lambda^r = \{\lambda' : \exists \lambda \in \Lambda(\lambda' \preceq \lambda)\}$. *We say that* Λ *is* closed under time refinement, *or r-closed, iff* $\Lambda^r \subseteq \Lambda$.

A time sequence refines another if the former interleaves time observations between any two time observations of the latter. Refinement extends to traces by requiring that no actions be observed in the finer trace between two consecutive times of the coarser.

It is not difficult to prove that the refinement relation makes the space of all time sequences a complete meet semi-lattice, the meet of two time sequences ρ_1 and ρ_2 being given by the recursion $\rho(i+1) = min(\{\rho_1(j) > \rho(i), j \in \mathbb{N}\} \cup \{\rho_2(j) > \rho(i), j \in \mathbb{N}\})$ together with the base $\rho(0) = 0$. However, if one considers the space of all δ-time sequences $\{\tau_\delta : \delta \in \mathbb{R}_{>0}\}$, it is easy to see that a meet of τ_{δ_1} and τ_{δ_2} exists iff δ_1 and δ_2 are commensurable, i.e., there are $n, m \in \mathbb{N}_{>0}$ such that $\delta_1/n = \delta_2/m$, in which case the meet is τ_δ where δ is their greatest common divisor.

Functions between sets of actions *(alphabet maps)* are useful for defining relationships between individual processes and the networks in which they operate.

Definition 3 (Projection and translation). *Let* $f:A \to B$ *be a function (alphabet map).*

- *For every* $\sigma \in (2^B)^\omega$, *we define* $\sigma|_f \in (2^A)^\omega$ *pointwise as* $\sigma|_f(i) = f^{-1}(\sigma(i))$ — *the* projection *of* σ *over* A. *If* f *is an inclusion, then we tend to write* $\_|_A$ *instead of* $\_|_f$ *(when applied to a trace,* $\_|_A$ *forgets the actions of* B *that are not in* A*).*
- *For every timed trace* $\lambda = \langle \sigma, \tau \rangle$ *over* B, *we define its projection over* A *to be* $\lambda|_f = \langle \sigma|_f, \tau \rangle$, *and for every timed property* Λ *over* B, $\Lambda|_f = \{\lambda|_f : \lambda \in \Lambda\}$ — *the* projection *of* Λ *to* A.
- *For every timed property* Λ *over* A, *we define* $f(\Lambda) = \{\langle \sigma, \tau \rangle : \langle \sigma|_f, \tau \rangle \in \Lambda\}$ — *the* translation *of* Λ *to* B.

We are particularly interested in translations defined by prefixing every element of a set with a given symbol. Such translations are useful for identifying in a network the machine to which an action belongs — we do not assume that machines have mutually disjoint alphabets. More precisely, given a set A and a symbol p, we denote by $(p._-)$ the function that prefixes the elements of A with 'p.'.

3 Heterogeneous Timed Asynchronous Relational Nets

We put forward a generalisation of the component algebra proposed in [6]. The main differences are that (1) we address networks of processes that operate over heterogeneous time, and (2) we use hypergraphs instead of simple graphs in order to account for multiple, not just peer-to-peer interactions. We start by detailing the communication model and then proceed to defining networks and investigating some of their properties.

3.1 Processes and Connections

Our communication model is asynchronous, interactions being based on the exchange of messages. We organise messages in sets that we call ports: a *port* is a finite set (of messages). Ports are communication abstractions that are convenient for organising networks of systems as formalised below. Every message belonging to a port has an associated *polarity*: $^-$ if it is an outgoing message (published at the port) and $^+$ if it is incoming (delivered at the port). Therefore, every port M has a partition $M^- \cup M^+$. For every port M we define its dual M^{op}, which is obtained by swapping the polarities of the messages in M, i.e., $M^{op^-} = M^+$ and $M^{op^+} = M^-$.

The actions of sending (publishing) or receiving (being delivered) a message m are denoted by $m!$ and m_i, respectively. More specifically, if M is a port, we define $A_{M^-} = \{m! : m \in M^-\}$, $A_{M^+} = \{m_i : m \in M^+\}$, and $A_M = A_{M^-} \cup A_{M^+}$ — the set of actions associated with M. Even if a process does not refuse the delivery of messages it can decide to discard them, e.g., if they arrive outside the expected protocol, and not all published messages can be guaranteed to be delivered to their destination.

Definition 4 (Process). *A process is a triple $P = \langle \delta, \gamma, \Lambda \rangle$ where: (1) $\delta \in \mathbb{R}_{>0}$ is the granularity of the clock of the process; (2) γ is a finite set of mutually disjoint ports; (3) Λ is the r-closure of a non-empty δ-timed property over $A_\gamma = \bigcup_{M \in \gamma} A_M$ defining the behaviour of the process.*

The fact that processes are r-closed means that they contain all possible interleavings of empty observations, thus capturing their behaviour in any possible environment. This notion of closure can be related to mechanisms that, such as stuttering [1], ensure that components do not constrain their environment.

We designate the process $\langle \delta, \{M\}, \Lambda^\delta(A_M)^r \rangle$ by $\square_M^\delta$. This is a process with a single port M that, at any time that is a multiple of its clock granularity, accepts any set of actions belonging to A_M, which henceforth is named RUN.

Our model of interaction is based on orchestrating the joint behaviour of a collection of parties, each of which defines a process; the same party may engage in different orchestrations. Each such orchestration is performed by another process – the orchestrator – that coordinates the joint behaviour of the other parties. Each party is connected to the orchestrator by what we call an attachment:

Definition 5 (Attachment). *An attachment is a triple* $\langle C, \xi, P \rangle$ *where* $C = \langle \delta_C, \gamma_C, \Lambda_C \rangle$ *and* $P = \langle \delta_P, \gamma_P, \Lambda_P \rangle$ *are processes and* ξ *is an injective map from* $M_C \in \gamma_C$ *to* $M_P \in \gamma_P$ *that reverses polarities, i.e.,* $\xi(M_C^+) \subseteq M_P^-$ *and* $\xi(M_C^-) \subseteq M_P^+$. *An attachment is* well formed *iff* δ_P *is a multiple of* δ_C. *We often use* ξ *to designate the whole attachment (triple) if the source and target processes are clear from the context.*

Notice that ξ translates A_{M_C} to A_{M_P} by switching publications and deliveries, i.e., $\xi(m_i) = \xi(m)!$ for $m \in M_C^+$ and $\xi(m!) = \xi(m)_i$ for $m \in M_C^-$. The condition that δ_P is a multiple of δ_C for the attachment to be 'well formed' reflects the fact that the source needs to be able to 'tick' (deliver and receive messages) in a way that is compatible with the target. Attachments are used for building connections:

Definition 6 (Connection). *A connection is a triple* $\Xi = \langle C, \gamma_F, \xi \rangle$ *where: (1)* C *is a process* $\langle \delta, \gamma, \Lambda \rangle$ *– the orchestrator of the connection; (2)* $\gamma_F \subseteq \gamma$ *consists of the ports that are 'free'; (3)* ξ *assigns to each* $M_i \in \gamma$ *a well-formed attachment* $\xi_i : M_i \to M_{P_i}$ *of* C *to a process* P_i *such that, (a) for every* $M_i \neq M_j$, $M_{P_i} \neq M_{P_j}$, *(b) for every* $M_i \in \gamma_F$, $P_i = \Box_{M_i^{op}}^{\delta}$ *and* ξ_i *is the identity.*

That is, a connection consists of a process that orchestrates interactions among a number of parties. Those parties are attached to the orchestrator, not directly to each other, thus making communication between parties to be asynchronous. Some of the ports of the orchestrator may be 'free', thus accounting for the ability of the connection to grow at run time by accepting new parties, i.e., connections may be open. Those free ports are attached to RUN. Each port of a party can only be used by at most one attachment, i.e., if a party plays different roles in the same connection, it does so via different ports. Because all the attachments in a connection need to be well formed, the clock granularity of each party P_i needs to be a multiple of that of the orchestrator C. Therefore, not all sets of processes can be interconnected: in order to be part of a connection, they need to have a common divisor.

3.2 Networks

Definition 7 (HT-ARN). *A heterogenous timed asynchronous relational net (HT-ARN)* α *consists of:*

- *A finite hypergraph* $\langle N, E \rangle$ *where* N *is a non-empty finite set of nodes and* E *is a finite set of hyperedges – each hyperedge is a non-empty set* $\{p_i \mid i=1..n\}$ *of nodes.*
- *A labelling function that assigns a process* $\alpha_p = \langle \delta_p, \gamma_p, \mathcal{A}_p \rangle$ *to every node* p *and a connection* $\Xi_c = \langle \alpha_c, \gamma_{cF}, \xi_c \rangle$ *to every hyperedge* c *such that:*
    - i) *For every hyperedge* c, Ξ_c *defines an onto mapping from* γ_c *to* c.
    - ii) *Each* ξ_{c_i} *is an attachment of* α_c *to* α_{p_i}.
    - iii) *If two hyperedges* c *and* d *share a node* p, *then the attachments* ξ_c *and* ξ_d *associated with* p *have different codomains, i.e., attach to different ports of* α_p.

We also define the following sets and mappings:

- A_α *is the alphabet associated with* α *– the union of the alphabets of the processes that label the nodes translated by prefixing all actions with the corresponding node.*

iv) For every $p \in N$, we denote by ι_p is the function that maps A_{γ_p} to A_α, which prefixes the actions of A_{γ_p} with p.

iiv) For every $c \in E$, we denote by ι_c is the function that maps A_{γ_c} to A_α. This function is such that, for every $p \in c$, $\iota_c(A_M) = \iota_p(\xi_p(A_M))$ where M is the source port of ξ_p. That is, actions of the orchestrator are translated through ξ_p to the attached process p (reversing polarities) and then according to ι_p.

$$- \Lambda_\alpha = \{\lambda \in \Lambda(A_\alpha) : \forall p \in N \cup E \ (\lambda|_{\iota_p} \in \Lambda_{\alpha_p})\}$$

Note that, for every $p \in N$, $(\_|_{\iota_p})$ first removes the actions that are not in the language $p.A_p$ and then removes the prefix p, and similarly for every $c \in E$. Therefore, the set Λ_α consists of all traces over the alphabet of the HT-ARN that are projected to traces of all its processes and channels:

$$\Lambda_\alpha = \bigcap_{p \in N \cup E} \iota_p(\Lambda_{\alpha_p})$$

We take this set to represent the behaviour of α. That is, the behaviour of the HT-ARN is given by the intersection of the behaviour of the processes at the nodes and the hyperedges (connections) translated to the language of the HT-ARN — this corresponds to what one normally understands as a parallel composition in trace-based models. Notice that, because the free ports of connections are labelled with run processes, only the non-free ports are relevant for the behaviour of the HT-ARN. Further notice that, when applied to a set of traces, the translations effectively open the behaviour of the processes to actions in which they are not involved.

As an example, consider a HT-ARN that models a heterogeneous system in which a bank clerk orchestrates a process that receives credit-requests, a process that gets information on risk from a database of clients, and a process that handles approved credit requests. As depicted in Fig. 1, its hypergraph has nodes $c: CreditRequest$, $d: ClientsDB$, $m: CreditMgr$ and r:RUN, and the hyperedge $\{c, d, m, r\}:\langle Clerk, \{P_k^4\}, id\rangle$ where:

- *CreditRequest* is a process that has a single port through which it sends *creditReq* and *accept*, and receives *approved*, *denied* and *transferDate*. This process starts by sending a *creditReq* and waits ten time units for receiving *approved* or *denied*. In the first case it sends *accept* and waits fifty time units for receiving *transferDate*. The granularity δ_c of its clock is 0.5.
- *ClientsDB* is a process that has a single port through which it receives *getClientRisk* and sends *clientRiskValue* and *clientRiskUnknown*. When the first *getClientRisk* is delivered, it takes no more than seven time units to publish either *clientRiskValue* or *clientRiskUnknown*. The granularity of its clock is 0.2.
- *CreditMgr* has a single port through which it receives *processCredit* and sends *expectedDate*. When the first *processCredit* is delivered, it takes no more than four time units to publish *expectedDate*. The granularity of its clock is 0.3.
- *Clerk* is a process with four ports: $P_k^1, P_k^2, P_k^3, P_k^4$. For instance, in port P_k^1, it receives messages *creditReq* and *accept* and sends the messages *approved*, *denied* and *transferDate*. After the delivery of the first *creditReq* on P_k^1, it publishes *getClientRisk* on P_k^2 within five time units; then it waits ten time units for the delivery of *clientRiskValue* or *clientRiskUnknown* in the same port. If the risk of the transaction is known, this is enough for making a decision and sending *approved* or *denied* in port P_k^1; if not, it publishes *getRisk* on P_k^4 within five time units and

waits twenty time units for the delivery of *riskValue*. After sending *approved* (if ever), *Clerk* waits forty time units for the delivery of *accept*, upon which it sends *processCredit* on P_k^3 within two time units and waits for *expectedDate*; when this happens, it sends *transferDate* within two time units on P_k^1. The granularity δ_k of its clock is 0.1.

– RUN is $\square_{P_k^4 op}^{0.1}$ and *id* is a set with four identity attachments (this is because, for ease of presentation, we have picked the same names in every pair of connected ports).

The fact that the port P_k^4 is free is represented in Fig. 1 by the grey shadow.

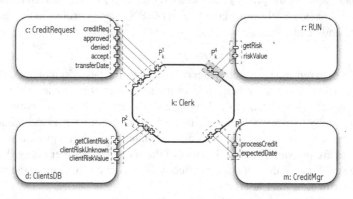

Fig. 1. A HT-ARN consisting of a connection with a free port and three processes

It is also important to note that, although the existence of a connection between two processes implies that the clock of the orchestrator is a common divisor of those of the processes, it is not necessary that a common divisor exists for all clock granularities of a HT-ARN. However, a common divisor exists for all clock granularities of every sub-net that is connected (i.e., one in which every pair of processes is linked via a path of connections). In particular, if a HT-ARN is a connected hypergraph, this means that it can be implemented over (or simulated by) a single processor.

As in [6], two HT-ARNs can be composed through the ports that are still available for establishing further interconnections, i.e., not connected to any other port, which we call *interaction-points*.

Definition 8 (Interaction-point). *An interaction-point of a HT-ARN α is a pair $\langle v, M \rangle$ such that $v \in N_\alpha$ is a node and either (1) $M \in \gamma_v$ is one of its ports and v is not attached through M to any hyperedge — what we call a* process interaction-point, *or (2) v belongs to an hyperedge $c_v \in E_\alpha$, M is a free port of Ξ_{c_v} and v is attached to M — what we call a* connection interaction-point. *We denote by J_α the collection of interaction-points of α.*

We can interconnect two HT-ARNs by merging process interaction-points with connection interaction-points via attachments that are well-formed:

Definition 9 (Composition of HT-ARNs). *Let α and β be two HT-ARNs with disjoint sets of nodes and θ be a family of wires between α and β, where a wire is a triple*

$$\theta_i = \langle\langle v_i, M_{c_{v_i}}\rangle, \xi_i, \langle p_i, M_{p_i}\rangle\rangle$$

such that, either

1. *$\langle v_i, M_{c_{v_i}}\rangle$ is a connection interaction-point of α, $\langle p_i, M_{p_i}\rangle$ is a process interaction-point of β and $\langle\alpha_{c_{v_i}}, \xi_i : M_{c_{v_i}} \to M_{p_i}, \beta_{p_i}\rangle$ is a well-formed attachment, or*
2. *$\langle v_i, M_{c_{v_i}}\rangle$ is a connection interaction-point of β, $\langle p_i, M_{p_i}\rangle$ is a process interaction-point of α and $\langle\beta_{c_{v_i}}, \xi_i : M_{c_{v_i}} \to M_{p_i}, \alpha_{p_i}\rangle$ is a well-formed attachment,*

with mutually-disjoint sets of interaction points. We define the HT-ARN $\alpha\|_\theta\beta$ as follows:

- *Its hypergraph is $\langle N, E\rangle$ where N is obtained from $N_\alpha \cup N_\beta$ by removing the nodes corresponding to the connection interaction-points, and E is obtained from $E_\alpha \cup E_\beta$ by replacing, for each attachment $\xi_i : M_{c_{v_i}} \to M_{p_i}$, the node v_i by p_i in c_{v_i}.*
- *Its node-labelling function γ coincides with γ_α or γ_β on the remaining nodes.*
- *Its hyperedge-labelling function Ξ is as $\Xi_\alpha \cup \Xi_\beta$ except that, for each attachment $\xi_i : M_{c_{v_i}} \to M_{p_i}$, the attachment of the run process at M_{c_v} is replaced with ξ_i and $M_{c_{v_i}}$ is removed from the set of free ports of $\Xi_{c_{v_i}}$.*

In order to illustrate composition of HT-ARNs, consider a HT-ARN that is obtained from the HT-ARN depicted in Fig. 1 by replacing the node c:*CreditRequest* by r':RUN′ and making free the port P_k^1, where RUN′ is the process $\square_{P_k^1 op}^{0.1}$. The HT-ARN presented in Fig. 1 is the composition of that HT-ARN and an atomic HT-ARN defined by c:*CreditRequest* through a wire ξ that connects the interaction-point $\langle r', P_k^1\rangle$ of the first HT-ARN to $\langle c, P_k^{1op}\rangle$, the single interaction-point of the latter. The wire ξ is built over the function between the two ports that keeps the names and only reverses polarities. This defines a well-formed attachment because δ_c is a multiple of δ_k.

4 Consistency

The joint consistency of the processes and the orchestrators operating in a HT-ARN is an important property because it ensures that their implementations can work together.

Definition 10 (Consistent HT-ARN). *A HT-ARN α is said to be consistent if $\Lambda_\alpha \neq \emptyset$.*

In [6], we defined a sub-algebra of (un-timed) ARNs that are consistent and closed under composition. The characterisation of this sub-algebra relied on the closure operator induced by the Cantor topology over action sequences. The same closure operator can be defined over timed traces but, for the purpose of separating the properties required of the action sequences from those of the time sequences and the way they can be checked over automata (which we do in [3]), it is useful to consider other notions of closure.

We can use the Cantor topology over $(2^A)^\omega$ to define a notion of closure relative to a fixed time sequence:

Definition 11 (Closure relative to time). *A timed property Λ is closed relative to time or, simply, t-closed, iff, for every $\tau \in \Lambda_{time}$, Λ_τ is closed. A t-closed HT-ARN is one in which all processes that label nodes or hyperedges (connections) are t-closed.*

Processes that are closed relative to time define safety properties in the usual un-timed sense: over a fixed time sequence, which cannot be controlled by the processes, the violation of the property can be checked over a finite trace. It is also easy to prove that:

Proposition 12. *Let α be a* HT-ARN: *(a) Λ_α is r-closed; (b) if α is t-closed, so is Λ_α.*

The first follows from the fact that all processes are r-closed by construction. The second follows from the fact that the intersection of t-closed properties is also t-closed.

A property that was found to be relevant in [6] for characterising consistent (un-timed) asynchronous relational nets concerns the ability to make joint progress. In the timed version, we need to take into account the way time itself progresses.

Definition 13 (Progress-enabled). *For every* HT-ARN *α and time sequence τ, let*
$$\Pi_{\alpha_\tau} = \{\pi \in (2^{A_\alpha})^* : \forall p \in N \cup E \ (\pi|_{\iota_p} \in \Lambda^f_{\alpha_{p_\tau}})\}$$
We say that α is progress-enabled *in relation to τ iff*
$$\epsilon \in \Pi_{\alpha_\tau} \text{ and } \forall \pi \in \Pi_{\alpha_\tau} \ \exists A \subseteq A_\alpha((\pi \cdot A) \in \Pi_{\alpha_\tau})$$
We say that α is progress-enabled *iff there is a time sequence τ such that α is progress-enabled in relation to every $\tau' \preceq \tau$.*

The set Π_{α_τ} consists of all the segments that the processes can jointly engage in across the time sequence τ. Notice that if Π_{α_τ} is not empty, τ is a refinement of a δ_{α_p}-time sequence for every node or edge p of α. Furthermore, because the intersection of A with the alphabet of any process can be empty, being progress-enabled does not require all parties to actually perform an action.

By itself, being progress-enabled does not guarantee that a HT-ARN is consistent: moving from finite to infinite behaviours requires the analysis of what happens 'at the limit'. However, if we work with t-closed properties, the limit behaviour will remain within the HT-ARN:

Theorem 14. *A* HT-ARN *is consistent if it is t-closed and progress-enabled.*

We now show how HT-ARNs can be guaranteed to be progress-enabled by construction: we identify atomic HT-ARNs that are progress-enabled and prove that the class of progress-enabled HT-ARNs is closed under composition. We start by remarking that, given a process P, the HT-ARN that consists of a single node labelled with P is progress-enabled in relation to at least a δ-time sequence and all its refinements, and therefore is progress-enabled. The same applies to any HT-ARN that consists of a finite set of unconnected processes — in fact, this generalises to any finite juxtaposition of progressed-enabled HT-ARNs (or, indeed, consistent HT-ARNs); the challenge is in checking that progress-enabled HT-ARNs are closed under composition because composition connects HT-ARNs, i.e., it creates connected components.

In [6], we gave criteria for the composition of two (un-timed) progress-enabled ARNs to be progress-enabled based on the ability of processes to buffer incoming messages – being 'delivery-enabled'. In a timed domain, it becomes necessary to identify time sequences across which all parties can work together. Given a HT-ARN and one of its interaction-points $\langle v, M \rangle$, we define the set $D_{\langle v,M \rangle}$ of deliveries that can be made at that point — $D_{\langle v,M \rangle} = \{v.m_i : m \in M^+\}$ if $\langle v, M \rangle$ is a process interaction-point and $\{v.m! : m \in M^+\}$ otherwise. Notice that in the latter case $\langle v, M \rangle$ is a connection interaction-point and deliveries to that point (in M) are publications by v.

Definition 15 (Delivery-enabled HT-ARN). *A* HT-*ARN* $\alpha = \langle P, C, \delta, \gamma, \Lambda \rangle$ *is delivery-enabled in relation to one of its interaction-points* $\langle v, M \rangle \in I_\alpha$ *if, for every* $B \subseteq D_{\langle v, M \rangle}$, $\tau \in \Lambda_{time}$ *and* $(\pi \cdot A) \in \Pi_{\alpha_\tau}$ *such that* $\tau(|\pi|)$ *is a multiple of* δ_v *(i.e., the process at* v *makes a step),* $(\pi \cdot B \cup (A \setminus D_{\langle v, M \rangle})) \in \Pi_{\alpha_\tau}$ *(i.e., the process at* v *accepts the deliveries in* B *instead of those in* A.)

That is, being delivery-enabled at an interaction point requires any joint segment of the HT-ARN over a time sequence to be extensible with any set of messages delivered at that interaction-point. Note that in the case of a connection interaction-point, being delivery-enabled means that the orchestrator of the connection is ready to accept publications at the node v. Also note that being delivery-enabled does not interfere with the decision to publish messages: $B \cup (A \setminus D_{\langle v, M \rangle})$ retains all the publications in A.

Finally, we need to make sure that the processes that orchestrate connections can work together with the processes that they interconnect, i.e., that they do not force the delivery of messages when the processes cannot receive them:

Definition 16 (Cooperative connections). *Let* $\Xi = \langle C, \gamma_F, \xi \rangle$ *be a connection with* $C = \langle \delta, \gamma, \Lambda \rangle$ *and, for every attachment* $\xi_i : M_i \to M_{P_i}$ *of* C *to a process* P_i, *let* $E_i = \{m! : m \in M_i^-\}$. *The connection is said to be* cooperative *if, for every* $\tau \in \Lambda_{time}$ *and for every* ξ_i, *if* $(\pi \cdot A) \in \Lambda_\tau^f$ *and* $\tau(|\pi|)$ *is not a multiple of* δ_{P_i} *then* $\pi \cdot (A \setminus E_i) \in \Lambda_\tau^f$.

That is, if after π the connection wants to make a delivery when a process is not in sync, there is an alternative path from π where no delivery is made at that time. Notice that, because δ_{P_i} is a multiple of δ, publications are always made in sync with the orchestrator. Therefore, in the context of a delivery-enabled HT-ARN, if $\tau(|\pi|)$ is not a multiple of δ_{P_i}, $\pi \cdot \emptyset \in \Lambda_\tau^f$.

Theorem 17. *Let* α *be a composition of progress-enabled* HT-*ARNs through a family of wires with mutually-disjoint sets of interaction points i.e.,*

$$\alpha = (\alpha_1 \;\Big\|_{\langle \langle v_i, M_{c_{v_i}} \rangle, \xi_i, \langle p_i, M_{p_i} \rangle \rangle}^{i=1\ldots n} \alpha_2)$$

where each $\langle \langle v_i, M_{c_{v_i}} \rangle, \xi_i, \langle p_i, M_{p_i} \rangle \rangle$ *is a wire between* α_1 *and* α_2. *If the connections involved in* θ *(those that label the hyperedges* c_{v_i}*) are cooperative and the* HT-*ARNs are delivery-enabled in relation to the interaction-points being connected, then* α *is progress-enabled.*

Therefore, the proof that a HT-ARN is progress-enabled can be reduced to checking that individual processes and orchestrators are delivery-enabled in relation to their interaction points. To guarantee that the HT-ARN is consistent, it is sufficient to choose processes and orchestrators that are t-closed (implement safety properties). All the checking can be done at design time, not at composition time.

5   A Compositional Theory for HT-ARNs

In this section, we discuss a logic that supports the specification of timed properties as defined in Section 2 and defines a specification theory for our component algebra.

Several extensions of LTL have been proposed to express and reason about real time, among which Metric Temporal Logic (MTL)[10]. MTL works over timed traces and has been studied extensively in relation to important properties such as decidability. The formulas of MTL are built from a set of atomic propositions A using Boolean connectives and time-constrained versions of the until operator of the form $\mathcal{U}_I$ where $I \subseteq [0, \infty)$ is an interval with endpoints in $\mathbb{Q}_{\geq 0} \cup \{\infty\}$.

$$\phi ::= a \mid \neg\phi \mid \phi \supset \phi \mid \phi \, \mathcal{U}_I \, \phi$$

Our purpose is to be able to use such a logic to define a process through a collection Φ of sentences over the language A_γ of the actions defined by the set γ of process ports, such that the behaviour of the process can be defined as $\{\lambda : \lambda \vDash \Phi\}$, i.e., the set of timed traces that satisfy all the sentences in Φ. We then want to use the inference mechanisms of the logic to be able to derive properties of processes and of HT-ARNs.

Because the behaviour of a process is the r-closure of a non-empty δ-timed property (Def. 4), where δ is a clock granularity, we need to be able to define the process semantics of a collection Φ of sentences in such a way that it meets those requirements. In addition, because only t-closed processes can guarantee good properties of HT-ARNs such as consistency, we should restrict ourselves to a safety fragment.

Fragments of MTL have been characterised in which only safety properties can be expressed such as SAFETY-MTL[12], which requires that sentences are in negation normal form and all eventualities to be time-bounded:

$$\phi ::= a \mid \neg a \mid \phi \wedge \phi \mid \phi \vee \phi \mid \phi \, \mathcal{U}_I \, \phi \mid \phi \, \mathcal{R}_I \, \phi \mid \phi \, \mathcal{R} \, \phi$$

where I is bounded and $\mathcal{R}_I$ (resp. $\mathcal{R}$) is the dual of $\mathcal{U}_I$ (resp. $\mathcal{U}_{[0,\infty)}$) operator. In a time context, a safety property Λ is one that is *divergent safe*, i.e., for any timed trace λ, if for all $\pi < \lambda$ there is $\lambda' \in \Lambda$ such that $\pi < \lambda'$, then $\lambda \in \Lambda$. It is easy to see that divergent-safe properties are also t-closed, showing that SAFETY-MTL is adequate for our purposes.

However, the need to specify and reason about r-closed sets of timed traces requires the characterisation of an appropriate fragment of SAFETY-MTL. An alternative, which we take in this paper, is to adopt instead the continuous semantics of MTL. Although the continuous semantics renders MTL and SAFETY-MTL undecidable, it provides a much simpler specification logic for HT-ARNs. We are currently working on the identification of a suitable fragment of SAFETY-MTL with the pointwise semantics.

The models of a continuous semantics are expressed in terms of signals:

Definition 18 (Signal). *A signal for an alphabet A is a function $f : \mathbb{R}_{>0} \to 2^A$ with finite variability, that is, with only finitely many discontinuities in any finite amount of time. The semantics of* MTL *over signals is as follows:*

- $f, t \vDash a$ *iff* $a \in f(t)$
- $f, t \vDash \neg\phi$ *iff* $f, t \nvDash \phi$
- $f, t \vDash \phi_1 \supset \phi_2$ *iff if* $f, t \vDash \phi_1$ *then* $f, t \vDash \phi_2$
- $f, t \vDash \phi_1 \, \mathcal{U}_I \, \phi_2$ *iff there exists* $u \geq t$ *s.t.* $(u - t) \in I$, $f, u \vDash \phi_2$ *and, for all* $t < r < u, f, r \vDash \phi_1$
- $f \vDash \phi$ *iff* $f, 0 \vDash \phi$

Definition 19 (Signals vs timed traces). *Given an alphabet A: (1) a timed-trace $\lambda = \langle \sigma, \tau \rangle$ defines the signal f_λ where, for every i, $f_\lambda(\tau(i)) = \sigma(i)$ and $f_\lambda(t) = \emptyset$*

everywhere else; (2) a signal f and a time sequence τ define a timed trace $\lambda_f^\tau = \langle \sigma, \tau \rangle$ where $\sigma(i) = f(\tau(i))$. We use λ_f^δ to denote the δ-timed trace defined by f and τ_δ.

An important result is that all refinements of a given trace define the same signal:

Proposition 20. *Given timed-traces λ and λ', $\lambda' \preceq \lambda$ implies $f_{\lambda'} = f_\lambda$. It follows that, for every Φ, $\Lambda_\Phi = \{\lambda : f_\lambda \vDash \Phi\}$ is r-closed.*

This is why the continuous semantics provides a 'natural' specification logic for HT-ARNs: only r-closed properties can be specified.

Definition 21 (Process specification). *A specification of a process $\langle \delta, \gamma, \Lambda \rangle$ is $\langle A_\gamma, \Phi \rangle$ such that Φ is in SAFETY-MTL and $\Lambda \vDash \Phi$, i.e., for every $\lambda \in \Lambda$, $f_\lambda \vDash \Phi$.*

As an example consider again the process *CreditMgr* and suppose that its set of timed traces Λ_m is the r-closure of the set of 0.3-timed traces $\langle \sigma, \tau \rangle$ satisfying

$$\forall_{i \in \mathbb{N}} \left(processCredit_i \in \sigma(i) \wedge \forall_{j<i} processCredit_i \notin \sigma(j) \right) \Rightarrow$$
$$\exists_{k>i} \left(expectedDate! \in \sigma(k) \wedge \tau(k) - \tau(i) < 4 \wedge \forall_{j \neq k} expectedDate! \notin \sigma(j) \right)$$

It is not difficult to prove that, for every $\lambda \in \Lambda_m$,

$$f_\lambda \vDash processCredit_i \mathcal{R} (\neg processCredit_i \vee \Diamond_{<4} expectedDate!)$$

where $\Diamond_{<t} \phi$ abbreviates $(true \, \mathcal{U}_{[0,t)} \, \phi)$. This sentence specifies that *expectedDate* is published within four time units from the first delivery of *processCredit*.

Given now a clock granularity δ and a specification $\langle A_\gamma, \Phi \rangle$, we are interested to know if there is actually a process $\langle \delta, \gamma, \Lambda \rangle$ that it specifies, i.e., if $\langle A_\gamma, \Phi \rangle$ is 'δ-satisfiable'. Note that, because the set of processes that $\langle A_\gamma, \Phi \rangle$ specifies is closed under union, if the set is not empty it will admit a biggest process.

Consider $\Lambda_\Phi = \{\lambda : f_\lambda \vDash \Phi\}$. By Prop. 20, Λ_Φ is r-closed. However, Λ_Φ is not necessarily the r-closure of a set of δ-timed traces. Consider instead the set $\{\lambda : \lambda \in \Lambda^\delta(A_\gamma)$ and $f_\lambda \vDash \Phi\}^r$. To determine if the set is not empty, we would have to find a δ-timed trace λ such that $f_\lambda \vDash \Phi$. For that purpose, we could consider the δ-timed trace λ_g^δ for some $g \vDash \Phi$ (assuming that Φ is logically satisfiable). However, it is not immediate that $f_{\lambda_g^\delta} \vDash \Phi$. This is because g and $f_{\lambda_g^\delta}$ are not necessarily the same signal: λ_g^δ retains only the observations made at multiples of δ and $f_{\lambda_g^\delta}$ then constructs a signal that observes the empty set of actions at all other instants, which g may fail to do. Our approach is to construct a sentence $\mathbb{A}x_\delta$ such that $g \vDash \mathbb{A}x_\delta$ implies $g = f_{\lambda_g^\delta}$. We can then take the set $\Lambda_\Phi^\delta = \{\lambda_f^\delta : f \vDash \Phi \text{ and } f \vDash \mathbb{A}x_\delta\}^r$ and reduce the δ-consistency of $\langle A_\gamma, \Phi \rangle$ to the satisfiability of $\Phi \cup \{\mathbb{A}x_\delta\}$.

Proposition 22. $\Lambda_\Phi^\delta \vDash \Phi$.

Hence, if $\Phi \cup \{\mathbb{A}x_\delta\}$ is satisfiable, $\langle \delta, \gamma, \Lambda_\Phi^\delta \rangle$ is a process, actually the biggest process that is specified by $\langle A_\gamma, \Phi \rangle$, which we take as its denotation.

We detail now the construction of $\mathbb{A}x_\delta$. We introduce a new class of unary operators $\boxed{\delta}$ where $\delta \in \mathbb{Q}_{>0}$, which allow us to express that a sentence holds at all multiples of δ:

$$f, t \vDash \boxed{\delta} \phi \text{ iff for all } n \in \mathbb{N}, f, t + n \cdot \delta \vDash \phi$$

Notice that restricting δ to $\mathbb{Q}_{>0}$ is not a real limitation. On the one hand, a connected HT-ARN is such that all the clock granularities are commensurate, which means that we can convert them to rational numbers by dividing them by a common divisor. On the other hand, reasoning about HT-ARNs that are not connected is not relevant because disconnected components do not interfere with each other. Notice that, for r-closure, one simply needs a dense set of time granularities.

In the extended language, the sentence $\boxed{\delta}(\square_{<\delta} \wedge_{a\in A} \neg a)$ — where $\square_{<t} \phi$ is an abbreviation of $\neg(true\, \mathcal{U}_{[0,t)} \neg\phi)$ — expresses a key property of δ-timed traces: empty observations occur at all time instants that are not multiple of δ. We denote this sentence by $\mathbb{A}x_\delta$ and, more generally, given $B \subseteq A$, we use $\mathbb{A}x_\delta^B$ to denote $\boxed{\delta}(\square_{<\delta} \wedge_{a\in B} \neg a)$.

Proposition 23. $f_\lambda \vDash \mathbb{A}x_\delta$ if λ refines a δ-timed trace.

Note that, because $\mathbb{A}x_\delta$ is a safety property, we can conclude that Λ_Φ^δ is safe if we restrict Φ to SAFETY-MTL.

We are now interested in reasoning about properties of HT-ARNs. That is, given a HT-ARN α and a sentence ϕ in the language of A_α, we are interested in determining whether $\Lambda_\alpha \vDash \phi$, i.e., $f_\lambda \vDash \phi$ for every $\lambda \in \Lambda_\alpha$.

Theorem 24. Let α be a HT-ARN and, for every node (resp. hyperedge) p, let Φ_{α_p} be a specification of the process (resp. orchestrator) at p. Let

$$\Phi_\alpha = \bigcup_{p\in N\cup E} \iota_p(\Phi_{\alpha_p} \cup \mathbb{A}x_{\delta_{\alpha_p}}^{A_{\alpha_p}})$$

We have that $\Lambda_\alpha \vDash \phi$ if $\Phi_\alpha \vdash \phi$.

That is, to prove that ϕ expresses a property of α, it is sufficient to derive ϕ from specifications of the processes and orchestrators of α enriched with the corresponding $\mathbb{A}x_\delta$ axioms.

6 Concluding Remarks

In this paper, we have proposed a component algebra that extends the notion of asynchronous relational net developed in [6] to a wider class of systems that operate in a heterogeneous time domain: a HT-ARN is a multigraph of nodes, each with its own clock granularity, where processes execute, and hyperedges where interactions among sets of such processes are orchestrated. Every hyperedge also has its one clock granularity, which needs to be a divisor of the clock granularities of the nodes that it connects so that they can interact. This is important for modelling the software systems that are now starting to operate in cyberspace, where they can connect dynamically, i.e., at run time, to other systems. We provided compositionality results for ensuring the consistency of interconnections when performed at run time across different clock granularities. Contrarily to techniques that operate at design time (e.g., [2]), our results do not require changes to be performed on the processes that execute in such systems so that they can be interconnected, which would defeat the purpose of supporting dynamic binding.

Our algebra is based on timed traces, which allows us to abstract from the specificities of the different classes of automata that can be chosen as models of implementations and characterise at a higher level the topological properties of the languages generated by such automata that support our compositionality results. In a companion paper [3] we investigate a specific automata-based model of machines, which we intend to extend to networks of automata. Another area of further work concerns the logics that can support an interface algebra for HT-ARNs. Although we provided a version of SAFETY-MTL that can support the specification of HT-ARNs, we had to rely on a continuous semantics to enforce the required closure properties. The problem here is that MTL with a continuous semantics is undecidable; better decidability properties can be obtained by choosing instead a pointwise semantics (i.e., where the logic is interpreted directly over timed traces) [12]. Initial results suggest that a pointwise semantics can be developed for HT-ARNs, though at the cost of restricting the syntax. This is an area in which we are currently working, also capitalising on the automata-based models of processes that we have developed in [3].

References

1. Abadi, M., Lamport, L.: The existence of refinement mappings. Theor. Comput. Sci. 82(2), 253–284 (1991)
2. Benveniste, A., Caillaud, B., Carloni, L.P., Sangiovanni-Vincentelli, A.L.: Tag machines. In: EMSOFT, pp. 255–263. ACM (2005)
3. Delahaye, B., Fiadeiro, J.L., Legay, A., Lopes, A.: Heterogeneous timed machines. Technical report (October 2013) (submitted)
4. Delahaye, B., Fiadeiro, J.L., Legay, A., Lopes, A.: A timed component algebra for services. In: Beyer, D., Boreale, M. (eds.) FMOODS/FORTE 2013. LNCS, vol. 7892, pp. 242–257. Springer, Heidelberg (2013)
5. Díaz, G., Pardo, J.J., Cambronero, M.-E., Valero, V., Cuartero, F.: Verification of web services with timed automata. Electr. Notes Theor. Comput. Sci. 157(2), 19–34 (2006)
6. Fiadeiro, J.L., Lopes, A.: An interface theory for service-oriented design. Theor. Comput. Sci. 503, 1–30 (2013)
7. Forget, J., Boniol, F., Lesens, D., Pagetti, C.: A multi-periodic synchronous data-flow language. In: HASE, pp. 251–260. IEEE Computer Society (2008)
8. Guermouche, N., Godart, C.: Timed model checking based approach for web services analysis. In: ICWS, pp. 213–221. IEEE (2009)
9. Kazhamiakin, R., Pandya, P.K., Pistore, M.: Representation, verification, and computation of timed properties in web. In: ICWS, pp. 497–504. IEEE Computer Society (2006)
10. Koymans, R.: Specifying real-time properties with metric temporal logic. Real-Time Systems 2(4), 255–299 (1990)
11. Le, T.T.H., Passerone, R., Fahrenberg, U., Legay, A.: Tag machines for modeling heterogeneous systems. In: ACSD, pp. 186–195. IEEE Computer Society (2013)
12. Ouaknine, J., Worrell, J.: Safety metric temporal logic is fully decidable. In: Hermanns, H., Palsberg, J. (eds.) TACAS 2006. LNCS, vol. 3920, pp. 411–425. Springer, Heidelberg (2006)
13. Ponge, J., Benatallah, B., Casati, F., Toumani, F.: Analysis and applications of timed service protocols. ACM Trans. Softw. Eng. Methodol. 19(4) (2010)

Family-Based Performance Analysis
of Variant-Rich Software Systems

Matthias Kowal[1], Ina Schaefer[1], and Mirco Tribastone[2]

[1] Technische Universität Braunschweig, Germany
[2] University of Southampton, United Kingdom

Abstract. We study models of software systems with variants that stem from a specific choice of configuration parameters with a direct impact on performance properties. Using UML activity diagrams with quantitative annotations, we model such systems as a product line. The efficiency of a *product-based* evaluation is typically low because each product must be analyzed in isolation, making difficult the re-use of computations across variants. Here, we propose a *family-based* approach based on symbolic computation. A numerical assessment on large activity diagrams shows that this approach can be up to three orders of magnitude faster than product-based analysis in large models, thus enabling computationally efficient explorations of large parameter spaces.

1 Introduction

User-configurable parameters of software systems often have a critical impact on non-functional properties such as performance and energy consumption. For example, an elastic cloud-based application may dynamically change the number of active virtual machines depending on the current workload conditions, by setting appropriate threshold-based rules in the virtualization framework. In embedded systems, such as those employed in automation, there may be a trade-off between energy consumption due to increasing speeds and the capability to process jobs with given time constraints (e.g., [1]).

Run-time analysis can be conveniently employed to find the optimal configuration of parameters to automatically adapt to changing conditions. For instance, workloads on a web server may be subjected to day/night or week-day/weekend patterns. In this case, the availability of a software model can be particularly beneficial: When a new operating condition is detected in the system, a mathematical problem can be defined, whose solution gives the values of the user-tunable parameters that satisfy certain given criteria of optimality with respect to the current situation, for instance a performace/cost trade off. Typical solution methods essentially involve repeated analyses using different feasible configurations. This makes the analysis difficult when the evaluation of a single configuration is expensive and/or when the parameter space is large. In particular, applicability of the approach at run-time may be severely hindered if the time constraints for re-configurations and adaptations are stringent enough.

S. Gnesi and A. Rensink (Eds.): FASE 2014, LNCS 8411, pp. 94–108, 2014.

This paper proposes a framework for the efficient evaluation of software designs with large parameter spaces. We consider a class of UML activity diagrams (ADs) to model systems which can be reasonably described as workflow processes, such as real-world data-centers [2], service-oriented architectures (e.g., [3]), and automation systems [4]. To capture non-functional properties, ADs are augmented with performance-related annotations (such as the duration to execute an activity of an activity node) and interpreted as continuous-time Markov chains, along the lines of established routes in model-driven software performance engineering; see, for instance, [5] for a review and [6], [7], and [8], for related work about the automatic extraction of performance models from ADs. Our *performance-annotated ADs* (PAADs) are integrated with software product-line techniques to precisely capture variability aspects. More specifically, we consider a *delta-oriented* approach, where possibly many variants can be generated as a result of applying changes (i.e., *deltas*) to a *core* PAAD [9]. This is a novel application of delta modeling, which has so far been used to represent static variability of software architectures [10] and Java programs [11].

A straightforward solution technique requires a separate analysis of each variant—the so-called *product-based* (PB) evaluation. In this paper, we consider a *family-based* (FB) approach [12]. The configurable parameters of the model under study, inferred by the kinds of delta operations defined on the AD, are used for obtaining a solution in *symbolic* form. In this way, performance indices can be simply obtained by evaluating a polynomial expression that explicitly depends on the configurable parameters. The evaluation may become faster than the PB analysis, which is based on the numerical inversion of a matrix of size equal to the number of nodes in the PAAD. By numerical experimentation we show that our FB approach is up to three orders of magnitude faster than PB analysis, with a tendency to become increasingly more convenient as the model size grows. Although family-based product line analyses have been introduced for type checking [13–15] and model checking [16–18], for the first time this approach is considered for the efficient performance modeling of product lines.

Related work. This paper is most closely related to [19], where an approach based on parametric probabilistic model checking of software product lines models as annotated UML sequence diagrams is proposed. This leads to a symbolic expression that encodes the dependence of certain properties of interest from variables, in a manner which is analogous to ours. However, our work is different in that we consider properties of performance as opposed to reliability/energy. While, in principle, the model checking algorithm of [19] is also applicable to performance-related properties, it may not be efficient. This is due to the potentially massive state space size involved in typical performance models, which generally consider contention for resources by many users, unlike the single-user model in [19]. Under these conditions, the state space size grows (at worst) exponentially with the number of users, which can make symbolic computation infeasible. In our work, instead, this problem is basically circumvented by observing that the classes of models of our interest admit an efficient solution technique that does not necessitate state-space enumeration altogether.

In [20, 21], UML-annotated software product line designs are translated into layered queueing networks [22] and solved with a PB analysis. While layered networks are more expressive than our model, as, e.g. they capture simultaneous resource possession, they do not admit an efficient FB analysis.

Paper outline. Section 2 introduces Performance Annotated Activity Diagrams (PAADs). In Section 3, PAADs are integrated with the delta modeling approach to handle variability. In Section 4, we present our FB analysis. The experimental comparison between the FB and PB evaluation is reported in Section 5, followed by concluding remarks in Section 6.

2   Foundations

Graphically, a UML AD is visualized as a multipartite directed graph. The elements of interest in our modeling framework are categorized into three different groups: *action nodes* essentially describe the smallest possible event in an activity; *activity edges* connect the nodes, expressing possible paths of execution; and *control flow nodes* are used to model, for instance, conditional behavior. Throughout the paper, we shall use the neutral name of *job* to indicate an element (i.e., a *token*) that circulates through the nodes of an activity diagram. This is to be interpreted, e.g., as a user, service request, or a physical item, depending on the context of the specific model under consideration.

The following provides a formal definition of performance-annotated activity diagrams in a manner that is independent from the actual annotation mechanism that may be used in an implementation. A concrete realization is feasible, for instance with the MARTE profile (see [23]) and its PaStep stereotype (e.g., [24]).

Definition 1 (Performance-Annotated Activity Diagram). *Let $\mathcal{V}$ be the set of all nodes. A* performance-annotated activity diagram *(PAAD) is a tuple*

$$PAAD = (V, E, \lambda, \mu),$$

where $V \subseteq \mathcal{V}$, $E \subseteq V \times \mathbb{R}_{\geq 0} \times V$, $\lambda : V \to \mathbb{R}_{\geq 0}$, and $\mu : V \to \mathbb{R}_{>0}$.

This definition specifies a directed graph annotated with three distinct pieces of information. Each edge $e \in E$ has a non-negative real, giving the probability with which that path is taken by a job in the source node. Each node $v \in V$ is associated with a *rate*, $\mu(v)$, denoting the average speed at which a job is processed in v; $\lambda(v)$, instead, denotes the *workload*, the speed at which jobs arrive from the external world. This may model, for instance, users that issue invocations to the service described by the AD.

We wish to point out that Definition 1 does not explicitly consider initial, final, and merge nodes. Similarly to previous work [24], we argue that these are not necessary when an AD is to be interpreted as a performance model. For instance, Figure 1 shows a sample AD (left diagram), and its representation in our annotated PAAD format (right diagram), removing the nodes that are not supported and redirecting the edges appropriately. For instance, the initial

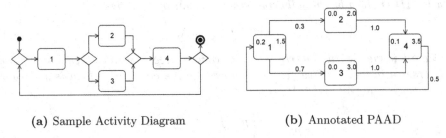

(a) Sample Activity Diagram   (b) Annotated PAAD

Fig. 1. Running example

node, which models the start of the activity, is replaced by a nonzero workload into node 1. This PAAD will be used as a running example throughout this paper. For each action node v, the top-left label gives $\lambda(v)$, the top-right label is $\mu(v)$, whereas the label in the middle indicates the node itself. The edges are instead labeled with their associated probabilities. For example, after an element is processed in node 4, it will return to node 1 with probability 0.5. Thus, with probability 0.5 it will leave the system. This captures the intended design in the AD diagram, where one outgoing edge of the decision node leads to a final state.

Of all the elements of UML ADs that are not used in Definition 1, we remark the absence of fork/join nodes. Unfortunately, their performance interpretation leads to models that do not enjoy efficient FB solutions. Although we leave further investigation of this matter to future work, we observe that Definition 1 allows us to capture models considered in the literature such as service-oriented systems (e.g., [25–27]) and manufacturing job-shops [1, 28].

We now provide conditions to be enjoyed by a PAAD to yield a meaningful performance model.

Definition 2 (Well-formedness). *A PAAD is well-formed if and only if the following conditions hold:*

i) There exists at least one $v \in V$ such that $\lambda(v) > 0$;
ii) For all $v \in V$ it holds that $\sum_{(v,p,v')\in E} p \leq 1$;
iii) For all $v, v' \in V$, for any $(v, p, v'), (v, q, v') \in E$ it holds that $p = q$;
iv) There exists at least one $v \in V$ such that $\sum_{(v,p,v')\in E} p < 1$.

Assumption i) is required to ensure that the model receives requests starting at least from one node. Assumption ii) corresponds to the natural interpretation of edge labels as probabilities. Assumption iii) requires that there is at most one directed edge between any two nodes, so that the probability with which node v' is visited after v is not ambiguously defined. Finally, iv) requires that, eventually, jobs leave the workflow. This is a necessary condition for a steady-state behaviour. Otherwise, the system would keep accumulating jobs.

The following definition permits the analysis of a (well-formed) PAAD. We call this *product-based evaluation* as it concerns a given, concrete PAAD, unlike *family-based evaluation*, which will be introduced later in the paper.

Definition 3 (Product-based evaluation). *The product-based evaluation of a PAAD is given by the following system of linear equations*

$$(I - P^T)\gamma = \lambda, \tag{1}$$

where I is the identity matrix, λ is the (column) vector with elements $\lambda(v)$. This is ordered in the same way as nodes appear in the matrix P, which is defined as $P = (p_{v,v'})$, for all $v, v' \in V$ with

$$p_{v,v'} = \begin{cases} p & \text{if } (v, p, v') \in E, \\ 0 & \text{otherwise.} \end{cases}$$

Finally, γ is the vector of unknowns, with elements denoted by $\gamma(v)$.

In essence, we are interpreting a PAAD as a continuous-time Markov chain that underlies a Jackson-type queueing network [28], by giving the following semantics. $\lambda(v)$ is the rate of arrival of jobs at the node v, which is assumed to be a Poisson process. Thus, for $\lambda(v) > 0$, $1/\lambda(v)$ is the inter-arrival time between two jobs, which is exponentially distributed. If $\lambda(v) = 0$, node v does not have exogenous arrivals and may only process jobs arriving from other nodes, according to the topology of the workflow. Jobs at action node v are served by a processing unit with rate $\mu(v) > 0$. Therefore, $1/\mu(v)$ is the average service demand of a job at node v. When the node is busy serving a job, the other jobs accumulate in an unbounded queue and are scheduled according to a first-in first-out discipline. P is the *routing probability matrix*, defining with which probability a job in node v, after being serviced, moves to any other node v'. Finally, γ gives the *effective* arrival rates, which take into account the actual traffic incoming at node v due to the exogenous arrival as well as to the feedback from other nodes. With obvious ordering, in our running example we have

$$P = \begin{bmatrix} 0.0 & 0.3 & 0.7 & 0.0 \\ 0.0 & 0.0 & 0.0 & 1.0 \\ 0.0 & 0.0 & 0.0 & 1.0 \\ 0.5 & 0.0 & 0.0 & 0.0 \end{bmatrix} \quad \lambda = \begin{bmatrix} 0.2 \\ 0.0 \\ 0.0 \\ 0.1 \end{bmatrix} \quad \mu = \begin{bmatrix} 1.5 \\ 2.0 \\ 3.0 \\ 3.5 \end{bmatrix} \tag{2}$$

Once the system (1) is solved for γ, the steady-state behavior of the network is completely characterized (e.g., [29]). Specifically, the following indices can be computed for any $v \in V$.

- $\gamma(v)$ is the *throughput*, i.e., the rate at which jobs are served at node v.
- The *utilization* of node v, denoted by $\rho(v)$, i.e., the probability that the node is busy serving jobs, is given by:

$$\rho(v) = \gamma(v)/\mu(v).$$

- The *queue length* at node v, denoted by $L(v)$, i.e., the number of jobs at node v including those in service, is given by

$$L(v) = \rho(v)/(1 - \rho(v)). \tag{3}$$

- Using Little's law, the *average response time* of jobs at node v, denoted by $W(v)$, is given by
$$W(v) = L(v)/\gamma(v).$$
Response times along paths of the PAAD can be computed similarly using the same law.

In our numerical evaluation in Section 5, we will consider the average queue length in the network as the metric of interest. This is simply obtained by computing $\sum_{v \in V} L(v)/|v|$. For instance, solving (2) yields

$$\gamma = \begin{bmatrix} 0.50 & 0.15 & 0.35 & 0.60 \end{bmatrix}^T$$

which leads to an average queue length of 0.23 customers in the steady state.

3   Variability of PAADs

In this section, we discuss how to model variability aspects of PAADs using delta modeling. Delta modeling is a modular, yet flexible variability modeling approach on the artifact level (in contrast to feature models which live on the requirements level) and allows capturing closed as well as open variant spaces. We consider a core PAAD and an associated set of *deltas* [9]. Each delta contains a set of basic operations to be performed on a PAAD, such as the addition and the removal of a node, or the modification of parameters such as the probabilities of an edge. Thus, applying a delta to the core yields a new PAAD *variant*, which has performance characteristics that can be numerically analyzed using the product-based evaluation in Definition 3.

In addition, from a core model with an associated set of deltas we generate a *150%-model*. This is an over-saturated variant representing the whole product line which, in general, does not correspond to a concrete variant of interest to the modeler. However, we define a solution method based on symbolic computation yielding an expression that directly relates a performance index (such as the average queue length) to all the model parameters that are at least altered once by any of the deltas. When such a symbolic expression is evaluated for the parameters of a specific variant, it returns the actual performance index for that variant. This allows the re-use of the same symbolic expression *for all variants*, unlike the numerical solution with product-based evaluation.

We start with defining all possible atomic delta operations on a PAAD.

Definition 4 (PAAD deltas). *A PAAD delta is a set of delta operations* $\delta \subseteq Op$, *where*

$$Op = \{ add\ (v_i, \lambda_i, \mu_i) \mid v_i \in \mathcal{V}, \lambda_i \geq 0, \mu_i \geq 0 \}$$
$$\cup\ \{ add\ (v_i, p_{ij}, v_j) \mid v_i, v_j \in \mathcal{V}, p_{ij} > 0 \} \cup \{ rem\ v \mid v \in \mathcal{V} \} \cup \{ rem\ e \mid e \in \mathcal{E} \}$$
$$\cup\ \{ mod\ \lambda(v_i)\ by\ \lambda_j \mid v_i \in \mathcal{V}, \lambda_j \geq 0 \} \cup \{ mod\ \mu(v_i)\ by\ \mu_j \mid v_i \in \mathcal{V}, \mu_j > 0 \}$$
$$\cup\ \{ mod\ (v_i, p_{ij}, v_j)\ by\ q_{ij} \mid (v_i, p_{ij}, v_j) \in \mathcal{E}, q_{ij} > 0 \}.$$

When an edge is added, its associated probability must be strictly positive. This is without loss of generality because an edge with probability zero essentially corresponds to the case where no edge at all is connecting two nodes. For the same reason, when a service rate or a probability are modified we require strictly positive values. This is not the case for arrival rates, so long as there exists at least a node with a positive arrival rate. The modification of values is a simplification since it can also be encoded by removing node or edge and adding it with the desired rate or probability, respectively.

For simplicity, in this paper we only consider a single delta to generate a PAAD variant. This is without loss of generality, since the effect of a set of deltas can be combined into a single composite delta by defining an appropriate delta composition operation. In order to ensure that the application of such a delta leads to a well-formed PAAD variant, we require that the delta is applicable and consistent. A delta is *applicable* to a PAAD if all elements (node, edge, rate or probability) which should be removed or modified exist and if all elements which are added do not exist. A delta is *consistent* if it adds, removes or modifies each element at most once [9]. Furthermore, a consistent delta ensures that are no dangling edges in the resulting PAAD. This means that removing a node also causes the removal of all resulting edges. Edges are never added between nodes that are removed in the delta. If a node of an added edge does not exist in the core PAAD, the necessary source and/or target edges are also added in the delta. However, there may be unreachable nodes in the resulting PAAD variant. This is not an issue for the well-formedness of the result.

As an example of delta modeling on PAADs, we consider deltas δ_1 and δ_2, defined as follows:

$$\delta_1 = \{\mathsf{rem}\ (4, 0.5, 1), \mathsf{add}\ (5, 0.1, 1.0), \mathsf{add}\ (4, 0.5, 5), \mathsf{add}\ (5, 1.0, 1)\},$$

$$\delta_2 = \{\mathsf{rem}\ (1, 0.3, 2), \mathsf{rem}\ (2, 1.0, 4), \mathsf{rem}\ 2, \mathsf{mod}\ (1, 0.7, 3)\ \mathsf{by}\ 1.0\}.$$

The following definition formalizes, in a straightforward way, how to obtain a variant by applying a delta to a PAAD. Figure 2 illustrates the application of δ_1 and δ_2 to the core model in Fig. 1.

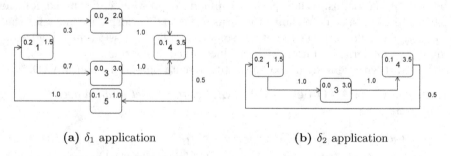

(a) δ_1 application   (b) δ_2 application

Fig. 2. Deltas applied to the core model in Figure 1

Definition 5 (PAAD delta application). *The application of an applicable and consistent delta $\delta \subseteq Op$ to a $PAAD = (V, E, \lambda, \mu)$ is defined by the function $PAAD' = apply(PAAD, \delta)$, where $PAAD' = (V', E', \lambda', \mu')$. It is recursively defined as follows.*

1. *Case $\delta = \emptyset$: $PAAD' = PAAD$.*
2. *Case: $\delta = \delta' \cup \delta'' \wedge \delta', \delta'' \in Op$: $PAAD' = apply(apply(PAAD, \delta'), \delta'')$.*
3. *Case: $\delta =$ add (v_i, λ_i, μ_i):*

$$V' = V \cup \{v_i\} \quad \lambda'(v) = \begin{cases} \lambda(v) & \text{if } v \neq v_i, \\ \lambda_i & \text{if } v = v_i, \end{cases} \quad \mu'(v) = \begin{cases} \mu(v) & \text{if } v \neq v_i, \\ \mu_i & \text{if } v = v_i. \end{cases}$$

4. *Case: $\delta =$ add (v_i, p_{ij}, v_j): $E' = E \cup \{(v_i, p_{ij}, v_j)\}$.*
5. *Case: $\delta =$ rem v: $V' = V \setminus \{v\}$.*
6. *Case: $\delta =$ rem e: $E' = E \setminus \{e\}$.*
7. *Case: $\delta =$ mod $\lambda(v_i)$ by λ_j: $\lambda'(v) = \begin{cases} \lambda(v) & \text{if } v \neq v_i, \\ \lambda_j & \text{if } v = v_i, \end{cases}$*
8. *Case: $\delta =$ mod $\mu(v_i)$ by μ_j: $\mu'(v) = \begin{cases} \mu(v) & \text{if } v \neq v_i, \\ \mu_j & \text{if } v = v_i, \end{cases}$*
9. *Case: $\delta =$ mod (v_i, p_{ij}, v_j) by q_{ij}: $E' = \big(E \setminus \{(v_i, p_{ij}, v_j)\}\big) \cup \{(v_i, q_{ij}, v_j)\}$.*

We now consider a *core* PAAD and a set of deltas Δ. We define the 150%-model as a special kind of PAAD which has all nodes and transitions that are introduced or modified by each $\delta \in \Delta$. As discussed, in general the 150%-model is not a valid PAAD variant, but it contains all the information to retrieve a variant resulting from the application of any $\delta \in \Delta$. The origin of a node or transition from the core model or a specific delta, where it is added, modified or removed, is traced by means of a labeling function $\mathcal{L}$, defined as follows.

Definition 6 (150%-model). *Let $PAAD_c = (V_c, E_c, \lambda_c, \mu_c)$ be the core model and Δ be a set of consistent and applicable deltas. Let $L = \{C\} \cup \{\underline{\delta}, !\underline{\delta} \mid \delta \in \Delta\}$, with $C \notin \Delta$, be the set of labels. The 150%-model is $PAAD_{150} = (V_{150}, E_{150}, \lambda_{150}, \mu_{150}, \mathcal{L})$, where:*

$V_{150} = V_c \cup \{v \mid \exists \delta \in \Delta : $ add $(v, \lambda_i, \mu_i) \in \delta\}$,

$E_{150} = E_c \cup \{(v_i, p_{ij}, v_j) \mid \exists \delta : $ add $(v_i, p_{ij}, v_j) \in \delta \vee $ mod (v_i, q_{ij}, v_j) by $p_{ij} \in \delta\}$,

λ_{150} and μ_{150} are partial functions of $V_{150} \times L$ defined as

$$\lambda_{150} : V_{150} \times L \to \mathbb{R}_{\geq 0}, \quad \lambda_{150}(v, l) = \begin{cases} \lambda_c(v) & \text{if } l = C \wedge v \in V_c, \\ \lambda_i & \text{if } l = \underline{\delta} \wedge \text{add } (v, \lambda_i, \mu_i) \in \delta, \\ \lambda_j & \text{if } l = \underline{\delta} \wedge \text{mod } \lambda(v_i) \text{ by } \lambda_j \in \delta, \\ 0 & \text{if } l = !\underline{\delta} \wedge \text{rem } v \in \delta, \end{cases}$$

$$\mu_{150} : V_{150} \times L \to \mathbb{R}_{\geq 0}, \quad \mu_{150}(v, l) = \begin{cases} \mu_c(v) & \text{if } l = C \wedge v \in V_c, \\ \mu_i & \text{if } l = \underline{\delta} \wedge \text{add } (v, \lambda_i, \mu_i) \in \delta, \\ \mu_j & \text{if } l = \underline{\delta} \wedge \text{mod } \mu(v_i) \text{ by } \mu_j \in \delta, \\ 0 & \text{if } l = !\underline{\delta} \wedge \text{rem } v \in \delta, \end{cases}$$

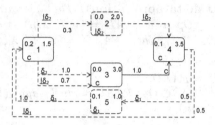

Fig. 3. 150%-model of the running example

and $\mathcal{L}$ is the labeling function *defined as*

$$\mathcal{L} : V_{150} \cup E_{150} \rightarrow 2^L,$$

$$\mathcal{L}(v) = \begin{cases} C & \text{if } v \in V_c, \\ \emptyset & \text{otherwise,} \end{cases} \cup \{\underline{\delta} \mid \textit{add } (v, \lambda_i, \mu_i) \in \delta\} \cup \{!\underline{\delta} \mid \textit{rem } v \in \delta\}.$$

$$\mathcal{L}(e) = \begin{cases} C & \text{if } e \in E_c, \\ \emptyset & \text{otherwise,} \end{cases} \cup \{\underline{\delta} \mid \textit{add } e \in \delta\} \cup \{!\underline{\delta} \mid \textit{rem } e \in \delta\}$$

$$\cup \{\underline{\delta} \mid \textit{mod } (v_i, q_{ij}, v_j) \textit{ by } p_{ij} \in \delta \wedge e = (v_i, p_{ij}, v_j)\}$$

$$\cup \{!\underline{\delta} \mid \textit{mod } (v_i, q_{ij}, v_j) \textit{ by } p_{ij} \in \delta \wedge e = (v_i, q_{ij}, v_j)\}.$$

In order to construct the 150%-model, we consider all nodes V_{150} which are either part of the core PAAD or are added in a delta. The set of edges E_{150} contains all edges from the core and all edges added by a delta. Since the probability of an existing edge can be modified by a delta, we add an edge with the new probability to the 150%-model. As a result, we have an edge with the previous probability and an edge with the modified one in the 150%-model. The domain of the functions λ_{150} and μ_{150} are pairs, where the first element indicates the node or edge that is labelled and the second pair specifies a delta label. The functions map onto the concrete value of the rate that the element has in that specific delta. Finally, the labeling function $\mathcal{L}$ is necessary in order to identify the core and the original PAAD variants in order to map the results of the FB analysis to the PAAD variants. Nodes have three possible labels: C means that the node is part of the core PAAD. Since deltas add or remove nodes, we use $\underline{\delta}$ to denote addition, and $!\underline{\delta}$ for removal. The labeling of edges is done in a similar way. The 150%-model of the running example is shown in Fig. 3. Nodes and edges occur only in the core model, e.g., $\mathcal{L}(v) = \{C\}$, are marked with solid lines; otherwise, dashed lines are used. The labels of the nodes are shown within the nodes in the bottom-left part.

4   Family-Based Evaluation

We now discuss the symbolic evaluation of the 150% model. This is accomplished, in essence, by taking a 150% model and associating a symbolic variable to each element that is varied in at least one delta. We use the following convention. We let $\mathcal{S}$ denote the set of all symbolic variables, whose elements are indicated by a superscript '*'.

Definition 7 (Family-based evaluation). *Let* $PAAD_{150}$ *be a 150% model. The* FB *evaluation* is given by the solution of

$$(I - P_s^T)\gamma_s = \lambda_s, \tag{4}$$

where:

$$\lambda_s : V_{150} \to \mathbb{R} \cup \mathcal{S}, \ \lambda_s(v) = \begin{cases} \lambda_{150}(v, C) & \text{if } \nexists l \in L \setminus \{C\} : \lambda_{150}(v, l) \text{ is defined.} \\ \lambda_v^* & \text{otherwise,} \end{cases}$$

$$\mu_s : V_{150} \to \mathbb{R} \cup \mathcal{S}, \ \mu_s(v) = \begin{cases} \mu_{150}(v, C) & \text{if } \nexists l \in L \setminus \{C\} : \mu_{150}(v, l) \text{ is defined.} \\ \mu_v^* & \text{otherwise,} \end{cases}$$

$$P_s = (p_{v,v'}^s)_{v,v' \in V_{150}}, \ p_{v,v'}^s = \begin{cases} q & \text{if } \exists e = (v, q, v') \in E_{150} \wedge \mathcal{L}(e) = \{C\}, \\ 0 & \text{if } \nexists e = (v, q, v') \in E_{150}, \\ p_{v,v'}^* & \text{otherwise.} \end{cases}$$

Informally, $\lambda_s(v)$ (and similarly, $\mu_s(v)$) treats as symbolic all the parameters that are changed by at least one delta operation. Else, the parameter is simply the concrete value assigned in the core model. Concrete probabilities $p_{v,v'}$ are assigned when two nodes are associated *only in the core model*, or when they are not associated at all. Otherwise, the symbolic variable $p_{v,v'}^*$ is used.

For an illustrative explanation, let us consider again our running example in Fig. 1 as core model and let us take $\Delta = \{\delta_a, \delta_b, \delta_c\}$, with

$$\delta_a = \{\text{mod } (1, 0.3, 2) \text{ by } 0.4, \ \text{mod } (1, 0.7, 3) \text{ by } 0.6\},$$
$$\delta_b = \{\text{mod } \lambda(1) \text{ by } 0.1\}, \quad \delta_c = \{\text{mod } \mu(4) \text{ by } 4.0\}.$$

For conciseness, we do not show the actual variants obtained through these deltas (which will have the same topology, but different concrete labels). By Definition 7, the FB evaluation is

$$P_s = \begin{bmatrix} 0.0 & p_{1,2}^* & p_{1,3}^* & 0.0 \\ 0.0 & 0.0 & 0.0 & 1.0 \\ 0.0 & 0.0 & 0.0 & 1.0 \\ 0.5 & 0.0 & 0.0 & 0.0 \end{bmatrix} \quad \lambda_s = \begin{bmatrix} \lambda_1^* \\ 0.0 \\ 0.0 \\ 0.1 \end{bmatrix} \quad \mu_s = \begin{bmatrix} 1.5 \\ 2.0 \\ 3.0 \\ \mu_4^* \end{bmatrix} \tag{5}$$

where $\mathcal{S} = \{p_{1,2}^*, p_{1,3}^*, \lambda_1^*, \mu_4^*\}$. As discussed in Section 2, P_s, λ_s, and μ_s characterize the performance of a PAAD. For instance, by using the formula (3), the average queue length (AQL) will be given by the following symbolic expression:

$$\text{AQL} = -\frac{20\lambda_1^* + 1}{80\lambda_1^* + 60p_{1,2}^* + 60p_{1,3}^* - 116} - \frac{p_{1,2}^*(20\lambda_1^* + 1)}{4(21p_{1,2}^* + 20p_{1,3}^* + 20\lambda_1^*p_{1,2}^* - 40)}$$
$$-\frac{10\lambda_1^*p_{1,2}^* + 10\lambda_1^*p_{1,3}^* + 1}{20\mu_4^*p_{1,2}^* - 40\mu_4^* + 20\mu_4^*p_{1,3}^* + 40\lambda_1^*p_{1,2}^* + 40\lambda_1^*p_{1,3}^* + 4}$$
$$-\frac{p_{1,3}^*(20\lambda_1^* + 1)}{4(30p_{1,2}^* + 31p_{1,3}^* + 20\lambda_1^*p_{1,2}^* - 60)}. \qquad (6)$$

Let us observe that assigning $p_{1,2}^* = 0.3$, $p_{1,3}^* = 0.7$, $\lambda_1^* = 0.2$, and $\mu_4^* = 3.5$ in the 150% model (5) corresponds to the model in (2), which is the product-based evaluation of a specific variant. Now, it holds that evaluating the symbolic expression (6) with such specific values yields 0.23, consistently with the product-based evaluation. The average queue lengths for the variants obtained by each of the deltas δ_a, δ_b, and δ_c, can be computed by evaluating *the same symbolic expression*, plugging in the appropriate concrete values related to each variant. Instead, as discussed, product-based evaluation does not allow the re-use of any computation because the solution based on matrix inversion is done numerically.

We are now left with showing that the symbolic evaluation with the appropriate concrete parameters of a variant always corresponds to the PB evaluation, i.e., the non-symbolic numerical analysis of a single variant in isolation. The following definition *concretizes* a 150% model with respect to a delta δ, i.e., it isolates the elements of the 150% model that are relevant for δ.

Definition 8 (Concretization). *Let $PAAD_{150}$ be a 150% model from a core $PAAD_c$ with a set of deltas Δ and with symbolic FB evaluation (4). A concretization of $PAAD_{150}$ for $\delta \in \Delta$ is given by $(I - P_k^T)\gamma_k = \lambda_k$, where*

$$\lambda_k = (\lambda_k(v))_{v \in V_{150}}, \quad \lambda_k(v) = \begin{cases} \lambda_{150}(v, \underline{\delta}) & \text{if defined,} \\ \lambda_{150}(v, C) & \text{if defined and } \lambda_{150}(v, \underline{\delta}) \text{ is not defined,} \\ 0 & \text{otherwise,} \end{cases}$$

$$P_k = (p_{v,v'}^k)_{v,v' \in V_{150}}, \quad p_{v,v'}^k = \begin{cases} p_{v,v'}^s & \text{if } p_{v,v'}^s \notin S, \\ p & \text{if } \exists e = (v, p, v') \in E_{150} \wedge \underline{\delta} \in \mathcal{L}(e), \\ 0 & \text{otherwise.} \end{cases}$$

The concretization yields a system of equations of the size of the 150% model. The next theorem is the desired, crucial result of consistency of this paper. It states that the FB symbolic solution, *restricted* to those nodes that are in the variant given by $apply(\text{PAAD}_c, \delta)$, corresponds to the PB evaluation of $apply(\text{PAAD}_c, \delta)$ itself.

Theorem 1 (Consistency). *Let $(I - P_a^T)\gamma_a = \lambda_a$ denote the PB evaluation of $(V_a, E_a, \lambda_a, \mu_a) = apply(PAAD_c, \delta)$, for $\delta \in \Delta$, and let $(I - P_k^T)\gamma_k = \lambda_k$ be the concretization of the 150% model $PAAD_{150}$ for δ. Furthermore, we define*

$$V^\delta = \left\{ v \in V_{150} : \left(C \in \mathcal{L}(v) \wedge \underline{!\delta} \notin \mathcal{L}(v)\right) \vee \underline{\delta} \in \mathcal{L}(v) \right\}.$$

It holds that i) $V^\delta = V^a$ and ii) $\gamma_a(v) = \gamma_k(v)$ and $\mu_a(v) = \mu_k(v)$, for all $v \in V^\delta$.

5   Numerical Experiments

We compared the FB symbolic analysis against the PB approach, where each configuration is solved numerically for a given concrete set of parameter values.

Our experimental set-up was as follows. We considered randomly generated 150% PAAD models with different numbers of nodes and different number of variables (i.e., the set of elements from $\mathcal{S}$) for their symbolic evaluation. This is motivated by the fact that, while PB evaluation has a cost which is at best quadratic with the number of nodes [29], the FB approach requires the evaluation of a polynomial expression. Thus, we wish to test the hypothesis that FB analysis is increasingly more convenient with larger networks, and to assess the impact of the number of variables on the length of such polynomials and thus on their evaluation time. Clearly, a trade-off must be struck between the degrees of freedom and the effectiveness of the FB approach, as the cost of such form of symbolic computation is clearly dependent on the number of variables [30]. Notice, however, that each symbol represents a parameter that takes values in the reals. Thus, even a *single variable* may represent *infinitely many variants*.

Let n denote the total number of nodes in the FB evaluation, i.e., $n = |V_{150}|$, p be the number of variables in the routing probability matrix (i.e., the number of symbols in P_s), m the number of variables in the service rates (the symbols in the range of the function in μ_s), and g the number of variables in the exogenous arrival rates (the symbols in the range of λ_s). For any given choice of (n, p, m, g), all the other parameters were randomly generated, with the service rates drawn uniformly at random in $[1.0; 20.0]$, and the arrival rates in the range $[0.0; 3.0]$. For instance, the symbolic evaluation (5) corresponds to a configuration $(n, p, m, g) = (4, 2, 1, 1)$, where the remaining concrete values shown in P_s, λ_s and μ_s would be generated randomly. In particular, the routing probability matrices generated in this way led to network topologies with densely connected nodes.

For each tuple (n, p, m, g), we considered 200 randomly generated variants which we analyzed with both the FB and the PB approach. We did so by randomly generating 200 tuples, each of length $p+m+g$, corresponding to a specific instantiation of the symbolic parameters. For the FB approach, each tuple was used to evaluate a symbolic expression of the average queue length such as (6); for the PB approach instead, the parameters were used to numerically solve the system of equations (1) for each variant.

We measured the wall-clock execution times for both FB and PB evaluation, repeated 5 times in order to reduce the noise in the measurements. The tests were implemented in Matlab version 7.9.0 (R2009b) using the *Symbolic Math Toolbox* for the FB evaluation, and the built-in functions for the solutions of systems of linear equations for the PB evaluation. The measurements were conducted on a machine with an Intel Core i7 2.66 GHz with 8 GB RAM.

Each line in Table 1 shows the overall execution times, averaged over the 5 tests, of both FB and PB across the 200 random variants, which represent the whole family for each configuration (n, p, m, g). We report the average speedup

Table 1. Numerical results

Variables				Runtimes (s)				Variables				Runtimes (s)			
n	p	m	g	FB	PB	PB/FB	PC	n	p	m	g	FB	PB	PB/FB	PC
4	1	0	0	0.011	0.049	4.47	0.545	142	1	0	0	0.016	6.540	397.34	5.425
4	0	1	0	0.004	0.043	10.78	0.185	142	0	1	0	0.005	8.107	1664.28	4.908
4	0	0	1	0.009	0.045	4.92	0.190	142	0	0	1	0.015	10.808	726.41	4.836
4	1	1	1	0.011	0.046	4.13	0.214	142	1	1	1	0.017	10.069	601.51	5.113
4	2	2	2	0.014	0.049	3.60	0.319	142	2	2	2	0.019	10.052	526.50	4.936
4	4	4	4	0.020	0.049	2.43	0.310	142	0	6	0	0.007	7.802	1191.79	5.137
24	1	0	0	0.011	0.066	5.96	1.141	142	4	4	4	0.026	10.985	429.83	4.942
24	0	1	0	0.004	0.063	14.60	1.124	302	1	0	0	0.019	19.186	1007.95	11.026
24	0	0	1	0.011	0.067	6.29	1.152	302	0	1	0	0.006	13.680	2292.46	11.192
24	1	1	1	0.013	0.068	5.04	1.244	302	0	0	1	0.018	13.399	728.73	11.050
24	2	2	2	0.016	0.068	4.31	1.100	302	1	1	1	0.021	19.520	909.12	11.591
24	0	6	0	0.007	0.065	9.94	1.004	302	2	2	2	0.024	19.459	820.30	11.214
24	4	4	4	0.099	0.070	0.70	1.904	302	0	6	0	0.006	13.896	2258.21	11.089
								302	4	4	4	0.030	14.879	495.06	11.718

PB/FB. The last column shows the pre-computation (PC) time taken to symbolically solve (4). These results allow us to make the following observations.

- We confirm that for any fixed choice of p, m, and g that we considered, larger values of n make FB increasingly more convenient, with speedups up to over 2000; see, for instance, the configurations $(4, 0, 1, 0)$, $(24, 0, 1, 0)$, $(142, 0, 1, 0)$, $(4, 1, 0, 0)$, and $(302, 1, 0, 0)$. This is because of the increasing cost of the solution of the system of linear equations for PB, while FB solves it symbolically only once and off-line.

- For fixed n, varying p, m, and g has an impact on speedup, since the higher the number of variables the larger the closed-form polynomial expression derived by the FB approach.

- For fixed n, not all other parameters affect the speedup in the same manner. In particular, compare the two cases $p = m = g = 2$ and $p = g = 0$, $m = 6$, for every given n. Both have the same number of variables (i.e., six), but the latter case consistently enjoys a better speedup. This is because the m variables do not appear in (1), thus for $m = 6$ the symbolic expressions of the solution (1) can be greatly simplified because it consists of only scalars. (The m variables will appear in the calculation for the queue lengths L_v.)

- FB evaluation is not always more effective than PB evaluation. In our study, this has occurred in smaller models (i.e., $n = 24$) with relatively high number of variables. In these cases, the polynomial expression turned out to be more difficult to analyze than the linear system of equations (for which Matlab is well-known to be optimized).

- The pre-computation time behaves well with the number of variables, in particular with respect to the p variables that are used in the solution of (1).

6 Conclusion

We have presented an efficient technique for model-based performance analysis of software product lines using a class of UML activity diagrams annotated with quantitative information. Our approach enables a family-based evaluation by means of symbolic computation, which has been shown to be up to three orders of magnitude faster than product-based analysis in large models.

Regarding future work, this paper can be extended in two directions. From a theoretical viewpoint, we will study extensions to other kinds of performance models that are amenable to analogous closed-form symbolic solutions. From a practical viewpoint, we plan an implementation integrated with UML CASE tools and an experimentation with run-time optimization of automation systems.

Acknowledgment. This work was partially supported by the DFG (German Research Foundation) under the Priority Programme SPP1593: Design For Future — Managed Software Evolution, and by the EU project QUANTICOL, 600708. The authors would like to thank Christian Prehofer for fruitful discussions.

References

1. Govil, M.K., Fu, M.C.: Queueing theory in manufacturing: A survey. Journal of Manufacturing Systems 18(3), 214–240 (1999)
2. Singh, R., Shenoy, P., Natu, M., Sadaphal, V., Vin, H.: Predico: A System for What-if Analysis in Complex Data Center Applications. In: Kon, F., Kermarrec, A.-M. (eds.) Middleware 2011. LNCS, vol. 7049, pp. 123–142. Springer, Heidelberg (2011)
3. Huhns, M., Singh, M.: Service-oriented computing: key concepts and principles. IEEE Internet Computing 9(1), 75–81 (2005)
4. Vogel-Heuser, B., Witsch, D., Katzke, U.: Automatic code generation from a UML model to IEC 61131-3 and system configuration tools. In: ICCA, pp. 1034–1039 (2005)
5. Balsamo, S., Di Marco, A., Inverardi, P., Simeoni, M.: Model-based performance prediction in software development: A survey. IEEE Trans. Software Eng. 30(5), 295–310 (2004)
6. Petriu, D.C., Shen, H.: Applying the UML performance profile: Graph grammar-based derivation of LQN models from UML specifications. In: Field, T., Harrison, P.G., Bradley, J., Harder, U. (eds.) TOOLS 2002. LNCS, vol. 2324, pp. 159–177. Springer, Heidelberg (2002)
7. Balsamo, S., Marzolla, M.: Performance evaluation of UML software architectures with multiclass queueing network models. In: WOSP, pp. 37–42 (2005)
8. López-Grao, J.P., Merseguer, J., Campos, J.: From UML activity diagrams to stochastic Petri nets: application to software performance engineering. SIGSOFT Softw. Eng. Notes 29(1), 25–36 (2004)
9. Schaefer, I.: Variability modelling for model-driven development of software product lines. In: VaMoS, pp. 85–92 (2010)

10. Haber, A., Kutz, T., Rendel, H., Rumpe, B., Schaefer, I.: Delta-oriented architectural variability using monticore. In: ECSA, pp. 6:1–6:10 (2011)
11. Schaefer, I., Bettini, L., Bono, V., Damiani, F., Tanzarella, N.: Delta-oriented programming of software product lines. In: Bosch, J., Lee, J. (eds.) SPLC 2010. LNCS, vol. 6287, pp. 77–91. Springer, Heidelberg (2010)
12. von Rhein, A., Apel, S., Kästner, C., Thüm, T., Schaefer, I.: The PLA model: on the combination of product-line analyses. In: VaMoS, pp. 14:1–14:8 (2013)
13. Apel, S., Kästner, C., Grösslinger, A., Lengauer, C.: Type safety for feature-oriented product lines. ASE 17(3), 251–300 (2010)
14. Delaware, B., Cook, W., Batory, D.: A Machine-Checked Model of Safe Composition. In: FOAL, pp. 31–35. ACM (2009)
15. Damiani, F., Schaefer, I.: Family-based analysis of type safety for delta-oriented software product lines. In: Margaria, T., Steffen, B. (eds.) ISoLA 2012, Part I. LNCS, vol. 7609, pp. 193–207. Springer, Heidelberg (2012)
16. Classen, A., Heymans, P., Schobbens, P.Y., Legay, A., Raskin, J.F.: Model checking lots of systems: Efficient verification of temporal properties in software product lines. In: ICSE. IEEE (2010)
17. Lauenroth, K., Pohl, K., Toehning, S.: Model checking of domain artifacts in product line engineering. In: ASE, 269–280 (2009)
18. Asirelli, P., ter Beek, M.H., Gnesi, S., Fantechi, A.: Deontic logics for modeling behavioural variability. In: VaMoS, Essen, Germany, pp. 71–76 (January 2009)
19. Ghezzi, C., Sharifloo, A.M.: Verifying non-functional properties of software product lines: Towards an efficient approach using parametric model checking. In: SPLC, pp. 170–174 (2011)
20. Tawhid, R., Petriu, D.C.: Towards automatic derivation of a product performance model from a UML software product line model. In: WOSP, pp. 91–102 (2008)
21. Tawhid, R., Petriu, D.C.: Automatic derivation of a product performance model from a software product line model. In: SPLC, pp. 80–89 (2011)
22. Franks, G., Al-Omari, T., Woodside, M., Das, O., Derisavi, S.: Enhanced modeling and solution of layered queueing networks. IEEE Trans. Software Eng. 35(2), 148–161 (2009)
23. Object Management Group: UML Profile for Modeling and Analysis of Real-Time and Embedded Systems (MARTE). Beta 1. OMG, OMG document number ptc/07-08-04 (2007)
24. Tribastone, M., Gilmore, S.: Automatic extraction of PEPA performance models from UML activity diagrams annotated with the MARTE profile. In: WOSP, pp. 67–78 (2008)
25. D'Ambrogio, A., Bocciarelli, P.: A model-driven approach to describe and predict the performance of composite services. In: WOSP, pp. 78–89 (2007)
26. Menascé, D., Dubey, V.: Utility-based QoS brokering in service oriented architectures. In: ICWS, pp. 422–430 (July 2007)
27. Marzolla, M., Mirandola, R.: Performance prediction of web service workflows. In: Overhage, S., Ren, X.-M., Reussner, R., Stafford, J.A. (eds.) QoSA 2007. LNCS, vol. 4880, pp. 127–144. Springer, Heidelberg (2008)
28. Jackson, J.R.: Jobshop-like queueing systems. Management Science 10(1), 131–142 (1963)
29. Stewart, W.J.: Probability, Markov Chains, Queues, and Simulation. Princeton University Press (2009)
30. Filieri, A., Ghezzi, C., Tamburrelli, G.: Run-time efficient probabilistic model checking. In: ICSE, pp. 341–350 (2011)

TouchCost: Cost Analysis of TouchDevelop Scripts

Pietro Ferrara[1,2], Daniel Schweizer[2], and Lucas Brutschy[2]

[1] IBM Thomas J. Watson Research Center, U.S.A.
[2] ETH Zurich, Switzerland
pietroferrara@us.ibm.com,
{daschwei@student,lucas.brutschy@inf}.ethz.ch

Abstract. TouchDevelop is a novel programming environment and language for mobile devices. These applications are typically developed by non-expert users, rather small, and published on the cloud. In this paper, we introduce TOUCHCOST, a new static analysis that infers the cost of loops in TouchDevelop programs. TOUCHCOST (i) infers numerical invariants through an existing generic analyzer, (ii) extracts cost relation systems, and (iii) solves them using an existing upper bound solver.

TOUCHCOST has been applied to all TouchDevelop scripts that are currently published on the cloud. Experimental results show that this tool is both scalable and precise. Studying the outputs of TOUCHCOST, we glimpse two major applications: (i) establishing at runtime the cost of a loop, and in case move its execution, and (ii) helping non-expert developers to debug their programs.

1 Introduction

In 2012 more mobile devices than personal computers and laptops have been sold [1,23]. The main characteristics of modern mobile devices are (i) an almost continuous connection to the cloud, (ii) relatively limited resources (e.g., computational power and battery), and (iii) various sensors and capabilities (e.g., GPS and camera). This technology shift has important consequences on programming languages and execution environments. In particular, they should take into account (i) novel input devices (e.g., touchscreens) when developing programs, and (ii) a runtime environment with limited local resources, but with (almost) continuous access to an extremely resourceful cloud infrastructure.

Microsoft TouchDevelop[1] [24] is a novel development environment and programming language for mobile applications. The main design principle of TouchDevelop is to allow one to develop mobile applications directly on mobile devices. In addition, TouchDevelop applications can be shared through the cloud infrastructure. Since its release in August 2011, more than 20.000 TouchDevelop scripts have been shared. Some of them became quite popular, and they have been downloaded and ran by thousands of users. Usually, TouchDevelop users are not expert developers, and the most part of the scripts are small [20].

---

[1] http://www.touchdevelop.com

S. Gnesi and A. Rensink (Eds.): FASE 2014, LNCS 8411, pp. 109–124, 2014.
© Springer-Verlag Berlin Heidelberg 2014

Static cost analysis [3] has been deeply studied, and it achieved significant results. The main goal of cost analysis is to compute statically (i.e., at compile time) and automatically (i.e., without any user annotation or interaction) the cost of a program. Its applications are extremely diverse.

Given this scenario, the main contribution of this work is TOUCHCOST, the application of static cost analysis to all existing TouchDevelop scripts to infer the cost of loops. As far as we know, TOUCHCOST is the first cost analysis that has been applied to a huge set (several thousands) of real programs. Given a TouchDevelop script, we apply an existing numerical domain [19] to infer numerical invariants. We then build up cost relation systems and pass them to PUBS [2], an up-to-date upper bound solver, obtaining loops' bounds.

TouchDevelop represents an ideal target for cost analysis since (i) TouchDevelop scripts are usually written by non-professional developers , and therefore debugging and optimizing them may improve significantly the quality and the efficiency of these programs, and (ii) these scripts run on mobile devices with limited resources and continuous access to an extremely resourceful cloud infrastructure, and therefore the information inferred by cost analysis may be adopted at runtime to reduce the amount of local resources consumed by the execution.

The analysis has been implemented and applied to all TouchDevelop scripts on the cloud containing loops. The experimental results show that the overall analysis is both scalable and precise. TOUCHCOST proves that existing engines for cost analyses are mature enough to be applied to real programs on a large scale. We have also investigated the results obtained by TOUCHCOST to propose possible applications of the inferred information. First of all, since mobile devices have limited local resources and often access to a resourceful cloud, the costs inferred by TOUCHCOST could be used to decide at runtime to move the execution to the cloud if there is a shortage of some local resources. In addition, TouchDevelop scripts are developed by novices, and particularly high or low costs expose bugs or possible misunderstandings of the developer. Therefore, we found out several published programs in which TOUCHCOST results can be useful for debugging.

The rest of the paper is structured as follows. In the rest of this Section, we will discuss some related work. Sections 2, 3, and 4 will recall the main existing components adopted by TOUCHCOST, that is, TouchDevelop, Sample, and PUBS, respectively. Section 5 will present the technical core of TOUCHCOST, while Section 6 will discuss the experimental results.

1.1   Related Work

Various tools performing cost and termination analyses have been formalized and developed. As far as we know, the COSTA system [3] represents the most advanced tool in the field of automatic cost analysis for object-oriented programming languages, and it includes the implementation of some recent research results on finding linear ranking functions [5]. This tool analyzes Java bytecode, and it relies on PUBS [2] to solve cost relation systems produced by extracting some numerical constraints from a Java bytecode program. TOUCHCOST relies on PUBS as well, but we deal with TouchDevelop code, and we apply a sound and relatively precise heap abstraction to the program. Instead, COSTA approximates the heap with the maximal length of the paths reachable from local variables. This approach is not precise enough for TouchDevelop programs since these heavily rely on the mobile environment approximated by the heap analysis. In particular, COSTA's heap abstraction would approximate the length of all the collections with their *maximal* length. For instance, it would not distinguish between the number of songs and the number of pictures in the mobile device.

Worst case execution time analyses (WCET) have been widely studied, implemented, and applied to industrial software [25]. WCET is focused on deriving realistic, platform-dependent timing information, and usually loop bounds are manually provided by the user [12]. Therefore, various analyses targeted the inference of loop bounds [17], but they target a specific platform, or type of loops, and in general they cannot straightforwardly applied to TouchDevelop scripts that heavily interact with the mobile environment.

Other work has been focused on the analysis of memory consumption [8], and on functional [6] and logic [11] programming. Instead, TOUCHCOST is aimed at targeting various types of costs, and it deals with TouchDevelop code, that is, with a language that mixes imperative and object-oriented constructs.

As far as we know, TOUCHCOST is the first automatic static cost analysis that has been applied to a wide set of mobile programs. Therefore, it represents the first extensive study on the application of cost analysis, and the experimental results (i) show that existing engines for these analyses can be applied to real programs on a large scale, and (ii) open new insights about possible applications of static cost analysis for mobile programs.

2   TouchDevelop

The core of TouchDevelop is a structured programming language designed to develop mobile applications directly on a mobile device. This language mainly mixes imperative and object-oriented features. A TouchDevelop program consists of a set of actions. Intuitively these correspond to methods in object-oriented programming languages. One of the most important design principles is to allow the developer to access all the main components of the mobile device (e.g., GPS sensors) through some standard libraries. Therefore, the API offers various predefined classes to access these components. The target audience of TouchDevelop is "everyone who might traditionally have been able to write a BASIC program on a regular keyboard and ordinary PC. This includes students and hobbyist programmers"[22]. In addition, TouchDevelop scripts can be shared through the cloud infrastructure. Currently, more than 20.000 scripts developed by more than 2.000 users have already been published.

Loops: The TouchDevelop programming language defines three distinct types of loops: while expr do block, for $0 \leq$ index $<$ expr do block, and foreach I in coll do block. The first type is a standard while loop. The for loop defines an index variable, and it increments this variable from 0 to expr. expr is evaluated only once at the beginning of the execution of the loop. The index variable is modified only by the implicit increment, and it cannot be changed in any other way. Finally, the foreach loop iterates over all elements which are part of a collection *before* starting the execution of the loop. Semantically, this is equivalent to taking a snapshot of the collection just before the execution of the loop, and to iterate over the elements of this snapshot.

Running Example: The program in Figure 1 is the running example we will adopt to explain how TOUCHCOST works. It contains a simple foreach loop, that iterates over all the pictures in the mobile device, prints them on the screen, and waits 1 second before showing the next picture. The loop is iterated n times, where n is the number of pictures contained in the mobile device. Note that we explicitly kept this example simple and minimal, since it will be used to show how TOUCHCOST works step by step in details.

```
action showPics() {
  foreach pic in media→pictures do {
    pic→post_to_wall;
    time→sleep(1);
  }
}
```

Fig. 1. The running example

3   Sample

Sample (Static Analyzer of Multiple Programming LanguagEs) [13,14] is a generic static analyzer based on the abstract interpretation theory [10]. Relying on compositional analyses, Sample combines various heap abstractions and value (e.g., numerical) domains. It has already been applied to various value analyses (e.g., strings [9], types [13], access permissions [15], and data leaking [26]). It supports some common numerical analyses through Apron [18], which is a library dedicated to the static analysis of the numerical variables. Additionally, some heap analyses are already part of Sample. In particular, [15] adopts a standard abstraction that binds each abstract reference to its allocation site, while [14] plugs a TVLA-based shape analysis.

First of all, Sample compiles source code to *Simple*, the internal language based on Control Flow Graphs (CFG). Sample contains compilers for Java, Scala, and TouchDevelop. The *Simple* program is then passed to the fixpoint engine together with a heap and a value analysis. This produces an abstract result over the CFG, that is, an entry and exit state for each statement of the program. This result is passed to a property checker that produces some alarms if the given property is not statically proved, or to an inference engine that produces some invariants (e.g., the access permissions required or guaranteed by a method [15]).

The TouchDevelop compiler was built both for TouchCost, and to apply various reliability analyses to TouchDevelop scripts.

Simple: *Simple* contains a minimal set of statements (mainly, variable's and field's assignments and accesses, object instantiations, and method calls), while conditional statements and loops are represented directly on the CFG. Each node in a CFG contains a list of (concatenated) statements, while edges may be weighted with a Boolean value or not. In particular, there is an edge from n_1 to n_2 if the first statement in n_2 may be executed directly after the last statement in n_1. We call an edge from n to some other node an out-edge of n. Weighted edges represents a conditional jump: the edge is traversed only if the expression evaluated by the last statement of the block is true or false depending on the edge's weight. Therefore, the out-edges of a block can be (i) one edge without any weight, (ii) two weighted edges (one with weight true and the other one false), or (iii) none to represent an exit point of the current action.

Loops: In *Simple*, the different TouchDevelop loops (namely, while, for, and foreach) are translated into specific CFG structures.

A while expr do block loop is translated to (i) an initial block where expr is evaluated with two out-edges, (ii) the true edge points to a node containing block, and this points back to the block evaluating expr, (iii) the false edge points to the block representing what is *after* the while loop.

for loops are translated in a similar way, initializing the counter to 0 before entering the loop, evaluating *once* the bound of the for loop before entering it, and incrementing the counter by one inside the loop body.

The foreach loop is equivalent to (i) taking a snapshot of the collection just before the execution of the loop, and (ii) iterating over the elements of this snapshot. The iterations are performed by incrementing a counter and accessing the elements contained in the snapshot of the collection.

Running Example: The code introduced in Figure 1 is compiled to the CFG in Figure 2. In particular, we can see that (i) the first block initializes i to zero and copies the collection, (ii) the block in the middle contains the loop guard, (iii) the block representing the body of the loop extracts the i-th element from the copy of the collection, execute the body of the foreach loop (that is, it prints the current picture), and increments i by one, and (iv) the false evaluation of the Boolean condition of the guard leads to exit of the action.

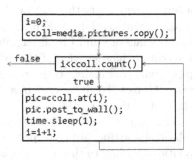

Fig. 2. The CFG of our running example

4   PUBS

TOUCHCOST adopts PUBS [2] to infer upper bounds on loops. In this Section, we briefly recall the main ingredients of PUBS. PUBS takes as input a cost relation system, and it returns an upper bound of the cost of this system.

Fist of all, we define the basic ingredients of cost relations. A *linear expression* has the form $\sum_{i=1}^{n} a_i * x_i + b$. A *linear constraint* is defined as $l_1 \le l_2$

where l_1 and l_2 are both linear expressions. A *guard* is a set of linear constraints, and it represents their conjunction. *Basic cost expression* e are then defined as follows:

e ::= r | nat(l) | e1 + e2 | e1 * e2 | log$_n$(e) | n^e | max(S) | e-r

where l is a linear expression, r is a real positive number, S is a set of basic cost expressions, nat(l) returns $\max(0, l)$.

These expressions are the basic blocks to define cost relations. A cost relation is a pair $\langle C(\overline{x}) = \mathtt{exp} + \sum_{i=1}^{k} D_i(\overline{y}_i), \phi \rangle$ where C and D_i are cost relation symbols (that is, symbols representing the costs of an action or a loop), exp is a basic cost expression, $\overline{x}$ and $\overline{y}_i$ are distinct variables, and ϕ is a guard. $C(\overline{x}) = \mathtt{exp} + \sum_{i=1}^{k} D_i(\overline{y}_i)$ will be called the *cost body* in the rest of this paper. Finally, a cost relation system is a set of cost relations.

Running Example: Consider now the running example we introduced in Figure 1, and in particular its CFG in Figure 2. For the sake of simplicity, let us suppose that the cost of one iteration of the loop body is 1. In addition, the cost relation system about this block should represent the fact that i is incremented by one, and in order to execute this block i < ccoll.count() must hold. All these facts are represented by the following cost relation:

$$\left\langle \begin{array}{c} C(\mathsf{old\_i}, \mathsf{pics\_count}) = 1 + C(\mathsf{i}, \mathsf{pics\_count}), \\ \{\mathsf{i} == \mathsf{old\_i} + 1, \mathsf{old\_i} < \mathsf{pics\_count}\} \end{array} \right\rangle$$

where C represents the cost of the foreach loop in terms of the initial value of i, pics_count the initial number of pictures in the mobile device, and old_i the initial value of i and i its final value. Instead, if i < ccoll.count() does not hold, the cost of the execution of the loop is zero: $\langle C(\mathsf{old\_i}, \mathsf{pics\_count}) = 0, \{\mathsf{old\_i} \geq \mathsf{pics\_count}\}\rangle$. Finally, we represent that, before entering the loop, i is equal to zero: $\langle C_l(\mathsf{pics\_count}) = C(0, \mathsf{pics\_count}), \{\mathsf{pics\_count} \geq 0\}\rangle$ where C_l represents the cost of the whole loop.

The goal of TOUCHCOST is to apply Sample to infer automatically these cost relations starting from the program in Figure 2. PUBS then solves these cost relations leading to the cost $nat(\mathsf{pics\_count})$, that is exactly the cost of our loop.

5   TouchCost

This Section presents the components developed in TouchCost to effectively apply the approach presented in the previous sections to TouchDevelop scripts.

Given a TouchDevelop action, TOUCHCOST (1) compiles it and augments its CFG, (2) applies Sample to this augmented CFG, (3) extracts from the abstract results a cost relation system for each loop, and (4) pass these cost relation systems to PUBS, obtaining their upper bounds.

5.1   Augmented Control Flow Graph (1)

Identifying Loops: First of all, given a control flow graph we have to identify the structures that represent loops. We traverse the control flow graph and we consider the edges that have two *deterministic* (that is, non-weighted) in-edges and two weighted out-edges (one true and one false). Such node is potentially the *initial* node of the loop. Then, starting from the out-edge labeled true, we check if there is a cyclic path coming back to this node. If this is the case, we have found a loop.

Augmenting the CFG: We need to infer relations between the entry and the exit values of variables. Unfortunately, a numerical domain usually does not infer such information, since the old value of a variable once this has been assigned. For instance, in the running example of Figure 1, once we increment i by one, we do not know that the value at the end of the loop is equal to the value at the beginning incremented by one. We have then to make a copy of all the variables modified inside a loop at the beginning of the loop body. For instance, the running example requires a cost relation that tells us that i at the end of the loop is equal to its initial value plus 1. So we introduce a variable old_i to represent the value of i at the beginning of the loop's body.

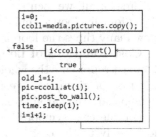

Therefore, for each loop in the CFG, we find all variables V that are assigned inside the loop, and we add a new assignment old_v := v at the beginning of the loop for each variable v ∈ V.

Running Example: Figure 3 depicts the augmented CFG we obtain for the CFG our running example of Figure 2.

Fig. 3. The augmented CFG

5.2   Sample's Analysis (2)

In order to run Sample on the augmented control flow graph, we have to instantiate the analysis with a heap and a numerical analysis.

Heap Analysis: Since TouchDevelop programs do not usually perform significant computation over the heap, and this rarely influences how many times loops are iterated, we apply a standard and efficient allocation-site based heap abstraction [4]. In addition, we build a precise model of the collections and the mobile environment (e.g., to distinguish the number of elements in the songs' collection from the pictures' collection).

Numerical Analysis: Sample has already been applied to various value analyses. Apron [18] is a library that provides a standard interface to various numerical domains, and it is plugged into Sample. In our analysis, we apply Linear equalities [19] to infer input-output relations that will be used to build up the cost relation system that is passed to PUBS.

Running Example: Consider the running example introduced in Figure 1. The heap analysis translates the method call ccoll.count() to the symbolic identifier we use to represent the number of elements in ccoll (represented by ccoll_count). This allows us to infer that the loop guard is i < ccoll_count. In addition, the heap semantics infers that ccoll_count == pics_count (where pics_count represents the number of pictures in the mobile device at the beginning of the execution), since ccoll is a copy of media.pictures, and the linear equalities domain infers that, inside the loop body after the increment of i, the constraint $i == \mathsf{old\_i} + 1$ holds.

Note that, even on this simple running example, we need a sound static analysis that defines the semantics of TouchDevelop APIs, and in particular of its data structures. For instance, we need to semantically track that when we copy media.pictures and we assign it to ccoll we have that ccoll_count $==$ pics_count.

5.3   Extracting Cost Relation Systems (3)

At the end of the analysis, Sample returns an abstract entry and exit state for each statement in the program. Using this information, we extract the cost relation systems that will be passed to PUBS.

First of all, we identify all the loops in the CFG as described in Section 5.1. Then for each loop we build up a cost relation system that is aimed at computing how many times the loop is iterated.

Cost Relations of Loops: We introduce two cost relation symbols for each loop: C_l represents the whole loop, while C represents the loop's iterations starting from a given state (e.g., after i iterations). The parameters of these two symbols are the variables involved in the guard of the loop, or in its body.

For the cost symbol C, the cost body adds the cost of one iteration of the loop body to the cost of the following iterations. The body of the loop could contain four different patterns of CFG structures, and they will be discussed in the following of this Section. For now, we suppose that the cost symbol representing block is provided by $cost(\mathsf{block})$. Formally, the cost body is then defined by $C(\overline{\mathsf{old\_x}}) = cost(\mathsf{block}) + C(\overline{\mathsf{x}})$, where $\overline{\mathsf{old\_x}}$ and $\overline{\mathsf{x}}$ represent a sequence of variables old_x and x, respectively. For all the variables that are not assigned in the loop body, we have that $\mathsf{old\_x} = \mathsf{x}$. For all the other variables, we try to extract an update rule from the information inferred by the linear equality domain after the last statement in the loop body.

Through the analysis introduced in Section 5.2 on the augmented CFG described in Section 5.1, the state inferred by Sample after the last statement in the loop body contains all the relations between the values of the variables at the beginning and at the end of the execution of one iteration of the loop. Since we have applied the linear equalities domain, we represent this state as a set of linear equalities. We want to extract from this set only the constraints that involve variables relevant to compute the cost of the loop. We also want to extract information that is (i) strong enough to infer the cost of the loop, and (ii) as little as possible to preserve the efficiency of the analysis. This means that we consider only the variables that influence how many times a loop is iterated.

We start from all the variables appearing in the loop guard. Then, for each of these variables, we try to find an update rule involving this variable. By update rule of variable x we mean a constraint that contains both x and old_x. Then, given a variable v, we consider all the equalities involving v and old_v. As a first try, we consider *only* the linear constraints that are fully described by v and old_v, that is, constraints of the form $\mathsf{v} == a * \mathsf{old\_v} + b$. Such constraints are often strong enough to infer the cost of the loop. If PUBS fails to compute the cost of the loop using these constraints, we consider all linear constraints of the form v $==$ expr, where expr is a linear expression containing old_v.

These update rules are plugged in the cost relation of C together with the loop guard b. Formally, the cost relation for C is defined by $\langle C(\overline{old\_x}) = cost(block) + C(\overline{x}), UR \cup \{b\}\rangle$ where UR represents the set of update rules we extracted, and $cost$ represents the cost symbol or variable of the loop body. This cost relation represents one iteration of the while loop. We add then a cost relation to represent when we exit from the loop. Formally, $\langle C(\overline{x}) = 0, \{!b\}\rangle$.

Finally, we have to introduce a cost relation to represent the whole execution of the loop. This is done by a cost relation that represents that the cost of the whole loop C_l is equal to the cost of the loop C when the parameters are the values of the variable before entering the loop for the first time. Therefore, for each variable v involved in the loop, we look at all linear constraints IV containing v that the numerical analysis inferred at the program point just before the loop. We then build up a cost relation $\langle C_l(\overline{x}) = C(\overline{x}), \{IV\}\rangle$.

Cost Relations of Other CFG Structures: Inside the loop body, we could have (i) one block, (ii) a sequence of blocks, (iii) a nested loop, or (iv) a conditional.

In the first case, we represent the cost of a single block with a *cost variable* (that is, the block at program point p is represented by a symbol c_p). A sequence of blocks is represented by the summation of the cost symbols of each block. For a nested loop, we extract the cost relations of the inner loop, and we use the cost symbol C_l to represent the whole inner loop in the body of the outer loop.

Finally, if we have a conditional, we introduce C_t to represent the true branch, and C_f for the false branch. Then we add (i) $\langle C_t(\overline{x}) = cost(block1), \{b\}\rangle$ to represent the true branch, (ii) $\langle C_f(\overline{x}) = cost(block2), \{!b\}\rangle$ to represent the false branch, and (iii) $\langle C_i(\overline{x}) = C_t(\overline{x}) + C_f(\overline{x}), \{\}\rangle$ to represent the whole if statement.

Boolean Conditions: Up to now, we have simplified the presentation by using b and $!b$ in the guards when dealing with loops and conditionals. Indeed, PUBS allows only linear relations in these guards. Therefore, we consider only the Boolean conditions of the following form:

```
c ::= true | false | e1 <op> e2 | ! c | c1 AND c2 | c1 OR c2
```

where e1 and e2 are linear expressions, and $< op > \in \{! =, ==, \geq, \leq\}$. All these conditions have to be translated into linear integer expressions to fulfill PUBS' syntax. true is translated to $1 == 1$, and false to $0 == 1$. expr1 <op> expr2 is already a linear expression, while ! c is translated to a positive form by using the De Morgan's laws if c is an AND or OR expression, by negating true or false, or by modifying <op> if the condition is a comparison of linear expressions. Linear integer conditions with $<$ or $>$ as comparison operators are translated to equivalent conditions with $\geq$ or $\leq$ as operators.

AND and OR conditions lead to several cost relations, since we cannot represent a conjunction or disjunction directly in PUBS guard. These are semantically equivalent to translate the conditions into equivalent CFG structures, and the cost relations for these structures are obtained as described in this Section previously.

Note that we may not be able to translate the original Boolean condition to integer linear relations that are supported by PUBS (e.g., if the original condition was not linear). In these cases, we simply omit the Boolean condition and its negation from the guards. In this way, we introduce some approximation (that is, the fact that a particular part of the code is executed only if the condition holds), but we preserve the soundness of the analysis.

Running Example: Consider now the running example of Figure 1. First of all, we have $\langle C(\text{old\_i}, \text{ccoll\_count}) = 0, \{\text{old\_i} \geq \text{ccoll\_count}\}\rangle$. This represents the situation in which the execution exit the loop. Instead, one iteration of the loop is represented by

$$\left\langle \begin{array}{c} C(\text{old\_i}, \text{ccoll\_count}) = c_b + C(\text{i}, \text{ccoll\_count}), \\ \{\text{i} = \text{old\_i} + 1, \text{old\_i} \leq \text{ccoll\_count} - 1\} \end{array} \right\rangle$$

In fact, the linear equalities domain infers that $\text{i} = \text{old\_i} + 1$, and c_b represents symbolically the cost of the loop body. In addition, the loop guard $\text{old\_i} < \text{ccoll\_count}$ is translated to $\text{old\_i} \leq \text{ccoll\_count} - 1$. Finally, the cost of the whole loop is

$$\left\langle \begin{array}{c} C_l(\text{i}, \text{ccoll\_count}) = C(\text{i}, \text{ccoll\_count}), \\ \{\text{i} == 0, \text{ccoll\_count} == \text{pics\_count}\} \end{array} \right\rangle$$

The numerical domain infers that initially $\text{i} == 0$ and $\text{ccoll\_count} == \text{pics\_count}$.

5.4   Using PUBS (4)

The last step of TOUCHCOST is to pass the cost relation systems we inferred for each loop to PUBS. The output of PUBS could be: (i) a sound upper bound of the given cost relation system, or (ii) a failure. In the second case, we do not know if this failure was due to some information that is not precisely tracked by PUBS, or if the analyzed loop may not terminate.

Running Example: PUBS returns $nat(\text{pics\_count})$ when we apply it to the cost relation system we inferred for our running example in Section 5.3. This is the exact cost of the loop, since it is iterated a number of times equal to the number of pictures we have in our mobile device (that is, pics_count).

6   Experimental Results

Table 1 reports the experimental results. We ran the experiments on an Intel Core 2 2.83Ghz QUAD CPU with 4GB RAM running Ubuntu 12.04. Column **Type** reports the script category we target. In particular, `all` denotes all the scripts published on the cloud before May, 16th 2013 containing loops, while the other categories refer to the scripts (always containing loops) that are tagged with the given name. Tags are used to categorize different types of scripts, and we used them to investigate how TOUCHCOST behaves when dealing with different types of scripts. Column **#scr.** reports the number of scripts, **LOC** the number of lines of code, **#loops** the number of loops, **Comp.** the number of

Table 1. Experimental results

Type	#scr.	LOC	#loops	Comp.	Prec.	St	TCt	Avg.LOC	Avg.St	Avg.TCt
all	5 405	1 222 250	19 035	13 403	70.4%	10 153	4 293	226	1.88	0.79
entertainment	164	42 485	553	419	75.8%	459	145	259	2.80	0.88
games	161	54 754	973	764	78.5%	749	274	340	4.65	1.70
libraries	129	23 548	405	236	58.3%	314	94	183	2.43	0.73
tools	82	22 460	374	132	35.3%	200	48	274	2.44	0.59
lifestyle	78	23 903	179	126	70.4%	135	55	306	1.73	0.70
music	59	9 163	149	100	67.1%	44	29	155	0.74	0.49
education	56	9 710	158	131	82.9%	71	25	173	1.27	0.45
gamelibraries	47	8 002	189	101	53.4%	237	47	170	5.04	1.00
Sample root	73	8 964	233	167	71.7%	94.4	56.9	123	1.29	0.78

loops for which TOUCHCOST computed the cost, **Prec.** the precision rate (that is, **Comp./#loops**), **St** the time spent by Sample to perform the heap and numerical analysis, **TCts** the time spent by TOUCHCOST to build up the cost relation systems and use PUBS to solve them, **Avg.LOC** the average number of lines of code per scripts, and **Avg.St** and **Avg.TCt** the average time of Sample and TOUCHCOST analysis per script, respectively. All the times are in seconds.

In this Section, we refer to the ratio **Comp./#loops** as the *precision* of the analysis. We have manually inspected the cost estimation inferred on the sample scripts (167 estimations on 230 loops, see Section 6.2), and we found out that we always inferred the most precise estimation for the loop. Therefore, we believe that this ratio is a good estimation of the precision of our analysis.

6.1 Global Performances and Precision

We first perform a quantitative analysis considering row all in Table 1. This benchmark consists of 5 405 scripts, and more than 1 million LOC. In terms of performances, the overall analysis (that is, **S t.+TC t.**) took 4h00'06" to analyze 1.222 KLOC (about 2.5 seconds per script). In terms of precision, TOUCHCOST inferred the cost of about 70% of the existing loops. On the one hand, this result underlines that, on average, TOUCHCOST automatically infers the cost of the most part of existing loops. On the other hand, different categories of scripts expose different levels of precision. For instance, games scripts are usually relatively big, and TOUCHCOST compute the cost of almost the 80% of the loops in these scripts. Instead, tools scripts seem to be more challenging, since the precision rate for this category is around 35%. In addition, one could expect that bigger scripts contain more complex code, and therefore TOUCHCOST is less precise on such scripts. Indeed, our experimental results show that there is no correlation between the length of the script and the precision of TOUCHCOST. For instance, gamelibraries scripts are smaller than the average, but the precision of TOUCHCOST is around 50%.

6.2 Precision on TouchDevelop Sample Scripts

We now inspect manually the precision of TOUCHCOST when dealing with TouchDevelop sample root scripts containing loops. TouchDevelop samples

```
action main() {
    // Initialize the board
    while true do {
        // Update the board
        time→sleep(0.01);
    }
}
```

(a) Script iuks

```
data _board : Board
data _bubbles : Sprite Set
data _touch : Sprite
action pop bubbles () {
    var p := _board→touch current
    _touch→set pos(p→x, p→y)
    foreach bubble in _touch→overlap
        with(_bubbles) do
        ...
}
```

(b) Script uigca

```
action TouchList (...) {
    var count := 0
    var b := true
    while b do {
        //Perform some computation
        count := count + 1
        if count = 5 then
            b := false
    }
}
```

(c) Script vrgt

```
action show(board: Board) {
    duration := 5;
    dt := time→now;
    while time→now→subtract(dt) < duration do {
        //Show something to the user
    }
}
```

(d) Script jhyg

```
action getConfCalls (s : DateTime, e : DateTime) {
    app := social →
        search_appointments(s, e);
    foreach a1 in app
    do {
        //Extracts information
    }
    //Build up the conference call
    //Call the people
}
```

(e) Script mpuj

```
action main() {
    b := true;
    while b do {
        code→play_round;
        b := wall →
        ask_boolean("Try␣again?", " ... ");
    }
}
```

(f) Script avpm

```
action b () {
    for 0 ≤ i < 999999 do {
        if i / 2 = math → floor(i / 2) then {
            wall →
                set background(colors → white)
            time → sleep(1) }
        else {
            wall →
                set background(colors → black)
            time → sleep(1) }
    }
}
```

(g) Script lypy

```
var len := 0
while len ≥ 0 do {
    ...
    len := len − 1
}
```

(h) Script hyax

Fig. 4. Case studies

(https://www.touchdevelop.com/pboj) contain a significant set of scripts developed by the TouchDevelop team to show the main features of this language. Row sample root in Table 1 reports the experimental results we obtained on these scripts. We analyzed 73 scripts (about 9.000 LOC). All together, these scripts contain 233 loops, and we failed to compute the cost of 66 loops.

Non-terminating Loops: First of all, we noticed that some of the loops are not necessarily terminating, and therefore the results of TOUCHCOST are precise. We have identified three main reasons of non-terminating loops.

User inputs: Some loops are iterated until the user provides a "good" input. Consider for instance script avpm[2] in Figure 4f. Action main iterates a while loop until the user says that he wants to stop. Statically, this loop may be non-terminating, since we do not know when the user will decide to stop.

while true *loops:* Another type of loops for which TOUCHCOST cannot compute their cost is represented by script iuks in Figure 4a. TouchDevelop provides a specific gameloop action that "is triggered by a timer approximately every 50

---

[2] The code of <script> is available at https://www.touchdevelop.com/<script>

milliseconds"[3]. Nevertheless, several users prefer to implement their own game loop iterators. In this way, they can establish exactly the triggering rate by adding a time→sleep statement inside the while loop.

Time constraints: Another recurrent pattern is exposed by script jhyg in Figure 4d. In this case, a loop is iterated during a given amount of time (e.g., 5 seconds). This is obtained by (i) recording the time just before entering the loop (variable dt), (ii) checking how much time is passed each time the loop is iterated, and (iii) exiting the loop if this subtraction exposes that that enough time (that is, at least duration seconds) has passed. Even though in this case we know that the loop will eventually terminate (since the time is always strictly increasing), we cannot know statically how many times the loop is iterated.

Approximation: There are some cases in which we fail to infer an upper bound on the number of iterations because of a too rough approximation. In particular, we identified two main sources of imprecision.

Collections: Figure 4b reports an excerpt of action popbubble of script uigca. This action is aimed at popping a bubble that is touched by the user. Therefore, it contains a foreach loop that iterates over the bubbles that overlaps with the existing bubbles. Unfortunately, the abstract semantics of Sprite.overlap in Sample is too imprecise, and we fail to infer any upper bound on this loop. Our experience shows that this situation is common to various scripts, and it is the main source of imprecision of TOUCHCOST. Therefore, we are currently working on more refined analyses for TouchDevelop analyses [7], and we expect it will fix this issue. Nevertheless, it will slow down the analysis, and we will have to study in which cases it is worth to apply more refined analysis.

Disjunctive information: In few cases TOUCHCOST fails to compute the cost of a loop because of complicated disjunctive invariants. One of these cases is the action TouchList of script vrgt sketched in Figure 4c. The loop is iterated 5 times, but this is obtained by (i) a Boolean flag b as loop guard, (ii) counting the number of iterations through a variable count, and (iii) setting b to true when count = 5. In order to compute that this loop is iterated 5 times, we would need to track disjunctive information through trace partitioning [21] that is already supported by Sample[16], and translate this information to a cost relation system.

6.3   Applications of TouchCost

Finally, we inspect the results of the analysis investigating some particular cases to study possible applications of TOUCHCOST. In particular, since TouchDevelop scripts are executed on mobile devices usually connected to the cloud, this information can be used at runtime to decide to move the execution to the cloud if the application is too expensive w.r.t. the available resources. In addition, TOUCHCOST provides useful information to debug programs of novice users.

Moving the Execution: We start by considering script mpuj in Figure 4e. This is the most popular script on the cloud: on May, 2013 it counted more than 2300 users and 40.000 runs. In addition, it is the evolution of slji, that counted more

---

[3] https://www.touchdevelop.com/help/events

than 450 users and 10.000 runs. This script extracts the conference calls from the calendar of the mobile device, and on request it dials the numbers of the people involved in the conference calls. It consists of 15 actions, and only getConfCalls contains a loop. Figure 4e sketches the main components of this action. The body of the loop extracts the subject and the location of the conference calls, and it builds up some strings to represent this information. TOUCHCOST infers that the loop is iterated a number of times equal to the number of elements contained in the collection returned by social→search_appointments(start, end). At compile time, the number of elements depends on start and end, two parameters of the action whose value is unknown. Instead, at runtime, when the action is called, we know the actual values of these two parameters. Then we can use this information to establish exactly how many times the loop is iterated when the action is called. So the runtime environment could decide to move the computation to the cloud if the loop requires (e.g., computational) resources that are not locally available. **Wrong Implementations and Bugs:** We then investigate some *extreme* costs. Since many TouchDevelop users are novices, they sometimes implement a functionality in the wrong way. A quite common example is a loop that is iterated an enormous number of times. Consider for instance the snippet of code in Figure 4g of `lypy`. This script is relatively popular, with more than 1000 runs and 100 users. Action b iterates 999 999 times a loop that changes the color of the background, and put the device to sleep for 1 second. The user intended to write an endless loop, and the cost analysis infers that the loop is iterated 999 999 times.

Finally, the cost information can expose some bugs as well. Script `hyax` contains three actions (Generate, Generate2, Generate3) that follow the pattern sketched in Figure 4h. TOUCHCOST correctly infers that the loop is iterated only once. This is definitely a bug, and even the various versions of this script (see scripts `fosieeps, nlqo`, and `lwnlb`) are all bugged. Generally, when TOUCHCOST infers that the loop is iterated only once, we may issue an alarm and ask the developer to check if this behavior is intended, or if it is a bug.

7   Conclusion

In this paper we presented TOUCHCOST, an automatic tool that combines a generic static analyzer (Sample) and an upper bound solver (PUBS) to automatically compute the cost of loops in TouchDevelop scripts. TOUCHCOST represents the first extensive application of automatic static cost analysis to real programs. The experimental results show that TOUCHCOST is both scalable and precise, and we envision possible applications of the inferred cost information. Mobile programs are a particularly appealing target for cost analysis, since they run on devices with limited local resources, but with a continuous access to the cloud.

Acknowledgments. Special thanks go to Samir Genaim for his support with PUBS, and Manuel Fähndrich and Nikolai Tillmann for their support with TouchDevelop.

References

1. http://www.businessinsider.com/the-future-of-mobile-slide-deck-2013-3
2. Albert, E., Arenas, P., Genaim, S., Puebla, G.: Closed-form upper bounds in static cost analysis. Journal of Automated Reasoning 46(2), 161–203 (2011)
3. Albert, E., Arenas, P., Genaim, S., Puebla, G., Zanardini, D.: Cost analysis of object-oriented bytecode programs. TCS 413(1), 142–159 (2012)
4. Andersen, L.O.: Program Analysis and Specialization for the C Programming Language. PhD thesis, DIKU, University of Copenhagen (1994)
5. Ben-Amram, A.M., Genaim, S.: On the linear ranking problem for integer linear-constraint loops. In: Proceedings of POPL 2013. ACM (2013)
6. Benzinger, R.: Automated higher-order complexity analysis. TCS 318, 79–103 (2004)
7. Bonjour, Y.: Must analysis of collection elements. Master's thesis, ETH Zurich (September 2013)
8. Braberman, V., Fernández, F., Garbervetsky, D., Yovine, S.: Parametric prediction of heap memory requirements. In: Proceedings of ISMM 2008. ACM (2008)
9. Costantini, G., Ferrara, P., Cortesi, A.: Static analysis of string values. In: Qin, S., Qiu, Z. (eds.) ICFEM 2011. LNCS, vol. 6991, pp. 505–521. Springer, Heidelberg (2011)
10. Cousot, P., Cousot, R.: Abstract interpretation: a unified lattice model for static analysis of programs by construction or approximation of fixpoints. In: Proceedings of POPL 1977. ACM (1977)
11. Debray, S.K., Lin, N.-W.: Cost analysis of logic programs. ACM Transactions on Programming Languages and Systems 15(5), 826–875 (1993)
12. Ferdinand, C., Heckmann, R., Theiling, H., Wilhelm, R.: Convenient user annotations for a wcet tool. In: Proceedings of WCET 2003 (2003)
13. Ferrara, P.: Static type analysis of pattern matching by abstract interpretation. In: Hatcliff, J., Zucca, E. (eds.) FMOODS/FORTE 2 2010, Part II. LNCS, vol. 6117, pp. 186–200. Springer, Heidelberg (2010)
14. Ferrara, P., Fuchs, R., Juhasz, U.: TVAL+: TVLA and value analyses together. In: Eleftherakis, G., Hinchey, M., Holcombe, M. (eds.) SEFM 2012. LNCS, vol. 7504, pp. 63–77. Springer, Heidelberg (2012)
15. Ferrara, P., Müller, P.: Automatic inference of access permissions. In: Kuncak, V., Rybalchenko, A. (eds.) VMCAI 2012. LNCS, vol. 7148, pp. 202–218. Springer, Heidelberg (2012)
16. Gabi, D.: Disjunction on demand. Master's thesis, ETH Zurich (2011)
17. Gustafsson, J., Ermedahl, A., Sandberg, C., Lisper, B.: Automatic derivation of loop bounds and infeasible paths for wcet analysis using abstract execution. In: Proceedings of RTSS 2006. IEEE Computer Society (2006)
18. Jeannet, B., Miné, A.: Apron: A library of numerical abstract domains for static analysis. In: Bouajjani, A., Maler, O. (eds.) CAV 2009. LNCS, vol. 5643, pp. 661–667. Springer, Heidelberg (2009)
19. Karr, M.: On affine relationships among variables of a program. Acta Informatica 6(2), 133–151 (1976)
20. Li, S., Xie, T., Tillmann, N., Moskal, M., de Halleux, J., Fahndrich, M., Burckhardt, S.: A comprehensive field study of end-user programming on mobile devices. Technical Report TR-2013-3, Microsoft Research (2013)
21. Mauborgne, L., Rival, X.: Trace partitioning in abstract interpretation based static analyzers. In: Sagiv, M. (ed.) ESOP 2005. LNCS, vol. 3444, pp. 5–20. Springer, Heidelberg (2005)

22. Tillmann, N., Moskal, M., de Halleux, J., Fahndrich, M.: Touchdevelop - programming cloud-connected mobile devices via touchscreen. Technical Report TR-2011-49, Microsoft Research (2011)
23. Tillmann, N., Moskal, M., de Halleux, J., Fahndrich, M., Bishop, J., Samuel, A., Xie, T.: Touchdevelop - app development on mobile devices. In: Proceedings of ITiCSE 2012. ACM (2012)
24. Tillmann, N., Moskal, M., de Halleux, J., Fahndrich, M., Burckhardt, S.: Touchdevelop - app development on mobile devices. In: Proceedings of FSE 2012, Demonstration. ACM (2012)
25. Wilhelm, R., Engblom, J., Ermedahl, A., Holsti, N., Thesing, S., Whalley, D., Bernat, G., Ferdinand, C., Heckmann, R., Mitra, T., Mueller, F., Puaut, I., Puschner, P., Staschulat, J., Stenström, P.: The worst-case execution-time problem. overview of methods and survey of tools. ACM Transactions on Embedded Computing Systems, 7(3) (2008)
26. Zanioli, M., Ferrara, P., Cortesi, A.: SAILS: static analysis of information leakage with Sample. In: Proceedings of SAC 2012. ACM (2012)

Efficient Incremental Static Analysis
Using Path Abstraction

Rashmi Mudduluru and Murali Krishna Ramanathan

Indian Institute of Science, Bangalore, India
{mudduluru.rashmi,muralikrishna}@csa.iisc.ernet.in

Abstract. *Incremental* static analysis involves analyzing changes to a
version of a source code along with analyzing code regions that are semantically affected by the changes. Existing analysis tools that attempt
to perform incremental analysis can perform redundant computations
due to poor abstraction. In this paper, we design a novel and efficient
incremental analysis algorithm for reducing the overall analysis time. We
use a *path abstraction* that encodes different paths in the program as a set
of constraints. The constraints encoded as boolean formulas are input to
a `SAT` solver and the (un)satisfiability of the formulas drives the analysis
further. While a majority of boolean formulas are similar across multiple
versions, the problem of finding their equivalence is *graph isomorphism
complete*. We address a relaxed version of the problem by designing efficient *memoization* techniques to identify equivalence of boolean formulas
to improve the performance of the static analysis engine. Our experimental results on a number of large codebases (upto 87 KLoC) show a
performance gain of upto 32% when incremental analysis is used. The
overhead associated with identifying equivalence of boolean formulas is
less (not more than 8.4%) than the overall reduction in analysis time.

1 Introduction

The adoption of static analysis tools for bug detection [4,20] in the software
development cycle has increased significantly in the past decade [5]. These tools
typically analyze the source code to find different kinds of bugs including null
pointer dereferences [9,12], resource leaks [18], concurrency bugs [5] and security flaws [19]. Software testing can be ineffective because it requires significant
manual effort to write good test cases to detect complex bugs. In contrast, static
analysis tools [13,20] can detect deep interprocedural defects on even rare execution paths *automatically* resulting in their increased use in software organizations. However, the time taken for static analysis to analyze the entire codebase
can be quite high. This has resulted in the design of a number of techniques to
reduce the analysis time [13,2].

In many organizations, each build goes through an automated software testing
process. If static analysis is integrated into the build system and the process is
time consuming, it can result in the unavailability of fresh testable binaries.
To address this, if the analysis is decoupled with the build process, the defects

S. Gnesi and A. Rensink (Eds.): FASE 2014, LNCS 8411, pp. 125–139, 2014.

eventually found by the static analysis will anyway *invalidate* the automated testing. This is because the defects detected by the analysis need to be fixed and automated testing needs to happen subsequently. Therefore, a practical mode of using static analysis is to integrate them into the nightly build [13]. As a result, the problem of improving the efficiency of static analysis has gained significance. Many approaches for improving the efficiency of static analyses [20,13,2] exploit the underlying parallelism in analyzing the code. For example, some functions can be analyzed concurrently to reduce the overall analysis time.

A state of the art static analysis tool that is based on the above paradigm is SATURN [20]. It is a path sensitive, interprocedural and a highly scalable static analysis tool that has its foundations on boolean satisfiability and models the programs being analyzed as a set of boolean constraints where the entire program behaviour including path information is encoded by the constraints. Each program point is represented as a boolean combination of these constraints. To check a property at a given program point, SATURN converts the boolean formula representing the program point into its conjunctive normal form and invokes a SAT solver on the formula. Thus, the problem of detecting bugs is reduced to that of checking the satisfiability of the boolean constraints at various program points. SATURN also has a parallel implementation of their analysis which distributes independent functions across multiple cores.

While parallelization of static analysis is a necessary first step in improving its scalability, there are other avenues for reducing the analysis time. An unexploited avenue of improvement is the reanalysis of unchanged source code. Programmers typically make only a few source code changes for every revision. *Incremental analysis* involves analyzing the modified parts of the source code and its dependencies. In practice, McPeak *et al* [13] show that incremental analysis is very effective in reducing the overall analysis time on revisions of the codebase.

We observe that the constraints, generated by SATURN, across successive versions are mostly the same because a majority of the codebase is unchanged. A minor change in a function only results in modification to a subset of these constraints. Because these constraints are not necessarily coupled to a function, many boolean constraints solved by the SAT solver are common across multiple functions within the same version of the codebase.

Recently, incremental static analysis techniques have been proposed for different applications [22,17,11,21,13]. For example, McPeak *et al* [13] propose an incremental static analysis tool for bug detection that abstracts a function in terms of a work unit. If the work unit is unchanged, then the result of analyzing the work unit from the previous run of the static analysis is used. We believe that this abstraction is coarse-grained and has many limitations. Firstly, a minor change in the work unit which does not necessarily affect the static analysis results can indeed cause a reanalysis of the work unit. Secondly, the work unit abstraction results in all paths within a function (including semantically independent paths) being coupled together and therefore prevents reusability of analysis results on unaffected paths. Finally, this abstraction does not leverage the potential reusability of results within the same version of the codebase. In this paper, we explore the possibility of using a *path abstraction* for designing incremental analysis which is fine grained and does not suffer from the above limitations.

We leverage the path abstraction properties of SATURN to build an incremental static analysis tool, named iSATURN, which addresses the limitations of work unit abstraction for performing incremental analysis. When iSATURN analyzes the source code initially, it *memoizes* the boolean constraints that are input to the SAT solver and the associated results from the solver. The number of symbols in a boolean formula can be significantly high. To reduce the overhead with hashing the entire boolean formula, we pick a subset of the symbols *deterministically*, hash it and use it as a key to identify the formula and its results. We store the memoized results in a highly efficient key-value database. In any subsequent analysis, the solver is not invoked if the database lookup for the boolean formula succeeds. The reduction in the number of invocations to the solver reduces the overall analysis time. Moreover, as these formulas are function agnostic, memoized results of boolean formulas solved earlier in the run can be reused appropriately.

We have implemented our approach on top of the SATURN analysis framework. We use BerkeleyDB [16] for storing the memoized results. Our experiments on multiple versions of large codebases show that the path based abstraction for performing incremental analysis reduces the overall analysis time upto 32%. More importantly, the results observed with the incremental static analysis is exactly the same as the results obtained using a full analysis.

We make the following technical contributions in this paper:

1. We leverage the path based abstraction of static analysis tools to design a novel and scalable incremental static analysis.
2. We implement our approach on top of the SATURN analysis framework to analyze C programs.
3. We analyze multiple versions of large (upto 87 KLoC) open source codebases showing upto 32% reduction in analysis time when compared to the overall analysis time of SATURN.

2   Motivation

In this section, we motivate our problem by using examples to illustrate the inefficiencies with existing static analysis engines. Figure 1 shows the implementation of function gunzip_file in two successive versions of busybox. Assume the application of a static analysis tool (e.g., SATURN) to identify null pointer dereferences [1]. Consider the program point corresponding to line number 135 in busybox v0.60.4. At this point, SATURN generates boolean constraints to check the satisfiability of conditions, unzip(in_file, out_file) == 0 and path == NULL. The first condition is a conditional that is present in the code and the second condition corresponds to the static analysis check to identify the feasibility of a null pointer at that point. Now, consider the program point corresponding to busybox v0.60.4

```
74 static int gunzip_file (const char *path, int flags)
75 {
    ....
133 if (unzip(in_file, out_file) == 0) {
134 /* Success, remove .gz file */
135   delete_path = path;
136   if (flags & gunzip_verbose) {
137     fprintf(stderr, "OK\n");
138   }
    ....
}
```

busybox v0.60.5

```
74 static int gunzip_file (const char *path, int flags)
75 {
    ....
133 if (unzip(in_file, out_file) == 0) {
134 /* Success, remove .gz file */
135   if ( !(flags & gunzip_to_stdout ))
136     delete_path = path;
137   if (flags & gunzip_verbose) {
138     fprintf(stderr, "OK\n");
139   }
    ....
}
```

Fig. 1. Illustrative Example: Function `gunzip_file` in two versions of `busybox`

line number 136 in `busybox v0.60.5` (right side of Figure 1). For this version, the boolean constraints generated to check the satisfiability of the conditions include `unzip(in_file, out_file) == 0`, `!(flags & gunzip_to_stdout)` and `path == NULL`. Obviously, the boolean constraints at the program point under consideration will *differ* for these two versions. Interestingly, the boolean constraints will *only* differ on paths that have either changed syntactically or are semantically dependent on the changed syntactic paths. In the above example, out of the 94 boolean formulas in the function that are checked for satisfiability, only 39 (40%) boolean formulas in the newer version differ from the original set. We observe that eliminating the redundant computation of checking boolean satisfiability can improve the performance of static analysis. Existing static analysis tools [13,20] will reanalyze the entire function. Our design of a more fine grained incremental analysis technique enables our tool, `iSATURN`, to effectively eliminate redundant computations.

Not surprisingly, our mechanism for improving the performance of static analysis also benefits analyzing the same version. Consider the code fragments for the functions `md5_get_result` and `md5_init` from `bftpd v3.1` shown in Figure 2. In line 244 of `md5_get_result`, the first parameter, `md5_p` to the function is dereferenced and there is a corresponding boolean formula associated with this

```
239 static void md5_get_result(const md5_t *md5_p, void *result)
240 {
241   md5_uint32 hold;
242   void *res_p = result;
243
244   hold = SWAP(md5_p->md_A);
245   memcpy(res_p, &hold, sizeof(md5_uint32));
246   res_p = (char *)res_p + sizeof(md5_uint32);
    ....
}
```

```
282 void md5_init(md5_t *md5_p)
283 {
284   md5_p->md_A = 0x67452301;
285   md5_p->md_B = 0xefcdab89;
    ....
}
```

Fig. 2. Illustrative Example: Commonality across two functions in the same version (`v3.1`) of `bftpd`

program point. Similarly, there is a boolean formula associated with dereferencing the first parameter md5_p of function md5_init at line 284. In our analysis, we observe that these two boolean formulas are exactly the same as these dereferences happen unconditionally and therefore the SAT solver need not be invoked twice unnecessarily. We observe similar *collisions* of boolean formulas within the same version of the program across multiple benchmarks.

3   Background

For completeness, we provide a brief overview of SATURN [20]. The framework provided by SATURN translates a C program into a set of boolean constraints. It has rules for modelling common C constructs like integers, pointers, conditionals, etc. For example, integers are encoded as their binary representations. Consider the statement: (c == 10)? s1 : s2; Here, statement s1 is executed if c has the value 10. So the boolean constraint that encodes the condition under which s1 is executed is (B(c) == 1010), where B(c) is the binary representation of the integer c. For s2, the constraint will be $\neg(B(c) == 1010)$.

Any property checker (e.g., null pointer analyzer, leak detector, etc.) is encoded as a set of finite state properties and plugged into this framework. This is accomplished by expressing the property checkers as a set of inference rules. For example, one such inference rule could state that given the premises (i) a pointer variable X points to another variable Y and (ii) at program point P, expression E evaluates to X hold, the conclusion "E evaluates to Y" holds [1]. If the property being checked is aliasing, then the function summary is inferred by checking the satisfiability of constraints obtained in conjunction with these properties and the primitive constraints generated by SATURN. Consequently, bug detection is reduced to checking if the error state is reachable. This checking is done with the help of SAT queries [1].

Interprocedural analysis is achieved by using function summaries. Function summaries represent the state of the function at its exit with respect to the property being checked. For example, if an argument is dereferenced within a function, and the property that is under consideration is null pointer dereference, then the function summary corresponding to the function will carry the fact that the argument to the function is dereferenced. For a more detailed exposition of SATURN, we refer the reader to [20].

To illustrate the working of how the null analysis in SATURN detects bugs, consider the example shown in Figure 3. SATURN performs bottom up analysis [13] by default. In this example, the function bar is analyzed before main. The boolean formulas generated by the null analysis for the function bar encode the constraints shown in Figure 4. The constraints on the left correspond to the true branch of the if condition and those on the right correspond to the else branch. When the function bar is analyzed, all these boolean formulas are satisfiable. Eventually, when main is analyzed, the function summary for bar is available. Among other facts, this summary contains the fact that if flag is not equal to 0, then the variable var is certainly dereferenced. This information

```
char *p1, *p2;                  void main(int args)
void bar(int flag)              {
{                                   p2 = 0;
   char var;                        bar(1);
   var = (!flag? *p1 : *p2);     }
}
```

Fig. 3. Illustrative example to describe bug detection in SATURN

1. arg(0) == 0 & p1 == 0   1. arg(0) != 0 & p1 != 0
2. arg(0) == 0 & p1 != 0   2. arg(0) != 0 & p2 == 0
3. arg(0) == 0 & p2 != 0   3. arg(0) != 0 & p2 != 0

Fig. 4. Boolean constraints for function bar() from Figure 3

along with the currently known facts, p2 = 0 and flag = 1 results in the null dereference bug being detected.

4   Design

In this section, we describe the overall architecture of our approach and subsequently describe the incremental analysis in detail.

4.1   Architecture

Figure 5 shows the overall architecture of iSATURN. CIL [15], the frontend C parser, parses the program and generates abstract syntax trees (ASTs) [13]. These ASTs are encoded as a set of predicates representing program relations. A database is created for each function that stores these predicates as a key value pair. These databases are known as syntax databases [1].

SATURN [20] consults the syntax databases and generates boolean constraints depending on the property being checked. In doing so, the path information is also encoded in the boolean constraints. While generating constraints, SATURN uses the predicates in the syntax databases to infer conditions under which a

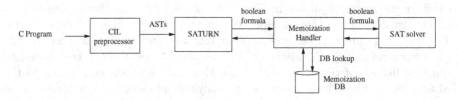

Fig. 5. Architecture of iSATURN

program point is reachable, thereby generating precise path information. SATURN thus performs an analysis of the memory model to generate path sensitive boolean formulas. These formulas are passed to a SAT solver [8] in their conjunctive normal forms. The results from the SAT solver help SATURN in generating the function summaries and error reports. The summary of a function represents all the states of the function at its exit with respect to the property being checked. Based on the results from the SAT solver, SATURN infers the predicates that are feasible for a function and generates function summaries [1].

In our tool, iSATURN, we introduce a memoization database before the invocation of the SAT solver. We choose BerkeleyDB [16], a high performance key value store for this purpose. The memoization database tracks the boolean formulas solved by the SAT solver and the corresponding results. Therefore, in iSATURN, we first check whether the results for a boolean formula are already present in the memoization database. We define the presence of the boolean formula as a *hit* and the absence as *miss*. In case of a hit, the SAT solver is not invoked and the results from the database are returned rightaway. Otherwise, the SAT solver is invoked as usual. We find that across successive versions, the number of calls to the SAT solver decreases significantly due to the repetitive nature of the boolean formulas being generated.

4.2   Equivalence of Boolean Formulas

We hypothesize that elimination of redundant invocations of the SAT solver to check the satisfiability of the boolean formulas can help improve the performance of the static analysis engine. By reusing the results of the solved boolean formulas, the analysis time can be decreased significantly. While stated simply, there are significant challenges to bringing this idea to fruition. To reuse the results, we need to identify the equivalence of boolean formulas.

Boolean Formula Structural Equivalence Problem: For two boolean formulas,

1. $\phi_1 = (a_{11} \lor a_{12} \lor ....a_{1i}) \land (a_{21} \lor a_{22} \lor ....a_{2j}) \land .... \land (a_{n1} \lor a_{n2} \lor ....a_{nk})$
2. $\phi_2 = (b_{11} \lor b_{12} \lor ....b_{1l}) \land (b_{21} \lor b_{22} \lor ....b_{2m}) \land .... \land (b_{n1} \lor b_{n2} \lor ....b_{np})$

ideally the two CNF formulas are equivalent, if there exists some permutation of the clauses and some permutation of the literals within these clauses resulting in a one to one mapping of variables in these formulas. More specifically, let the clauses of ϕ_1 be denoted as cl_1, cl_2, ..., cl_n. Now consider the following transformations on ϕ_1:

1. $\phi_1' = cl_1' \land cl_2' \land ... \land cl_n'$, where $(cl_1', cl_2'..., cl_n')$ is a permutation of $(cl_1, cl_2, ..., cl_n)$
2. $\phi_1'' = (a_{11}'' \lor a_{12}'' \lor ....a_{1l}'') \land (a_{21}'' \lor a_{22}'' \lor ....a_{2m}'') \land ... \land (a_{n1}'' \lor a_{n2}'' \lor ....a_{np}'')$, where $(a_{i1}'', a_{i2}'', ..., a_{ik}'')$ is a permutation of literals in cl_i'

If the variables in ϕ_1'' can be renamed such that the resulting formula becomes equal to ϕ_2, then the two formulas ϕ_1 and ϕ_2 are structurally equivalent.

Any truth assignment to the variables of ϕ_1 can also be applied to the corresponding variables in ϕ_2. For example, the following two boolean CNF formulas are structurally equivalent:

1. $\psi_1 = (a \vee \neg b \vee c) \wedge (d \vee a \vee b)$
2. $\psi_2 = (z \vee w \vee x) \wedge (w \vee y \vee \neg x)$

Permuting the clauses of ψ_1, we get $\psi_1' = (d \vee a \vee b) \wedge (a \vee \neg b \vee c)$. Further, permuting the literals of the second clause in ψ_1' results in $\psi_1'' = (d \vee a \vee b) \wedge (a \vee c \vee \neg b)$. There is a one to one correspondence between the variables of ψ_1'' and ψ_2 (i.e) (a, b, c, d) corresponds to (w, x, y, z). Any satisfying truth assignment of (a, b, c, d) for ψ_1 can also be applied to (w, x, y, z) in ψ_2 respectively.

Theorem 1. *The boolean CNF formula structural equivalence problem is graph isomorphism complete [3].*

Proof. The problem of determining equivalence of CNF formulas is reducible to that of graph isomorphism in polynomial time [3].

If we make the approach of considering equivalence of formulas more conservative by foregoing the permutation of clauses and literals in defining the equivalence of CNF formulas, then the approach has a polynomial time complexity. More specifically, for two CNF formulas,

1. $\phi_3 = (a_{11} \vee a_{12} \vee ....a_{1i}) \wedge (a_{21} \vee a_{22} \vee ....a_{2j}) \wedge .... \wedge (a_{n1} \vee a_{n2} \vee ....a_{nk})$
2. $\phi_4 = (b_{11} \vee b_{12} \vee ....b_{1i}) \wedge (b_{21} \vee b_{22} \vee ....b_{2j}) \wedge .... \wedge (b_{n1} \vee b_{n1} \vee ....b_{nk})$

the formulas are said to be equivalent if there exists a one to one mapping of variables such that the literals in ϕ_3 can be renamed as those in ϕ_4 at their corresponding positions. This conservative technique gives fewer number of hits than the original boolean CNF formula equivalence problem. In other words, it may miss some formulas that are actually equivalent because of the permutations of the clauses and the literals within. As a result, ψ_1 and ψ_2 given above would not be considered equivalent in this approach. However, in this approach, the following two boolean formulas are considered equal:

1. $\psi_3 = (a \vee \neg b \vee c) \wedge (d \vee a \vee b)$
2. $\psi_4 = (w \vee \neg x \vee y) \wedge (z \vee w \vee x)$

ψ_3 and ψ_4 are considered equivalent in this approach because there is a one to one correspondence between their clauses, and within each clause, each variable of ψ_3 can be mapped to the variable at the corresponding position in ψ_4.

Nevertheless, even this conservative approach does not necessarily scale because it involves canonical renaming of variables and their comparison. In order to rename a variable, we need to maintain a mapping of the variables' names and their new names. For each variable, we check if it has already been renamed. If not, we assign it a new name in a canonical manner. This has to be done for every literal in every clause. This results in a quadratic complexity in the total number of literals in the formula.

Therefore, we consider the most practical approach to compare the formulas. Here, two formulas are considered equivalent only if they are exactly the same. This approach reduces the number of formulas that are syntactically equivalent and results in more invocations of the SAT solver than is necessary. Surprisingly, our experimental results shows that the number of hits even with this technique is significantly high and helps improve the performance of static analysis.

5 Implementation

Algorithm 1. Memoization Handler

Input: $\phi = (c_{11} \vee c_{12} \vee \dots c_{1i}) \wedge (c_{21} \vee c_{22} \vee \dots c_{2j}) \wedge \dots \wedge (c_{n1} \vee c_{n2} \vee \dots c_{nk})$
Output: SAT or UNSAT
1: $\text{Num}_c(\phi)$: number of clauses in ϕ
2: $\text{Num}_l(\psi)$: number of literals in ψ
3: $H(i_1, i_2, .., i_m)$: MD5 hash of concatenation of $i_1, i_2, ..., i_m$
4: **if** $\text{Num}_c(\phi) < K$ **then**
5:     key $\leftarrow$ $H(...H(H(c_{11}, c_{12}, ..., c_{1i}),(c_{21}, c_{22}, ..., c_{2j})),....,(c_{n1}, c_{n2}, ..., c_{nk}))$
6: **else**
7:     key $\leftarrow$ ""
8:     index $\leftarrow$ 1
9:     **for** each clause ψ in ϕ **do**
10:         pos $\leftarrow$ index mod $(\text{Num}_l(\psi))$
11:         key $\leftarrow$ $H($key,$H($literal at position **pos** in $\psi))$
12:         index $\leftarrow$ index + 1
13:     **end for**
14:     value $\leftarrow$ memdb_lookup(key)
15:     **if** value is found **then**
16:         return the value
17:     **else**
18:         result $\leftarrow$ SAT_solver(ϕ)
19:         memdb_store(key,result)
20:         return result
21:     **end if**
22: **end if**

In our implementation, we use BerkeleyDB [16], a highly efficient key value store to memoize the formulas and their results. If the formulas include a lot of literals, memoizing the boolean formulas as strings is highly inefficient. In practice, because SATURN encodes programs as boolean constraints and maintains precise path information down to the level of bits, these boolean formulas tend to be very large. For example, in our experimental setup, for benchmarks of about 7 KLoC, we observe that the maximum number of clauses is 7000 and the maximum number of literals within each clause is 100 approximately.

We address the above problem by employing an efficient hashing technique to store the formulas. Given a boolean formula $(c_{11} \vee c_{12} \vee \dots c_{1i}) \wedge (c_{21} \vee c_{22} \vee \dots c_{2j}) \wedge \dots \wedge (c_{n1} \vee c_{n2} \vee \dots c_{nk})$, we store $H(..H(H(c_{11}, .., c_{1i}),(c_{21}, .., c_{2j})), .., (c_{n1}, .., c_{nk}))$

as the key, where $H(a, b)$ denotes the hash of concatenation of a and b. We employ the MD5 algorithm [7] for hashing which ensures that every key is 128 bits long.

To optimize the implementation further and to leverage the large size of the boolean formulas, we also employ a *deterministic sampling* approach to generate the key for every boolean formula. Instead of using the complete formula to generate the hash, the hash is based on picking a predetermined literal from each clause. The hash function used is $H(...H(H(c_{1a}), c_{2b}), ..., c_{nk})$, where n is the number of clauses in the formula, c_{ij} denotes the jth literal of ith clause, where $j = i \mod f(i)$ and $f(i)$ is the number of literals in i^{th} clause. The complete algorithm is shown in Algorithm 1.

In Algorithm 1, for formulas with number of clauses less than K, lines 4 and 5 generate the key for database lookup by hashing the entire SAT formula. For the remaining formulas, lines 9 to 13 generate the key by hashing the sampled literals from each clause in the SAT formula. The rest of the algorithm describes how the generated key is used in database lookup. Upon a hit, the result stored in the DB is returned. Otherwise, the SAT solver is invoked and the result is returned after storing it against the generated key in the memoization DB.

Though the deterministic sampling may result in two unequal formulas being matched, the probability of such a scenario is very low. More specifically, the probability of two distinct formulas being considered equivalent due to sampling will happen if the sampled literal from each clause matches. The probability of two distinct formulas matching because of deterministic sampling is $\Pi_{i=1}^{n} 1/f(i)$. For sufficiently large n and $f(i)$, we deploy the sampling technique and for smaller values, we use the complete approach. In our experimental results, we also empirically verify across a number of benchmarks that deterministic sampling does not result in two distinct formulas being considered equivalent.

6   Experimental Results

We conduct our experiments on an Ubuntu 12.04 desktop equipped with 3.5 GHz Intel core i7 processor and 16 GB RAM. We use BerkeleyDB version 5.3.21 to store the SAT formulas and their results. We use the null pointer dereference analysis to show the scalability of our approach. We believe that the conclusions drawn from the experiments can be extended to other interprocedural analyses as well. We use five open source benchmarks for our experiments. busybox is a collection of utilities for embedded systems, openssh uses the SSH protocol to provide secure communication sessions over a network, gzip is used for compression and decompression of files and bftpd is a flexible FTP server. We use two different versions of gzip (gzip(A) and gzip(B)) to show that the performance of our approach is also dependent on the kinds of changes made across the versions.

Table 1 provides the list of benchmarks used and the statistics associated with the benchmarks including the number of lines of code and the number of formulas that need to be solved by the static analysis engine. The number of lines of code varies from 5 KLoC to 88 KLoC approximately. The number of formulas varies

Table 1. Benchmarks used in our experiments and associated statistics

Benchmark	Version 1	Version 2	KLoC		Number of formulas	
			version 1	version 2	version 1	version 2
busybox	0.60.4	0.60.5	75.5	75.8	48198	48388
openssh	20130823	20130830	87.7	87.9	106305	106305
bftpd	3.1	3.2	5.2	5.2	9638	9704
gzip(A)	1.2.4	1.2.4a	8.0	8.0	51363	51363
gzip(B)	1.3.2	1.3.3	9.2	9.2	56210	56210

Table 2. Comparison of performance between SATURN and iSATURN

Benchmark	version 1			version 2			Memory overhead percentage[*]
	T_S (secs)	T_I (secs)	Overhead percentage	T_S (secs)	T_I (secs)	Improvement percentage	
busybox	333	358	7.5	337	228	32	0.83
openssh	661	717	8.4	664	455	31.4	1.11
bftpd	65	66	1.5	65	58	10.7	0.22
gzip(A)	2811	2987	6.2	2891	2069	28.4	0.66
gzip(B)	7071	7309	3.3	7212	6734	6.6	0.7

T_s : Analysis time with SATURN.
T_I : Analysis time with iSATURN.
[*]Memory overhead of iSATURN over SATURN.

from 9638 for bftpd to 106305 for openssh. In scenarios where the number of formulas is the same across versions (Example: openssh, gzip(A), gzip(B)), we will show later that they are not necessarily the same set of formulas.

Table 2 presents a comparison of iSATURN and SATURN in analyzing the five benchmarks. For each version of the benchmark, we analyze it using both the tools. The choice of SAT formulas that are sampled and not cached completely by iSATURN depends on the structure of the formula being considered. Specifically, while converting the SAT formulas into their CNF forms and simplifying them, SATURN has a way of putting the clauses into either one group or two groups. Typically, when the clauses are put into two groups, the number of clauses in the first group is very large and we sample the literals from the clauses of this group. We run the analysis to fixpoint or 20 iterations, whichever completes earlier. We also do not consider analyzing functions[1] that timeout due to implementation issues in SATURN itself. In the first version, there will be overhead associated with iSATURN because the results pertaining to the boolean formulas are being stored in the database. This overhead varies from 1.5 to 8.4%. Subsequently, when the second version of the benchmark is analyzed by both the tools, iSATURN shows a performance improvement of upto 32% for busybox. This performance gain can be obtained across multiple runs of the program on the same version or any subsequent version. We also observe that in bftpd, the size of the SAT

---

[1] The number of formulas that timeout is less than 3.5%.

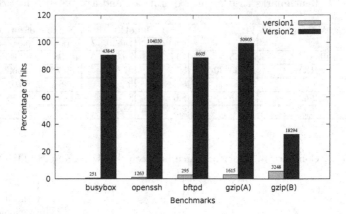

Fig. 6. Percentage of hits across versions. The number on top of the bars represents the actual number of hits.

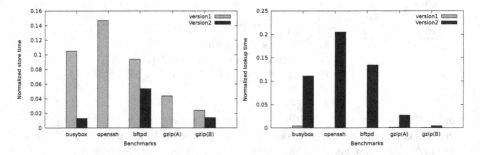

Fig. 7. Normalized store time   **Fig. 8.** Normalized lookup time

formulas does not exceed 2502 clauses and it has the least overhead during the analysis in the first version (1.5%). On the other hand, analysis of `openssh` generates formulas with the number of clauses as high as 22839 but the overhead is relatively small (8.4%). The last column in table 2 shows that the memory overhead incurred by `iSATURN` over `SATURN` is negligible.

Figure 6 shows the benchmarks on the X axis and number of hits on the Y axis. Recall that a hit happens whenever the formula that needs to be solved has its results stored in the database. While analyzing successive versions of the codebase, the number of hits increases significantly. With increase in the number of hits, the reduction in the overall analysis time is prominent. Furthermore, we also observe that the database lookup succeeds even when analyzing the same version. For example, while analyzing the first version of `gzip(B)`, we notice a non trivial (3248) number of hits.

Figure 7 compares the normalized time of storing the SAT formulas and their results across versions. The time to store the formulas and the results does not exceed 15% of the overall analysis time and is negligible in many cases.

Figure 8 shows the normalized lookup time across versions. The lookup time also does not exceed 20% of the overall analysis time. Using a more efficient key value store can reduce these overheads even further.

The results show that the techniques used here can be employed to improve efficiency of applications where a number of SAT formulas need to be solved and many of them are equivalent as described here. However, in applications where the precise equivalence of SAT formulas is essential, the sampling technique should not be employed.

7   Related Work

McPeak *et al* [13] propose a solution for the problem of incremental static analysis and provide a solution. One of the fundamental limitations of their approach is that the incremental analysis is based on a coarse grained work unit. Therefore, even a minor modification to a function which does not necessarily change the outcome of static analysis can result in the function being re-analyzed. In other words, their approach does not fully exploit semantically equivalent paths. Furthermore, even while analyzing the same version, the avenues for reducing redundancy is not explored comprehensively. Our approach is complementary to their approach. For functions where the approach of [13] suggests a reanalysis, iSATURN can be used to reduce the redundancy.

Recently, memoization has been applied to improve efficiency of symbolic execution and model checking. Yang *et al* [22] propose memoized symbolic execution, where a trie data structure is used to represent symbolic paths generated during a symbolic run. Subsequent symbolic runs of the program use the information stored in the trie to avoid re-execution of unaffected paths. Person *et al* [17] describe techniques to direct the symbolic execution using changes across different versions of a program. Path conditions affected by code changes are computed and are used to explore execution paths in the affected parts of the program. Lauterburg *et al* [11], show how state space exploration can be made incremental by memoizing information about states that are unaffected by changes across program versions. Similarly, Yang *et al* [21] propose regression model checking where data from previous versions helps to avoid checking some state spaces that are safe in the current version. It uses test suites to identify paths in a CFG that are modified in the current version and thereby prunes states that are safe. Our approach differs from these techniques as it aims at improving the efficiency of static analysis approaches that depend on solving SAT queries to detect bugs.

In approaches that attempt to improve performance of static analysis, parallelism in the code being analyzed is exploited to achieve speedup [2,14]. These approaches bank upon additional cores to achieve speedup and are agnostic pertaining to the incremental nature of the source code. In contrast, our approach gives performance benefits with the existing resources alone.

There are a variety of static analysis tools available that target specific kinds of bugs [18,19]. Techniques based on model checking [4,6] may find more bugs accurately but are not scalable for large programs. These approaches focus mainly on finding bugs more precisely but do not attempt to address the incremental nature of software.

Incremental analysis requires that the tool identify parts of the code that have been syntactically and semantically affected by code changes. Impact analysis identifies the impact of a change on a program [10]. It has been used in the context of testing to identify tests that need to be executed after a code change. Static analysis requires the identification of parts of code that need to be reanalyzed in the incremental setting. In our approach, we analyze only the paths that are affected by code changes in the context of the property being checked.

8 Conclusions

In this paper, we identify the problem of redundant computations performed by existing state of the art static analysis engines. The redundancy exists due to the incremental nature of software development. We leverage this characteristic of software development to build a scalable static analysis that stores and uses previous analysis results effectively. We have implemented a tool, iSATURN, on top of SATURN, a state of the art static analysis engine. Our experimental results on large codebases (upto 87 KLoC) show that iSATURN reduces the overall analysis time upto 32%.

Acknowledgements. We thank Alex Aiken and Isig Dillig for answering our questions related to SATURN. We also thank Ananth Grama, Mehmet Koyuturk and Deepak D'Souza for providing useful pointers.

References

1. Aiken, A., Bugrara, S., Dillig, I., Dillig, T., Hackett, B., Hawkins, P.: An overview of the saturn project. In: Proceedings of the 7th ACM SIGPLAN-SIGSOFT Workshop on Program Analysis for Software Tools and Engineering, pp. 43–48. ACM (2007)
2. Albarghouthi, A., Kumar, R., Nori, A., Rajamani, S.: Parallelizing top-down interprocedural analyses. In: Proceedings of the 33rd ACM SIGPLAN Conference on Programming Language Design and Implementation, pp. 217–228. ACM (2012)
3. Ausiello, G., Cristiano, F., Laura, L.: Syntactic isomorphism of cnf boolean formulas is graph isomorphism complete. In: Electronic Colloquium on Computational Complexity (ECCC), vol. 19, p. 122 (2012)
4. Ball, T., Rajamani, S.: Automatically validating temporal safety properties of interfaces. In: Dwyer, M.B. (ed.) SPIN 2001. LNCS, vol. 2057, pp. 103–122. Springer, Heidelberg (2001)
5. Bessey, A., Block, K., Chelf, B., Chou, A., Fulton, B., Hallem, S., Henri-Gros, C., Kamsky, A., McPeak, S., Engler, D.: A few billion lines of code later: using static analysis to find bugs in the real world. Commun. ACM 53(2), 66–75 (2010)
6. Beyer, D., Henzinger, T.A., Jhala, R., Majumdar, R.: The software model checker blast. International Journal on Software Tools for Technology Transfer 9(5-6), 505–525 (2007)

7. Deepakumara, J., Heys, H.M., Venkatesan, R.: Fpga implementation of md5 hash algorithm. In: Canadian Conference on Electrical and Computer Engineering, vol. 2, pp. 919–924. IEEE (2001)
8. Een, N., Sörensson, N.: Minisat: A sat solver with conflict-clause minimization. Sat, 5 (2005)
9. Hovemeyer, D., Pugh, W.: Finding more null pointer bugs, but not too many. In: Proceedings of the 7th ACM SIGPLAN-SIGSOFT Workshop on Program Analysis for Software Tools and Engineering, pp. 9–14. ACM (2007)
10. Jashki, M.-A., Zafarani, R., Bagheri, E.: Towards a more efficient static software change impact analysis method. In: Proceedings of the 8th ACM SIGPLAN-SIGSOFT Workshop on Program Analysis for Software Tools and Engineering, PASTE 2008, pp. 84–90. ACM (2008)
11. Lauterburg, S., Sobeih, A., Marinov, D., Viswanathan, M.: Incremental state-space exploration for programs with dynamically allocated data. In: Proceedings of the 30th International Conference on Software Engineering, pp. 291–300. ACM (2008)
12. Livshits, V.B., Lam, M.S.: Tracking pointers with path and context sensitivity for bug detection in c programs. In: ACM SIGSOFT Software Engineering Notes, vol. 28, pp. 317–326. ACM (2003)
13. McPeak, S., Gros, C.-H., Ramanathan, M.K.: Scalable and incremental software bug detection. In: Proceedings of the 2013 9th Joint Meeting on Foundations of Software Engineering, ESEC/FSE 2013, pp. 554–564 (2013)
14. Mendez-Lojo, M., Mathew, A., Pingali, K.: Parallel inclusion-based points-to analysis. In: Proceedings of the ACM International Conference on Object Oriented Programming Systems Languages and Applications, OOPSLA 2010, pp. 428–443 (2010)
15. Necula, G.C., McPeak, S., Rahul, S.P., Weimer, W.: Cil: Intermediate language and tools for analysis and transformation of c programs. In: Nigel Horspool, R. (ed.) CC 2002. LNCS, vol. 2304, pp. 213–228. Springer, Heidelberg (2002)
16. Olson, M.A., Bostic, K., Seltzer, M.I.: Berkeley db. In: USENIX Annual Technical Conference, FREENIX Track, pp. 183–191 (1999)
17. Person, S., Yang, G., Rungta, N., Khurshid, S.: Directed incremental symbolic execution. ACM SIGPLAN Notices 47(6), 504–515 (2012)
18. Torlak, E., Chandra, S.: Effective interprocedural resource leak detection. In: 2010 ACM/IEEE 32nd International Conference on Software Engineering, vol. 1, pp. 535–544. IEEE (2010)
19. Wassermann, G., Su, Z.: Sound and precise analysis of web applications for injection vulnerabilities. In: Proceedings of the 2007 ACM SIGPLAN Conference on Programming Language Design and Implementation, PLDI 2007, pp. 32–41 (2007)
20. Xie, Y., Aiken, A.: Scalable error detection using boolean satisfiability. In: POPL 2005: Proceedings of the 32nd ACM SIGPLAN-SIGACT Symposium on Principles of Programming Languages, pp. 351–363 (2005)
21. Yang, G., Dwyer, M.B., Rothermel, G.: Regression model checking. In: IEEE International Conference on Software Maintenance, ICSM 2009, pp. 115–124. IEEE (2009)
22. Yang, G., Păsăreanu, C.S., Khurshid, S.: Memoized symbolic execution. In: Proceedings of the 2012 International Symposium on Software Testing and Analysis, pp. 144–154. ACM (2012)

Type-Based Taint Analysis for Java Web Applications

Wei Huang, Yao Dong, and Ana Milanova

Rensselaer Polytechnic Institute

Abstract. Static taint analysis detects information flow vulnerabilities. It has gained considerable importance in the last decade, with the majority of work focusing on dataflow and points-to-based approaches.

In this paper, we advocate *type-based taint analysis*. We present SFlow, a context-sensitive type system for secure information flow, and SFlow-Infer, a corresponding worst-case cubic inference analysis. Our approach effectively handles reflection, libraries and frameworks, features notoriously difficult for dataflow and points-to-based taint analysis.

We implemented SFlow and SFlowInfer. Empirical results on 13 real-world Java web applications show that our approach is scalable and also precise, achieving false positive rate of 15%.

1 Introduction

Information flow vulnerabilities are one of the most common security problems according to OWASP [14]. A common information flow vulnerability is SQL injection, shown in the example in Fig. 1 (adapted from [9]).

```
1  HttpServletRequest request = ...;
2  Statement stat = ...;
3  String user = request.getParameter("user");
4  StringBuffer sb = ...;
5  sb.append("SELECT * FROM Users WHERE name = ");
6  sb.append(user);
7  String query = sb.toString();
8  stat.executeQuery(query);
```

Fig. 1. SQL Injection Example

In this example, the user parameter of the HTTP request is obtained through request.getParameter("user") and stored in variable user, which is later appended to an SQL query string and sent to a database for execution: stat.executeQuery (query). At a first glance, this code snippet is unremarkable. However, if a malicious end-user supplies the user parameter with the value of "John OR 1 = 1", the unauthorized end-user can gain access to the information of all other users, because the WHERE clause always evaluates to true. Other information flow vulnerabilities include cross-site scripting (XXS), HTTP response splitting, path traversal and command injection [9].

S. Gnesi and A. Rensink (Eds.): FASE 2014, LNCS 8411, pp. 140–154, 2014.

Static taint analysis detects information flow vulnerabilities. It automatically detects flow from untrusted *sources* to security-sensitive *sinks*. In the example in Fig. 1, the return value of HttpServletRequest.getParameter() is a source, and the parameter p of Statement.executeQuery(String p) is a sink.

Research on static taint analysis for Java web applications has largely focused on dataflow and points-to-based approaches [5, 9, 18–20]. One issue with these approaches is that they usually rely on context-sensitive points-to analysis, which is expensive and non-modular (i.e., it requires a whole program). Arguably the toughest issue is dealing with reflection, libraries (JDK and third-party), and frameworks (Struts, Spring, Hibernate, etc.), features notoriously difficult for dataflow and points-to analysis and yet ubiquitous in Java web applications.

In this paper, we advocate *type-based taint analysis*. Specifically, we present SFlow, a context-sensitive type system for secure information flow, and SFlow-Infer, a corresponding worst-case cubic inference analysis. We leverage the inference and checking framework we built in previous work [6], which we have used to infer and check object ownership [6] and reference immutability [8].

Our inference is modular and compositional. It is modular in the sense that it can analyze any given set of classes L. Unknown callees in L are handled using appropriate defaults. Callers of L can be analyzed separately and composed with L without reanalysis of L. The inference requires annotations *only on sources and sinks*. Once the sources and sinks are built into annotated libraries, web applications are analyzed *without any input from the user*. The modularity of the inference allows for the effective handling of libraries and frameworks. Our approach handles reflective object creation as well. This is possible because SFlow does not require abstraction of heap objects; instead, it models flow from one variable to another through subtyping. To the best of our knowledge, this is the first type-based taint analysis for Java web applications, as well as the first analysis that is low polynomial and yet precise.

The paper makes the following contributions:

- SFlow, a context-sensitive type system for secure information flow.
- SFlowInfer, a novel, cubic inference analysis for SFlow.
- Effective handling of reflective object creation, libraries and frameworks.
- An empirical evaluation on Java web applications of up to 126kLOC, comprising 473kLOC in total.

The rest of the paper is organized as follows. Sect. 2 describes the SFlow type system and Sect. 3 describes the inference analysis. Sect. 4 describes techniques for handling of reflection, libraries and frameworks. Sect. 5 presents the empirical evaluations. Sect. 6 discusses the related work, and Sect. 7 concludes the paper.

2   SFlow Type System

This section first describes the basic type qualifiers in SFlow (Sect. 2.1) followed by the extension for context sensitivity (Sect. 2.2). It proceeds to formalize SFlow (Sect. 2.3), and combine SFlow with reference immutability (Sect. 2.4).

2.1   SFlow Qualifiers

There are two basic type qualifiers in SFlow: tainted and safe.

- tainted: A variable x is tainted, if there is flow from a source to x. Sources, e.g., the return value of ServletRequest.getParameter(), are annotated as tainted.
- safe: A variable x is safe if there is flow from x to a sensitive sink. Sinks, e.g., the parameter p of Statement.executeQuery(String p), are annotated as safe.

SFlow disallows flow from tainted sources to safe sinks. Therefore, we define the following subtyping hierarchy[1]:

$$\text{safe} <: \text{tainted}$$

where $q_1 <: q_2$ denotes q_1 is a subtype of q_2 (q is also a subtype of itself: $q <: q$). Thus, assigning a safe variable to a tainted one is allowed:

> **safe** int s = ...;   **tainted** int t = s;

but assigning a tainted variable to a safe one is disallowed:

> **tainted** int t = ...;   **safe** int s = t; // *type error!*

In the SQL injection example in Fig. 1, the return value of getParameter() is annotated as tainted, and the parameter of executeQuery(String p) is annotated as safe, as they are a source and a sink, respectively. The other variables are tainted:

```
2   ...
3   tainted String user = request.getParameter("user");
4   tainted StringBuffer sb = ...;     // it includes the tainted user
5   sb.append("SELECT * FROM Users WHERE name = ");
6   sb.append(user);
7   tainted String query = sb.toString();
8   stat.executeQuery(query);          // type error!
```

Since it is not allowed to assign the tainted query to the safe parameter of executeQuery(String p), statement 8 does not type-check, resulting in a type error. The type error signals an information flow violation.

2.2   Context Sensitivity

Context sensitivity is crucial to the typing precision of SFlow. Note that in the context-insensitive typing above, methods append and toString must be typed as follows (code throughout the paper makes parameter this explicit):

> **tainted** StringBuffer append(**tainted** StringBuffer this, **tainted** String s) {...}
> **tainted** String toString(**tainted** StringBuffer this) {...}

Such context-insensitive typing is imprecise, because it types the return value of toString as tainted. Consider the example in Fig. 2. query at line 7 is not tainted by any input, but it is *typed* tainted because the return value of toString is of type tainted. Therefore, the program is rejected, even though it is safe.

SFlow achieves context sensitivity by making use of a polymorphic type qualifier, poly, and *viewpoint adaptation*.

---

[1] Note that this is the desired subtyping. Unfortunately, this subtyping is not always safe, as we discuss in detail in Sect. 2.4.

```
1  String user = request.getParameter("user");
2  StringBuffer sb1 = ...; StringBuffer sb2 = ...;
3  sb1.append("SELECT * FROM Users WHERE name = ");
4  sb2.append("SELECT * FROM Users WHERE name = ");
5  sb1.append(user);
6  sb2.append("John");
7  String query = sb2.toString();
8  stat.executeQuery(query);
```

Fig. 2. Context sensitivity example

– poly: The poly qualifier expresses context sensitivity. poly is interpreted as tainted in some invocation contexts and as safe in other contexts.

The subtyping hierarchy becomes

safe <: poly <: tainted

and append and toString are typed as follows:

poly StringBuffer append(**poly** StringBuffer this, **poly** String s) {...}
poly String toString(**poly** StringBuffer this) {...}

The poly qualifiers must be interpreted according to invocation context. Intuitively, the role of *viewpoint adaptation* (which we elaborate upon shortly), is to interpret the poly qualifiers according to the invocation context. In Fig. 2, poly is interpreted as tainted at call sb1.append(user), and as safe at call sb2.append ("John"). As a result, the tainted argument in the call through sb1 does not propagate to sb2; thus, query at line 7 is typed safe, and the type error at line 8 is avoided.

The type of a poly field f is interpreted in the context of the receiver at the field access. If the receiver x is tainted, then x.f is tainted. If the receiver x is safe, then x.f is safe. An instance field can be tainted or poly, but it cannot be safe; this is necessary to ensure soundness.

Viewpoint adaptation is a concept from Universe Types [3]. Viewpoint adaptation of a type q' from the viewpoint of another type q, results in the adapted type q''. This is written as $q \triangleright q' = q''$. Viewpoint adaptation adapts fields, formal parameters, and method return values from the viewpoint of the receiver at the field access or method call.

The viewpoint adaptation operation is as follows:

$$\_ \triangleright \text{tainted} = \text{tainted} \qquad \_ \triangleright \text{safe} = \text{safe} \qquad q \triangleright \text{poly} = q$$

The underscore denotes a "don't care" value. Qualifiers tainted and safe do not depend on the viewpoint (context). Qualifier poly depends on the viewpoint; in fact, it adapts to that viewpoint (context).

2.3 Typing Rules

Fig. 3 shows the typing rules over a syntax in "named form", where the results of field accesses, method calls, and instantiations are immediately stored in a variable. Without loss of generality, we assume that methods have parameter this,

$$\frac{\text{(TNEW)}}{\Gamma \vdash x = \text{new } q \text{ C}} \quad \Gamma(x) = q_x \quad q <: q_x$$

$$\frac{\text{(TWRITE)}}{\Gamma \vdash y.\text{f} = x} \quad \Gamma(y) = q_y \quad typeof(\text{f}) = q_f \quad \Gamma(x) = q_x \quad q_x <: q_y \triangleright q_f$$

$$\frac{\text{(TASSIGN)}}{\Gamma \vdash x = y} \quad \Gamma(x) = q_x \quad \Gamma(y) = q_y \quad q_y <: q_x$$

$$\frac{\text{(TREAD)}}{\Gamma \vdash x = y.\text{f}} \quad \Gamma(y) = q_y \quad typeof(\text{f}) = q_f \quad \Gamma(x) = q_x \quad q_y \triangleright q_f <: q_x$$

$$\frac{\text{(TCALL)}}{\Gamma \vdash x = y.\text{m}(z)} \quad \begin{array}{l} \Gamma(y) = q_y \quad typeof(\text{m}) = q_{\text{this}}, q_p \rightarrow q_{\text{ret}} \quad \Gamma(x) = q_x \quad \Gamma(z) = q_z \\ q_y <: q_y \triangleright q_{\text{this}} \quad q_z <: q_y \triangleright q_p \quad q_y \triangleright q_{\text{ret}} <: q_x \end{array}$$

Fig. 3. Typing rules. Function *typeof* retrieves the SFlow types of fields and methods, Γ is a type environment that maps variables to SFlow qualifiers.

and exactly one other formal parameter. The SFlow type system is *orthogonal* to (i.e., independent of) the Java type system, which allows us to specify typing rules over type qualifiers q alone.

The rules create subtyping constraints at explicit assignments (e.g., x = y, x = y.f) and at implicit assignments (e.g., assignments from actual arguments to formal parameters). The rules for field access, (TREAD) and (TWRITE), adapt the field f from the viewpoint of the *receiver* y, and create the expected subtyping constraints. The rule for method call, (TCALL), adapts formal parameters this and p and return value ret from the viewpoint of the *receiver* y, and creates the subtyping constraints that capture flows from actual arguments to formal parameters, and from return value to the left-hand-side of the call assignment.

Let us return to the example in Fig. 2. Method append is polymorphic, i.e., it is typed as follows:

poly StringBuffer append(**poly** StringBuffer this, **poly** String s) {...}

Let sb1 be typed tainted. The call at line 5, namely sb1.append(user), accounts for the following constraint (for brevity, for the rest of the paper, we typically use only the variable, e.g., user, instead of the more verbose q_{user}):

$$\text{user} <: \text{s1} \triangleright \text{s} \quad \equiv \quad \text{user} <: \text{s1} \triangleright \text{poly} \quad \equiv \quad \text{user} <: \text{s1}$$

Since user and s1 are tainted, the call at line 5 type-checks. Now let sb2 be typed safe. The call at line 6, sb2.append("John"), accounts for constraint:

$$\text{"John"} <: \text{s2} \triangleright \text{s} \quad \equiv \quad \text{"John"} <: \text{s2} \triangleright \text{poly} \quad \equiv \quad \text{"John"} <: \text{s2}$$

Since string constant "John" and s2 are both safe, this type-checks as well. In the first context of invocation of append we interpreted poly s as tainted, while in the second context, we interpreted it as safe.

Method overriding is handled by the standard constraints for function subtyping. If m$'$ overrides m we require $typeof(\text{m}') <: typeof(\text{m})$ and thus,

$$(q_{\text{this}_{m'}}, q_{p_{m'}} \rightarrow q_{\text{ret}_{m'}}) \quad <: \quad (q_{\text{this}_m}, q_{p_m} \rightarrow q_{\text{ret}_m})$$

This entails $q_{\text{this}_m} <: q_{\text{this}_{m'}}$, $q_{p_m} <: q_{p_{m'}}$, and $q_{\text{ret}_{m'}} <: q_{\text{ret}_m}$.

As it is evident from these typing rules, we consider only explicit flows (i.e., data dependences). To the best of our knowledge, all effective static taint analyses [1,2,5,9,18–20] forgo implicit flows.

2.4 Composition with Reference Immutability

The reader has likely noticed that subtyping safe $<$: poly $<$: tainted is not always sound. Suppose the field f of class A is poly in the following example:

```
tainted B tf = ...;    safe A s = ...;
tainted A t = s;       // because of safe <: tainted
t.f = tf;              // t.f is tainted
safe B sf = s.f;       // s.f is safe, unsafe flow!
```

The program type-checks, but the tainted variable tf flows to safe variable sf. This is the known problem of subtyping in the presence of mutable references, also known as the issue with Java's covariant arrays [13].

The standard solution is to disallow subtyping for references [16]. This solution demands two sets of qualifiers, safe $<$: poly $<$: tainted for simple types (e.g., int,char), and Safe, Poly, Tainted for reference types. While subtyping is allowed for simple types, it is disallowed for reference types. Unfortunately, disallowing subtyping for reference types leads to imprecision, i.e., the type system rejects valid programs. It amounts to using *equality constraints* as opposed to subtyping constraints, and thus, propagating safe and tainted qualifiers bi-directionally, resulting in often unnecessary propagation [11].

We propose a solution using reference immutability, which allows limited subtyping and improves precision. It is a theorem that subtyping is safe when the reference on the left-hand-side of the assignment is an *immutable reference*, that is, the state of the referenced object, including its transitively reachable state, *cannot be mutated through this reference.*

We compose SFlow with ReIm, a reference immutability type system we developed in previous work [8]. We run ReImInfer [8], ReIm's inference tool, and obtain ReIm types for all variables. If the ReIm type of the left-hand-side of an assignment is readonly, i.e., it is guaranteed that this left-hand-side is immutable, we use a subtyping constraint in SFlow. Otherwise, i.e., if the ReIm type is not readonly, we use an equality constraint. For example, at (TREAD) x = y.f, if x is readonly, we use constraint $q_y \triangleright q_f <: q_x$; otherwise, we use constraint $q_y \triangleright q_f = q_x$. Due to space constraints, we do not describe the details of the type system. The dynamic semantics and soundness proof can be found in the accompanying technical report [7]. This composition approach achieves at least 20% precision improvement over the standard approach as shown in our previous work [11].

3 Type Inference

Type inference derives a *valid typing*, i.e., an assignment of qualifiers to program variables that type-checks with the rules in Fig. 3. If inference succeeds, then the program is safe, i.e., it is guaranteed that there is no flow from a source to a sink. If it fails, then a valid typing does not exist, meaning that there could be unsafe flow from a source to a sink.

Type inference leverages the framework we developed in [6]. It first computes a *set-based solution S*, which maps variables to *sets* of potential type qualifiers.

The key novelty over [6] is the use of *method summary constraints*, which refine the set-based solution, and help derive a valid typing.

3.1 Set-Based Solution

The set-based solution is a mapping S from variables to sets of qualifiers. The variables in the mapping can be (1) local variables, (2) parameters (including this), (3) fields, and (4) method returns. For example, $S(x) = \{poly, safe\}$ denotes the type of variable x can be poly, or safe, but not tainted. Programmer-annotated variables, including annotated library variables, are initialized to the singleton set that contains the programmer-provided qualifier. In SFlow, all sources and sinks are programmer-provided, i.e., sources and sinks are annotated as tainted and safe, respectively. Fields are initialized to $S(f) = \{tainted, poly\}$. All other variables are initialized to the maximal set of qualifiers, i.e., $S(x) = \{tainted, poly, safe\}$.

The inference creates constraints for all program statements according to the typing rules in Fig. 3. It takes into account ReIm: if the left-hand-side of the assignment is readonly, the inference creates a subtyping constraint; otherwise, it creates an equality constraint. Consider (TREAD) x = y.f. If x is readonly, the inference creates constraint $q_y \triangleright q_f <: q_x$; otherwise, it creates an equality constraint $q_y \triangleright q_f = q_x$. In the latter case, the inference actually creates two subtyping constraints that are equivalent to the equality constraint. In the above example, it creates $q_y \triangleright q_f <: q_x$ and $q_x <: q_y \triangleright q_f$.

Subsequently, the set-based solver iterates over these constraints, and runs SOLVECONSTRAINT(c) for each constraint c. SOLVECONSTRAINT(c) removes infeasible qualifiers from the set of variables that participate in c. It works as follows (for a more formal description, see [6]). Consider x = y.f again, and suppose x is readonly, thus creating the sole subtyping constraint $q_y \triangleright q_f <: q_x$. Suppose that before processing this constraint, we have $S(x) = \{poly\}$, $S(y) = \{tainted, poly, safe\}$, and $S(f) = \{tainted, poly\}$. The solver removes tainted from $S(y)$ because there do not exist $q_f \in S(f)$ and $q_x \in S(x)$ that satisfy $q_y \triangleright tainted <: q_x$. Similarly, tainted is removed from $S(f)$. After processing the constraint, S is updated to $S(x) = \{poly\}$, $S(y) = \{poly, safe\}$, and $S(f) = \{poly\}$. If the infeasible qualifier is the last element in $S(x)$, SOLVECONSTRAINT(c) keeps this qualifier in $S(x)$, and reports a *type error* at c (we keep the qualifier in order to produce better error reports: a type error x{tainted} <: y{safe} is more informative than x{} <: y{safe}).

The set-based solver iterates over the constraints and refines the sets until it reaches a fixpoint. There are two possible outcomes: (1) there are no type errors, and (2) there are one or more type errors. If the set-based solver arrives at type errors, this means that the programmer-provided sources and sinks are inconsistent, and the program cannot be typed. In other words, a type error indicates that there could be unsafe flow from a source to a sink.

Consider the Aliasing5 example from Ben Livshits' Stanford SecuriBench Micro benchmarks[2] in Fig. 4. foo is safe when b1 and b2 refer to distinct StringBuffer

---

[2] http://suif.stanford.edu/~livshits/work/securibench-micro/

```
1   void doGet(A this, ServletRequest request, ServletResponse response) {
2       StringBuffer buf = ...;
3       this.foo(buf,buf,request,response);
4   }
5   void foo(A this, StringBuffer b1, StringBuffer b2,
6           ServletRequest req, ServletResponse resp) {
7       String url = req.getParameter("url");
8       b1.append(url);
9       String str = b2.toString();
10      PrintWriter writer = resp.getWriter();
11      writer.print(str);
12  }
```

Line 3: $\boxed{\text{buf} = \text{this}_{doGet} \rhd \text{b1}}$ $\boxed{S(\text{buf}) = \{\text{tainted}\}}$

Line 4: $\boxed{\text{buf} <: \text{this}_{doGet} \rhd \text{b2}}$ $\boxed{S(\text{b2}) = \{\text{tainted}, \text{poly}\}}$

Line 7: $\boxed{\text{req} \rhd \textbf{tainted} <: \text{url}}$ $\boxed{S(\text{url}) = \{\text{tainted}\}}$

Line 8: $\boxed{\text{url} <: \text{b1} \rhd \textbf{poly}}$ $\boxed{S(\text{b1}) = \{\text{tainted}\}}$

Line 9: $\boxed{\text{b2} \rhd \textbf{poly} <: \text{str}}$ $\boxed{S(\text{str}) = \{\text{tainted}, \text{poly}\}}$

Line 11: $\boxed{\text{str} <: \text{writer} \rhd \textbf{safe}}$ $\boxed{\text{TYPE ERROR!}}$

Fig. 4. Aliasing5 example from Stanford SecuriBench Micro. The frame box beside each statement shows the corresponding constraints the statement generates. The oval boxes show propagation during the set-based solution. The constraint at 7 forces url to be tainted, and the constraint at 8 forces b1 to be tainted. The constraint at 3 forces buf to be tainted and the one at 4 forces b2 to be tainted or poly (i.e., the set-based solver removes safe from b2's set). The constraint at 9 then forces str to be tainted or poly. There is a TYPE ERROR at writer.print(str).

objects. However, when b1 and b2 are aliased, foo creates dangerous flow from source req.getParameter to a sink, the parameter of PrintWriter.print. Note that the constraint at line 3 is an equality constraint: b1 is mutated at b1.append(url), ReIm infers b1 as mutable, and hence the equality constraint. The set-based solver reports a type error at statement 11; the constraint at 11 is unsatisfiable as it requires that str is safe, which contradicts the finding that str is {tainted, poly}.

3.2 Valid Typing

The set-based solver removes many infeasible qualifiers and in many cases, it discovers type errors. In our experience, the set-based solver, which is worst-case quadratic and linear in practice, discovers the vast majority of type errors, and therefore it is useful on its own. Unfortunately, when the set-based solver terminates without type errors, it is unclear if a valid typing exists or not, and therefore, there is no guarantee of safety. The question is, how do we extract a valid typing, or conversely, show that a valid typing does not exist?

The key idea is to compute what we call *method summary constraints*, which remove additional qualifiers from the set-based solution. These constraints reflect the relations (subtyping or equality) between formal parameters (including this) and return values (ret). Such references are usually "connected" indirectly, e.g. this and ret can be connected through two constraints this <: x and x <: ret. Note that intuitively, the subtyping relation reflects flow: there is flow from this to x, there is flow from x to ret, and due to transitivity, there is flow from this to ret. Once we have computed the relations between formal parameters and return values of a method m, we connect the actual arguments to the left hand sides of the call assignment at calls to m. The computation of method summary constraints

```
 1: procedure RUNSOLVER
 2:   repeat
 3:     for each c in C do
 4:       SOLVECONSTRAINT(c)
 5:       if c is qₓ <: q_y ▷ q_f and S(f) is {poly} then        ▷ Case 1
 6:         Add qₓ <: q_y into C
 7:       else if c is qₓ ▷ q_f <: q_y and S(f) is {poly} then     ▷ Case 2
 8:         Add qₓ <: q_y into C
 9:       else if c is qₓ <: q_y then                            ▷ Case 3
10:         for each q_y <: q_z in C do add qₓ <: q_z to C end for
11:         for each q_w <: qₓ in C do add q_w <: q_y to C end for
12:         for each q_w <: q_a ▷ qₓ and q_a ▷ q_y <: q_z in C do   ▷ Case 4
13:           Add q_w <: q_z to C
14:         end for
15:       end if
16:     end for
17:   until S remains unchanged
18: end procedure
```

Fig. 5. Computation of method summary constraints. C is the set of constraints, it is initialized to the set of constraints for program statements, derived as described in Sect. 3.1 (recall that each equality constraint is written as two subtyping constraints). S is initialized to the result of the set-based solver. Cases 1 and 2 add $q_x <: q_y$ into C because $q_y \triangleright \text{poly}$ always yields q_y. Case 3 adds constraints due to transitivity; this case discovers constraints from formals to return values. Case 4 adds constraints between actual(s) and left-hand-side(s) at calls: if there are constraints $q_w <: q_a \triangleright q_x$ (flow from actual to formal) and $q_a \triangleright q_y <: q_z$ (flow from return value to left-hand-side), and also $q_x <: q_y$ (flow from formal to return value, usually discovered by Case 3), Case 4 adds $q_w <: q_z$. Note that line 4 calls SOLVECONSTRAINT(c): the solver infers new constraints, which remove additional infeasible qualifiers from S. This process repeats until S stays unchanged.

is presented in Fig. 5. As an example, consider the following code snippet:

```
class A {                    A y = ...;
  String f;                  PrintWriter writer = ...;
  String get()               String x = y.get();  y <: y ▷ this   y ▷ ret <: x
  {return this.f;}  this ▷ f <: ret    writer.print(x);   x <: writer ▷ safe
}
```

where generated constraints are shown in the frame boxes beside statements. The set-based solver yields $S(x) = \{\text{safe}\}$, $S(y) = \{\text{tainted}, \text{poly}, \text{safe}\}$, $S(\text{this}) = \{\text{poly}, \text{safe}\}$, $S(\text{ret}) = \{\text{poly}, \text{safe}\}$, and $S(f) = \{\text{poly}\}$. Case 2 in Fig. 5 creates this <: ret. This entails y ▷ this <: y ▷ ret since viewpoint adaptation preserves subtyping [11]. Case 3 combines this with constraints y <: y▷this and y▷ret <: x, yielding a new constraint y <: x. Because tainted and poly are not subtypes of safe, SOLVECONSTRAINT removes them from $S(y)$, and $S(y)$ becomes {safe}.

RUNSOLVER terminates either (1) with type errors, or (2) without type errors, just as the set-based solver. When it terminates without errors, SFlow-Infer types each variable x by picking the *maximal* element of $S(x)$, according to the following preference ranking: tainted > poly > safe. This *maximal typing* almost always type-checks. In the above example, typing $\Gamma(\mathsf{x}) = \Gamma(\mathsf{y}) =$ safe, $\Gamma(\mathsf{this}) = \Gamma(\mathsf{ret}) = \Gamma(\mathsf{f}) =$ poly type-checks; in contrast, the maximal typing extracted from the set-based solution, does not type-check. In our experiments, the maximal typing always type-checks, except for 2 constraints in one benchmark, jugjobs. It is a theorem that even if it does not type-check, the program is still safe, i.e., there is no flow from sources to sinks. We confirmed this for the 2 constraints in jugjobs.

The inference is dominated by the algorithm in Fig. 5, which has worst-case complexity of $O(n^3)$, where n is the size of the program (see [7] for details).

4 Handling of Reflection, Libraries and Frameworks

Reflection, libraries (standard and third-party) and frameworks (e.g., Struts, Spring, Hibernate) are the bane of static taint analysis. Yet they are ubiquitous in Java web applications. The type-based approach we espouse, handles these features safely and effortlessly.

Reflective Object Creation. Use of reflective object creation in web applications is widespread. Ignoring it, as some static analyses do, renders a static analysis useless. Consider the use of newInstance():

```
X x = (X) Class.forName("someInput").newInstance();
x.f = a;        // a is tainted, comes from source
y = x;
b = y.f;        // b is safe, flows to sink
```

If a points-to-based static analysis fails to handle newInstance(), the points-to sets of x and y will be empty, and the flow from a to b will be missed. On the other hand, handling of reflective object creation is difficult, expensive and often unsound.

We handle reflective object creation with newInstance() safely and effortlessly. The key is that SFlow tracks dependences between variables through subtyping, which *obviates the need to abstract heap objects*. It can be shown that, roughly speaking, if x flows to y, then x <: y holds. In the above example, x <: y holds and subsequently a <: b holds. SFlowInfer reports a type error caused by the flow from tainted a to safe b.

Libraries. Our inference analysis is modular. Thus, it can analyze any given set of classes L. If there is an unknown callee in L, e.g. a library method whose source code is unavailable, the analysis assumes typing poly, poly $\rightarrow$ poly for the callee. This typing conservatively propagates tainted arguments to the receiver and left-hand-side of the call assignment. Similarly, it propagates a safe left-hand-side to the receiver and arguments at the call. E.g., String.toUpperCase() is typed as

    poly String toUpperCase(**poly** String this)

At call s2 = s1.toUpperCase() we have constraint s1 ▷ poly <: s2 or equivalently s1 <: s2. Thus, a tainted s1 propagates to s2, and a safe s2 propagates to s1.

We apply the poly, poly $\rightarrow$ poly typing to all methods in the standard library, third-party libraries (e.g., apache-tomcat, xalan) and frameworks, with several exceptions described in the next section.

Frameworks. Most Java web applications are built on top of one or more *frameworks* such as Struts, Spring, Hibernate, and etc. The problem with these frameworks is twofold. First, they contain "hidden" sources and sinks, i.e., sources and sinks deep in framework code that affect the public API. For example, Hibernate (version 2.1) contains a public method Session.find(String s), where s flows to query at sink prepareStatement(query). This happens deep in the code of Hibernate. We run a version of our inference analysis and "lift" such hidden sources and sinks to the return values and parameters of the public methods they affect. In the above example, Session.find() is typed as

> **poly** List find(**poly** Session this, **safe** String s)

Callers to find() in application code must handle the argument of find() as safe, otherwise it may lead to an SQL injection vulnerability as described by Livshits and Lam [9]. To the best of our knowledge, no other taint analysis attempts to "lift" these "hidden" sources and sinks in the frameworks.

Second, these frameworks rely heavily on reflection and callbacks, which must be handled in the analysis. These are notorious issues for dataflow and points-to based analysis, which usually relies on reachability analysis. Our type-based analysis handles these features with the method overriding constraints.

As an illustrating example, Struts defines framework classes ActionForm and Action and method Action.execute(ActionForm form). The application built on top of Struts defines numerous xxxForm classes extending ActionForm, and numerous xxxAction classes extending Action. Framework code performs the following (roughly):

1. Action a = (Action) Class.forName("inputClass").newInstance(); a instantiates one user-defined xxxAction class.
2. ActionForm f = (ActionForm) Class.forName("inputForm").newInstance(); similarly, this instantiates one user-defined xxxForm class.
3. Framework populates the xxxForm object with *tainted* values from sources.
4. Framework calls a.execute(f), a callback to user-defined xxxAction.execute.

In our type-based analysis Action.execute() is typed as

> execute(**poly** Action this, **tainted** ActionForm form)

The method overriding constraints (recall Sect. 2.3) propagate tainted to the form parameter of each execute method in user-defined subclasses. As a result, all values retrieved through get methods from forms in user code are tainted, which accurately reflects that the xxxForm object is populated with tainted values.

5   Empirical Results

SFlow and SFlowInfer are implemented within our type inference framework [6, 8], which is built on top of the Checker Framework (CF) [15]. The type inference framework, including SFlow and SFlowInfer, is publicly available at http://code.google.com/p/type-inference/.

The implementation is evaluated on 13 relatively large Java web applications, used in previous work [9,18,20]. We run SFlowInfer on these benchmarks on a

Benchmark	#Line	Time (s)	[Parameter,SQL]			[Parameter,XSS]		
			Type-1	Type-2	FP	Type-1	Type-2	FP
blojsom	12830	15.1	0	0	0 (0%)	0	0	0 (0%)
blueblog	4139	7.5	0	0	0 (0%)	0	0	0 (0%)
friki	1843	4.5	0	0	0 (0%)	0	0	0 (0%)
gestcv	7422	10.1	1	0	0 (0%)	0	8	2 (20%)
jboard	17405	22.2	3	0	0 (0%)	0	0	0 (0%)
jspwiki	83329	126.9	0	0	25 (100%)	73	12	20 (19%)
jugjobs	4044	18.7	0	0	0 (0%)	0	0	0 (0%)
pebble	42542	50.3	0	0	0 (0%)	2	0	0 (0%)
personalblog	9943	17.6	6	0	0 (0%)	3	21	2 (8%)
photov	126886	640.2	46	0	0 (0%)	0	0	0 (0%)
roller	81171	213.4	0	0	0 (0%)	21	2	0 (0%)
snipsnap	73295	87.3	0	0	3 (100%)	1	0	0 (0%)
webgoat	8474	9.6	10	0	0 (0%)	0	0	0 (0%)
Average					(**15%**)			(**4%**)

Fig. 6. Inference results for [*Parameter, SQL*] and [*Parameter, XSS*]. **Time** shows the running times of SFlowInfer for [*Parameter, SQL*] in seconds; running times for other configurations are essentially the same. The multicolumns show numbers of **Type-1**, **Type-2**, and False-positive (**FP**) type errors for the two configurations; note that a large number of benchmarks have 0 type errors, i.e., they are proven safe.

server with Intel® Xeon® CPU X3460 @2.80GHz and 8 GB RAM (the maximal heap size is set to 2 GB). The software environment consists of Oracle JDK 1.6 and the Checker Framework 1.1.5 on GNU/Linux 3.2.0.

Experiments. We use the sources and sinks described in detail in Livshits and Lam [9,10]. In addition, we use 59 sources and sinks in API methods of Struts, Spring, and Hibernate, discovered as described in Sect. 4. There are 3 categories of sources [9]: *Parameter manipulation*, *Header manipulation*, and *Cookie poisoning*. There are 4 categories of sinks [9]: *SQL injection*, *HTTP splitting*, *Cross-site scripting (XSS)*, and *Path traversal*. These sources and sinks are added to the annotated JDK, Struts, Spring, and Hibernate, which is easily done with the CF. Once these annotated libraries are created, individual web applications are analyzed without any input from the user. We run the benchmarks with all 12 configurations. However, for space reasons, we report only on 2 configurations: [*Parameter manipulation*, *SQL*] and [*Parameter manipulation*, *XSS*].

Fig. 6 presents the sizes of the benchmarks as well as the running times of SFlowInfer in seconds. The running times attest to efficiency — for all but 1 benchmark, the analysis completes in less than 4 minutes; we believe that these running times can be improved.

We examined the type errors reported by SFlowInfer, and classified them as **Type-1**, **Type-2**, or False-positive (**FP**). **Type-1** errors reflect direct flow from a source to a sink. The following code, adapted from webgoat, is a Type-1 error:

```
String u = request.getParameter("user");
String s = "SELECT * FROM users WHERE name = '" + u;
stat.executeQuery(s);
```

Tool Name	AppScan Source	Fortify SCA	FlowDroid	SFlowInfer
$\sqrt{}$, higher is better	14	17	26	28
$\times$, lower is better	5	4	4	9
$\bigcirc$, lower is better	14	11	2	0
Precision $p = \sqrt{}/(\sqrt{} + \times)$	74%	81%	86%	76%
Recall $r = \sqrt{}/(\sqrt{} + \bigcirc)$	50%	61%	93%	100%
F-measure $2pr/(p + r)$	0.60	0.70	0.89	0.86

Fig. 7. Summary of comparison with other taint analysis tools ($\sqrt{}$ = correct warning, $\times$ = false warning, $\bigcirc$ = missed flow)

Type-2 errors reflect key-value dependences. The following code, adapted from personalblog, is a Type-2 error:

```
HashMap map = ...; PrintWriter out = ...;
String id = request.getParameter("id");
User user = (User) map.get(id);
out.print(user.getName());
```

The tainted id is used as a key to retrieve the user from the map, then user.getName() is sent to a safe sink (the parameter of PrintWriter.print()). This is a dangerous flow according to the semantics of noninterference, because the tainted value of the key affects the value of the safe sink. We classified as **FP** all errors that would not lead to flow violations. Most false positives are due to our conservative assumption about unknown libraries, e.g., that a tainted argument always propagate to the left-hand-side (see Sect. 4). The results are presented in Fig. 6. Additional results and nontrivial examples of type errors can be found in [7].

Comparison. Direct comparison with TAJ [20], F4F [18], and ANDROMEDA [19] is impossible because the analysis tools are proprietary, and therefore unavailable. Instead, we run SFlowInfer on DroidBench [5], which is a suit of 39 Android apps, and compare with three other taint analysis tools – AppScan Source [2], Fortify SCA [1], and FlowDroid [5], using the results presented by Fritz et al. [5]. The comparison with AppScan Source is an indirect comparison with TAJ, F4F, and ANDROMEDA, because these analyses are built into AppScan Source.

For space reasons, Fig. 7, which borrows the format from Fritz et al. [5], only presents the summary of the comparison. Detailed comparison results can be found in our technical report [7]. Although SFlowInfer performs slightly worse in terms of precision (due to the conservativeness of the type system), it outperforms all other tools in terms of recall, i.e. it detects more vulnerabilities than all other tools. Commercial tools AppScan Source and Fortify SCA detect less than 61% of all vulnerabilities, while SFlowInfer detects 100%. FlowDroid, which targets Android apps, not Java web applications, is more precise than SFlowInfer. This is because it uses a flow-sensitive analysis, which unfortunately can be costly.

6   Related Work

Unfortunately, we cannot include all related work on information flow control. More related work is discussed in the accompanying technical report [7].

The most closely related to ours is the work by Shankar et al. [17]. They present a type system for detecting string format vulnerabilities in C programs. The type system has two type qualifiers, tainted and untainted; polymorphism is not part of the core system. They include a type inference engine built on top of CQual [4]. CQual relies on dependence graphs built using points-to analysis. In contrast, SFlow and SFlowInfer handle polymorphism naturally, as it is built into the type system using the poly qualifier and viewpoint adaptation. In addition, we compose with reference immutability, thus improving precision significantly. SFlow and SFlowInfer handle reflection and frameworks seamlessly.

Tripp et al. [20] present TAJ, a points-to-based taint analysis for industrial applications. In order to handle Struts, TAJ treats all Action classes as entry points. In addition, it simulates the passing of all subclasses of ActionForm to Action.execute, by generating a constructor, which assigns tainted values to all fields of the subclasses. In contrast, our inference analysis handles Struts by annotating the ActionForm parameter of Action.execute as tainted. Our handling is simpler and equally precise. Finally, according to Sridharan et al. [18], TAJ's reflection modeling is not scalable. In contrast, our type-based analysis does not need abstract objects, and handles reflection seamlessly and safely.

Livshits and Lam [9] present a static analysis based on a scalable and precise points-to analysis. In contrast, our inference analysis is type-based and modular. Similarly to TAJ, they handle reflection by trying to infer the value of string s at forName(s).newInstance() calls. In addition, Livshits and Lam's analysis does not handle frameworks, which are essential for web applications.

Sridharan et al. [18] present F4F, a system for taint analysis of framework-based web applications. In order to handle frameworks, F4F analyzes the application code and XML configuration files to construct a specification, which summarizes reflection and callback-driven behavior. In contrast, our analysis handles frameworks by inferring or adding annotations to sources and sinks in the frameworks, which propagate to user code through subtyping. Tripp et al. [19] present ANDROMEDA, a demand-driven analysis that improves on F4F.

Volpano et al. [21] and Myers [12] present type systems for secure information flow. These systems are substantially more complex and powerful than SFlow. They focus on type checking and do not include type inference, or include only local type inference. In contrast, SFlowInfer handles large web applications.

7   Conclusions

We have presented SFlow, a context-sensitive type system for secure information flow, and SFlowInfer, the corresponding cubic inference analysis. Our approach handled reflective object creation, libraries and frameworks safely and effectively. Experiments on 13 Java web applications showed that SFlowInfer is scalable and precise.

Acknowledgements. We thank the anonymous reviewers for their helpful feedback. This work was supported by NSF Career Award CCF-0642811 and a Google Faculty Research Award (February 2013).

References

1. HP fortify static code analyzer (2013),
   http://www8.hp.com/us/en/software-solutions/
   software.html?compURI=1338812#.Uk4YZWRhsyk
2. IBM security AppScan (2013),
   http://www-03.ibm.com/software/products/us/en/appscan/
3. Dietl, W., Müller, P.: Universes: Lightweight ownership for JML. Journal of Object Technology 4(8), 5–32 (2005)
4. Foster, J.S., Fähndrich, M., Aiken, A.: A theory of type qualifiers. In: PLDI, pp. 192–203 (May 1999)
5. Fritz, C., Arzt, S., Rasthofer, S., Bodden, E., Bartel, A., Klein, J., le Traon, Y., Octeau, D., McDaniel, P.: Highly precise taint analysis for Android applications. EC SPRIDE Technical Report TUD-CS-2013-0113 (2013),
   http://www.bodden.de/pubs/TUD-CS-2013-0113.pdf
6. Huang, W., Dietl, W., Milanova, A., Ernst, M.D.: Inference and checking of object ownership. In: Noble, J. (ed.) ECOOP 2012. LNCS, vol. 7313, pp. 181–206. Springer, Heidelberg (2012)
7. Huang, W., Dong, Y., Milanova, A.: Type-based taint analysis for Java web applications. Rensselaer Polytechnic Institute Technical Report RPI-CS-13-02 (2013),
   http://www.cs.rpi.edu/~huangw5/docs/RPI-CS-13-02.pdf
8. Huang, W., Milanova, A., Dietl, W., Ernst, M.D.: ReIm & ReImInfer: Checking and inference of reference immutability and method purity. In: OOPSLA, pp. 879–896 (2012)
9. Livshits, V.B., Lam, M.S.: Finding security vulnerabilities in Java applications with static analysis. In: USENIX Security (2005)
10. Livshits, V.B., Lam, M.S.: Finding security vulnerabilities in Java applications with static analysis. Technical Report. Stanford University (2005),
    http://suif.stanford.edu/~livshits/papers/tr/webappsec_tr.pdf
11. Milanova, A., Huang, W.: Composing information flow type systems with reference immutability. In: FTfJP (2013)
12. Myers, A.C.: JFlow: Practical mostly-static information flow control. In: POPL, pp. 228–241 (1999)
13. Myers, A.C., Bank, J.A., Liskov, B.: Parameterized types for Java. In: POPL (1997)
14. OWASP. Top ten project (2013),
    https://www.owasp.org/index.php/Category:OWASP_Top_Ten_Project
15. Papi, M.M., Ali, M., Correa Jr., T.L., Perkins, J.H., Ernst, M.D.: Practical pluggable types for Java. In: ISSTA, pp. 201–212 (2008)
16. Sampson, A., Dietl, W., Fortuna, E.: EnerJ: Approximate data types for safe and general low-power computation. In: PLDI, pp. 164–174 (2011)
17. Shankar, U., Talwar, K., Foster, J.S., Wagner, D.: Detecting format string vulnerabilities with type qualifiers. In: USENIX Security (2001)
18. Sridharan, M., Artzi, S., Pistoia, M., Guarnieri, S., Tripp, O., Berg, R.: F4F: Taint analysis of framework-based web applications. In: OOPSLA, pp. 1053–1068 (2011)
19. Tripp, O., Pistoia, M., Cousot, P., Cousot, R., Guarnieri, S.: ANDROMEDA: Accurate and scalable security analysis of web applications. In: Cortellessa, V., Varró, D. (eds.) FASE 2013. LNCS, vol. 7793, pp. 210–225. Springer, Heidelberg (2013)
20. Tripp, O., Pistoia, M., Fink, S.J., Sridharan, M., Weisman, O.: TAJ: Effective taint analysis of web applications. In: PLDI, pp. 87–97 (2009)
21. Volpano, D., Smith, G., Irvine, C.: A sound type system for secure flow analysis. Journal of Computer Security, 167–187 (1996)

Mining the Categorized Software Repositories to Improve the Analysis of Security Vulnerabilities

Alireza Sadeghi, Naeem Esfahani, and Sam Malek

Department of Computer Science
George Mason University
{asadeghi,nesfaha2,smalek}@gmu.edu

Abstract. Security has become the Achilles' heel of most modern software systems. Techniques ranging from the manual inspection to automated static and dynamic analyses are commonly employed to identify security vulnerabilities prior to the release of the software. However, these techniques are time consuming and cannot keep up with the complexity of ever-growing software repositories (e.g., Google Play and Apple App Store). In this paper, we aim to improve the status quo and increase the efficiency of static analysis by mining relevant information from vulnerabilities found in the categorized software repositories. The approach relies on the fact that many modern software systems are developed using rich *application development frameworks (ADF)*, allowing us to raise the level of abstraction for detecting vulnerabilities and thereby making it possible to classify the types of vulnerabilities that are encountered in a given category of application. We used open-source software repositories comprising more than 7 million lines of code to demonstrate how our approach can improve the efficiency of static analysis, and in turn, vulnerability detection.

Keywords: Security Vulnerability, Mining Software Repositories, Software Analysis.

1 Introduction

According to the Symantec's Norton report [1], in 2012 the annual financial loss due to cybercrime exceeded $110 billion globally. An equally ominous report from Gartner [2] predicts 10 percent yearly growth in cybercrime-related financial loss through 2016. This growth is partly driven by the new security threats targeted at emerging platforms, such as Google Android and Apple iPhone, that provision vibrant open-access software repositories, often referred to as *app markets*.

By providing a medium for reaching a large consumer market at a nominal cost, app markets have leveled the software industry, allowing small entrepreneurs to compete head-to-head against prominent software development companies. The result has been a highly vibrant ecosystem of application software, but the paradigm shift has also given rise to a whole host of security

S. Gnesi and A. Rensink (Eds.): FASE 2014, LNCS 8411, pp. 155–169, 2014.

issues [1]. Numerous culprits are at play here, and some are not even technical, such as the general lack of an overseeing authority in the case of open markets and inconsequential punishment for those caught provisioning applications with vulnerabilities or malicious capabilities.

From the standpoint of application security, the state-of-the-practice needs to move away from the reactive model of patching the security vulnerabilities to proactive model of catching them prior to product release [3]. One approach is to manually inspect the security of application software prior to its release, which is an expensive and error-prone process. Alternatively, as a step toward addressing the above issues, static code analysis is gaining popularity for automatically finding security problems in application software [4].

While more efficient than manual inspection, the ability to improve the efficiency of static code analysis is gaining prominence for two reasons: (1) App market operators and overseeing authorities need to employ source code analysis techniques in large scale. On September 26, 2012 Android team unveiled that Google Play hosts 675,000 apps [5]. In less than 10 months, the number of apps in Google Play hit 1,000,000, meaning that more than 1,000 apps were added per day during that time period. On top of this, thousands of apps are updated every day that also need to be analyzed. (2) Recent research [6] has shown the benefit of continuously running static analysis tools in *real-time* and as programmers are developing the code, thereby helping them catch vulnerabilities earlier in the development phase. In such settings, even a slight improvement in efficiency is highly desirable and sought-after.

An opportunity to tackle this issue is presented by the fact that software products are increasingly organized into categorized repositories, where each item is mapped to a flat or hierarchical category. Some examples are SourceForge for open source and Google Play for Android applications. Other than facilitating the users in searching and browsing, categorized repositories have shown to be good predictors of the common features found within software of a particular category [7].

In this paper, we explore the utility of categorized repositories in informing the security inspection and analysis of software applications. The fact that the majority of apps provisioned on such repositories are built using a common *application development framework (ADF)* presents us with an additional opportunity. The information encoded in the source code of software developed on top of an ADF (e.g., Android) is richer than information encoded in the source code of traditional software (e.g., one developed from scratch in Java or C++). The reason for this is that an app developed on top of an ADF leverages libraries, services, and APIs provisioned by the ADF that disclose a significant amount of information about the app's behavior/functionality. This information can be used for various purposes, including security assessment, since many of the security issues encountered in modern software are due to the wrong usage of ADF [1]. In this paper, we show how this information can be used to build a predictor for vulnerabilities one may find in the app of a particular category.

This result is important, as it allows us to improve the efficiency of static analysis techniques for security assessment of software.

Running all possible static analysis rules, which encode patterns of vulnerability one may find in the code, on an application software is a time consuming and resource intensive process. For instance, in our experiments, in some cases it took up to 5.4 hours and 1.3 hours to statically analyze a single Java and Android application, respectively. Given an app belonging to a given category, we are able to use our predictor to focus the analysis on the vulnerabilities that are commonly encountered in that category. The predictor helps us pick and apply the static analysis rules that are empirically shown to be effective for the different categories of apps.

Our experimental results for Android apps that make extensive use of a particular ADF have been very positive. Our approach improved the efficiency of static analysis in the case of Android apps by 68%, while keeping the vulnerability detection rate at 100%. The results are useful, although not as significant, for plain Java applications that do not make use of any ADF, leading to efficiency improvement of 37%, while 4% of vulnerabilities are missed.

The remainder of this paper is organized as follows. Section 2 provides the required background as well as motivation for this work. Section 3 outlines the overview of our approach, while Section 4 describes the details. Sections 5 and 6 describe the research experimental setup, results, and analysis. Section 7 outlines the threats to validity of our experiments. Finally, the paper concludes with a discussion of related research and our future work.

2   Background and Motivation

Static analysis entails analysis of computer software without actually executing the software. While static analysis techniques originated in the compiler community for optimization of source code [8], they have found new applications in the past decade, as they have also shown to be effective for finding vulnerabilities in the source code [4]. Due to the complexity of statically reasoning about source code, static analysis is usually performed on an abstract model of code, such as control flow or data flow. The type of analysis done depends on the types of vulnerabilities that one aims to find. In this research, we have used three static analysis techniques for detecting vulnerabilities in Android apps: content, data flow, and control flow analysis

Content analysis deals with the pre-specified values that are known to create vulnerabilities in a program. By detecting "bad" content, the vulnerability can be discovered and prevented. For instance, a well-known attack against any phone app with communication capabilities is to trick that app to communicate (e.g., call, text message, etc.) with premium-rate numbers, which can be prevented by detecting the pattern of premium-rate numbers.

Data flow analysis considers the flow of information in the system tracking how data from input sources, such as phone identification, user input, and network interface lead to to output sinks. Data flow analysis is an effective approach

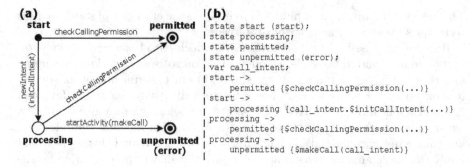

Fig. 1. An example of a sequence pattern used by control flow analysis to detect privilege escalation vulnerability: (a) state model representing the pattern and (b) realization of the pattern as a rule in Fortify

for detection of information leak or malicious input injection vulnerabilities by identifying unsafe sinks and input values respectively. Android apps have plenty of vulnerabilities that can be detected by this approach. In a recent study, Enck et al. [9] found that about 17% of the top free Android apps on the Google Play market transmit private user information, such as the phone's ID or location information over the web. They also reported that some apps log this private information to the phone's shared log stream, which is accessible to other apps running on the phone.

Control flow analysis entails processing the sequence of program execution, such as method calls. When a vulnerability can be modeled as a sequence of actions, we use control flow analysis. In this case, static analysis determines whether program execution can follow a certain sequence of actions that lead to a vulnerable status. For instance, control flow analysis can be used to detect privilege escalation in Android apps. Privilege escalation occurs when a malicious app exploits a second app to access resources that it does not have permission.

Fig. 1a depicts a control flow sequence pattern that we have developed for detecting privilege escalation vulnerability. Control flow sequence patterns model the transition of the system from a start state to two final states (one for error and one for success) through several possible intermediate states. The error state in Fig. 1a is a result of a flow in the program, where *startActivity* occurs without checking the permission of the calling application (by calling *checkCallingPermission* method). Fig. 1b shows the realization of this pattern as a rule in Fortify Static Code Analysis environment [10].

Fortify is a powerful static analysis tool, however, there are plenty of analysis tools that could reveal different kinds of vulnerabilities. Ware and Fox [11], used eight different static analysis tools (namely Checkstyle [12], Eclipse TPTP [13], FindBugs [14], Fortify [10], Jlint [15], Lint4j [16], PMD [17], and QJ-Pro [18]) to identify the vulnerabilities in Java projects. Then they compared the result of using these tools side-by-side. Among 50 distinct vulnerabilities detected by combination of eight tools, no individual tool could detect more than 27 distinct items. This implies that using a single tool increases the chance of missing vulnerabilities (i.e., having false negatives). Therefore, one should apply various

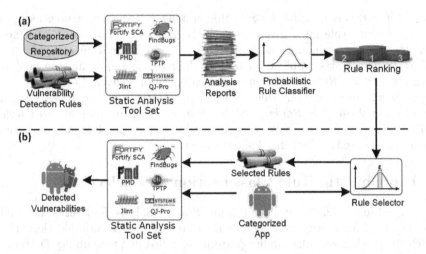

Fig. 2. Overview of the approach: (a) rank rules and (b) efficient vulnerability analysis

tools with many detection rules. However, this affects the analysis time and hampers the efficiency. This is exactly the challenge that we are aiming to resolve in this paper. In the next section, we provide an overview of our approach, which prioritizes the rules based on the likelihood of detecting vulnerabilities. Applying rules based on their priorities improves the efficiency of static analysis.

3 Approach Overview

Fig. 2 depicts an overview of our approach. *Categorized Repository* of software applications is the first input to our framework. In this repository, each application is labeled with a predefined class or category. Here, we assume such categorized applications can be gathered from on-line repositories (e.g., F-Droid and SourceForge) without any classification effort. Otherwise, machine learning techniques could be used to find the category of each application [7].

The second input to our framework is *Vulnerability Detection Rules*, which define the interesting patterns in the source code. Since our research focus is on security issues, we are interested in the rules that define patterns of vulnerability in the code.

Static Analysis Tool Set inspects the code repository and looks for any instance that matches the patterns defined in the rules. The result is an *Analysis Report*. *Analysis Report* consists of all locations in the code that are detected as potential vulnerabilities. Static analysis recurs for each application in the repository and generates the corresponding report.

The generated list of latent vulnerabilities for a categorized repository of applications serves as our training data set. Given this data, the *Probabilistic Rule Classifier* ranks each vulnerability based on its frequency in the *Analysis Report*. In this regard, *Probabilistic Rule Classifier* applies conditional probability to find the likelihood of occurrence of each vulnerability in each category.

The result of this is *Rule Ranking*. In this ranking, a frequency score is assigned to each security rule for a given category. Higher score means that it is more likely for the corresponding rule to detect a vulnerability in that category.

Fig. 2b depicts the application of *Rule Ranking* in improving the analysis of vulnerabilities. *Rule Selector* uses the category of a given *Categorized App* and picks the most efficient rules from *Vulnerability Detection Rules* for that category based on *Rule Ranking*. *Static Analysis Tool Set* uses *Selected Rules* to efficiently analyze the *Categorized App* and detect its possible vulnerabilities, which are reported as *Detected Vulnerabilities*.

4   Probabilistic Rule Classification and Selection

As depicted in Fig. 2, the result of running Static Analysis Tool Set is the Analysis Report. This report contains the application's source code locations that match the predefined vulnerability patterns specified in Vulnerability Detection Rules. The tool set tries all the rules and finds all matches in the source code. However, some of the rules may not match at all. We depict the set of all Vulnerability Detection Rules as R and the set of rules where at least one match has been found for them as M. If we know these rules upfront, we can improve the efficiency of static analysis by removing the irrelevant rules (i.e., $\overline{M} = R - M$). We call this rule reduction.

We can extend our definition by considering the categorical information. Applications categorized in the same class have some common features implemented by similar source code patterns and API calls to common libraries [7]. Consequently, it is more likely for a set of applications in a given category $c \in C$ (where C is the set of all categories) to have common vulnerabilities. We use this insight and extend our definition as follows: M_c is the set of rules that are matched at least once inside an application with category c.

It takes only one false positive to include the corresponding rule r in M_c. As the number of projects in the category and the number of files in the projects increases, it becomes more likely for all the rules to be included in M_c due to false positives, hence M_c converges to R. In other words, for each rule some kind of matching (which may be a false positive) is found. This is the problem with simply checking the membership of rule r in M_c as the binary measure of relevance of rule r to category c. We need a measure that expresses the likelihood of rule r being relevant to a given category c. This is the classical definition of conditional probability of $P(r|c)$. Calculating this value helps us to confine the static analysis rules for each application category to the rules that detect widespread vulnerability in that category.

By applying Bayes Theorem [19] to the Analysis Reports (recall Fig. 2), we can calculate $P(r|c)$, indicating the probability of a given rule matching an application from a category:

$$P(r|c) = \frac{P(c|r) \times P(r)}{P(c)} \tag{1}$$

Here, $P(c)$ is the probability of an application belonging to a category c, calculated via dividing the number of applications belonging to category c by the total number of applications under study. $P(r)$ is the probability of a rule r matching, calculated via dividing the number of matches for rule r by the total number of matches for all rules on all applications. Finally, $P(c|r)$ is the probability that a given application category c have the rule r matching, calculated via dividing the total number of times applications of category c were matched with rule r by the total number of matches for applications of that category.

As we described earlier $P(r|c)$ is used by the Rule Selector to reduce the number of rules used in static analysis. We can exclude a rule r from the static analysis of an application belonging to category c, when $P(r|c) \leq \epsilon$, where ϵ is a user-defined threshold indicating the desired level of rule reduction. We indicate the set of excluded rules for category c as E_c, and in turn, assess the reduction in the number of rules for category c as following:

$$Reduction_c = (|E_c|/|R|) \times 100 \qquad (2)$$

The value selected for the threshold presents a trade-off between the reduction of rules (i.e., the improvement in efficiency) and the coverage of static analysis. As more rules are removed, the static analysis is done faster, but the coverage decreases, increasing the chances of missing a vulnerability in the code. We will discuss the selection of threshold in Section 6.

5 Experiment Setup

The first step for using our approach is to populate Categorized Repository and Vulnerability Detection Rules (depicted as the two inputs in Fig. 2) with a set of application (denoted as set App) and a set of rules (recall R from Section 4), respectively. In this section, we describe how we collected App and R for our evaluation purposes and set up the experiments. We evaluated our approach on applications developed using Java and Android (as a representative ADF).[1]

We considered applications with two characteristics in the evaluation process: categorized and open-source. The first characteristic is the basis of our hypothesis and almost all App repositories (e.g., F-Droid and Google Play) support it. The second characteristic is based on the requirements of some static analysis tools (e.g., Fortify) and manual inspection. Among the available repositories, the best candidates for Java and Android are Source Forge and F-Droid, respectively. The additional benefit of using Source Forge and F-Droid together is that they have categorized the applications very similarly, allowing us to compare the results from these repositories. Table 1 shows the number of applications gathered from each category. We depict the set of applications in the same category c as App_c. Categories with two labels (one in parentheses) indicate alternative category

---

[1] Research artifacts and experimental data are available at
http://www.sdalab.com/projects/infovul

Table 1. Number of application in each category

C_ID	Category	Java	Android
c1	Business-Enterprise	47	-
c2	Communications (Phone)	55	14
c3	Development	54	17
c4	Game	30	51
c5	Graphics	29	-
c6	Home-Education	51	21
c7	Internet	30	53
c8	Multimedia (Audio-Video)	51	51
c9	Navigation	-	32
c10	Office	-	101
c11	Reading	-	17
c12	Science-Engineering	42	-
c13	Security-Utilities	17	-
c14	System	35	95
c15	Wallpaper	-	8
Total Number of Applications		441	460

Table 2. Experiment environment statistics

Experiment Stats	Java	Android
Total Lines of Code	6,166,755	1,360,881
Number of Categories	11	11
Number of Exclusive Rules	156	50
Total Number of Vulnerabilities	38,312	2,633

names used in the two repositories. For instance, the *Multimedia* category in Android, is called *Audio/Video* category in Java.

We used HP Fortify [10] as the main static analysis tool (recall *Static Analysis Tool Set* from Fig. 2). While Fortify provides a set of built-in rules for various programming languages, it also supports customized rules, which are composed by third-parties for specific purposes. For Java we utilized built-in rules provided by Fortify, while for Android we used rules provided by Enck et al. [9]. However, as we mentioned in Section 2, a single tool has a high chance of missing some of the vulnerabilities. Hence, we also used FindBugs [14], Jlint [15], and PMD [17] to reinforce the static analysis and reduce the false negative rate.

We ran Static Analysis Tool Set with the inputs discussed above to detect vulnerabilities in the experiments and prepare Analysis Report. The results are summarized in Table 2. We then fed the Analysis Report to Probabilistic Rule Classifier to calculate the Rule Ranking for each category. Before delving into the effects of this ranking on the static analysis, which is presented in Section 6, we provide some additional insights about the generated Analysis Report in this section. To that end, we extracted the detected vulnerabilities in each category from Analysis Reports to profile the applications in our study. However, since the number of applications under study in each category (i.e., $|App_c|$) are

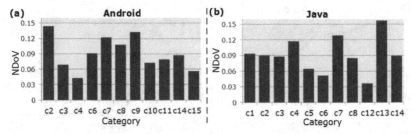

Fig. 3. Normalized Density of Vulnerabilities ($NDoV$) based on application categories for different domains: (a) Android and (b) Java

different, the raw measurements are misleading. Therefore, we define the *Density of Vulnerability* (DoV_c) metric for a given category c as follows:

$$DoV_c = \frac{\sum_{r \in R} \sum_{a \in App_c} |V_{r,a}|}{|App_c|} \qquad (3)$$

Here, $V_{r,a}$ is the set of vulnerabilities in the application a, which are detected by applying rule r. Since the total number of vulnerabilities may be different for Android and Java, the DoV_c is not comparable between the two domains. Therefore, we define *Normalized Density of Vulnerability* ($NDoV_c$) for a given category c as follows:

$$NDoV_c = \frac{DoV_c}{\sum_{c \in C} DoV_c} \qquad (4)$$

Fig. 3, which is practically the probability distribution of the vulnerabilities in the two experiments, presents $NDoV_c$ values for Android and Java domains. In Android domain, *Communication* (c2) and *Game* (c4) are the most vulnerable and safest categories respectively. This result is reasonable, as the applications in the *Communication* category call many security-relevant APIs (e.g., *Telephony*), while applications in the *Game* category mostly call benign APIs (e.g., *Graphic*). We observe similar trends for Java domain, where *Security-Utilities* (c13) and *Science-Engineering* (c12) have the highest and lowest vulnerability rates, respectively. The results show that the different categories have starkly different levels of vulnerability.

6 Evaluation

The ultimate contribution of our research is to improve the efficiency of software security analysis. Therefore, evaluation of our approach entails measuring the efficiency improvement from using the suggested ranking. Additionally, we want to investigate our hypothesis that the abstractions afforded by ADF indeed enable further efficiency gains.

As you may recall from Section 4, the value of ϵ presents a trade-off between the reduction of rules and the coverage of static analysis. If ϵ is too low, reduction, and in turn, improvement in efficiency would be insignificant. On the other

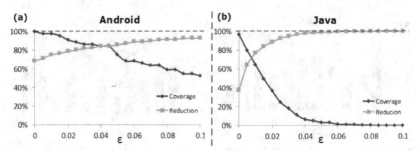

Fig. 4. The overall reduction vs. the overall coverage of the remaining rules for: (a) Android and (b) Java

hand, if ϵ is too high, the chance of missing detectable vulnerabilities in static analysis increases. We have already described how we exclude rules (recall E_c from Section 4) and assess rule reduction for a given category c (recall Equation 2). Coverage of the remaining rules (i.e., $\overline{E}_c = R - E_c$) for a given category c represents the percentage of the vulnerabilities detected in that category by only using the rules that are not excluded and is defined as follows:

$$Coverage_c = \frac{\sum_{r \in \overline{E}_c} \sum_{a \in App_c} |V_{r,a}|}{\sum_{r \in R} \sum_{a \in App_c} |V_{r,a}|} \times 100 \tag{5}$$

Fig. 4 shows the overall reduction and coverage of all categories for various ϵ values in Android and Java domains. We calculated these values using 10-Fold Cross Validation technique [20]. We partitioned the set of apps under study into 10 subsets with equal size and used them to conduct 10 independent experiments. In each experiment, we treated 9 subsets as the training set and the remaining subset as the test set. Recall from Table 2 that our data set comprised of 441 Java and 460 Android applications. We calculated $Reduction_c$ and $Coverage_c$ values for each test set based on the $P(r|c)$ values learned from the corresponding training set. Then, we calculated the intermediate reduction and coverage for each experiment as the weighted average of $Reduction_c$ and $Coverage_c$ values; the weights were assigned proportional to the number of applications fallen in category c for that experiment. Finally, we calculated the overall reduction and coverage as the average of intermediate reduction and coverage values obtained from the 10 experiments.

According to Fig. 4, in Android domain, with $\epsilon = 0$ (i.e., when only the rules with learned detection probability of 0 are excluded), reduction is 68%, while coverage is at 100%, meaning that all vulnerabilities that are detectable using all of the rules in our experiment are indeed detected. In other words, the remaining 32% of the rules are as powerful as all of the rules in detecting all of the vulnerabilities and achieving 100% coverage. However, in Java domain, the results are significantly different as reduction with $\epsilon = 0$ is 37%. Additionally, the remaining 63% of rules can only provide 96% coverage. In other words, they . are not as powerful as all of the rules in detecting Java vulnerabilities.

These results support our hypotheses. They emphasize the effectiveness of our probabilistic ranking as we could achieve full coverage of Android vulnerabilities with 68% reduction of unnecessary rules. In our experiments, no rule was excluded from all categories. This implies that every rule is useful, but, may be unnecessary in some categories. Moreover, as we expected, the use of ADF has a positive influence on the effectiveness of our approach. This is because the rules specified in terms of ADF are at a level of abstraction that lend themselves naturally to positive or negative correlation with a particular application category. The results show that in the domains where ADFs are heavily used, our approach could be used to significantly improve the performance of static analysis by removing the irrelevant rules.

The divergence of coverage and reduction in Java domain is very high compared to Android domain. The loss of coverage with $\epsilon = 0.04$ for Android is 16%, while for Java the loss is 93%. This clearly shows that our approach is most effective in domains where an ADF is used for the implementation of application software. As a result, in the remainder of evaluation, we focus on the results obtained in Android domain.

Table 3 provides the detailed results of experiments for Android apps when $\epsilon = 0$. The number of excluded rules (i.e., $|E_c|$) in the categories varies between 24 to 43 rules out of total 50 vulnerability detection rules. In other words, $Reduction_c$ is between 48% to 86% for different categories that leads to the average reduction of 68%, as shown before in Fig. 4a.

Table 3 presents the average and 95% confidence interval for the analysis time of an Android app in each category. Here, $Uninformed$ column corresponds to the time spent for source code analysis if all vulnerability detection rules (i.e., R) are applied, while $Informed$ is when unnecessary rules (i.e., E_c) are excluded from the analysis procedure. The last column in Table 3 shows the significant time savings by pruning the useless rules from source code analysis. From the last row of the table, we can see that our approach on average achieves a 67% speed up compared to the uninformed approach of simply analyzing the source code for all types of vulnerability.

Table 3. Analysis time for Android apps for $\epsilon = 0$

Android Category	Rule Exclusion $|E_c|$	$Reduction_c$	Analysis Time (mins) Uninformed	Informed	Saved Analysis Time (mins)
Development	43	86	43.48±8.3	6.09±1.16	37.39±7.14
Education	35	70	59.29±17.76	17.79±5.33	41.5±12.43
Game	39	78	48.92±4.94	10.76±1.09	38.16±3.85
Internet	33	66	49.83±6.65	16.94±2.26	32.89±4.39
Multimedia	29	58	60.47±11.22	25.4±4.71	35.07±6.51
Navigation	31	62	44.61±8.25	16.95±3.14	27.66±5.12
Office	30	60	44.25±4.11	17.7±1.64	26.55±2.46
Phone	30	60	70.36±22.47	28.14±8.99	42.21±13.48
Reading	40	80	62.4±18.25	12.48±3.65	49.92±14.6
System	24	48	47.17±11.93	24.53±6.2	22.64±5.73
Wallpaper	42	84	44.27±12.04	7.08±1.93	37.19±10.12
All categories	34	68	52.28±11.45	16.54±3.62	35.74±7.83

7 Threats to Validity

With regard to the internal threats, there is one issue. Since we needed access
to open source applications for our experiments, the training set was limited
to 460 open-source Android apps, which is small in comparison to 700,000 (not
necessarily open source) apps currently available on Google Play. However, since
we have covered almost all available categories that exist in Google Play with
a similar app distribution, our experimental app set could be considered as an
admissible representation of the global Android app market. Extending our study
to a larger set of applications is likely to improve the accuracy of our approach.

An external threat is related to our non-overlapping decisive app categoriza-
tion method. In this research, we have assumed each app belongs to a single
prespecified category. This is a reasonable assumption as many app markets
(e.g., F-Droid as well as Google Play) assign an app to one category. But when
software repositories allow an application to belong to multiple categories, an
app may possess the features, and thus vulnerabilities of more than one category.
Our approach in its current form is not applicable to such settings. For this we
would need to precede our approach with a preprocessing step in which we first
determine the category that best matches the characteristics of an application,
or alternatively provide a probabilistic measure of confidence with which the
application belongs to a particular category.

8 Related Work

Prior research could be classified into two thrusts: (1) security vulnerability
prediction and (2) Android security threats and analysis techniques. In this
section, we review the prior literature in light of our approach.

The goal of the first thrust of research is to inform the process of security
inspection by helping the security analyst to focus on the parts of the system
that are likely to harbor vulnerabilities. While most prior approaches on vulnerability prediction are platform-independent and try to predict the occurrence
of vulnerability regardless of the application domain [21–23], some have focused
on a specific platform or domain, such as Android [24] or Microsoft Windows
vulnerabilities [25].

An Important distinction between our work and the prior research is the
features of application software that are selected for prediction. Some vulnerability prediction approaches are based on various software metrics. For example
Scandariato and Walden [24] have considered a variety of source code metrics,
including size, complexity and object-oriented metrics, Shin et al. [23] have applied complexity, code churn, and developer activity metrics, and Zimmermann
et al. [25] have used the same metrics together with coverage and dependency
measures. Some other vulnerability prediction approaches have considered the
raw source code and applied text retrieval techniques to extract the features.
For example, Hovsepyan et al. [21] have transferred Java files into feature vectors, where each feature represents a word of the source code, while Neuhaus

et al. [22] have not included all of the words in the source code in the analysis, and instead established a correlation between vulnerabilities, imports, and function calls.

In our research, we took advantage of categorized software repositories to predict the potential vulnerabilities of an application. In contrast to the prior work, we have used meta-data of apps (i.e., category), which is predefined and does not require any preprocessing techniques, together with the information obtained through static analysis of the code. We believe our approach complements the prior research, as it presents an alternative method of detecting and classifying presence of vulnerabilities.

The second thrust of research has studied Android security threats and analysis techniques at different levels of system stack, from operating system level [26, 27] to application level [9, 27–29]. However, in most cases, Android architecture and its security model have been the main focus of the study [26–28], as opposed to the vulnerabilities that arise in the application logic. Shabtai et al. [26] have clustered security threats based on their risk, described the available security mechanism(s) to address each threat, and assessed the mitigation level of described solutions. Enck et al. [27] have enumerated security enforcement of Android at two levels: system level and inter-component communication level. They have developed a tool, named Kirin, to check the compliance of described security mechanism with Android apps. Enck et al. [9] have also investigated vulnerabilities of 1,100 Android apps by using static analysis. In this regard, they have provided a set of vulnerability detection rules, which we have used in our research.

A body of prior research has tried to automate the security testing of Android apps. Mahmood et al. [28] suggested a whitebox approach for testing Android apps on the cloud, where test cases are generated through lightweight program analysis. In another research, Gilbert at el. [29] suggested AppInspector, which tracks and logs sensitive information flows throughout app's possible execution paths and identifies security or privacy violations. Unlike our work, all prior research has implicitly assumed that various vulnerabilities have the same likelihood, and consequently tackled them with equal priority. Our research complements prior research by prioritizing the order in which vulnerabilities are analyzed and tested.

9 Conclusion

The ability to streamline the security analysis and assessment of software is gaining prominence, partly due to the evolving nature of the way in which software is provisioned to the users. We identified two new sources of information that when mined properly present us with a unique opportunity to improve the state-of-the-art (1) meta-data available in the form of application category on such repositories, and (2) vulnerabilities specific to the wrong usage of *application development framework (ADF)*.

In summary, the contributions of our work are as follows: (1) We were able to derive a strong correlation between software categories and security vulnerabilities, in turn allowing us to eliminate the vulnerabilities that are irrelevant for a given category. Most notably, we showed that we can achieve 68% reduction in the vulnerability detection rules, while maintaining 100% coverage of the detectable vulnerabilities in Android. (2) We developed a probabilistic method of ranking the rules to improve the efficiency and enable prioritization of static analysis for finding security vulnerabilities. (3) We empirically demonstrated the benefits of ADF in the security vulnerability assessment process. An app developed on top of an ADF leverages libraries, services, and APIs provisioned by the ADF that disclose a significant amount of information about the app's behavior/functionality. We showed how this information can be used to predict vulnerabilities one may find in the app of a particular category.

As part of our future work, we are interested to extend the research to situations in which an app belongs to more than one category. In addition, in this research we focused on vulnerabilities, which are unintentional mistakes providing exploitable conditions that an adversary may use to attack a system. However, another important factor in security analysis is malicious capabilities, which are intentionally designed by attackers and embedded in an app. Hence, as a complement of this research, we plan to mine the categorized software repositories to improve the malware analysis techniques.

Acknowledgements. This work was supported in part by awards W911NF-09-1-0273 from the US Army Research Office, D11AP00282 from the US Defense Advanced Research Projects Agency, and CCF-1252644 and CCF-1217503 from the US National Science Foundation.

References

1. Symantec Corp.: 2012 norton study (2012)
2. Gartner Inc.: Gartner reveals top predictions for IT organizations and users for 2012 and beyond (2011)
3. McGraw, G.: Testing for security during development: why we should scrap penetrate-and-patch. In: Are We Making Progress Towards Computer Assurance? Proceedings of the 12th Annual Conference on Computer Assurance, COMPASS 1997, pp. 117–119 (1997)
4. McGraw, G.: Automated code review tools for security. Computer 41, 108–111 (2008)
5. Android: Official blog (officialandroid.blogspot.com)
6. Muslu, K., et al.: Making offline analyses continuous. In: Int'l Symp. on the Foundations of Software Engineering, Saint Petersburg, Russia, pp. 323–333 (2013)
7. Linares-Vsquez, M., et al.: On using machine learning to automatically classify software applications into domain categories. Empirical Software Engineering, 1–37 (2012)
8. Binkley, D.: Source code analysis: A road map. In: Int'l Conf. on Software Engineering, Minneapolis, Minnesota, pp. 104–119 (2007)
9. Enck, W., et al.: A study of android application security. In: Proceedings of the 20th USENIX Security Symposium, vol. 2011 (2011)

10. HP Enterprise Security: (Static application security testing)
11. Ware, M.S., Fox, C.J.: Securing java code: heuristics and an evaluation of static analysis tools. In: Proceedings of the 2008 Workshop on Static Analysis, SAW 2008, Tucson, Arizona, pp. 12–21. ACM (2008)
12. Checkstyle: Enforce coding standards (checkstyle.sourceforge.net)
13. Eclipse: Eclipse test & performance tools platform project, http://www.eclipse.org/tptp
14. Hovemeyer, D., Pugh, W.: Finding bugs is easy. ACM Sigplan Notices 39, 92–106 (2004)
15. Jlint: Find bugs in java programs (jlint.sourceforge.net)
16. Lint4j: Lint4j overview, http://www.jutils.com
17. PMD: Source code analyzer (pmd.sourceforge.net)
18. QJ-Pro: Code analyzer for java (qjpro.sourceforge.net)
19. Bertsekas, D.P., Tsitsiklis, J.N.: Introduction to Probability, 2nd edn. Athena Scientific (2008)
20. Tan, P.N., et al.: Introduction to Data Mining, 1st edn. Addison Wesley (2005)
21. Hovsepyan, A., et al.: Software vulnerability prediction using text analysis techniques. In: Proceedings of the 4th International Workshop on Security Measurements and Metrics, pp. 7–10 (2012)
22. Neuhaus, S., et al.: Predicting vulnerable software components. In: Proceedings of the 14th ACM Conference on Computer and Communications Security, pp. 529–540 (2007)
23. Shin, Y., et al.: Evaluating complexity, code churn, and developer activity metrics as indicators of software vulnerabilities. IEEE Transactions on Software Engineering 37, 772–787 (2011)
24. Scandariato, R., Walden, J.: Predicting vulnerable classes in an android application. In: Proceedings of the 4th International Workshop on Security Measurements and Metrics, pp. 11–16 (2012)
25. Zimmermann, T., et al.: Searching for a needle in a haystack: Predicting security vulnerabilities for windows vista. In: 2010 Third International Conference on Software Testing, Verification and Validation (ICST), pp. 421–428 (2010)
26. Shabtai, A., et al.: Google android: A comprehensive security assessment. IEEE Security & Privacy 8, 35–44 (2010)
27. Enck, W., et al.: Understanding android security. IEEE Security & Privacy 7, 50–57 (2009)
28. Mahmood, R., et al.: A whitebox approach for automated security testing of android applications on the cloud. In: 2012 7th International Workshop on Automation of Software Test (AST), pp. 22–28 (2012)
29. Gilbert, P., et al.: Vision: automated security validation of mobile apps at app markets. In: Proceedings of the Second International Workshop on Mobile Cloud Computing and Services, pp. 21–26 (2011)

Modularizing Early Architectural Assumptions in Scenario-Based Requirements

Dimitri Van Landuyt and Wouter Joosen

iMinds-DistriNet, KU Leuven
Celestijnenlaan 200A,
B-3001 Leuven, Belgium
{dimitri.vanlanduyt,wouter.joosen}@cs.kuleuven.be

Abstract. Early architectural assumptions (EAAs) are initial assumptions about the architectural solution that are made already during requirements elicitation. Such EAAs are inherently present when applying requirements engineering methods and techniques situated at the transition to architecture, for example those adhering to the Twin Peaks model to software engineering.

In the current state-of-the-art, early architectural assumptions (EAAs) are documented implicitly, and they are tangled within and scattered across heterogeneous requirement artifacts. This makes it hard to distinguish EAAs from actual requirements, analyze their relevance, and bring them in relation to architectural decisions taken in later development stages. As a consequence, early development activities in the transition to architecture are hindered by the lack of explicit support for EAAs.

In this paper, we address this problem in the context of scenario-based requirements (use cases and quality attribute scenarios). We present a system meta-model for EAAs, and provide an aspect-oriented requirements language that allows the instantiation of EAAs in terms of use case-level pointcuts. We employ our prototype implementation of above-mentioned techniques to evaluate and illustrate the benefits of making EAAs explicit in the early stages of development, specifically in terms of modularity and requirements navigability.

1 Introduction

It is widely accepted that in practical software development, there is seldomly a clear-cut dichotomy between requirements engineering and architectural design, but that, in order to achieve an easier transition and faster convergence to the final architecture, these activities are often intertwined. This is called the Twin Peaks model to software engineering [18].

One consequence of this is that requirements —which exist in the problem space– are inherently affected or based upon initial architectural assumptions — solution-space elements. These early assumptions are architectural in nature, in the sense that they exist in different architectural views: some assumptions are about the structural decomposition of the architecture, some about the system's behavior, some about the deployment configuration, etc. It is in the intrinsic

S. Gnesi and A. Rensink (Eds.): FASE 2014, LNCS 8411, pp. 170–184, 2014.

nature of software engineering activities in the transition to architecture that they rely on some early-defined, pre-assumed system abstractions. We call these *early architectural assumptions* (EAAs). In earlier work [29], we have argued that making such early assumptions is indeed an effective technique to converge more quickly to a suitable architectural solution.

In the current state-of-the-art, early architectural assumptions (EAAs) are documented implicitly. Specifically in the context of scenario-based requirements, they are embedded in natural language descriptions, and it takes substantial analytic effort to (i) identify and understand them, (ii) distinguish them from actual stakeholder requirements or technical constraints, and (iii) understand their often subtle interactions. Furthermore, we have seen that EAAs have a crosscutting impact on the different requirements: they are scattered across scenarios and tangled with each other within these scenarios. This inherent characteristic of EAAs has been pointed out by Nusebeih who argues that crosscutting influences between requirements can mostly be observed *"when elements of a solution also begin to be explored"* [19].

For these reasons, implicit early architectural assumptions have a negative impact on the development activities at the transition from requirements to architecture. Specifically, activities involving change impact analysis and trade-off analysis such as the Architecture Trade-off Analysis Method (ATAM) [12]) and Attribute-Driven Design (ADD) [32,2] are hindered by badly modularized and implicit EAAs [30] as they increase the required analytic effort to understand and manipulate the requirement body.

In this paper, we address these problems in the context of scenario-based requirements (use cases [9] and quality attribute scenarios [2]). Specifically, we create an EAA model which acts as a knowledge repository of explicit early-defined system abstractions. This EAA model is promoted as a key enabler to achieve a smooth transition to architecture. To increase the robustness and expressivity of EAA definitions and to address their crosscutting nature, we introduce and employ an expressive use case-level pointcut language called AspectU+.

Additionally, we present prototype implementation of these techniques, and we leverage this prototype to evaluate the presented solutions. Specifically, we present detailed development scenarios from a realistic case study, a car crash management system (CMS) [13,11], and we focus on illustrating the benefits of having an explicit EAA model in the transition to architecture.

This paper is structured as follows: Sect. 2 presents the problem statement. Subsequently, Sect. 3 presents a set of techniques for modularizing EAAs in the context of scenario-based requirements. Then, Sect. 4 evaluates our results. Sect. 5 discusses related work and finally, Sect. 6 concludes this paper.

2   Problem Statement

We motivate our work in the context of a realistic case study, a crisis management system (CMS) for resolving car crashes (e.g. by dispatching tow trucks, ambulance, rescue workers, . . .), the requirements of which are scenario-based in nature. QAS 1 presents a (shortened) performance quality attribute scenario related to the calculation or revision of car crash resolution strategies. Specifically, it prescribes how the system should react in the case when too much new information arrives, giving rise to many strategy (re-)calculations in parallel; i.e. by shifting some of the calculation requests to a replica instance of the strategy calculation component.

QAS 1 Performance. Strategy calculation and revision

[..] the rate of newly-arriving information exceeds the throughput of strategy revisions and initial strategy calculations, especially in the case that many strategy calculations are executed in parallel, for example in case of multiple related accidents (e.g. a pile-up).

- **Source:** Witness, Service Provider or Information Service
- **Stimulus:** New car crashes reported by Witness, new information received from the Information Service or Service Provider.
- **Artifact:** (sub-)system responsible for strategy (re-)calculation
- **Environment:** Normal execution mode.
- **Response:** 'Overload' mode: requests are forwarded to a next instance of the sub-system:
  - when processing new information, the CMS assesses whether this new information gives rise to a strategy revision. In overload mode, the request is sent to the replica instance.
  - when entering a new dossier, the initial strategy is selected by the Coordinator. In overload mode, the request is sent to the replica instance.
- **Response Measure:**
  - the system goes into 'overload' mode when the response time > 500 ms for a given strategy (re-)calculation job.

Upon analysis, it is clear that this scenario has been written with a number of early architectural assumptions (EAAs) in mind: (i) the algorithms used to calculate strategies will not be light-weight (and thus it is realistic to imagine a situation of system overload); (ii) initial strategy calculation and strategy revision will be done by one and the same component; (iii) this component will be easily replicated, and there will at least be two replicas in total; and (iv) the system or its middleware will have the ability to monitor the throughput of strategy calculation jobs, and redirect requests dynamically.

These assumptions are fundamentally different from other requirement artifacts such as use cases, domain models, glossaries, and most importantly, they are architectural in nature: the first assumption is about the performance characteristics of the selected algorithms while the second is an assumption about the structural decomposition of the system. The third is an assumption about the deployment configuration of the CMS, while the fourth is about the selected technologies and platforms on which the CMS is to be built.

Due to the inherently implicit nature of these EAAs (embedded in requirements), it is hard to assess (without additional analysis) (i) that these are in fact assumptions and not constraints or requirements imposed by the stakeholders, (ii) whether or not these EAAs are made after thoughtful (architectural) analysis, and if so, (iii) what the underlying rationale was, and (iv) whether these

EAAs are contradicted or reinforced by other assumptions (perhaps documented in different scenarios).

The software architect —when handed these requirements— must assess whether these EAAs are desirable, realistic and technically feasible. Perhaps the architect decides to reject some assumptions, and this in turn might lead to consistency problems, as it is unclear what the impact of that decision might be on the other requirements, on the other architectural assumptions and decisions. This is worsened by the large number of inherent yet subtle interdependencies between (the EAAs and) the different architectural drivers, often crosscutting in nature. To illustrate this, we extend the example of QAS 1 with the *"Revise current strategy"* use case, which involves the revision of a currently executing car crash resolution strategy (presented in Use Case 1). When comparing the description of the strategy revision algorithm in step 2 of Use Case 1 with QAS 1, it becomes clear that some of the assumptions made during the creation of QAS 1 have been influenced directly by this use case (e.g. the first EAA highlighted above about the complexity of the strategy calculation and revision algorithms).

Use Case 1. The *'Revise current strategy'* use case

- **Id/name:** Revise current strategy
- **Primary actor:** Coordinator, CMS
- **Basic Flow:**
  1. The Coordinator indicates that he wants to revise the current strategy for an ongoing car crash [..] by selecting an ongoing car crash dossier.
  2. The CMS calculates and proposes a number of car crash resolution strategies and indicates for each of these strategies, the price, the expected time duration and the risks associated with these. The CMS takes into account possible dependencies between individual missions, missions that have already been executed, the availability of the external service providers and emergency services already at the scene.
  3. The Coordinator selects the desired strategy.
  4. The CMS registers the revised strategy in the car crash dossier.
  5. The CMS informs the involved external service providers [..] about their new or updated missions.
- **Alternative Scenario:**
  3B. The CMS only comes up with one strategy, continue with step 4.

Problem Statement. A more detailed problem statement has been derived and presented in earlier work [29]. This problem statement is summarized below:

1. EAAs are documented **implicitly** in scenario-based requirements;
2. EAA definitions are scattered across scenario-based requirements and tangled with other EAA definitions: **bad modularity** of EAAs;
3. EAAs typically have a **crosscutting** influence on other requirements.

3 Modularizing EAAs in Scenario-Based Requirements

In this section, we provide a set of techniques to modularize early architectural assumptions (EAAs) in the context of scenario-based requirements (use cases and quality attribute scenarios). Sect. 3.1 presents our system meta-model for expressing EAAs. Then, Sect. 3.2 discusses our technique to instantiate EAAs in terms of use-case level pointcuts. Subsequently, Sect. 3.3 describes the role of EAAs in the quality attribute scenario authoring process.

3.1   System Meta-model for EAAs

As the goal is to define a system meta-model suitable for documenting EAAs in quality attribute scenarios, we have analyzed the quality attribute scenario creation guidelines presented in [2]. Specifically, we selected the most common system concepts used in quality attribute scenarios and we removed synonyms, in order to keep the resulting meta-model minimal and light-weight. The result is presented in Fig. 1.

EAAs in quality attribute scenarios typically refer to functional requirements and fragments of functionality, which are in our case described as use cases. To capture and document these semantic interdependencies, we instantiate EAAs in terms of use case steps (or collections thereof). As use case modeling in general aligns best to a behavioral architectural view, the key behavioral concepts (`Message`, `Request`, `Response` and `Event`) are instantiated directly from use case steps. Based on these elements, the remaining concepts (`Interaction`, `Function`, `Subsystem`, `Channel` and `Node`) can be derived. Table 1 below provides a detailed description of the meta-model concepts and provides syntax to instantiate EAAs in terms of use case (fragments).

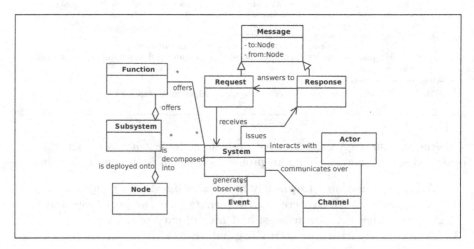

Fig. 1. The meta-model for expressing early architectural assumptions (EAAs)

Table 1. Detailed description of the meta-model concepts and Java-like constructor syntax for instantiating EAAs

---

Message. In general, every use case step corresponds to a message. It represents a trigger or an action relevant to the system. A message is always directed, from a one Subsystem to another. The following syntax is used to instantiate messages:

```
Message(UseCaseStep step);
```

Request and Response. Conceptually, requests and responses are refinements of the more generic message. The messages sent by any actor other than the system are considered requests, while the use case steps directed from the system are called responses. The constructor syntax to instantiate these elements is as follows:

```
Request(UseCaseStep step); // pre: (!step.getActor().getName().equals("System"))
```

```
Response(UseCaseStep step); // pre: (step.getActor().getName().equals("System"))
```

Event. In essence, an event is a certain path through a use case, or a subset thereof. The necessary precondition is that an event consists of consecutive use case steps. The constructor syntax for instantiating an Event is presented below:

```
Event(UseCaseStep[] steps); // pre: (steps.size()>1 and steps are subsequent)
```

Interaction. An interaction is defined as a single couple of consecutive Request-Responses instances. Therefore, the constructor for an Interaction is as follows:

```
Interaction(Request req, Response resp); // pre: resp.answersTo(req)
```

Function. The concept of a function overlaps slightly with that of an Event, in the sense that a function realizes or executes a certain Event path. It represents how the system reacts or behaves, given a certain trigger or request. To instantiate a concrete function, the following syntax is used:

```
Function(Event event); // pre: event starts with a Request, and the consecutive steps
conceptually belong together
```

Subsystem. Similarly, a subsystem is defined by referring to the Function(s) offered by it. It is possible to formulate the assumption that several related Functions are offered by one single Subsystem, and therefore to instantiate a specific subsystem, the following syntax is offered:

```
Subsystem(Function[] functions);
```

Channel. Channels are defined by one or more interactions between the system and one or more actors. Potentially, many different interactions may occur over a single channel, or separate channels (e.g. a control channel or a data channel). It is possible to merge several interactions over one channel. To instantiate a Channel, the following syntax is offered:

```
Channel(Interaction[] interaction); // pre: the same actors are involved in each
interaction
```

Node. Finally, a node represents a physical machine. We refer to a node by referring to one or more subsystems deployed to it. Nodes are instantiated as follows:

```
Node(Subsystem[] subsystems); // pre: subsystems.size >=1
```

3.2   EAA Instantiation in Terms of Use Case-Level Pointcuts

A straightforward strategy to instantiate the early architectural assumptions (EAAs) would involve referring directly to specific use case steps. However, as this would introduce tight coupling between the EAA model and the use case model (due to their often crosscutting interrelations), this strategy would not adequately address Problem #3 defined in Sect. 2. Therefore, we present an alternative instantiation strategy that involves referring to use case steps (or collections thereof) by means of pointcut expressions.

First, we introduce a use case-level pointcut specification language (PSL) called AspectU+. This PSL allows capturing the crosscutting nature of the EAAs in a more expressive manner. Then, we define some EAAs from the running example of Sect. 2 in terms of AspectU+ pointcuts.

AspectU+. Sillito et al. [24] have already proposed a use case-level PSL called AspectU, which is primarily meant for composition of functional aspects to use case models. However, this PSL is limited in the sense that it does not fully exploit the semantics and structural conventions behind use case modeling. For example, in AspectU it is not possible to match all steps in which a certain actor is involved, or the set of responses to a certain step (which includes main steps and steps from alternative scenarios). Nonetheless, these are useful constructs for defining EAAs.

Table 2. AspectU+ primitive pointcuts

Primitive pointcut	description
usecase(*ucname*)	selects all use case steps from the use cases whose names match *ucname* (incl. alternate scenarios)
main(*ucname*)	selects only the use case steps from the main scenario of the use cases whose names match *ucname*
extension(*ucname*)	selects only the use case steps from the alternate or extension scenarios of the use cases whose names match *ucname*)
steps(*id*)	selects specific steps that match the *id* expression
actorsteps(*id*)	selects the use case steps that are performed by the actors whose names match *id*
responses(*steps*)	selects the use case steps in response to the steps in *steps*
operators: and (&&), or (||), not (!)	(*prefix* notation)
define: name := *expression*	

Therefore, we have extended the AspectU PSL to serve our needs[1], and we call the resulting language AspectU+. Note that pointcut expressions specified in AspectU remain fully compatible to pointcut expressions in AspectU+, but not vice versa. Table 2 presents the syntax of the AspectU+ language. The rows of this table that are colored in grey present our extension to AspectU [24]. String matching in AspectU+ is done by means of regular expressions.

---

[1] This is a minimal extension, as we only extend AspectU for pragmatic reasons; i.e. to illustrate the feasibility of the method presented in this paper.

Below, we present one EAA from the motivating example of Sect. 2. Specifically, we model the `strategyRevision` event using the Java-like constructor syntax introduced in Sect. 3.1. To refer to use case steps or collections thereof, we provide an AspectU+ pointcut expression as the parameter to the `Event` constructor (placed between curly brackets). This pointcut refers to the use case whose name matches to the '`.*Revise.*strategy.*`' regular expression, and more specifically, the steps in the main flow of this use case (`main(''.*'')`)). In the CMS use cases, this matches to steps 1–5 of the *"Revise current strategy"* use case (Use Case 1).

`strategyRevision := Event(`	1
`{ &&(usecase(".*Revise.*strategy.*"),`	2
`main(".*")) });`	3

3.3 Authoring Quality Attribute Scenarios with EAAs

During the quality attribute scenario elicitation and authoring process, the requirements engineer has to be aware of the centrally defined EAA model. This model will aid him in making explicit key assumptions about the system. Whenever such an assumption has to be made (for example, *initial strategy calculation and strategy revision will be done by one and the same component*), he first has to verify whether these assumed system elements —for example, the `strategyRevision` event— have already been defined in the EAA model. If so, he can simply refer to these elements. If not, he first has to introduce them in the EAA model, possibly by reusing or building upon already-existing model elements or pointcuts.

QAS 2 Performance. Strategy calculation

– [..] **Response:** 'Overload' mode: requests are forwarded to a next instance of the sub-system:
  - when processing new information (`processingNewData`), the CMS assesses whether this new information gives rise to a strategy revision (`strategyRevision`). In overload mode, the request is sent to the replica instance.
  - when entering a new dossier (`newDossierEntered`), the initial strategy is selected by the Coordinator (`strategyCalculation`). In overload mode, the request is sent to the replica instance.

QAS 2 presents the Response part of QAS 1 from Sect. 2 after re-factoring. We have introduced annotations (presented in a `typewriter` font and between brackets) that refer to the EAAs. For example, we introduced a direct reference to the `strategyRevision` event defined in Sect. 3.2. In our experience, EAAs are most common in the *"Stimulus"*, *"Response"*, and *"Response Measure"* fields of a quality attribute scenario.

Clearly, the main goal of our approach is not to re-factor existing quality attribute scenarios after the fact, but to support the authoring process itself. This is in line with the view that the EAA model will act as a central knowledge repository during requirements engineering, in which and from which the relevant interrelations between the different requirement artifacts can be documented and derived.

4 Evaluation and Discussion

We have evaluated the presented approach in the context of the Crisis Management System (CMS) case study. In total, the case study requirements comprise (i) 13 detailed use cases, and (ii) in total, eighteen quality attribute scenarios, specifically 6 availability, 6 performance and 6 modifiability scenarios. While the use cases originate from the original case study [13], the quality attribute scenarios have been derived from textual software quality descriptions in [13]. Further details on the followed process to obtain these requirements can be found in [28]. Throughout Sect. 3, we have illustrated the method over a very small subset of this case study. Note that the requirements presented in this paper are in fact highly simplified versions of those from the case study.

First, Sect. 4.1 discusses our prototype implementation. Then, Sect. 4.2 evaluates our results in terms of the modularity of early architectural assumptions (EAAs). Finally, Sect. 4.3 discusses how the existence of an explicit EAA model improves the navigability of the requirements body.

4.1 Prototype Implementation

We have developed a prototype implementing the proposed techniques[2] for modularizing EAAs in scenario-based requirements. The tool can be used for querying the EAA model and navigating the interdependencies between the different requirement artifacts. To this end, it provides a web front-end and the interrelations between EAAs and quality attribute scenarios (which we represented earlier as annotations) are shown by the prototype as hyperlinks. The prototype evaluates the pointcut expressions on demand. It offers a fully implemented pointcut parser and evaluator for the AspectU+ pointcut language. An EAA is presented by showing its AspectU+ pointcut expression, the concrete use case steps which are the concrete join points for that pointcut (as hyperlinks) and the quality attribute scenarios referring to the EAA (also as hyperlinks). The screenshot in Fig. 2(a) illustrates this for the running example of the strategyCalculation EAA. When displaying a specific use case, the tool automatically adds hyperlinks referring to the EAAs for which that use case offers join points.

In addition, the tool offers an environment to create and test AspectU+ pointcut expressions, of which Fig. 2(b) presents a screenshot. During the construction of an AspectU+ expression, the expression is evaluated over the use case model and the matching use case-level join points are presented.

In future work, we plan to refine and integrate this tool into requirements engineering tools such as the UCEd [26] which offer a more rigorous approach

---

[2] The source code of this prototype and further implementation details can be found on http://people.cs.kuleuven.be/~dimitri.vanlanduyt/eaa/

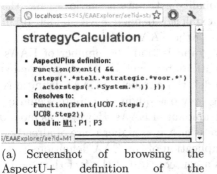
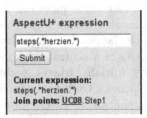

(a) Screenshot of browsing the AspectU+ definition of the strategyCalculation EAA

(b) Screenshot of creating and testing AspectU+ expressions

to use case and domain modeling, and architecture creation tools such as the SEI's ArchE [25] to impose EAAs as actual architectural constraints during architectural design.

4.2   Modularity of EAAs

In this part of the evaluation, we focus on the modularity of early architectural assumptions (EAAs). Specifically, we have applied scattering metrics [7] (i.e. based of the number of recurring EAA definitions) on the requirements of the CMS, and we compare the cases with and without an explicit EAA model.

To ensure comparability of both sets of quality attribute scenarios, we started with the 18 existing quality attribute scenarios of the CMS, and re-factored these incrementally by moving the EAAs one by one to the EAA model, reusing already-existing definitions wherever possible. Fig. 2 depicts this process. The X-axis shows the order in which quality attribute scenarios are selected and re-factored, while the Y-axis shows the number of distinct EAA definitions. The grey curve represents the case without an EAA model —thus scattering and

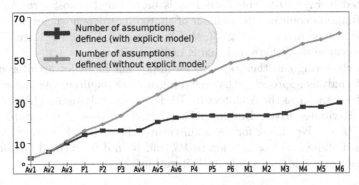

Fig. 2. The number of EAAs defined over time, with and without creating an EAA model

tangling EAAs within and across quality attribute scenarios— and the black curve represents the case with an explicitly defined EAA model, or in other words, the black curve plots the size of the EAA model.

The main observation from this graph is that the number of EAAs grows linearly with the number of quality attribute scenarios. However, when specifying the EAAs in a central EAA model, the number of EAAs definitions grows sub-linearly. Initially, when covering only one quality attribute scenario ($Av1$), both approaches introduce the same amount of EAAs. However, as more quality attribute scenarios are covered, there is clearly a higher reuse of already-defined EAAs. This is an indication that duplication of the EAA definitions (scattering and tangling) is avoided and this is a consequence of the fact that many of the system-level assumptions suitable for one quality attribute scenario also proved suitable for others. In total, this reduction of duplication has led to the definition of 29 EAAs in the centrally defined model, as opposed to 62 EAA definitions scattered across and hard-coded within the 18 quality attribute scenarios, a reduction of 53%.

4.3   Requirement Navigability and the Transition to Architecture

We now illustrate how an explicit EAA model facilitates the navigation[3] of requirement bodies in the transition to architecture. Fig. 3(a) presents a dependency graph that has been derived directly from the EAA definitions. In addition to the requirements already presented in Sect. 2, it depicts three additional use cases and a second quality attribute scenario ($P3$) (about to the performance of the back-end system in the CMS). It shows the (otherwise implicit) relations between these requirements, made explicit on the one hand by means of explicit annotations, and on the other hand by means of AspectU+ pointcuts.

From this dependency graph, we have defined a distance function between two requirements that measures how closely related they are in terms of shared EAA references. These distance measurements can then be used to cluster the set of requirements. An example hierarchical clustering of the CMS requirements is presented in Fig. 3(b). This clustering is based on the most straightforward distance function counting the number of shared interdependencies between the requirements (the arrows in Fig. 3(a)). For example, $P1$ and $P3$ are clustered together because they share multiple EAA definitions.

Such a clustering can then serve as an important input for architecture creation and analysis approaches that rely on grouping requirements and architectural trade-offs, such as the Architecture Trade-off Analysis Method (ATAM) [12]) and the Attribute-Driven Design (ADD) [32,2] process. For example, when selecting $P1$ as a key driver for the architecture, the architect can automatically be informed about its close relation to $P3$, and both drivers could be addressed together (for example, in a single ADD iteration).

---

[3] And as a direct consequence, the consistency management and traceability of requirements.

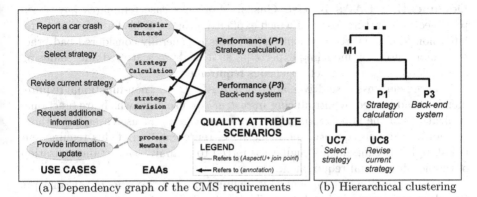

(a) Dependency graph of the CMS requirements   (b) Hierarchical clustering

Fig. 3. Illustration of how explicit EAAs improve the navigability of the CMS requirements

5 Related Work

First, we discuss related work in the domain of Early Aspects (Aspect-Oriented Requirement and Architecture approaches). Then, we zoom in specifically on existing methods and techniques that involve documenting EAAs within use cases. Finally, we discuss related work in the domain of architectural knowledge management.

Early Aspects. Chitchan et al. have presented their semantics-based composition approach of [4,31] which enables annotating requirements with semantic information obtained with natural language processing techniques. COMPASS further elaborates upon this approach by mapping the semantic compositions to initial AO architecture diagrams [3]. As such, this work traces key concepts in requirements specification towards architecture, facilitating consistency management between architecture and requirements.

The generic AORE model presented by Rashid et al. [20] supports the separation of crosscutting requirements and the identification of crosscutting influences between requirement-level aspects. As such, this enables the identification of critical trade-offs well before architectural design. In addition to this work, Moreira et al. [17] advocate a multi-dimensional approach to separation of concerns in requirements engineering that supports architectural trade-off analysis based on the notion of the *compositional intersection* between the stakeholder concerns.

Many additional AORE approaches focus on identifying and representing the crosscutting influences of non-functional requirements on system functionalities [16,23,27].

Although these approaches are related in terms of the techniques used, the key difference is that these do not explicitly disambiguate between requirements and assumptions. In future work, we will further explore the instantiation of our techniques in the context of these AORE approaches.

Documenting EAAs in Use Cases. Many use case templates have been proposed in literature, some of which explicitly propose fields for referring to related non-functional requirements [15,6]. This is generally considered bad practice among use case modeling experts [5] as it leads to scattered and confusing cross-references between heterogeneous requirements.

In Jacobson's use case-driven approach to AOSD [10], non-functional requirements are addressed by introducing *infrastructure* use cases which are functional realizations of the non-functional requirement (e.g. *log-in* use cases for authentication). As a consequence, the higher-level representation of this requirement is lost and the requirements engineer is forced to commit to a certain realization of the non-functional requirement.

Another common technique involves defining project glossaries of key concepts (which might correspond to EAAs). The main disadvantage of these techniques is a consequence of their disconnect from the other requirement artifacts.

Architectural Assumptions. In their seminal work about architectural mismatch [8], Garlan et al. have demonstrated that implicit architectural assumptions are one major factor impeding effective reuse and evolution of code- and architecture-level artifacts. This is related to *architectural decay* [21]. Roeller et al. [22] propose an approach for retro-actively discovering such architectural assumptions in existing software systems and documenting them. Zschaler et al. [33] have extensively studied *aspect assumptions*. These are all instances of architectural assumptions. However, the main difference to the assumptions targeted in this paper is that we focus on *early* architectural assumptions; i.e. those assumptions made about the system during requirement elicitation and in the transition phases to architecture.

Architectural knowledge management [1,14] focuses on making explicit key architectural assumptions. Again, these approaches focus on *late architectural assumptions* (solution-space assumptions). Given the potentially large impact of EAAs on the architecture and its creation processes, it is nonetheless important to also investigate architectural knowledge management in the context of EAAs. To our knowledge, no other approaches exist with this explicit focus.

6   Conclusion

In the development activities at the transition from requirements to architecture, the requirements engineer often makes *early architectural assumptions* (EAAs); i.e. initial assumptions about key properties or characteristics of the envisioned architectural solution. The inherently implicit nature of EAAs and the lack of modularization thereof has been shown to hinder key architectural design activities [29].

To address this, we have presented a set of techniques to modularize EAAs in the context of scenario-based requirements. These EAAs are stored in a central knowledge repository —the EAA model— which we consider to be a missing link in the transition from requirements to architecture. The crosscutting nature of EAAs is tackled by employing aspect-oriented requirements engineering techniques and we define EAAs in terms of requirement-level pointcut expressions. This work addresses some of the research challenges in the domain of architectural knowledge management. As a general trend, the focus shifts from purely documenting the architectural solutions (end products) to documenting the architectural creation processes themselves (i.e., the intermediate results, design decisions, design rationale, etc), and this well before actual architectural design decisions may have been taken.

Acknowledgements. This research is partially funded by the Research Fund KU Leuven.

References

1. Ali Babar, M., Dingsyr, T., Lago, P., Van Vliet, H.: Software Architecture Knowledge Management: Theory and Practice. Springer (2009)
2. Bass, L., Clements, P., Kazman, R.: Software Architecture in Practice, 2nd edn. Addison-Wesley (2003)
3. Chitchyan, R., Pinto, M., Rashid, A., Fuentes, L.: Compass: Composition-centric mapping of aspectual requirements to architecture. In: Rashid, A., Akşit, M. (eds.) Transactions on AOSD IV. LNCS, vol. 4640, pp. 3–53. Springer, Heidelberg (2007)
4. Chitchyan, R., Rashid, A., Rayson, P., Waters, R.: Semantics-based composition for aspect-oriented requirements engineering. In: Barry, B.M., de Moor, O. (eds.) AOSD. ACM ICPS, vol. 208, pp. 36–48. ACM (2007)
5. Cockburn, A.: Writing Effective Use Cases. Addison-Wesley Professional (January 2000)
6. Coleman, D.: A use case template: Draft for discussion (1998)
7. Eaddy, M., Aho, A., Murphy, G.C.: Identifying, assigning, and quantifying crosscutting concerns. In: Proceedings of the First International ACoM Workshop, ACoM 2007, p. 2 (2007)
8. Garlan, D., Allen, R., Ockerbloom, J.: Architectural mismatch, or, why it's hard to build systems out of existing parts. In: Proceedings of the 17th ICSE Conference, pp. 179–185 (April 1995)
9. Jacobson, I., Griss, M., Jonssson, P.: Software Reuse: Architecture, Process and Organization for Business Success. Addison-Wesley (1997)
10. Jacobson, I., Ng, P.-W.: Aspect-Oriented Software Development with Use Cases, 1st edn. Addison-Wesley (December 2004)
11. Katz, S., Mezini, M., Kienzle, J. (eds.): Transactions on Aspect-Oriented Software Development VII. LNCS, vol. 6210. Springer, Heidelberg (2010)
12. Kazman, R., Klein, M., Barbacci, M., Longstaff, T., Lipson, H., Carriere, J.: The architecture tradeoff analysis method. In: Proceedings of the Fourth IEEE International Conference on Engineering of Complex Computer Systems, ICECCS 1998, pp. 68–78 (1998)
13. Kienzle, J., Guelfi, N., Mustafiz, S.: Crisis Management Systems: A Case Study for Aspect-Oriented Modeling. Transactions on Aspect-Oriented Software Development 7, 1–22 (2010)
14. Kruchten, P., Lago, P., van Vliet, H.: Building up and reasoning about architectural knowledge. In: Hofmeister, C., Crnković, I., Reussner, R. (eds.) QoSA 2006. LNCS, vol. 4214, pp. 43–58. Springer, Heidelberg (2006)

15. Malan, R., Bredemeyer, D.: Functional requirements and use cases: System has properties (2005)
16. Moreira, A., Araújo, J.A., Brito, I.: Crosscutting quality attributes for requirements engineering. In: Proceedings of the 14th International Conference on Software Engineering and Knowledge Engineering, SEKE 2002, pp. 167–174. ACM, New York (2002)
17. Moreira, A., Rashid, A., Araújo, J.: Multi-dimensional separation of concerns in requirements engineering. In: RE, pp. 285–296. IEEE Computer Society (2005)
18. Nuseibeh, B.: Weaving together requirements and architectures. IEEE Computer 34(3), 115–117 (2001)
19. Nuseibeh, B.: Crosscutting requirements. In: Proceedings of the 3rd International Conference on Aspect-Oriented Software Development, AOSD 2004, pp. 3–4. ACM, New York (2004)
20. Rashid, A., Moreira, A., Araújo, J.: Modularisation and composition of aspectual requirements. In: AOSD 2003: Proceedings of the 2nd International Conference on Aspect-Oriented Software Development, pp. 11–20. ACM, New York (2003)
21. Riaz, M., Sulayman, M., Naqvi, H.: Architectural decay during continuous software evolution and impact of 'design for change' on software architecture. In: Ślęzak, D., Kim, T.-h., Kiumi, A., Jiang, T., Verner, J., Abrahão, S. (eds.) ASEA 2009. CCIS, vol. 59, pp. 119–126. Springer, Heidelberg (2009)
22. Roeller, R., Lago, P., van Vliet, H.: Recovering architectural assumptions. Journal of Systems and Software 79(4), 552–573 (2006)
23. Rosenhainer, L.: Identifying crosscutting concerns in requirements specifications (2004)
24. Sillito, J., Dutchyn, C., Eisenberg, A.D., De Volder, K.: Use case level pointcuts. In: Odersky, M. (ed.) ECOOP 2004. LNCS, vol. 3086, pp. 246–268. Springer, Heidelberg (2004)
25. U. Software Engineering Institute (SEI) (Carnegie Mellon). Arche, architecture expert design assistant, http://www.sei.cmu.edu/architecture/tools/arche/
26. Some, S.S.: Use cases based requirements validation with scenarios. In: IEEE International Conference on Requirements Engineering, pp. 465–466 (2005)
27. Tekinerdogan, B., Moreira, A., Araujo, J., Clements, P.: Presented papers: finding aspects in requirements with theme/doc (2004)
28. Van Landuyt, D., Truyen, E., Joosen, W.: Discovery of stable abstractions for aspect-oriented composition in the car crash management domain. In: Katz, S., Mezini, M., Kienzle, J. (eds.) Transactions on AOSD VII. LNCS, vol. 6210, pp. 375–422. Springer, Heidelberg (2010)
29. Van Landuyt, D., Truyen, E., Joosen, W.: Documenting early architectural assumptions in scenario-based requirements. In: Proceedings of the Joint 10th Working IEEE/IFIP Conference on Software Architecture & 6th European Conference on Software Architecture (2012)
30. Van Landuyt, D., Truyen, E., Joosen, W.: On the modularity impact of architectural assumptions. In: Proceedings of the 2012 NEMARA Workshop, NEMARA 2012, pp. 13–16 (2012)
31. Weston, N., Chitchyan, R., Rashid, A.: Formal semantic conflict detection in aspect-oriented requirements. Requir. Eng. 14, 247–268 (2009)
32. Wojcik, R., Bachmann, F., Bass, L., Clements, P.C., Merson, P., Nord, R., Wood, W.G.: Attribute-driven design (add), version 2.0. Technical report, Software Engineering Institute (November 2006)
33. Zschaler, S., Rashid, A.: Aspect assumptions: a retrospective study of aspectj developers' assumptions about aspect usage. In: Proceedings of the Tenth International Conference on AOSD 2011, pp. 93–104. ACM (2011)

Semantically Configurable Analysis of Scenario-Based Specifications

Barak Cohen and Shahar Maoz

School of Computer Science, Tel Aviv University, Israel

Abstract. Scenarios, represented using variants of sequence diagrams, are popular means to specify systems requirements. Live sequence charts (LSC), is a formal and expressive scenario-based specification language, which has been extensively studied over the last decade. Careful reading of the LSC literature, however, reveals many variations and ambiguities in the semantics of LSC, as it is used by different authors in different contexts. Moreover, different works define their semantics of LSC using different means. This variability, in both language features and means of semantics definition, creates a challenge for researchers and tool developers.

In this paper we address this challenge by investigating semantically configurable analysis. We define and formalize the variability in the semantics of LSC using a feature model and develop an analysis technique that can be instantiated to comply with each of its legal configurations. Thus, the analysis is semantically configured and its results change according to the semantics induced by the selected feature configuration. The work is implemented and demonstrated using examples. It advances the state-of-the-art in the area of scenario-based specifications and provides an example for a formal and automated approach to handling semantic variability in modeling languages.

> *"... the world don't move to the beat of just one drum..."*
> *Diff'rent Strokes (1978)*

1 Introduction

Scenarios, represented using variants of sequence diagrams, are popular means to specify systems requirements. A scenario tells a 'short story' of interaction between system and environment entities. Live sequence charts (LSC), originally presented by Damm and Harel [4], is a formal and expressive scenario-based specification language. LSC has been extensively studied over the last decade in the context of execution and synthesis (e.g., [9,12,17,24,29,31,38]), in the context of consistency checking and formal verification (e.g., [6,11,22,25]), specification mining and testing (e.g., [26]), expressive power and standardization (e.g., [5,13,14,23,28,39]). Moreover, several tools which support various analyses that involve the LSC language have been developed by different research

S. Gnesi and A. Rensink (Eds.): FASE 2014, LNCS 8411, pp. 185–199, 2014.

groups, including, e.g, PlayGo [15], the Modal Transition System Analyzer [7], and ScenarioTools [10,37].

Careful reading of the LSC literature, however, reveals many variations and ambiguities in the semantics of LSC, as it is used by different authors in different contexts, for different purposes and in different tools. Moreover, different works define their semantics of LSC using different means, e.g., by transformation to temporal logic formulas, by describing an execution mechanism (play-out), by translation into various types of automata, etc. This variability, in both language features and means of semantics definition, creates a challenge for researchers and tool developers.

In this paper we address this challenge by investigating *semantically configurable analysis of LSC*. First, we define and formalize the variability in the semantics of LSC, as it is found in the literature, using a feature model: each configuration that the feature model permits, induces a different semantics mapping (over the same domain). Second, we develop a parametrized analysis technique that can be instantiated to comply with every legal configuration of the feature model. Thus, the resulting analysis, e.g., verification or synthesis, is semantically configured and its results change according to the semantics induced by the selected feature configuration.

There are several advantages to using a feature model to describe a language's semantic variability. First, the feature model provides a means to formally structure the various semantic choices; this supports human comprehension of the semantics, allows comparison of different variants, and, significantly, enables the parsing required in order to support an automatically configurable analysis. Second, the use of a feature model provides a formal means to define logical dependencies between the semantic choices, e.g., mutual exclusion, implication etc. This is indeed necessary, because not all theoretically possible combinations induce well-defined and useful semantics that are found in the literature.

To present the semantics of LSC in our work, we chose a single, uniform semantic domain — traces of events — and a uniform formalism — alternating one pair Streett automata (see e.g., [8]), which is expressive enough to faithfully support the representation of all variants we have found in the literature. This uniform representation enables human comprehension and comparison between variants, and serves as a basis for building semantically configurable automated analysis tools.

Our feature model for the semantics of LSC consists of 19 features. One feature, for example, relates to whether the LSC should be interpreted universally or existentially. Another feature relates to the question of whether the chart's semantics is tolerant or strict with regard to partial-order violations by events that appear in it. One feature relates to the semantics of pre-charts in existential charts, a set of features differentiates between invariant, and iterative modes of interpretation, a set of features relates to the use of environment assumptions, and another set of features differentiates between true and interleaving modes of concurrency. Each feature is formally defined as part of the LSC semantics

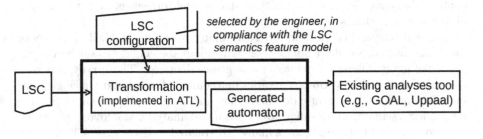

Fig. 1. The architecture of our solution to semantically configurable analysis of LSC

definition. The feature model organizes the different features so that each of its configurations induces a specific overall semantics.

The semantic mapping itself is realized using a model-to-model (M2M) transformation. The input for the transformation consists of (1) an LSC and (2) a valid configuration of the feature model. The output is an automaton, which can be used as input for downstream analysis tools. An overview of the architecture of our solution is shown in Fig. 1.

Our work is fully automated and implemented in a prototype Eclipse plug-in, where one can edit an LSC, select a semantic configuration, and generate an automaton corresponding to the LSC semantics according to the chosen configuration. For LSC editing we use components from PlayGo [15]. For feature model definitions and implementation of feature selection we use components from FeatureIDE [20]. The M2M transformation is implemented in ATL [19].

The remainder of the paper is organized as follows. Sect. 2 discusses related work. Sect. 3 provides an overview and an example. Sect. 4 describes the LSC language and the feature model of its semantics. Sect. 5 presents our technique for semantically configurable analysis. Sect. 6 presents the implementation and a discussion. Sect. 7 concludes.

2   Related Work

The question of how to deal with semantic variability in a modeling language has been investigated before. Several works by Atlee et al., e.g., [35,36], used *template semantics* to configure the semantics of state machines, and demonstrated configured translations of state machines into SMV and into Java. Different from these works, we use a feature model to model semantic variability. Moreover, these works relate to state machine models while our present work focuses on scenario-based models.

Cengarle et al. [2] have presented a taxonomy of variability mechanisms in language definitions syntax and semantics, and demonstrated the use of feature diagrams to model possible variants. The present work builds on these previous ideas while focusing on semantic variability, specifically, semantic mapping variability (rather than syntactic variability) and on its application to semantically configurable analysis, specifically demonstrated and implemented in the context of live sequence charts.

A recent survey [34] has explored the many meanings of UML 2 sequence diagrams. Indeed, we share similar concerns about the challenges set by the existence of many different semantics for sequence diagrams. The survey, however, does not formalize the various semantics mathematically and under a single, uniform formalism as a semantic domain. Thus, unlike our work, it cannot provide a basis for a semantically configurable automated analysis. Moreover, the survey does not focus on LSC and ignores many LSC-related works (e.g., [24,39]), whose semantics we do cover in this paper.

Many previous works provide various analyses for LSC, e.g., formal verification, specification mining, and synthesis (e.g., [9,24,26,32,39]). To the best of our knowledge, none of the works in the LSC literature supports variability-based semantically configurable analysis.

Most recently, the second listed author et al. [30] presented semantically configurable consistency checking of class and object diagrams. The work motivates the use of feature models to support semantically configurable analysis. It uses a feature model to specify variations in the semantics of CDs and ODs, and a parameterized translation of CDs and ODs to Alloy, which is expressive enough to support all the considered variants. This work has inspired us to apply a similar solution to address the challenge of variability in the semantics of LSC.

3   Example and Overview

We use a simple example as an overview of our work. The description is partial and semi-formal. We refer back to this example later in the paper.

We consider a single small LSC, related to the vending machine specification presented in [31,32]. The LSC OnHeatRequest (Fig. 2, left) consists of one environment lifeline (heater) and two system lifelines, representing the system's panel and thermometer. The minimal event of the LSC is a cold heat message that is sent from the panel to the heater. It is followed by two hot messages, with no particular order between them: (1) the panel's own lockPanel message, and (2) the heater's reachMax message to the thermometer.

We define the semantics of an LSC by translation to an automaton. The language accepted by the automaton consists of the runs that satisfy the LSC.

The construction of the automaton consists of a common part and a variable part. The common part (marked in black in Fig. 2, right) includes the states (one for each LSC cut) and the transitions induced by the unwinding of the LSC's partial order. The variable part, marked in several colors according to the corresponding semantic features, consists of (1) additional transitions, (2) a reject state, (3) a quantification on the initial state, and (4) an acceptance condition.

For example, for a universal semantics, the red transitions and reject state are added on top of the common construction. For the choice between a strict and a tolerant interpretation, the purple or the orange transitions are added. To support true concurrency rather than interleaving semantics, the green transitions

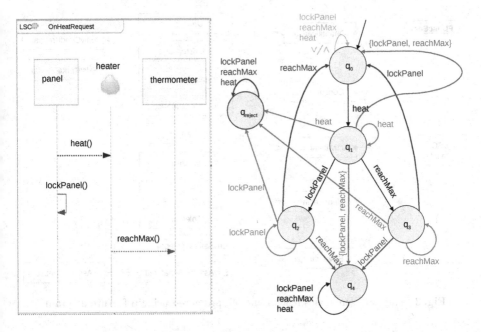

Fig. 2. An example LSC and a sketch of a corresponding automaton. The automaton sketch is color-coded based on the LSC semantics feature model: the common parts are black while the parts corresponding to selected semantic features are marked in different colors, one color per feature.

are added. The choice of whether to consider environment assumptions changes the acceptance condition (not shown in Fig. 2).

Characterizing and formalizing the required variability, and showing how it is implemented in a single, configurable analysis solution, are the challenges we address in this paper.

4   LSC Semantics Variability

We start off with an overview of LSC's common syntax and semantics. We then describe the feature model that organizes LSC's semantic variability.

4.1   Live Sequence Charts Common Syntax and Semantics

A live sequence chart consists of a set of lifelines and messages, depicted in the concrete syntax using vertical lines and arrows between them. Message send and receive events are placed in the intersection of messages and lifelines. On each lifeline, events are fully ordered from top to bottom. Events appearing on different lifelines are not ordered, except that a receive event cannot happen before its corresponding send event. Thus, the LSC syntax induces a partial order over events. This partial order is common to all LSC variants found in the

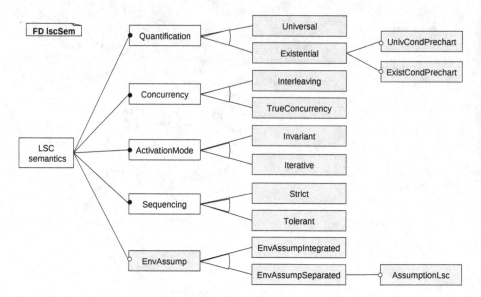

Fig. 3. The LSC semantics feature model, presented using a feature diagram

literature (and in fact also to all message sequence charts and UML sequence diagrams variants).

Another common syntactic feature of all LSC variants is message temperature, which can be either hot or cold. In the concrete syntax, the temperature is reflected by the message's color, red or blue.

These syntax and semantics are common to all LSC variants found in the literature. Next we discuss the semantic variants found in the literature and the feature model we use to formalize and structure them.

4.2   The LSC Semantic Variability Feature Model

A feature model describes a structured set of features and their logical dependencies [1,3]. Feature models are commonly used in the area of software product lines. They may be visually represented using feature diagrams, which are basically and-or trees, extended with textual cross-tree logical constraints. Here we use a feature model to formalize variability in the semantics of LSC. The model includes several cross-tree logical constrains. In the feature diagrams we use the standard notation: for mandatory features, a line ending with a filled circle; for alternative features of which exactly one must be selected (xor), an empty slice covering the lines leading to the different alternatives.

Our feature model consists of 19 features, as shown in the feature diagram in Fig. 3. Roughly, a valid feature configuration of this model specifies whether the semantics is universal or existential (with the kind of pre-chart specified), invariant or iterative, of true concurrency or interleaving, using strict or tolerant sequencing, and whether the semantics includes environment assumptions.

Some of these features have sub-features. Each of the features and sub-features represents a semantic choice used in one or more works from the LSC literature, as we detail next.

The Universal vs. Existential semantic choice was first presented in [4] and appeared in almost all works (although many works support only the universal variant). An existential LSC specifies an interaction example and requires that at least one system run exhibits the events appearing in it (in compliance with the partial order specified by the chart). A universal LSC specifies a rule that all system runs are expected to satisfy. A run satisfies a universal LSC iff each time the LSC is activated its hot enabled messages eventually occur, or an enabled cold message is violated.

A pre-chart appeared already in [4]. Many works use an LSC variant with pre-chart, but not all (e.g., [9,31]). When a pre-chart is used in an existential LSC, two variants are found: one variant, introduced in [4] and called in our feature model existential conditional pre-chart (ExistCondPrechart), states that there should be at least one system run in which if the pre-chart is traversed successfully, then the main chart is fulfilled as well. Another variant with a stronger interpretation requires that whenever the pre-chart is fulfilled there is at least one execution from that point on that satisfies the main chart. This semantic variant is defined in [39] and called in our feature model universal conditional pre-chart (UnivCondPrechart)

The model of concurrency assumed by an LSC may vary. Almost all works use an Interleaving interpretation, where no two events happen at the same point in time. Some works, e.g., [4,22], however, do allow true concurrency (TrueConcurrency).

The kind of sequencing is another distinction found in the literature. Two sequencing kinds are considered: Strict and Tolerant. According to the strict interpretation, events that appear in the chart but are not currently enabled cause a violation. According to the tolerant interpretation, these events do not cause a violation. In all variants, the chart's sequencing ignores events not appearing in the chart. Almost all works use strict sequencing. Tolerant sequencing is formalized and investigated in [16].

The mode of activation is another variation found in the literature. We consider two activation modes from the literature: Invariant and Iterative. In invariant activation mode, every occurrence of a minimal event activates the chart. In iterative mode, a chart is not activated if it is currently active (so at most one instance of the chart may be active at each point in time). The invariant mode is used in many works, e.g., [4,6,13,22,39]. The iterative mode is used in other works, e.g., [10,22,24].

Finally, the use of liveness environment assumptions is another variation point in the LSC literature. Some works make a distinction between environment and system lifelines, which is reflected in the LSC semantics; when the environment violates its assumptions, the system is no longer required to fulfill its guarantees. An integrated variant, which allows to specify environment assumptions and system guarantees in a single LSC, is presented in [31] and used in [15].

A variant where assumptions must appear in separate LSCs is presented in [9,22] and used in [10]. However, while most works do make a syntactic distinction between environment and system lifelines, many of them, e.g., [13,17,39], do not support liveness environment assumptions.

Cross-Tree Constraints. To complete the feature model, we add to the feature diagram cross-tree logical constraints that define dependencies between the different features, for us, the semantic choices, e.g., mutual exclusion, implication etc. This is indeed necessary, because, as we have found, not all theoretically possible combinations (feature configurations) induce well-defined and useful semantics (which appeared in the literature). Specifically, we use two cross-tree constraints:

$$\text{EnvAssump implies Universal} \tag{1}$$

$$\text{not (UnivCondPrechart and ExistCondPrechart)} \tag{2}$$

We add constraint 1 because the provisional behavior specified by an existential semantics is too weak to be useful as an assumption on the environment's behavior (*"The quantification is always universal, because assumptions express universal constraints on the behavior of the environment"*, [21, p. 196]). Indeed, in the literature all works that support environment assumptions (e.g., [9,31]) support only universal LSCs. We add constraint 2 because a pre-chart in an exististial LSC may have either a universal conditional semantics or an existential conditional semantics, but not both.

Overall, our feature model contains 19 features, 5 of which are core features, i.e., features that are included in all configurations. The model has 56 valid configurations. The complete feature model we have defined is available in [27], in formats compliant with S.P.L.O.T [33] and with FeatureIDE [20], to allow others to inspect it and use it.

5   Semantically Configurable Analysis

We start with a short overview of the target formalism we use as the semantic domain for LSC. We then describe the model-to-model transformation we have defined to support semantically configurable analysis.

5.1   Alternating One Pair Streett Automata

The key to the semantically configurable analysis is a transformation to a single, uniform formalism, in our case, an alternating one pair Streett automaton [8].

Roughly, an alternating automaton's transition function maps a state and an alphabet symbol to a positive Boolean expression over states. It thus allows expressing both non-determinism (disjunction) and concurrency (conjunction). A Streett acceptance condition consists of a set of pairs of bad and good sets of states; a run is accepted iff for each pair, if it visits the bad set infinitely often it also visits the good set infinitely often.

For our purposes of representing the semantics of all LSC variants found in the literature, a simpler automaton is sufficient. Specifically, we need only one pair $(F, E) \subseteq Q^2$ of bad and good sets of states for the Streett acceptance condition, and we can limit quantification to the automaton's initial state (and in the case of pre-chart to at most one more state).

In addition to an LSC, the input for the transformation includes one valid configuration of the LSC semantics feature model described in Sect. 4. We now describe the transformation as it is implemented in ATL [19]. We use the LSC presented earlier in Sect. 3 as a running example.

5.2   Overview of the Transformation

The ATL transformation uses three meta models: (1) for LSC (input), (2) for a semantics configuration (input), and (3) for an alternating one pair Streett automaton (output). As the transformation is quite complex we use many ATL helpers, to define required data structures and functions.

Most importantly, the transformation uses two kinds of rules: **common rules**, which are invoked based on the LSC input model only and apply to all variants (e.g., construct the unwinding structure based on the partial order), and **feature specific rules**, which are invoked based on the input feature model configuration (rule per feature, see details below).

The notions of unwinding structure, cut and the events it induces, etc. are common to all LSC variants, see, e.g., [13]. For lack of space we do not repeat their definition here and do not show the common transformation rules. The complete transformation is available from [27]. Here we focus only on the feature specific rules.

5.3   Handling Semantic Variability: Feature Specific Rules

Handling variability is technically realized using feature specific rules. Below we show how some of the features are handled and demonstrate the application of the rules to the example LSC shown in Sect. 3.

Universal vs. Existential. List. 1.1 shows two rules. The rule universal (lines 1-13) matches the feature Universal in the configuration Conf. It stores the universal quantification enumerator in a global variable and if a pre-chart exists it connects its unwinding structure to the main chart's unwinding structure. In addition, it generates transitions that represent the LSC's successful traversal. Next, it creates a reject state, turns it into a sink vertex and adds it to the set F of the acceptance condition. Finally, it sets the set E of the acceptance condition to include all cold states. The rule is applied iff the input configuration includes the feature Universal.

For example, in Fig. 2, the resulting contribution of the rule universal is marked in red: it consists of the transitions going from states q_2 and q_3 to state q_0 as well as the additional state q_{reject} and its self-transition. With this construction, a run that starts $(heat, reachMax, lockPanel)$ returns to the initial state q_0, ready for another activation of the LSC.

```
1  rule universal {
2    from f  :  Conf!Universal
3    do {
4      self.initialStateQuant  <- #Universal;
5      if (self.isPrechartSet)
6        self.joinCharts();
7      self.generateBackTransitions();
8      self.generateRejectState();
9      self.selfTrans(self.mappedSymbols, self.rejectState);
10     self.addToFstates(self.rejectState);
11     for (state in self.unwindingStructureStates) {
12       if (self.isCold(state))
13         self.addToEstates(state);}}}
14 rule existential {
15   from f  :  Conf!Existential
16   do {
17     self.initialStateQuant  <- #Existential;
18     self.ignoreTemperature  <- true;
19     self.connectAcceptingSinkState();}}
```

Listing 1.1. ATL rules to support existential and universal semantics

The rule `existential` (lines 14-19) matches the feature `Existential` in the configuration `Conf`. It stores the existential quantification enumerator in a global variable and instructs the transformation to ignore message temperature. It is applied iff the input configuration includes the feature `Existential`.

As an example, in Fig. 2, the resulting contribution of the rule `existential` is marked in blue: it consists of the transitions going from states q_2 and q_3 to state q_4. After applying this rule, a run that starts $(heat, reachMax, lockPanel)$ reaches the state q_4 and stays there forever.

Invariant vs. Iterative. List. 1.2 shows two rules. The rule `invariant` (List. 1.2 lines 1-9) matches the feature `Invariant` in the configuration `Conf`. It creates a self-transition (loop) on the initial state, labeled with all used alphabet symbols, and sets the quantification on the transitions outgoing the initial state to the quantification stored by the `universal / existential` rules. If a pre-chart is present, it sets the quantification on transitions outgoing the initial state of the main chart in a similiar manner. It is applied iff the input configuration includes the feature `Invariant`.

Fig. 2 demonstrates the contribution of the rule `invariant`: a self-transition on q_0 and a quantification on q_0's outgoing transitions (marked in light blue). For instance, in combination with universal strict semantics, a run that starts $(heat, heat)$ branches out to three states: q_0, q_1 and q_{reject}, representing three copies of the LSC.

The rule `iterative` (List. 1.2 lines 10-13) matches the feature `Iterative` in the configuration `Conf`. It creates self-transitions on the initial state, for all symbols that do not yet appear on any outgoing transition from the initial state. It is applied iff the input configuration includes the feature `Iterative`.

```
1  rule invariant {
2    from f: Conf!Invariant
3    do {
4      self.selfTransMappedSymbols(self.initialState);
5      self.initialState.quantification <-
6              self.initialStateQuant;
7      if (self.isPrechartSet)
8        self.prechartToMainState.quantification <-
9              self.prechartToMainStateQuant;}}
10 rule iterative {
11   from f: Conf!Iterative
12   do {
13     self.selfTransUnboundedSymbols(self.initialState);}}
```

Listing 1.2. ATL rules to support invariant and iterative semantics

Strict vs. Tolerant. List. 1.3 shows two rules. The rule `strict` (lines 1-7) matches the feature `Strict` in the configuration `Conf`. It iterates over the states in the unwinding structure and for each state creates outgoing transitions either to the initial state or to the reject state, in correspondence to the messages causing violations in it. It is applied iff the input configuration includes the feature `Strict`.

Fig. 2 shows the contribution of the rule `strict` in the context of universal semantics. It includes three transitions going from $q1, q2$ and $q3$ to q_{reject} (marked in purple). For instance, all the runs that start $(heat, heat)$ visit q_{reject} and stay there forever.

The rule `tolerant` (lines 8-12) matches the feature `Tolerant` in the configuration `Conf`. It iterates over the states in the unwinding structure and for each state generates a self-transition that carries all the symbols that are included in any outgoing transition. It is applied iff the input configuration includes the feature `Tolerant`.

The contribution of the rule `tolerant` is depicted in Fig. 2: three self-transitions on the states $q1, q2$ and $q3$ (marked in orange). For instance, in this case the infinite word $(heat, heat, reachMax, lockPanel)^\omega$ is accepted by both in universal and existential semantics.

Environment Assumptions. List. 1.4 shows two rules. The rule `assumptionLsc` (lines 1-5) matches the feature `AssumptionLsc` in the configuration `Conf`. It sets the set E of the acceptance condition to include all states. It is applied iff the input configuration includes the feature `AssumptionLsc`.

The rule `envAssumpIntegrated` (lines 6-16) matches the feature `EnvAssump-Integrated` in the configuration `Conf`. It sets the set F of the acceptance condition to include all cold-environment-hot-system states and the set E of the acceptance condition to include all cold-system states. It is applied iff the input configuration includes the feature `EnvAssumpIntegrated`. In the example shown in Fig. 2, in the context of universal semantics and in the case where the feature `EnvAssump` is not selected, the acceptance condition is set to $F = Q$

```
1  rule strict {
2    from f: Conf!Strict
3    do {
4      for (state in self.unwindingStructureStates) {
5        if (state <> self.initialState and
6            state <> self.acceptingSinkState)
7          self.violatingTrans(state);}}}
8  rule tolerant {
9    from f: Conf!Tolerant
10   do {
11     for (state in self.unwindingStructureStates) {
12       self.addUnboundedSymbolsToSelfTrans(state);}}}
```

Listing 1.3. ATL rules to support tolerant and strict semantics

```
1  rule assumptionLSC {
2    from f: Conf!assumptionLSC
3    do {
4      for (state in Automaton!State.allInstances()) {
5        self.E_states <- self.E_states.including(state);}}}
6  rule envAssumpIntegrated {
7    from f: Conf!envAssumpIntegrated
8    do {
9      self.F_states <- Set{};   self.E_states <- Set{};
10     if (not self.rejectState.oclIsUndefined())
11       self.F_states <- Set{self.rejectState};
12     for (state in self.unwindingStructureStates) {
13       if (self.isCEHS(self.matchingCut(state)))
14         self.F_states <- self.F_states.including(state);
15       else if (self.isCS(self.matchingCut(state)))
16         self.E_states <- self.E_states.including(state);}}}
```

Listing 1.4. ATL rules to support assumptions

(the complete set of states) and $E = \{q_0, q_4\}$. In the case where the features
EnvAssump and EnvAssumpIntegrated are selected, the acceptance condition is
set to $F = \{q_3, q_{reject}\}$ and $E = \{q_0, q_2, q_4\}$.

6   Implementation, Validation, and Discussion

Implementation. We have created a prototype implementation of our work,
packaged as an Eclipse plug-in. For the representation of the LSC semantics
feature model and the selection of valid configurations we use components from
FeatureIDE [20]. For editing LSCs we use the UI and APIs of PlayGo [15]. The
M2M transformation is implemented in ATL [19]. The prototype plug-in together
with several examples is available from [27].

Validation. We validated our solution as follows. First, we implemented tests
that iterate and apply all possible configurations of the feature model to a set of

non-trivial LSCs, and check various properties of the resulting automata (e.g., the existence of a specific self-transition etc.). The tests are available from [27].

Second, we used the output of our solution as input for GOAL [40] (a Graphical Tool for ω-Automata and Logics), and thus executed several usage scenarios, including (1) verifying an automaton against a property LSC, (2) checking the consistency of an LSC specification, while applying several, different semantic configurations. Details of these examples of usage scenarios are available from [27].

Choice of Variability Modeling Language. Our choice of feature diagrams as a variability modeling language was motivated by its wide use in the literature, its tool support (we use FeatureIDE [20]) and its expressive power, which is good enough for our purposes. Considering other means to model variability in our context, e.g., the Common Variability Language (CVL) [18], is outside the scope of this paper.

Choice of Target Formalism. Our choice of alternating one pair Streett automata as the target formalism for the semantics definition was motivated by its expressive power, which covers all variants found in the literature. Alternatively, one may use a Buchi acceptance condition, however, we consider this to be less intuitive for the variants involving environment assumptions.

Choice of Transformation Language. Our choice of ATL for the implementation of the model-to-model transformation was motivated by its tool and standard support. It allowed us to create a rather high-level readable code that reflects the one-to-one mapping between features and rules.

Set of Supported LSC Language Constructs. Our current work supports a limited set of LSC constructs, which excludes, e.g., asynchronous messages, conditions, and various interaction fragments (alternatives, loops). The semantics of some of these constructs does not seem to vary in the literature, but they are defined and used so they are necessary for a more comprehensive solution.

7   Conclusion

In this paper we have investigated the idea of semantically configurable analysis in the context of live sequence charts. We formalized semantic variability in LSC using a feature model and presented a semantically configurable fully automated analysis solution based on a transformation to an alternating one pair Streett automaton, capable of expressing all semantic variants found in the literature. The work was implemented in an Eclipse plug-in and demonstrated with examples.

We consider the following possible future work. First, our current work focuses on semantic variability and thus considers a set of LSC variants that share a core syntax. One may extend our work to also explore and model syntactic variability for LSC. Second, we consider integrating our semantically configurable analysis with existing tools that are using LSC, such as PlayGo [15] and ScenarioTools [10,37].

The paper continues our previous work on semantically configurable analysis [30] and is part of our larger project on investigating formal and automated ways to handling variability in modeling languages syntax and semantics.

References

1. Batory, D.S.: Feature models, grammars, and propositional formulas. In: Obbink, H., Pohl, K. (eds.) SPLC 2005. LNCS, vol. 3714, pp. 7–20. Springer, Heidelberg (2005)
2. Cengarle, M.V., Grönniger, H., Rumpe, B.: Variability within modeling language definitions. In: Schürr, A., Selic, B. (eds.) MODELS 2009. LNCS, vol. 5795, pp. 670–684. Springer, Heidelberg (2009)
3. Czarnecki, K., Eisenecker, U.: Generative Programming Methods, Tools, and Applications. Addison-Wesley (2000)
4. Damm, W., Harel, D.: LSCs: Breathing Life into Message Sequence Charts. Formal Methods in System Design 19(1), 45–80 (2001)
5. Damm, W., Toben, T., Westphal, B.: On the expressive power of live sequence charts. In: Reps, T., Sagiv, M., Bauer, J. (eds.) Wilhelm Festschrift. LNCS, vol. 4444, pp. 225–246. Springer, Heidelberg (2007)
6. Damm, W., Westphal, B.: Live and let die: LSC-based verification of UML-models. In: de Boer, F.S., Bonsangue, M.M., Graf, S., de Roever, W.-P. (eds.) FMCO 2002. LNCS, vol. 2852, pp. 99–135. Springer, Heidelberg (2003)
7. Fischbein, D., D'Ippolito, N., Sibay, G., Uchitel, S.: Modal Transition System Analyzer (MTSA), http://sourceforge.net/projects/mtsa/ (accessed September 2013)
8. Grädel, E., Thomas, W., Wilke, T. (eds.): Automata, Logics, and Infinite Games. LNCS, vol. 2500. Springer, Heidelberg (2002)
9. Greenyer, J., Brenner, C., Cordy, M., Heymans, P., Gressi, E.: Incrementally synthesizing controllers from scenario-based product line specifications. In: ESEC/SIGSOFT FSE, pp. 433–443. ACM (2013)
10. Greenyer, J., Brenner, C., Manna, V.P.L.: The ScenarioTools Play-Out of Modal Sequence Diagram Specifications with Environment Assumptions. ECEASST 58 (2013)
11. Greenyer, J., Sharifloo, A.M., Cordy, M., Heymans, P.: Efficient consistency checking of scenario-based product-line specifications. In: RE, pp. 161–170. IEEE (2012)
12. Harel, D., Kugler, H.: Synthesizing state-based object systems from LSC specifications. Int. J. Found. Comput. Sci. 13(1), 5–51 (2002)
13. Harel, D., Maoz, S.: Assert and negate revisited: Modal semantics for UML sequence diagrams. Software and Systems Modeling 7(2), 237–252 (2008)
14. Harel, D., Maoz, S., Segall, I.: Some results on the expressive power and complexity of LSCs. In: Avron, A., Dershowitz, N., Rabinovich, A. (eds.) Trakhtenbrot/Festschrift. LNCS, vol. 4800, pp. 351–366. Springer, Heidelberg (2008)
15. Harel, D., Maoz, S., Szekely, S., Barkan, D.: PlayGo: towards a comprehensive tool for scenario based programming. In: ASE, pp. 359–360. ACM (2010)
16. Harel, D., Marelly, R.: Come, let's play - scenario-based programming using LSCs and the play-engine. Springer (2003)
17. Harel, D., Segall, I.: Synthesis from scenario-based specifications. J. Comput. Syst. Sci. 78(3), 970–980 (2012)
18. Haugen, Ø., Møller-Pedersen, B., Oldevik, J., Olsen, G.K., Svendsen, A.: Adding standardized variability to domain specific languages. In: SPLC, pp. 139–148. IEEE Computer Society (2008)

19. Jouault, F., Allilaire, F., Bézivin, J., Kurtev, I.: ATL: A model transformation tool. Sci. Comput. Program. 72(1-2), 31–39 (2008)
20. Kästner, C., Thüm, T., Saake, G., Feigenspan, J., Leich, T., Wielgorz, F., Apel, S.: FeatureIDE: A tool framework for feature-oriented software development. In: ICSE, pp. 611–614 (2009)
21. Klose, J.: Live sequence charts: a graphical formalism for the specification of communication behavior. PhD thesis, University of Oldenburg (2003)
22. Klose, J., Toben, T., Westphal, B., Wittke, H.: Check it out: On the efficient formal verification of live sequence charts. In: Ball, T., Jones, R.B. (eds.) CAV 2006. LNCS, vol. 4144, pp. 219–233. Springer, Heidelberg (2006)
23. Kugler, H., Harel, D., Pnueli, A., Lu, Y., Bontemps, Y.: Temporal logic for scenario-based specifications. In: Halbwachs, N., Zuck, L.D. (eds.) TACAS 2005. LNCS, vol. 3440, pp. 445–460. Springer, Heidelberg (2005)
24. Larsen, K.G., Li, S., Nielsen, B., Pusinskas, S.: Scenario-based analysis and synthesis of real-time systems using Uppaal. In: DATE, pp. 447–452. IEEE (2010)
25. Li, S., Balaguer, S., David, A., Larsen, K.G., Nielsen, B., Pusinskas, S.: Scenario-based verification of real-time systems using Uppaal. Formal Methods in System Design 37(2-3), 200–264 (2010)
26. Lo, D., Maoz, S.: Scenario-based and value-based specification mining: better together. Autom. Softw. Eng. 19(4), 423–458 (2012)
27. LSC semantic variability supporting materials, http://smlab.cs.tau.ac.il/lscvar/
28. Maoz, S.: Polymorphic scenario-based specification models: semantics and applications. Software and Systems Modeling 11(3), 327–345 (2012)
29. Maoz, S., Harel, D., Kleinbort, A.: A compiler for multimodal scenarios: Transforming LSCs into AspectJ. ACM Trans. Softw. Eng. Methodol. 20(4), 18 (2011)
30. Maoz, S., Ringert, J.O., Rumpe, B.: Semantically configurable consistency analysis for class and object diagrams. In: Whittle, J., Clark, T., Kühne, T. (eds.) MODELS 2011. LNCS, vol. 6981, pp. 153–167. Springer, Heidelberg (2011)
31. Maoz, S., Sa'ar, Y.: Assume-guarantee scenarios: Semantics and synthesis. In: France, R.B., Kazmeier, J., Breu, R., Atkinson, C. (eds.) MODELS 2012. LNCS, vol. 7590, pp. 335–351. Springer, Heidelberg (2012)
32. Maoz, S., Sa'ar, Y.: Counter play-out: executing unrealizable scenario-based specifications. In: ICSE, pp. 242–251. IEEE / ACM (2013)
33. Mendonça, M., Branco, M., Cowan, D.D.: S.P.L.O.T.: software product lines online tools. In: OOPSLA Companion, pp. 761–762 (2009)
34. Micskei, Z., Waeselynck, H.: The many meanings of UML 2 Sequence Diagrams: a survey. Software and Systems Modeling (SoSyM) 10(4), 489–514 (2011)
35. Niu, J., Atlee, J.M., Day, N.A.: Template semantics for model-based notations. IEEE Trans. Software Eng. 29(10), 866–882 (2003)
36. Prout, A., Atlee, J.M., Day, N.A., Shaker, P.: Code generation for a family of executable modelling notations. Software and Systems Modeling 11(2), 251–272 (2012)
37. ScenarioTools, http://www.scenariotools.org/ (accessed September 2013)
38. Sibay, G.E., Braberman, V.A., Uchitel, S., Kramer, J.: Synthesizing modal transition systems from triggered scenarios. IEEE Trans. Software Eng. 39(7), 975–1001 (2013)
39. Sibay, G.E., Uchitel, S., Braberman, V.A.: Existential live sequence charts revisited. In: ICSE, pp. 41–50. ACM (2008)
40. Tsay, Y.-K., Chen, Y.-F., Tsai, M.-H., Wu, K.-N., Chan, W.-C.: GOAL: A Graphical Tool for Manipulating Büchi Automata and Temporal Formulae. In: Grumberg, O., Huth, M. (eds.) TACAS 2007. LNCS, vol. 4424, pp. 466–471. Springer, Heidelberg (2007)

Formal Verification of Medical Device User Interfaces Using PVS[*]

Paolo Masci[1,**], Yi Zhang[2], Paul Jones[2],
Paul Curzon[1], and Harold Thimbleby[3]

[1] School of Electronic Engineering and Computer Science
Queen Mary University of London, United Kingdom
{paolo.masci,pc}@eecs.qmul.ac.uk
[2] Center for Device and Radiological Health,
U.S. Food and Drug Administration, Silver Spring, Maryland, USA
{yi.zhang2,paul.jones}@fda.hhs.gov
[3] FIT Lab, Future Interaction Technology Laboratory
Swansea University, United Kingdom
harold@thimbleby.net

Abstract. We present a formal verification approach for detecting design issues related to user interaction, with a focus on user interface of medical devices. The approach makes a novel use of configuration diagrams proposed by Rushby to formally verify important human factors properties of user interface implementation. In particular, it first translates the software implementation of user interface into an equivalent formal specification, from which a behavioral model is constructed using theorem proving; human factors properties are then verified against the behavioral model; lastly, a comprehensive set of test inputs are produced by exploring the behavioral model, which can be used to challenge the real interface implementation and to ensure that the issues detected in the behavior model do apply to the implementation.

We have prototyped the approach based on the PVS proof system, and applied it to analyze the user interface of a real medical device. The analysis detected several interaction design issues in the device, which may potentially lead to severe consequences.

Keywords: Software verification, Medical devices, User interfaces.

1   Introduction

In many countries, manufacturers of medical devices are required to assure reasonable safety and effectiveness of software in their devices; they have to provide adequate evidence to support this before their device can be placed on the market [1]. When considering the safety of a medical device, human factors issues

---

[*] The rights of this work are transferred to the extent transferable according to title 17 U.S.C. 105.

[**] Corresponding author.

S. Gnesi and A. Rensink (Eds.): FASE 2014, LNCS 8411, pp. 200–214, 2014.
© Springer-Verlag Berlin Heidelberg 2014

that include the human-device interface are critical. We refer to the part of a device that the user receives information from and provides information to as *the user interface*. Software in the device that contributes to the behavior of this interface we refer to as *user interface software*. User interface software defines the way in which a device supports user actions (e.g., the effect of clicking a (Start) button) and provides feedback (e.g., rendering error messages on the device's display) in response to events.

The development of user interface software, or more generally, the interaction design of medical devices, is not standardized in the industry. Instead, each device manufacturer crafts its own device interaction design. A number of reports (such as [27]) have asserted that manufacturers typically address human factors issues within their user interface software in an ad hoc manner, rather than using rigorous design and evaluation techniques. Part of the reason lies in the fact that human factors specialists are usually involved too late in the software development process, if at all. These specialists typically base their analysis upon methods like heuristic evaluation [10], which require the availability of a fairly complete user interface prototype. As a result, it is often too late and too expensive to find and correct an interaction design flaw. Software engineers, on the other hand, do not have effective means to identify human factors related flaws in a software implementation, if such flaws are inherited from system-level design and defined in software requirements and design specifications.

The reality described above, as well as the fact that many manufactures reuse legacy code to develop new devices, makes it necessary to verify interaction design flaws after a user interface is implemented. However, dosing so can be expensive and time-consuming. It is more desirable and cost-effective if such flaws can be detected and weeded out early on (e.g. at the design stage). Rigorous development techniques, such as model-based design [13,22], can help to achieve this objective, if integrated into the development life-cycle.

In this paper, we focus on user interface software in medical devices, and present a formal approach for detecting design issues in such software. The approach translates the source-code implementation of user interface software into a formal specification. Theorem proving is then used to generate from this specification a behavioral model of the software. This model captures the control structure and behavior of the software related to handling user interactions. During this process, theorem proving is also used to prove that important human factors principles are satisfied by (all reachable states of) the model, or otherwise to detect potential interaction design issues. The behavioral model generated is also exhaustively explored to derive a suite of test input sequences that can expose the detected interaction design issues, if any, in the implementation of the user interface software.

The contributions of the paper are as follows. (i) We present a formal approach to generate and verify behavioral models of user interface software. The approach is based on a novel use of configuration diagrams [23]. (ii) We describe a case study based on a real medical infusion pump. The presented approach is demonstrated within PVS [20] for a C++ implementation of the device user interface software. Our approach was successful in detecting multiple interaction design issues from the implementation of the user interface software of the subject pump, many of which could potentially cause severe consequences.

The reason that we chose infusion pumps as a representative class of medical devices for study is because many infusion pumps suffer from poor human factors design. In fact, 87 models of infusion pumps were recalled in the US alone between 2005 and 2009. Human factors issues were among the primary causes for these recalls [6].

The present work builds on our previous research on the verification of medical device user interfaces [11,14–16,22] and on user interface prototyping [19]. These previous efforts have demonstrated that formal methods can be used to identify human factors issues in reverse-engineered models of medical devices. This paper presents an approach that continues our previous work, and extends rigorous analysis to source code implementations of real user interfaces.

2   Example Results from Formal Source Code Analysis

To better illustrate the usefulness of our approach, we first explain the results of applying it to analyze the user interface implementation of a real infusion pump. In this case study, the details of which are introduced in section 4, our approach detected four interaction issues listed below. These issues cause the pump to either overlook user errors or interpret input numbers in an erroneous way. In either situation, unexpected numbers may be used to configure the pump, which can potentially cause serious clinical consequences (e.g., a lethal dose of drug is infused to the patient, because the amount of drug to be infused is mistakenly configured as an extremely large number).

Valid Input Key Sequences Are Incorrectly Registered without the User's Awareness. The pump mistakenly discards the decimal point in input key sequences for fractional numbers between [100.1, 1200). For example, the input key sequence $\boxed{1}\,\boxed{0}\,\boxed{0}\,\boxed{\bullet}\,\boxed{1}$ is registered as 1001 without any warning or error message. This issue arises because of a constraint imposed in a routine of the pump's software: numbers above or equal to 100 cannot have a fractional part. Due to this constraint, the pump erroneously ignores the decimal point in the key sequence $\boxed{1}\,\boxed{0}\,\boxed{0}\,\boxed{\bullet}\,\boxed{1}$, and registers it as 1001. This issue opens the possibility that a user commits a missing decimal point error and accidentally inputs a value ten times larger than the intended one (an out-by-ten error).

Inappropriate Feedback is Given to the User for Error Conditions. The pump produces an inappropriate error message for fractional numbers between [120.1, 1200). For example, the pump rejects the input key sequence $\boxed{2}\,\boxed{0}\,\boxed{0}$ $\boxed{\bullet}\,\boxed{1}$ with the error message *"HIGH"* even if the range of accepted values is (0, 1200]. The reason for this issue is because the pump erroneously ignores the decimal point in the key sequence and registers the number as 2001, which is beyond the permitted range. What the pump should have reported is a message like *"The input value 200.1 should not have a fractional part"*. Even though the pump rejects the key sequence for ⟨2⟩⟨0⟩⟨0⟩⟨•⟩⟨1⟩, it accepts key sequences for integers on either side of 200.1. Without appropriate feedback, the user might not understand why keying a number within the range limits supported by the device is rejected, and could erroneously reach the conclusion that the device is malfunctioning.

Ill-Formed Input Key Sequences Are Silently Accepted without the User's Awareness. For instance, the sequence ⟨9⟩⟨•⟩⟨9⟩⟨•⟩⟨1⟩ is accepted and registered as 9.91 with the second decimal point silently discarded. This invalid input sequence might be the result of a user error in reality. For example, the user intends to input the value of 99.1, but due to issues like inattention, he/she presses an unnecessary ⟨•⟩ between two ⟨9⟩ keys. Accepting such invalid key sequences could allow user errors to go undetected. The safe and correct way of handling such invalid sequences is to halt user interaction and return a warning message.

Digits after Decimal Point Silently Discarded without the User's Awareness. For instance, the pump mistakenly registers the input key sequence ⟨1⟩⟨0⟩⟨•⟩⟨0⟩⟨9⟩ as 10, as opposed to the intended 10.09. The reason for this issue is because the pump software automatically limits the accuracy of numbers to one decimal digit for values between [10, 100).

Notably, we used input sequences like the above to challenge another infusion pump from a different manufacturer. Similar design issues were observed for the same input sequences. This suggests that such design flaws may be common to different implementations of user interface software. Therefore, fixing defects presented in this paper can result in significant improvement in the safety of infusion pumps [29], and possibly other devices that incorporate interactive data entry software (such as ventilators and radiation therapy systems).

3   The Approach

Our approach, as depicted in figure 1, starts with translating the source code of user interface software of medical devices into a formal specification acceptable to the PVS theorem prover. A behavioral model is then extracted, in a mechanized manner, from the formal specification using PVS and configuration diagrams. Theorem proving is also applied to the behavioral model to verify its compliance to human factor design principles. Lastly, the behavioral model is exhaustively explored to generate a suite of test key sequences that expose interaction design issues of the original device.

3.1   From C++ Code to PVS Specifications

PVS is a well known industrial-level theorem prover that enables mechanized verification of potentially infinite-state systems. It is based on a typed higher-order logic, and its specification language has many features similar to those of C++. These similarities between the two languages make it possible to devise a set of guidelines for translating (a subset of) C++ programs into PVS specifications, with the semantics of the original C++ programs preserved.

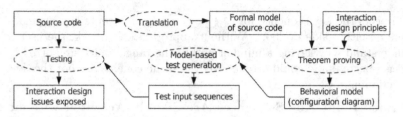

Fig. 1. Overview of our approach for verifying user interface software

Our approach adopts the following guidelines to manually translate C++ programs into PVS specifications. These guidelines provide a systematic approach for the translation:

- Conditional and iterative statements in C++ are straightforwardly translated to their counterparts in the PVS specification language;
- Computation in C++, which is typically defined as instructions modifying the values of variables of objects, is emulated in PVS with the assistance of a record type, namely state. In type state, each field is defined to record the value of a member variable in C++. Thus, computation over C++ variables can be translated as updating the fields of state accordingly. Type state is then passed to all PVS functions for reference and update;
- C++ functions are emulated in PVS as higher-order functions with the same function arguments, while local variables in C++ functions are emulated using the PVS LET-IN construct that binds expressions to local names;
- Class inheritance in C++ is translated by introducing a field in the structure that translates (the state variables of) the base class.

Data types in C++, such as float and integer, can be mimicked in PVS using subtyping [25], a PVS language mechanism that restricts the data domain of types. For instance, the subtype {x: real | x >= FLOAT_MIN AND x <= FLOAT_MAX} checks if a real-typed variable has value within the range from FLOAT_MIN to FLOAT_MAX. In many cases, subtyping is sufficient to check whether a behavioral model correctly captures all boundary conditions encountered by the C++ implementation. Furthermore, PVS includes a standard library that emulates C++ data types such as lists and strings, as well as common C++ library functions such as strcmp.

It is worth pointing out that, the translation of C++ programs benefits from the strong type-checking mechanism in PVS. That is, if data types declared in the PVS specifications are consistent with those in the C++ code, PVS can assist in detecting type errors in the C++ code. With appropriate subtypes, it is also possible to conduct more sophisticated type checking using PVS to detect common coding errors in C++, such as null pointer dereferences, use-before-def errors, and out-of-bound array accesses.

Currently, the translation of C++ programs in our approach considers only basic C++ constructs. The translation of complex C++ features, such as passing function parameters by reference, is left for future work, as it is not needed for our case study.

3.2 Generation of Behavioral Models from PVS Specifications

Safe user interface design for medical devices needs to comply with important human factors principles, such as consistency of actions, feedback, mode clarity, and ability to undo. As shown in [12], such principles can be formalized as properties that must always be˙satisfied by a device. Our approach formalizes such principles as invariants that the behavioral model of user interface software in medical devices must satisfy.

We use in a novel way configuration diagrams, first proposed in [23], to extract the behavioral model from the PVS specification of user interface software, and to prove invariants of interest against the model. The intuition of configuration diagrams is that, proving an invariant G can be facilitated by using a strengthening invariant A, where A is given as a disjunction of properties $A = A_1 \vee \cdots \vee A_k$. Then, instead of proving G, the proof is done on $G \wedge A$, or, equivalently, $(G \wedge A_1) \vee \cdots \vee (G \wedge A_k)$. Properties A_i need not to be invariants, which makes them easier to define. Sub-properties $C_i = G \wedge A_i$ are referred to as *configurations*.

All configurations encountered during the analysis can be organized as a configuration diagram, which is a labeled graph where each node corresponds to a configuration, each edge represents a possible transition between configurations, and the labels marked on the edges denote conditions that enable transitions.

Our approach follows the following mechanized process, also presented in [23], to construct configuration diagrams for PVS specifications:

1. Invent a configuration C_1; Use the theorem prover to verify that C_1 is reachable from the initial state and C_1 satisfies the property being verified.
2. Identify the conditions that trigger outgoing transitions from C_1, and use the theorem prover to check if the disjunction of these conditions is *true*. This ensures that all possible cases are covered.
3. For each condition identified in (2), use the theorem prover to perform a symbolic execution for one step from C_1. This returns a new configuration C_2, an already existing configuration, or a variant of an existing one. If new configurations are obtained, check them against the property being verified.
4. Repeat steps (2) and (3) until no new configuration is encountered.

An example of using configuration diagrams to extract and verify behavioral models can be found in sub-sections 4.3 and 4.4.

3.3 Generation of Test Input Sequences

In many modern medical devices user interaction is carried out by clicking buttons. Test cases to (the user interface of) these devices can therefore be given in the form of a sequence of key presses that the user performs to operate the devices. The effectiveness of using input key sequences to analyze the user interface of medical devices has been demonstrated in [5], where key sequences reflecting arbitrary user strategies were generated to assess the sensitivity of infusion pumps to unnoticed key slip errors.

In our approach, however, key sequences are generated from configuration diagrams, and used as test cases to challenge the real implementation of user interface software. That is, an analyst can watch the execution of the implementation based on the generated key sequences, so as to confirm whether or not it actually possesses the design issues detected in its behavioral model.

To generate key sequences from a configuration diagram, our approach traverses the diagram and identifies user actions associated with its transitions. Formally, a *walk* in a configuration diagram is a sequence $n_0 \xrightarrow{e_{01}} n_1 \xrightarrow{e_{12}} n_2 \ldots$, where n_i is a node in the diagram, and e_{ij} is an edge connecting node n_i to n_j. By collecting user actions (key presses in our case) marked on each edge e_{ij} in a walk, one can produce a sequence of key presses that can be used as a test case.

3.4 Discussion

Most of the model construction and proof tasks in our approach are automated by PVS and *grind*, a powerful decision procedure included in PVS, which repeatedly applies definition expansion, propositional simplification, and decision support to assist the analysis [26]. Human intervention is required only for two purposes: 1) guide PVS to prune irrelevant details away from the analysis, in order to avoid case-explosion and keep the generated configuration diagram compact; and 2) guide PVS to decompose theorems into sub-theorems. More specifically, the analyst needs to select or modify control conditions of the behavioral model suggested by PVS. PVS then checks if the selected or modified ones cover all possible model execution paths.

It should be noted that, even though human intervention demands skills and expertise with PVS, the level of human involvement required by our approach does promote active thinking for the analyst, giving her/him deep insights into the software's control structure and behavior. Because of this active involvement, it is possible to identify (the root cause of) issues and their fixes before the analysis is complete [23].

Lastly, the key point of generating useful key sequences, as in traditional software test generation, is to ensure that the key sequences derived from the configuration diagram achieve full coverage of the diagram. This ensures that the generated key sequences represent all possible user interactions that user interface software may encounter. Our approach currently realizes the generation of test sequences based on manual browsing of configuration diagrams. But it can certainly be extended with effective model based test generation techniques (e.g. [28]), to automate the exploration of (large-scale) configuration diagrams and the generation of comprehensive test key sequences from them.

4 Case Study: Analyzing a Real-World Infusion Pump

To evaluate the effectiveness of our approach, we applied it to the user interface implementation of a real infusion pump[1]. It should be noted that, in the study

---

[1] The identity of the pump is concealed for confidentiality reasons, even though it is no longer marketed in US. Also, the information presented in this section is obfuscated.

Fig. 2. Layout of the infusion pump user interface under study

we had access to the source code of the user interface software, but we did not have access to the design documentation of the pump, nor the library objects its implementation referenced. Admittedly, the absence of library code may cause inaccuracy of verification (e.g., design issues are falsely detected or omitted). Fortunately, the design issues detected in this study, as reported in section 2, were confirmed as genuine and caused by the subject implementation.

4.1 Overview of the User Interface under Study

Figure 2 illustrates the general layout of the user interface considered in the study. Keys relating to the data entry system are labeled, while the others are left blank for simplicity. By understanding the pump implementation, we comprehended its behavior, which is summarized as follows.

Digit Keys. During data entry, the software accepts one key press at a time and calculates new values to be rendered on the display according to the following rules: (i) if a decimal point key has not been registered, then the new value is obtained by adding ten times the current displayed value and the value associated with the digit key clicked. For instance, if the display is 1 and a click on ⑦ is registered, then the new value is $10 \times 1 + 7 = 17$; (ii) if a decimal point key has been registered, the value is obtained by adding the current displayed value and the value associated with the clicked digit times $10^{-(\text{decimalDigits} + 1)}$, where decimalDigits is the current number of decimals of the displayed value. Thus if the display is 17. and a click on ② is registered, the new value is $17 + 2 \times 10^{-1} = 17.2$; (iii) the display is updated to the calculated value only if:

- The new value is in the range 0–1200;
- The maximum decimal precision of the new value does not exceed
  - 2 decimal digits if the new value is less than 10; or
  - 1 decimal digit if the new value is within [10, 100); or
  - 0 decimal digits if the new value is equal to or greater than 100.

A key that causes the calculated value to violate the above constraints puts the software into an error mode, in which user interaction is halted, and a warning message is displayed.

Decimal Point Key. The pump registers decimal points only when the current displayed value is less than 100 and a decimal point has not been previously registered. Otherwise, the decimal point key click is discarded.

Clear Key. If the software is not in the error mode, the initial state is restored (i.e., the displayed value is reset to 0); otherwise, the error mode is cleared and the most recent valid state is restored.

4.2   Translation of the C++ Implementation

The portion of the implementation under study was a C++ class, the body of which consists of approximately 2,000 lines of code. This class defines the pump's behavior of handling key presses on the number pad, and managing feedback rendered on its display.

The first step of analysis was to translate the C++ class into PVS specifications, in which the guidelines given in section 3.2 were followed.

Listing 1.1. PVS specification of the software's state variables

```
1 state: TYPE = [# display: {s: string | s'length < DISP_BUFF_SIZE},
2                 dispval: float,
3                 pointRegistered: bool,
4                 decimalDigits  : {i: int | i >= 0 AND i <= 2}
5                 errorMode      : bool #]
```

State Variables. A record type, *state*, is defined to correspond to (the structure of) the C++ class in the implementation. Listing 1.1 illustrates the definition of *state*, in which every field is defined for one member variable of the C++ class. In particular, the *display* field stores the string to be rendered on the display; the *dispval* field is a float number that stores the current legal value registered by the pump; *pointRegistered* is a Boolean field that indicates whether or not the decimal point has been registered; the *decimalDigits* field records the number of decimal digits of the currently registered value; and *errorMode* is a Boolean that is set to true when the software is in the error mode. The predicate subtype associated with the *display* field is used to restrict the string length, while the subtype for *decimalDigits* is to enforce constraints on the number of decimal digits. Both of these subtypes are consistent with the constraints imposed by the original code.

Listing 1.2. PVS specification of decimal point

```
1 pointClicked(st: state): state =
2  if(NOT errorMode(st) & NOT pointRegistered(st) & dispval(st) < 100)
3  then st WITH [ pointRegistered := TRUE,
4                 display := strcat(display(st), ".") ] else st endif
```

Decimal Point. Function *pointClicked*, as shown in listing 1.2, translates the code that handles decimal point clicks. It takes the software's current state (*st*) as parameter, and updates the device's display by invoking *strcat* (a simulation of the counterpart C++ function) to concatenate the pieces to be displayed. A PVS's WITH construct is used to update two fields of *st* when it is not in the error mode; or leave *st* unchanged otherwise.

Digit Keys. Function *digitClicked* translates the code that handles digit keys. The parameter *key* of type KEY_CODE specifies the identifier of the key (each key is given a unique identifier whose value corresponds to the key label). Listing 1.3 provides the definition of *digitClicked*, where a LET-IN construct is used to create local bindings to simulate local variables used in the implementation. When a digit key is clicked, the new display value is computed and stored in variable *tmp* (line 3 in Listing 1.3). If the new value meets the range and precision constraints, the display and other relevant state variables are updated with this value (lines 5-12 and 16-18); otherwise a warning message is displayed (lines 14-15). Function *sprintf* is called to reproduce the behavior of the corresponding C++ function, which outputs the string to be displayed.

Listing 1.3. PVS specification of digit keys

```
1 digitClicked(key: KEY_CODE)(st: state): state =
2 if(NOT errorMode(st)) then LET
3    tmp: double = dispval(st),
4    (tmp, st) = if(dotRegistered(st)) then
5        if(decimalDigits(st) < MAX_DECIMAL_DIGITS
6            & ((tmp < 100 & decimalDigits(st) = 0)
7              OR (tmp < 10 & decimalDigits(st) = 1))) then LET
8            PPdecimalDigits = decimalDigits(st) + 1,
9            tmp = tmp + key * pow10(-1 * PPdecimalDigits)    IN
10           (tmp, st WITH [ decimalDigits := PPdecimalDigits ])
11       else (tmp, st) endif
12   else (tmp * 10 + key, st) endif IN
13 if(tmp > MAX_VALUE)
14 then st WITH [ errorMode := true,
15               display := strcpy(display(st),message(TOO_HIGH))]
16 else st WITH [ dispval := tmp,
17               display := sprintf(display(st), "%*.*f", 0,
18               decimalDigits(st),tmp)] endif else st endif
```

Clear Key. Function *clearClicked*, shown in Listing 1.4, translates the code segment that handles the Clear key clicks. When a click on the Clear key is detected and the software is not in the error mode, *clearClicked* restores the initial state. Otherwise, it clears the error by setting *errorMode* to false, and updates the display with the last legal value stored in *dispval*.

Listing 1.4. PVS specification of clear key

```
1 clearClicked(st: state): state =
2   if(NOT errorMode(st))
3   then st WITH [ dispval := 0, display := "0",
4                  pointRegistered := false, decimalDigits := 0  ]
5   else st WITH [ errorMode := false,
6                  display := sprintf(display(st), "%*.*f", 0,
7                  decimalDigits(st),dispval(st))] endif
```

4.3   Verification Using Configuration Diagrams

The human factors principles that we attempted to verify against the pump implementation included: **consistency**, asserting that the same user actions

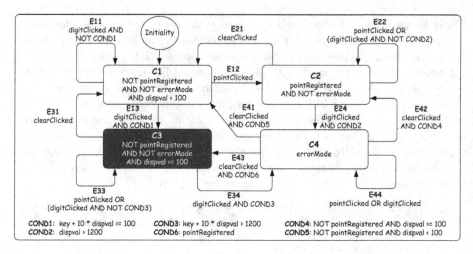

Fig. 3. Configuration diagram regarding the *consistency* of decimal point clicks

(in this case, key clicks) should produce the same results in logically equivalent situations; and **feedback**, which ensures that the user is provided with sufficient information on what actions have been done and what result has been achieved.

Given different aspects of the pump's behavior, these two principles can be instantiated differently. Take the handling of decimal point clicks for example. We instantiated these two principles, for this specific aspect of the pump's behavior, as predicate decimal_point_pred (see Listing 1.5)[2]. This predicate essentially asserts that, no matter what current state (*st*) the pump has, when the decimal point key is clicked, the pump should enter into a new state *st_prime*, in which either the decimal point is registered (variable *pointRegistered* is set true), or the error mode is triggered (*errorMode* is true).

Listing 1.5. Predicate decimal_point_pred in PVS

```
1  decimal_point_pred(st: state): bool =
2      LET st_prime = pointClicked(st)
3         IN (pointRegistered(st_prime) OR errorMode(st_prime))
```

Predicate decimal_point_pred defines a safe way to manipulate decimal point clicks. Based on this predicate, a behavioral model was constructed for the infusion pump under study, by applying the procedure presented in section 3.2 to the PVS translation of its implementation. Simultaneously, the proof that the pump satisfies decimal_point_pred was accomplished within the PVS theorem prover by checking this predicate against all reachable states of the behavioral model under all possible input key sequences.

The behavioral model illustrated in figure 3, in the form of a configuration diagram, was constructed as the result of our analysis effort. After proving twenty

---

[2] Instantiation of the principles with respect to other aspects of the pump's behavior can be carried out similarly.

theorems during the model construction process, we verified that the infusion pump violates predicate decimal_point_pred (an example of such violation is shown in section 4.4). Please refer to section 2 for an explanation of the verification results, and to [17] for more details on the generation of the configuration diagram and the proof process.

4.4   Generation of Test Input Sequences

As discussed in section 3.3, a comprehensive set of key sequences can be generated as test cases to the device implementation by exploring all *walks* in its configuration diagram.

Consider generating test cases from the configuration diagram in figure 3. At the beginning, the pump satisfies C_1: the decimal point is not registered; its user interface is not in the error mode; the display value is less than 100. This is visualized in the diagram as an edge from a default node **Initiality** to C_1.

Outgoing edges from C_1 are labeled with the combination of conditions and user actions that can lead the pump into a new configuration. Note that only conditions and user actions related to the verification of desired properties are considered. For example, only the following combinations can trigger the pump to exit from configuration C_1: a decimal point is pressed (E_{12} in figure 3); or, a digit key is pressed when COND1 holds (E_{13} in figure 3), where COND1 asserts that the new display value is greater than or equal to 100.

The trace $C_1 \xrightarrow{E_{13}} C_3 \xrightarrow{E_{33}} C_3 \xrightarrow{E_{33}} C_3$ represents a walk in this configuration diagram. This walk stands for a class of possible user interaction scenarios, one of which can be: start from C_1 when the display value is 10; key $\boxed{0}$ is pressed, and the model moves to C_3 as a digit key is pressed and COND1 is satisfied; key $\boxed{\bullet}$ is pressed, and the model stays in C_3. Lastly, key $\boxed{1}$ is pressed.

An example of sequence of key presses that can be extracted from the above example walk is $\boxed{1}\boxed{0}\boxed{0}\boxed{\bullet}\boxed{1}$, which exposes an interaction design flaw: the pump silently discards the decimal point. In particular, when the prefix $\boxed{1}\boxed{0}\boxed{0}$ $\boxed{\bullet}$ of this sequence is fed to the pump, the model will stay in configuration C_3, in which predicate *pointRegistered* is false indicating that the decimal point is not registered, and predicate *errorMode* is also false indicating that no warning message is provided to the user.

Following the above process, we generated test cases that exposed the interaction design flaws presented in section 2. These test cases were used to check the infusion pump under study, and confirmed that the detected design flaws did exist in its implementation.

5   Related Work

The work presented in the paper is based on configuration diagrams, originally introduced by Rushby to verify safety properties of potentially infinite-state systems [23]. For such systems, formal verification requires either a direct proof through deductive mechanized methods (e.g., theorem proving), or justification of an abstraction that downscales the system so that it can be verified through exhaustive state exploration (using model checking for example). In contrast, our approach uses configuration diagrams in a novel way to identify interaction design issues in software. In particular, we use configuration diagrams to extract and verify a behavioral model of the software specifying how the software manages the interactions with the user.

Several approaches have been proposed to use model checking to verify user interface implementations[3]. For example, Rushby [24] used model checkers Murϕ and SAL to verify mode confusion in a cockpit; Rukšėnas et al [21] used SAL to identify post-completion errors in infusion pumps; Campos and Harrison used IVY/NuSMV to analyze infusion pumps against properties such as consistency, visibility, and feedback [4, 11]; and in our own work, we used SAL and Event-B/Rodin to analyze the data entry system of infusion pumps for their predictability [15, 16] and other safety properties identified by FDA [22].

The main limitation of using model checking to analyze user interface design/implementations lies in that, one has to wisely balance the complexity of the models constructed for user interface and the fidelity of these models to the original design/implementation. On one hand, the constructed models cannot be too complex to be analyzable (within reasonable time cost) [3, 9, 12]. This is why abstraction has to be used to eliminate irrelevant details away from the models. On the other hand, it is often difficult to find appropriate types of abstraction, so as to preserve necessary details of the user interface for verification. Therefore, model checkers often use too coarse abstraction to extract models from the real design/implementation, resulting in excessive spurious counterexamples (i.e., counterexamples representing behaviors that do not exist in the real design/implementation) to be reported.

Even though counterexample guided techniques, such as [2,7,8], can be used to guide model checkers to refine and optimize the abstraction, such techniques still demand significant effort from the analysts to first decide if a counterexample is genuine or spurious. Unfortunately, with respect to analyzing user interface software for its human factors properties, no general solution has been proposed to assist analysts in making such decisions.

In contrast to model checking driven approaches, our approach defines a general method for model construction based on theorem proving and configuration diagrams. It avoids the difficulty of finding an appropriate level of abstraction that ensures the accuracy and fidelity of the constructed behavioral models. However, the behavioral models constructed by our approach can also be verified by model checkers for their human factors properties.

6   Conclusions

A rigorous and effective approach for formally verifying the source code implementation of user interface software in medical devices has been presented.

---

[3] It is worth noting that model-checking can be used in the design phase as a "high-level debugger" of designs. However, this requires a different approach to modeling, such as that illustrated in [22].

The case study shows that this approach can detect interaction design issues in real implementations that might lead to critical safety consequences. These issues exist because of a combination of design features in user interface software, each of which is not problematic individually. Interestingly, we fed the test cases generated by the approach to another infusion pump made by a different manufacturer, and observed similar design issues.

The case study presented only formally analyzed a portion of the software implementation of the subject infusion pump. As a result, only part of the configuration diagram was developed, and only part of the proofs generated by PVS were formally proved. However, even with this partially completed formal analysis, real issues were identified. This suggests that our approach has the potential to assess and improve the quality and safety of user interface software in medical devices even before their complete implementation is available.

Once human factors properties are assured using PVS, the specification can be used to rapidly prototype a new user interface design in which the identified interaction design issues have been addressed. In fact, PVS provides a component called PVSio-web [19] that helps developers to define the layout of a user interface; and a component called PVSio [18] that enables interactive execution of specifications defining the behavior of the user interface, and a ground evaluator that automatically compiles these specifications into executable code.

Acknowledgments. We thank Michael Harrison for his invaluable suggestions and comments on the paper and the support of CHI+MED (Computer-Human Interaction for Medical Devices, EPSRC research grant [EP/G059063/1]).

References

1. AAMI Medical Device Software Committee. Medical device software risk management. AAMI Tech. Rep. TIR32:2004 (2004)
2. Ball, T., Cook, B., Das, S., Rajamani, S.K.: Refining approximations in software predicate abstraction. In: Jensen, K., Podelski, A. (eds.) TACAS 2004. LNCS, vol. 2988, pp. 388–403. Springer, Heidelberg (2004)
3. Bolton, M.L., Bass, E.J.: Formally verifying human-automation interaction as part of a system model: Limitations and tradeoffs. Innovations in Systems and Software Engineering 6(3), 219–231 (2010)
4. Campos, J.C., Harrison, M.D.: Modelling and analysing the interactive behaviour of an infusion pump. Electronic Communications of the EASST (2011)
5. Cauchi, A., Gimblett, A., Thimbleby, H., Curzon, P., Masci, P.: Safer 5-key number entry user interfaces using differential formal analysis. In: BCS-HCI (2012)
6. Center for Devices and Radiological Health, US Food and Drug Administration. White Paper: Infusion Pump Improvement Initiative (2010)
7. Clarke, E., Grumberg, O., Jha, S., Lu, Y., Veith, H.: Counterexample-guided abstraction refinement. In: Emerson, E.A., Sistla, A.P. (eds.) CAV 2000. LNCS, vol. 1855, pp. 154–169. Springer, Heidelberg (2000)
8. Dwyer, M.B., Tkachuk, O., Visser, W., et al.: Analyzing interaction orderings with model checking. In: ASE 2004, pp. 154–163. IEEE Computer Society (2004)
9. Gelman, G.E., Feigh, K.M., Rushby, J.: Example of a complementary use of model checking and agent-based simulation. In: SMC 2013. IEEE (2013)

10. Ginsburg, G.: Human factors engineering: A tool for medical device evaluation in hospital procurement decision-making. Journal of Bio. Informatics 38(3) (2005)
11. Harrison, M.D., Campos, J.C., Masci, P.: Reusing models and properties in the analysis of similar interactive devices. Innovations in Systems and Software Engineering, 1–17 (2013)
12. Harrison, M.D., Masci, P., Campos, J.C., Curzon, P.: Automated theorem proving for the systematic analysis of interactive systems. In: FMIS 2013 (2013)
13. Jetley, R., Purushothaman Iyer, S., Jones, P.L.: A formal methods approach to medical device review. Computer 39(4), 61–67 (2006)
14. Masci, P., Curzon, P., Harrison, M.D., Ayoub, A., Lee, I., Thimbleby, H.: Verification of interactive software for medical devices: PCA infusion pumps and FDA regulation as an example. In: EICS 2013. ACM Digital Library (2013)
15. Masci, P., Rukšėnas, R., Oladimeji, P., Cauchi, A., Gimblett, A., Li, Y., Curzon, P., Thimbleby, H.: On formalising interactive number entry on infusion pumps. Electronic Communications of the EASST 45 (2011)
16. Masci, P., Rukšėnas, R., Oladimeji, P., Cauchi, A., Gimblett, A., Li, Y., Curzon, P., Thimbleby, H.: The benefits of formalising design guidelines: a case study on the predictability of drug infusion pumps. Innovations in Systems and Software Engineering, 1–21 (2013)
17. Masci, P., Zhang, Y., Curzon, P., Harrison, M.D., Jones, P., Thimbleby, H.: Verification of software for medical devices in PVS. CHI+MED Tech. Rep. (2013), http://www.chi-med.ac.uk/researchers/bibdetail.php?docID=656
18. Munoz, C.: Rapid prototyping in PVS. National Institute of Aerospace, Hampton, VA, USA, Tech. Rep. NIA, 3 (2003)
19. Oladimeji, P., Masci, P., Curzon, P., Thimbleby, H.: PVSio-web: A tool for rapid prototyping device user interfaces in PVS. In: FMIS 2013 (2013)
20. Owre, S., Rajan, S., Rushby, J., Shankar, N., Srivas, M.: PVS: Combining specification, proof checking, and model checking. In: Alur, R., Henzinger, T.A. (eds.) CAV 1996. LNCS, vol. 1102, pp. 411–414. Springer, Heidelberg (1996)
21. Rukšėnas, R., Curzon, P., Blandford, A.E., Back, J.: Combining human error verification and timing analysis: A case study on an infusion pump. Formal Aspects of Computing (2013) (in press)
22. Rukšėnas, R., Masci, P., Harrison, M.D., Curzon, P.: Developing and verifying user interface requirements for infusion pumps: A refinement approach. In: FMIS 2013 (2013)
23. Rushby, J.: Verification diagrams revisited: Disjunctive invariants for easy verification. In: Emerson, E.A., Sistla, A.P. (eds.) CAV 2000. LNCS, vol. 1855, pp. 508–520. Springer, Heidelberg (2000)
24. Rushby, J.: Using model checking to help discover mode confusions and other automation surprises. Reliability Engineering & System Safety 75(2), 167–177 (2002)
25. Shankar, N., Owre, S.: Principles and pragmatics of subtyping in PVS. In: Bert, D., Choppy, C., Mosses, P.D. (eds.) WADT 1999. LNCS, vol. 1827, pp. 37–52. Springer, Heidelberg (2000)
26. Shankar, N., Owre, S., Rushby, J., Stringer-Calvert, D.: PVS prover guide. Computer Science Laboratory, vol. 1, pp. 11–12. SRI International, Menlo Park (2001)
27. Story, M.F.: The FDA perspective on human factors in medical device software Development. In: IQPC Software Design for Medical Devices Europe (2012)
28. Thimbleby, H.: Press on: Principles of Interaction Programming. Mit Press (2007)
29. Thimbleby, H., Cairns, P.: Reducing number entry errors: solving a widespread, serious problem. Journal of the Royal Society Interface 7(51), 1429–1439 (2010)

Sound Control Flow Graph Extraction from Incomplete Java Bytecode Programs

Pedro de Carvalho Gomes, Attilio Picoco, and Dilian Gurov

KTH Royal Institute of Technology, Stockholm, Sweden

Abstract. The modular analysis of control flow of incomplete Java byte-code programs is challenging, mainly because of the complex semantics of the language, and the unknown inter-dependencies between the available and unavailable components. In this paper we describe a technique for incremental, modular extraction of control flow graphs that are provably sound w.r.t. sequences of method invocations and exceptions. The extracted models are suitable for various program analyses, in particular model-checking of temporal control flow safety properties. Soundness comes at the price of over-approximation, potentially giving rise to false positives reports during verification. Still, our technique supports incremental refinement of the already extracted models, as more components code becomes available. The extraction has been implemented as the CoNFLEx tool, and test-cases show its utility and efficiency.

1 Introduction

The main obstacle to the formal verification of software is the size of its state space. A standard approach to address this problem is to construct an abstract model of manageable size and to perform the verification over the model. Ideally, the abstraction should come with a formal argument that it is property-preserving for the class of properties of interest, otherwise the verification results cannot be trusted. *Control flow graphs* (CFGs) are among the most commonly used software models, where nodes represent the program's control points, while edges represent the transfer of control between the points.

In this paper we present a framework for the extraction of CFGs from the available components of *incomplete Java bytecode* (JBC) *programs*. That is, programs where the implementation of some components is not yet available. Typical situations when one has to deal with incomplete programs are systems under development, or systems depending on third-party software. In the latter case, it is common that the source code of the third-party software never becomes available, which motivates our choice to analyze Java bytecode.

We extract CFGs that are *sound* w.r.t sequences of method invocations and exceptions. Such models are useful for many static analyses, especially for the formal verification of temporal control flow safety properties. Previous techniques have been proposed to analyze incomplete JBC programs [6,16]; however they are admittedly unsound. To the best of our knowledge, our framework is the first to soundly analyze the control flow of incomplete programs.

S. Gnesi and A. Rensink (Eds.): FASE 2014, LNCS 8411, pp. 215–229, 2014.

The challenges to soundly analyze control flow from incomplete JBC programs are twofold. The first are the *object-oriented* features of JBC. For instance, *virtual method calls* (VMC) and exceptions impose difficulties. The second are the unknown inter-dependencies between available and yet unavailable software components. For instance, it is hard to estimate the control flow caused by exception propagation, or to determine precisely the possible receivers of a VMC.

We define our framework by generalizing a previous algorithm from Amighi *et al.* [2] for complete JBC programs that uses a transformation into an intermediate bytecode representation (BIR) [12]. The transformation into BIR allows the *precise* estimation of a significant subset of the implicit (e.g., division by zero) exceptions, and of explicit (with `athrow` instruction) exceptions.

The inter-dependencies involving yet unavailable components are captured by means of *user-provided interfaces*. Our approach is conservative, and assumes that unavailable methods may propagate any exception. This results in significant over-approximation, but the user may alleviate it by specifying in the method's interface the exceptions it should never propagate.

Still, valid global properties may fail to be established, giving rise to so-called *false positives*. The algorithm mitigates this by allowing the *incremental refinement* of previously extracted CFGs, as more code becomes available. This is accomplished by decoupling the intra- and inter-procedural exceptional flow analysis. So, properties that could not be verified in the more abstract CFGs may be established over the refined CFGs.

The framework defines formally the constraints to instantiating yet unavailable code, needed to ensure the soundness of the already generated CFGs w.r.t. sequences of method invocations and exceptions. Further, we prove the *correctness* of our extraction. First, we show that the extracted CFGs from the available components are supergraphs of the ones extracted from the same components by the algorithm for complete programs. Then, we connect this with previously established results to conclude that the CFGs extracted with the present algorithm are also sound w.r.t. the JBC behavior (as defined by the JVM), as long as the specified constraints are respected. Therefore, already established behavioral or structural properties are thus guaranteed to still hold.

We have implemented our technique as the CoNFLEx tool. It features caching of previous analyses, necessary for the incremental refinement, and matching of newly arriving code against their interface specifications. Our experimental results confirm the intuitive expectation that the over-approximations impact significantly the size of the CFGs. Also, the results show that CoNFLEx is efficient, and performs a light-weight extraction of CFGs.

Organization. Section 2 describes the program models on which we base our technique, and the transformation into the BIR. Section 3 motivates our work by presenting a compositional verification technique that benefits directly from our results. Section 4 describes our framework to analyze incomplete programs, and outlines a correctness argument. Section 5 describes the implementation of our approach, and presents experimental results. Section 6 discusses related work, while Section 7 draws conclusions and outlines directions for future work.

2   Preliminaries

In this section we briefly present the program model, and give an overview of the BIR language, both necessary to define our CFG extraction algorithm.

2.1   Program Model

We define CFGs, following Huisman *et al.* [13], as *Kripke structures* with transition labels, where nodes represent program control points, and the edges represent how instructions shift control between the points. The atomic propositions associated with nodes contain information about the control address, possible exceptions, and returns. We use the following notational convention: $\circ_m^p$ denotes a normal non-return control node in the address p of method m, $\bullet_m^{p,x}$ an exceptional non-return control node with exception x, while $\circ_m^{p,r}$ and $\bullet_m^{p,x,r}$ a normal and an exceptional return node, respectively.

Edge labels are either method signatures m corresponding to invocation instructions, or the special label ε signifying any other type of instruction. This choice is made here because of our interest in the possible sequences of method invocations (expressed as temporal safety properties), but the program model can be adapted to other needs as well. API methods are not considered a part of the program, and are thus labeled by ε. However, the propagated exceptions declared in the signature with **throws** are taken into account.

Let METH and EXCP be the sets of all method signatures and exceptions, respectively. We now define formally CFGs as a collection of method graphs.

Definition 1 (Method Graph). *A method graph for method $m \in M$ over sets $M \subseteq$ METH and $E \subseteq$ EXCP is a pair $\mathcal{G}_m = (\mathcal{M}_m, \mathbb{E}_m)$, where $\mathcal{M}_m = (V_m, L_m, \to_m, A_m, \lambda_m)$ is a labeled Kripke structure, with V_m the set of control nodes of m, $A_m = \{m, r\} \cup E$ the set of atomic propositions, and $L_m = M \cup \{\varepsilon\}$ the set of transition labels. We require that $m \in \lambda_m(v)$ for all $v \in V_m$, and for all $x, x' \in E$, if $\{x, x'\} \subseteq \lambda_m(v)$ then $x = x'$ (i.e., every control node is tagged with the method signature it belongs to and with at most one exception). $\mathbb{E}_m \subseteq V_M$ is the (non-empty) set of entry control points of m.*

Every control flow graph $\mathcal{G}$ is equipped with an *interface* $I = (I^+, I^-, I^e)$, written $\mathcal{G} : I$, specifying the (disjoint) sets of *provided* and (externally) *required* methods, and the set $I^e \subseteq I^+ \times E$ of potentially propagated exceptions by the provided methods. We say a CFG is *closed* if there are no (externally) required methods; we say it is *open* otherwise. CFG *composition* is defined as the disjoint union $\uplus$ of their method graphs. Interface composition is defined as $I_1 \cup I_2 = (I_1^+ \cup I_2^+, (I_1^- \cup I_2^-)\backslash(I_1^+ \cup I_2^+), I_1^e \cup I_2^e)$.

Example 1 (CFG). Figure 1a shows a simple program to check the parity of an integer. It is presented in Java source (rather than bytecode), to help the comprehension. The program has three methods. The method **main** calls **parseInt** to convert the input string into an integer, then calls **even**. Notice that **parseInt** is a method from the Java API, and is not considered a part of the program. However, its signature declares that it may propagate a `NumberFormatException`, and this must be taken into account in the analysis. The method `odd` potentially throws an `ArithmeticException`.

The implementation of method `even` is not available. We specify it with the interface $I_{even} = (\{even\}, \{odd\}, \{\})$. It declares that the method may call itself or `odd`, and does not propagate any exceptions. It is represented in the code by the empty-bodied method, and the Java annotation `GhostComponent`.

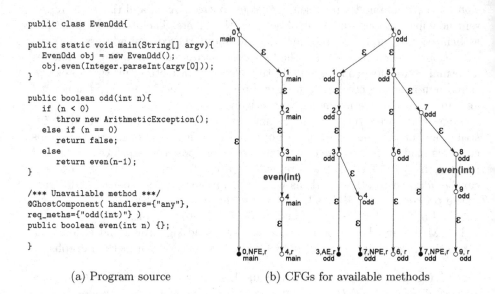

```
public class EvenOdd{

public static void main(String[] argv){
    EvenOdd obj = new EvenOdd();
    obj.even(Integer.parseInt(argv[0]));
}

public boolean odd(int n){
    if (n < 0)
        throw new ArithmeticException();
    else if (n == 0)
        return false;
    else
        return even(n-1);
}

/*** Unavailable method ***/
@GhostComponent( handlers={"any"},
req_meths={"odd(int)"} )
public boolean even(int n) {};

}
```

(a) Program source   (b) CFGs for available methods

Fig. 1. Example of Incomplete Java program

Figure 1b shows the CFGs for the available methods `main` and `odd`. The nodes are tagged with the method's signature and a control address. Entry nodes are depicted as usual by incoming edges without source. There are three exceptional nodes in the CFG, which represent points in which program control is taken over by the JVM to take care of the exception. These three are also return nodes (i.e., tagged with the atomic proposition r), and indicate the propagation of the respective exception by the method. The invocations of methods `even` and `odd` are represented by call edges. The invocation of `parseInt`, however, which is a method from the Java API, is not represented by a call edge. Further, the method's signature declares that a `NumberFormatException` (NFE) is potentially propagated, and this is reflected by an edge to $\bullet_{main}^{0,NFE,r}$.

2.2   Bytecode Intermediate Representation

The BIR language is an intermediate representation of Java bytecode developed at INRIA Rennes [12]. The main difference with JBC is that BIR instructions are stack-less. That is, instructions do not operate over values stored on the operand stack. Instead, a JBC method is translated into BIR by symbolically executing the bytecode, using an abstract stack. This stack is used to reconstruct expression trees and to connect instructions to its operands. We give a brief overview of the BIR language. However, we omit the details of the transformation from JBC to BIR; for a full account we refer to [12]. Figure 2a shows the BIR syntax.

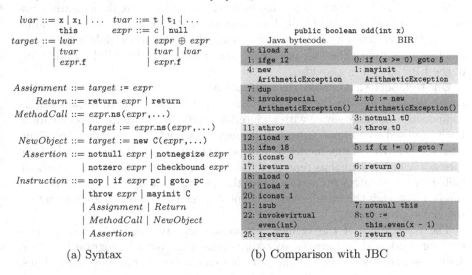

(a) Syntax   (b) Comparison with JBC

Fig. 2. The BIR language

The transformation into BIR simplifies the analysis of exceptional control flow. It identifies *implicit* exceptions by inserting special assertions before the instructions that can potentially raise the exception, as defined by the JVM specification [18]. For example, the transformation inserts a [notnegsize *expr*] assertion before instructions that might raise a NegativeArraySizeException. If the assertion holds, meaning that *expr* does not evaluate to negative a number, it behaves as a [nop], and control flow passes to the next instruction. If the assertion fails, control flow is passed to the exception handling mechanism. Moreover, the BIR transformation connects the *explicit* exceptions, raised by athrow, to their types in the [throw *target*] instruction. Now, data-flow analysis can estimate the possible types of the *target* variable.

Example 2 (JBC and BIR Comparison). Figure 2b shows the JBC and BIR versions of method odd() from Figure 1a. The different shades indicate the reconstruction of expression trees, and the collapsing of instructions by the transformation. The BIR method has a local variable (x), which is also present in the JBC, and a newly introduced variable (t0). Notice that the argument for the method invocation and the operand to the [if] instruction are reconstructed expression trees. The [notnull] instruction asserts that NullPointerException can potentially be raised at this program point.

3   Motivation

The motivation for the present work is to support the formal verification of in-complete JBC programs. Typical scenarios of incomplete programs are systems under development, or systems that depend on third-party software. Two exam-ples are an ATM system that depends on the code from users' smart-cards, or ERP systems, which are typically modular. It is desirable that the available com-ponents are checked against global properties in advance. Then, the only pending task is the verification of the missing code, which should be light-weight, and can be delayed until the user inserts the smart-card into the ATM, or a module of the ERP system is provided.

One technique that enables the verification of incomplete programs is the com-positional principle developed by Gurov *et al.* [11]. There, unavailable software components are represented with an interface and a local temporal specification. Both are used to compute a so-called *maximal model*, i.e., a model that simu-lates the behavior of any model that respects the interface and satisfies the local specification, and can thus represent the unavailable component when checking global temporal safety properties. Once the missing code becomes available, it is checked to match the interface and the local specification. If it does, this entails the global properties.

The correctness of the verified temporal safety properties is only guaran-teed for models that *soundly* over-approximate the actual program behavior. Soundness, however, comes at the price of excessive over-approximations. Thus, potentially giving rise to false positives. To alleviate this problem, we aim to a model extraction strategy that is *incremental*: whenever more code arrives, the existing model can be refined, and the false positive may now be provable.

Example 3 (Compositional Verification). Suppose we want to verify two global properties over the available code from the incomplete program in Figure 1. Let ϕ_1 be defined informally as "if an `ArithmeticException` is raised within a method, it must be either caught locally, or by the immediate caller method", and ϕ_2 be the same property, but for an `ArrayStoreException`.

We define the local property ψ_{even} for the missing method `even` informally as "after calling `odd`, `even` must terminate normally", and construct the maximal CFG for ψ_{even} and I_{even}. Also, we extract the CFGs from the available methods `main` and `odd`, and compose them with the maximal CFG for `even`.

The global property ϕ_1 is checked against the composed model, and it turns out to hold. Thus, once the implementation of `even` is provided, we simply ex-tract its CFG, and check it against the local property ψ_{even}. If it holds, the cor-rectness of the program is established w.r.t. ϕ_1. Also the property ϕ_2 is checked over the same composed model. However, ϕ_2 does not hold since neither the interface, nor the local property restrict an `ArrayStoreException` from being raised by `even`. Still, it may be a false positive: once the code of `even` becomes available, we may extract its CFG, refine the previously extracted CFGs, com-pose them, and re-check the property.

4 CFG Extraction Framework

In this section we outline the theoretical definitions of the framework for extraction of CFGs from incomplete JBC programs, and summarize the soundness argument. For the complete definitions and results we refer to [4].

4.1 Incomplete JBC Programs and Extraction Algorithm

We model incomplete JBC programs as *open environments*, following Freund and Mitchell's definition of *closed environment* for complete JBC programs [10]. An open environment Γ_o is defined in Figure 3 as the union of partial mappings from method references, class names and **interface** names to their respective definitions. We write **interfaces** (in typewrite font) to distinguish it from the CFG interfaces introduced in Section 2.1. An important aspect of the definition is that it contains all information about the type hierarchy. Thus, we can enumerate the set of exception types from a given open environment.

The difference from the modeling of complete programs is that in open environments a method body (i.e., **code**) may be empty. Also, entries in the **handlers** have a special meaning for empty methods. They represent the exception types that cannot be propagated by the method's implementation, once provided.

$$\Gamma^I : \textit{IFace-Name} \rightharpoonup \left\langle \begin{array}{l} \textbf{interfaces} : \textit{set of IFace-Name} \\ \textbf{method} : \textit{set of IFace-Method-Ref} \end{array} \right\rangle$$

$$\Gamma^C : \textit{Class-Name} \rightharpoonup \left\langle \begin{array}{l} \textbf{super} : \textit{Class-Name} \\ \textbf{interfaces} : \textit{set of IFace-Name} \\ \textbf{fields} : \textit{set of Field-Ref} \end{array} \right\rangle \qquad \Gamma_o = \Gamma^I \cup \Gamma^C \cup \Gamma^M$$

$$\Gamma^M : \textit{Method-Ref} \rightharpoonup \left\langle \begin{array}{l} \textbf{code} : \textit{Instruction}^* \\ \textbf{handlers} : \textit{Handler}^* \end{array} \right\rangle$$

Fig. 3. Open environment of a JBC/BIR program

Open environments also model the BIR version of incomplete programs. The differences to the JBC version is the **code** array, translated syntactically to BIR instructions, and **handlers**, which has the addresses of the exception handlers mapped to the respective BIR addresses. We use the common modeling as open environments to define the CFG extraction indirectly. First we transform JBC into BIR; then extract CFGs from the intermediate representation. Here we focus on the latter transformation; for the former, we refer again to [12].

The $o\mathcal{G}$ algorithm extracts CFGs from the available methods of an open environment. It iterates over the instructions array of a method m and produces, for every program counter **pc** and corresponding instruction i, a set of edges $o\mathcal{G}_m^{\text{pc},i}$ together with the associated nodes. Figure 4 shows the necessary auxiliary functions, and the extraction rules for $o\mathcal{G}$, grouped by their BIR instruction type.

$$MCA(\text{C.ns}) = \begin{cases} \{\ c'.\text{ns} \mid c' \text{ is the closest super-type s.t. } c'.\text{ns} \in dom(\Gamma^M)\} \\ \cup\ \{\ c.\text{ns} \mid c <: \text{C} \wedge c.\text{ns} \in dom(\Gamma^M)\ \} & \text{if call is virtual} \\ \{\ \text{C.ns}\ \} & \text{otherwise} \end{cases}$$

$$\mathcal{H}_m^{\text{pc},x,l} = \begin{cases} \{\ (o_m^{\text{pc},x}, l, \bullet_m^{\text{pc},x,r})\ \} & \text{if } h_m^{\text{pc},x} = undef \\ \{\ (o_m^{\text{pc}'}, l, \bullet_m^{\text{pc},x}), (\bullet_m^{\text{pc},x}, \varepsilon, o_m^{\text{pc}'})\ \} & \text{if } h_m^{\text{pc},x} = \text{pc}' \end{cases}$$

$$\mathcal{N}_m^{\text{pc},n} = \begin{cases} \bigcup_{\{x \mid \bullet_n^{\text{pc}',x,r} \in \mathcal{G}(n)\}} \mathcal{H}_m^{\text{pc},x,n} & \text{if } \Gamma^M[m] \text{ is available} \\ \bigcup_{x \in E_{\Gamma_o} - \Gamma_o^m[n].\text{handlers}} \mathcal{H}_m^{\text{pc},x,n} & \text{otherwise} \end{cases}$$

$$o\mathcal{G}_m^{\text{pc},i} = \begin{cases} \{(o_m^{\text{pc}}, \varepsilon, o_m^{\text{pc}+1})\} & \text{if } i \in Assignment \cup \{[\text{nop}],[\text{mayinit}]\} \\ \{(o_m^{\text{pc}}, \varepsilon, o_m^{\text{pc}+1}), (o_m^{\text{pc}}, \varepsilon, o_m^{\text{pc}'})\} & \text{if } i = [\text{if } expr \text{ pc}'] \\ \{(o_m^{\text{pc}}, \varepsilon, o_m^{\text{pc}'})\} & \text{if } i = [\text{goto pc}'] \\ \{(o_m^{\text{pc}}, \varepsilon, o_m^{\text{pc},r})\} & \text{if } i \in Return \\ \bigcup_{\{x \mid x <: X\}} \mathcal{H}_m^{\text{pc},x,\varepsilon} & \text{if } i = [\text{throw } X] \\ \{(o_m^{\text{pc}}, \varepsilon, o_m^{\text{pc}+1})\} \cup \mathcal{H}_m^{\text{pc},\chi_i,\varepsilon} & \text{if } i \in Assertion \\ \{(o_m^{\text{pc}}, \text{C}, o_m^{\text{pc}+1})\} \cup \mathcal{H}_m^{\text{pc,NPE,C}} \cup \mathcal{N}_m^{\text{pc,C}} & \text{if } i \in NewObject \\ \bigcup_{n \in MCA(\text{n})} \{(o_m^{\text{pc}}, n, o_m^{\text{pc}+1})\} \cup \mathcal{N}_m^{\text{pc},n} & \text{if } i \in MethodCall \end{cases}$$

Fig. 4. CFG extraction from incomplete BIR

Let $h_m^{\text{pc},x}$ denote the first handler (if any) in the exception table of method m (with the same entries as the JBC table, but with control points relating to BIR instructions) for the exception of type (or subtype of) x at position pc. The function $\mathcal{H}_m^{\text{pc},x,l}$ produces edges related to exception handling, determined by the value of $h_m^{\text{pc},x}$. If there is a handler for x at pc in m, it returns two edges: one from a normal node to an exceptional node, and another one from the exceptional node to the normal node tagged with the handler's initial control point pc'; otherwise, it returns an edge to an exceptional return node. The label l is either the signature of a callee method that propagates the exception, or ε, if the exception is raised within the method. The function χ_i simply returns the exception type associated to a BIR assertion i.

The definition of $o\mathcal{G}_m^{\text{pc},i}$ is sub-divided into two parts. The *intra-procedural* analysis extracts for every method an initial CFG, based solely on its instruction array and its exception table. Based on these CFGs, the *inter-procedural* analysis computes the functions $\mathcal{N}_m^{\text{pc},n}$, which return exceptional edges for exceptions propagated by calls to method n. The functions for inter-dependent methods are thus mutually recursive, and are computed in a fixed-point manner.

The $o\mathcal{G}$ algorithm is a generalization from the $\mathcal{G}$ algorithm, proposed by Amighi *et al.* [2] for complete programs. It introduces two significant modifications. The first one is w.r.t. virtual method call resolution. The $\mathcal{G}$ algorithm is parametrized by a sound VMC resolution algorithm. However, standard VMC algorithms, such as the *Rapid Type Analysis* (*RTA*) [3], are defined for complete programs only, and may provide unsound estimation in the absence of code. We therefore fix the VMC resolution algorithm to our *Modular Class Analysis* (*MCA*), which is a generalization of the *Class Hierarchy Analysis* (*CHA*) [7]. *MCA* soundly over-approximates the possible receivers to methods with the same signature (ns) from sub-types and from the closest super-type of the static type (C) that are either provided or declared to be missing (given by function *dom*). The second modification concerns the function $\mathcal{N}$ that computes the control flow caused by exception propagation. In this case, when the callee method is unavailable, the set of exceptions that are propagated is defined as all exception types, excluding those annotated by the user in handlers to be never propagated.

4.2 Correctness of o$\mathcal{G}$

The main purpose of the transformation above is to extract CFGs from the available components of incomplete JBC programs that are sound for any instantiation of the missing code. CFGs that preserve this property entails the verification of global temporal safety properties, as explained in Section 3. Further, the transformation allows the extracted CFGs to be refined incrementally as more component code becomes available, until completion of the system.

Theoretically, both purposes are supported through a *refinement pre-order* on open environments, as defined below. Notice that closed environments for complete programs are simply open environments where all method bodies are provided, and are thus minimal w.r.t. the pre-order.

Definition 2 (Environment Refinement). *Let Γ_o and Γ_o' be open environments. We say that environment Γ_o refines environment Γ_o', written $\Gamma_o \preceq \Gamma_o'$, if the following conditions hold:*

(i) *method references, class names and interface names defined in Γ_o' must also be in Γ_o;*

(ii) *an interface in Γ^I contain the same methods, and extend a subset of the interfaces in $\Gamma^{I'}$;*

(iii) *classes in Γ^C have the same super-class, implement a subset of the interfaces in of the same classes in $\Gamma^{C'}$;*

(iv) *a method in Γ_o' must have a superset of the handlers of Γ_o' if it is unavailable in both environments, it must have the same code and handlers if it is implemented in both environments, or the method implementation Γ_o cannot propagate exceptions declared in Γ_o'.handlers, where it was unavailable.*

We say that Γ implements Γ_o whenever $\Gamma \preceq \Gamma_o$ and Γ is closed.

The refinement of a method which is unavailable in both environments entails that in Γ_o it propagates at most the same set of exceptions as in Γ_o'. Thus, a CFG extraction from Γ_o' must have over-approximated the set of propagated exceptions involving the method. In the refinement which a method is implemented in both environments, there cannot be changes; otherwise, the method graph extracted from Γ_o' would not soundly over-approximate the method graph from Γ_o. The refinement of a missing method in Γ_o', which is implemented in Γ_o, simply guarantees that it respects its interface w.r.t. propagated exceptions.

The following result states that, when applied to closed environments, the algorithm for open environments reduces to the one for closed environments with MCA as the virtual method call resolution algorithm.

Theorem 1. *Let Γ be a closed environment, and $\mathcal{G}_{MCA}$ be the instantiation of $\mathcal{G}$ with MCA. Then $\mathcal{G}_{MCA}(\Gamma) = o\mathcal{G}(\Gamma)$.*

The next result establishes *monotonicity* of CFG extraction w.r.t. refinement.

Theorem 2. *Let Γ_o and Γ'_o be open environments, and m be the signature of a method available on both. Then $\Gamma_o \preceq \Gamma'_o$ implies $o\mathcal{G}(m, \Gamma_o) \subseteq o\mathcal{G}(m, \Gamma'_o)$.*

The proofs of the above theorems are available in [4], due to space limitation. These results ensure *soundness* of the CFG extraction w.r.t. temporal safety properties, by virtue of several results established earlier. Here we briefly outline the soundness argument; for the full account the reader is referred to [2,11]. First, subgraph inclusion of CFGs entails *structural simulation* between CFGs in terms of a simulation relation between the nodes of the two graphs. Next, structural simulation in turn entails *behavioral simulation* in terms of a simulation relation between the behavioral configurations induced by the two graphs by means of pushdown systems ([11, Th. 36]). Third, temporal safety properties are preserved (backwards) under behavioral simulation ([11, Cor. 17]). These three results guarantee preservation of temporal safety properties under refinement of open environments. Together with the soundness result for $\mathcal{G}$ established in [2] and Theorem 1 above, we obtain soundness of $o\mathcal{G}$.

As more code becomes available, not only the temporal safety properties that were already verified over the previously extracted CFGs are guaranteed to still hold if the CFGs are re-extracted (and so, refined), but new properties can be established. The problem of potential *false positives*, intrinsic to sound over-approximation, can thus be alleviated through CFG re-extraction. We have designed our framework in a way that the intra-procedural analysis is preserved, as long as the implementation is not changed. Therefore, the incremental analysis upon the arrival of previously unavailable code produces a refined model due to the fewer over-approximations w.r.t. exceptional flow.

5   The ConFlEx Tool

In this section we describe the implementation of the CFG extraction algorithms described in Section 4. First we describe some practical aspects of the implementation, and then provide experimental data that validate our tool.

5.1   Implementation

We have implemented both the algorithm for complete and for incomplete programs as the *Control Flow Extractor* tool (ConFlEx). It is based on Sawja [12], a library for the static analysis of Java bytecode. We have tailored SAWJA to address our needs. First, we have instrumented the BIR transformation to soundly provide the possible exceptions raised explicitly by throw instructions.

Moreover, SAWJA supports only the analysis of complete programs. Thus, we have lifted it to support open environments. On top of it, we have implemented the check of the refinement relation. Missing methods and their interfaces are provided as dummy methods with annotations. We have defined a template in Java annotation, named GhostComponent, to represent the interface of missing methods. Figure 1a shows the source code of an annotated missing method. It declares that the method even may call odd, or itself, and may not propagate exceptions. Here the keyword any denotes the set of all exception types. After compiling, the annotation is accessible as meta-data in the JBC .class file.

Finally, we have implemented the extraction rules from the BIR representation, as in defined in Figure 4. As described in Section 4.2, the intra-procedural analysis always produces the same set of triples if a method's implementation is not altered. Thus, we have implemented the caching of edges produced in the intra-procedural analysis. The caching allows us to perform the incremental extraction of the newly arrived component. Still, the inter-procedural analysis has to be recomputed.

5.2   Experimental Results

We validate our tool by using real-world Java applications to emulate incomplete Java bytecode systems. We choose three large, existing complete JBC applications, and replace the implementation of some of the classes with annotated methods. Then, we re-introduce the implementations incrementally, to mimic the arrival of code.

In the initial configuration, we replace the implementations of the methods of four classes with annotated methods. We perform the analysis of the resulting incomplete environment and cache the intra-procedural analysis. Next, we refine the incomplete program by re-inserting three of the four classes removed in configurations 2 and 3. For the former we reuse the cached results from configuration 1, while for the latter we perform a completely new analysis, for the purposes of assessing the impact of caching intra- results. Then, configuration 4 represents the completion of the incomplete system from set 2. The next two configurations 5 and 6 are performed over the original closed programs, with MCA, and RTA to investigate the impact of the chosen VMC resolution algorithm on the size of the resulting CFGs. Table 1 shows the experimental data. All tests have been made on an Intel i3 2.27 GHz with 4GB of RAM.

We can draw several conclusions from the experimental results. First, we observe that the number of unavailable components has a significant impact on the size of the over-approximations. For instance, configuration 1, where four classes are missing and thus has fewer instructions, produces larger CFGs than configurations 2 and 3, where a single class is missing. This can be explained partially by the excessive over-approximation of the exceptional control flow.

Table 1. Experimental results for CONFLEX

Configuration	VMC	Reused results	Missing classes	# of JBC instructions	# of Nodes	# of Edges	Time (ms) Intra	Inter
Jasmin								
1		no	4	25440	53467	54285	1256	339
2		yes	1	30377	35684	36228	291	109
3	MCA	no	1	30377	35684	36228	1540	104
4		yes	0	32223	34411	35052	49	104
5		no	0	32223	34411	35052	1554	85
6	RTA	no	0	30930	27267	27717	690	35
Java-Cup								
1		no	4	30042	76511	77345	1799	512
2		yes	1	33354	76798	77649	567	427
3	MCA	no	1	33354	76798	77649	2098	518
4		yes	0	35422	45455	46328	66	151
5		no	0	35422	45455	46328	2126	141
6	RTA	no	0	32049	32097	32509	983	45
JFlex								
1		no	4	52336	118414	119868	6396	877
2		yes	1	55972	77174	78678	960	631
3	MCA	no	1	55972	77174	78678	7227	407
4		yes	0	60417	72154	73175	115	181
5		no	0	60417	72154	73175	7219	177
6	RTA	no	0	53474	53956	54777	1676	76

Next, we see that the choice of VMC resolution algorithm has a serious impact on the CFG size. For example, in the analysis of the complete JFlex, MCA (configuration 5) produces 43% more nodes as compared to RTA (configuration 6). One reason is that RTA performs reachability analysis and eliminates dead code, and thus, the extraction is performed over fewer instructions. Further, a more precise estimation of receivers to virtual calls results in fewer call edges. Consequently, fewer nodes and edges relate to potentially propagated exceptions.

The caching of intra-procedural analysis, and consequent incremental extraction, leads to significant speed-up when compared to a whole new analysis. Also, the fixed-point computation in the inter-procedural analysis proves to be lightweight in practice, and contributes to a small fraction of the total time. This makes CONFLEX suitable for extracting CFGs in a context where the verification must be light-weight, such as in the ATM example mentioned in Section 3.

We do not provide comparative data with other extraction tools, such as Soot [16] or Wala [14] because this would demand the implementation of similar extraction rules from their intermediate representations. However, experimental results from SAWJA [12] show that it outperforms Soot in all tests w.r.t. the transformation into their respective intermediate representations, and outperforms Wala w.r.t. virtual method call algorithms. Thus, CONFLEX clearly benefits from using SAWJA and BIR. Also, to the best of our knowledge, CONFLEX is the first control flow analysis tool that supports incremental CFG extraction.

6 Related Work

The present work combines several aspects of program analysis, namely *soundness* w.r.t. sequences of method invocations and exceptions, *precision* w.r.t exceptional flow, and *modularity* and *incrementally* of the analysis of JBC. To the best of our knowledge, no previous work has addressed all these aspects together.

The present algorithm is modular in its essence. It analyzes components individually, as long as the interfaces for the missing components are provided. This strategy is described by Cousot and Cousot [5], and called *separate analysis*. However, a "pure" modular analysis, in the sense that each component is analyzed in isolation, would not take advantage of the inter-dependencies among the available components, and can lead to excessive over-approximation of the exceptional flow. In our case, we take inter-dependencies into account, and the isolated analyses are made incrementally.

Bandera [9] is a pioneering tool to generate abstract models from Java source programs. It is built on top of the Soot framework [16], and uses its intermediate language Jimple, in a similar fashion as CoNFLEx uses Sawja and BIR. It provides several features, such as output for multiple model checkers, and some static analyses. In comparison to CoNFLEx, Bandera is a versatile tool, which provides an integrated framework to program checking. However, it cannot analyze incomplete programs, and it does not address exceptional flows.

Dagenais and Hendren [6] present *partial program analysis* (PPA), a technique to build a typed intermediate representation from an incomplete program. It has been implemented in Soot, and also uses Jimple as its IR. The technique performs other analysis than control flow. Also, it is less restrictive and does not constrain the class hierarchy. However, it is admittedly unsound. Wala [14], another framework for the analysis of JBC, can also analyze partial programs. However, it ignores any side-effects from calls to unavailable methods. Thus, it is also unsound.

Ali and Lhotk [1] present a modular algorithm to generate call graphs from applications, without analyzing the API for possible call-backs. They assume that the API was coded in separation, and does not have knowledge about the application. Thus, call-backs are only possible to the application methods that overwrite a method from the API. Unfortunately this assumption is not valid for unavailable components, since developers have full knowledge of the application. The authors validate their algorithm empirically over a set of benchmarks. Thus, there is no formal argument about the soundness of their approach.

Several works propose different exception analyses. Our algorithm follows the approach of Jo and Chang [15] to extract CFGs by decoupling the intra- and inter-procedural analyses of exceptional control flow. However, they do not discuss implicit exceptions, nor address virtual method calls. Li *et al.* [17] present a framework for the extraction of CFGs *and* the model-checking of exceptional safety properties. The CFG extraction does not compute inter-procedural exceptional flow; instead, it uses a model checker to traverse the state-space. This approach requires exploration to be bounded, and is thus unsound.

7 Conclusion

We have presented a framework to extract control flow graphs from the available components of incomplete Java bytecode programs. It generalizes a previous algorithm for complete JBC programs that is defined through a transformation into an intermediate representation, and has been proven to produce sound CFGs, simulating the JVM behavior of the original programs. Our algorithm is modular in its essence. However, for higher precision, we perform the analysis of all available components together, and support the incremental refinement of the extracted CFGs as more components become available. The extracted CFGs are proven to be sound w.r.t. sequences of method invocations and exceptions. The extracted models are thus suitable for several program analyses, in particular model-checking of temporal control flow safety properties.

We have implemented the framework as the CONFLEX tool. The experimental results show that the over-approximations necessary to generate sound models (in the presence of unavailable components) have a considerable impact on the size of the extracted control flow graphs. Moreover, the over-approximations may give rise to false positive reports. CONFLEX alleviates this by providing support for the incremental refinement of the extracted models, as soon as more code becomes available. This shows the utility of CONFLEX to generate sound CFGs for incomplete programs with few missing components.

Future Work. Our framework constrains the components and how they relate w.r.t. the class hierarchy, and is limited to programs for which we know all components in advance. Our goal is to extend our analysis to truly open Java bytecode programs, where any number of components may be added in some regulated fashion. One idea is to follow the idea of *lazy parsing*, as introduced in [8]. There, instead of bounding *a priori* the unavailable components of a system, the analysis generates the constraints that the unavailable components have to fulfill to guarantee the soundness of any previous analyses.

Acknowledgments. We thank Musard Balliu, Roberto Guanciale and Siavash Soleimanifard for their valuable comments.

References

1. Ali, K., Lhoták, O.: Application-only call graph construction. In: Noble, J. (ed.) ECOOP 2012. LNCS, vol. 7313, pp. 688–712. Springer, Heidelberg (2012), http://dx.doi.org/10.1007/978-3-642-31057-7_30
2. Amighi, A., de Carvalho Gomes, P., Gurov, D., Huisman, M.: Sound control-flow graph extraction for java programs with exceptions. In: Eleftherakis, G., Hinchey, M., Holcombe, M. (eds.) SEFM 2012. LNCS, vol. 7504, pp. 33–47. Springer, Heidelberg (2012)
3. Bacon, D.F., Sweeney, P.F.: Fast static analysis of C++ virtual function calls. In: OOPSLA, pp. 324–341 (1996)

4. de Carvalho Gomes, P., Picoco, A.: Sound extraction of control-flow graphs from open java bytecode systems. Tech. rep., KTH Royal Institute of Technology (2012), http://urn.kb.se/resolve?urn=urn:nbn:se:kth:diva-104076
5. Cousot, P., Cousot, R.: Modular static program analysis. In: Nigel Horspool, R. (ed.) CC 2002. LNCS, vol. 2304, pp. 159–178. Springer, Heidelberg (2002)
6. Dagenais, B., Hendren, L.: Enabling static analysis for partial java programs. SIGPLAN Not. 43(10), 313–328 (2008)
7. Dean, J., Grove, D., Chambers, C.: Optimization of object-oriented programs using static class hierarchy analysis. In: Olthoff, W. (ed.) ECOOP 1995. LNCS, vol. 952, pp. 77–101. Springer, Heidelberg (1995)
8. Dovland, J., Johnsen, E.B., Owe, O., Steffen, M.: Lazy behavioral subtyping. The Journal of Logic and Algebraic Programming 79(7), 578–607 (2010), The 20th Nordic Workshop on Programming Theory (NWPT 2008)
9. Dwyer, M.B., Hatcliff, J., Joehanes, R., Laubach, S., Păsăreanu, C.S., Zheng, H., Visser, W.: Tool-supported program abstraction for finite-state verification. In: Proceedings of the 23rd International Conference on Software Engineering, ICSE 2001, pp. 177–187. IEEE Computer Society, Washington, DC (2001)
10. Freund, S.N., Mitchell, J.C.: A type system for the Java bytecode language and verifier. J. Autom. Reason. 30, 271–321 (2003)
11. Gurov, D., Huisman, M., Sprenger, C.: Compositional verification of sequential programs with procedures. Information and Computation 206(7), 840–868 (2008)
12. Hubert, L., Barré, N., Besson, F., Demange, D., Jensen, T., Monfort, V., Pichardie, D., Turpin, T.: Sawja: Static Analysis Workshop for Java. In: Beckert, B., Marché, C. (eds.) FoVeOOS 2010. LNCS, vol. 6528, pp. 92–106. Springer, Heidelberg (2011)
13. Huisman, M., Aktug, I., Gurov, D.: Program models for compositional verification. In: Liu, S., Araki, K. (eds.) ICFEM 2008. LNCS, vol. 5256, pp. 147–166. Springer, Heidelberg (2008)
14. IBM: T.J. Watson Libraries for Analysis (2012), http://wala.sourceforge.net/
15. Jo, J.-W., Chang, B.-M.: Constructing control flow graph for java by decoupling exception flow from normal flow. In: Laganá, A., Gavrilova, M.L., Kumar, V., Mun, Y., Tan, C.J.K., Gervasi, O. (eds.) ICCSA 2004. LNCS, vol. 3043, pp. 106–113. Springer, Heidelberg (2004), http://dx.doi.org/10.1007/978-3-540-24707-4_14
16. Lam, P., Bodden, E., Lhoták, O., Hendren, L.: The Soot framework for Java program analysis: a retrospective. In: Cetus Users and Compiler Infrastructure Workshop, Galveston Island, TX (October 2011)
17. Li, X., Hoover, H.J., Rudnicki, P.: Towards automatic exception safety verification. In: Misra, J., Nipkow, T., Sekerinski, E. (eds.) FM 2006. LNCS, vol. 4085, pp. 396–411. Springer, Heidelberg (2006)
18. Lindholm, T., Yellin, F., Bracha, G., Buckley, A.: The java virtual machine specification. java se 7 edition. Tech. Rep. JSR-000924, Oracle (2012)

Verifying Class Invariants in Concurrent Programs

Marina Zaharieva-Stojanovski and Marieke Huisman

University of Twente, the Netherlands

Abstract. Class invariants are a highly useful feature for the verification of object-oriented programs, because they can be used to capture all valid object states. In a sequential program setting, the validity of class invariants is typically described in terms of a *visible state semantics*, i.e., invariants only have to hold whenever a method begins or ends execution, and they may be broken inside a method body. However, in a concurrent setting, this restriction is no longer usable, because due to thread interleavings, any program state is potentially a visible state.

In this paper we present a new approach for reasoning about class invariants in multithreaded programs. We allow a thread to explicitly break an invariant at specific program locations, while ensuring that no other thread can observe the broken invariant. We develop our technique in a permission-based separation logic environment. However, we deviate from separation logic's standard rules and allow a class invariant to express properties over shared memory locations (the *invariant footprint*), independently of the permissions on these locations. In this way, a thread may break or reestablish an invariant without holding permissions to all locations in its footprint. To enable modular verification, we adopt the restrictions of Müller's ownership-based type system.

1 Introduction

In object-oriented programs, class invariants are typically used to express properties about the object's state that should hold throughout the object's life cycle. However, in practice it is often impossible to maintain the invariant continuously. For example, for an invariant that expresses a relation between fields x and y, $x == y$, when x is updated, y must also be updated, and both updates can not be done atomically. Therefore, invariant theory should provide for the possibility that a class invariant is temporarily *broken* at specific program parts.

In the sequential setting, the theory about invariant validity is well-developed; in essence, class invariants only have to hold in the program's *visible states*, i.e., in pre- and poststates of public methods [17]. In particular, if a class invariant I holds in a method's prestate, the method must end in a state satisfying I.

However, in the setting of multithreading programs, this approach can not be carried over directly. Due to possible interference between parallel threads, any program state may be *visible*. For example, when the field x in the invariant above is updated, any other thread might observe this change and the broken invariant. This problem is sometimes called a *high-level data race* [2].

S. Gnesi and A. Rensink (Eds.): FASE 2014, LNCS 8411, pp. 230–245, 2014.
© Springer-Verlag Berlin Heidelberg 2014

Therefore, this paper defines an approach to define validity of class invariants in a multithreaded setting. Our approach supports explicit *breaking of invariants*, under the condition that other threads can not see that the invariant is broken. We build our technique on *permission-based separation logic* [4], using a Java-like language. However, in contrast to standard separation logic, we explicitly make a distinction between *state formulas*, which describe a property about the shared state, and *resource formulas*, which describe when a thread holds a permission to access a certain location. We ensure modular verification using the restrictions from *ownership-based type systems* [7].

Our approach works as follows. A class invariant is specified as a condition on the shared memory. For each class invariant, we maintain a token that indicates whether the class invariant can be inspected. This token can be split and combined: if a thread has the complete token, it can *break* the invariant; otherwise it can only *use* it. Breaking the invariant is done by executing a (specification-only) unpack statement. When a thread reestablishes the invariant, the token to inspect the invariant becomes available again for other threads to break or inspect the invariant. This behaviour is modeled by a (specification-only) pack statement. Thus, within the unpacked segment, a thread is free to do whatever it wants with the class invariant, as our verification approach ensures that no other thread can observe the invariant in parallel.

To guarantee that class invariants can be verified in a modular way, when a class invariant is broken, a thread is not allowed to obtain any new permissions anymore. In particular, if a thread requires a lock to change any of the fields associated to the invariant, it should obtain this lock before breaking the invariant. This requirement shows that there is close connection between the locking strategy and the functional invariant properties that can be maintained in an application. Further, it is important that with our approach, a thread does not need to have all access permissions that are associated with the invariant, but only the access permissions needed to break the invariant; all other variables are implicitly assumed to be unchanged. Moreover, our technique does allow creating new (helper) threads when an invariant is broken; however, these threads need to be finished and joined before the invariant is reestablished again.

The main contribution of this paper is a sound modular technique for verification of class invariants in multithreaded programs, which:

- is flexible and permissive, because it allows a thread to break an invariant without holding all permissions associated to the invariant property; and
- reveals the connection between locking policy and invariant properties that can be maintained.

The motivation and applicability of our approach is illustrated on several examples. Its implementation as part of the VerCors tool set is under development.

Outline. We begin by introducing a short overview of permissions in separation logic, Sec. 2. Next, in Sec. 3 we present the main concepts of our approach, which is further formalised in Sec. 4. Sec. 5 reviews others approaches that tie in with our work. Finally, in Sec. 6 we summarise our work and discuss our future plans.

2 Background

This paper builds on Parkinson's work on separation logic for Java-like programs [21], and its extension by Haack *et al.* [11] for concurrency.

Separation logic [23] is an extension of Hoare Logic [12] for reasoning about separate parts of the heap. The base of this logic is the binary *separating conjunction* operation: $P*Q$ describes that P and Q hold for disjoint parts of the heap. O'Hearn shows that separation logic is also convenient for reasoning about multithreaded programs [19]. To allow parallel reads of the same data, basic separation logic is extended with *fractional permissions* [4]. Permission π is a value in the domain $(0, 1]$. At any point in time, a thread holds a number of permissions on locations. If a thread has a write permission for a certain location, i.e., the value 1, it is allowed to change this location. If a thread has a fractional permission, i.e., a fraction less than 1, then it may only read this location. Permissions can be split and combined, to change between read and write permissions. The soundness of this logic ensures that the sum of all threads' permissions for a certain location never exceeds 1, which guarantees data-race freedom. The predicate $\mathsf{Perm}(x.f, \pi)$ indicates that $x.f$ points to a location for which the actual thread has a permission π. Permission expressions are combined with the *separating conjunction* operation.

Parkinson adapts separation logic for object-oriented concepts in a Java-like language [21]. He proposes *abstract predicates* [20] to provide abstraction. Later, Haack *et al.* extended this logic to show how to reason about multithreaded Java-like programs [11] that include reentrant locks and dynamic thread creation. For each lock, a *resource invariant* is specified, i.e., an abstract predicate describing which permissions are stored in the lock. A newly created lock is still fresh and not ready to be acquired. The thread must first execute the commit command on the lock, which transfers the permissions from the thread to the lock and changes the lock's state to initialized. Any thread then may acquire the initialized lock to get the resource invariant (except for reentrant acquiring). Upon final release of the lock, the thread returns the resource invariant back to the lock.

3 Verification Methodology for Class Invariants

This section gives a conceptual understanding of our methodology, presented from two different aspects. First, we discuss how we model the *invariant protocol*, i.e., when an invariant may be assumed, and how it can be broken and reestablished. Then, we describe how our method supports modular verification.

3.1 Class Invariant Protocol

We assume that class invariants express properties over non-static class fields. Thus, a class invariant I defined in a class C is always associated with a particular object v of class C, we write $v.I$. We call the set of locations referred to by an invariant $v.I$ the *footprint of* $v.I$, denoted $\mathsf{fp}(v.I)$ (formally defined in Sec. 4).

Assuming a Class Invariant. Our technique should guarantee absence of high-level data races; therefore, it should control access to the invariant's footprint. To provide this control, to every invariant $v.I$, we associate a special abstract predicate $\text{holds}(v.I, 1)$, distributed as a token among the threads. The intuitive meaning of this predicate is the following: when a thread holds a predicate $\text{holds}(v.I, \pi), \pi > 0$, it may assume that the invariant $v.I$ holds; if $\pi = 1$, the running thread may additionally break the invariant. The predicate might be divided among different threads by using the following equivalence:

$$\text{holds}(v.I, \pi) * - * \text{holds}(v.I, \pi/2) * \text{holds}(v.I, \pi/2)$$

This approach guarantees that: 1) a class invariant $v.I$ is stable and all threads that hold a token $\text{holds}(v.I, \pi)$ may rely on $v.I$'s correctness; or 2) *at most one* thread has the token $\text{holds}(v.I, 1)$ and no other thread may assume $v.I$.

Breaking a Class Invariant. Inspired by the work of Leino *et al.* [14], we explicitly specify the segment in the program where an invariant property might be violated: for an invariant $v.I$, specification command $\text{unpack}(v.I)$ must be executed at the beginning of such a segment, and $\text{pack}(v.I)$ at its end. The segment between both commands is called an *unpacked segment of $v.I$*. A special case is object initialisation: the program segment between the end of v's construction and the first execution of the $\text{pack}(v.I)$ command is also $v.I$'s unpacked segment.

The $\text{unpack}(v.I)$ command consumes the token $\text{holds}(v.I, 1)$, and issues a predicate $\text{unpacked}(v.I, 1)$ (*breaking token*). This token serves as a license for the thread to break the invariant $v.I$. Once all updates are done, the running thread must reestablish the validity of $v.I$ and call the $\text{pack}(v.I)$ command, which trades the $\text{unpacked}(v.I, 1)$ token for the $\text{holds}(v.I, 1)$ token. The $\text{unpack}(v.I)$ command is always followed by $\text{pack}(v.I)$ within the same method and executed by the same thread. This thread is called *a holder* of the unpacked segment.

Lst. 1 illustrates the use of an unpacked segment: a class Point, represents a point lying on or above the line $y = -x$. Since method move() updates the fields x and y to which invariant I refers, these updates must happen within an unpacked segment of I. (The annotation safe at line 7 is discussed next.)

Restrictions to Unpacked Segments. We showed how a thread obtains permission to modify an invariant footprint location $p.f$. Once $p.f$ is assigned, we say that $p.f$ is in a *critical state* until the end of the unpacked segment. More precisely:

Definition 1. *(Critical state of a location) Let $v.I$ be an invariant, $p.f$ a location, such that $p.f \in \text{fp}(v.I)$, and let $p.f$ be assigned inside an unpacked segment of $v.I$. Then, any program execution state between the assignment and the end of the unpacked segment is a* critical state *for $p.f$.*

To prevent a thread to observe a broken invariant, a location in a critical state must not be publicly exposed. Therefore, within an unpacked segment we forbid the running thread to release permissions and make them accessible to other threads. Concretely, within an unpacked segment, we allow only safe

```
   class Point {
2    int x; int y;
     //@ invariant I : this.x + this.y >= 0;
4      //...constructors
     //@ requires holds(this.I,1) * Perm(this.x,1) * Perm(this.y,1);
6    //@ ensures holds(this.I,1) * Perm(this.x,1) * Perm(this.y,1);
     /*@ safe @*/ void move() {
8              // the invariant I may now be assumed because of the holds token
     {holds(this.I,1) * Perm(this.x,1) * Perm(this.y,1) * this.I}
10     //@ unpack(this.I);      // trades holds token for unpacked token
     {unpacked(this.I,1) * Perm(this.x,1) * Perm(this.y,1) * this.I}
12     this.x = this.x − 1;    // the invariant I is broken
       this.y = this.y + 1;    // the invariant I can now be reestablished
14   {unpacked(this.I,1) * Perm(this.x,1) * Perm(this.y,1) * this.I}
       //@ pack(this.I);         // trades unpacked token for holds token
16   {holds(this.I,1) * Perm(this.x,1) * Perm(this.y,1)}
     }}
```

Lst. 1. Unpacked segment of a class invariant

commands, i.e., commands that exclude any lock-related operation (acquiring, releasing or committing a lock). This means that all permissions used in the unpacked segment must be obtained before the segment begins. A safe command may call only safe methods, i.e., methods composed of safe commands only. These methods are specified with the optional modifier safe (see Lst. 1, line 7).

We allow forking a safe thread, i.e., threads with a safe $run()$ method, under the condition that the thread must be joined within the unpacked segment. We call these threads *local to the segment*. A safe thread may further fork other safe threads. The breaking token might be shared among all local threads of the unpacked segment, and thus, they might all update different locations of the invariant footprint in parallel. For this purpose, we define the following axiom:

$$\mathsf{unpacked}(v.I, \pi) * - * \mathsf{unpacked}(v.I, \pi/2) * \mathsf{unpacked}(v.I, \pi/2)$$

Lst. 2 shows a modified version of the move method (from Lst. 1) that can not be verified since acquiring/releasing a lock is used within the unpacked segment.

Object Initialisation. In our language, object initialisation (the object constructor) is divided into two steps: 1) *object construction* creates an empty object v (all v's fields get a default value), and gives the running thread write permission for each of v's fields and a token $\mathsf{unpacked}(v.I, 1)$ for each invariant $v.I$. 2) the init method follows obligatorily after object construction, where object fields are initialised. Additionally, for every invariant $v.I$, the $\mathsf{pack}(v.I)$ is called by default at the end of the init method. Hence, at the end of v's initialisation, all v's invariants hold, and therefore, v is a valid object.

```
   Lock lock;  // resource invariant: Perm(x, 1) * Perm(y,1);
 2 //@ requires holds(this.I,1);
   //@ ensures holds(this.I,1);
 4 void move(){
   //@ unpack(this.I); //trades holds token for unpacked (breaking) token
 6 lock.lock(); //invalid call (permissions to x and y must be gained before unpacking)
   t.fork();      //another thread t may get half of the breaking token to modify x
 8 updateY();       //for updating y another method is called, which must be safe
   lock.unlock();  // invalid call, must happen after packing
10 t.join();         //t is a safe thread, thus joining must be before packing
   //@ pack(this.I);
12 }
```

Lst. 2. Restrictions to unpacked segments

A verified program with our approach is free of *high-level data races*. This is expressed by the following theorem:

Theorem 1. *(High-level data race freedom) If a value p.f is in a critical state s of an unpacked segment S of an invariant v.I, then any thread that is neither holder nor a local thread of S can not access p.f.*

Proof. See [25].

As discussed initially, a thread that holds a token $\mathsf{holds}(v.I, \pi), \pi > 0$ may use the invariant $v.I$. This is justified by the following theorem:

Theorem 2. *(Use of a class invariant) An invariant v.I holds in a program state in which the running thread t holds the predicate* $\mathsf{holds}(v.I, \pi)$, $\pi > 0$.

Proof. See [25].

Lst. 3 extends the program with the `Point` class (see Lst. 1) to show how a class invariant may be used for verifying a client class. The main thread creates initially a valid `Point` object s for which the invariant $s.I$ holds $(s.x + s.y >= 0)$ and obtains the token $\mathsf{holds}(s.I, 1)$ (lines 3,4). The thread then forks a set of new threads (lines 5-9), passing each of them a reference to s and part of the holds token. Each forked thread has a task to create a sequence of new points at specific locations calculated from the location of s (line 21). To prove that each new `Point` p is a valid object $(p.x + p.y >= 0)$ (line 24), each thread uses the class invariant $s.I$, which is guaranteed by the token $\mathsf{holds}(s.I, \pi)$.

To conclude, we summarise the rules that define the invariant protocol:

R1 (*Assuming*). A thread t may assume (use) a class invariant $v.I$ if t holds the predicate $\mathsf{holds}(v.I, \pi), \pi > 0$.

R2 (*Breaking*). A thread t may write on a location $p.f$ if apart from holding a write permission to $p.f$, it holds a breaking token $\mathsf{unpacked}(v.I, \pi), \pi > 0$ for each invariant $v.I$ that refers to $p.f$, *i.e.*, $p.f \in \mathsf{fp}(v.I)$.

```
   class DrawPoints {                    14  class Task {
 2 void create(){                            Point s; int k;
   Point s = new Point (0, 0);          16  // ... constructors
 4 //holds(s.l,1) is produced               //@ requires holds(s.l. π) * ... ;
   for (int k = 1; k<=10; k++){         18  //@ ensures holds(s.l. π) * ... ;
 6 Task t = new Task(s, k);                  void run(){
   //each t gets part of holds token    20  for (int i = 1; i < 10; i ++) {
 8 t.fork();                                 int x = s.x+i; int y = s.y+ki;
   }                                     22  //s.l holds(because of the holds token)
10 //join Task threads                       //use s.l to validate p.l
   } }                                   24  Point p = new Point(x, y);
12                                           draw(p);
                                         26  } } }
```

Lst. 3. Using a class invariant for verifying a client class

R3 (*Reestablishing*). An invariant $v.I$ must have been reestablished when pack($v.I$) is executed.

R4 (*Exchanging tokens*). The token unpacked($v.I$, 1) is produced at v's construction; commands unpack($v.I$) and pack($v.I$) exchange the holds($v.I$, 1) token for the unpacked($v.I$, 1) token, and vice versa.

3.2   Modular Verification

As a second step, we discuss the additional properties needed to support modular verification. In the prestate of the assignment to a location $p.f$, rule **R2** requires a breaking token for all invariants that refer to $p.f$. However, in the context (class) where the assignment happens, not all invariants in the program are known. To support modularity, the breaking token is only explicitly checked for the invariants of the object p. Additionally, it is guaranteed that this token is implicitly held for all other invariants. We use Müller's *ownership type system* [7], which is strongly connected to modular verification of invariants [18,3,16,8].

Ownership-Based Types. The ownership type system organises the objects in the heap in an *ownership tree*, where each object has one *owner* (either the root of the tree, or another object in the heap). We say that each ancestor of an object p in the tree is p's *transitive owner*. The position of the object p in the tree is determined on p's creation, with an attached required modifier from the set {rep, peer, rd} where: peer indicates that r has the same owner as the object this; rep specifies that r is owned by this, and rd(readonly) is any other relation. Additionally, the self modifier is used for references that point to the this object. An array a of object references has an additional modifier to define the relation of each element $a[i]$ with the this reference (see Lst. 4, line 2). When an object changes its context, for example, via transfer as a method parameter, the type of the new reference is determined by applying the *viewpoint adaptation* function ▷ (see [25]). For example, if the this reference owns r, while r owns x, the type of the reference $r.x$ in the context of this is rep ▷ rep = rd.

Additionally, the following discipline is imposed in the program: writing to a field $p.f$ or a call to a *non-pure* method (i.e. with side-effects) with a receiver p is forbidden when p has a modifier rd. In this way, each object controls all updates that happen in its transitively owned objects. This guarantees the following:

RO. If a field $p.f$ is modified in a method m, for each transitive owner o of p, the call stack contains a method invocation where o is a receiver.

We require that all class invariants in the program are *ownership admissible*:

Definition 2. *A class invariant $v.I$ is ownership admissible if it expresses properties over fields $p_1.p_2...p_n.f$, where $n \geq 1$, $v == p_1$ and p_i is a rep field in the class of p_{i-1} ($i = 2..n$).*

Verification Technique via Ownership Types. Based on Def. 2, we observe the following: for a location $p.f$, an invariant $v.I$ may refer to $p.f$ only if $v == p$ or v is a transitive owner of p. Our verification technique suggests that before assigning to a location $p.f$, it is enough to require a breaking token only for the invariants of the object p ($p.I$) that refer to $p.f$. If an invariant $v.I$, where v is a transitive owner of p, refers to $p.f$, then the rule **RO** ensures that assignment of $p.f$ is preceded by a method call where v is a receiver. To support modular verification, the check that the actual thread holds a breaking token for $v.I$ should therefore be a requirement of the method call where object v is a receiver. More precisely, we replace the rule **R2** listed above with the following two rules:

R2' A precondition for assigning a field $p.f$ requires a token unpacked$(p.I, \pi)$ $(\pi > 0)$ for each invariant I of the object p that refers to $p.f$.
R2'' A precondition for invoking a method m that assigns a field $p.f$ requires the token unpacked$(\text{this}.I, \pi)(\pi > 0)$ for each invariant I of the this object that refers to $p.f$.

To establish **R2''**, the contract of the called method m should provide information to the caller about the locations it assigns to. In permission-based separation logic, assigning to a location $p.f$ in m requires a write permission $\pi = 1$ for $p.f$. The caller can identify the locations assignable by m from the precondition formula $\mathsf{Pre_m}$: this is the set of locations for which $\mathsf{Pre_m}$ requires a write permission, denoted $\mathsf{wrt(Pre_m)}$ (see [25]). However, π might also be obtained by acquiring a lock during the execution of m. We ensure that this scenario is not possible. In particular, if a location $p.f$ is in the footprint of an invariant $v.I$, $p.f$ should not be protected by a lock object that is transitively owned by v, because this would mean that other threads might observe a broken invariant (see the example below). This restriction is imposed by the following rule (the used functions are defined in [25]):

RL $\forall I \in \mathsf{inv}(C)$; $\forall f \in \mathsf{relFld}(C)$; $\mathsf{fld}(I) \cap \mathsf{fldResInv}(\mathsf{classOf}(f)) = \emptyset$

The rule is translated as: for any invariant I defined in a class C, and a field f *relevant* to C, the set of fields that appear in I is disjoint from the set of fields

```
   class PointsSet {
2      rep rep Point[] points = new rep rep Point[100];
       //@ Invariant I₁:  (∀int i: 0 <=i<100) (points[i].x <= 10) * (points[i].y <= 10);
4      //@ requires holds(this.I₁, 1) * Perm(points[i].x, 1) * Perm(points[i].y, 1)
       //@ ensures holds(this.I₁, 1) * Perm(points[i].x, 1) * Perm(points[i].y, 1)
6      void moveAt(int i) {
         //@ unpack(this.I₁);  // trades the holds token for unpacked token
8        if (points[i].y <= 9) {
       //required unpacked token for I₁ (as points[i].x, points[i].y ∈ wrt(Pre_move)∩fp(I₁))
10       points[i].move(); }
         //@ pack(this.I₁);  // trades the unpacked token for holds token
12     } }
```

Lst. 4. Modular verification

that appear in the resource invariant definition in the class of f. A field f is *relevant* to a class C if it may be expressed as a $p_1.p_2., ...p_n.f$, where p_1 is a rep field defined in C, and p_i is a rep or peer field in the class of $p_{i-1}, i = 2..n, n >= 1$.

In Lst. 4, we extend our program (from Lst. 1) to illustrate modular verification. Class PointsSet represents a set of points that lie within a predefined area. When calling the method move()(line 10), the caller provides a breaking token for its own invariants that move() might break (in this case invariant I_1). After the call to move(), invariant I_1 is reestablished (line 11), even though the actual thread has permissions to the ith array element only; our approach ensures that the other locations in fp(I_1) are stable until the end of the unpacked segment.

Fields x and y from class Point are relevant to the PointsSet class and used in I_1; hence, Rule **RL** forbids a lock that protects x and/or y to be transitively owned by a PointsSet object. This is necessary: if permissions to x and y could be obtained by a lock in Point, other threads might observe that I_1 is broken. To avoid this, the lock would have to be already acquired before the unpacked segments for I_1, but this would violate modularity. The example shows that the invariants that can be maintained strongly depend on the locking strategy used.

4   Formalisation

We formalise our approach using a Java-like concurrent language. The formalisation is mainly inspired by Haack *et al.* [11]. We concentrate on those points that are relevant for class invariants. For other concepts, e.g., those associated to locks, we only provide some basic intuition to make the paper self-contained.

4.1   Language

Fig. 1 shows the grammar of our language. With $\overline{x}$ we define sequences of x, while $x?$ represents an optional x. A class is composed of fields, methods, predicates, and class invariants. The special predicate *res_inv* is associated to a lock

$cl \in$ Class $\qquad ::=$ class C $\{fd * md * inv * pd*\}$

$fd \in$ Field $\qquad ::= T f$

$md \in$ Method $\qquad ::= spec\ T\ m(\overline{V}\ \overline{x})\{c\}$

$spec \in$ MethSpec $::=$ requires F ensures F pure? safe?

$pd \in$ Predicate $\qquad ::=$ pred $P = F_{res}(P \neq res\_inv)$ | pred $res\_inv = F_{res}$

$inv \in$ Invariant $\qquad ::=$ Invariant $I : F_{inv}$

$c \in$ Command $\qquad ::= v$ (return value or null in case of type void)

$\qquad\qquad\qquad\qquad$ | $T\ x; c$ | $x = v; c$ | $x = op(\overline{v}); c$ | $x = v.f; c$

$\qquad\qquad\qquad\qquad$ | $x =$ new $rtype\ C; c$ | $(x = v.m(\overline{v}); c$ | if v.then c else $c; c$

$\qquad\qquad\qquad\qquad$ | $v.f = v; c$ | $v.$lock$(); c$ | $v.$commit$(); c$ | $v.$unlock$(); c$

$\qquad\qquad\qquad\qquad$ | $v.$fork$(); c$ | $v.$join$(); c$ | unpack$(v.I); c$ | pack$(v.I); c$

$F \in$ Formula $\qquad ::= e$ | Perm$(v.f, \pi)$ | $\pi.P$ | $F \oplus F$ | $(qt\ T\ \alpha)F$

$\qquad\qquad\qquad\qquad$ | holds$(v.I, \pi)$ | unpacked$(v.I, \pi)$ | $e.$fresh$()$ | $e.$initialized$()$

$F_{res} \in$ Formula$_{res}$ $::= e$ | Perm$(v.f, \pi)$ | $\pi.P$ | $F_{res} \oplus F_{res}$ | $(qt\ T\ \alpha)(F_{res})$ | holds$(v.I, \pi)$

$F_{inv} \in$ Formula$_{inv}$ $::= e_{inv}$ | $(qt\ T\ \alpha)(F_{inv})$ | $F_{inv} \oplus F_{inv}$

$e \in$ Exp $\qquad ::= \pi$ | $v.f$ | v | $op(\overline{e})$

$e_{inv} \in$ Exp$_{inv}$ $\qquad ::= v_1.v_2...v_n.f$ | $op(\overline{e_{inv}})$

$T, U, V \in$ Type $\qquad ::=$ void | int | bool | perm | $(rtype, C)$

$rtype \in$ RefType $\qquad ::=$ rep | peer | self | rd

$\pi \in$ SpecVal $\qquad ::= \alpha$ | v | 1 | split(π) (1/2 of a fractional permission π)

$u, v, w \in$ Val $\qquad ::=$ null | n | b | o | x

$\oplus \in \{*, \wedge, \vee\} \qquad op \in$ Op $\supseteq \{==, !, \wedge, \vee, \Rightarrow\} \qquad qt \in \{\exists, \forall\}$

$n \in$ int $\qquad b \in \{$true, false$\} \qquad x, y, z \in$ Variables $\qquad o, p \in$ ObjectId

Fig. 1. Language Syntax

object, and is used to describe the resources that the lock protects. Methods may be declared as pure and/or safe, as explained below. The set of commands is extended with the specification commands pack$(v.I)$ and unpack$(v.I)$.

Specification Formulas. We distinguish three types of specification formulas: i) *Standard formulas F*, expressed in permission-based separation logic and used to specify methods. Predicates holds and unpacked, and fresh and initialized are special tokens that describe the state of a class invariant or a lock, respectively. ii) *Resource invariant formulas* F_{res}, used to express the res_inv predicate. They are more restrictive than F: F_{res} must not use the special tokens unpacked, fresh and initialized.

iii) *State formulas* F_{inv}, first-order logic formulas, used to specify class invariants and describe properties over shared memory locations only. Thus, their syntax does not include the predicate Perm$(v.f, \pi)$ or any of the special tokens. We define the invariant footprint fp$(v.I)$ by induction of the structure of $v.I$:

$$\text{fp}(v_1.v_2..v_n.f) = \{v_1, v_1.v_2, ..., v_1...v_n.f\} \quad \text{fp}(op(\overline{e_{inv}})) = \bigcup_{e \in \overline{e_{inv}}} \text{fp}(e)$$

$$\text{fp}(F_{inv_1} \oplus F_{inv_2}) = \text{fp}(F_{inv_1}) \cup \text{fp}(F_{inv_2}) \quad \text{fp}((qt\ \alpha\ T)(F_{inv})) = \bigcup_{v \in T \setminus \{\alpha\}} \text{fp}(F_{inv}[v/\alpha])$$

Types. A type of an object reference in our language is represented as a tuple $T = (rtype, C)$. The first component, T^1, is a type modifier from the set

RefType $= \{$rep, peer, self, rd$\}$, while the second, T^2, represents the object's class. Consequently, two references pointing to the same object might have different reference types if they are in a different context. In this paper we do not present the typing rules of the language; rules that represent constraints imposed by the ownership type system are listed in [25].

Safe and Pure Commands. Above, we introduced the notion of safe commands. For a safe command c the predicate safe(c, V) holds, where V is a set that keeps track of all identifiers of threads that are forked and expected to be joined. The V parameter is used to capture that threads forked within a safe command c, must also be joined within c. For a method m defined as safe $T\ m(\overline{V}\ \overline{i})\ \{c\}$, the relation safe$(m)$ holds iff safe$(c, [])$ holds. A safe method is annotated with the optional modifier safe. We define inductively the set of safe commands.

safe(v, V) $\Leftrightarrow$ true
safe(c, V) $\Leftrightarrow$ false,   if $c \in \{v.\mathsf{lock}(), v.\mathsf{unlock}(), v.\mathsf{commit}()\}$
safe$(c; c_1, V)$ $\Leftrightarrow$ safe(c_1, V),   if $c \in \{T\ x,\ x = v,\ x = v.f,\ v.f = v,$
                  $x = op(\overline{v}),\ \mathsf{new}\ rtype\ C,\ \mathsf{unpack}(v.I),\ \mathsf{pack}(v.I)\}$
safe$(x = v.m(\overline{v}); c, V)$ $\Leftrightarrow$ safe$(m) \wedge$ safe(c, V)
safe$(v.\mathsf{fork}(); c, V)$ $\Leftrightarrow$ safe$(c, V \cup \{v\})$
safe$(v.\mathsf{join}(); c, V)$ $\Leftrightarrow$ safe$(c, V \setminus \{v\})$
safe$(\mathsf{if}\ v\ \mathsf{then}\ c_1\ \mathsf{else}\ c_2; c,\ V)$ $\Leftrightarrow$ safe$(c_1, []) \wedge$ safe$(c_2, []) \wedge$ safe(c, V)

Our method uses also the notion of pure commands, i.e., commands that do not make any changes to the shared state (defined in [25]). Pure methods are composed of pure commands and specified with the optional modifier pure.

4.2   Hoare Triples

Fig. 2 shows the Hoare triples relevant to our approach (for the complete list of rules see [11]). We use: $\circledast_i F_i$ to abbreviate a separation conjunction of all formulas F_i; PointsTo$(v.f, \pi, w)$ to abbreviate Perm$(v.f, \pi) \wedge v.f == w$; functions fld$(C)$ and inv(C) to represent respectively the set of fields and invariants in the class C; df(T) for the default value of type T; wrt(F) for the set of locations for which F expresses a write permission (all defined formally in [25]).

The rule (New) shows that construction of object v produces an unpacked token for each invariant of v, and a write permission for each field of v. Rules (Set) and (MethCall) encode **R2'** and **R2"** (see Sec. 3.2); they ensure that the breaking token is a condition for breaking the invariant $v.I$. Rules (Pack) and (Unpack) describe the invariant protocol and encode **R3** and **R4** (see Sec. 3.1). Finally, the rule (RuleInv) shows that the token holds$(v.I, \pi)$ provides the actual thread the right to use the invariant $v.I$ (as justified by Theorem 2 in Sec 3.1).

4.3   Semantics

We define a program state as: $st \in$ State $=$ Heap $\times$ ThreadPool $\times$ LockTable. A Heap models the shared memory: $h \in$ Heap $=$ ObjId $\mapsto$ Type$\times$ (FieldId $\mapsto$ Value).

(New)
$$\{\mathsf{true}\}$$
$$v = \mathsf{new\ rtype\ } C$$
$$\{ \circledast_{Tf \in \mathsf{fld}(C)} \mathsf{PointsTo}(v.f, 1, \mathsf{df}(T^1)) * \circledast_{I \in \mathsf{inv}(C)} \mathsf{unpacked}(v.I, 1) \}$$

(Set)
$$\frac{v : V}{\begin{array}{c} \{v \neq \mathsf{null} * \mathsf{PointsTo}(v.f, 1, u) * \circledast_{I \in \mathsf{inv}(V^2), v.f \in \mathsf{fp}(v.I)} \mathsf{unpacked}(v.I, \pi) \} \\ v.f = w; \\ \{ \mathsf{PointsTo}(v.f, 1, w) * \circledast_{I \in \mathsf{inv}(V^2), v.f \in \mathsf{fp}(v.I)} \mathsf{unpacked}(v.I, \pi) \} \end{array}}$$

(MethCall)
$$\frac{md ::= \mathsf{requires\ } F \mathsf{\ ensures\ } F' \mathsf{\ safe?\ pure?\ } T\ m(\overline{U}\ \overline{u})\{c\} \quad \mathsf{this} : V}{\begin{array}{c} \{u \neq \mathsf{null} * F * \circledast_{I \in \mathsf{inv}(V^2), \mathsf{wrt}(F) \cap \mathsf{fp}(\mathsf{this}.I) \neq \emptyset} \mathsf{unpacked}(\mathsf{this}.I, \pi) \} \\ x = u.m(\overline{i}) \\ \{\exists\ T\alpha)(\alpha == x * F') * \circledast_{I \in \mathsf{inv}(V^2), \mathsf{wrt}(F) \cap \mathsf{fp}(\mathsf{this}.I) \neq \emptyset} \mathsf{unpacked}(\mathsf{this}.I, \pi) \} \end{array}}$$

(Unpack)
$$\{\mathsf{holds}(v.I, 1)\}\ \mathsf{unpack}(v.I)\{\mathsf{unpacked}(v.I, 1) * v.I\}$$

(Pack)
$$\{\mathsf{unpacked}(v.I, 1) * v.I\}\ \mathsf{pack}(v.I)\ \{\mathsf{holds}(v.I, 1)\}$$

(RuleInv)
$$\frac{\{\mathsf{holds}(v.I, \pi) * v.I\}\ c\ \{F\}}{\{\mathsf{holds}(v.I, \pi)\}\ c\ \{F\}}$$

Fig. 2. Hoare triples

The ThreadPool component describes all threads that operate on the heap: $ts \in$ ThreadPool = ObjId $\mapsto$ Thread, where each thread contains its own local memory and a command to execute, $t \in$ Thread = Stack $\times$ Cmd. The LockTable expresses for every lock whether it is free, or it is acquired by a thread a certain number of times: $l \in$ LockTable = ObjId $\mapsto$ free $\uplus$ (ObjId $\times$ $\mathbb{N}$). Operationally, the two specification commands unpack$(v.I)$ and pack$(v.I)$ are no operations. The small-step operational semantics of the other commands is standard, see [11].

Semantics of Formulas. The specification formulas are interpreted using the semantics relation $\Gamma \vdash \mathcal{E}, \mathcal{R}, s \models F$, which expresses validity of the formula F in a type environment Γ, a predicate environment $\mathcal{E}$ and a stack s, given a resource $\mathcal{R}$. Type environment Γ is a partial function of type ObjId $\cup$ Var $\mapsto$ Type that maps each object or variable to its type, while $\mathcal{E}$ maps each predicate symbol to an appropriate relation that represents its definition. For details see [11].

The resource $\mathcal{R}$ is an abstraction of a program state represented by an 8-tuple, $\mathcal{R} = (h, \mathcal{P}, \mathcal{J}, \mathcal{L}, \mathcal{F}, \mathcal{I}, \mathcal{U}, \mathcal{T})$, where each component describes part of the state: i) h represents the heap: ObjId $\mapsto$ Type$\times$(FieldId $\mapsto$ Val) ii) $\mathcal{P}$ is a permission table that stores permissions to object fields from the heap (ObjId $\times$ FieldId $\mapsto$ [0, 1]); iii) $\mathcal{J}$ is a join table (ObjId $\mapsto$ [0, 1]), where $\mathcal{J}(t)$ represents how much of the postcondition of a thread t is given to other forked threads; iv) $\mathcal{L}$ is an abstraction of the lock table, which maps each thread to the set of locks that it holds; v) $\mathcal{F}$ keeps a set of fresh locks; vi) $\mathcal{I}$ keeps a set of initialized locks; vii) $\mathcal{U}$ keeps the parts of the unpacked tokens for each invariant; and analogously viii) $\mathcal{T}$ keeps the holds tokens. Both components $\mathcal{U}$ and $\mathcal{T}$ are defined as functions ObjId $\times$ InvId $\mapsto$ [0, 1].

We define a *compatibility* binary relation ($\#$) and a *resource joining operation* ($*$) over resources. Compatibility ensures that two different threads always observe the abstract state as two compatible resources, $\mathcal{R}\#\mathcal{R}'$: the object fields that are common for the heaps in $\mathcal{R}$ and $\mathcal{R}'$ are mapped to the same value; the sum of permissions for a location in $\mathcal{R}$ and $\mathcal{R}'$, or the sum of the parts of the special tokens (holds and unpacked) for an invariant in both resources never exceeds 1; etc. The intuitive meaning of the operation $\mathcal{R}*\mathcal{R}'$ is joining (summing) both resources. For example, $\mathcal{R}*\mathcal{R}'$ contains all permissions from both resources or all tokens from both resources. The definition of the $\#$ and $*$ is component-wise. We give the formal definitions for the structure ($\#,*$) for the components $\mathcal{U}$ and $\mathcal{T}$, while for the others we refer to [11].

$$\mathcal{U}\#\mathcal{U}' \Leftrightarrow \forall i \in \mathsf{dom}(\mathcal{U}) \cap \mathsf{dom}(\mathcal{U}'). \ \mathcal{U}(i) + \mathcal{U}'(i) \leq 1 \quad (\mathcal{U}*\mathcal{U}')(i) = \mathcal{U}(i) + \mathcal{U}'(i)$$
$$\mathcal{T}\#\mathcal{T}' \Leftrightarrow \forall i \in \mathsf{dom}(\mathcal{T}) \cap \mathsf{dom}(\mathcal{T}'). \ \mathcal{T}(i) + \mathcal{T}'(i) \leq 1 \quad (\mathcal{T}*\mathcal{T}')(i) = \mathcal{T}(i) + \mathcal{T}'(i)$$

Below we define that the specification formula $\mathsf{holds}(v.I, \pi)$ holds for a resource $\mathcal{R}$ if the part of the holds token for the invariant $v.I$ in $\mathcal{R}$ is at least π. The validity of the $\mathsf{unpacked}(v.I, \pi)$ formula is defined analogously. The semantics of a class invariant $v.I$ is expressed as a validity of the representation formula of $v.I$, i.e., F_{inv}.

$$\Gamma \vdash \mathcal{E}, (h, \mathcal{P}, \mathcal{J}, \mathcal{L}, \mathcal{F}, \mathcal{I}, \mathcal{U}, \mathcal{T}), s \models \mathsf{holds}(v.I, \pi) \Leftrightarrow \mathcal{T}(v.I) \geq \pi$$
$$\Gamma \vdash \mathcal{E}, (h, \mathcal{P}, \mathcal{J}, \mathcal{L}, \mathcal{F}, \mathcal{I}, \mathcal{U}, \mathcal{T}), s \models \mathsf{unpacked}(v.I, \pi) \Leftrightarrow \mathcal{U}(v.I) \geq \pi$$
$$\Gamma \vdash \mathcal{R} = \mathcal{E}, (h, \mathcal{P}, \mathcal{J}, \mathcal{L}, \mathcal{F}, \mathcal{I}, \mathcal{U}, \mathcal{T}), s \models v.I(I = F_{\mathsf{inv}}) \Leftrightarrow \Gamma \vdash \mathcal{E}, \mathcal{R}, s \models F_{\mathsf{inv}}$$

As our language contains *state formulas*, not all locations in the partial heap must be 'framed' by a positive permission (unlike in standard permission-based separation logic). For a sound resource $\mathcal{R} = (h, \mathcal{P}, \mathcal{J}, \mathcal{L}, \mathcal{F}, \mathcal{I}, \mathcal{U}, \mathcal{T})$ we require:

$$\forall p \in \mathsf{dom}(h), f \in \mathsf{dom}(h(p)_2), \mathcal{P}(p,f) > 0 \ \vee$$
$$(\exists v.I \in \mathsf{dom}(\mathcal{T}) \ p.f \in \mathsf{fp}(v.I) \wedge (\mathcal{T}(v.I) > 0 \vee \mathcal{U}(v.I) > 0))$$

The rule states that if a location $p.f$ is not protected by a read permission ($\mathcal{P}(p,f) = 0$), then it must be protected by (a part of) the holds or unpacked token ($\mathcal{T}(v.I) > 0 \vee \mathcal{U}(v.I) > 0$), for an invariant $v.I$ that refers to $p.f$. This ensures that the location $p.f$ is stable and might not be modified by other threads.

5   Related Work

The early work on verification of class invariants in sequential programs [17,15] is unsound for more complex data structure, for example if an invariant captures properties over different objects. Later, Poetzsch-Heffter [22] and Huizing *et al.* [13] presented sound techniques that do not restrict the invariant definition or the program itself; however, both approaches are not modular.

Müller *et al.* [18] propose two sound techniques for modular reasoning: the *ownership technique* and the less restrictive *visibility technique*. Both concepts, as well as Lu *et al.*'s modular technique [16], are designed for ownership-based type systems. These techniques are captured in Drossopoulou *et al.*'s abstract unified framework [9]. Although it is stated that this abstract framework should be suitable to model class invariants in a concurrent setting, the framework has never been applied on a concrete verification technique for concurrent programs.

Weiß models class invariants with a boolean model field *inv* [24]. Their validity is checked only on demand. Specifications use *inv* explicitly where needed, while this.*inv* is implicitly generated in each method pre- and postcondition.

We are not aware of much work done on verification of class invariants for multithreaded programs. Comparable to our approach is Jacobs *et al.*'s technique [14] for verifying multithreaded programs with class invariants, using the *Boogie methodology* [3] for sequential programs. However, this technique allows a thread to break an invariant of an object only if it completely owns this object. Instead, with our technique, breaking a class invariant is independent of permissions on heap memory. This ensures a broader applicability of our technique.

A different approach for modular verification of object invariants in concurrent programs is proposed by Cohen [6], implemented in VCC [5]. Each object is assigned a two-state invariant expressing the required relation between any two consecutive states of execution that has to be respected by every state update in the program. Modular verification of multithreaded programs with class invariants is also supported by the static checker Calvin [10]. However, both methodologies do not allow breaking of a class invariant in the program.

6   Conclusion and Future Work

We introduced a sound and modular approach for verifying class invariants in multithreaded Java-like programs in a permission-based separation logic setting. We do, however, deviate from the standard rules in separation logic: we impose that class invariants may express properties only over state and thus, their definition is free of permission expressions. We allow a thread to explicitly break an invariant, and we ensure that no other thread can observe the invalidated object's state. Moreover, breaking and reestablishing an invariant is allowed without holding all permissions associated to the invariant. This makes our technique broadly applicable. To achieve modularity, we restrict our technique to ownership-based type systems only. The method requires simple specifications support.

For future work, we plan to integrate our technique in the VerCors tool [1], and to use it to verify data structures from the *java.util.concurrency* package. We plan to extend the concept to support class inheritance, to allow more permissive invariants with model methods and/or abstract predicates, to allow more fine-grained permission handling. as well as to support *history constraints*.

Acknowledgments. We thank Christian Haack and Stefan Blom for their useful feedback. This work was supported by ERC grant 258405 for the VerCors project.

References

1. Amighi, A., Blom, S., Huisman, M., Zaharieva-Stojanovski, M.: The VerCors project: setting up basecamp. In: PLPV, pp. 71–82 (2012)
2. Artho, C., Havelund, K., Biere, A.: High-level data races. Softw. Test., Verif. Reliab. 13(4), 207–227 (2003)
3. Barnett, M., DeLine, R., Fähndrich, M., Leino, K.R.M., Schulte, W.: Verification of object-oriented programs with invariants. Journal of Object Technology 3(6), 27–56 (2004)
4. Bornat, R., Calcagno, C., O'Hearn, P., Parkinson, M.: Permission accounting in separation logic. In: Palsberg, J., Abadi, M. (eds.) POPL, pp. 259–270. ACM (2005)
5. Cohen, E., Dahlweid, M., Hillebrand, M., Leinenbach, D., Moskal, M., Santen, T., Schulte, W., Tobies, S.: VCC: A practical system for verifying concurrent C. In: Berghofer, S., Nipkow, T., Urban, C., Wenzel, M. (eds.) TPHOLs 2009. LNCS, vol. 5674, pp. 23–42. Springer, Heidelberg (2009)
6. Cohen, E., Moskal, M., Schulte, W., Tobies, S.: Local verification of global invariants in concurrent programs. In: Touili, T., Cook, B., Jackson, P. (eds.) CAV 2010. LNCS, vol. 6174, pp. 480–494. Springer, Heidelberg (2010)
7. Dietl, W., Müller, P.: Universes: Lightweight ownership for JML. Journal of Object Technology 4(8), 5–32 (2005)
8. Dietl, W., Müller, P.: Object ownership in program verification. In: Clarke, D., Noble, J., Wrigstad, T. (eds.) Aliasing in Object-Oriented Programming. LNCS, vol. 7850, pp. 289–318. Springer, Heidelberg (2013)
9. Drossopoulou, S., Francalanza, A., Müller, P., Summers, A.J.: A unified framework for verification techniques for object invariants. In: Vitek, J. (ed.) ECOOP 2008. LNCS, vol. 5142, pp. 412–437. Springer, Heidelberg (2008)
10. Flanagan, C., Freund, S.N., Qadeer, S., Seshia, S.A.: Modular verification of multithreaded programs. Theor. Comput. Sci. 338(1-3), 153–183 (2005)
11. Haack, C., Huisman, M., Hurlin, C., Amighi, A.: Permission-based separation logic for Java, 201x. Conditionally accepted for LMCS
12. Hoare, C.A.R.: An axiomatic basis for computer programming. Commun. ACM 12(10), 576–580 (1969)
13. Huizing, K., Kuiper, R.: Verification of object oriented programs using class invariants. In: Maibaum, T. (ed.) FASE 2000. LNCS, vol. 1783, pp. 208–221. Springer, Heidelberg (2000)
14. Jacobs, B., Piessens, F., Leino, K.R.M., Schulte, W.: Safe concurrency for aggregate objects with invariants. In: SEFM, pp. 137–147 (2005)
15. Liskov, B., Guttag, J.: Abstraction and specification in program development. MIT Press, Cambridge (1986)
16. Lu, Y., Xue, J.: Validity invariants and effects. In: Ernst, E. (ed.) ECOOP 2007. LNCS, vol. 4609, pp. 202–226. Springer, Heidelberg (2007)
17. Meyer, B.: Object-Oriented Software Construction, 2nd edn. Prentice-Hall (1997)
18. Müller, P., Poetzsch-Heffter, A., Leavens, G.T.: Modular invariants for layered object structures. Sci. Comput. Program. 62(3), 253–286 (2006)
19. O'Hearn, P.W.: Resources, concurrency, and local reasoning. Theor. Comput. Sci. 375(1-3), 271–307 (2007)
20. Parkinson, M., Bierman, G.: Separation logic, abstraction and inheritance. In: Principles of programming languages (POPL 2008), pp. 75–86. ACM (2008)
21. Parkinson, M.J.: Local reasoning for Java. Technical Report UCAM-CL-TR-654, University of Cambridge, Computer Laboratory (November 2005)

22. Poetzsch-Heffter, A.: Specification and Verification of Object-Oriented Programs. PhD thesis, Habilitation thesis, Technical University of Munich (1997)
23. Reynolds, J.: Separation logic: A logic for shared mutable data structures. In: 17th IEEE Symposium on LICS 2002, pp. 55–74. IEEE Computer Society (2002)
24. Weiß, B.: Deductive Verification of Object-Oriented Software: Dynamic Frames, Dynamic Logic and Predicate Abstraction. PhD thesis, Karlsruhe Institute of Technology (2011)
25. Zaharieva-Stojanovski, M., Huisman, M.: Verifying class invariants in concurrent programs. Technical Report TR-CTIT-13-10, Centre for Telematics and Information Technology, University of Twente (2014)

Automatic Program Repair by Fixing Contracts*

Yu Pei, Carlo A. Furia, Martin Nordio, and Bertrand Meyer

Chair of Software Engineering, ETH Zurich, Switzerland
firstname.lastname@inf.ethz.ch

Abstract. While most debugging techniques focus on patching implementations, there are bugs whose most appropriate corrections consist in fixing the specification to prevent invalid executions—such as to define the correct input domain of a function. In this paper, we present a fully automatic technique that fixes bugs by proposing changes to contracts (simple executable specification elements such as pre- and postconditions). The technique relies on dynamic analysis to understand the source of buggy behavior, to infer changes to the contracts that emend the bugs, and to validate the changes against general usage. We have implemented the technique in a tool called SpeciFix, which works on programs written in Eiffel, and evaluated it on 44 bugs found in standard data-structure libraries. Manual analysis by human programmers found that SpeciFix suggested repairs that are deployable for 25% of the faults; in most cases, these contract repairs were preferred over fixes for the same bugs that change the implementation.

1 Introduction

A software *bug* is the manifestation of a discrepancy between specification and implementation: program behavior (implementation) deviates from expectations (specification). Correcting a bug may thus require changing implementation, specification, or both. In fact, there is a significant number of bugs [3] whose most appropriate correction is changing the specification to rectify the expectations about what the implementation ought to do. For example, a function max computing the maximum value of a set of integers is undefined if the set is empty; we could change max's implementation to return a special value when called on an empty set, but the best thing to do is disallowing such calls altogether by specifying them invalid. However, since specifications are often informal or implicit at best, debugging techniques normally modify implementations rather than specifications. In particular, fully automatic fixing—which has made substantial progress in recent years [13, 20, 21] (see Section 5 for more references)—has focused on suggesting repairs to implementations, thus failing to provide the best corrections in cases where the ultimate source of failure is incorrect specification.

This paper presents a fully automatic technique that fixes bugs by rectifying specifications. Our technique targets programs with *contracts*—simple specification elements in the form of executable assertions. A program execution that violates some contract reveals a bug; to fix it, the technique suggests changes to the contracts that prevent the violation from being triggered. We have prototyped the technique in a tool called

---

* Work partially supported by ERC grant CME/291389; by SNF grants LSAT/200020-134974 and ASII/200021-134976; and by Hasler-Stiftung grant #2327.

S. Gnesi and A. Rensink (Eds.): FASE 2014, LNCS 8411, pp. 246–260, 2014.
© Springer-Verlag Berlin Heidelberg 2014

SpeciFix, which works on programs with contracts written in Eiffel. (However, the same technique is implementable in any language supporting some form of contracts.) SpeciFix is completely automatic: its only required input are programs with simple contracts. In an experimental evaluation, we applied SpeciFix to 44 bugs of Eiffel's standard data-structure libraries. SpeciFix suggested repairs for 42 of these bugs; more significant, 11 of the bug repairs are genuine corrections of quality sufficient to be deployable. A small trial with human programmers confirmed this assessment and often found the fixes produced by SpeciFix preferable to fixes for the same bugs that modified the implementation rather than the contracts.

Fixing contracts relies on extracting specification elements based on the actual behavior of the implementation. This is superficially similar to the problem of *inferring* (or mining) specifications—a well-established research area that produced numerous landmark results (e.g., [4, 8]; see Section 5 for more references). While SpeciFix uses inference techniques as one of its components, suggesting changes to an existing specification to correct a bug is more delicate business than just inferring specifications. Changing contracts is changing the design of an API as experienced by its clients. In the example of max, adding a precondition that requires that the set be non empty makes all client code of max responsible for satisfying the requirement upon calling max. Therefore, we must make sure that the suggested contract changes have a limited impact on a potentially infinite number of clients.

The SpeciFix technique presented in this paper uses a combination of heuristics to validate possible specification fixes with respect to their impact on client code. It discards fixes that invalidate previously passing test cases; to avoid overfitting, it runs every candidate fix through a regression testing session that generates (completely automatically, using our testing framework AutoTest) new executions; and it ranks all fixes that pass regression by preferring those that are the least restrictive. The empirical evaluation in Section 4 indicates that these heuristics work well in practice for the bugs we considered. Notably, there is a significant fraction of bugs whose appropriate fix is a change to the specification; in those cases, SpeciFix can often generate useful fixes.

Section 2 demonstrates the idea of fixing specifications by means of an actual example from the standard Eiffel implementation of array-based circular lists. Section 3 presents the technique implemented in SpeciFix, starting with an overview of its components (Figure 3) followed by a detailed description of each of them. For brevity, we use the name "SpeciFix" to denote both the fixing technique presented in this paper and its prototype implementation. The evaluation in Section 4 presents experiments where we applied SpeciFix to 44 faults in standard data-structure libraries. Section 5 discusses the essential related work; and Section 6 concludes and outlines future work.

2   SpeciFix in Action

Let us briefly demonstrate how SpeciFix works using an example from the experimental evaluation of Section 4. The example targets a bug of routine (method) duplicate in class CIRCULAR, which is the standard Eiffel library implementation of circular array-based lists.

To understand the bug, Figure 1 illustrates a few details of CIRCULAR's API. Lists are numbered from index 1 to index count (an attribute denoting the list length), and

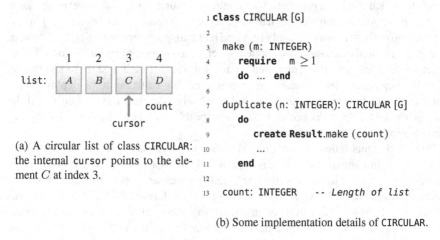

(a) A circular list of class CIRCULAR: the internal cursor points to the element C at index 3.

```
1  class CIRCULAR [G]
2
3      make (m: INTEGER)
4          require  m ≥ 1
5          do ... end
6
7      duplicate (n: INTEGER): CIRCULAR [G]
8          do
9              create Result.make (count)
10             ...
11         end
12
13     count: INTEGER    -- Length of list
```

(b) Some implementation details of CIRCULAR.

Fig. 1. Example and some API details of circular lists in Eiffel

include an internal cursor that may point to any element of the list. Routine duplicate takes a single integer argument n, which denotes the number of elements to be copied; called on a list object list, it returns a new instance of CIRCULAR with at most n elements copied from list starting from the position pointed to by cursor. Since we are dealing with circular lists, the copy wraps over to the first element. For example, calling duplicate (3) on the list in Figure 1a returns a fresh list with elements $\langle C, D, A \rangle$ in this order.

The implementation of duplicate is straightforward: it creates a fresh CIRCULAR object **Result** (line 9 in Figure 1b); it iteratively copies n elements from the current list into **Result**; and it finally returns the list attached to **Result**. The call to the creation procedure (constructor) make on line 9 allocates space for a list with count elements; this is certainly sufficient, since **Result** cannot contain more elements than the list that is duplicated. However, CIRCULAR's creation procedure make includes a precondition (line 4 in Figure 1b) that only allows allocating lists with space for at least one element (**require** m ≥ 1). This sets off a bug when duplicate is called on an empty list: count is 0, and hence the call on line 9 triggers a violation of make's precondition. Testing tools such as AutoTest detect this bug automatically by providing a concrete test case that exposes the discrepancy between implementation and specification.

How should we fix this bug? Figure 2 shows three different possible repairs, all of which we can generate completely automatically. An obvious choice is patching duplicate's implementation as shown in Figure 2a: if count is 0 when duplicate is invoked, allocate **Result** with space for *one* element; this satisfies make's precondition in all cases. Our AutoFix tool [17, 20] targets fixes of *implementations* and in fact suggests the patch in Figure 2a.

The fix that changes the implementation is acceptable, since it makes duplicate run correctly, but it is not entirely satisfactory: CIRCULAR's implementation looks perfectly adequate, whereas the ultimate source of failure seems to be incorrect or inadequate *specification*. A straightforward fix is then adding a precondition to duplicate that

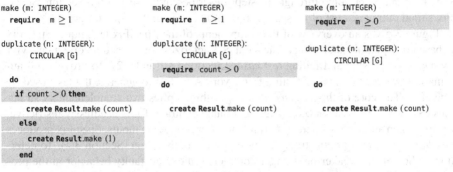

Fig. 2. Three different fixes for the bug of Figure 1. Changed or added lines are highlighted.

only allows calling it on non-empty lists. Figure 2b shows such a fix, which *strengthens* duplicate's precondition thus invalidating the test case exposing the bug. The strengthening fix has the advantage of being textually simpler than the implementation fix, and hence also probably simpler for programmers to understand. However, both fixes in Figures 2a and 2b are partial, in that they remove the source of faulty behavior in duplicate but they do not prevent similar faults—deriving from calling make with $m = 0$—from happening. A more critical issue with the specification-strengthening fix in Figure 2b is that it may break clients of CIRCULAR that rely on the previous weaker precondition.[1] There are cases—such as when computing the maximum of an empty list—where strengthening produces the most appropriate fixes; in the running example, however, strengthening arguably is not the optimal strategy.

A look at make's implementation (not shown in Figure 1b) would reveal that the creation procedure's precondition $m \geq 1$ is unnecessarily restrictive, since the routine body works as expected also when executed with $m = 0$. This suggests a fix that *weakens* make's precondition as shown in Figure 2c. This is arguably the most appropriate correction to the bug of duplicate: it is very simple, it fixes the specific bug as well as similar ones originating in creating an empty list, and it does not invalidate any clients of CIRCULAR's API. The SpeciFix tool described in this paper generates both specification fixes in Figures 2b and 2c but ranks the weakening fix higher than the strengthening one. More generally, SpeciFix outputs specification-strengthening fixes only when they do not introduce bugs in available tests, and it always prefers the least restrictive fixes among those that are applicable.

3   How SpeciFix Works

SpeciFix works completely automatically: its only input is an Eiffel program annotated with simple contracts (pre- and postconditions and class invariants) which constitute its

---

[1] Note that this strengthening does not introduce new bugs; it just shifts the responsibility for the fault from duplicate to its clients.

specification. After going through the steps described in the rest of this section, Speci-Fix's final output is a list of fix suggestions for the bugs in the input program.

Figure 3 gives an overview of the components of the SpeciFix technique. SpeciFix is based on dynamic analysis, and hence it characterizes correct and incorrect behavior by means of passing and failing *test cases* (Sections 3.1 and 3.2). To provide full automation, we use the random testing framework AutoTest to generate the tests used by SpeciFix. The core of the *fix generation* algorithm applies two complementary strategies (Section 3.3): weaken (i.e., relax) a violated contract if it is needlessly restrictive; or strengthen an existing contract to rule out failure-inducing inputs. SpeciFix produces *candidate fixes* using both strategies, possibly in combination (Section 3.4). To determine whether the weaker or stronger contracts remove all faulty behavior in the program, SpeciFix runs candidate fixes through a *validation* phase (Section 3.5) based on all available tests. To avoid overfitting, some tests are generated initially but used only in the validation phase (and not directly to generate fixes). If multiple fixes for the same fault survive the validation phase, SpeciFix outputs them to the user *ordered* according to the strength of their new contracts: weaker contracts are more widely applicable, and hence are ranked higher than more restrictive stronger contracts (Section 3.5).

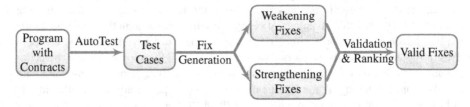

Fig. 3. An overview of how SpeciFix works. Running AutoTest on an input Eiffel program with contracts produces a collection of test cases that characterize correct and incorrect behavior. With the goal of correcting faulty behavior, the fix generation algorithm builds candidate fixes using two strategies: weakening and strengthening the existing contracts. The candidate fixes enter a validation phase where they must pass all valid test cases; valid fixes are ranked—the weaker the new contracts the higher the ranking—and presented as output.

3.1   Test Cases

A *test case* (or just "test") t consists of a call of some routine r with actual arguments $a_1, \ldots, a_n$ on a target object a_0, written $t : a_0.r(a_1, \ldots, a_m)$; we refer to r as t's *outermost* routine. For instance, if list is the list of Figure 1a and emp is an instance of empty CIRCULAR list, list.duplicate(3) and emp.duplicate(1) are two tests.

Let $\mathcal{S}$ be a set of program states. The execution of a test t starts with routine r's body executing from an initial state $s_0 \in \mathcal{S}$. In general, r's body may call another routine r_1 from a state s_1, which in turn calls another r_2 from a state s_2, and so on until the test terminates.[2] Therefore, a test t uniquely defines a *trace* ρ_t as the sequence

$$\rho_t \;=\; s_0\, r_0\, s_1\, r_1 \cdots s_{n-1}\, r_{n-1}\, s_n\, r_n \tag{1}$$

---

[2] To avoid dealing with nonterminating programs, we forcibly terminate tests that are still running after a timeout.

of state snapshots when nested routines are called or return. Precisely, for $j = 0, \ldots, n$, a pair $s_j r_j$ denotes either that routine r_j begins execution from state s_j, that is s_j is the *pre-state* of a nested call; or that routine r_j returns to the caller from state s_j, that is s_j is the *post-state* of a nested call. Since t is a call to r at the outermost level, $r_0 = r$; call traces ignore intermediate states other than pre- and post-states. The sequence $\kappa_t = r_0 r_1 \cdots r_{n-1} r_n$ containing only routine names in ρ_t is the *call sequence* determined by t. For example, the test emp.duplicate(1) determines the trace x_0 duplicate x_1 make where x_0 is the initial state and x_1 is the state when calling make on line 9 in Figure 1b; the test terminates then with a contract violation. The other test list.duplicate(3) determines the trace y_0 duplicate y_1 make y_2 make y_3 duplicate where y_0 is the initial state, y_1 is the state when calling make, y_2 is the state when make returns, and y_3 is the state when duplicate and the whole test terminates.

In SpeciFix, we generate test cases automatically using AutoTest—Eiffel's random test generator. However, if manually-written test cases are available, they can also be supplied to SpeciFix to supplement the automatically generated tests; the extra input may improve the quality of the final output.

3.2   Contracts, Correctness, and Faults

Contracts are simple specification elements made of assertions including preconditions (**require**), postconditions (**ensure**), and class invariants (**invariant**). We denote by P_r and Q_r the pre- and postcondition of a routine r. In this work, we focus on changing pre- and postconditions only; thus, we use the term *specification* to collectively denote pre- and postconditions, and use the terms "specification" and "contracts" as synonyms.

Given an assertion A (pre- or postcondition) and a program state $s \in \mathcal{S}$, we say that A *holds* at s (or, equivalently, that s satisfies A) if A evaluates to **True** under state s; if this is the case, we write $s \models A$. Since contracts are executable, we can evaluate any assertion at any program state reached during a concrete execution.

Contracts provide an operational criterion to classify test cases into invalid, passing, and failing. A test case t is *valid* if the initial state s_0 of the trace ρ_t is such that it satisfies r's precondition, that is $s_0 \models P_r$; otherwise t is *invalid*. An invalid test case for routine r does not tell us anything about r's correctness, since every invocation of r should satisfy r's precondition to be acceptable. A valid test case t is *passing* if, for every $j = 1, \ldots, n$, state s_j in t's trace ρ_t satisfies the following: if s_j is the pre-state of a call to r_j then $s_j \models P_{r_j}$; and if s_j is the post-state of a call to r_j then $s_j \models Q_{r_j}$. In words, every nested call performed during the computation of r starts in a state that satisfies the called routine's precondition and terminates in a state that satisfies the called routine's postcondition when it returns. A valid test case is *failing* if it is not passing, that is if it eventually reaches a state that violates some pre- or postcondition; the violation terminates test case execution. The test list.duplicate(3) is passing because the call to duplicate terminates without violating any contract (and produces the correct result). The other test emp.duplicate(1) is valid but failing: the nested call to make does not satisfy make's precondition m ≥ 1 on line 4 in Figure 1b because count $= 0 < 1$ in an empty list.

A failing test case t reveals a *fault* (informally called bug in the introduction) in routine r, namely a discrepancy between implementation and specification (the violated contract). Conversely, a passing test case documents a legitimate usage of routine r with respect to its specification. Two failing test cases t_1, t_2 identify the *same fault* if their call sequences κ_1, κ_2 are the same (and hence they violate the same assertion).

3.3 Weakening vs. Strengthening

Let t be a failing test case with trace ρ_t as in (1); $r = r_0$ is the outermost routine of t, and r_n is the routine whose contract violation triggers the fault. Assuming the implementation of all routines $r_0, \ldots, r_n$ is correct, we should change the contracts of $r_0, r_1, \ldots, r_n$ to fix the fault exposed by t. There are two ways to do that:

Strengthening: strengthen r's precondition to disallow t's input. Strengthening makes t invalid and thus prevents the call sequence that led to the violation of r_n's contract.
Weakening: weaken r_n's contract to allow t's execution to continue past r_n. If the execution can continue without triggering other errors, weakening makes t passing.

If applicable, weakening is in principle preferable to strengthening, because the former does not risk breaking clients by introducing more stringent conditions for correctly calling r. Strengthening is, however, always applicable, whereas weakening may not work if r_n's correct execution depends on the weakened contract. Even in the cases where weakening makes t passing without triggering any new fault, it may be that the absence of new faults is just a result of the rest of the specification being inaccurate or incomplete. For example, weakening the precondition of a function max to work on lists of any size (including empty lists) may not trigger any faults simply because max has no postcondition, and hence there is no automatic way of finding out that the value returned for empty lists is inconsistent.

In practice, SpeciFix prefers the least restrictive fixes (i.e., weakening) but always tries both weakening and strengthening in combination. Another observation is that strengthening only the outermost routine's precondition often is too *ad hoc*, since it corresponds to a partial change of API assumptions which may be inconsistent with the way other routines are used. Therefore, SpeciFix tries to collectively strengthen all routines $r_0, \ldots, r_{n-1}$ to disallow fault-inducing input at every call site. Indeed, the experiments of Section 4 show that strengthening leads to many useful and correct fixes in practice.

3.4 Fix Generation

A run of SpeciFix targets a specific fault of some routine r. This is characterized by a set $\mathcal{F}_r$ of failing test cases all of which have r as outermost routine and identify the same fault—the violation of contract A_n (pre- or postcondition) of routine r_n. To characterize correct behavior, SpeciFix also inputs a set $\mathcal{P}_r$ of passing test cases which have r as outermost routine. Based on this, SpeciFix builds a set Φ of candidate fixes through the following steps, illustrated on the running example.

Build weakening assertions Ω **for** r_n. Let $\tilde{r}_n$ be r_n with A_n relaxed to True. Generate fresh sets $\tilde{\mathcal{P}}$ and $\tilde{\mathcal{F}}$ of passing and failing test cases for $\tilde{r}_n$. Based on them, determine the sets $\mathcal{I}^{\tilde{\mathcal{P}}}$ and $\mathcal{I}^{\tilde{\mathcal{F}}}$ of dynamic *invariants* respectively holding in all passing tests $\widetilde{\mathcal{P}}$ and in all failing tests $\widetilde{\mathcal{F}}$ (Section 3.6 describes the dynamic invariant detection process). Let $\Omega = \{\omega \mid \omega \in \mathcal{I}^{\widetilde{\mathcal{P}}}$ and $\neg\omega \in \mathcal{I}^{\widetilde{\mathcal{F}}}\}$ be a set of weakening assertions, which characterize the minimal requirements for a test of $\widetilde{r}_n$ to be passing and not failing. In the example, make works without errors when $m \geq 0$, whereas it fails when $m < 0$; thus $\Omega = \{m \geq 0\}$.

Build weakening fixes W. For each $\omega \in \Omega \cup \{\text{False}\}$, build the weakening fix f obtained by replacing A_n with $A_n \vee w$ in r_n. Add f to the set W of weakening fixes. Adding **False** to Ω determines a dummy fix which is used to build purely strengthening fixes in the next step. In the example, W contains a weakening fix f_w corresponding to the one in Figure 2c, and a dummy fix f_0 where make's precondition has been "weakened" with **False** (hence it is unchanged).

Validate weakening fixes. For each $f \in W$, if f passes all tests in $\mathcal{P}_r \cup \mathcal{F}_r$ then add f to the set Φ of candidate fixes without modifications, and remove it from W. In the example, f_w passes validation and is added to Φ. f_0 is instead the unchanged program in Figure 1b, and hence it stays in W.

Build strengthening assertions Σ_k for r_k. For each $f \in W$ that did not pass validation, determine the sets $\mathcal{I}_k^P$ and $\mathcal{I}_k^F$ of dynamic *invariants* currently holding in all pre-states of the calls to r_k respectively in the passing tests $\mathcal{P}_r$ and in the failing tests $\mathcal{F}_r$; k ranges over the subset of $\{0, \ldots, n-1\}$ for which s_k is a pre-state ($s_k r_k$ appears in the traces). Let $\Sigma_k = \{\sigma \mid \sigma \in \mathcal{I}_k^P$ and $\neg\sigma \in \mathcal{I}_k^F\}$ be the corresponding sets of strengthening assertions, which characterize the minimal additional requirements for a test to pass through r_k without failing. In the example, duplicate correctly calls make precisely when count > 0; thus, $\Sigma_0 = \{\text{count} > 0\}$.

Build strengthening fixes. For each combination $\langle \sigma_0, \ldots, \sigma_{n-1} \rangle \subseteq \Sigma_0 \times \cdots \times \Sigma_{n-1}$ of strengthening assertions, build the strengthening fix ϕ obtained by replacing each precondition P_{r_k} of routine r_k with $P_{r_k} \wedge \sigma_k$, for all applicable k. Add ϕ to the set Φ of candidate fixes. In the example, the dummy fix f_0 is turned into a valid fix ϕ_0 by strengthening duplicate's precondition as count > 0.

Candidates. The output of the fix generation phase is a set Φ of fix candidates. The candidates are filtered and ranked as explained in the following section.

3.5 Fix Validation and Ranking

Validation. The purpose of the *validation* phase is to ascertain which of the candidate fixes in Φ remove the fault under analysis. To this end, SpeciFix runs every fix candidate $f \in \Phi$ through all available tests for r; f is *valid* if it still passes all originally passing tests, and it also passes all originally failing tests that have not become invalid.

The dual risk of unsoundness for validation based on a finite number of test cases is *overfitting*: a fix may pass validation but be unusable in a general context, because it introduces specification changes that harm usages of the API different from those exercised by the test cases used to generate the fix. To reduce the risk of overfitting, SpeciFix uses only half of the originally generated test cases to generate the candidate fixes. Then, the validation phase uses *all* available tests for the routine under analysis, not only those in $\mathcal{P}_r$ and $\mathcal{F}_r$ used to generate fixes. This increases the likelihood that the validated fixes are applicable beyond the specific cases that drove fix generation.

Ranking. Not all valid fixes are equally desirable: all else being equal, we prefer those that introduce the least changes to the specification, and that make invalid the fewest test cases. SpeciFix ranks valid fixes to reflect these criteria, and only reports the top five fixes for each fault. This approach is a good compromise between the contrasting needs of exposing programmers to a limited number of fixes—which they have to understand and validate—and of retaining fixes that fall behind in the ranking even if they are of high quality, due to the imperfect precision of the ranking heuristics.

The ranking heuristics is based on two elements: number of invalidated tests and the strength of the new contracts. A fix f consists of a collection $\langle A_0, \ldots, A_n \rangle$ of new contracts for the routines $r_0, \ldots, r_n$; each A_k $(0 \leq k \leq n)$ is either a pre- or a postcondition and may be weaker, stronger, or unchanged with respect to the original program. Given two valid fixes f_1, f_2, let A_k^1, A_k^2 be their new contracts for the same routine r_k. We say that A_k^1 is *not stronger than* A_k^2, written $A_k^1 \preceq A_k^2$, if A_k^1 holds whenever A_k^2 holds; precisely, we determine strength based on executing all available tests for r: $A_k^1 \preceq A_k^2$ iff every test that is valid for A_k^1 (i.e., a test that leads to executions where A_k^1 is evaluated and holds) is also valid for A_k^2 (i.e., A_k^2 is evaluated and holds). This generalizes to an ordering between fixes by lexicographic generalization of $\preceq$ on tuples $\langle A_0, \ldots, A_n \rangle$. The ordering is partial because the sets of valid test cases for f_1 and for f_2 may be non-comparable. The final ranking orders fixes according to the $\preceq$ relation and, for incomparable fixes, ranks higher those that determine the higher number of valid (and hence passing) tests.

In the running example, the weakening fix in Figure 2c ranks higher than the strengthening fix in Figure 2b: all test cases with count > 0 are equivalent for the two fixes, but the test cases with count $= 0$ are valid only for the weakening fix.

3.6 Dynamic Invariants and State Abstraction

SpeciFix infers invariants at program states dynamically by observing the behavior during concrete executions. Dynamic invariant inference (see Section 5) has become a standard technique of dynamic analysis. Using the notation of Section 3.1, we can define an invariant at the entry of routine r_k as an assertion I such that $s_k \models I$ for every test t whose trace ρ_t includes the snapshot $s_k r_k$ where s_k is a pre-state; the invariant at routine exit is defined similarly with respect to post-states.

Invariant inference in SpeciFix must cater to the specific needs of fixing contracts. To this end, we abstract the concrete program state by a number of predicates that include public queries (i.e., routines or attributes giving a value characterizing object state) as well as any subexpressions of the available contracts.

4 Experimental Evaluation

We performed a preliminary evaluation of the behavior of SpeciFix by applying it to 44 bugs of production software. The overall goal of the evaluation is corroborating the expectation that, for bugs whose "most appropriate" correction is fixing the specification, SpeciFix can produce repair suggestions of good quality. A more detailed evaluation taking into account aspects such as robustness and readability of the produced fixes belongs to future work.

4.1   Experimental Setup

We selected 10 of the most widely used data-structure classes of the EiffelBase (rev. 92914) and Gobo (rev. 91005) libraries—the two major Eiffel standard libraries. While these are the same classes used in the experimental evaluation of AutoFix [20], we did not attempt a direct comparison for different reasons. First, some of the bugs used in AutoFix have been fixed in the latest library versions, and hence they are not reproducible. Second, AutoFix and SpeciFix are complementary approaches: our experience with AutoFix suggested that there is a substantial fraction of bugs whose most appropriate correction is fixing the specification, and it is precisely on those that we expect SpeciFix to work successfully. Third, running SpeciFix on the very same input as AutoFix would limit the generalizability of the evaluation results; instead, we want to evaluate the behavior of SpeciFix in standard conditions and avoid overfitting.

All the experiments ran on a Windows 7 machine with a 2.6 GHz Intel 4-core CPU and 16 GB of memory. We ran AutoTest for one hour on each of the 10 classes in Table 4. This automatic testing session found 44 unique faults consisting of pre- or postcondition violations. We ran SpeciFix on each of these faults individually, using only half of the test cases (randomly picked among those generated for each fault in the one-hour session) to generate the fixes and all of them in the validation phase (Section 3.5). The right-hand side of Table 4 reports, for each class, the total number of test cases used by SpeciFix, and the total time for testing (the initial one-hour sessions plus additional calls to AutoTest to generate tests for relaxed routines used to infer the weakening assertions Ω, as described in Section 3.4) and fixing. The average figures *per fault* are: 106.4 minutes of testing time and 7.2 minutes of fixing time (minimum: 4.1 minutes, maximum: 30 minutes, median 6.2 minutes). The testing time dominates since AutoTest operates randomly and thus generates many test cases that will not be used (such as passing tests of routines without faults).

Table 4. Classes used in the experiments; for each class we report: lines of code LOC, number #R of routines, number #P of assertions in preconditions, number #Q of assertions in postconditions, and number #C of assertions in the class invariant. In the right-hand side, we report the number #F of faults targeted by the experiments, the total number of test cases (passing #$\mathcal{P}$ and #$\mathcal{F}$ failing) used by SpeciFix, the $\mathcal{T}_t$ minutes spent running AutoTest on routines of the class, and the $\mathcal{T}_f$ minutes spent running SpeciFix (net of testing time) on faults of the class.

CLASS	LOC	#R	#P	#Q	#C	#F	#$\mathcal{P}$	#$\mathcal{F}$	$\mathcal{T}_t$	$\mathcal{T}_f$
ACTIVE_LIST	2165	139	91	121	25	2	212	210	240	23
ARRAY	1474	101	70	110	10	9	850	555	900	72
ARRAYED_CIRCULAR[3]	1907	133	80	92	23	3	320	234	360	17
ARRAYED_SET	2346	146	118	131	26	6	554	432	720	34
DS_ARRAYED_LIST	2862	168	219	173	15	3	132	89	240	15
DS_HASH_SET	3159	171	154	140	20	1	14	60	120	5
DS_LINKED_LIST	3497	162	207	166	13	3	360	25	360	25
LINKED_LIST	1995	109	70	91	23	0	–	–	60	–
LINKED_SET	2347	122	99	101	26	4	416	70	480	22
TWO_WAY_SORTED_SET	2856	141	118	118	31	13	1260	655	1260	106
TOTAL	24608	1392	1226	1243	212	44	4118	2330	4680	319

---

[3] Shortened to CIRCULAR in Section 2.

4.2 Results

Evaluating the effectiveness of repairs that modify contracts is a somewhat subtle issue, since it ultimately involves what is a design choice: changing API specification. Related work on automatic repair (see Section 5) has rarely, if ever,[4] assessed the quality and *acceptability* for human programmers of the produced fixes beyond running standard regression test suites. To this end, in previous work [17,20] we introduced the notions of *valid* and *proper* fix: any fix that passes all the available tests is valid (and hence every fix output by SpeciFix is valid), but only those that manual inspection reveals to satisfactorily remove the real source of failure without introducing other bugs are classified as *proper*. Even if the line between proper and improper might be fuzzy in some corner cases, we could normally confidently classify fixes into proper and improper based on our familiarity with the code base under analysis.

We use the same classification criterion in the evaluation of fixes produced by Speci-Fix: Table 5 lists the total number of faults for which SpeciFix generated valid or proper fixes (and ranked them in the top 5 positions: we ignore fixes that rank lower).

> *For 25% of the faults, SpeciFix produced fixes that manual inspection revealed to satisfactorily remove the real source of failure.*

Table 5. Fixes built by SpeciFix. For each TYPE of fault, the left-hand side of the table reports the number #F of faults of that type input to SpeciFix, and for how many of those faults SpeciFix built (at least one) VALID or PROPER fixes. The right-hand side reports the total number of *fixes* produced in each category; the same fault may have multiple valid or proper fixes. Columns ALL list all fixes in each category, followed by a breakdown into purely weakening (WEAK), purely strengthening (STRONG), and mixed (involving BOTH strengthening of some contract and weakening of some other).

TYPE OF FAULT	#F	VALID	PROPER	VALID FIXES				PROPER FIXES			
				ALL	WEAK	STRONG	BOTH	ALL	WEAK	STRONG	BOTH
Precondition violation	22	22	7	77	23	30	24	13	1	12	0
Postcondition violation	22	20	4	71	56	13	2	7	3	4	0
TOTAL	44	42	11	148	79	43	26	20	4	16	0

The percentage of proper fixes (25% of faults) is similar to that obtained in the work with AutoFix; but the high percentage of valid fixes (over 90%) requires some explanation. Obtaining valid contract fixes is easy if only poor-quality tests are available. One can always strengthen preconditions to invalidate failing test cases (or, conversely, weaken failing postconditions to trivially pass tests): since SpeciFix validates fixes based on the available test cases, which in turn are only as good as the contracts of the class (beyond those directly targeted by the fix), such straightforward fixes yield valid repairs for classes equipped with very weak and incomplete contracts. This does not mean that such fixes are always improper; in fact, 80% of all proper fixes strengthen preconditions: it is only when it is combined with very poor specification (especially class invariants) that fixing may lead to improper fixes. Furthermore, despite being not

---

[4] The only exception we are aware of is [13].

directly deployable, the valid but improper fixes produced by SpeciFix are still very valuable as debugging aids, since they clearly highlight the failure-inducing inputs.

Acceptability Trial. In order to get more confidence in the capability of SpeciFix to produce proper, acceptable fixes from a programmer's perspective, we conducted a small trial involving 4 PhD students (henceforth, the "subjects") in our group. The subjects were quite familiar with the Eiffel language and its standard libraries, but had not been involved in the work on SpeciFix or AutoFix. To keep the workload small, we randomly selected only 8 out of the 11 faults for which SpeciFix produced proper fixes, and submitted them to the subjects: for each fault, we produced one failing test case (randomly picked among those produced by AutoTest) and up to 3 fixes produced by SpeciFix. In order to compare the acceptability of specification and implementation fixes, we also included up to 2 proper implementation fixes for each of 5 faults (out of 8) produced using AutoFix. For each fault, the subjects: (1) declared which fixes they considered acceptable (i.e., they "correct the fault while not introducing new faults", as in our definition of "proper"); and (2) ordered the fixes in decreasing order of quality.

See the extended version of this paper for detailed results. The highlights: all subjects but one agreed with our assessment of proper fixes; the subjects unanimously preferred a contract fix over an implementation fix for 3 of the 5 faults that had both kinds of fix. The subject who disagreed about proper fixes still agreed that the contract fixes for 6 out of 8 faults are proper. With the proviso that its small scale does not warrant arbitrary generalizations, the trial demonstrates substantial agreement with our assessment of proper fixes; and suggests that, if a fault can be fixed with a contract fix, SpeciFix has a chance of building a high-quality one.

> *Programmers found most proper fixes produced by SpeciFix acceptable and often preferable to fixes for the same bugs that change the implementation.*

4.3   Limitations and Threats to Validity

Limitations. The main limitation to the applicability of SpeciFix is that it requires contracts. On the one hand, it requires a language where contracts are expressible; this is an obvious consequence of the technique's goals and is not severely restrictive since many languages support some form of notation for contracts (e.g., JML for Java and Code-Contracts for C#). On the other hand, SpeciFix works well only on classes that come already equipped with *some* contracts of decent quality. Class invariants (which SpeciFix does not change but only assumes) are particularly useful to ensure that the test cases generated represent reasonable usage, so that validation (Section 3.5) is precise. Despite being often weak and largely incomplete, the kinds of contracts Eiffel programmer write have been sufficient to get good experimental results; but in future work we will investigate how SpeciFix performance improves if it is given more expressive contracts [18].

Threats to Validity. The most significant threat to *external* validity—concerning the generalizability of our experimental results—comes from limiting the experiments to data-structure classes. This is a limitation partly inherited from the usage of AutoTest to generate test cases; AutoTest is meant for unit testing and hence works more easily with classes with a clearly defined interface such as data structures. In future work, we plan to experiment with other kinds of program (as we already did successfully with Auto-Fix [17]) and possibly with manually-written test cases. Another threat comes from the small number of subjects used in the trial (Section 4.2), and the fact that they all were graduate students. We acknowledge that the trial only gives a preliminary assessment, and more user studies are needed to ensure generalizability.

Threats to *internal* validity—concerning the proper execution of our experiments—include repeatability. Since SpeciFix uses AutoTest to generate test cases, and the performance of AutoTest is affected by chance, different runs may yield different results. Based on our previous extensive experience with using AutoTest's test cases for dynamic analysis [17–20], we expect AutoTest behavior to be predictable over the testing time allotted in our experiments; therefore, this threat is unlikely to be significant. Since SpeciFix produces many valid but not proper fixes, an issue is how much effort is required to identify the improper fixes. While we have no hard evidence about this, even improper fixes succinctly characterize the failure-inducing inputs, and hence they are still useful as debugging aids. Furthermore, contract fixes are normally quite simple, arguably easier to read than implementation fixes; all subjects in the trial spent on average around two minutes to classify each contract fix, which seems to indicate an acceptable overhead. More experiments are also needed to determine the sensitivity of SpeciFix to what fraction of the tests are used for generation vs. validation.

5   Related Work

SpeciFix is a novel technique in the recently emerging area of automatic program repair, whose most important contributions we briefly review below. Dynamic invariant inference is one of the specific techniques used in SpeciFix; we also discuss fundamental related work in this area.

Automatic Program Repair.   Source-code repair aims to remove buggy behavior from a program by changing its implementation. GenProg [21] is one of the first and most successful techniques for source-code repair. It uses genetic programming to mutate a faulty program into one that satisfies a given set of test cases. GenProg has been evaluated [14] using various open-source programs, showing that it can produce many non-trivial fixes. GenProg works on programs without annotations; however, it requires a regression test suite as part of its input.

Other work has applied different techniques to the problem of source-code repair, with the goal of improving the applicability and acceptability of the produced repairs; for example, by deploying machine-learning techniques [2, 12, 13], constraint-based approaches [10, 16], and finite-state abstractions [7]. These techniques also normally require a regression test suite as part of their input.

In previous work, we developed AutoFix [17, 20], an automatic tool that suggests fixes of implementations written in Eiffel and annotated with simple contracts. Contracts dispense with the need for a regression test suite, as one can be generated as needed through automatic testing. SpeciFix's technique can be seen as the dual to AutoFix's: the latter assumes contracts correct to fix implementations, whereas the former assumes implementations correct to fix contracts.

Invariant Inference. Invariant inference techniques learn assertions that hold for a given implementation. These techniques are naturally classified in *static* and *dynamic*. Static techniques analyze the source code to infer specification elements. Since inferring all but the simplest classes of properties is undecidable, static techniques are usually sound but incomplete. Abstract interpretation is a fundamental framework for static invariant inference [4], which has been applied in many different contexts.

SpeciFix relies instead on *dynamic* techniques for invariant inference. These summarize properties that are invariant over multiple runs of a program; their advantage over static techniques is that dynamic approaches do not require a sophisticated analytical framework and are applicable to the whole programming language: they work on anything that can be executed. While dynamic techniques provide no guarantees of soundness or completeness, they work quite well in practice. Dynamic invariant inference has been pioneered by the Daikon tool [8]. Daikon uses a pre-defined set of templates describing common relations among program variables. Much work has been done to extend and improve the Daikon approach; for example to support object-oriented features [5], and to infer complex and often complete postconditions [19]. The dynamic approach has also been applied to other kinds of specifications such as finite-state behavioral specifications [1, 6, 15, 22] and algebraic specifications [9, 11].

6 Conclusions and Future Work

We presented an automatic technique that fixes programming bugs by rectifying *specifications* in the form of simple contracts (pre- and postconditions). In an experimental evaluation, we ran SpeciFix on 44 bugs of Eiffel standard data-structure libraries. An evaluation by human programmers indicates that SpeciFix produced fixes of quality sufficient to be deployed for 25% of the bugs.

We now have complementary techniques to fix bugs either by changing the implementation (such as in our previous work on AutoFix [17, 20]) or by changing the specification (using SpeciFix presented in this paper). Therefore, the main goal of future work is to apply both fixing approaches in combination, and in particular to develop automatic heuristics to decide whether the "best" fix for a given bug involves changing implementation, specification, or both.

Availability. The SpeciFix source code, and all data and results cited in this article, are available at: http://se.inf.ethz.ch/research/specifix/.

Acknowledgments. Thanks to Alexey Kolesnichenko, Nadia Polikarpova, Andrey Rusakov, and Julian Tschannen for participating in the trial (Section 4.2).

References

1. Ammons, G., Bodík, R., Larus, J.R.: Mining specifications. In: POPL, pp. 4–16 (2002)
2. Arcuri, A.: Evolutionary repair of faulty software. Applied Soft Computing 11(4), 3494–3514 (2011)
3. Ciupa, I., Pretschner, A., Oriol, M., Leitner, A., Meyer, B.: On the number and nature of faults found by random testing. Softw. Test., Verif. Reliab. 21(1), 3–28 (2011)

4. Cousot, P., Halbwachs, N.: Automatic discovery of linear restraints among variables of a program. In: POPL, pp. 84–96 (1978)
5. Csallner, C., Smaragdakis, Y.: Dynamically discovering likely interface invariants. In: ICSE, pp. 861–864 (2006)
6. Dallmeier, V., Lindig, C., Wasylkowski, A., Zeller, A.: Mining object behavior with ADABU. In: WODA, pp. 17–24 (2006)
7. Dallmeier, V., Zeller, A., Meyer, B.: Generating fixes from object behavior anomalies. In: ASE, pp. 550–554. IEEE (2009)
8. Ernst, M.D., Cockrell, J., Griswold, W.G., Notkin, D.: Dynamically discovering likely program invariants to support program evolution. IEEE TSE 27(2), 99–123 (2001)
9. Ghezzi, C., Mocci, A., Monga, M.: Synthesizing intensional behavior models by graph transformation. In: ICSE, pp. 430–440 (2009)
10. Gopinath, D., Malik, M.Z., Khurshid, S.: Specification-based program repair using SAT. In: Abdulla, P.A., Leino, K.R.M. (eds.) TACAS 2011. LNCS, vol. 6605, pp. 173–188. Springer, Heidelberg (2011)
11. Henkel, J., Reichenbach, C., Diwan, A.: Discovering documentation for Java container classes. IEEE TSE 33(8), 526–543 (2007)
12. Jeffrey, D., Feng, M., Gupta, N., Gupta, R.: BugFix: a learning-based tool to assist developers in fixing bugs. In: ICPC, pp. 70–79. IEEE (2009)
13. Kim, D., Nam, J., Song, J., Kim, S.: Automatic patch generation learned from human-written patches. In: ICSE, pp. 802–811. IEEE (2013)
14. Le Goues, C., Dewey-Vogt, M., Forrest, S., Weimer, W.: A systematic study of automated program repair: Fixing 55 out of 105 bugs for $8 each. In: ICSE, pp. 3–13. IEEE (2012)
15. Lorenzoli, D., Mariani, L., Pezzè, M.: Automatic generation of software behavioral models. In: ICSE, pp. 501–510 (2008)
16. Nguyen, H.D.T., Qi, D., Roychoudhury, A., Chandra, S.: SemFix: program repair via semantic analysis. In: ICSE, pp. 772–781. IEEE (2013)
17. Pei, Y., Wei, Y., Furia, C.A., Nordio, M., Meyer, B.: Code-based automated program fixing. In: ASE, pp. 392–395. ACM (2011)
18. Polikarpova, N., Furia, C.A., Pei, Y., Wei, Y., Meyer, B.: What good are strong specifications? In: ICSE, pp. 257–266. ACM (2013)
19. Wei, Y., Furia, C.A., Kazmin, N., Meyer, B.: Inferring better contracts. In: ICSE, pp. 191–200. ACM (2011)
20. Wei, Y., Pei, Y., Furia, C.A., Silva, L.S., Buchholz, S., Meyer, B., Zeller, A.: Automated fixing of programs with contracts. In: ISSTA, pp. 61–72. ACM (2010)
21. Weimer, W., Nguyen, T., Le Goues, C., Forrest, S.: Automatically finding patches using genetic programming. In: ICSE, pp. 364–374. IEEE (2009)
22. Xie, T., Martin, E., Yuan, H.: Automatic extraction of abstract-object-state machines from unit-test executions. In: ICSE, pp. 835–838. IEEE (2006)

Dynamic Package Interfaces

Shahram Esmaeilsabzali[1,*], Rupak Majumdar[2], Thomas Wies[3],
and Damien Zufferey[4,**]

[1] University of Waterloo
[2] MPI-SWS
[3] NYU
[4] MIT CSAIL

Abstract. A hallmark of object-oriented programming is the ability to perform computation through a set of interacting objects. A common manifestation of this style is the notion of a *package*, which groups a set of commonly used classes together. A challenge in using a package is to ensure that a client follows the implicit protocol of the package when calling its methods. Violations of the protocol can cause a runtime error or latent invariant violations. These protocols can extend across different, potentially unboundedly many, objects, and are specified informally in the documentation. As a result, ensuring that a client does not violate the protocol is hard.

We introduce *dynamic package interfaces (DPI)*, a formalism to explicitly capture the protocol of a package. The DPI of a package is a finite set of rules that together specify how any set of interacting objects of the package can evolve through method calls and under what conditions an error can happen. We have developed a dynamic tool that automatically computes an approximation of the DPI of a package, given a set of abstraction predicates. A key property of DPI is that the unbounded number of configurations of objects of a package are summarized finitely in an abstract domain. This uses the observation that many packages behave monotonically: the semantics of a method call over a configuration does not essentially change if more objects are added to the configuration. We have exploited monotonicity and have devised heuristics to obtain succinct yet general DPIs. We have used our tool to compute DPIs for several commonly used Java packages with complex protocols, such as JDBC, HashSet, and ArrayList.

1 Introduction

Modern object-oriented programming practice uses packages to encapsulate components, allowing programmers to use these packages through well-defined application programming interfaces (APIs). While programming languages such as Java and C# provide a clear specification of the static APIs of a package in terms of classes and their (typed) methods, there is usually no specification of the implicit *protocol* that constrains the temporal ordering of method calls on different objects. If the protocol is limited to a single object of a single class, it can be specified in form of a state machine whose states are the abstract states of the object and whose edges are the invocations of its

---

* Shahram Esmaeilsabzali was at MPI-SWS when this work was done.
** Damien Zufferey was at IST Austria when this work was done.

S. Gnesi and A. Rensink (Eds.): FASE 2014, LNCS 8411, pp. 261–275, 2014.
© Springer-Verlag Berlin Heidelberg 2014

methods [2, 14, 16]. For example, a lock object has two states: locked and unlocked. While in the unlocked (resp. locked) state, a call to the lock (resp. unlock) method takes it to the locked (resp. unlocked) state. Any other method call results in an error. The notion of state-machine interfaces has been studied extensively, and there are many tools to generate interfaces using static or dynamic techniques [2, 9, 13, 15]. However, existing notions of state machines on object states must be generalized when considering a package. First, the internal state of an object should be considered in the context of the internal states of other objects; e.g., in the Java Database Connectivity (JDBC) package, a `Statement` object can execute safely only if its corresponding `Connection` object is open. Second, the execution of a method on an object can change the internal state of other objects in the environment; e.g., calling the `executeQuery` method on a JDBC `Statement` object closes its corresponding open `ResultSet` object. Finally, the protocol can constrain the states and transitions of *unboundedly* many interacting objects; e.g., considering a collection object and its iterators, modifying the collection directly invalidates *all* of its iterators.

The problem of generalizing interfaces from single to multiple objects has been studied recently [10–12]. However, what is missing is a clear definition of what constitutes an interface in the presence of unboundedly many objects on the heap. Our first contribution is the introduction of *dynamic package interface* (DPI), which allows to capture the protocol of a package in a succinct manner. The DPI of a package is a set of *rules*, each of which specifies the effect of a method call on an object within an abstract *configuration* of objects. An abstract configuration denotes an unbounded number of concrete configurations of objects from a package. A rule has a *source* and a *destination* configuration, together with a *mapping* that specifies how the objects in the source change to the objects in the destination.

Our first technical ingredient is a representation of abstract configurations using *nested graphs* [17]. In a nested graph, a subgraph can be marked to be repeatable, and repetitions can be nested. Nested graphs naturally represent unbounded heap configurations. For example, Figure 1 shows a (two-level) nested graph representing an open JDBC `Connection` object with its many corresponding closed `Statement` objects, each with many closed `ResultSet` objects.

Our second ingredient is an abstract semantics of Java-like languages over the domain of nested graphs that is monotonic (in fact, the abstract transition system is *well-structured* [1]): if a method can be called in a "smaller" configuration, it can be also called in a "larger" configuration, with the resulting configurations maintaining the relationship. Monotonicity enables us to define the DPI rules of a package only over its *maximal* abstract configurations, letting each rule subsume infinitely many similar "smaller" rules. We prove that the set of maximal configurations has a finite representation, and thus the DPI of a package has a finite number of rules [6].

Our second contribution is a dynamic analysis technique to compute an approximation of the DPI of a package directly from the source code. Our tool explores the usage scenarios of a package by running a *universal client* that in each of its finite number of steps, nondeterministically, either creates a new object or invokes a method of an existing object. Each step of the universal client results in a rule. The universal client can end up computing hundreds or thousands of distinct rules, which makes the resulting DPI practically not useful. The challenge is to generalize these rules to obtain a compact DPI by exploiting similarity. Often, a pair of rules for the same method are incomparable only because their sources and destinations are slightly different. For example, in one rule for the close method of the Statement class, the source configuration has closed ResultSet objects but not an open one, and vice versa, another rule might have an open ResultSet object but not closed ones. It makes sense, however, to combine these two rules because the effect of the two rules are essentially the same: the Statement object and its open ResultSet object are closed.

We have devised three heuristics that generalize a set of explored rules into a smaller, more general set. Our *extrapolation* heuristic compares the configurations of different rules and deduces whether the configuration of a certain rule can be expanded by repeating part of it based on the repetitions observed in the configurations of other rules. Our *merge* heuristic combines two rules that are based on similar method invocations into one rule. Our *exception isolation* heuristic combines two similar exception rules into one. While merging is similar to the union of the two rules, exception isolation is closer to an intersection that isolates the root cause of an exception. Our heuristics are all grounded in the monotonicity property of our abstract semantics.

We have used our tool to compute the DPIs of Java packages such as JDBC (26 rules), HashSet (16 rules), and ArrayList (15 rules). The rules of these DPIs can be traced to their documentation, as well as to the programming errors discussed in online discussion groups. Our tool more often than not computes the expected number of rules for these packages, but not all these rules are the most general ones. Our tool never computes a rule that is not consistent with the behaviour of a package. This is an indication that our heuristics are effective.

A more formal treatment of our work can be found in the technical reports [5, 6].

2   Overview and Outline

We now explain the notion of DPI, and describe the main steps that our tool carries out to compute the DPI of a package. We use Java Database Connectivity (JDBC), a package that provides database connectivity, as our running example.

We consider four commonly-used classes of JDBC and their methods. The Driver-Manager class allows to create a new connection to a database by invoking its static getConnection method. The string parameter of the method specifies the type of database, its address, and the needed credentials to access it. A Connection object can serve multiple Statement objects, each of which can be used to read or change the content of the database. The createStatement method of the Connection class creates a new Statement object. SQL commands and queries are executed through the execute and executeQuery methods of the Statement class. Both methods accept a string argument that is an SQL statement. The executeQuery method returns a new ResultSet object, which is a collection of rows retrieved from the database; the next method can be used to traverse these rows. A Connection, Statement, or ResultSet object is *open* initially, but can be closed via their corresponding close methods. Invoking the executeQuery method on a Statement object causes an open ResultSet object that references it to be closed, while creating a new open ResultSet object. If an object, or one of the objects that it references directly or transitively, is closed, invoking a non-close method on it would raise an exception.

2.1 System Input

Besides the names of classes and the signatures of their methods, our tool receives a set of abstraction predicates over the attributes of the classes. A predicate is either *scalar*, defined over the simple, non-reference attributes of the classes, or *reference*, determining which objects of a class are related to which objects of another class via a certain reference attribute. For simplicity, we assume these predicates are input by the user, but standard techniques based on Boolean methods and reference-valued fields in classes can be used to identify these predicates [15].

For example, in JDBC, the Statement class has an active attribute that determines whether it is open or not. This attribute is a unary scalar predicate, but in general a scalar predicate may read multiple fields from referenced objects. We also use the applicationConnection field of the Statement class to define a reference predicate that determines which Statement object points to which Connection object. We define similar scalar predicates for the Connection and ResultSet classes, which determine whether their objects are open or closed. We also define a reference predicate that determines which ResultSet objects reference which Statement objects.

We require that the set of reference attributes do not create a cycle when evaluated over objects: i.e., when objects are considered as nodes and the true valuations of reference attributes as directed edges, the resulting graph is acyclic. This is necessary as some of our algorithms rely on computing the topological ordering of heap-related graphs. This requirement can be relaxed: it is possible to allow the more general class of the depth-bounded graphs [6].

2.2 Nested Object Graphs

The enabling technique that allows us to compute a succinct, general DPI for a package is the ability to model a *heap configuration*, i.e., a set of concrete (e.g., Java) objects in the heap that reference each other, as a *nested object graph*.

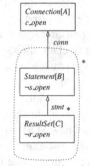

A nested object graph is a labeled, directed graph whose subgraphs can be marked as repeatable. The nodes of a nested object graph represent objects and its directed edges represent references between the objects. The nodes and edges of the graph are labelled according to the input scalar and reference abstraction predicates, respectively. When a subgraph of a nested object graph is marked as *repeatable*, it denotes that arbitrary-many sets of objects similar to the objects in the subgraph can exist in the heap. Repetition can be nested, and hence the name "nested object graph." As an example, the nested object graph in Figure 1 repre-

Fig. 1. A nested object graph

sents all possible heap configurations consisting of an open Connection object with zero or more (in fact, possibly unboundedly many) closed Statement objects, each of which has zero or more closed ResultSet objects. Repetitions are specified via "*" next to nodes or subgraphs. Node C, for example, which represents the ResultSet objects, is marked repeatable in a nested manner: each group of repeatable ResultSet objects is associated with a Statement object, which itself is marked as repeatable via the "*" next to the subgraph specified by the dotted line. The repetition structure of a nested object graph is captured by assigning *nesting levels* to the nodes of the graph. The larger the nesting level is, the more levels of repetition it belongs to [6]. For example, the nesting levels of nodes *A*, *B*, and *C* in Figure 1 are 0, 1, and 2, respectively.

2.3 DPI Rules

The *dynamic package interface* (DPI) of a package is a set of *rules*, each of which represents a family of method calls. A *rule* for a method call essentially specifies how a certain family of similar method calls change the shape of their corresponding heaps. A rule consists of:

– A *source* and a *destination* nested object graph, which represent all possible concrete heap configurations before and after the method call;
– A *source* and a *destination cast nested object graph*, each of which is a nested object graph some of whose nodes are labelled with *roles*, such as "callee", "parameter_0", and "new"; these graphs represent the heap configurations that are directly, in the sense that we will make clear, involved in the method call;
– An *object mapping*, which maps the nodes of the source nested object graph to the nodes of the destination nested object graph, possibly non-deterministically; and
– A *role mapping*, which maps the nodes of the source cast nested object graph to the nodes of the destination cast nested object graph; a node that is labelled by a role is mapped deterministically, but other nodes could be mapped non-deterministically.

Each tuple in the object mapping or the role mapping is annotated with *multiplicity* information that specifies how many of the concrete objects represented by the source node are transferred to the destination node: *one* or *many*. The semantics of the computation of object mapping and role mapping of a rule should ensure that a concrete object is either mapped via the role mapping or the object mapping, but not both.

As an example, Figure 2 shows the rule that our system computes for executeQuery method calls that raise no exceptions. The rule specifies that an open ResultSet is closed when its corresponding Statement object performs executeQuery; instead, a new ResultSet object is created. Figure 2(a) specifies the role mapping of the rule, via dotted arrows that connect the nodes in the source cast nested object graph to the nodes in the destination cast nested object graph. The "callee" and "new" labels determine the callee and the newly created objects, respectively. Figure 2(b) specifies the object mapping of the rule via dotted arrows that, for the sake of brevity, connect the subgraphs of the nested object graphs. While in this rule the object mapping does not specify any change in its corresponding objects, in general that is not the case. Both nested object graphs and cast nested object graphs of the rule exhibit repetitions. It is this ability to express unbounded number of concrete heap configurations that allows us to compute general, yet concise rules.

Exception Rules. When a method call does not raise any exception, we are looking for general rules with the largest possible nested object graphs (because it captures more

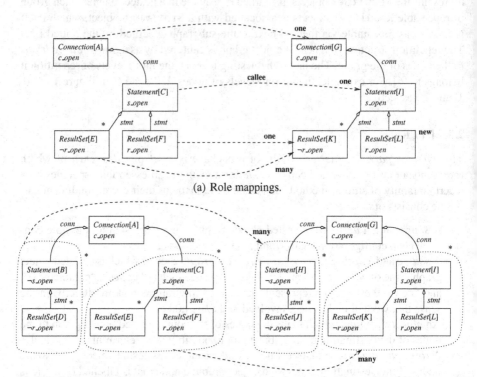

(a) Role mappings.

(b) Object mappings. An arrow over a nested subgraph denotes that the nodes of its source are mapped to their isomorphic nodes in the destination.

Fig. 2. The most general rule for `executeQuery`, with no exception

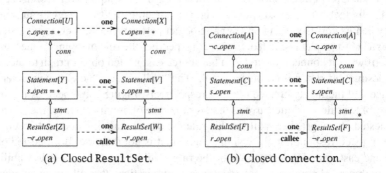

(a) Closed `ResultSet`.   (b) Closed `Connection`.

Fig. 3. The two most general rules for `next` with `ResultSet not open` exception

---

Algorithm 1. *ComputeDPI*

Input: A set of classes and methods and a set of abstraction predicates
Result: A set of general rules, *Rules*, each of which represents a family of method calls
1 *Rules* = ∅;
2 **while** ¬*Threshold* **do**
3 | Pick a snapshot, a concrete Java object, execute one of its methods;
4 | Compute, r, the corresponding rule of the method call;
5 | **if** *there is no $r' \in$ Rules that "covers" r* **then** *Rules = Rules* ∪ {r};
6 **end**
7 Remove any $r \in$ *Rules* that is "covered" by another rule;
8 Extrapolate $r \in$ *Rules* using $r' \in$ *Rules*, when possible; prune rules that are covered by r;
9 Merge all pairs of mergeable rules in *Rules*;
10 Isolate all pairs of similar exception rules in *Rules*;

---

concrete cases). On the other hand, when a call raises an exception, it is desirable to have the smallest rule that isolates the cause of the exception. Furthermore, for exception rules, we use a ternary logic that assigns an unknown value "*" to a predicate of an object when the evaluation of the predicate does not affect whether the exception will be raised or not. These characterizations of the most general rules for a method call are inspired by the monotonic semantics that we have developed for object-oriented programs [6]. For a safe method call, it should be possible to replicate its result in a context with more objects. For a method call with an exception, there is no context with more objects that can avoid the exception.

Figure 3 shows the two rules that our tool computes for the `next` method when it raises the `ResultSet not open` exception. In Figure 3(a), the "*" values for the *s_open* and *c_open* predicates denote that regardless of whether the corresponding statement or connection objects of a `Resultset` object are open or not, the method call over the `Resultset` raises the exception when it is closed. Figure 3(b) shows the case when the `Resultset` is actually open, but its corresponding `Connection` is not. These rules point out succinctly the root cause of a bug discussed in an Apache forum.[1]

2.4 Computation Stages

Creating a rule from a specific method call is only the first step to compute a DPI. Algorithm 1 outlines the main steps that our tool takes to compute succinct DPIs.

The first stage of the algorithm (lines 1-7) is the *exploration stage*, in which a *universal client* non-deterministically explores the behaviour of the package. Each step of the universal client is recorded using a *source* and a *destination snapshot*, each of which is a set of Java objects in the heap. The result of each step of the universal client is a rule. If a new rule is *covered* by another already-explored rule, it is considered redundant and discarded (line 5). Intuitively, a rule r' covers rule r if r' subsumes the behaviour of r by having "larger" elements. The exploration stage continues until a maximum number

---

[1] https://issues.apache.org/jira/browse/DERBY-5545

of redundant rules are encountered. After this threshold is reached, the redundant rules in the set of explored rules are removed (line 7).

After the exploration stage, we apply three heuristics to the set of explored rules. Our *extrapolation* heuristic generalizes a rule by expanding its (cast) nested object graphs into more general graphs that represent more heap configurations. Our *merge* heuristic combines a pair of similar rules into one. Similarly, the *exception isolation* heuristic combines a pair of similar exception rules. These heuristics decrease the number of distinct explored rules of a DPI substantially; e.g., in the case of JDBC, from about 2000 distinct rules to 26 final rules.

3   Method Calls and Rules

From a Method Call to a Rule. A key step in computing a rule from a method call is to derive the source and destination nested object graphs and cast nested object graphs of a rule from the source and destination snapshots of the method call. The object mapping and role mapping of a rule are simply computed by tracking how objects change from the source to the destination snapshot, and ensuring that if an object is mapped by the role mapping it is not mapped by the object mapping. The computation of nested object graphs is the same for source and destination snapshots, except that a destination snapshot can have newly created objects. For the sake of brevity, at below, we assume that we deal with the source (cast) nested object graph of a rule.

The corresponding snapshot of a cast nested object graph consists of the callee object, actual parameter objects, and all other objects that transitively reach these objects through their references, as well as all objects that are transitively reached from these objects through their references. The corresponding snapshot of a nested object graph consists of all objects in the cast nested object graph plus all objects that can reach these objects transitively. To compute these snapshots, we use the input reference predicates. Next, we describe how to compute a nested object graph.

The first step is to turn the snapshot into a directed labelled graph by using the input scalar and reference predicates. We call such a graph a *heap graph*. Figure 4(a) shows a heap graph corresponding to 9 JDBC objects, using the predicates described in Section 2. Each node of the graph is labelled with the name of its class, the evaluations of its scalar predicates, as well as a unique id that is enclosed inside a pair of brackets. Each edge of the heap graph is labelled with the name of its corresponding reference predicate. Figure 4(b) is another heap graph resulting from the invocation of method executeQuery on the Java object that the node with id 4 in Figure 4(a) represents. The nodes with the same identifiers in the two graphs represent the same Java objects.

The second step is to reduce a heap graph to a nested object graph. The idea is that if an object or a pattern for a set of interconnected objects appears more than once, then it is marked as repeatable. The reduction from a heap graph to a nested object graph can be considered as a bisimulation reduction: two nodes in a heap graph are equivalent iff they have the same evaluations for their scalar predicates, and furthermore, they mimic one another by reaching equivalent nodes following their similar reference edges. Figure 5 shows two nested object graphs that our tool computes for the heap graphs in Figure 4. Repetition of a single node is denoted just by a "*" next to it. Repetition of a subgraph

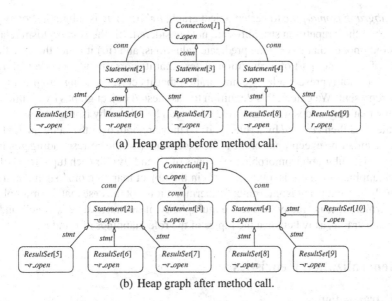

(a) Heap graph before method call.

(b) Heap graph after method call.

Fig. 4. Two heap graphs for invocation of `executeQuery` on object 4

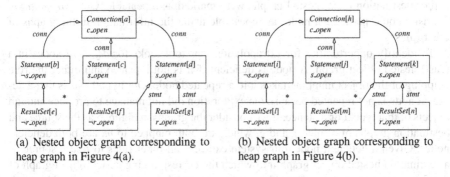

(a) Nested object graph corresponding to heap graph in Figure 4(a).

(b) Nested object graph corresponding to heap graph in Figure 4(b).

Fig. 5. Two nested object graphs

(not shown in this figure) is denoted by a dotted line around the subgraph together with a "*"; e.g., as in Figure 2(b). The nodes of the nested object graphs are graphically similar to heap graphs except that they are shown by solid rectangles and they are labelled with alphabetic ids. As examples of repetition, node e in Figure 5(a) is the equivalence class for the nodes 5, 6, and 7 in Figure 4(a), and node m in Figure 5(b) is the equivalence class for the nodes 8 and 9 in Figure 4(b).

The computation of a cast nested object graph is similar. The difference is that two objects of the snapshot that have roles cannot be mapped to the same equivalence class.

Rule Coverage Relation. In order to determine whether a rule covers another rule, we need to compare their corresponding (cast) nested object graphs. A nested object graph, *ng*, is *subgraph isomorphic* to nested object graph, *ng'* if: (i) *ng* is subgraph isomorphic to *ng'* when their repetition structures are not considered; (ii) the isomorphism relation relates only nodes that have same predicate valuations; and (iii) it is not the case that a node *v'* of *ng'* is not part of a repetition pattern that its corresponding node *v* of *ng* is; i.e., *ng* does not represent a heap configuration that its corresponding subgraph in *ng'* cannot represent. We extend this definition to cast nested object graphs by additionally requiring that only nodes with same role labels can be related by isomorphism.

A rule, *r*, is then *covered* by a rule, *r'*, if: (i) they are both over the same method; (ii) both raise either no exceptions, or the same exception; (iii) the corresponding graphs of *r* are pairwise subgraph isomorphic to the ones of *r'*; and (iv) for each tuple (u, v) of the object mapping of *r* there is a tuple (u', v') in the object mapping of *r'* such that *u* and *u'*, as well as *v* and *v'* are isomorphic; furthermore, it is not the case that the multiplicity of the former tuple is "many" while the multiplicity of the latter tuple is "one"; and (v) similar constraints as iv between the tuples of the role mappings of *r* and *r'*.

4 Generalization Heuristics

4.1 Extrapolation

Sometimes a rule could have covered many other rules if certain nodes in its source and/or destination (cast) nested graphs were marked as repeatable. Our *extrapolation* heuristic could mark such nodes as repeatable using the information in the graphs of other rules.

To identify opportunities for extrapolation, our tool looks for *deficient* nodes in a (cast) nested object graph. A node is deficient if it is not repeated and either the role mapping or the object mapping takes it to a repeated node. Our hypothesis is that a deficient node is not repeated because the exploration did not manage to produce enough objects of that type. For instance, if we consider the graphs in Figure 5 as the source and destination graphs of a rule , *f* and *g*, which are both mapped to *m*, are both deficient nodes. Given a deficient node, our system explores all other rules to find a source or a destination nested object graph into which the corresponding nested object graph of the deficient node can be *embedded* w.r.t. the subgraph isomorphism relation. If according to the embedding the node corresponding to the deficient node in the other graph is repeated, then the deficient node will be marked as repeatable too. In our example, our tool can find an embedding relation that leads to the extrapolation of *f*. However, *g* cannot be extrapolated. Indeed, each JDBC `Statement` object cannot have more than one open `ResultSet` object.

Repetition is propagated to all nodes pointing to the extrapolated node, in order to ensure that there is no non-repeated node pointing to a node that is marked as repeatable. Lastly, the multiplicities of mappings might need to be adjusted to ensure that a node that is marked as repeatable is not mapped only once via a "one" multiplicity. The extrapolation heuristic is applied to all rules after the exploration stage, and then all redundant rules are removed.

4.2 Merging

While the extrapolation stage prunes a substantial number of rules, there may still be a large number of rules in a DPI, e.g., thousands of rules for JDBC. The reason is that different rules for the same method might have explored different instances of heaps that have incomparable sets of objects, and there are various exception cases. To further reduce the number of the rules, we have developed the *merging* heuristic, which combine sets of related rules into one.

To check whether two rules can be merged, we compare a part of their cast nested object graphs that we call the *upward* part. The upward part of a cast nested object graph is its subgraph that consists of the set of nodes that are labelled by roles plus the nodes that are reached from these nodes. A pair of rules are *mergeable* if: (i) the upward parts of their source and destination cast nested object graphs are pairwise isomorphic; and (ii) their role mappings restricted to the upward parts are similar and over isomorphic nodes. For a mergeable pair of rules, the merge heuristic essentially first computes their union and then performs a reduction over the resulting source and destination nested object graphs of the resulting rule. The reduction replaces a nested object graph with its smallest subgraph that simulates all other subgraphs of the original graph. This reduction is in the spirit of *downward closed* graphs where a nested object graph not only represents all heap instances arising from the repetition of its repeatable subgraphs, but also represents any graph which is a subgraph of those – hence the term "downward closed" [5]. Finally, the role mapping and object mapping of the resulting rule are adjusted according to the reduction. As an example, assuming that the nested object graphs in Figure 5 belong to a rule, then node c in Figure 5(a), for instance, would be mapped to node C in Figure 2(b) during the merge operation. Similar to the extrapolation heuristic, the multiplicities of mappings might need to be adjusted.

4.3 Exception Isolation

While the merge heuristic corresponds to the union of a set of rules, the *exception isolation* heuristic corresponds to the intersection of a set of exception rules. This heuristic deals only with the cast nested object graphs; the nested object graphs are discarded. For a pair of rules that raise the same exception and whose cast nested object graphs are isomorphic when their scalar abstraction predicates are not considered, this heuristic essentially combines the corresponding nodes of the cast nested object graphs of the two rules via a ternary logic. If the values of a predicate are different, the unknown value, denote by "*", is chosen. Nested object graphs of the rules are not useful because often when an exception is raised the states of the corresponding objects of these graph do not change. Furthermore, we are interested in identifying the smallest contexts in which an exception can raise.

5 System

Figure 6 shows the high-level architecture of our system, implemented in Java. The arrows specify the high-level information communicated between the components.

Fig. 6. The main components of the system

The *Package Abstraction* component provides the information about the input package. It consists of a set of classes whose methods provide the names of classes of the package under study, their methods, and predicate abstractions. These classes use Java reflection to obtain these information. Furthermore, there are classes that provide the actual parameters for the method calls of the universal client; these parameters have random values.

The *Package Explorer* component implements the exploration stage of Algorithm 1. To implement the snapshots whose objects can be accessed throughout the exploration, our tool maintains the corresponding trace of method calls that resulted in the snapshot. To call a method of an object of a snapshot, our tool recreates the entire snapshot by replaying its corresponding trace. Cloning or saving an object, in general, would not work, as not all classes implement these methods. A recreated snapshot has similar objects as the original snapshot, assuming that, as far as the abstraction predicates are concerned, method calls are deterministic. To relate the objects in a snapshot to the objects in its replayed copy, we use a notion of *logical id* for each of the objects of the snapshots; objects that have the same logical ids are treated as copy of one another.

To ensure that our exploration does not prematurely identify objects as non-repeatable in a rule, we use a repetitive object creation scheme in our exploration: if a creator method is chosen to be executed, we invoke the method $n > 1$ number of times consecutively, and only after that compute the rule with respect to the snapshot before consecutive method calls and the snapshot after that. Also, after the initial exploration stage, to achieve a good coverage, similar to other approaches [3], our system ensures that all possible method calls on all objects of all rules in the repository are executed and their corresponding rules are stored in the repository.

The *Heuristics* component implements the algorithms in Section 4. We use the graph data structures in the JGraphT library to implement our graph algorithms.

Limitations. While we expect our tool to work in a straightforward manner on packages that solely work on the heap (e.g., Java collections), for packages that work with external components, the Package Abstraction part is more complex, because an environment needs to be set up. Also, the feasibility of the replay mechanism should be considered. These limitations are inherent to dynamic approaches.

6   Experiences

We have used our tool to compute the DPI of three Java packages: JDBC, ArrayList, and HashSet. While our tool usually identifies the expected set of rules for the DPI, some of these rules could, in principle, be more general. The converse, however, has never happened in our experiments. A rule computed by our tool always corresponded to an actual behaviour of the package.

Table 1. Duration and number of rules after different stages in computing DPIs of three packages. Information, except for the last column, correspond to average values of five runs.

Package	Threshold #	Time (min:sec) Exploration	Extrapolation	Merging	Isolation	#Rules Exploration	Extrapolation	Merging	Isolation
ArrayList	200000	010:37	000:03	000:00	000:00	572	299	29	15 (once 14)
HashSet	200000	168:26	000:23	000:01	000:00	1140	503	34	16
JDBC	1200	032:01	000:57	000:05	000:00	2465	2370	29	26 (twice 25)

Table 1 shows the results of our experiments for each of these packages. The measurements for each package are for the average of five runs on a dual-core CPU Windows 7 desktop machine with 8 GB of RAM. In all our experiments, we have set JVM options to use 5GB of physical memory. For each package, Table 1 presents the time taken and the number of rules after each stage of the computation, namely after the exploration, extrapolation, merge, and exception isolation phases.

JDBC. In Section 2, we already presented some of the rules of the DPI of JDBC. In our experiments, the universal client connects to a local Apache Derby database. We use a key-value table that is manipulated through INSERT, DELETE, and SELECT SQL commands with random values, via JDBC. We are thus assuming that the DPI of the JDBC package is independent of the schema of databases to which it connects. This is justified by our interest in determining the relationship of interacting objects of a package, and not its interaction with external components. Increasing the threshold value to larger than 1200 would cause out-of-memory exceptions. Our tool computed 26 rules in three out of five runs; in the other two runs, it computes 25 rules. The missing rule in both cases was the rule for the close method when called over an open ResultSet that is connected to a closed Statement and a closed Connection.

ArrayList. We consider two classes of ArrayList: Array and its internal class Itr, which implements Java Iterator. Besides the methods of these classes that create objects, we consider the Add method of Array, and the next and remove methods of Itr. We provide a reference predicate, *iter_of*, to the system, denoting which Itr object belongs to which Array object. We provide four scalar predicates to the system: *empty* $\equiv$ *size > 0*, which determines whether an Array object is empty or not, *nextCalled* $\equiv$ *lastRet $\neq$ −1*, which determines whether the remove method of an Itr object can be called (i.e., if next has been called), *mover* $\equiv$ *size > cursor*, which determines whether an Itr has traversed all members of its corresponding Array or not, and *sync* $\equiv$ *modCount = expectedModCount*, which determines whether an Array object and an Itr object agree on their version numbers (i.e., if the Array object has been modified by another Itr object). Lastly, we use integers as the domain of Array.

Our tool computed 15 rules that cover all possible behaviour of ArrayList. It once missed computing the rule for next when called on an iterator whose all predicates are true and remain true after the method call. Figure 7 shows the object mapping of one of the three rules that our tool computes for the remove method in one of our experiments.

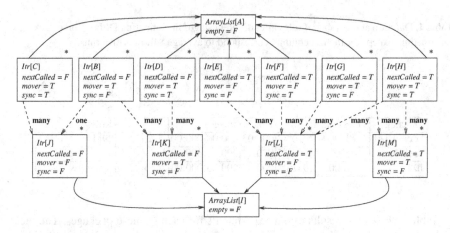

Fig. 7. The object mapping of a rule for `remove` method of `ArrayList`. "*T*" and "*F*" represent *true* and *false*, respectively. For clarity, the reference edges are not labelled with *iter_of*.

The role mapping, not shown here, changes only the *nextCalled* predicate of the callee iterator object whose all scalar predicates are true. This rule is interesting because it demonstrates that the object mapping of a rule can be non-deterministic. The rule could have been more general, however. First, in the source nested object graph, the object with *nextCalled = false*, *mover = false*, and *sync = false* is missing. Second, the object mapping from *B* to *J* could have had multiplicity "many". And lastly, there could have been an object mapping from *D* to *L* with multiplicity "many" denoting that some of the mover, sync objects whose *nextCalled* is false become non-movers.

HashSet. The DPIs of `HashSet` and `ArrayList` are computed using similar predicates, but `HashSet` uses a `HashMap` class internally, instead of a resizable array. The DPIs of two package are also somewhat different. The main difference is that the `add` method of `HashSet` does not change the heap if its input parameter is duplicate; thus, there is an extra rule that captures this behaviour. Another difference is that the *mover* predicate of an `Iterator` object of a `HashSet` only correctly denotes whether it has traversed all elements of its corresponding `HashSet` if its *sync* predicate is true. This is because unlike an `ArrayList` object, whose iterator objects maintain an index of the underlying array of the `ArrayList` object, the iterators of a `HashSet` objects needs to traverse the underlying hash table of its internal `HashMap` object. Lastly, computing the DPI of `HashSet` takes significantly longer than `ArrayList`'s, both because of their different underlying data structures and because significantly more reflections are needed when evaluating the abstraction predicates of `HashSet`.

7   Conclusion

We have introduced the notion of dynamic package interfaces (DPI). DPIs provide a succinct way to describe valid usage patterns for a package. The DPI of a package is a set of rules, each of which specifies the effect of a method call over a general configuration of a set of objects. We have developed a dynamic tool that computes an approximation of the DPI of a Java package automatically, given a set of abstraction predicates. The rules of such a DPI generalize the usual examples used in the documentation of the Java package and can be traced to problems discussed in online forums.

A DPI captures both the *inter*-object aspects of the dynamic behaviour of the classes of a package, as well as the *intra*-object aspects of individual classes of the package, relative to a set of scalar and reference predicates, even when unboundedly many objects interact.[2] In contrast, previous dynamic techniques primarily focus on either deriving intra-object specifications for one object or deriving finite state machines that capture the interaction pattern of a finite number of objects [3, 7, 8, 11–13].

References

1. Abdulla, P.A., Cerans, K., Jonsson, B., Tsay, Y.K.: General decidability theorems for infinite-state systems. In: LICS '96. pp. 313–321. IEEE (1996)
2. Alur, R., Černý, P., Madhusudan, P., Nam, W.: Synthesis of interface specifications for Java classes. In: POPL'05. pp. 98–109. ACM (2005)
3. Dallmeier, V., Knopp, N., Mallon, C., Hack, S., Zeller, A.: Generating test cases for specification mining. In: ISSTA. pp. 85–96. ACM (2010)
4. Damm, W., Harel, D.: LSCs: Breathing life into message sequence charts. Formal Methods in System Design 19(1), 45–80 (2001)
5. Esmaeilsabzali, S., Majumdar, R., Wies, T., Zufferey, D.: Dynamic package interfaces - extended version. CoRR abs/1311.4934 (2013)
6. Esmaeilsabzali, S., Majumdar, R., Wies, T., Zufferey, D.: A notion of dynamic interface for depth-bounded object-oriented packages. CoRR abs/1311.4615 (2013)
7. Ghezzi, C., Mocci, A., Monga, M.: Synthesizing intensional behavior models by graph transformation. In: ICSE. pp. 430–440. IEEE (2009)
8. Henkel, J., Reichenbach, C., Diwan, A.: Discovering documentation for java container classes. IEEE Trans. Software Eng 33(8), 526–543 (2007)
9. Henzinger, T., Jhala, R., Majumdar, R.: Permissive interfaces. In: Wermelinger, M., Gall, H. (eds.) ESEC/SIGSOFT FSE. pp. 31–40. ACM (2005)
10. Nanda, M., Grothoff, C., Chandra, S.: Deriving object typestates in the presence of inter-object references. In: OOPSLA. pp. 77–96. ACM (2005)
11. Nguyen, T.T., Nguyen, H.A., Pham, N.H., Al-Kofahi, J.M., Nguyen, T.N.: Graph-based mining of multiple object usage patterns. In: ESEC/SIGSOFT FSE. pp. 383–392. ACM (2009)
12. Pradel, M., Jaspan, C., Aldrich, J., Gross, T.: Statically checking API protocol conformance with mined multi-object specifications. In: ICSE'12. pp. 925–935. IEEE (2012)
13. Pradel, M., Gross, T.R.: Automatic generation of object usage specifications from large method traces. In: ASE. pp. 371–382. IEEE Computer Society (2009)
14. Strom, R.E., Yemini, S.A.: Typestate: A programming language concept for enhancing software reliability. IEEE Transactions on Software Engineering 12(1), 157–171 (Jan 1986)
15. Wasylkowski, A., Zeller, A.: Mining temporal specifications from object usage. Autom. Softw. Eng. 18(3-4), 263–292 (2011)
16. Whaley, J., Martin, M., Lam, M.: Automatic extraction of object-oriented component interfaces. In: ISSTA. pp. 218–228 (2002)
17. Wies, T., Zufferey, D., Henzinger, T.: Forward analysis of depth-bounded processes. In: FOSSACS. LNCS, vol. 6014, pp. 94–108. Springer (2010)

---

[2] We use the terms "inter-object" and "intra-object" in a similar sense as in OO design [4].

SMT-Based Checking of SOLOIST
over Sparse Traces

Marcello Maria Bersani[1], Domenico Bianculli[2], Carlo Ghezzi[1], Srđan Krstić[1],
and Pierluigi San Pietro[1]

[1] DEEP-SE group - DEIB - Politecnico di Milano, Italy
{bersani,ghezzi,krstic,sanpietr}@elet.polimi.it
[2] SnT Centre - University of Luxembourg, Luxembourg
domenico.bianculli@uni.lu

Abstract. SMT solvers have been recently applied to bounded model checking and satisfiability checking of metric temporal logic. In this paper we consider SOLOIST, an extension of metric temporal logic with aggregate temporal modalities; it has been defined based on a field study on the use of specification patterns in the context of the provisioning of service-based applications. We apply bounded satisfiability checking to perform trace checking of service execution traces against requirements expressed in SOLOIST. In particular, we focus on sparse traces, i.e., traces in which the number of time instants when events occur is very low with respect to the length of the trace.

The main contribution of this paper is an encoding of SOLOIST formulae into formulae of the theory of quantifier-free integer difference logic with uninterpreted function and predicate symbols. This encoding paves the way for efficient checking of SOLOIST formulae over sparse traces using an SMT-based verification toolkit. We report on the evaluation of the proposed encoding, commenting on its scalability and its effectiveness.

1 Introduction

Bounded satisfiability checking [23] (BSC) is a verification technique that complements bounded model checking [9] (BMC): instead of a customary operational model (e.g., a state-transition system) used in BMC, BSC supports the analysis of a *descriptive model*, denoted by a set of temporal logic formulae. With BSC, verification tasks become suitable instances of the satisfiability problem for quite large formulae (written in a certain logic), which comprehend the model of the system to analyze as well as the requirement(s) to verify. BSC has been successfully applied in the context of metric temporal logics and implemented in ZOT [23], a verification toolset based on SAT- and SMT-solvers, developed within our group.

In this paper we apply BSC to trace checking for the language SOLOIST (*SpecificatiOn Language fOr servIce compoSitions inTeractions*) [8], a metric temporal logic with new, additional temporal modalities that support aggregate operations on events occurring in a given time window. SOLOIST has been defined based on the results of a field study [7] on the type of property specification patterns used to express requirements in the context of service-based applications. The study—performed by some of the authors in collaboration with an industrial partner—analyzed more than 900 requirements

S. Gnesi and A. Rensink (Eds.): FASE 2014, LNCS 8411, pp. 276–290, 2014.
© Springer-Verlag Berlin Heidelberg 2014

specifications, extracted both from research papers and industrial data, and led to the identification of a new class of specification patterns, in addition to the ones already known in literature [13,17]. The new class of patterns is specific to the domain of service provisioning and contains seven patterns, among which there are: *average response time* (hereafter referred to as S1), *count of the number of events* (S2), *average/maximum number of events* (S3/S4).

SOLOIST can be used to specify both functional and quality-of-service requirements of the interactions of a composite service with its partner services. As for the verification of properties expressed in SOLOIST, in [8] we first presented a translation of SOLOIST into LTL that, under certain assumptions, guaranteed its decidability based on well-known results in temporal logic. Nevertheless, this translation was only a proof of concept and was not meant to be used for implementing efficient verification procedures. In subsequent work [18], some of the authors described an approach for performing *trace checking*[1] of service execution traces against requirements expressed in SOLOIST. The approach in [18] defined the *trace checking* problem in terms of the BSC problem for metric temporal logic, where the descriptive model of system executions is represented by traces, while properties are expressed in SOLOIST; in particular, it translates SOLOIST into CLTLB($\mathscr{D}$) [4], an extension of PLTLB (Propositional Linear Temporal Logic with both future and past modalities) augmented with atomic formulae over a constraint system $\mathscr{D}$; the resulting CLTLB($\mathscr{D}$) formula is then checked by ZOT. The main limitation of the approach presented in [18] is that it does not scale well when the trace to check is *sparse*, i.e., when the number of time instants in which events occur is very low with respect to the length of the trace. Notice that the case of sparse traces is *not rare* in the logs of service-based applications. For example, the log used for the *Business Process Intelligence Challenge 2012 (BPIC 2012)* [12] was taken from a Dutch Financial Institute; it contains 13087 traces, whose average number of time instants in which events occur is 20.0347: this represents (on average) the 0.003% of the total number of time instants.

The main contribution of this paper is a new encoding of SOLOIST, targeting formulae of quantifier-free difference logic with uninterpreted function and predicate symbols (QF-EUFIDL), for which there exist efficient decision procedures to be used with SMT solvers. As confirmed by the experimental evaluation we detail in the paper, this new encoding targeting QF-EUFIDL proves to be scalable and effective for checking SOLOIST formulae over sparse traces.

Related Work. There are only few approaches that deal with the verification of properties involving aggregate modalities. Basin et al. [2] define an extension of metric first-order temporal logic that supports aggregation. The language can express aggregate properties over the values of the parameters of relations (corresponding to system events), while SOLOIST expresses aggregate properties on the occurrences of the events. Finkbeiner et al. [15] describe an approach to collect statistics over run-time executions. They use LTL extended with the capability to compute aggregate properties of the trace. However, this specification language provides only limited support for timing information; unlike SOLOIST, it cannot express properties on a certain subset of an

---

[1] Trace checking is also called *trace validation* [20] or *history checking* [14].

execution trace. This work is also related to approaches for SAT/SMT-based trace checking and bounded model checking, which is usually done over properties expressed in conventional temporal logics. For example, the SAT-based approach for bounded model checking proposed in [24] verifies Metric Temporal Logic (MTL) properties of discrete timed automata. SMT-based techniques like those proposed in [5,6,16] deal with verification of MTL over real-valued words.

The rest of the paper is structured as follows. Section 2 provides a brief introduction to SOLOIST and QF-EUFIDL. The main contribution of the paper is presented in Sect. 3, where we present the encoding of SOLOIST into QF-EUFIDL over a finite temporal structure and assess its complexity. Section 4 reports on the evaluation of an implementation of the proposed encoding, performed to assess its scalability and effectiveness. Section 5 gives some concluding remarks.

2 Background

2.1 SOLOIST at a Glance

In this section we provide a brief overview of SOLOIST; for the rationale behind the language and a detailed explanation of its semantics see [8].

The syntax of SOLOIST is defined by the following grammar:

$$\phi ::= p \mid \neg\phi \mid \phi \wedge \phi \mid \phi \mathsf{U}_I \phi \mid \phi \mathsf{S}_I \phi \mid \mathfrak{C}^K_{\bowtie n}(\phi) \mid \mathfrak{U}^{K,h}_{\bowtie n}(\phi) \mid \mathfrak{M}^{K,h}_{\bowtie n}(\phi) \mid \mathfrak{D}^K_{\bowtie n}(\phi, \phi)$$

where $p \in \Pi$, with Π being a finite set of atoms; I is a nonempty interval over $\mathbb{N}$; n, K, h range over $\mathbb{N}$; $\bowtie \in \{<, \leq, \geq, >, =\}$. We restrict the arguments ϕ of modalities $\mathfrak{C}, \mathfrak{U}, \mathfrak{M}, \mathfrak{D}$ to atoms in Π.

The U_I and S_I modalities are, respectively, the metric "Until" and "Since" operators. Additional temporal modalities can be derived using the usual conventions; for example "Always" is defined as $\mathsf{G}_I \phi \equiv \neg(\top \mathsf{U}_I \neg \phi)$ and "Eventually in the Past" as $\mathsf{P}_I \phi \equiv \top \mathsf{S}_I \phi$, where $\top$ means "true". The remaining modalities are called *aggregate* modalities and are used to express the specification patterns S1–S4 mentioned above. The $\mathfrak{C}^K_{\bowtie n}(\phi)$ modality states a bound (represent by $\bowtie n$) on the number of occurrences of an event ϕ in the previous K time instants: it expresses pattern S2. The $\mathfrak{U}^{K,h}_{\bowtie n}(\phi)$ (respectively, $\mathfrak{M}^{K,h}_{\bowtie n}(\phi)$) modality expresses a bound on the average (respectively, maximum) number of occurrences of an event ϕ, aggregated over the set of right-aligned adjacent non-overlapping subintervals within a time window K; it corresponds to pattern S3 (respectively, S4), as in "the average/maximum number of events per hour in the last ten hours". A subtle difference in the semantics of the $\mathfrak{U}$ and $\mathfrak{M}$ modalities is that $\mathfrak{M}$ considers events in the (possibly empty) tail interval, i.e., the leftmost observation subinterval whose length is less than h, while the $\mathfrak{U}$ modality ignores them. The $\mathfrak{D}^K_{\bowtie n}(\phi, \psi)$ modality expresses a bound on the average time elapsed between a pair of specific adjacent events ϕ and ψ occurring in the previous K time instants; it can be used to express pattern S1.

The formal semantics of SOLOIST is defined on timed ω-words [1] over $2^\Pi \times \mathbb{N}$. A timed sequence $\tau = \tau_1 \tau_2 \ldots$ is an infinite sequence of values $\tau_i \in \mathbb{N}$ with $\tau_i > 0$ satisfying $\tau_i < \tau_{i+1}$, for all $i \geq 1$, i.e., the sequence increases strictly monotonically.

$$
\begin{aligned}
(w,i) &\models p & &\text{iff } p \in \sigma_i \\
(w,i) &\models \neg\phi & &\text{iff } (w,i) \not\models \phi \\
(w,i) &\models \phi \wedge \psi & &\text{iff } (w,i) \models \phi \wedge (w,i) \models \psi \\
(w,i) &\models \phi S_I \psi & &\text{iff for some } j < i, \tau_i - \tau_j \in I, (w,j) \models \psi \text{ and for all } k, j < k < i, (w,k) \models \phi \\
(w,i) &\models \phi U_I \psi & &\text{iff for some } j > i, \tau_j - \tau_i \in I, (w,j) \models \psi \text{ and for all } k, i < k < j, (w,k) \models \phi \\
(w,i) &\models \mathfrak{C}^K_{\bowtie n}(\phi) & &\text{iff } c(\tau_i - K, \tau_i, \phi) \bowtie n \text{ and } \tau_i \geq K \\
(w,i) &\models \mathfrak{U}^{K,h}_{\bowtie n}(\phi) & &\text{iff } \frac{c(\tau_i - \lfloor \frac{K}{h} \rfloor h, \tau_i, \phi)}{\lfloor \frac{K}{h} \rfloor} \bowtie n \text{ and } \tau_i \geq K \\
(w,i) &\models \mathfrak{M}^{K,h}_{\bowtie n}(\phi) & &\text{iff } \max\left\{ \bigcup_{m=0}^{\lfloor \frac{K}{h} \rfloor} \{c(lb(m), rb(m), \phi)\} \right\} \bowtie n \text{ and } \tau_i \geq K \\
(w,i) &\models \mathfrak{D}^K_{\bowtie n}(\phi, \psi) & &\text{iff } \frac{\sum_{(s,t) \in d(\phi, \psi, \tau_i, K)} (\tau_t - \tau_s)}{|d(\phi, \psi, \tau_i, K)|} \bowtie n \text{ and } \tau_i \geq K
\end{aligned}
$$

where $c(\tau_a, \tau_b, \phi) = |\{s \mid \tau_a < \tau_s \leq \tau_b \text{ and } (w,s) \models \phi\}|$, $lb(m) = \max\{\tau_i - K, \tau_i - (m+1)h\}$, $rb(m) = \tau_i - mh$, and $d(\phi, \psi, \tau_i, K) = \{(s,t) \mid \tau_i - K < \tau_s \leq \tau_i \text{ and } (w,s) \models \phi, t = \min\{u \mid \tau_s < \tau_u \leq \tau_i, (w,u) \models \psi\}\}$

Fig. 1. Formal semantics of SOLOIST

A timed ω-word over alphabet 2^Π is a pair (σ, τ) where $\sigma = \sigma_1 \sigma_2 \dots$ is an infinite word over 2^Π and τ is a timed sequence. A timed language over 2^Π is a set of timed words over the same alphabet. Notice that there is a distinction between the integer position i in the timed ω-word and the corresponding timestamp τ_i. Figure 1 defines the satisfiability relation $(w,i) \models \phi$ for every timed ω-word w, every position $i \geq 0$ and for every SOLOIST formula ϕ. For the sake of simplicity, hereafter we express the $\mathfrak{U}$ modality in terms of the $\mathfrak{C}$ one, based on this definition: $\mathfrak{U}^{K,h}_{\bowtie n}(\phi) \equiv \mathfrak{C}^{\lfloor \frac{K}{h} \rfloor \cdot h}_{\bowtie n \cdot \lfloor \frac{K}{h} \rfloor}(\phi)$, which can be derived from the semantics in Fig. 1.

We remark that the version of SOLOIST presented here is a restriction of the original one in [8]: to simplify the presentation in the next sections, we dropped first-order quantification on finite domains and limited the argument of the $\mathfrak{D}$ modality to only one pair of events; as detailed in [8], these assumptions do not affect the expressiveness of the language.

2.2 QF-EUFIDL

The target language of our encoding is a quantifier free integer difference logic formula with uninterpreted function and predicate symbols (QF-EUFIDL). Since trace checking only deals with finite traces, we require the outcome of the encoding to be a QF-EUFIDL formula that is satisfiable if and only if there exists a *finite* timed word that satisfies the translated SOLOIST formula. Such a logic combines decision procedures from two theories, namely theory of equality and uninterpreted functions and theory of integer difference logic. This combination is shown to be decidable, and the satisfiability problem is NP-complete, according to Nelson-Oppen Theorem [21]. Well-formed QF-EUFIDL formulae conform to the following grammar: $\phi ::= p \mid t = t \mid \neg\phi \mid \phi \vee \phi$, with $t ::= v \mid f(t, \dots, t)$, where p is an atomic proposition, v is a variable and f is a function. An example is $f(x) = y \wedge x = g(y) \wedge (\neg p \vee q)$, where x and y are variables while p and q are atomic propositions. The decision procedure for this logic combines SAT solving (for the propositional formulae) with an algorithm that checks equalities by building a tree representation of their equivalence classes. Integer difference Logic is a restriction of the theory of linear arithmetic and can be represented with the structure

$(\mathbb{Z}, =, (<_d)_{d\in\mathbb{Z}})$, for which decidability has been proven in [11]; each $<_d$ is a binary relation defined as $x <_d y \leftrightarrow x < y + d$, and notations like $x < y, x \leq y, x \geq y, x > y$ and $x = y + d$ are abbreviations for $x <_0 y, x <_0 y \vee x = y, \neg(x <_0 y), \neg(x <_0 y \vee x = y)$ and $y <_{d-1} x \wedge x <_{d+1} y$, respectively.

Although LTL with arithmetical constraints is proved [11] undecidable over infinite words, and QF-EUFIDL involves variables over discrete infinite domains, our particular use is bounded, because we deal with finite words; hence, the decidability is retained.

3   Encoding SOLOIST into QF-EUFIDL

SOLOIST can be seen as MTL over discrete time, enriched with aggregate modalities. MTL satisfiability checking over discrete time [23] can be efficiently performed by reducing semantics of U_I and S_I to suitable propositional formulae which take advantage from the information about the metric over time defined by I. In [23], however, authors consider ω-words as models for MTL formulae without timestamps. Therefore, the temporal structure required to translate the semantics of a formula such as $\top U_{[10,10]}\phi$ is at least as long as ten discrete positions, because no timing information is available from the model. In this paper, we devise a new way to represent information about timing constraints defined in metric temporal modalities (including the aggregate ones); this is an improvement on the method proposed in [23]. The encoding presented afterwards is an extension of the one defined in [3], which allows one to capture timed ω-words. As a consequence, models do not require as many discrete positions as needed to build the discrete temporal structure in [23], because the measure of time distances is realized through arithmetical variables that store how much time elapses among consecutive discrete positions. Intuitively, by adding an arithmetical variable $\tau \in \mathbb{N}$ measuring the elapsed time, formula $\top U_{[10,10]}\phi$ holds at position i if, for instance, at position $i+1$, ϕ holds and the time τ elapsed between position i and position $i+1$ is equal to 10. To realize this counting mechanism with variables and arithmetical operators, we require a language that incorporates arithmetics, hence our choice of QF-EUFIDL as the target language of our encoding.

We use the following QF-EUFIDL structure $(\mathbb{Z}, F, P, V, =, <)$ where F contains functions of the form $f : \mathbb{Z}_0^+ \to \mathbb{Z}$. Each function represents arithmetical variable used in the encoding. Set P contains boolean functions of the form $p : \mathbb{Z}_0^+ \to \{\top, \bot\}$; each of them represents a predicate whose value is defined over a nonnegative integer domain. Set V is a subset of F containing nullary functions returning a value from $\mathbb{Z}$. Using this structure we can define a finite representation of models of SOLOIST formulae. Since our structure is ordered, let $0, 1, 2, \ldots, H$ be a finite linear order, with H corresponding to the length of the finite prefix of the timed ω-word satisfying a SOLOIST formula. The linear order represents a temporal structure and since it is a subset of the domain of both the predicates from P and the functions from F, we can interpret them as having "time dependent" values. On the other hand, we can interpret elements of V as being time invariant, i.e., have constant value over the linear order.

In the encoding, we use the notation $[\![X]\!]$ to denote any additional predicate introduced in P to represent an entity X. We denote with $|X|$ an additional arithmetical variable in F representing an arithmetical entity X. We use $[\![X]\!]_i$ and $|X|_i$ as a shorthand for $[\![X]\!](i)$ and $|X|(i)$, respectively. The truth of $[\![X]\!]_i$ is interpreted as entity X holding at time instant i in an execution trace (or, equivalently, a timed word).

We assume SOLOIST formulae to be in *positive normal form* (PNF). The PNF of a formula is an equivalent formula where negation may only occur on atoms, i.e., atomic propositions (see [22]). PNF can be obtained by propagating the negation towards the atoms, by means of converting a negated operator into its dual version and negating its operand(s). To do so, we introduce the connective $\vee$, dual of $\wedge$, as well as the dual versions of all temporal modalities. The dual of U_I is *"Release"* R_I: $\phi\mathsf{R}_I\psi \equiv \neg(\neg\phi\mathsf{U}_I\neg\psi)$; the dual of S_I is *"Trigger"* T_I: $\phi\mathsf{T}_I\psi \equiv \neg(\neg\phi\mathsf{S}_I\neg\psi)^2$. A negation in front of one of the $\mathfrak{C}^K_{\bowtie n}, \mathfrak{U}^{K,h}_{\bowtie n}, \mathfrak{M}^{K,h}_{\bowtie n}, \mathfrak{D}^K_{\bowtie n}$ modalities becomes a negation of the relation denoted by the $\bowtie$ symbol, hence no dual version is needed for them.

Let Φ be a SOLOIST formula in PNF. Its encoding is a set of QF-EUFIDL constraints over the predicates from P and functions from F. We introduce a predicate $[\![\varphi]\!]$ for each subformula φ of Φ.

We first define the constraints for timing information. As defined in Sect. 2, the temporal structure contains an integer timestamp. An arithmetical variable $|\tau|$ denotes the absolute time at positions $i = 0\ldots H$. Let $\mathscr{C}_{time}$ be the conjunction of the following constraints:

Position i	Timing information	Description	
$0\ldots H-1$	$|\tau|_i < |\tau|_{i+1}$	strict monotonicity	(1)

Next, we define constraints for atomic propositions and propositional operators; their conjunction is denoted as $\mathscr{C}_{prop}$ (where $\leftrightarrow$ stands for a double implication):

Position i	Propositional operators	Description	
$0\ldots H$	$[\![p]\!]_i \leftrightarrow p(i)$	atomic propositions	
$0\ldots H$	$[\![\neg p]\!]_i \leftrightarrow \neg p(i)$	negation	(2)
$0\ldots H$	$[\![\phi \wedge \psi]\!]_i \leftrightarrow [\![\phi]\!]_i \wedge [\![\psi]\!]_i$	conjunction	

Notice that for any sub-formula of the form $\phi \wedge \psi$ in a SOLOIST formula Φ we add in the resulting encoding, instances of formulae from the third row of (2). This encoding completely conforms to the one in [9].

As for the modality U_I, we add to the encoding, for any subformula of the form[3] $\phi\mathsf{U}_{(a,b)}\psi$ in Φ, the following formulae, denoted as $\mathscr{C}_{temp-until}$:

Position i	Temporal operator	Description	
$0\ldots H-1$	$[\![\phi\mathsf{U}_{(a,b)}\psi]\!]_i \leftrightarrow \bigvee_{k=i+1}^{H}([\![\psi]\!]_k \wedge$ $a < |\tau|_k - |\tau|_i \wedge |\tau|_k - |\tau|_i < b \wedge \bigwedge_{p=i+1}^{k-1}[\![\phi]\!]_p)$	"Until"	(3)
H	$[\![\phi\mathsf{U}_{(a,b)}\psi]\!]_H \leftrightarrow \bot^.$	"Until" at position H	

---

[2] Note that the strict semantics of U_I and S_I preserve the duality of R_I and T_I also on finite words.

[3] A closed interval $[a,b]$ over $\mathbb{N}$ can be expressed as an open one of the form $(a-1,b+1)$.

This is a straightforward encoding of the semantics of the "*Until*" operator. The disjunction in the first row represents a case split on all possible future time instants with respect to i. For each such time instant k a conjunction is created with $[\![\psi]\!]_k$ stating that ψ subformula has to hold at time instant k; moreover, ϕ needs to hold in all instants from $i + 1$ to $k - 1$, i.e., $\bigwedge_{p=i+1}^{k-1}[\![\phi]\!]_p$. Formula $(a < |\tau|_k - |\tau|_i) \wedge (|\tau|_k - |\tau|_i < b)$ enforces the timing constraint of the $\mathsf{U}_{(a,b)}$ modality, i.e., if $\tau_k - \tau_i \in (a,b)$.

The case for the S_I modality is similar to the above. For any sub-formula of the form S_I in Φ we add to the encoding the following formulae, denoted as $\mathscr{C}_{temp-since}$:

Position i	Temporal operator	Description
0	$[\![\phi\mathsf{S}_{(a,b)}\psi]\!]_0 \leftrightarrow \bot$	"Since" at position 0
1...H	$[\![\phi\mathsf{S}_{(a,b)}\psi]\!]_i \leftrightarrow \bigvee_{k=0}^{i-1}([\![\psi]\!]_k \wedge$ $a < |\tau|_i - |\tau|_k \wedge |\tau|_i - |\tau|_k < b \wedge \bigwedge_{p=k+1}^{i-1}[\![\phi]\!]_p)$	"Since"

(4)

The conjunction of all formulae from $\mathscr{C}_{temp-until}$ and $\mathscr{C}_{temp-since}$ is denoted as $\mathscr{C}_{temp}$.

The $\mathfrak{C}$ modality expresses a bound on the number of occurrences of a certain event in a given time window; in the encoding, it comes natural to use arithmetical variables as counters of the events. For each subformula of the form $\mathfrak{C}^K_{\bowtie n}(\phi)$, we add an arithmetical variable $|c_\phi|$ to F, constrained with the following formulae:

Position i	$\mathfrak{C}$ modality constraints	Description
0	$|c_\phi|_0 = 0$	initialization
0...H − 1	$[\![\phi]\!]_i \rightarrow (|c_\phi|_{i+1} = (|c_\phi|_i + 1))$	ϕ occurs at i
0...H − 1	$\neg[\![\phi]\!]_i \rightarrow (|c_\phi|_{i+1} = |c_\phi|_i)$	ϕ does not occur at i

(5)

The constraint in the first row initializes the arithmetical variable to zero at time instant 0. The following H constraints (in the second row) force $|c_\phi|$ to increase by 1 at time instant $i + 1$, if ϕ occurs at time instant i. The last H constraints from the third row refer to the opposite situation: when there is no occurrence of the event ϕ at time instant i, the value of $|c_\phi|_{i+1}$ is constrained to have the same value as $|c_\phi|_i$. Let us denote, for a $\mathfrak{C}$ modality that has ϕ as a sub-formula, the conjunction of these constraints as $\mathscr{C}_{c-cons}(\phi)$. Besides $\mathscr{C}_{c-cons}(\phi)$, we add to the encoding, for each $i = 0...H$, the following constraints, denoted as $\mathscr{C}_{c-form}(\phi)$:

$$[\![\mathsf{C}^K_{\bowtie n}(\phi)]\!]_i \leftrightarrow \bigvee_{z=0}^{min\{i,K\}} |c_\phi|_{i+1} - |c_\phi|_{i-z} \bowtie n \wedge |\tau|_i - |\tau|_{i-z-1} > K \wedge |\tau|_i - |\tau|_{i-z} \leq K$$

This formula characterizes each time instant i of the temporal structure in which the $\mathfrak{C}$ modality is true. The disjunction is a case split for each position z in the past with respect to the current position i. Notice that, if $K > i$ we need to consider all previous positions in the temporal structure; otherwise, it is enough to consider K previous time instants, since in the worst case all timestamps can increase by at least one. Each case is a conjunction where sub-formula $|\tau|_i - |\tau|_{i-z-1} > K \wedge |\tau|_i - |\tau|_{i-z} \leq K$ determines the correct position on the left side of the time window, while $|c_\phi|_{i+1} - |c_\phi|_{i-z} \bowtie n$ checks that the $\mathfrak{C}$ modality holds in the considered time window.

As for the $\mathfrak{M}$ modality, for each subformula of the form $\mathfrak{M}_{\bowtie n}^{K,h}(\phi)$, we introduce the same arithmetical variable $|c_\phi|$ and the constraint $\mathscr{C}_{c-cons}(\phi)$ (now denoted $\mathscr{C}_{m-cons}(\phi)$) as for the $\mathfrak{C}$ modality. Additionally, we add arithmetical variables $|p_0|\ldots|p_{\lfloor\frac{K}{h}\rfloor+1}|$ to the set F for each $\mathfrak{M}$ modality sub-formula of Φ. The encoding of the $\mathfrak{M}$ modality depends on the operator $\bowtie$; for example, when the comparison operator is "<" we have the following constraints, denoted $\mathscr{C}_{m-form}(\phi)$:

$$[\![M_{<n}^{K,h}(\phi)]\!]_i \leftrightarrow \bigwedge_{y=0}^{\lfloor\frac{K}{h}\rfloor} \left(\bigvee_{z=0}^{min\{i,h\cdot(y+1)\}} (|p_{y+1}|_i = |c_\phi|_{i+1} - |c_\phi|_{i-z} \wedge |p_{y+1}|_i - |p_y|_i < n\wedge \right.$$
$$\left. |\tau|_i - |\tau|_{i-z-1} > (y+1)\cdot h \wedge |\tau|_i - |\tau|_{i-z} \le (y+1)\cdot h)\right) \wedge |p_0|_i = 0$$

In this formula, in each conjunct y we perform a case split, similar to the case of the $\mathfrak{C}$ modality, but with a different time window: $(y+1)\cdot h$. We assign the result of counting to the variable $|p_{y+1}|$ in each conjunct. Therefore, values $|p_0|_i \ldots |p_{\lfloor\frac{K}{h}\rfloor+1}|_i$ contain the number of occurrences of ϕ in time windows $0, h, 2h, \ldots, \lfloor\frac{K}{h}\rfloor\cdot h, K$ with respect to position i, respectively. With subformula $|p_{y+1}|_i - |p_y|_i < n$, we check that in each observation subinterval with respect to i there is a bounded number of occurrences. The other cases of $\bowtie$ can be defined in a similar way.

The $\mathfrak{D}$ modality expresses a bound on the average distance between the occurrences of a pair of events in a given time window. Since events can occur multiple times in the temporal structure, a pair of events (ϕ, ψ) may have multiple instances. We call a pair of the form $([\![\phi]\!]_i, [\![\psi]\!]_j)$ an instance if there is an occurrence of event ϕ at time instant i and an occurrence of event ψ at time instant j, with $i < j$. We call such instance open at time instant q if $i \le q < j$. Otherwise, the instance is closed at time instant q. The distance of a closed pair instance is $j - i$; for an open pair at time instant q, the distance is $q - i$. A time window defined for a $\mathfrak{D}_{\bowtie n}^K(\phi, \psi)$ (sub-)formula evaluated at time instant q is bounded by the time instants $q + 1$ and $q - K + 1$. It has a left-open (respectively, right-open) pair in position q of a temporal structure, if there is an open instance of (ϕ, ψ) at time instant $q - K + 1$ (respectively, $q + 1$). Depending on whether a $\mathfrak{D}$ modality (sub-)formula contains either (left- and/ or right-) open pairs or none, there are four distinct cases to take into account for the encoding.

For each subformula of the form $\mathfrak{D}_{\bowtie n}^K(\phi, \psi)$, we add to F five arithmetical variables:

- $|g_{\phi,\psi}|$: it assumes value 1 in the time instants following an occurrence of ϕ and is reset to 0 after an occurrence of ψ. It acts as a flag denoting the time instants during which the event pair instance is open.
- $|h_{\phi,\psi}|$: in each time instant, it contains the number of previously seen closed pair instances. It is increased after every occurrence of ψ.
- $|s_{\phi,\psi}|$: At each time instant, its value corresponds to the sum of distances of all previously occurred pair instances. It is increased every time instant when either $|g_{\phi,\psi}|$ is 1 or ϕ holds.
- $|a_{\phi,\psi}|$: it keeps track of the sum of the distances of all previously occurred closed pair instances.
- $|b_{\phi,\psi}|$: it has the values that will be assumed by variable $|s_{\phi,\psi}|$ at the next occurrence of ψ (more details below).

	ϕ	ψ	ϕ	φ	ψ	ϕ	ψ
τ	2	5	9	12	14	17	19
$g_{\phi,\psi}$	0	1	0	1	1	0	1
$h_{\phi,\psi}$	0	0	1	1	1	2	2
$s_{\phi,\psi}$	0	3	3	6	8	8	10
$a_{\phi,\psi}$	0	0	3	3	3	8	8
$b_{\phi,\psi}$	3	3	8	8	8	10	10

Fig. 2. Example of trace for the $\mathfrak{D}$ modality, with the corresponding arithmetical variables used in the encoding

Variables $|a_{\phi,\psi}|$, $|b_{\phi,\psi}|$, and $|h_{\phi,\psi}|$ are directly used in the encoding of the $\mathfrak{D}$ modality (sub-)formulae, while variables $|g_{\phi,\psi}|$ and $|s_{\phi,\psi}|$ are helper variables, used to determine the values of the other variables. Figure 2 shows a portion of a trace and the values assumed by these variables: the uppermost row shows instants where *atoms* ϕ, ψ, and φ hold; the second row shows the value of $|\tau|$ at each time instant; the other rows show the values of the variables at each time instant.

For each $\mathfrak{D}^K_{\bowtie n}(\phi,\psi)$ modality sub-formula we define the set of constraints $\mathscr{C}_{d-cons}(\phi,\psi)$:

Position i	$\mathfrak{D}$ modality constraints	Description
0	$|g_{\phi,\psi}|_0 = 0 \wedge |h_{\phi,\psi}|_0 = 0 \wedge |a_{\phi,\psi}|_0 = 0 \wedge |s_{\phi,\psi}|_0 = 0$	variable initialization
0	$[\![B_{eq}]\!]_0$	$|b_{\phi,\psi}|$ initialization
$0 \dots H-1$	$[\![\phi]\!]_i \to (|g_{\phi,\psi}|_{i+1} = 1 \wedge |s_{\phi,\psi}|_{i+1} = |s_{\phi,\psi}|_i + (|\tau|_{i+1} - |\tau|_i) \wedge$ $|h_{\phi,\psi}|_{i+1} = |h_{\phi,\psi}|_i \wedge |a_{\phi,\psi}|_{i+1} = |a_{\phi,\psi}|_i)$	ϕ occurs at i
$0 \dots H-1$	$[\![\psi]\!]_i \to (|g_{\phi,\psi}|_{i+1} = 0 \wedge |h_{\phi,\psi}|_{i+1} = |h_{\phi,\psi}|_i + 1 \wedge$ $|a_{\phi,\psi}|_{i+1} = |s_{\phi,\psi}|_i \wedge |s_{\phi,\psi}|_{i+1} = |s_{\phi,\psi}|_i \wedge$ $|b_{\phi,\psi}|_i = |s_{\phi,\psi}|_i \wedge [\![B_{eq}]\!]_{i+1})$	ψ occurs at i
$0 \dots H-1$	$\neg[\![\phi]\!]_i \wedge \neg[\![\psi]\!]_i \to (|g_{\phi,\psi}|_{i+1} = |g_{\phi,\psi}|_i \wedge |h_{\phi,\psi}|_{i+1} = |h_{\phi,\psi}|_i \wedge$ $|a_{\phi,\psi}|_{i+1} = |a_{\phi,\psi}|_i \wedge$ $(|g_{\phi,\psi}|_i = 1 \to |s_{\phi,\psi}|_{i+1} =$ $|s_{\phi,\psi}|_i + (|\tau|_{i+1} - |\tau|_i)) \wedge$ $|g_{\phi,\psi}|_i = 0 \to |s_{\phi,\psi}|_{i+1} = |s_{\phi,\psi}|_i))$	neither ϕ nor ψ occurs at i

(6)

The formula in the first row of (6) initializes all variables at time instant 0 except $|b_{\phi,\psi}|$. In the second row we introduce a new predicate $[\![B_{eq}]\!]$; it has the following constraints:

Position i	$[\![B_{eq}]\!]$ predicate constraints	Description
$0 \dots H-1$	$[\![B_{eq}]\!]_i \leftrightarrow [\![\psi]\!]_i \vee ((|b_{\phi,\psi}|_{i+1} = |b_{\phi,\psi}|_i) \wedge [\![B_{eq}]\!]_{i+1})$	propagation of value of $|b_{\phi,\psi}|$
H	$[\![B_{eq}]\!]_H \leftrightarrow \top$	last state constraint

(7)

These constraints force the values of the variables $|b_{\phi,\psi}|_i$ to stay the same in all the consecutive time instants until the first occurrence of ψ or until the end of the trace; the second constraint in (7) deals with traces without occurrences of ψ.

The third constraint in (6) determines the value of variables in the next time instant, upon occurrence of an event ϕ at time instant i. Variable $|g_{\phi,\psi}|_{i+1}$ is set to 1; variable $|s_{\phi,\psi}|_{i+1}$ is incremented by $|\tau|_{i+1} - |\tau|_i$ with respect to value of the variable $|s_{\phi,\psi}|_i$; variables $|h_{\phi,\psi}|_{i+1}$ and $|a_{\phi,\psi}|_{i+1}$ are constrained not to change with respect to value of their counterparts at time instant i. The fourth constraint determines how the variables are updated when an event ψ occurs at time instant i: variable $|g_{\phi,\psi}|_{i+1}$ is set to 0; variables $|b_{\phi,\psi}|_i$, $|a_{\phi,\psi}|_{i+1}$, and $|s_{\phi,\psi}|_{i+1}$ are set to be equal to $|s_{\phi,\psi}|_i$. Moreover, $[\![B_{eq}]\!]_{i+1}$ is constrained to hold, forcing values of $|b_{\phi,\psi}|_j$ to stay the same in all the consecutive time instants $j > i$, until the next occurrence of ψ. The constraints in the fifth row of (6) cover the cases when neither ϕ nor ψ occur at time instant i. In these cases the values of variables $|g_{\phi,\psi}|_{i+1}$, $|h_{\phi,\psi}|_{i+1}$, and $|a_{\phi,\psi}|_{i+1}$ are constrained to have the same value as in their counterparts at i, variable $|b_{\phi,\psi}|_{i+1}$ is unconstrained, while for $|s_{\phi,\psi}|_{i+1}$ we need to distinguish two separate cases. If the last event of the pair is ϕ (denoted by $|g_{\phi,\psi}|_i = 1$), then value of $|s_{\phi,\psi}|_{i+1}$ is $|s_{\phi,\psi}|_i$ incremented by $|\tau|_{i+1} - |\tau|_i$, otherwise it is just $|s_{\phi,\psi}|_i$.

For any sub-formula of the form $D^K_{\bowtie n}\{(\phi,\psi)\}$ evaluated at time instant i, we add to the encoding the constraint $\mathscr{C}_{d-form}(\phi,\psi)$:

$$[\![D^K_{\bowtie n}(\phi,\psi)]\!]_i \leftrightarrow \bigvee_{z=0}^{min\{i,K\}} \left((\texttt{if}^4(|g_{\phi,\psi}|_{i-z} = 1) \text{ then } \left(\frac{|a_{\phi,\psi}|_{i+1} - |b_{\phi,\psi}|_{i-z}}{|h_{\phi,\psi}|_{i+1} - |h_{\phi,\psi}|_{i-z-1}} \bowtie n \right) \right.$$
$$\left. \text{else } \left(\frac{|a_{\phi,\psi}|_{i+1} - |a_{\phi,\psi}|_{i-z}}{|h_{\phi,\psi}|_{i+1} - |h_{\phi,\psi}|_{i-z}} \bowtie n \right) \right)$$
$$\wedge |\tau|_i - |\tau|_{i-z-1} > K \wedge |\tau|_i - |\tau|_{i-z} \leq K)$$

In the above formula, the outer disjunction considers all positions that are z time instants in the past with respect to i (i.e., $i - z$) and checks, for each of them, if they fit into the time window using the $|\tau|_i - |\tau|_{i-z-1} > K \wedge |\tau|_i - |\tau|_{i-z} \leq K$ formula. If one position does, the rest of the formula considers whether there is an *open* (ϕ,ψ) pair instance at that position which is captured by the $|g_{\phi,\psi}|_{i-z} = 1$ formula. In such a case, we compute the total delay between all pair instances within the time window by subtracting variable $|b_{\phi,\psi}|$ from $|a_{\phi,\psi}|$ at the appropriate positions. Since the value of $|b_{\phi,\psi}|$ at each position contains the value of $|s_{\phi,\psi}|$ at the position of the next occurrence of ψ, we effectively ignore the delay of the left-open pair. Otherwise, we use variable $|a_{\phi,\psi}|$, since it contains the delay from the last *closed* pair instance. Fractions in this formula are used for the sake of clarity, however the actual formula conforms to IDL due to the fact that n is a constant and $\frac{A}{B} = n$ can be written as $A = \underbrace{B + B + \ldots + B}_{n \text{ times}}$.

The final QF-EUFIDL formula obtained from the encoding of the input SOLOIST formula Φ is the following conjunction of (possibly empty) formulae, which is supplied to the SMT solver: $[\![\Phi]\!]_0 \wedge \mathscr{C}_{time} \wedge \mathscr{C}_{prop} \wedge \mathscr{C}_{temp} \wedge \mathscr{C}_c \wedge \mathscr{C}_m \wedge \mathscr{C}_d$, where $\mathscr{C}_c \leftrightarrow \mathscr{C}_{c-cons} \wedge \mathscr{C}_{c-form}$, $\mathscr{C}_m \leftrightarrow \mathscr{C}_{m-cons} \wedge \mathscr{C}_{m-form}$ and $\mathscr{C}_d \leftrightarrow \mathscr{C}_{d-cons} \wedge \mathscr{C}_{d-form}$.

---

[4] "$\texttt{if } A \texttt{ then } B \texttt{ else } C$" can be written as $(A \wedge B) \vee (\neg A \wedge C)$.

Complexity. We provide an estimation of the size of the QF-EUFIDL formula corresponding to a temporal or aggregating modality of SOLOIST. Although the syntactic complexity of the translation is already known in the case of standard LTL temporal modalities (e.g., [9]), we still provide a measure for U_I and S_I, since we rely on an ad-hoc encoding.

Let us consider first $\phi U_I \psi$; the case for $\phi S_I \psi$ is similar. At position $0 \le i \le H$, the formula in (3) has size $\mathscr{O}(H - i)^2$. We have then $\sum_{i=0}^{H} \mathscr{O}(H - i)^2 < \mathscr{O}(H^3)$.

Let μ be the maximum constant occurring in the SOLOIST formula and in the trace. One variable $|c_\phi|$ is required for all formulae $\mathfrak{C}_{\bowtie n}^K(\phi)$ with the same argument ϕ. In the worst case, we introduce one variable for each one. At position $0 \le i \le H$, formula $[\![C_{\bowtie n}^K(\phi)]\!]_i$ has size $\mathscr{O}(i)$. We have then $\sum_{i=0}^{H} \mathscr{O}(\log(\mu)i) < \mathscr{O}(\log(\mu)H^2)$. The $\mathfrak{U}$ modality is defined through $\mathfrak{C}$ and, therefore, inherits the same syntactic complexity.

Encoding of formula $\mathfrak{M}_{\bowtie n}^{K,h}(\phi)$ requires one variable $|c_\phi|$. We can reuse variable c_ϕ if in the original SOLOIST formula there are $\mathfrak{M}$ formulae or $\mathfrak{C}$ formulae with the same argument ϕ. Moreover, for each $\mathfrak{M}$ we need also $\lfloor \frac{K}{h} \rfloor + 1$ arithmetical variables $|p_0| \dots |p_{\frac{K}{h}}|$. In the worst case, we introduce $\lfloor \frac{K}{h} \rfloor + 2$ variables for each formula $\mathfrak{M}_{\bowtie n}^{K,h}(\phi)$. At position $0 \le i \le H$, formula $[\![M_{\bowtie n}^{K,h}(\phi)]\!]_i$ has size $\mathscr{O}(\log(\mu)\frac{K}{h} \cdot i)$. We have then $\sum_{i=0}^{H} \mathscr{O}(\log(\mu)\frac{K}{h}i) < \mathscr{O}(\log(\mu)\frac{K}{h}H^2)$.

The set of formulae translating $\mathfrak{D}$ is defined by the conjunction of formulae in (6) and (7) in addition to constraint $\mathscr{C}_{d-form}$. For each formula $\mathfrak{D}$ we introduce five variables related to the pair (ϕ, ψ). The size of formulae in (6) and in (7) is $\mathscr{O}(H)$. Constraint $\mathscr{C}_{d-form}$ requires a more careful analysis; notice that its size depends on the parameter n because of the way formula $\frac{q}{b} < n$ is expanded. At position $0 \le i \le H$, formula $[\![D_{\bowtie n}^K(\phi, \psi)]\!]_i$ has size $\mathscr{O}(\log(\mu)in)$. Then, the complexity for $\mathfrak{D}$ is obtained by $\sum_{i=0}^{H} \mathscr{O}(\log(\mu)in) < \mathscr{O}(\log(\mu)nH^2)$.

The size of the QF-EUFIDL encoding of a SOLOIST formula of length λ is $\mathscr{O}(\lambda \log(\mu)(H^3 + \frac{K}{h}H^2 + nH^2))$, as the number of sub-formulae is polynomial in λ, whereas the size of the encoding of a trace is $\mathscr{O}(\log(\mu)H)$. In the worst-case, $K = H, h = 1$, hence the overall size of the QF-EUFIDL formula encoding a trace checking problem is $\mathscr{O}(\lambda \log(\mu)H^3)$. Finally, we notice that the complexity of trace checking SOLOIST formulae is NP-complete. In fact, since size is polynomial and satisfiability of QF-EUFIDL is NP-complete, then the complexity of solving one instance of the problem is NP; NP-hardness may easily obtained by reducing SAT to trace checking SOLOIST formulae.

4   Evaluation

We implemented the encoding as a Common Lisp plugin for the ZOT verification toolset[5]. Before reporting the results of the evaluation of the implementation of the proposed encoding, we first define a metric to characterize the degree of sparseness for the execution traces to be checked. Let ξ be the number of valid time instants in a trace, i.e., the instants in which at least one event occurs. This number corresponds to the number of positions in a timed word modeling the trace. Let ν denote the number of

---

[5] http://code.google.com/p/zot/

non-valid time instants, i.e., those where no event occurs. Notice that, in timed words, these events are abstracted away by using timestamps. We can use the total length of a trace $\xi + v$ to compute the degree of sparseness as $\varsigma = \frac{\xi}{\xi+v}$.

Scalability. To show how scalable the proposed encoding is with respect to the parameters mentioned in Sect. 3, we synthesized traces using the PLG (Process Log Generator) tool [10]. This tool can generate traces that conform to the business logic of the process given in input, varying the trace length and the number of valid time instants. We used a variant of the *ATMFrontEnd* business process example from the JBoss jBPM distribution; this process provides customers with some operations to interact with their bank account, such as `query-balance`, `withdraw`, and `deposit`. For space reasons we only report the evaluation of checking properties expressed using the $\mathfrak{C}$ and $\mathfrak{D}$ modalities. We considered the two properties P1: "The number of `query-balance` operations performed in the last 10 minutes is less than 10" and P2: "The average response time of the `query-balance` operation is less than n seconds in the last 6 hours", which can be expressed in SOLOIST as $\mathfrak{C}^{600}_{<10}(QB_s)$ and $\mathfrak{D}^{21600}_{<n}(QB_s, QB_e)$, respectively. Notice that we express time in seconds and use events QB_s and QB_e to denote, respectively, the start and the end of operation `query-balance`.

For both modalities we consider as parameter the number of valid time instants ξ, i.e., the length H of the temporal structure; for the $\mathfrak{D}$ modality we also consider the varying bound n. The plots in Fig. 3a show quadratic increase in memory usage and time with respect to the number of valid time instants, as anticipated in Sect. 3. In addition, the plots in Fig. 3b show that parameter n does not affect the computational time and space. Although in the complexity analysis we theoretically determined that the size of the encoding for the $\mathfrak{D}$ modality linearly depends on n, the evaluation showed that in the actual implementation this does not happen, because the SMT decision procedure supports natively the use of multiplication of terms by a constant. This allows us to write a more concise encoding for $\mathfrak{D}$ modality in $\mathcal{O}(H^2)$.

Application to a Realistic Example. We have applied our approach also to a realistic example, a sample service composition called ACME BOT [19], whose monitoring data are available[6] as part of the "S-Cube Use Case Repository". We reconstructed 9796 execution traces, based on the monitoring data of the corresponding service composition instances. On each of these traces, we performed trace checking with respect to two simple properties, one containing the $\mathfrak{C}$ modality, and the other the $\mathfrak{D}$ modality. In the first case, trace checking took on average 0.672s with a standard deviation of 0.035s and used on average 125.7MB of memory with 0.476MB standard deviation; for the checks with the $\mathfrak{D}$ modality, it took on average 0.813s with 0.032s standard deviation and used on average 127.7MB of memory with 0.476MB standard deviation. On average, each trace had 31.5 valid time instants and a total length of 39341.3; the average degree of sparseness was then 0.08%. This example shows that our approach can efficiently check properties of realistic service compositions.

---

[6] http://scube-casestudies.ws.dei.polimi.it/index.php/

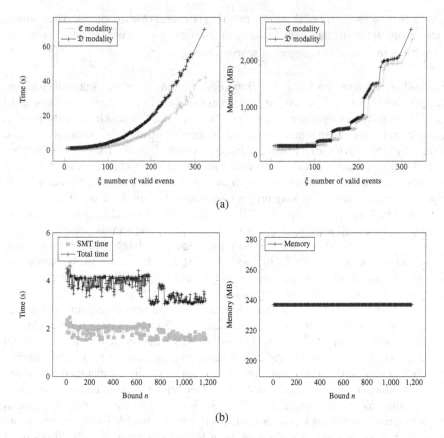

Fig. 3. Scalability of the encoding with respect to: (a) the number of valid time instants ξ in the trace, in the case of the $\mathfrak{C}$ and $\mathfrak{D}$ modalities; (b) bound n, in the case of the $\mathfrak{D}$ modality

Discussion and Trade-Offs. As you can see from Fig. 3a, our approach can support the checking of traces containing up to 300 valid time instants, using up to 2GB of memory. The strength of the approach is that the number of non-valid time instants in the trace does not affect its scalability. In principle, we can deal with traces of arbitrary length, with varying degrees of sparseness, and still use up to 2GB of memory if the trace contains at most 300 valid time instants. The realistic example described above as well as the process log of the BPI challenge mentioned earlier show that execution traces with a limited number of valid time instants and a low degree of sparseness can be very common in enterprise service-based applications. We compared the performance of the approach proposed in this paper with a previous, not-optimized implementation [18] based on CLTLB($\mathscr{D}$); for the evaluation, we varied the degree of sparseness in the traces and their total length $\xi + \nu$. The approach in [18] does not keep track of timing information and therefore has to enumerate both valid and non-valid time instants. Figure 4 shows the results of this comparison, in terms of time and memory usage: the black line shows the scalability of the approach based on CLTLB($\mathscr{D}$) from [18], while the seven gray lines correspond to the QF-EUFIDL-based approach presented in this

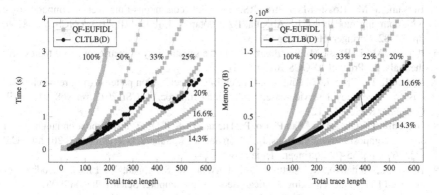

Fig. 4. Tradeoff between the trace checking approach based on CLTLB($\mathscr{D}$) [18] and the one based on the QF-EUFIDL encoding, with respect to the degree of sparseness of the trace

paper, applied to traces with different degrees of sparseness (100%, 50%, 33%, 25%, 20%, 16.6%, and 14.3%, from left to right, respectively). The results show that the approach presented in this paper is more efficient than the one presented in [18] when the degree of sparseness of input traces is less than 25%.

5   Conclusions

We have shown how trace checking for SOLOIST can be reduced to an existential satisfiability problem for the QF-EUFIDL logic, which can be solved with efficient decision procedures using SMT verifiers. We motivate our approach with two case studies and provide complexity analysis as well as practical evaluation. In the future, we plan to collaborate with an industrial partner, to apply our trace checking approach to more examples of realistic execution traces.

Acknowledgments. This work has been supported by the European Community under the IDEAS-ERC grant agreement no. 227977-SMScom and by the National Research Fund, Luxembourg (FNR/P10/03).

References

1. Alur, R., Dill, D.L.: A theory of timed automata. Theoreotical Computer Science 126(2), 183–235 (1994)
2. Basin, D., Klaedtke, F., Marinovic, S., Zălinescu, E.: Monitoring of temporal first-order properties with aggregations. In: Legay, A., Bensalem, S. (eds.) RV 2013. LNCS, vol. 8174, pp. 40–58. Springer, Heidelberg (2013)
3. Bersani, M.M., Frigeri, A., Morzenti, A., Pradella, M., Rossi, M., San Pietro, P.: Bounded reachability for temporal logic over constraint systems. In: Proc. of TIME 2010, pp. 43–50. IEEE Computer Society (2010)
4. Bersani, M.M., Frigeri, A., Rossi, M., San Pietro, P.: Completeness of the bounded satisfiability problem for constraint LTL. In: Delzanno, G., Potapov, I. (eds.) RP 2011. LNCS, vol. 6945, pp. 58–71. Springer, Heidelberg (2011)

5. Bersani, M.M., Rossi, M., Pietro, P.S.: Deciding continuous-time metric temporal logic with counting modalities. In: Abdulla, P.A., Potapov, I. (eds.) RP 2013. LNCS, vol. 8169, pp. 70–82. Springer, Heidelberg (2013)
6. Bersani, M.M., Rossi, M., San Pietro, P.: On the satisfiability of metric temporal logics over the reals. In: Proc. of AVOCS 2013 (2013)
7. Bianculli, D., Ghezzi, C., Pautasso, C., Senti, P.: Specification patterns from research to industry: a case study in service-based applications. In: Proc. of ICSE 2012, pp. 968–976. IEEE Computer Society (2012)
8. Bianculli, D., Ghezzi, C., San Pietro, P.: The tale of SOLOIST: a specification language for service compositions interactions. In: Păsăreanu, C.S., Salaün, G. (eds.) FACS 2012. LNCS, vol. 7684, pp. 55–72. Springer, Heidelberg (2013)
9. Biere, A., Heljanko, K., Junttila, T.A., Latvala, T., Schuppan, V.: Linear encodings of bounded LTL model checking. Logical Methods in Computer Science 2(15) (2006)
10. Burattin, A., Sperduti, A.: PLG: A framework for the generation of business process models and their execution logs. In: Muehlen, M.z., Su, J. (eds.) BPM 2010 Workshops. LNBIP, vol. 66, pp. 214–219. Springer, Heidelberg (2011)
11. Demri, S., D'Souza, D.: An automata-theoretic approach to constraint LTL. Inf. Comput. 205(3), 380–415 (2007)
12. van Dongen, B.: BPI challenge 2012 (2012),
http://dx.doi.org/10.4121/uuid:3926db30-f712-4394-aebc-75976070e91f
13. Dwyer, M.B., Avrunin, G.S., Corbett, J.C.: Property specification patterns for finite-state verification. In: Proc. of FMSP 1998, pp. 7–15. ACM (1998)
14. Felder, M., Morzenti, A.: Validating real-time systems by history-checking TRIO specifications. ACM Trans. Softw. Eng. Methodol. 3(4), 308–339 (1994)
15. Finkbeiner, B., Sankaranarayanan, S., Sipma, H.: Collecting statistics over runtime executions. Form. Method Syst. Des. 27, 253–274 (2005)
16. Kindermann, R., Junttila, T.A., Niemelä, I.: Bounded model checking of an MITL fragment for timed automata. CoRR abs/1304.7209 (2013)
17. Konrad, S., Cheng, B.H.C.: Real-time specification patterns. In: Proc. of ICSE 2005, pp. 372–381. ACM (2005)
18. Krstić, S.: Verification of quantitative properties of service-based applications. Master's thesis, Politecnico di Milano (December 2012)
19. Leitner, P., Hummer, W., Dustdar, S.: A Monitoring Data Set for Evaluating QoS-Aware Service-Based Systems. In: Proc. of PESOS 2012, pp. 67–68 (2012)
20. Mrad, A., Ahmed, S., Hallé, S., Beaudet, É.: BabelTrace: A collection of transducers for trace validation. In: Qadeer, S., Tasiran, S. (eds.) RV 2012. LNCS, vol. 7687, pp. 126–130. Springer, Heidelberg (2013)
21. Nelson, G., Oppen, D.C.: Simplification by cooperating decision procedures. ACM Trans. Program. Lang. Syst. 1(2), 245–257 (1979)
22. Pradella, M., Morzenti, A., San Pietro, P.: The symmetry of the past and of the future: bi-infinite time in the verification of temporal properties. In: Proc. of ESEC-FSE 2007, pp. 312–320. ACM (2007)
23. Pradella, M., Morzenti, A., San Pietro, P.: Bounded satisfiability checking of metric temporal logic specifications. ACM Trans. Softw. 20, 1–20 (2013)
24. Wozna-Szczesniak, B., Zbrzezny, A.: Checking MTL properties of discrete timed automata via bounded model checking. In: CS&P, vol. 1032, pp. 469–477. CEUR-WS.org (2013)

An Online Validator for Provenance: Algorithmic Design, Testing, and API

Luc Moreau, Trung Dong Huynh, and Danius Michaelides

Electronics and Computer Science, University of Southampton

Abstract. Provenance is a record that describes the people, institutions, entities, and activities involved in producing, influencing, or delivering a piece of data or a thing. The W3C Provenance Working group has just published the PROV family of specifications, which include a data model for provenance on the Web. The working group introduces a notion of valid PROV document whose intent is to ensure that a PROV document represents a consistent history of objects and their interactions that is safe to use for the purpose of reasoning and other kinds of analysis. Valid PROV documents satisfy certain definitions, inferences, and constraints, specified in PROV-CONSTRAINTS. This paper discusses the design of ProvValidator, an online service for validating provenance documents according to PROV-CONSTRAINTS. It discusses the algorithmic design of the validator, the complexity of the algorithm, how we demonstrated compliance with the standard, and its REST API.

Keywords: provenance, prov, validation.

1 Introduction

Provenance is a record that describes the people, institutions, entities, and activities involved in producing, influencing, or delivering a piece of data or a thing [1]. (Such a record is encoded in a PROV*document* [2].) The W3C Provenance Working group has just published the PROV family of specifications [3], which include a data model for provenance on the Web (PROV-DM [1]).

PROV comprises a notion of *valid* document [2]. A valid PROV document is one that represents a consistent history of objects and their interactions that is safe to use for the purpose of logical reasoning and other kinds of analysis. Valid PROV documents satisfy certain definitions, inferences, and constraints, specified in PROV-CONSTRAINTS [2]. There are several issues related to PROV-CONSTRAINTS that motivate this work: we discuss them now.

By design, PROV-CONSTRAINTS provides a logic specification of what valid provenance is. This gives implementors the opportunity to design their own implementation, allowing them to meet the requirements set by their applications. To be compliant with PROV-CONSTRAINTS, implementations are expected to produce the same results. In essence, compliance with PROV-CONSTRAINTS is established by observational equivalence with the specification.

S. Gnesi and A. Rensink (Eds.): FASE 2014, LNCS 8411, pp. 291–305, 2014.

PROV-CONSTRAINTS relies on inference rules that lend themselves to implementation by rule-based languages. However, such a paradigm is not an option for some implementors (for instance, having to work with an imperative language or having to control memory management). Furthermore, rule-based specifications do not make explicit the execution order and the type of data structures that are required. Thus, an open research question is the formulation of an algorithm for PROV validation that could be readily adopted by implementors.

In PROV-CONSTRAINTS, not all inferences are necessary for validating documents. Instead, some simply exist because they are considered useful. While this goal helps understand what is meant by provenance, it does not help implementors determine what is essential to implement in a validator.

PROV-CONSTRAINTS does not analyse the complexity of the problem of validity of provenance documents. Understanding this complexity would be useful since provenance documents can become very big, especially those generated by distributed applications with many nodes that run for a very long time.

PROV-CONSTRAINTS is concerned with specifying whether a provenance document is valid. Hence, from this perspective, the outcome of validity checking is a simple yes/no answer. We argue that the validation procedure can also output useful information, which can be exploited by other provenance-processing tools. For instance, the order of events underpinning a provenance document may be useful for Gantt chart plotting applications.

Finally, a question relevant to practitioners is how such validation-checking facility can be accessed. In the context of the Web, exposing such a functionality as a REST service, which can be exploited by browser-based user interfaces or specific applications, would be desirable.

This paper provides answers to these questions, as summarized by its contributions: *(i)* An algorithm to validate provenance; *(ii)* An analysis of its complexity; *(iii)* A REST API for validating provenance graphs, but also accessing validation by-products. Doing so, the paper identifies those essential inferences to save the effort of future validator implementors. Finally, we discuss ProvValidator, an implementation of this algorithm, its exposition as a REST service, and its testing.

Notation Convention. We refrain from copying the text of definitions, inference rules, and constraints of PROV-CONSTRAINTS; instead, we refer to them using the following notations DEF 1, INF 5, CON 50, for definitions, inferences, and constraints respectively. In the electronic version of this paper, they directly link to the corresponding entries in the PROV-CONSTRAINTS specification.

2   A Brief Introduction to PROV

PROV is a family of specifications [3] for representing provenance on the Web. It includes a conceptual data model, PROV-DM [1], which can be mapped and serialized to different technologies. There is an OWL2 ontology for PROV, allowing mapping of PROV to RDF, an XML schema for provenance, and a textual representation for PROV.

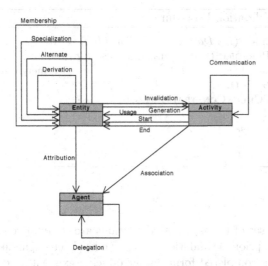

Fig. 1. PROV-DM UML Classes and Associations (simplified view)

Figure 1 summarises PROV-DM [1]. There are three classes: entities (the data or things for which we want to express provenance), activities (representing what happens in systems), and agents (bearing responsibility for things and activities). These three classes can be related with some relations.

1. Derivation view: entities may be derived from others (Derivation).
2. Responsibility view: agents may be responsible for other entities (Attribution), for activities (Association), or for other agents (Delegation).
3. Process view: activities may have used entities (Usage), and vice-versa entities may have been generated by activities (Generation). Furthermore, activities can be informed by other activities (Communication). Activities can be started and ended by entity triggers (Start and End).
4. Alternate and Membership views: entities may have alternates and specializations; entities may be collections with members.

In reality, relations are not necessarily binary, but may involve more instances and may also contain *attributes* such as time information. Table 1 (in Section 3.1) summarizes a textual notation for the model.

3   Validation Algorithm

The overall validation procedure is described in Algorithm 1. It consists of three steps: *(i)* perform the inferences that are relevant to validation;   *(ii)* merge terms;   *(iii)* finally, if successful, check constraints.   We discuss these steps in turn.

Our approach relies on a type system and well-formed terms to deal with illegal situations (many of the so-called impossibility rules in PROV-CONSTRAINTS). First, we present the terms that are accepted by PROV-DM.

Algorithm 1. Validation Procedure

1: **function** VALIDATE($D : Document, T : TypeMap$) $\Rightarrow$ true|fail
2:     $D_1, T_1 \leftarrow$ PERFORMRELEVANTINFERENCES(D, T)
3:     $res \leftarrow$ MERGETERMS(D_1, T_1)   ▷ merge can succeed or fail
4:     **if** $res = D_2, U_2$ **then**
5:         **return** CHECKCONSTRAINTS(D_2, U_2)
6:     **else**
7:         **return** $false$
8:     **end if**
9: **end function**

3.1   Terms

A document is a set of terms, whose definitions are summarized in Table 1. We assume here that, prior to validation, each term has been expanded[1] (**DEF 3**) and has been put in a completed form, by introducing existential identifiers, where appropriate, for optional term identifiers (**DEF 1**) and for optional placeholders (**DEF 4**). For derivation and association, we consider two variants of these terms, when placeholders are unknown; with these terms, **CON 51** is enforced.

There are a few further points worth noting. First, identifiers occur in the first position of terms. Second, entity, activity, and agent statements include a ground identifier specified by the provenance asserter. For relations, their identifiers may be grounded or existential variables (noted with the symbol ν). Finally, time is not a PROV term, but occurs in several of them; hence, its listing in Table 1.

PROV allows for optional extra attributes to be added to terms (see **DEF 2**). For the purpose of validation, they can simply be ignored, except for prov:type, which affects type checking. So, in the interest of space, we have also dropped them from Table 1. We assume a map of types T populated as follows: $v \in T[\alpha]$ whenever the term with identifier α contains an attribute-value pair prov:type=v (this caters for EmptyCollection in **CON 50**). Furthermore, we determine the type of identifiers for entities, activities, and agents, as follows. For every occurrence of variable α^e in a term, $ent \in T[\alpha^e]$; for every α^a occurring in a term, $act \in T[\alpha^a]$; for every α^{ag} occurring in a term, $ag \in T[\alpha^a]$ (cf. **CON 50**).

We also support bundles [1], which are named sets of terms occurring at the top-level of documents. Due to space limitation, we do not discuss them. Bundles are treated by PROV-CONSTRAINTS as mini-documents that can be validated independently.

3.2   Relevant Inferences

PROV-CONSTRAINTS specifies inferences that potentially affect the outcome of the merging (Section 3.3) and constraint checking procedures (Section 3.4), but also inferences that have no impact on the outcome of the validation procedure. Algorithm 2 specifies the former, whereas Section 3.5 discusses the latter.

---

[1] Expansion makes explicit optional arguments ommitted in PROV concise notation.

Algorithm 2. Inference Procedure

1: **function** PERFORMRELEVANTINFERENCES($D : Document, T : Type$)
2: $\quad\quad\quad\quad\quad\quad \Rightarrow Document \times Type$
3: $\quad$ **for** *any* α *such that* $relation(\alpha, \ldots) \in D$ **do** $\qquad\qquad\qquad$ ▷ CON 50
4: $\quad\quad T \leftarrow T[\alpha \rightarrow \{typeof(relation)\} \cup T[\alpha]]$
5: $\quad$ **end for**
6: $\quad$ **for** *any* α^e *such that* $ent(\alpha^e) \in D$ **do** $\qquad\qquad\qquad\qquad$ ▷ INF 7
7: $\quad\quad$ **if** $\nexists \, \alpha^g, \alpha^a, \alpha^t \, gen(\alpha^g, \alpha^e, \alpha^a, \alpha^t) \in D$ **then**
8: $\quad\quad\quad D \leftarrow D \cup \{gen(\nu^g, \alpha^e, \nu^a, \nu^t)\}$ with fresh ν^g, ν^a, ν^t
9: $\quad\quad$ **end if**
10: $\quad\quad$ **if** $\nexists \, \alpha^i, \alpha^a, \alpha^t \, inv(\alpha^i, \alpha^e, \alpha^a, \alpha^t) \in D$ **then**
11: $\quad\quad\quad D \leftarrow D \cup \{inv(\nu^i, \alpha^e, \nu^a, \nu^t)\}$ with fresh ν^i, ν^a, ν^t
12: $\quad\quad$ **end if**
13: $\quad$ **end for**
14: $\quad$ **for** *any* $\alpha^a, \alpha_1^t, \alpha_2^t$ *such that* $act(\alpha^a, \alpha_1^t, \alpha_2^t) \in D$ **do** $\qquad$ ▷ INF 8
15: $\quad\quad$ **if** $\nexists \, \alpha^s, \alpha^e, \alpha_1^a, \alpha^t \, start(\alpha^s, \alpha^a, \alpha^e, \alpha_1^a, \alpha^t) \in D$ **then**
16: $\quad\quad\quad D \leftarrow D \cup \{start(\nu^s, \alpha^a, \nu^e, \nu_1^a, \nu^t)\}$ with fresh $\nu^s, \nu^e, \nu_1^a, \nu^t$
17: $\quad\quad$ **end if**
18: $\quad\quad$ **if** $\nexists \, \alpha^n, \alpha^e, \alpha_1^a, \alpha^t \, end(\alpha^n, \alpha^a, \alpha^e, \alpha_1^a, \alpha^t) \in D$ **then**
19: $\quad\quad\quad D \leftarrow D \cup \{end(\nu^n, \alpha^a, \nu^e, \nu_1^a, \nu^t)\}$ with fresh $\nu^n, \nu^e, \nu_1^a, \nu^t$
20: $\quad\quad$ **end if**
21: $\quad$ **end for**
22: $\quad$ **for** any $\alpha_1^s, \alpha_1^{en}$ such that $\qquad\qquad\qquad\qquad$ **do** $\qquad$ ▷ INF 9,INF 10
$\quad\quad\quad\quad (start(\,\alpha_1^s, \alpha_1^a, \alpha_1^e, \alpha_2^a, \alpha_1^t) \in D$
$\quad\quad\quad\quad or \; end(\alpha_1^{en}, \alpha_1^a, \alpha_1^e, \alpha_2^a, \alpha_1^t), \in D)$
$\quad\quad\quad\quad and \; \nexists \alpha^g, \alpha^t, gen(\alpha^g, \alpha_1^e, \alpha_2^a, \alpha^t) \in D$
23: $\quad\quad T \leftarrow T[\nu^g \rightarrow \{gen\}]; D \leftarrow D \cup \{gen(\nu^g, \alpha_1^e, \alpha_2^a, \nu^t)\}$ with fresh ν^g, ν^t
24: $\quad$ **end for**
25: $\quad$ **for** any α^d such that $der(\alpha^d, \alpha_1^e, \alpha_2^e, \alpha^a, \alpha^g, \alpha^u) \in D$ **do** $\qquad$ ▷ INF 11
26: $\quad\quad D \leftarrow D \cup \{gen(\alpha^g, \alpha_1^e, \alpha^a, \nu_1^t), use(\alpha^u, \alpha^a, \alpha_2^e, \nu_2^t)\}$ with fresh ν_1^t, ν_2^t
27: $\quad$ **end for**
28: $\quad$ **for** any α^{del} such that $del(\alpha^{del}, \alpha_1^{ag}, \alpha_2^{ag}, \alpha^a) \in D$ **do** $\qquad$ ▷ INF 14
29: $\quad\quad$ **if** $assoc(\alpha_1^{as}, \alpha^a, \alpha_1^{ag}, \alpha_1^e), assoc(\alpha_2^{as}, \alpha^a, \alpha_2^{ag}, \alpha_2^e) \notin D$ **then**
$\quad\quad\quad\quad for \; some \; \alpha_{1,2}^{as}, \alpha_{1,2}^e$
30: $\quad\quad\quad D \leftarrow D \cup \{assoc(\nu_1^{as}, \alpha^a, \alpha_1^{ag}, \nu_1^e), assoc(\nu_2^{as}, \alpha^a, \alpha_2^{ag}, \nu_2^e)\}$
31: $\quad\quad\quad\quad$ with fresh $\nu_1^{as}, \nu_1^e, \nu_2^{as}, \nu_2^e$
32: $\quad\quad\quad T \leftarrow T[\nu_1^e \rightarrow \{ent\}][\nu_2^e \rightarrow \{ent\}][\nu_1^{as} \rightarrow \{assoc\}][\nu_2^{as} \rightarrow \{assoc\}]$
33: $\quad\quad$ **end if**
34: $\quad$ **end for**
35: $\quad$ **for** any $\alpha_1^e, \alpha_2^e, \alpha_3^e$ such that $spec(\alpha_1^e, \alpha_2^e), spec(\alpha_2^e, \alpha_3^e) \in D$ **do** $\quad$ ▷ INF 19
36: $\quad\quad D \leftarrow D \cup \{spec(\alpha_1^e, \alpha_3^e)\}$
37: $\quad$ **end for**
38: $\quad$ **for** any α_1^e, α_2^e such that $spec(\alpha_1^e, \alpha_2^e), ent(\alpha_2^e) \in D$ **do** $\qquad$ ▷ INF 21
39: $\quad\quad D \leftarrow D \cup \{ent(\alpha_1^e)\}; T \leftarrow T[\alpha_1^e \rightarrow T[\alpha_1^e] \cup T[\alpha_2^e]]$
40: $\quad$ **end for**
41: $\quad$ **for** any α_1^e, α_2^e such that $mem(\alpha_1^e, \alpha_2^e) \in D$ **do**
42: $\quad\quad T \leftarrow T[\alpha_1^e \rightarrow T[\alpha_1^e] \cup \{nonEmptyCollection\}]$
43: $\quad$ **end for**
44: $\quad$ **return** D, T
45: **end function**

Table 1. Terms, Term Types, and Variable Types

identifier type	ground identifier	existential variable	pattern variable	term	type
Entity	id^e	ν^e	α^e	$ent(id^e)$	ent
Activity	id^a	ν^a	α^a	$act(id^a)$	act
Agent	id^{ag}	ν^{ag}	α^{ag}	$ag(id^{ag})$	ag
Generation	id^g	ν^g	α^g	$gen(\alpha^g, id^e, \alpha^a, \alpha^t)$	gen
Usage	id^u	ν^u	α^u	$use(\alpha^u, id^e, \alpha^a, \alpha^t)$	use
Invalidation	id^i	ν^i	α^i	$inv(\alpha^g, id^e, \alpha^a, \alpha^t)$	inv
Start	id^s	ν^s	α^s	$start(\alpha^s, id^a, \alpha^e, \alpha^a, \alpha^t)$	start
End	id^n	ν^n	α^n	$end(\alpha^e, id^a, \alpha^e, \alpha^a, \alpha^t)$	end
Derivation	id^d	ν^d	α^d	$der(\alpha^d, id^e, id^e, \alpha^a, \alpha^g, \alpha^u)$	der
				$der_\perp(\alpha^d, id^e, id^e)$	der $_\perp$
Association	id^{as}	ν^{as}	α^{as}	$assoc_\perp(\alpha^{as}, id^a, \alpha^{ag})$	assoc $_\perp$
				$assoc(\alpha^{as}, id^a, \alpha^{ag}, \alpha^e)$	assoc
Delegation	id^d	ν^d	α^d	$del(\alpha^d, id^{ag}, id^{ag}, \alpha^a)$	del
Attribution	id^{at}	ν^{at}	α^{at}	$attr(\alpha^{at}, id^e, id^{ag})$	attr
Communication	id^c	ν^c	α^c	$comm(\alpha^c, id^a, id^e)$	comm
Influence	id^{inf}	ν^{inf}	α^{inf}	$infl(\alpha^{inf}, id, id)$	infl
Specialization				$spec(id^e, id^e)$	spec
Alternate				$alt(id^e, id^e)$	alt
Membership				$mem(id^e, id^e)$	mem
time	t	ν^t	α^t		

In Algorithm 2, lines 3–5, 23, 32, 39, and 42 update type information. Lines 6–21 ensure that all events relevant to the graph are made explicit: each entity is accompanied by generation and invalidation events, and each activity accompanied by start and end events. INF 9 and INF 10 (lines 22–24) ensure the presence of a generation event *gen* for every trigger α_1^e in *start* and *end* events. INF 11 (lines 25–27) links α^g, α^u in a derivation event *der* to corresponding generation and usage events, gen, use. INF 14 ensures that a delegation's activity is associated with both its agents (lines 28–34). INF 19 (lines 35–37) computes the transitive closure of specialization *spec*. INF 21 (lines 38–40) propagates types through specializations. Lines 41–43 infer the type *nonEmptyCollection* for any collection that has members. This type is introduced by this algorithm to enforce CON 56 by means of the type system (see Section 3.4).

These inferences are applied till saturation. The algorithm's termination can be explained as follows.

- Lines 6–21 process a finite set of $ent(\alpha^e), act(\alpha^a)$ in a finite document D.
- Lines 22–24 process a finite set of start/end events.
- Lines 25–27 process a finite set of der events.
- Lines 28–34 process a finite set of del events.
- Lines 35–37 compute a transitive closure over a finite set of spec relations.
- Lines 38–40 process a finite set of spec tuples.
- Lines 41–43 process a finite set of mem relations.

So, the total number of iterations is bounded. We also note that at no point in these inferences, we infer terms from which previous inferences could have derived further terms.

3.3 Term Merging

MERGETERMS (see Algorithm 3) ensures that events that must satisfy a uniqueness constraint are merged (lines 4–28); to this end, merging requires unification [4]. If successful, the resulting document is in a "quasi-normal form". Such a quasi-normal form is essentially equivalent to PROV-CONSTRAINTS normal form, except for some inferences that have not been carried out (see Section 3.5).

Algorithm 3. Term Merging Procedure

1: **function** MERGETERMS($D : Document, T : TypeMap$)
2:                   $\Rightarrow Document \times UObject \mid$ fail
3:     $U \leftarrow \langle \emptyset, T \rangle$
4:     **repeat**
5:         $U_p \leftarrow U$
6:         **if** $relation(\alpha, \alpha_{1,1}, \alpha_{1,2}, \ldots), relation(\alpha, \alpha_{2,1}, \alpha_{2,2}, \ldots) \in D$ **then**
7:             $U \leftarrow unify^*(\{\alpha_{1,1} = \alpha_{2,1}, \alpha_{1,2} = \alpha_{2,2}, \ldots\}, U)$ ▷ CON 22, CON 23
8:         **end if**
9:         **if** $gen(\alpha_1^g, \alpha^e, \alpha_1^a, \alpha_1^t), gen(\alpha_2^g, \alpha^e, \alpha_2^a, \alpha_2^t) \in D$ **then**   ▷ CON 24
10:             $U \leftarrow unify^*(\{\alpha_1^g = \alpha_2^g, \alpha_1^a = \alpha_2^a, \alpha_1^t = \alpha_2^t\}, U)$
11:         **end if**
12:         **if** $inv(\alpha_1^i, \alpha^e, \alpha_1^a, \alpha_1^t), inv(\alpha_2^i, \alpha^e, \alpha_2^a, \alpha_2^t) \in D$ **then**   ▷ CON 25
13:             $U \leftarrow unify^*(\{\alpha_1^i = \alpha_2^i, \alpha_1^a = \alpha_2^a, \alpha_1^t = \alpha_2^t\}, U)$
14:         **end if**
15:         **if** $start(\alpha_1^s, \alpha_1^a, \alpha_1^i, \alpha_2^a, \alpha_1^t), start(\alpha_2^s, \alpha_1^a, \alpha_2^i, \alpha_2^a, \alpha_2^t) \in D$ **then**   ▷ CON 26
16:             $U \leftarrow unify^*(\{\alpha_1^s = \alpha_2^s, \alpha_1^i = \alpha_2^i, \alpha_1^t = \alpha_2^t\}, U)$
17:         **end if**
18:         **if** $end(\alpha_1^n, \alpha_1^a, \alpha_1^i, \alpha_2^a, \alpha_1^t), end(\alpha_2^n, \alpha_1^a, \alpha_2^i, \alpha_2^a, \alpha_2^t) \in D$ **then**   ▷ CON 27
19:             $U \leftarrow unify^*(\{\alpha_1^n = \alpha_2^n, \alpha_1^i = \alpha_2^i, \alpha_1^t = \alpha_2^t\}, U)$
20:         **end if**
21:         **if** $start(\alpha_1^s, id_1^a, \alpha_1^i, \alpha_2^a, \alpha_1^t), act(id_1^a, \alpha_2^t, \alpha_3^t) \in D$ **then**   ▷ CON 28
22:             $U \leftarrow unify^*(\{\alpha_1^t = \alpha_2^t\}, U)$
23:         **end if**
24:         **if** $end(\alpha_1^s, id_1^a, \alpha_1^e, \alpha_2^a, \alpha_1^t), act(id_1^a, \alpha_2^t, \alpha_3^t) \in D$ **then**   ▷ CON 29
25:             $U \leftarrow unify^*(\{\alpha_1^t = \alpha_3^t\}, U)$
26:         **end if**
27:         $D \leftarrow applySubstitution(U, D)$
28:     **until** $U = U_p$ or $U =$ fail
29:     **if** $U =$ fail **then**
30:         **return** fail
31:     **else**
32:         **return** D, U
33:     **end if**
34: **end function**

The algorithm's termination can be explained as follows. Lines 4–28 can only generate a finite number of different bindings $\alpha_1 = \alpha_2$, since α_1, α_2 have to occur in a finite document D, and no new variable is generated by this algorithm. So, the number of iterations is bounded.

Term merging relies on unification, where the existential variables are considered as logical variables; for the purpose of validation of provenance terms, we require full unification [4], except for the fact that variables only occur at the top-level of PROV terms and cannot be nested in expressions. In Algorithm 4, the meaning of $U \in UObject$ is now explicit: it pairs up bindings B and a type map T.

3.4   Constraint Checking

Algorithm 5 is concerned with checking the applicable constraints. First, in lines 4–5, reflexive cases of specialization are rejected. Second, leveraging all the type inferences performed in previous steps, lines 6–10 detect type impossibility cases. They are all encoded in Table 2, where the presence of a cross in cell $conflict(\tau_1, \tau_2)$ indicates that τ_1 and τ_2 are conflicting types to which no variable is allowed to be simultaneously assigned. Finally, lines 11–14 detect violations of ordering constraints.

PROV-CONSTRAINTS defines an order between events, as opposed to an order between time instants. Thus, Ordering constraints checking relies on a two-dimensional matrix $order$ indicating whether two events, identified by α_1 and α_2, are ordered by a "strictly precede" ($order[\alpha_1, \alpha_2] = 2$) or by a "precede" ($order[\alpha_1, \alpha_2] = 1$) relation, or unordered ($order[\alpha_1, \alpha_2] = 0$). The table $order$ is initialized with value 0. The following indicates how the $order$ table is assigned values, according to PROV-CONSTRAINTS.

Constraint	Ordering Relation
CON 30, CON 31, CON 32, CON 33, CON 34, CON 35, CON 36, CON 37, CON 38, CON 39, CON 40, CON 41, CON 43, CON 44, CON 45, CON 46, CON 47, CON 48, CON 49	$order[\alpha_1, \alpha_2] = 1$
CON 42	$order[\alpha_1, \alpha_2] = 2$

Next, the transitive closure for the ordering relations is computed by a variant of Floyd-Warshall algorithm [5], using the rule below.

$$if\ order[\alpha_1, \alpha_2] = x,\ for\ some\ x > 0$$
$$and\ order[\alpha_2, \alpha_3] = y,\ for\ some\ y > 0$$
$$then\ order[\alpha_1, \alpha_3] \leftarrow \max(order[\alpha_1, \alpha_3], x, y)$$

This rule ensures that a strict precedence between two events is also recorded between sequence of events involving these two. The algorithm is further adapted to work on a sparse matrix representation suitable for provenance graphs.

3.5   Validation-Neutral Inferences

It is safe to ignore some inference rules, referred to as validation-neutral (VN) inferences. VN inferences are such that, for any document D, MERGETERMS

Algorithm 4. Unification Procedure

1: **function** UNIFY$^*(\{\alpha^x = \alpha^y\} \cup A, U)$
2:     **return** UNIFY$^*(A, \text{UNIFY}(\alpha^x, \alpha^y, U))$
3: **end function**
4: **function** UNIFY$^*(\emptyset, U)$
5:     **return** U
6: **end function**
7: **function** UNIFY(α^x, α^y, U)
8:     **if** $U = $ fail **then return** fail
9:     **end if**
10:    **if** $\alpha^x = \alpha^y$ **then return** U
11:    **end if**
12:    **if** α^x is an existential variable ν^x **then**
13:        **return** $unifyVar(\nu^x, \alpha^y, U)$
14:    **end if**
15:    **if** α^y is an existential variable ν^y **then**
16:        **return** $unifyVar(\nu^y, \alpha^x, U)$
17:    **else**
18:        **return** fail   ▷ Two distinct ground value
19:    **end if**
20: **end function**
21: **function** UNIFYVAR$(\nu, \alpha^y, U))$
22:    **if** $\nu = \alpha^y$ **then return** U
23:    **end if**
24:    **if** $bound(\nu, U)$ **then**
25:        **return** UNIFYVAR$(lookup(\nu, U), \alpha^y, U)$
26:    **end if**
27:    **if** α^y is a variable ν^y and $bound(\nu^y, U)$ **then**
28:        **return** UNIFYVAR$(\nu, lookup(\nu^y, U), U)$
29:    **else**
30:        **return** EXTEND(ν, α^y, U) ▷ α^y is an unbound variable or a ground value
31:    **end if**
32: **end function**
33: **function** EXTEND(ν, α^y, U)
34:    $\langle B, T \rangle \leftarrow U$
35:    $B' \leftarrow B[\nu \rightarrow \alpha^y]$
36:    **if** α^y is a variable ν^y **then**
37:        $T' \leftarrow T[\nu \rightarrow T(\nu) \cup T(\nu^y)][\nu^y \rightarrow T(\nu) \cup T(\nu^y)]$
38:    **else**
39:        $T' \leftarrow T$
40:    **end if**
41:    **return** $\langle B', T' \rangle$
42: **end function**

Algorithm 5. Checking Constraints Procedure

1: **function** CHECKCONSTRAINTS($D : Document, U : UObject$)
2:     $\Rightarrow$ true|fail
3:     $B, T \leftarrow U$
4:     **if** $spec(\alpha^e, \alpha^e) \in D$ **then return** fail   ▷ CON 52
5:     **end if**
6:     **if** $\tau_1, \tau_2 \in T[\alpha]$ for some α in D **then**   ▷ CON 53, CON 54, CON 55, CON 56
7:         **if** $conflict(\tau_1, \tau_2)$ **then**
8:             **return** fail
9:         **end if**
10:     **end if**
11:     $order \leftarrow inferOrderingRelation(D)$
12:     $order \leftarrow transitiveClosure(order)$
13:     **if** $order[\alpha, \alpha] = 2$ for some α **then return** fail
14:     **end if**
15:     **return** true
16: **end function**

---

succeeds for D if and only if MERGETERMS succeeds for the document obtained by application of VN-inferences to D. Furthermore, application of VN-inferences do not entail ordering constraints that cannot be found otherwise. Below, we list the VN-inferences, and why they can be ignored.

INF 5: the new Generation and Usage events for a new entity always satisfy all ordering constraints.

INF 6: ordering constraints CON 35 can be inferred from CON 33, CON 34, and by transitivity of the ordering relation.

INF 13: the ordering constraints related to Attribution (CON 48) imply the ordering constraints related to Association (CON 47).

INF 15: can be ignored since there is no ordering constraint on Influence.

Likewise, INF 12, INF 16, INF 17, INF 18, INF 20 can be ignored since there is no ordering constraints on Alternate.

4   Complexity Analysis

In this section, we establish that the validation process is polynomial. Specifically, VALIDATE is $O(N^3)$, where N is the size of document D. To establish this result, we analyze the complexity of the various steps of the algorithm. We use the superscripts of Figure 1 to denote the number of terms of that type. For instance, we write $f = O(e)$ to say that f grows asymptotically no faster than the number of entities e (itself bounded by N).

PERFORMRELEVANTINFERENCES is $O(N^3)$ (see Algorithm 2).

Lines 3–5 $O(N)$ by iterating over all elements and relations;
Lines 6–21 $O(e) + O(a) = O(N)$ by iterating over entities and activities;
Lines 22–24 $O(s) + O(en) = O(N)$ by iterating over all starts and ends;
Lines 25–27 $O(d) = O(N)$ by iterating over all derivations;

Table 2. Conflicting Types $conflict(\tau_1, \tau_2)$

	entity	activity	agent	generation	usage	communication	start	end	invalidation	derivation	derivation$_\perp$	revision	quotation	primarySource	attribution	association	association$_\perp$	delegation	influence	bundle	collection	emptyCollection	person	organization	softwareAgent	nonEmptyCollection
entity		X		X	X	X	X	X	X	X	X	X	X	X	X	X	X	X	X							
activity	X			X	X	X	X	X	X	X	X	X	X	X	X	X	X	X	X	X	X	X				X
agent				X	X	X	X	X	X	X	X	X	X	X	X	X	X	X	X	X	X	X				
generation	X	X	X		X	X	X	X	X	X	X	X	X	X	X	X	X	X		X	X	X	X	X	X	X
usage	X	X	X	X		X	X	X	X	X	X	X	X	X	X	X	X	X		X	X	X	X	X	X	X
communication	X	X	X	X	X		X	X	X	X	X	X	X	X	X	X	X	X		X	X	X	X	X	X	X
start	X	X	X	X	X	X		X	X	X	X	X	X	X	X	X	X	X		X	X	X	X	X	X	X
end	X	X	X	X	X	X	X		X	X	X	X	X	X	X	X	X	X		X	X	X	X	X	X	X
invalidation	X	X	X	X	X	X	X	X		X	X	X	X	X	X	X	X	X		X	X	X	X	X	X	X
derivation	X	X	X	X	X	X	X	X	X		X				X	X	X	X		X	X	X	X	X	X	X
derivation$_\perp$	X	X	X	X	X	X	X	X	X	X					X	X	X	X		X	X	X	X	X	X	X
revision	X	X	X	X	X	X	X	X							X	X	X	X		X	X	X	X	X	X	X
quotation	X	X	X	X	X	X	X	X							X	X	X	X		X	X	X	X	X	X	X
primarySource	X	X	X	X	X	X	X	X							X	X	X	X		X	X	X	X	X	X	X
attribution	X	X	X	X	X	X	X	X	X	X	X	X	X			X	X	X		X	X	X	X	X	X	X
association	X	X	X	X	X	X	X	X	X	X	X	X	X	X			X	X		X	X	X	X	X	X	X
association$_\perp$	X	X	X	X	X	X	X	X	X	X	X	X	X	X	X			X		X	X	X	X	X	X	X
delegation	X	X	X	X	X	X	X	X	X	X	X	X	X	X	X	X				X	X	X	X	X	X	X
influence	X	X	X																	X	X	X	X	X	X	X
bundle		X		X	X	X	X	X	X	X	X	X	X	X	X	X	X	X	X							
collection		X		X	X	X	X	X	X	X	X	X	X	X	X	X	X	X	X							
emptyCollection		X		X	X	X	X	X	X	X	X	X	X	X	X	X	X	X	X							X
person				X	X	X	X	X	X	X	X	X	X	X	X	X	X	X	X							
organization				X	X	X	X	X	X	X	X	X	X	X	X	X	X	X	X							
softwareAgent				X	X	X	X	X	X	X	X	X	X	X	X	X	X	X	X							
nonEmptyCollection		X		X	X	X	X	X	X	X	X	X	X	X	X	X	X	X	X			X				

Lines 28–34 $O(del) = O(N)$ by iterating over all delegations;

Lines 35–37 $O(spec^3) = O(N^3)$ by computing a transitive closure over the specialization edges;

Lines 38–40 $O(spec^2) = O(N^2)$ by iterating over the transitive closure of specialization edges;

Lines 41–43 $O(mem) = O(N)$ by iterating over membership edges.

Specialization-related inferences aside, each inference adds 2 terms at most to the document; with $O(N)$ inferences, the resulting document remains $O(N)$. In the worst case, a transitive closure over specialization can result in a quadratic number of terms. In practice, we observe that specialization is relatively infrequently used, and that specializations do not form long chains[2]. So, assuming[3] that $spec \ll N$, it is reasonable to conclude that the *average* inferred document is $O(N)$.

---

[2] It is in fact revisions of entities that potentially create long derivation chains, each entity in the chain being a specialization of one general entity.

[3] This does not hold for the corner case consisting of a document of N specializations.

The complexity of UNIFY is bounded by the number of bindings (see Algorithm 4).

Lines 21–32 $O(|U|)$: worst case is proportional to the number of bindings;
Lines 33–42 $O(1)$: constant time operation.

MERGETERMS is $O(N^2)$ (see Algorithm 3). Worst case binding size is when all variables are to be unified; binding size is proportional to document size.

Lines 6–8 $O(edges \times N)$: worst case scenario, all edges have the same identifier and need to be merged;
Lines 9–11 $O(g \times N)$: worst case scenario, all generation edges have the same entity identifier and need to be merged;
Lines 12–14 $O(i \times N)$: similar worst case scenario for invalidations;
Lines 15–17 $O(s \times N)$: similar worst case scenario for starts;
Lines 18–20 $O(en \times N)$: similar worst case scenario for ends;
Lines 21–23 $O(max(s,a) \times N)$: similar worst case scenario for starts or activities;
Lines 24–26 $O(max(en,a) \times N)$: similar worst case scenario for ends or activities;
Line 27 $O(N^2)$ since *applySubstitution* applies $O(N)$ substitutions, on average, each costing $O(N)$, on average.

The cost of checking constraints is $O(N^3)$ (see Algorithm 5). Let γ be the number of different types.

Lines 4–5 checking this impossibility constraint is $O(spec)$;
Lines 6–10 identifying conflicting pairs of types for each statement is $O(\gamma \times \gamma \times N) = O(N)$;
Lines 11–14 The size of *order* is $O(N^2)$, the number of ordering constraints directly inferred is $O(N)$, and the transitive closure computation is $O(N^3)$.

5 Testing and Establishing Compliance with PR

ProvValidator is a Java-based implementation of the algorithm presented in this paper. In order to make sure ProvValidator covers all the specified constraints, we collated a test suite containing 168 unit test cases for specific constraints.[4]

A test case here is a provenance document that is expected to pass or fail a validity check. Hence, the result from validating a test case can be either PASS for a valid provenance document or FAIL for an invalid one. Out of 168 test cases, there are 101 PASS cases and 67 FAIL cases, covering all constraints in the PROV-CONSTRAINTS specification (excluding the inferences). The test suite was reviewed by the W3C Provenance working group and was adopted by the group as the way to establish a validator implementation's compliance with PROV-CONSTRAINTS.

As shown in the PROV implementation report [6], ProvValidator fully covers the PROV-CONSTRAINTS specification by passing all the specified test cases.

---

[4] The full test suite is available at
https://dvcs.w3.org/hg/prov/raw-file/default/testcases/process.html,
which also summarizes the coverage of various constraints by its test cases.

6   Validator API

ProvValidator is deployed as a Web service accessible from http://provenance.ecs.soton.ac.uk/. This section discusses how the validation algorithm was exposed by means of a REST API.

In designing an API to expose the validator functionality, we wanted to tackle a number of requirements. First, the API should be easy to use and accessible on the Web. Second, we would be providing a web-based front-end but also expect other tools to interact with the facility. Third, the validation-checking process generates a number of by-products (e.g., ordering matrix, quasi-normal form) that may be of use to other tools, and therefore need to be exposed. Thus, we chose to expose the API as a RESTful web service. In such services, the API's focus is on exposing information as resources, how the information is represented, and the use of the verbs of the HTTP protocol to interact with the service [7].

The primary input to the validation process is a document containing PROV statements. The validator supports a variety of representations of PROV: PROV-N, PROV-XML, various formats of RDF, PROV-JSON. Documents are submitted to the service via the POST HTTP verb to the URL: /documents/ . The body of the POST request is the PROV document and the Content-type HTTP header is used to indicate which representation is being used. In addition, to facilitate easy integration with web-pages, posting of standard HTML form data is also supported; here provenance documents can be submitted inline, by a URL or using the HTML form file upload mechanism. If the document is syntactically correct, a new resource for the document is created, with a URL following the schema /documents/{id} where {id} is an identifier. This resource represents the provenance document loaded by the service. In a hierarchical fashion, we further expose a number of other resources that are generated by the validation process (see Table 3).

Our API makes use of content negotiation in situations where there are multiple representations of an information resource [8]; then, we issue HTTP 303 See Other responses to redirect the client to the correct URL for the representation they requested. For example, a client's request for /documents/{id} with an Accept: text/provenance-notation header is redirected to /documents/{id}.provn.

Table 3. Resources in the REST API. We use ∗ to indicate a resource that supports content negotiation.

∗ /documents/	all the provenance documents
∗ /documents/{id}	a provenance document
∗ /documents/{id}/validation/report	a report generated by VALIDATE
/documents/{id}/validation/report/{part}	a section of the validation report
∗ /documents/{id}/validation/matrix	the *order* matrix
∗ /documents/{id}/validation/normalForm	the quasi-normal form

The validation report is a document in XML format that indicates whether a PROV document validated; if not, it also lists problematic statements to help users identify and fix issues. The quasi-normal form and the *order* matrix are the two by-products of the validation process that are made available.

7   Related Work

Two other validators for PROV have been publicly reported in [6]. Paul Groth's prov-check[5], and James Cheney and Stephen Cresswell's checker.pl[6]. The first is based on SPARQL queries, whereas the second is Prolog based. SPARQL queries lend themselves to the implementation of rules, by means of insert statement, however, it is challenging to implement merging of terms with SPARQL only. On the other hand, Prolog comes with rules and unification and therefore handles easily term merging. While their source code is publicly available, it is not directly integrated in a software release that is readily installable. There is also a commercial implementation which reportedly[7] implements aspects of provenance validation using some extensions to OWL-based reasoning.

The PROV-CONSTRAINTS specification was designed with a view to deploying services on the Web supporting this PROV document validation. Several validators exist for other Web technologies. The W3C validator[8] checks the markup validity of Web documents in HTML, XHTML, SMIL, MathML. W3C Jigsaw[9] is a CSS validation service. The Manchester Validator [10] validates OWL ontologies. Finally, W3C also hosts an RDFa validator[11].

The PROV-CONSTRAINTS specification builds upon [9] providing a semantics for OPM [10], a precursor to and subset of PROV.

8   Conclusion

In this paper, we have presented an algorithm for provenance validation. It relies on a minimum set of inferences that have to be performed prior to validation, and on type checking to detect most impossible situations. We expose the algorithm functionality, and validation by-products such as the ordering matrix and quasi-normal form of a document through a REST API.

In this paper, we have also investigated the complexity of the validation process. Inferences are established to be linear in the size of the document to validate. Merging terms is quadratic in its size. This is really a worst case situation: it is indeed possible to generate provenance documents that do not require any

---

[5] Prov-check: https://github.com/pgroth/prov-check

[6] Checker: https://github.com/jamescheney/prov-constraints

[7] http://semtechbizsf2013.semanticweb.com/
sessionPop.cfm?confid=70&proposalid=5118

[8] http://validator.w3.org/

[9] http://jigsaw.w3.org/css-validator/

[10] http://owl.cs.manchester.ac.uk/validator/

[11] http://www.w3.org/2012/pyRdfa/Validator.html

merging of terms. Finally, checking ordering constraints is cubic in the document size, due to the computing of a transitive closure of some precedence relation; however, it has been shown that it can be implemented efficiently.

Future work will investigate functionality that leverages the validation by-products, including editors of valid provenance and visualization of (in)valid provenance; the presented framework could also be extended with domain specific constraints capable of checking provenance even further.

Acknowledgements. Thanks to the Provenance Working Group members; the co-authors of PROV-CONSTRAINTS, James Cheney, Paolo Missier, Tom De Nies; other implementors of PROV-CONSTRAINTS Paul Groth, James Cheney, and Stephen Cresswell. This work is funded in part by the EPSRC SOCIAM (EP/J017728/1) and ORCHID Projects (EP/I011587/1), the FP7 SmartSociety Project (600854), and the ESRC estat2 (ES/K007246/1).

References

1. Moreau, L., Missier, P., Belhajjame, K., B'Far, R., Cheney, J., Coppens, S., Cresswell, S., Gil, Y., Groth, P., Klyne, G., Lebo, T., McCusker, J., Miles, S., Myers, J., Sahoo, S., Tilmes, C. (eds.): PROV-DM: The PROV Data Model. W3C Recommendation REC-prov-dm-20130430, World Wide Web Consortium (October 2013)
2. Cheney, J., Missier, P., Moreau, L., Nies, T.D. (eds.): Constraints of the PROV Data Model. W3C Recommendation REC-prov-constraints-20130430, World Wide Web Consortium (October 2013)
3. Groth, P., Moreau, L. (eds.): PROV-Overview. An Overview of the PROV Family of Documents. W3C Working Group Note NOTE-prov-overview-20130430, World Wide Web Consortium (April 2013)
4. Norvig, P.: Correcting a widespread error in unification algorithms. Softw. Pract. Exper. 21(2), 231–233 (1991)
5. Cormen, T.H., Stein, C., Rivest, R.L., Leiserson, C.E.: Introduction to Algorithms, 2nd edn. McGraw-Hill Higher Education (2001)
6. Huynh, T.D., Groth, P., Zednik, S. (eds.): PROV Implementation Report. W3C Working Group Note NOTE-prov-implementations-20130430, World Wide Web Consortium (April 2013)
7. Fielding, R., Gettys, J., Mogul, J., Frystyk, H., Berners-Lee, T.: Hypertext transfer protocol – http/1.1. Rfc2068, World Wide Web Consortium (January 1997), http://www.w3.org/Protocols/Specs.html
8. Jacobs, I., Walsh, N.: Architecture of the world wide web, volume one. Technical report, World Wide Web Consortium (2004)
9. Kwasnikowska, N., Moreau, L., Van den Bussche, J.: A formal account of the open provenance model (December 2010) (under review)
10. Moreau, L., Clifford, B., Freire, J., Futrelle, J., Gil, Y., Groth, P., Kwasnikowska, N., Miles, S., Missier, P., Myers, J., Plale, B., Simmhan, Y., Stephan, E., Van den Bussche, J.: The open provenance model core specification (v1.1). Future Generation Computer Systems 27(6), 743–756 (2011)

Comparator: A Tool for Quantifying Behavioural Compatibility

Meriem Ouederni[1], Gwen Salaün[2], Javier Cámara[3], and Ernesto Pimentel[4]

[1] Toulouse INP, IRIT, France
[2] Grenoble INP, Inria, France
[3] Institute for Software Research, Carnegie Mellon University, USA
[4] Department of Computer Science, Universidad de Málaga, Spain

Abstract. We present Comparator, a tool that measures the compatibility between two behavioural interfaces. Comparator can be used as a stand-alone Web application, and is also integrated into a model-based adaptation toolbox.

1 Introduction

Context. Building new applications by composing existing software components or Web services is now mainstream. However, this task remains error-prone, especially when reusing stateful components accessed through their behavioural interfaces. Techniques and tools are therefore necessary to support this composition task, and to make sure that the new system will behave correctly, avoiding undesired behaviours such as deadlocks.

Model. In this work, we assume that component interfaces are described using their interaction protocols represented by *Symbolic Transition Systems* (STSs) which are Labelled Transition Systems extended with value-passing (parameters coming with messages). In particular, a STS is a tuple (A, S, I, F, T) where A is an alphabet which corresponds to the set of labels, S is a set of states, $I \in S$ is the initial state, $F \subseteq S$ is a nonempty set of final states, and $T \subseteq S \times A \times S$ is the transition relation. Note that a *label* is either the (internal) τ action or a tuple (m, d, pl) where m is the message name, d indicates the communication direction (either an emission ! or a reception ?), and pl is either a list of typed data terms if the label corresponds to an emission, or a list of typed variables if the label is a reception. STSs can be easily derived from higher-level description languages such as Abstract BPEL for instance where such abstractions were used for verification, composition or adaptation of Web services.

Contributions. In this tool paper, we present Comparator, a tool supporting the composition task by analysing the behavioural interfaces of the components to be composed. Comparator accepts as input two behavioural interfaces described using STSs. We assume that both STSs interact *wrt.* a synchronous communication model. Our tool indicates whether the interfaces can interoperate correctly. Otherwise, it provides three outputs: a detailed compatibility measure for all

S. Gnesi and A. Rensink (Eds.): FASE 2014, LNCS 8411, pp. 306–309, 2014.
© Springer-Verlag Berlin Heidelberg 2014

states in both STSs, a list of mismatches, and a global compatibility measure. Comparator can be used as a stand-alone application through a Web interface. It is also integrated into ITACA [2], a toolbox for model-based adaptation.

2   Quantifying Behavioural Compatibility

Interfaces are compatible if they interact successfully with no mismatch *wrt.* a criterion set on their observable actions. This criterion is called compatibility notion, *e.g.*, *unspecified receptions* where all reachable emissions can be received in the other STS, and *unidirectional complementarity* where all actions in one STS have a matching in the other STS [3].

In this section, we overview the main ideas behind our measure computation. All the theoretical background for identifying possible mismatches and measuring the compatibility of two STSs is presented in [4]. The computation process accepts as input two protocols $STS_1 = (A_1, S_1, I_1, F_1, T_1)$ and $STS_2 = (A_2, S_2, I_2, F_2, T_2)$ and computes a compatibility degree for each global state, *i.e.*, each couple of states (s_1, s_2) with $s_1 \in S_1$ and $s_2 \in S_2$. All compatibility scores range between 0 and 1, where 1 means a perfect compatibility. Our approach is parameterised by a compatibility notion, that is, we measure how far the two interfaces are from being compatible *wrt.* this compatibility notion.

To measure the compatibility of two STSs, we compute the compatibility degree for all possible global states in two steps. We first compute a static compatibility based on the comparison of state nature (*i.e.*, initial, final, or none of them), labels, and types of exchanged parameters. These measures are then used to quantify the behavioural compatibility taking the label ordering into account and the structure of both STSs. The second step returns the compatibility measure for all global states in both STSs. State compatibility is based on the fact that two states are compatible if their preceding and succeeding neighbouring states are compatible, where the preceding and succeeding neighbours of state s' in transitions (s, l, s') and (s', l', s'') are respectively the states s and s''. Hence, in order to measure the compatibility degree of two protocols, we consider an iterative approach which propagates the compatibility degree from one state to all its neighbours. This process is called compatibility flooding and works using a double propagation (forward and backward).

3   Online Comparator Tool

Our approach for measuring the protocol compatibility degree has been fully implemented in a tool called Comparator. We encoded it in Python 2.6 using Eclipse 3.5.1 as programming IDE. The tool accepts as input two XML files corresponding to the interfaces, and a compatibility notion used as comparison criterion. Comparator returns the compatibility matrix, the mismatch list, and the global compatibility degree, which indicates how compatible the two interfaces are. The implementation of our proposal is highly modular, thus facilitating its extension with other compatibility notions. In order to make our Comparator tool widely available to any potential users, we implemented a Web interface [1] so that anyone can use and run it online (Fig. 1).

Experimental Results. We validated our tool on about 110 real-world examples, *e.g.*, a car rental service, a travel booking system, a medical management system, or an online email service. Some of these examples are available online [1] to illustrate the results returned by our compatibility measure. Note that Comparator computes the compatibility degree of quite large systems (*e.g.*, interfaces with hundreds of states and transitions) in a reasonable time (a few minutes).

Evaluation. We evaluate our tool accuracy using precision and recall metrics [5], which estimate how much our measure meets the expected result. Precision measures the matching quality (number of false positive matches) and is defined as the ratio of the number of correct state matches found out of the total of state matches found. Recall is the coverage of the state matching results and is defined as the ratio of the number of correct state matches found out of the total of all correct state matches in the two protocols. An effective measure must produce high precision and recall values. We have computed these metrics for the examples of our database using both UC and UR notions. We assume (s_1, s_2) is a correct match if the state $s_1 \in S_1$ has the highest compatibility degree with $s_2 \in S_2$ among those in S_2. Our measuring process yields a precision and recall of 100% for compatible protocols. Our empirical analysis also showed the good quality of our approach for comparing incompatible protocols. For instance, the study of the car rental service [1] produces a precision and recall equal to 85% and 95%, respectively. We applied the same evaluation to a flight advice system [1] which helps travellers to find flight information. This yields a precision and a recall equal to 91% and 100%, respectively. We measured precision and recall for the other examples of our dataset as well, and our study revealed very high values for both metrics (more than 90% in average).

4   Application to Model-Based Adaptation of Web Services

Our compatibility degree results have some straightforward applications for, *e.g.*, service selection, ranking, and adaptation. We focus in the rest of this section on software adaptation [6]. Adaptation aims at computing an intermediate component or *adaptor* to resolve mismatches existing between services interacting with each other. An adaptor is built from abstract descriptions, *a.k.a* adaptation contracts, specifying how the involved services can successfully interact together for fulfilling some specific requirements in spite of the mismatches existing in their interfaces. The Comparator tool was integrated into a graphical environment, called ACIDE, for the interactive specification of adaptation contracts. This module belongs to a complete framework, called ITACA, dedicated to the design and synthesis of adaptors for Web services [2].

ACIDE includes a graphical representation of STSs and a visualization of their *ports*. Each label on the STS corresponds to a port in the graphical description.

Ports include a data port for each parameter contained in the parameter list of the label. Correspondences between STSs are represented as port bindings and data port bindings. Starting from the graphical representation, the architect can specify these bindings by successively connecting ports and data ports. The resulting collection of bindings is the adaptation contract.

Our compatibility measure can be used in different ways to specify the adaptation contract in ACIDE. Firstly, it is possible to automatically generate port bindings for labels that perfectly match. Secondly, the designer can also select a state (label, resp.) in one protocol, and Comparator returns the best state (label, resp.) matching in the other protocol. For instance, Fig. 2 shows the state-based matching results when the designer selects state number 2 in the top left STS and compares it with all the states in the client STS on the right.

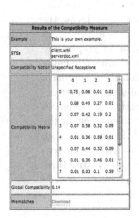

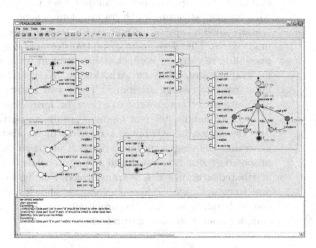

Fig. 1. Online Comparator   **Fig. 2.** State-based matching in ACIDE

References

1. Comparator Web Page,
   http://ouederni.perso.enseeiht.fr/10-comparator-tool.html
2. Cámara, J., Antonio Martín, J., Salaün, G., Cubo, J., Ouederni, M., Canal, C., Pimentel, E.: ITACA: An Integrated Toolbox for the Automatic Composition and Adaptation of Web Services. In: Proc. of ICSE 2009, pp. 627–630. IEEE (2009)
3. Durán, F., Ouederni, M., Salaün, G.: A Generic Framework for N-Protocol Compatibility Checking. SCP 77(7-8), 870–886 (2012)
4. Ouederni, M., Salaün, G., Pimentel, E.: Measuring the Compatibility of Service Interaction Protocols. In: Proc. of SAC 2011, pp. 1560–1567. ACM (2011)
5. Salton, G., McGill, M.J.: Introduction to Modern Information Retrieval. McGraw-Hill, New York (1983)
6. Yellin, D.M., Strom, R.E.: Protocol Specifications and Component Adaptors. ACM Trans. Program. Lang. Syst. 19(2), 292–333 (1997)

Transformation of Attributed Structures with Cloning*

Dominique Duval[1], Rachid Echahed[2], Frederic Prost[2], and Leila Ribeiro[3]

[1] LJK - Université de Grenoble
[2] LIG - Université de Grenoble
[3] INF - Universidade Federal do Rio Grande do Sul

Abstract. Copying, or cloning, is a basic operation used in the specification of many applications in computer science. However, when dealing with complex structures, like graphs, cloning is not a straightforward operation since a copy of a single vertex may involve (implicitly) copying many edges. Therefore, most graph transformation approaches forbid the possibility of cloning. We tackle this problem by providing a framework for graph transformations with cloning. We use attributed graphs and allow rules to change attributes. These two features (cloning/changing attributes) together give rise to a powerful formal specification approach. In order to handle different kinds of graphs and attributes, we first define the notion of attributed structures in an abstract way. Then we generalise the sesqui-pushout approach of graph transformation in the proposed general framework and give appropriate conditions under which attributed structures can be transformed. Finally, we instantiate our general framework with different examples, showing that many structures can be handled and that the proposed framework allows one to specify complex operations in a natural way.

1 Introduction

Graph structures and graph transformation have been successfully used as foundational concepts of modelling languages in a wide range of areas related to software engineering. Such a success mainly stems from the intuitive and pictorial features of graphs which ease the writing as well as the understanding of specifications. Several ways to define graph transformation rules have been proposed (see e.g., [22,12,14] for a survey). We can distinguish two main approaches: The algorithmic approach which is rather pragmatic and defines graph transformation rules by means of the algorithms used to transform the graphs (e.g.[3]) and the algebraic approach which is more abstract (e.g. [15]). This latter borrows notions from category theory to define graph transformation rules. The most popular algebraic approaches are the double pushout (DPO) [15,7] and the single pushout (SPO) [13].

* This work has been partially funded by projects CLIMT (ANR-11-BS02-016), TGV (CNRS-INRIA-FAPERGS/156779 and 12/0997-7), VeriTeS (CNPq/FAPERGS 11/2016-2 and 485048/2012-4) and PLATUS (CNPq 306843/2010-2).

S. Gnesi and A. Rensink (Eds.): FASE 2014, LNCS 8411, pp. 310–324, 2014.

Very often, graph structures are endowed with attributes. Such attributes, which enrich nodes and edges with data values, have been proven very useful to enhance the expressiveness of visual modelling frameworks (see, e.g., UML diagrams). These attributes can be simple names of an alphabet (labels) or elaborated expressions of a given language. Several investigations tackling attributed graph transformations have been proposed in the literature, see e.g. [19,18,4,11,20,16]. These proposals follow the so-called double pushout approach to define graph transformation steps. This approach can be used in many applications (see e.g. [7]) but it forbids actions which consist in cloning nodes together with their incident edges (merging of nodes is also usually forbidden). Moreover, this approach also prevents the application of rules that erase a node when there are edges connected to this node in the graph that represents the state (erasing nodes is only possible if all connected arcs are explicitly deleted by the rule). However, there are applications in which these restrictions of DPO would lead to rather complex specifications. For instance, duplicating or erasing some component may be very useful in the development process of an architecture, and should be a simple operation. Also, making a security copy of a virtual machine in a cloud (for fault-tolerance reasons) is a very reasonable operation, as well as switching down a (physical) machine from the infrastructure of a cloud. To model such situations we may profit from cloning/merging as basic operations in a formalism. But we certainly need to use attributed structures to get a suitable formalism for real applications. In this paper, we propose a framework that has both the ability to model cloning/merging of entities in a natural way, and also the feature of using attributes together with the graphs.

To develop our proposal, we follow a more recent approach of graph transformation known as the sesqui-pushout approach (SqPO) [6]. This latter is a conservative extension of DPO with some additional features such as deletion or cloning.

A rule is defined, as in the DPO approach, by means of a span of the form $(l : L \leftarrow K \rightarrow R : r)$ where the morphisms l and r are not necessarily monos. The fact that l is not mono allows one to duplicate some nodes and edges. Notice that most proposals dealing with attributed graphs assume l to be mono. A rewrite step can be depicted as follows where the left square is a final pullback complement and the right square is a pushout. The intuition is analogous to the DPO approach: the left square specifies what is removed (and also what is cloned) by the rule application and the right square creates the new items. The difference, besides allowing non injective rules, is that when applying the rule the so called dangling condition does not need to be checked: if there are edges in G connected to nodes in the image of m that is deleted by the rule, these edges are automatically removed by the rule application. In DPO, in such a situation a rule would not be applicable.

$$
\begin{array}{ccccc}
L & \xleftarrow{\quad l \quad} & K & \xrightarrow{\quad r \quad} & R \\
\downarrow{\scriptstyle m} & (FPBC) & \downarrow{\scriptstyle d} & (PO) & \downarrow{\scriptstyle h} \\
G & \xleftarrow{\quad l_1 \quad} & D & \xrightarrow{\quad r_1 \quad} & H
\end{array}
$$

Sesqui-pushout: $G \overset{\text{sqpo}}{\Longrightarrow} H$

In order to consider different kinds of graphs and attributes, we present our approach in a general setting. That is to say, we consider structures of the form $\widehat{G} = (G, A, \alpha)$ made of an object G whose elements may be attributed, an object A defining attributes and a partial function α which assigns to some elements of G attributes in A. The fact that α is partial turns out to be very useful to write transformation rules that change the attributes of some elements of G (see, e.g. [17,4]). We do not assume G to be necessarily a graph nor do we assume A to be necessarily an algebra. We thus elaborate a framework which can be instantiated with different kinds of structures and attributes fulfilling some criteria we introduce in this paper. Therefore we can handle different graphs with various kinds of attributes (algebras, lambda-terms, finite labels, syntactic theories, etc.). Similar objectives, with different outcome, have been recently investigated in [16] for the DPO approach.

The rest of the paper is organized as follows. The next section introduces the category of attributed structures and provides some definitions which may help the understanding of the paper. Section 3 recalls briefly the useful definitions regarding the sesqui-pushout approach. Then, Section 4 shows how to lift SqPO rewriting in the context of attributed structures. Sections 5 and 6 illustrate our approach through some examples while related work are discussed in Section 7. Concluding remarks are given in Section 8. The missing proofs may be found in [10].

2   Attributed Structures

In this section we define the notion of attributed structures and set some notations.

Structures. Let $\mathbf{G}$ be a category and $S : \mathbf{G} \to \mathbf{Set}$ a functor from $\mathbf{G}$ to the category of sets. For instance, $\mathbf{G}$ may be the category of graphs $\mathbf{Gr}$ [22] and S may be either the *vertex* functor V defined by $V(G) = V_G$ and $V(g) = g_V$, or the *edge* functor E defined by $E(G) = E_G$ and $E(g) = g_E$, or the functor $V + E$ which maps each graph G to the disjoint union $V_G + E_G$ and each morphism $g : G_1 \to G_2$ to the map $g_V + g_E$.

Attributes. Let $\mathbf{A}$ be a category and $T : \mathbf{A} \to \mathbf{Set}$ a functor from $\mathbf{A}$ to the category of sets. For instance, $\mathbf{A}$ may be the category $\mathbf{Alg}(\Sigma)$ of Σ-algebras [23] for some signature $\Sigma = (S, \Omega)$, or more generally the category $\mathbf{Mod}(Sp)$ of models of an equational specification $Sp = (\Sigma, E)$, made of a signature Σ and a set of equations E. Then the functor $T : \mathbf{A} \to \mathbf{Set}$ may be such that $T(A) = \sum_{s \in S} A_s$, i.e., T maps each Σ-algebra A to the disjoint union of its carriers, or more generally $T(A) = \sum_{s \in S'} A_s$ for some fixed subset S' of S. In the following, we sometimes write Fx instead of $F(x)$ when a functor F is applied to an object or a morphism x.

Definition 1. *The category of* attributed structures $\mathbf{AttG}$ *(with respect to the functors S and T) is the comma category $(S \downarrow T)$. Thus, an attributed structure is a triple $\widehat{G} = (G, A, \alpha)$ made of an object G in $\mathbf{G}$, an object A in $\mathbf{A}$ and a* map $\alpha : S(G) \to T(A)$ *(in Set) ; and a morphism of attributed structures* $\widehat{g} : \widehat{G} \to \widehat{G'}$, *where* $\widehat{G} = (G, A, \alpha)$ *and* $\widehat{G'} = (G', A', \alpha')$, *is a pair* $\widehat{g} = (g, a)$ *made of a morphism* $g : G \to G'$ *in* **G** *and a morphism* $a : A \to A'$ *in* **A** *such that* $\alpha' \circ Sg = Ta \circ \alpha$ *(in Set).*

$$
\begin{array}{ccc}
\widehat{G} & & G \\
\widehat{g}\downarrow & = & g\downarrow \\
\widehat{G'} & & G'
\end{array}
\qquad
\begin{array}{ccc}
SG & \xrightarrow{\alpha} & TA \\
Sg\downarrow & = & \downarrow Ta \\
SG' & \xrightarrow{\alpha'} & TA'
\end{array}
\qquad
\begin{array}{c}
A \\
\downarrow a \\
A'
\end{array}
$$

Partial Maps. Let **Part** be the category of sets with partial maps, which contains **Set**. A partial map f from X to Y is denoted $f : X \rightharpoonup Y$ and its domain of definition is denoted $\mathcal{D}(f)$. The partial order between partial maps is denoted $\leq$, it endows **Part** with a structure of 2-category. By composing S and T with the inclusion of **Set** in **Part** we get two functors $S_p : \mathbf{G} \to \mathbf{Part}$ and $T_p : \mathbf{A} \to \mathbf{Part}$.

Definition 2. *The category of* partially attributed structures **PAttG** *(with respect to the functors S and T) is defined as follows. A partially attributed structure is a triple $\widehat{G} = (G, A, \alpha)$ made of an object G in* **G**, *an object A in* **A** *and a partial map $\alpha : S_p(G) \rightharpoonup T_p(A)$ (in* **Part***) ; and a morphism of partially attributed structures $\widehat{g} : \widehat{G} \to \widehat{G'}$, where $\widehat{G} = (G, A, \alpha)$ and $\widehat{G'} = (G', A', \alpha')$, is a pair $\widehat{g} = (g, a)$ made of a morphism $g : G \to G'$ in* **G** *and a morphism $a : A \to A'$ in* **A** *such that $\alpha' \circ S_p g \geq T_p a \circ \alpha$ (in* **Part***).*

$$
\begin{array}{ccc}
\widehat{G} & & G \\
\widehat{g}\downarrow & = & g\downarrow \\
\widehat{G'} & & G'
\end{array}
\qquad
\begin{array}{ccc}
S_pG & \xrightarrow{\alpha} & T_pA \\
S_pg\downarrow & \geq & \downarrow T_pa \\
S_pG' & \xrightarrow{\alpha'} & T_pA'
\end{array}
\qquad
\begin{array}{c}
A \\
\downarrow a \\
A'
\end{array}
$$

Such a morphism of partially attributed structures is called strict *when* $\alpha' \circ S_p(g) = T_p(a) \circ \alpha$.

Remark 1. Clearly, **AttG** is a full subcategory of **PAttG** and every morphism in **AttG** is a strict morphism in **PAttG**. The subcategory **AttG** of **PAttG** is called the subcategory of *totally attributed structures.*

Definition 3. *A morphism of (partially) attributed structure $\widehat{g} : \widehat{G} \to \widehat{G'}$ preserves attributes if $\widehat{G} = (G, A, \alpha)$, $\widehat{G'} = (G', A, \alpha')$ and $\widehat{g} = (g, id_A)$ for some object A in* **A**.

Notations. We will omit the subscript p in S_p and T_p. Let (G, A, α) be a (partially) attributed structure, the notation $x : t$ means that $x \in S(G), t \in T(A)$ and $\alpha(x) = t$ (i.e., x has t as attribute), and the notation $x : \perp$ means that $x \in S(G)$, $x \notin \mathcal{D}(\alpha)$ (i.e., x has no attribute). Let (G, A, α) and (G', A', α') be attributed structures, let $g : G \to G'$ in **G** and $a : A \to A'$ in **A**, then

$(g, a) : (G, A, \alpha) \to (G', A', \alpha')$ is a morphism of attributed structures if and only if for all $x \in S(G)$ and $t \in T(A)$ $x : t \implies g(x) : a(t)$. Let (G, A, α) and (G', A', α') be partially attributed structures, let $g : G \to G'$ in $\mathbf{G}$ and $a : A \to A'$ in $\mathbf{A}$, then $(g, a) : (G, A, \alpha) \to (G', A', \alpha')$ is a morphism of partially attributed structures if and only if for all $x \in SG$ and $t \in TA$ $x \in \mathcal{D}(\alpha) \implies g(x) \in \mathcal{D}(\alpha')$ and then $x : t \implies g(x) : a(t)$, and (g, a) is strict if and only if for all $x \in SG$ and $t \in TA$ $x \in \mathcal{D}(\alpha) \iff g(x) \in \mathcal{D}(\alpha')$, and then $x : t \implies g(x) : a(t)$. The notation $x : \bot$ can be misleading: of course we can extend $a : TA \to TA'$ as $a : TA + \{\bot\} \to TA' + \{\bot\}$ by setting $a(\bot) = \bot$, but then it is *false* that $x : t \implies g(x) : a(t)$ for each $x \in SG$ and $t \in TA + \{\bot\}$. In fact, for each morphism of partially attributed structures (g, a) we have $g(x) : \bot \implies x : \bot$, and it is only when g is strict that in addition $x : \bot \implies g(x) : \bot$.

Definition 4. *The* underlying structure *functor is the functor* $U_{\mathbf{G}} : \mathbf{PAttG} \to \mathbf{G}$ *which maps an attributed structure* (G, A, α) *to the object* G *and* (g, a) *to the morphism* g. *The* underlying attributes *functor is the functor* $U_{\mathbf{A}} : \mathbf{PAttG} \to \mathbf{A}$ *which maps an attributed structure* (G, A, α) *to the object* A *and* (g, a) *to the morphism* a.

3   Sesqui-Pushouts

In this section we briefly recall the definition of sesqui-pushout (SqPO) rewriting, introduced in [6]. A sesqui-pushout rewriting step is made of a final pullback complement (FPBC) followed by a pushout (PO). The definitions of FPBC and SqPO are reminded here, in any category $\mathbf{C}$. The initiality property of POs and the finality property of FPBCs imply that POs, FPBCs and SqPOs are unique up to isomorphism, when they exist.

Definition 5. *The* final pullback complement *(FPBC) of a morphism* $m_L : L \to G$ *along a morphism* $l : K \to L$ *is a pullback (PB) (below on the left) such that for each pullback (below on the right)*

$$
\begin{array}{ccc}
L & \xleftarrow{\quad l \quad} & K \\
{\scriptstyle m_L}\downarrow & (PB) & \downarrow{\scriptstyle m_K} \\
G & \xleftarrow{\quad l_1 \quad} & D
\end{array}
\qquad\qquad
\begin{array}{ccc}
L & \xleftarrow{\quad l' \quad} & K' \\
{\scriptstyle m_L}\downarrow & (PB) & \downarrow{\scriptstyle m'} \\
G & \xleftarrow{\quad l_1' \quad} & D'
\end{array}
$$

and each morphism $f : K' \to K$ *such that* $l \circ f = l'$ *there is a unique morphism* $f_1 : D' \to D$ *such that* $l_1 \circ f_1 = l_1'$ *and* $f_1 \circ m' = m_K \circ f$.

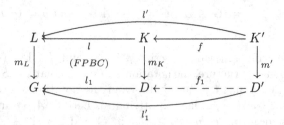

Definition 6. *The* sesqui-pushout *of a morphism* $m_L : L \to G$ *along a span of morphisms* $(l : L \leftarrow K \to R : r)$ *is the FPBC of* m_L *along* l *followed by the PO of* m_K *along* r *(see diagram below).*

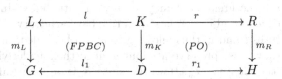

A comparison of SqPO with DPO and SPO approaches can be found in [6], where it is stated that "*Probably the most original and interesting feature of sesqui-pushout rewriting is the fact that it can be applied to non-left-linear rules as well, and in this case it models the cloning of structures.*"

In the category of graphs, under the assumption that $m_L : L \to G$ is an inclusion, the result of the sesqui-pushout can be described as follows [6, Section 4.1], [9]. With respect to a rule $(l : L \leftarrow K \to R : r)$, let us call *tri-node* a triple (n_L, n_K, n_R) where n_L, n_K and n_R are nodes in L, K and R respectively and where $n_L = l(n_K)$ and $n_R = r(n_K)$. Since m_L is an inclusion, L is a subgraph of G. Let $\overline{L}$ be the subgraph of G made of all the nodes outside L and all the vertices between these nodes. Let $\widetilde{L}$ be the set of edges outside L with at least one endpoint in L (called the *linking edges*), so that G is the disjoint union of L, $\overline{L}$ and $\widetilde{L}$. Then, up to isomorphism, m_R is an inclusion and H is obtained from G by replacing L by R and by "gluing R and $\overline{L}$ in H according to the way L and $\overline{L}$ are glued in G", which means precisely that H is the disjoint union of R, $\overline{L}$ and the following set $\widetilde{R}$ of linking edges (see [9] for more details):

- if n is a node in R and p a node in $\overline{L}$, there is an edge from n to p in $\widetilde{R}$ for each tri-node (n_L, n_K, n_R) with $n_R = n$ and each edge from n_L to p in $\widetilde{L}$;
- if n is a node in $\overline{L}$ and p a node in R, there is an edge from n to p in $\widetilde{R}$ for each tri-node (p_L, p_K, p_R) with $p_R = p$ and each edge from n to p_L in $\widetilde{L}$;
- if n and p are nodes in R, there is an edge from n to p in $\widetilde{R}$ for each tri-node (n_L, n_K, n_R) with $n_R = n$, each tri-node (p_L, p_K, p_R) with $p_R = p$ and each edge from n_L to p_L in $\widetilde{L}$.

4   Attributed Sesqui-Pushout Rewriting

In this section we define rewriting of attributed structures based on sesqui-pushouts, then we construct such SqPOs from SqPOs of the underlying (non-attributed) structures.

Definition 7. *Given an object A of $\mathbf{A}$, a* rewriting rule with attributes in A *is a span $(\widehat{l} : \widehat{L} \leftarrow \widehat{K} \to \widehat{R} : \widehat{r})$, or simply $(\widehat{l}, \widehat{r})$, made of morphisms $\widehat{l}$ and $\widehat{r}$ in* $\mathbf{PAttG}$ *which preserve attributes and such that $\widehat{L}$ and $\widehat{R}$ are totally attributed structures. A* match *for a rule $(\widehat{l}, \widehat{r})$ in an attributed structure $\widehat{G}$ is a morphism $\widehat{m} = (m, a) : \widehat{L} \to \widehat{G}$ in* $\mathbf{AttG}$ *such that the map Sm is injective. The* SqPO rewriting step *(or simply the* rewriting step*) applying a rule $(\widehat{l}, \widehat{r})$ to a match $\widehat{m}$ is the sesqui-pushout of $\widehat{m}$ along $(\widehat{l}, \widehat{r})$ in the category* $\mathbf{PAttG}$.

From the definition above, a rewrite rule is characterised by (i) the object A of attributes, (ii) the attributed structures $\widehat{L}$, $\widehat{K}$ and $\widehat{R}$ and (iii) the span of structures $(l : L \leftarrow K \rightarrow R : r)$. A match $\widehat{m}$ must have an injective underlying morphism of structures but it may modify the attributes. In contrast, the morphisms $\widehat{l} = (l, id_A)$ and $\widehat{r} = (r, id_A)$ in a rule have arbitrary underlying morphisms of structures l and r, thus allowing items to be added, deleted, merged or cloned, but they must preserve attributes since their underlying morphism on attributes is the identity id_A. However, since $\widehat{K}$ is only partially attributed, any element $x \in SK$ without attribute may be mapped to $l(x) : a$ in $\widehat{L}$ and to $r(x) : a'$ in $\widehat{R}$ with $a \neq a'$. Thus the assignment of attributes to vertices/edges may change in the transformation process.

In the following when (m, a) is a match we often assume that Sm is an inclusion, rather than any injection; in this way the notations are simpler while the results are the same, since all constructions (PO, PB, FPBC) are up to isomorphism.

The construction of a sesqui-pushout in **PAttG** can be made in two steps: first a sesqui-pushout in **G**, which depends only on the properties of the category **G**, then its lifting to **PAttG**, which does not depend any more on **G**. Moreover, this lifting is quite simple: since the morphisms l and r do not modify the attributes, it can be proved that m_K and m_R have the same underlying morphism on attributes as m_L. This is stated in Theorem 1.

Theorem 1. *Let us assume that the functors $U_{\mathbf{G}} : \mathbf{PAttG} \rightarrow \mathbf{G}$, $U_{\mathbf{A}} : \mathbf{PAttG} \rightarrow \mathbf{A}$, $S : \mathbf{G} \rightarrow \mathbf{Set}$ and $T : \mathbf{A} \rightarrow \mathbf{Set}$ preserve PBs and that the functor S preserves POs. Let $(\widehat{l} : \widehat{L} \leftarrow \widehat{K} \rightarrow \widehat{R} : \widehat{r})$ be a rewriting rule and $\widehat{m_L} = (m_L, a) : \widehat{L} \rightarrow \widehat{G}$ a match. If diagram Δ (below on the left) is a SqPO rewriting step in $\mathbf{G}$ then diagram $\widehat{\Delta}$ (below on the right) is a SqPO rewriting step in $\mathbf{PAttG}$ and (m_R, a) is a match.*

$$
\Delta : \qquad\qquad\qquad\qquad\qquad \widehat{\Delta} :
$$

$$
\begin{array}{ccccc}
L & \xleftarrow{\;l\;} & K & \xrightarrow{\;r\;} & R \\
{\scriptstyle m_L}\downarrow & {\scriptstyle (FPBC)} & {\scriptstyle m_K}\downarrow & {\scriptstyle (PO)} & \downarrow{\scriptstyle m_R} \\
G & \xleftarrow{\;l_1\;} & D & \xrightarrow{\;r_1\;} & H
\end{array}
\qquad
\begin{array}{ccccc}
\widehat{L} & \xleftarrow{(l,id_A)} & \widehat{K} & \xrightarrow{(r,id_A)} & \widehat{R} \\
{\scriptstyle (m_L,a)}\downarrow & {\scriptstyle (FPBC)} & {\scriptstyle (m_K,a)}\downarrow & {\scriptstyle (PO)} & \downarrow{\scriptstyle (m_R,a)} \\
\widehat{G} & \xleftarrow{(l_1,id_{A_1})} & \widehat{D} & \xrightarrow{(r_1,id_{A_1})} & \widehat{H}
\end{array}
$$

Proof. Since a sesqui-pushout is a FPBC followed by a PO, this proof relies on similar results about the lifting of FPBCs and the lifting of POs (see [10]).

Let us summarize what may occur for an element $x \in SD$. If $x \notin SK$ then only one case may occur:
$$
l_1(x) : t_1 \longleftarrow\!\!\!| \; x : t_1 \longmapsto r_1(x) : t_1
$$

If $x \in SK$ then two cases may occur:

$$
\begin{array}{ccc}
l(x) : t \longleftarrow\!\!\!| & x : t \longmapsto & r(x) : t \\
\downarrow & \downarrow & \downarrow \\
l_1(x) : a(t) \longleftarrow\!\!\!| & x : a(t) \longmapsto & r_1(x) : a(t)
\end{array}
\qquad
\begin{array}{ccc}
l()x : t \longleftarrow\!\!\!| & x : \bot \longmapsto & r(x) : t' \\
\downarrow & \downarrow & \downarrow \\
l_1(x) : a(t) \longleftarrow\!\!\!| & x : \bot \longmapsto & r_1(x) : a(t')
\end{array}
$$

5   Graph Transformations with Simply Typed λ-terms as Attributes

In this section we consider simply typed λ-terms as attributes. The choice of the λ-calculus can be motivated by the possibility to perform higher-order computations (functions can be passed as parameters). We refer to [2] for more details concerning the simply-typed λ-calculus, though basic notions of λ-calculus are enough to understand the example provided in this section.

First, let us choose the categories $\mathbf{G}$ and $\mathbf{A}$ and the functors S and T. Let $\mathbf{G} = \mathbf{Gr}$ be the category of graphs. Let $S : \mathbf{G} \to \mathbf{Set}$ be the functor which maps each graph to the disjoint union of its set of vertices and its set of edges. We define the category $\mathbf{A}$ as the category where objects are sets $\Lambda(X)$ of simply typed λ-terms, à la Church, built over variables in X. For the sake of simplicity we only consider one base type ι. Simply typed λ-terms in $\Lambda(X)$, noted t, and types, noted τ, are defined inductively by: $\tau :: = \iota \mid \tau \to \tau$ and $t :: = x \mid (t\ t) \mid \lambda x^\tau.t$ with $x \in X$. A morphism m from $\Lambda(X)$ to $\Lambda(X')$ is totally defined by a substitution from X to $\Lambda(X')$. The functor $T : \mathbf{A} \to \mathbf{Set}$ is such that $T(\Lambda(X))$ is the set of normal forms of elements in $\Lambda(X)$. Other choices for T are possible, for instance $T(\Lambda(X))$ could be chosen to be $\Lambda(X)$ itself. However in this case there would be no reduction in the attributes while rewriting. With the definitions as above, the functors $U_{\mathbf{G}} : \mathbf{PAttG} \to \mathbf{Gr}$, $U_{\mathbf{A}} : \mathbf{PAttG} \to \mathbf{A}$, $S : \mathbf{Gr} \to \mathbf{Set}$ and $T : \mathbf{A} \to \mathbf{Set}$ preserve pullbacks, and S preserves pushouts.

Graph transformations can be coupled with λ-term evaluation. For instance, a vertex, n, of a right-hand side, R, of a rule may be attributed with a λ-term, t, containing free variables which occur in the left-hand side L. A match, σ of such a rule instantiates the free variables. Firing the rule will result in (i) the computation of the normal form of the λ-term $\sigma(t)$ and (ii) its attribution to the image of vertex n in the resulting transformed graph. Below we give an example of such a rule and illustrate it on the graph λG.

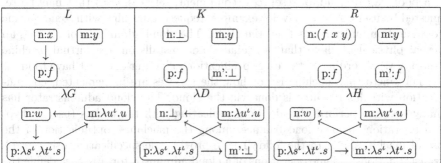

Graph morphisms are represented via vertex name sharing, and $U_{\mathbf{A}}$ can be deduced from them (for instance attribute x in L is instantiated by attribute w in λG because of the match on vertex n, likewise f is instantiated by $\lambda s^\iota.\lambda t^\iota.s$ and y is instantiated by $\lambda u^\iota.u$). In this example several features of our framework are underlined. First, notice that vertex m in L is cloned, as a structure, into m and m'. This cloning of structure implies that the edges incident to m in λG

are to be duplicated for m and m' in λH. As for attributes, the example shows that the structure can be cloned while the attributes can be changed (this is the case for the attribute of vertex m'). The edge between vertices n and p is erased since it is matched and is not present in K nor in R. Furthermore, the attribute of n in R shows a higher-order computation. Via the match, f is substituted by the function $\lambda s^{\iota}.\lambda t^{\iota}.s$ and is applied to the instances of x and y. In λH the attribute of n is the normal form of $(\lambda s^{\iota}.\lambda t^{\iota}.s\ w\ \lambda u^{\iota}.u)$ which is w. Attributes can be easily copied, e.g., f occurs twice in R. Finally, attributes of a vertex can be modified thanks to the partiality of the attribution in K. It is witnessed on vertices n and even m' which is a clone of m. In fact m' clones only the incident edges of m, one would have to write $m': y$ to copy the attribute of m as well. Free variables are used to provide arguments of lambda-terms. This allows us to simulate the attribute dependency relation introduced in [5].

6   Graph Transformations with Attributes Defined Equationally: Administration of Cloud Infrastructure

In this section we explore how our framework allows us to take into account attributed graph transformations with attributes built over equational specifications. First we instantiate the definition with appropriate categories and functors, and then model an example.

Let the category $\mathbf{G}$ and functor $S : \mathbf{G} \to \mathbf{Set}$ be defined as in section 5. Let $T : \mathbf{A} \to \mathbf{Set}$ be the functor which maps each model of $Sp = (\Sigma, E)$, with $\Sigma = (S, \Omega)$, to the disjoint union of the carriers sets A_s for s in some given set of sorts S. With the definitions as above, the functors $U_{\mathbf{G}} : \mathbf{PAttG} \to \mathbf{Gr}$, $U_{\mathbf{A}} : \mathbf{PAttG} \to \mathbf{Mod}(Sp)$, $S : \mathbf{Gr} \to \mathbf{Set}$ and $T : \mathbf{Mod}(Sp) \to \mathbf{Set}$ preserve pullbacks, and S preserves pushouts.

Cloud Computing is very popular nowadays [1]. The general idea is that there is a pool, called cloud, of resources (equipment, services, etc.) that may be requested by users. A user may, for example, request a machine with some specific configuration and services from the cloud. The cloud administrator chooses an actual physical machine that is available and installs on it a virtual machine (short VM) according to the user specification. The user does not have to know neither where this machine is nor how the services are implemented, communication with his machine is done via the cloud. The cloud administrator has many tasks to perform, besides communicating with the clients (users). Typical operations involve load balance among the machines, optimisation of the use of machines, etc. In the following we provide the specification using graph transformations of some operations of a cloud administrator. First we define the static structure, defining data types and the states of the system (as attributed graphs), and then we define the operations (as rules). Since the purpose of this case study is to show the use of our framework, we will not describe a complete set of attributes and rules needed to specify the behaviour of a cloud administrator, but concentrate on those parts that make explicit use of the features of the approach.

6.1 Cloud Administration: Static Part

To model this scenario, we will use graphs with many attributes. The approach presented in the previous sections could be easily extended to families of attributes. Alternatively, one could use just one record attribute, but we prefer the former representation since the specification becomes more readable. The attributes that will be used are:

Vertex Attributes: nodeType, represent the different entities involved in this system, that is, cloud administrator, users, machines and virtual machines. In the graphical notation, this attribute will be denoted by a corresponding image (, , and , resp.); ident, models the identifier of the vertex; size, denotes the size of the machine and virtual machine; free, describes the amount of unused space in a machine; type, describes the type of a virtual machine (as a simplification, we assumed that there is a set of standard virtual machines that may be requested by users, identified by their types); config, this models the internal configuration of the cloud administrator, probably this would be a set of tables and variables describing the current state of machines and virtual machines;

Edge Attributes: edgeType, some arcs will represent physical relations (like a cloud administrator is connected to all machines monitored by it) or "knows"-relations (like a user may know a cloud administrator) and others will represent messages that are sent in the system. Messages will be denoted by dashed arrows, all other relations will be solid edges; type, analogous to the types of vertices; id, used in messages that require a parameter (identifier of a virtual machine).

The data types used in the state graph are defined in specification $Cloud\_Sp$ (Figure 1). This specification includes sorts for booleans and natural numbers with usual operations and equations, sort T for the different types of virtual machines, and a sort C to describe configurations of a cloud administrator. Such configurations are records containing the current status of the cloud. Due to space limitations, we will not define details of configurations, just use some basic operations (equations will be also omitted).

For example, the graph **G1** depicted in Fig. 2 describes two users and one cloud administrator that knows one machine, $M1$, and two types of virtual machines, $T1$ and $T2$. Actually, the administrator stores the images of the corresponding virtual machines such that, when a request is done, it creates a copy of this image in an available machine. Images are modelled by a special identifier (0). There are also two request messages, one from each user.

6.2 Cloud Administration: Dynamic Part

Figure 2 also shows some rules that describe the behaviour of the cloud administrator. Rule **CreateVM** models the creation of a new virtual machine. This may happen when there is a request from a user (dashed edge in **L1**) having as

```
Cloud_Sp :
sorts B, N, C,T
opns
        . . .                                boolean operators...
        . . .                                natural numbers operators...
        newId: C × N → B                     checks whether an id is not used in a config
        enoughSpace: C × N → B               checks if there is enough space in a config
        newVM: C × N × N × N × T → C         includes a new virtual machine in a config
        replVM: C × N × N → C                replicates a virtual machine in a config
        newMch: C × N × N ×Nat → C            includes a new machine in a config
        mergeMch: C × N × N → C              merges two machines in a config
        replicateAdm?: C → B                 checks whether a new administrator is needed
eqns
        . . .
```

Fig. 1. Specification *Cloud_Sp*

attribute the type of virtual machine that is created and the cloud administrator has a corresponding image and a machine to install this VM. Some additional constraints over the attributes are modelled by equations (written below the rule): the identifier that will be used for the new VM is fresh ($newId(c, idVM)$), there is enough free space in the chosen machine ($nVM \leq f$)[1]. The remaining equations describe the values that some attributes will receive when this rule is applied: variable f' depicts the amount of free space in the machine after the installation of the new VM, and c' is the updated configuration of the could administrator. Note that the two instances of the VM in **K1** are copies of the corresponding vertex in **L1**, just the identifier attribute in the second copy is left undefined, the attributes *config* and *free* are also undefined, since their values will change. Finally, in **R1**, this second copy is updated with the new identifier ($idVM$) and it is installed in the machine and sent to the user, and the attributes of the cloud administrator and machine are updated accordingly. Application of this rule to graph **G1** is given by the span $G1 \leftarrow D \rightarrow G2$ on top of Fig. 2.

Rule **replicateVM** creates a copy (replica) of a VM in another physical machine. This operation is important for fault tolerance reasons. When this rule is applied, all references to the original VM will also point to the new VM. The configuration of the cloud administrator is updated because any change in one virtual machine must now be propagated to its copy. Rule **replicateAdm** is used to replicate the cloud administrator itself. This kind of operation may be necessary, for example, when the number of clients becomes too large or for dependability reasons. The rule that specifies the operation has an equation that checks whether this replication is needed ($replicateAdm?(c)$). In case this is true in the current configuration, the administrator is copied and the two configurations (the original and the copy) are updated (because now they must

---

[1] To enhance readability, when working with boolean expressions in equations, we omit the right side of the equation. For example, we write simply $newId(c, Id)$ instead of $newId(c, Id) = \text{true}$.

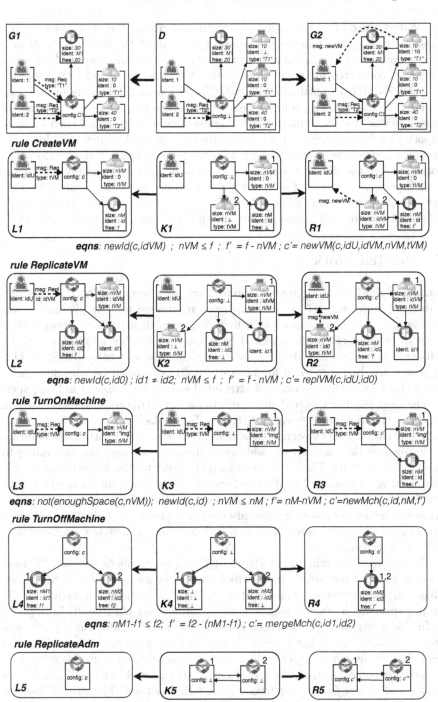

Fig. 2. Graph and Rules of the Cloud Administrator

know that some synchronisation is needed to perform the operations). Since these are copies, they manage the same machines and VMs, but now clients may send requests to either of the administrators (when this rule is applied, all edges that were connected to one administrator will also be connected to the copy).

Rules **TurnOnMachine** and **TurnOffMachine** model the creation and deletion of machines in the system. We assumed that there is an unlimited number of machines that may be connected to the system, and thus there is a need for more capacity ($not(enoughSpace(c, nVM)$ is true), a new machine may be added. We specified a simple version of turning off a machine by merging the vertices that correspond to two different machines. This can be done if the administrator notices that there is enough free space in one machine to accommodate VMs that are in another machines ($nM1 - f1 \leq f2$ is true). When this rule is applied, all VMs that were in both machines will end up in the machine with identifier $id2$.

7   Related Work

Various definitions of attributed graphs have been proposed in the literature. Labelled graphs, e.g. [17], where attributes are limited to a simple set of a vocabulary, could be considered as a first step towards attributed graphs. Such a set of vocabulary can be replaced by a specific, possibly infinite, set (of attributes) such as integers yielding particular definition of attributed graphs. This approach has been proposed for instance in [21] and could be considered as a particular case of the definition of attributed graphs we proposed in this paper.

The most popular way to define the data part in attributed graphs is based on algebraic specifications, see e.g. [19,18,4,11]. E-Graphs [11] is one of the principal contribution in this perspective, where an attributed graph gathers, in addition to its own vertices and edges, additional vertices and edges corresponding to the attribution part. The latter vertices correspond to possible attribution values. Such vertices might be infinite whenever the set of attributes is infinite. An attribution edge goes from a vertex or an edge of the considered graph to an attribution vertex. Attribution edges are used to represent graphically attribution functions. Due to the representation of each attribute as a vertex, an E-graph is infinite in general.

To overcome the infinite structures of E-graphs, Symbolic graphs [20] have been proposed. They are E-graphs which have variables as attributes. Such variables can be constrained by means of first order logic formulae. Hence a symbolic graph represents in concise way a (possibly infinite) set of (ground) E-graphs.

In this paper, we have proposed a general definition of attributed structures where the data part is not necessarily specified as an algebra. Our approach is very close to the recent paper by U. Golas [16] where an attributed graph is also defined as a tuple (G, A, α) where G is a given structure, A consists of attribution values and α is a *family* of partial attribution functions. The main difference with our proposal lies in the consideration of attribution functions α. For sake of simplicity, we considered simply partial functions for α. Generalization to families of functions as in [16] is straightforward.

Besides the variety of definitions of attributed graphs as mentioned above, attributed graph transformation rules have been based mainly on the double pushout approach which departs from the sesquipushout approach we have used in our framework. For a comparison of the double and the sesquipushout approaches we refer the reader to [6]. As far as we are aware of, the present paper presents the first study of attributed graph transformations following the sesquipushout approach and thus featuring the possibility of vertex and edge cloning in presence of attributes. Thanks to partial morphisms, rules allow also deletion and change of attributes.

8 Conclusion

In this paper we presented an approach to transformations of attributed structures that allows cloning and merging of items. This approach is based on the SqPO approach to graph transformations, and thus also allows deletion in unknown context. Concerning the attributes, our framework is general in the sense that many different kinds of attributes can be used (not just algebras, as in most attributed graph transformation definitions) and allows that rules change the attributes associated to vertices/edges. The resulting formalism is very interesting and we believe that it can be used to provide suitable specifications of many classes of applications like cloud computing, adaptive systems, and other highly dynamically changing systems.

As future work, we plan to develop more case studies to understand the strengths and weaknesses of this formalism for practical applications. We also want to study analysis methods. Since we are allowing non-injective rules, great part of the theory of graph transformations can not be used directly and we need to investigate which results may hold. Concerning verification of properties, we intent to extend the analysis of graph transformations using theorem provers [8] to attributed SqPO-rewriting.

References

1. Armbrust, M., Fox, A., Griffith, R., Joseph, A.D., Katz, R., Konwinski, A., Lee, G., Patterson, D., Rabkin, A., Stoica, I., Zaharia, M.: A view of cloud computing. Commun. ACM 53(4), 50–58 (2010)
2. Barendregt, H., Dekers, W., Statman, R.: Lambda Calculus with Types. Cambridge University Press (2013)
3. Barendregt, H., van Eekelen, M., Glauert, J., Kenneway, R., Plasmeijer, M.J., Sleep, M.: Term graph rewriting. In: de Bakker, J.W., Nijman, A.J., Treleaven, P.C. (eds.) PARLE 1987. LNCS, vol. 259, pp. 141–158. Springer, Heidelberg (1987)
4. Berthold, M.R., Fischer, I., Koch, M.: Attributed graph transformation with partial attribution (2002)
5. Boisvert, B., Féraud, L., Soloviev, S.: Typed lambda-terms in categorical attributed graph transformation. In: Procs of AMMSE 2011. EPTCS, vol. 56, pp. 33–47 (2011)
6. Corradini, A., Heindel, T., Hermann, F., König, B.: Sesqui-pushout rewriting. In: Corradini, A., Ehrig, H., Montanari, U., Ribeiro, L., Rozenberg, G. (eds.) ICGT 2006. LNCS, vol. 4178, pp. 30–45. Springer, Heidelberg (2006)

7. Corradini, A., Montanari, U., Rossi, F., Ehrig, H., Heckel, R., Löwe, M.: Algebraic approaches to graph transformation - part I: Basic concepts and double pushout approach. In: Handbook of Graph Grammars, pp. 163–246 (1997)

8. da Costa, S.A., Ribeiro, L.: Verification of graph grammars using a logical approach. Sci. Comput. Program. 77(4), 480–504 (2012)

9. Duval, D., Echahed, R., Prost, F.: Graph transformation with focus on incident edges. In: Ehrig, H., Engels, G., Kreowski, H.-J., Rozenberg, G. (eds.) ICGT 2012. LNCS, vol. 7562, pp. 156–171. Springer, Heidelberg (2012)

10. Duval, D., Echahed, R., Prost, F., Ribeiro, L.: Transformation of attributed structures with cloning (extended version). CoRR, abs/1401.2751 (2014)

11. Ehrig, H., Ehrig, K., Prange, U., Taentzer, G.: Fundamental theory for typed attributed graphs and graph transformation based on adhesive hlr categories. Fundam. Inform. 74(1), 31–61 (2006)

12. Ehrig, H., Engels, G., Kreowski, H.-J., Rozenberg, G. (eds.): Handbook of Graph Grammars and Computing by Graph Transformations, vol. 2: Applications, Languages and Tools. World Scientific (1999)

13. Ehrig, H., Heckel, R., Korff, M., Löwe, M., Ribeiro, L., Wagner, A., Corradini, A.: Algebraic approaches to graph transformation - part ii: Single pushout approach and comparison with double pushout approach. In: Handbook of Graph Grammars, pp. 247–312 (1997)

14. Ehrig, H., Kreowski, H.-J., Montanari, U., Rozenberg, G. (eds.): Handbook of Graph Grammars and Computing by Graph Transformations, vol. 3: Concurrency, Parallelism and Distribution. World Scientific (1999)

15. Ehrig, H., Pfender, M., Schneider, H.J.: Graph-grammars: An algebraic approach. In: 14th Annual Symposium on Foundations of Computer Science (FOCS), The University of Iowa, USA, October 15-17, pp. 167–180. IEEE (1973)

16. Golas, U.: A general attribution concept for models in $\mathcal{M}$-adhesive transformation systems. In: Ehrig, H., Engels, G., Kreowski, H.-J., Rozenberg, G. (eds.) ICGT 2012. LNCS, vol. 7562, pp. 187–202. Springer, Heidelberg (2012)

17. Habel, A., Plump, D.: Relabelling in graph transformation. In: Corradini, A., Ehrig, H., Kreowski, H.-J., Rozenberg, G. (eds.) ICGT 2002. LNCS, vol. 2505, pp. 135–147. Springer, Heidelberg (2002)

18. Heckel, R., Küster, J.M., Taentzer, G.: Confluence of typed attributed graph transformation systems. In: Corradini, A., Ehrig, H., Kreowski, H.-J., Rozenberg, G. (eds.) ICGT 2002. LNCS, vol. 2505, pp. 161–176. Springer, Heidelberg (2002)

19. Löwe, M., Korff, M., Wagner, A.: An algebraic framework for the transformation of attributed graphs. In: Sleep, R., Plasmeijer, M., van Eekelen, M. (eds.) Term Graph Rewriting: Theory and Practice, ch. 14, pp. 185–199. John Wiley & Sons Ltd. (1993)

20. Orejas, F., Lambers, L.: Symbolic attributed graphs for attributed graph transformation. ECEASST 30 (2010)

21. Plump, D., Steinert, S.: Towards graph programs for graph algorithms. In: Ehrig, H., Engels, G., Parisi-Presicce, F., Rozenberg, G. (eds.) ICGT 2004. LNCS, vol. 3256, pp. 128–143. Springer, Heidelberg (2004)

22. Rozenberg, G. (ed.): Handbook of Graph Grammars and Computing by Graph Transformations, vol. 1: Foundations. World Scientific (1997)

23. Sannella, D., Tarlecki, A.: Foundations of Algebraic Specification and Formal Software Development. EATCS Monographs on theoretical computer science. Springer (2012)

Implementing Graph Transformations in the Bulk Synchronous Parallel Model

Christian Krause[1], Matthias Tichy[2], and Holger Giese[3]

[1] SAP Innovation Center, Potsdam, Germany
christian.krause01@sap.com
[2] Chalmers | University of Gothenburg, Sweden
matthias.tichy@cse.gu.se
[3] Hasso Plattner Institute, University of Potsdam
holger.giese@hpi.uni-potsdam.de

Abstract. Big data becomes a challenge in more and more domains. In many areas, such as in social networks, the entities of interest have relational references to each other and thereby form large-scale graphs (in the order of billions of vertices). At the same time, querying and updating these data structures is a key requirement. Complex queries and updates demand expressive high-level languages which can still be efficiently executed on these large-scale graphs. In this paper, we use the well-studied concepts of graph transformation rules and units as a high-level modeling language with declarative and operational features for transforming graph structures. In order to apply them to large-scale graphs, we introduce an approach to distribute and parallelize graph transformations by mapping them to the Bulk Synchronous Parallel (BSP) model. Our tool support builds on Henshin as modeling tool and consists of a code generator for the BSP framework Apache Giraph. We evaluated the approach with the IMDB movie database and a computation cluster with up to 48 processing nodes with 8 cores each.

1 Introduction

Graph-based modeling and analysis becomes relevant in an increasing number of domains including traditional business applications such as supply chain management and product lifecycle management, but also in non-traditional application areas such as social network analysis and context-aware search [1]. In many of these areas, there is a trend towards collecting more data with the effect that the big-data dimension of the graph processing problem becomes a limiting factor for existing modeling and analysis approaches. On the one hand, there is a demand for high-level, declarative modeling languages that abstract from the basic underlying graph operations such as traversals and node and edge manipulations. On the other, these high-level, declarative modeling languages must be executed efficiently also on large-scale graphs (in the size of billions of vertices and edges).

In the last decades, the theory of graph transformations (see, e.g., [2]) evolved to a very active field both on the foundational and the application side. Graph transformations provide high-level modeling concepts for graph processing with both declarative and operational parts. However, most of their today's applications are, e.g., in model management, model transformation and software architectures where only

S. Gnesi and A. Rensink (Eds.): FASE 2014, LNCS 8411, pp. 325–339, 2014.
© Springer-Verlag Berlin Heidelberg 2014

recently issues with big models have been started to get addressed (e.g., [3]). Because of this and the fact that graph transformations are algorithmically challenging, little effort has been taken so far to make the concepts usable also for big data problems. Specifically, the recent work on large-scale graph processing focuses on relatively simple graph queries for vertex-labeled graphs [4,5,6,3]. While these approaches support distribution of large-scale graphs on several compute nodes in a cluster and parallelized execution of queries, the expressive power of these approaches is very limited (see the discussion of related work in Section 2). On the other hand, distribution of graphs in the area of graph transformations is currently only considered for modeling purposes [7], but not for physically distributing large-scale graphs on several machines. Thus, the high expressive power of graph transformations can currently not be used to solve big data problems which rely on truely parallel and distributed graph processing.

To make the high-level modeling concepts of graph transformations available for processing of large-scale graphs, we map the concepts of (declarative) transformation rules and (operational) transformation units [8] to the bridging model *Bulk Synchronous Parallel* (BSP) [9] which provides an abstraction layer for implementing parallel algorithms on distributed data. Thereby, we enable the use of the expressive language concepts of graph transformations for solving big data problems. In our prototypical tool suppport we use the Henshin [10] graph transformation language and tool to specify transformation rules and units. We have implemented a code generator which takes Henshin models as input and generates code for the BSP-based framework Apache Giraph [11]. Giraph builds on the infrastructure of Apache Hadoop [12] which implements the MapReduce [13] programming model. Our choice for BSP and Giraph was driven by fact that they provide the required support and infrastructure for transparent distribution and parallelization including load-balancing. We use a synthetic and a real-data example to show the feasability and the scalability (horizontal and vertical) of our approach. We also define modeling concepts tailored for parallel graph processing.

Organization. The rest of this paper is organized as follows. In Section 2 we compare our approach to existing work in this area. In Section 3 we give an overview of the relevant background. Section 4 describes our mapping of graph transformation to the BSP model and run-time optimizations. Section 5 contains an experimental evaluation. Section 6 discusses conclusions and future work.

2   Related Work

An algorithm for subgraph matching on large-scale graphs deployed on a distributed memory store is introduced in [4]. The approach is limited to vertex-labeled graphs without attributes and edge labels. More advanced matching conditions such as negative application conditions are not supported and transformations are also not considered. These restrictions apply also to the work on distributed graph pattern matching in [5] and [6]. Moreover, only graph simulations (as opposed to subgraph-isomorphy checking) are considered which are less powerful but can be checked in quadratic time.

The distributed graph transformation approach developed by Taentzer [7] focuses on the modeling of distributed graphs and transformations, but not on physical distribution on several machines. This is also the case for the parallel graph transformation approach for modeling Timed Transition Petri Nets in [14]. Parallelizing (incremental) graph pattern matching and graph transformations is discussed in [15]. Again, the approach does not consider distributing a large-scale graph on a cluster of compute nodes and therefore also does not support horizontal scalability. Furthermore, all matches are stored in memory and thus the approach does not scale for large graphs with a high number of matches due to the memory restrictions. Large-scale graph processing based on a mapping to an in-memory relational database is discussed in [1]. Scalability is not investigated here. Early results on distributed and massive parallel execution of graph transformations on similar sized graphs are shown in [3]. However, it is unclear which type of matching conditions are supported and how the approach scales for rules with a high number of partial matches as in our example.

Blom et al. present a distributed state space generation approach for graph transformations [16] based on LTSmin [17]. In contrast to our work, the framework does not allow to distribute the graph over a cluster. Instead the clients store complete states and send newly created states to itself or other clients for further subsequent generation. This approach is not applicable to large-scale graphs targeted in our work. State space generation for graphs of this size is neither our target nor reasonable.

Besides Giraph [11], Pregel [18] is another implementation of the Bulk Synchronous Parallel model on graph data. An architectural difference is that Giraph builds upon the MapReduce [13] framework Apache Hadoop [12] which is widely used and available.

3   Background

3.1   Graph Transformations with Transformation Units

Our modeling concepts build on the theory of algebraic graph transformations for typed, attributed graphs [2]. Specifically, we consider directed graphs with vertex and edge types, and primitive-typed vertex attributes. Transformations for these graphs are defined using declarative transformation rules and procedural transformation units [8,10].

In our approach, we consider transformation rules as graphs extended with stereotypes for vertices and edges, and conditions and calculations on attribute values. We use the following vertex and edge stereotypes: 《preserve》, 《delete》, 《create》, 《require》 and 《forbid》. Applying a rule consists of finding a match of the rule in the host graph and performing the operations indicated by the stereotypes. The stereotypes 《require》 and 《forbid》 have special meanings and are used for defining positive and negative application conditions (PACs and NACs), respectively. For attributes, we use expressions to constrain the allowed values and to calculate new values.

Transformation units are a means to define control-flows for transformations. We consider here a subset of the transformation unit types supported by the Henshin [10] model transformation tool. An *iterated unit* executes another unit or rule a fixed number of times. A *loop unit* executes a rule as long as possible, i.e., until no match is found. A *sequential unit* executes a list of units or rules in a fixed order. An *independent unit* nondeterministically selects one rule or unit from a set of rules or units and executes it.

Parallel Execution Semantics

In this paper, all rule applications are maximum parallel, i.e., rules are by default applied to *all* found matches in the host graph. The rationale behind this is to enforce parallelism

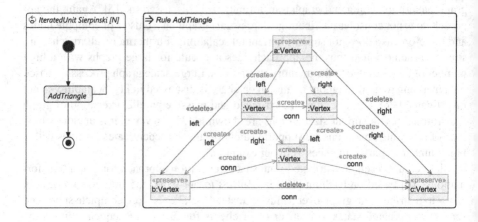

Fig. 1. Iterated unit and rule for constructing Sierpinski triangles of depth N

already at the modeling level. This is necessary in order to actually parallelize the execution of the transformations at run-time. Also, we assume that for any two overlapping matches during the parallel application, the graph modifications are conflict-free, e.g., if a vertex is preserved in one match, it cannot be deleted in another match. Different rules are applied in the order as specified in Henshin, e.g., sequentially in a sequential unit. Regarding transformation units, we note that we do not consider any transactional behavior, i.e., there is no rollback on unsuccessful execution of subunits.

Example 1 (Sierpinski triangle). Fig. 1 shows an example of a transformation unit and a rule for constructing Sierpinski triangles modeled using Henshin. The transformation unit on the left is an iterated unit which executes the rule **AddTriangle** on the right N times. Since in our semantics in every iteration the rule is applied in parallel to all matches, executing the transformation unit on a 3-vertex triangle generates the full Sierpinski triangle of depth N.

3.2 Bulk Synchronous Parallel (BSP) on Graphs

Bulk Synchronous Parallel (BSP) is a bridging model for implementing parallel algorithms which was developed by Leslie Valiant in the 1980s [9]. Nowadays, BSP is a popular approach for efficiently processing large-scale graph data. Implementations of BSP for graph data include Apache Giraph [11] which is used at Facebook to analyze social networks, and Pregel [18], a graph processing architecture developed at Google. In both of these frameworks BSP is used as computational model for implementing highly parallel algorithms on very large graphs distributed in a cluster, that supports both horizontal and vertical scaling.[1] Standard examples of BSP applications are com-

---

[1] Horizontal scaling (*scale-out*) refers to adding nodes to a compute cluster. Vertical scaling (*scale-up*) refers to adding resources, e.g., main memory or processing cores, to single nodes.

puting shortest paths and the well-known PageRank algorithm which is used to rank websites in search results.

Algorithms following the BSP bridging model must adhere to a specific scheme. In particular, any algorithm implemented in BSP is executed as a series of *supersteps*. In a superstep, every vertex in the graph can be either active or inactive. A superstep constitutes a unit of computation and interaction consisting of four components:

1. **Master computation:** Single computation executed centrally on a master node, mainly used for bookkeeping and orchestrating the vertex computations.
2. **Vertex computation:** Concurrent computation executed locally for every active vertex of the graph. This part can be highly parallelized.
3. **Communication:** During the vertex computation, vertices can send messages to other vertices, which will be available in the next superstep.
4. **Barrier synchronization:** Before the next superstep is started, the vertex computation and communication of the current superstep must be finished for all vertices.

The master computation can be seen as an initialization phase for every supersteps. In the parallel vertex computations, incoming messages are processed, local computations for the current vertex are performed, messages can be sent to other vertices, and the vertex can be requested to become inactive. Inactive vertices do not take part in the vertex computations of the next supersteps. However, an inactive vertex becomes active again if it receives a message. In a vertex computation, messages can be either send to adjacent vertices or vertices with known IDs. For instance, a received message can contain such a vertex ID. The final step of every superstep is a barrier synchronization. Specifically, the next superstep can be started only when all vertex computations and communications of the current superstep are finished. The BSP algorithm ends when all vertices are inactive.

In addition to the computation and communication, vertices can *mutate*, i.e. change, the graph during the vertex computation. It is important to note that –analogously to the communication– the effects of graph mutations are visible only in the next superstep.

Example 2 (BSP computation). Fig. 2 illustrates the run of an example BSP algorithm. In fact, is shows already an application of the graph transformation *AddTriangle* in Example 1 realized as a BSP computation. The run consists in total of 5 supersteps. In superstep I, vertex 0 sends the message [0] to vertex 1. In supersteps II and III this message is extended and first forwarded to vertex 2 and then back to vertex 0. Note that in I and II the messages are sent via the *l*- and *r*-edges, respectively, whereas in III vertex 2 extracts the vertex ID from the message in order to send it back to vertex 0. In superstep IV, no more messages are sent. Instead, a number of graph mutations are performed, specifically: 3 edges are removed, 3 new vertices and 9 new edges are created. The details of the mapping from transformations to BSP are explained in the Section 4.

In addition to the inter-vertex communication, vertices can also send data to dedicated, centrally managed *aggregators*. Aggregators process all received data items using an associative, commutative aggregation operation to produce a single value available to all vertices in the next superstep. We distinguish between *regular* and *persistent* aggregators, where the former are being reset in every superstep and the latter not. Using the

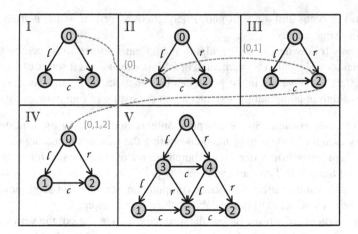

Fig. 2. Illustration of a BSP computation that realizes an application of the *AddTriangle* rule

sum of integers as aggregator operations, it is for instance possible to compute the total number of exchanged messages – either only for the last superstep (using a regular aggregator) or the total number for all previous supersteps (using a persistent aggregator).

4   Implementing Graph Transformations in BSP

Example 2 indicates already that the BSP model is generic and powerful enough to realize graph transformations with it. In this section, we show that this is in fact the case for arbitrary complex transformation rules and control-flows modeled using transformation units. We identified three main challenges in implementing graph transformations in BSP: 1) to realize the rule pattern matching with only local knowledge, 2) to coordinate the distributed and parallel execution of rules and transformation units, and 3) to deal with the complexity of the graph pattern matching problem. In addition, we propose the new concept of *attribute aggregators* to benefit from the parallelism not only in the execution phase, but also in the modeling. Finally, we discuss run-time optimizations of the graph pattern matching.

4.1   Graph Pattern Matching and Rule Applications

To apply a rule requires to find all its matches in the distributed graph using a parallel algorithm that is designed based on the BSP-principles. To this end, we propose to split up the matching process into a series of *local steps*[2]. In each local step, local constraints are checked and sets of partial matches are generated, extended or merged. After all constraints have been checked and the final set of matches has been computed, the rule can be applied by performing the required graph modifications in parallel.

The most performance-critical part of a rule is the pattern matching. For a given rule, we statically construct a search plan which defines the operations for every local step

---

[2] Local steps are relative to a specific rule; supersteps are defined for a complete transformation.

Listing 1.1. Simplified algorithm for search plan generation of connected graph patterns

```
1   /* Function for generating a search plan for a graph pattern.
2    * Input 'pattern' : a connected graph pattern to be searched.
3    * Output: search plan as list of edges.
4    */
5   generateSearchPlan(pattern) {
6      visited := ∅    // set of visited vertices
7      result := []    // search plan as list of edges
8      while (|visited| < |pattern.vertices|) {
9        traversals := ∅    // set of traversals as set of list of edges
10       for (start ∈ pattern.vertices)
11         if (start ∉ visited) {
12           t := dfsTraversal(start, visited)    // depth–first traversal stopping at visited vertices
13              traversals := traversals ∪ { t }
14         }
15       next := sup(traversals)    // select longest traversal
16       result := result++ next    // append to search plan
17       visited := visited ∪ next.vertices
18     }
19     return result
20  }
```

in the matching phase. A simplified version of the search plan generation algorithm is shown in Listing 1.1. For simplicity, we consider here only connected graph patterns with at least one edge. The algorithm generates a search plan in the form of a list of edges along which the matches are constructed. The algorithm iteratively builds maximal, ordered subgraphs of the pattern until the complete pattern is covered. The generated search plan starts with a depth-first traversal of the largest traversable subgraph of the pattern. The search plan continues with depth-first traversals of the remaining parts of the pattern, until the search plan contains the complete pattern graph. For example, the generated search plan for the *AddTriangle* rule in Fig. 1 is given by the following list of edges: $[(a - left \rightarrow b), (b - conn \rightarrow c), (a - right \rightarrow c)]$.

The list of edges generated by the search plan function is translated into a series of local steps. In such a local step, local constraints of a vertex, such as type information, attribute values, existence of edges and injectivity of matches are checked. During the pattern matching, a set of local matches is maintained and step-wise extended. The partial matches are forwarded as messages to either adjacent vertices (for extending a partial match by new bindings of nodes) or vertices that have been matched already (for checking an edge between bound objects or merging partial matches). When the complete search plan has been processed, the final set of matches is used to perform the rule modifications in parallel. Note that both the pattern matching as well as the graph modifications are executed in parallel in this model. A simplified version of the generated matching code for the *AddTriangle* rule is shown in Listing 1.2.

Listing 1.2. Simplified generated matching code for the *AddTriangle* rule

```
 1  /*
 2   * Generated matching function for the AddTriangle rule.
 3   * Input 'vertex': active vertex in the host graph.
 4   * Input 'matches': list of matches received in the current superstep.
 5   * Input 'step': currently executed local step.
 6   */
 7  matchAddTriangle(vertex, matches, step) {
 8    targets := ∅
 9    switch (step) {
10    0: if (vertex.value = TYPE_VERTEX ∧ |vertex.edges| ≥ 2) {     // matching vertex "a"
11         match := [vertex.id]
12         for (edge ∈ vertex.edges)
13           if (edge.value = TYPE_VERTEX_LEFT ∧ edge.target ∉ targets) {
14             sendMessage(edge.target, match)
15             targets = targets ∪ {edge.target}
16           }
17       }
18       break
19    1: if (vertex.value = TYPE_VERTEX ∧ |vertex.edges| ≥ 1)     // matching vertex "b"
20         for (match ∈ matches) {
21           if (vertex.id ∈ match) continue     // injectivity check
22           match := match ++ [vertex.id]
23           for (edge ∈ vertex.edges)
24             if (edge.value = TYPE_VERTEX_CONN ∧ edge.target ∉ targets) {
25               sendMessage(edge.target, match)
26               targets = targets ∪ edge.target
27             }
28         }
29       break
30    2: if (vertex.value = TYPE_VERTEX)     // matching vertex "c"
31         for (match ∈ matches) {
32           if (vertex.id ∈ match) continue     // injectivity check
33           match := match ++ [vertex.id]
34           sendMessage(match[0], match)
35         }
36       break
37    3: for (match ∈ matches)     // checking for "right" edge
38         for (edge : vertex.edges)
39           if (edge.value = TYPE_VERTEX_RIGHT ∧ edge.target = match[2]) {
40             applySierpinski(match)     // apply the rule w.r.t. the found match
41             break
42           }
43       break
44    }
45  }
```

Graph pattern elements with the stereotype ⟪require⟫ take a special role in our parallel graph transformation approach. The difference to the ⟪preserve⟫ stereotype is that the existence of the elements is checked, but they are not considered as part of the match. This is a useful modeling feature to avoid overlapping and conflicting matches. We give a specific example for this modeling concept in Section 5.

4.2 Transformation Units

Transformation units provide control-flow constructs to coordinate the execution of rules. In our BSP-based approach, transformation units are managed during the master computation. The master computation maintains a unit execution stack in the form of a persistent aggregator. The elements on this stack are pairs of unit or rule IDs and local step indizes. The unit ID is used to decide which unit or rule is active, and the local step determines the current execution phase in this unit or rule. In a rule, the local step defines the current stage in the matching phase. In a sequential unit, the local step is used to store the index of the currently executed subunit, and similarly for other unit types. In addition to the unit execution stack, we maintain a rule application counter in the form of a regular aggregator. It stores the number of rule applications in the last superstep and is required to decide when loop units should be terminated.

For an example of generated code for a transformation unit, we refer to the online resources provided for the example in Section 5.2.

4.3 Attribute Aggregators

In many graph transformation approaches, attribute values of vertices can be set during a rule application using an expression that takes as parameters other attribute values of matched vertices. These expressions are usually limited to the scope of a single match. In our approach, however, rule applications are always maximum parallel, i.e., always applied to all found matches. Since during a rule application all matches are readily available, we can define attribute calculations that are not limited to the scope of a single match, but a set of matches, potentially all of them.

To facilitate global attribute calculations, we introduce the concept of *attribute aggregators*, which are associative and commutative operations on attribute values (similarly to aggregation functions in relational databases). Specifically, we consider the following set of pre-defined attribute aggregators: COUNT, MIN, MAX, SUM and AVG which respectively count occurences, compute the minimum, the maximum, the sum and the average of numerical attribute values. We distinguish between local and global attribute aggregators. Global attribute aggregators use the attribute values of all found matches. In local attribute aggregators, if the aggregator is used in an attribute calculation of a vertex v in the rule and v is matched to a vertex x, then all matches where v is matched to x are used. We give an example of a local attribute aggregator in Section 5.2.

4.4 Run-Time Optimizations

The performance of the BSP-based graph transformations mainly depends on the efficiency of the match finding. The most effective way to improve it is to reduce the number of partial matches generated during the matching. We realized two optimizations.

Number of workers	2	4	6	8	10	12
Execution time (seconds) for levels 1–15	281.8	195.7	166.3	133.7	114.9	112.6
Execution time (seconds) for level 16	559.1	376.8	295.6	197.9	172.1	158.2
Execution time (seconds) for level 17	–	–	896.4	635.0	526.3	489.7

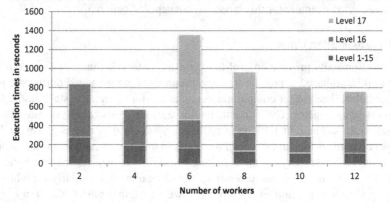

Fig. 3. Execution times of the iterated unit *Sierpinski* for different numbers of workers

To reduce the number of symmetric partial matches, we introduced a static analysis that finds symmetries in PACs. During the matching phase, symmetric matches to the PACs are automatically discarded. As a second approach to reduce the number of partial matches during the matching, we consider *segmentation*. The idea is to partition the vertices of the host graph into a set of disjoint segments. Each segment is individually examined during the matching phase. Specifically, the matching process starts with vertices from one of these segments and continues until all segments were used. Matches from previous segments are kept during the matching. Thus, we partially sequentialize the matching process to reduce the memory consumption for partial matches.

5   Evaluation

We used the Henshin [10] tool to model transformation rules and units and implemented a code generator that takes Henshin models as input and produces Java code for the BSP-framework Apache Giraph [11]. Except for the parallelism, the Giraph-based semantics of rules is the same as in the Henshin interpreter. We tested this using a test suite that currently consists of 15 non-trivial example transformations. We conducted our experiments on a small cluster consisting of 6 slave nodes, each of them with 120GB main memory and Intel Xeon® CPU with 24 cores at 2.30GHz, connected via InfiniBand. To investigate the horizontal and the vertical scalability, we varied the number of Giraph workers between 2 and 12 where we used a maximum number of 6 compute threads per worker. The speed improvements up to 6 workers are primarily horizontal scaling, whereas the speed improvements between 6 and 12 workers are vertical scaling effects.

5.1   Synthetic Example: Sierpinski Triangles

We use the iterated unit in Fig. 1 to construct the Sierpinski triangle of depth N. Note that the size of the result graph is exponential in N. Using our set-up of 6 slave nodes, we built the Sierpinski triangle of depth $N=17$ which consists of ≈ 194 million vertices and 387 million edges. One parallel rule application of the *AddTriangle* rule requires 4 local steps, totaling in 68 supersteps for the whole transformation for $N=17$, which required 12 minutes. Fig. 3 shows a comparison of the aggregated run-times of the transformation for different number of workers. The difference from 2 to 6 workers is a horizontal scaling effect, which is a speed-up of factor 1.9. The difference from 6 to 12 workers is a vertical scaling effect, which is an additional speed-up of factor 2. Note that for <6 workers we were only able to compute up to $N=16$ due to insufficient memory.

We also ran this example in the non-distributed, non-parallel interpreter of Henshin. The Henshin solution was still 25% faster than the 12-worker version of Giraph. We believe that this is due to the additional communication and coordination overhead of Giraph. Due to the memory limitations of one machine, the Henshin solution worked only up to $N=16$. Note that due to the exponential growth, the graph sizes and number of matches for $N=17$ is 3 times, and for $N=18$ already 9 times larger than for $N=16$.

5.2   Real-Data Example: Movie Database

As a real-data example, we used the IMDB movie database[3] dated July, 26th 2013. The database contains $924,054$ movies (we consider only movies and not TV series), $1,777,656$ actors, and $980,396$ actresses. We use the simplified metamodel / typegraph shown in Fig. 4, which contains classes for movies, actors and actresses. Additionally, we introduce the new class Couple, which references two persons. The goal of this transformation is that for every pair of actors / actresses which played together in at least three movies, we create a Couple object. This new couple object should contain references to all movies that the couple occurred in. Moreover, the couple has a numerical attribute to store the average rank of all movies the couple appeared in.

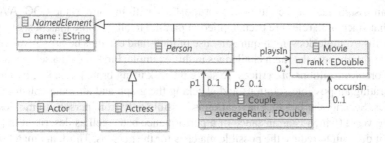

Fig. 4. Simplified and extended metamodel for IMDB movie dataset

We use the transformation rules and the sequential unit shown in Fig. 5 to solve this task. First, the rule *CreateCouple* generates Couple vertices for every pair of persons that played together in at least three movies. It is important to ensure that only one Couple vertex is created for every such pair. Thus, the movie vertices are matched as a PAC (using «require» stereotypes), i.e., their existence is checked but they are not

---

[3] Obtained from http://www.imdb.com/interfaces

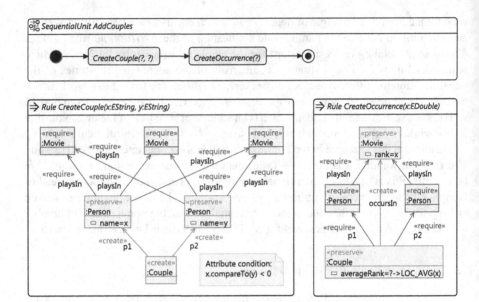

Fig. 5. Sequential unit and rules for adding couple nodes

considered as part of the matches. To avoid symmetric couples, we use an additional attribute condition that enforces a lexicographical order of the names of the two persons.

In the second part, the rule *CreateOccurrence* is used to add links between the newly created couple vertices and the movies they played in. Moreover, we use the local attribute aggregator LOC_AVG (see Section 4.3) to compute the average rank of all movies the couple occurred in. The expression averageRank=?→LOC_AVG(x) denotes an assignment of the attribute averageRank with the new value LOC_AVG(x). Note that since both rules are each applied in parallel to all possible matches, our solution to this example does not require any use of loops and can thus be fully parallelized.

We highlight here the main challenges in this example. First, the data set is too large (in the order of millions of vertices) to solve the task using brute force, i.e., by naively enumerating all possible solutions and checking the graph and attribute constraints of the rules. Second, the fact that navigation is possible only from persons to movies, but not vice versa (which is an instance of a performance bad smell as described in [19]), makes it difficult to reduce the possible matches for the persons. Third, the matching of the three movies is highly symmetrical and can cause an unnecessary high number of partial matches during the matching.

We generated code for this example transformation.[4] In this example, we benefit from the optimizations described in Section 4.4. This reduced the number of symmetric matches of the PACs by a factor of 6. However, the number of partial matches during the matching was still too high. Therefore, we also used segmentation with 100 segments.

---

[4] Models and generated source code available at
http://www.eclipse.org/henshin/examples.php?example=giraph-movies

Number of workers	2	4	6	8	10	12
Execution time (seconds) for 60% graph size	939	327	162	172	125	113
Execution time (seconds) for 80% graph size	2,273	757	376	378	295	253
Execution time (seconds) for 100% graph size	5,254	1,499	762	751	561	479

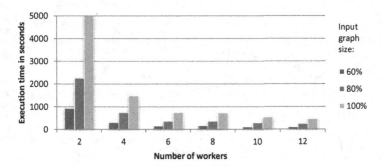

Fig. 6. Execution times of the couples example (2-movie version) in seconds

We executed the transformation on our 6-slave node cluster. The graph before the transformation had 3,635,741 vertices and 5,615,552 edges, and afterwards 5,328,961 vertices and 16,933,630 edges.[5] Because of the relatively high number of segments, the execution time was approx. 6 hours. In addition, we ran a variant of this transformation with only two common movies per couple where we did not require segmentation. Fig. 6 shows the execution times for this version. The overall performance improved by a factor of 11 when switching from 2 to 12 workers.

In addition to the small 6-node cluster, we ran this example (with two common movies) on a part of the Glenn cluster at Chalmers. In this set-up, each node uses 2 AMD Opteron® 6220 processors (8 cores each at 3GHz) with 32GB of main memory. For this benchmark, we varied the number of nodes between 5 and 24. For each node, we used 3 Giraph workers with 6 threads each. The memory was restricted for each Giraph worker to 10GB. Fig. 7 shows the resulting execution time averaged over 3 runs. On the left y-axis of the plot, the execution time per node is shown whereas on the right y-axis of the plot, the total execution time is shown. The latter is the product of the execution time and the number of nodes used in order to see how much total time of the cluster is used. Both figures show a good horizontal scalability until 14 nodes are used. Please note that during each evaluation run, the rest of cluster was also used by other jobs and thus could influence the results by network traffic. This is a possible explanation for the spike in the execution time for 20 nodes. More nodes still benefit the execution, but due to increasing fixed costs and communication overhead, the performance does not increase at the same rate.

Finally, we used the standard Henshin interpreter (version 0.9.10) to compute all matches of the *CreateCouple* rule on a single machine using dynamic EMF models. Henshin was not able to compute a single match for the same movie database as used in the other evaluations. This is because nested conditions, such as PACs and NACs, are

---

[5] We validated our transformation 1) using a 25-vertices test input graph, 2) by taking samples from the full output graph, and 3) using similar rules in our test suite.

Number of nodes	5	6	8	10	12	14	16	18	20	22	24
Execution time in seconds	1,220	866	666	587	518	453	430	401	440	387	373
Total node time in seconds	6,104	5,199	5,333	5,879	6,216	6,351	6,880	7,227	8,803	8,529	8,957

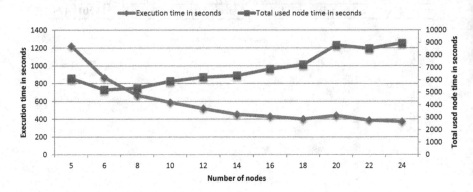

Fig. 7. Execution times of couples example (2-movie version) on the Glenn cluster at Chalmers

checked only after a match of the left-hand side of the rule has been found. Specifically, Henshin first fixes matches for the two Person vertices, and then checks the PACs. This matching approach boils down to a brute-force, which is only working for toy input graphs. In our experiments, also alternative models, such as with bidirectional references, nested rules or loop units, were not able to solve the task due to similar problems. Please note that this is mostly an inefficiency of the matching strategy of (this version of) the Henshin interpreter.

6   Conclusions and Future Work

Processing large-scale graph data becomes an important task in an increasing number of application domains. On the one hand, there is a demand for high-level, declarative query and transformation languages for graph data. On the other, the efficient processing of the large-scale graphs is a limiting factor for existing approaches. In this paper, we introduced an approach for the specification of graph querying and processing using graph transformation rules and units which provide a high-level modeling approach with declarative and operational parts. In order to efficiently apply them to large-scale graphs, we mapped graph transformation rules and units to the Bulk Synchronous Parallel model which allowed us to distribute the graphs and to parallelize their processing. We showed using a synthetic and a real-data example that the approach 1) provides new and high-level modeling features that are currently not available for large-scale graph processing, and 2) that the BSP solution provides both horizontal and vertical scalability for efficiently executing these models on large data graphs.

As future work, we plan to investigate more on new modeling features for parallel graph transformations and to optimize the execution in BSP. Concrete next steps involve more fine-tuning in the search plans and a dynamic segmentation approach which chooses the number of segments on-the-fly based on the current workload. In a different line of research we plan to define automatic ways to detect and resolve conflicting parallel matches. Both run-time checks and static analysis, e.g., using a variation of critical pair analysis seem to be relevant here. Finally, we plan to perform more benchmarks, e.g., using the graph transformation benchmark suite described in [20].

References

1. Rudolf, M., Paradies, M., Bornhövd, C., Lehner, W.: The graph story of the SAP HANA database. In: BTW 2013. LNI, vol. 214, pp. 403–420. GI (2013)
2. Ehrig, H., Ehrig, K., Prange, U., Taentzer, G.: Fundamentals of Algebraic Graph Transformation. Monographs in Theoretical Computer Science. An EATCS Series. Springer-Verlag New York, Inc., Secaucus (2006)
3. Izsó, B., Szárnyas, G., Ráth, I., Varró, D.: Incquery-d: Incremental graph search in the cloud. In: Proc. of BigMDE 2013. ACM (2013), doi:10.1145/2487766.2487772
4. Sun, Z., Wang, H., Wang, H., Shao, B., Li, J.: Efficient subgraph matching on billion node graphs. Proc. VLDB Endow. 5(9), 788–799 (2012)
5. Ma, S., Cao, Y., Huai, J., Wo, T.: Distributed graph pattern matching. In: Proc. WWW 2012, pp. 949–958. ACM (2012), doi:10.1145/2187836.2187963
6. Fard, A., Abdolrashidi, A., Ramaswamy, L., Miller, J.A.: Towards efficient query processing on massive time-evolving graphs. In: Proc. CollaborateCom 2012, pp. 567–574. IEEE (2012)
7. Taentzer, G.: Distributed graphs and graph transformation. Applied Categorical Structures 7(4), 431–462 (1999), doi:10.1023/A:1008683005045
8. Kreowski, H.J., Kuske, S.: Graph transformation units and modules. Handbook of Graph Grammars and Computing by Graph Transformation 2, 607–638 (1999)
9. Valiant, L.G.: A bridging model for parallel computation. Commun. ACM 33(8), 103–111 (1990), doi:10.1145/79173.79181
10. Arendt, T., Biermann, E., Jurack, S., Krause, C., Taentzer, G.: Henshin: Advanced concepts and tools for in-place EMF model transformations. In: Petriu, D.C., Rouquette, N., Haugen, Ø. (eds.) MODELS 2010, Part I. LNCS, vol. 6394, pp. 121–135. Springer, Heidelberg (2010)
11. Apache Software Foundation: Apache Giraph, http://giraph.apache.org
12. Apache Software Foundation: Apache Hadoop, http://hadoop.apache.org
13. Dean, J., Ghemawat, S.: MapReduce: simplified data processing on large clusters. Commun. ACM 51(1), 107–113 (2008), doi:10.1145/1327452.1327492
14. de Lara, J., Ermel, C., Taentzer, G., Ehrig, K.: Parallel graph transformation for model simulation applied to timed transition Petri nets. ENTCS 109, 17–29 (2004), Proc. GT-VMT 2004, doi:10.1016/j.entcs.2004.02.053
15. Bergmann, G., Ráth, I., Varró, D.: Parallelization of graph transformation based on incremental pattern matching. ECEASST 18 (2009)
16. Blom, S., Kant, G., Rensink, A.: Distributed graph-based state space generation. ECEASST 32 (2010)
17. Blom, S., van de Pol, J., Weber, M.: LTSMIN: distributed and symbolic reachability. In: Touili, T., Cook, B., Jackson, P. (eds.) CAV 2010. LNCS, vol. 6174, pp. 354–359. Springer, Heidelberg (2010)
18. Malewicz, G., Austern, M.H., Bik, A.J., Dehnert, J.C., Horn, I., Leiser, N., Czajkowski, G.: Pregel: a system for large-scale graph processing. In: Proc. SIGMOD 2010, pp. 135–146. ACM (2010), doi:10.1145/1807167.1807184
19. Tichy, M., Krause, C., Liebel, G.: Detecting performance bad smells for Henshin model transformations. In: Proc. AMT 2013. CEUR-WS.org (2013)
20. Varró, G., Schürr, A., Varró, D.: Benchmarking for graph transformation. In: VL/HCC, pp. 79–88. IEEE Computer Society (2005), doi:10.1109/VLHCC.2005.23

Modularizing Triple Graph Grammars Using Rule Refinement

Anthony Anjorin, Karsten Saller, Malte Lochau, and Andy Schürr

Technische Universität Darmstadt,
Real-Time Systems Lab, Germany
surname@es.tu-darmstadt.de

Abstract. Model transformation plays a central role in Model-Driven Engineering. In application scenarios such as tool integration or view specification, bidirectionality is a crucial requirement. Triple Graph Grammars (TGGs) are a formally founded, bidirectional transformation language, which has been used successfully in various case studies from different applications domains.

In practice, supporting the maintainability of TGGs is a current challenge and existing modularity concepts, e.g., to avoid pattern duplication in TGG rules, are still inadequate. Existing TGG tools either provide no support at all for modularity, or provide limited support with restrictions that are often not applicable.

In this paper, we present and formalize a novel modularity concept for TGGs: *Rule refinement*, which generalizes existing modularity concepts, solves the problem of pattern duplication, and enables concise, maintainable specifications.

Keywords: model transformation, triple graph grammars, modularity.

1 Introduction and Motivation

Model-Driven Engineering (MDE) is an established, viable means of coping with the increasing complexity of modern software systems, promising an increase in productivity, interoperability and a reduced gap between problem and solution domains. *Model transformation* plays a central role in MDE and *bidirectionality* is often a crucial requirement especially in application scenarios that require model synchronization such as tool integration and view specification [3].

Triple Graph Grammars (TGGs) [9] are a rule-based, formally founded technique of specifying a consistency relation between models in a source and target domain, which allows for bidirectional model transformation. TGG rules consist of patterns representing the precondition and postcondition of a change to a model and are fully declarative, i.e., no control flow or similar constructs can be used to specify exactly *how* the change should be realized. In contrast to, e.g., *programmed* graph transformations, TGGs, therefore, require a *rule* structuring mechanism to avoid redundancy, i.e., identical patterns in multiple rules. When TGGs with a considerable number of rules are required, supporting productivity and maintainability becomes crucial.

S. Gnesi and A. Rensink (Eds.): FASE 2014, LNCS 8411, pp. 340–354, 2014.

As initially presented by Klar et al. [7], a viable means of addressing these challenges is to avoid pattern duplication in TGG rules by reusing rule fragments. Existing modularity concepts [7,5], however, pose strong restrictions on the way rules can be reused. Examples for such restrictions include: (i) that the context of a basis rule (the rule to be reused by refining it appropriately) can only be extended but not changed, and (ii) a lack of support for multiple basis rules. Our observation is that these restrictions are too strong and thus prevent reuse in many cases, especially in combination with the limited support for modularity on the metamodel level provided by EMF/Ecore.

Our contribution in this paper is to:

1. Present a novel flexible concept of *rule refinement* for TGG rules as a generalization of previous work by Klar et al. [7] and Greenyer et al. [5]. This is done intuitively in Sect. 2 with a running example.
2. Compare our approach with [7,5] and explain in detail why the generalizations we suggest are necessary. This is done in Sect. 3, where we discuss related existing modularity concepts for TGGs and graph transformations.
3. Provide a comprehensive formalization of rule refinement in Sect. 4.

We conclude with a summary and an overview of areas of future work in Sect. 5.

2 Rule Refinements for TGGs

Our running example is inspired by the families to persons transformation example in the ATL transformation zoo[1]. It represents a tool integration scenario, e.g., between the residents registration office and the tax office of a city.

Figure 1 depicts the triple of *source*, *correspondence*, and *target* metamodels for the transformation, referred to as a *TGG schema*. The source metamodel (left of Fig. 1) comprises a FamilyRegister, which contains multiple Families. A Family consists of Members, which play the role of a son, father, mother, or daughter in the family as indicated by the *references* connecting Family with Member.

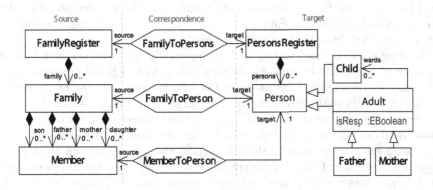

Fig. 1. TGG schema for the running example

---

[1] http://www.eclipse.org/atl/atlTransformations/#Families2Persons

The target metamodel (right of Fig. 1) comprises a PersonsRegister containing Persons. A Person is either a Child, or an Adult, i.e., a Father or Mother. Although the concept of a family is not explicitly present in the target metamodel, an Adult can be responsible for a number of children (isResp attribute in Adult and wards reference to Child) as this is relevant for tax calculation. The source and target metamodels are connected by a correspondence metamodel (hexagonal elements in Fig. 1) specifying which source and target types correspond to each other.

In addition to a TGG schema, a TGG consists of *TGG rules* that describe how triples of source, correspondence and target models are built-up simultaneously. Figure 2 depicts three of the seven rules implementing the families to persons transformation. A TGG rule consists of *elements* (nodes and edges). Nodes are depicted as label:Type, e.g., family:Family, while edges are depicted as Type without labels. Elements *created* by a TGG rule are depicted as green nodes/edges with a "++" markup, while *context* elements are depicted as black nodes/edges without any markup and must be present for the rule to be applied.

The TGG rule r_1: FamilyToPersonsRule creates a family register and a persons register simultaneously and connects them appropriately with a correspondence link. The TGG rules r_2: FamilyToFatherRule and r_3: MemberToFatherRule specify how fathers are handled: According to r_2, a family with a father Member corresponds to a Father in a PersonsRegister, if the Father is responsible for children (isResp := true in the node person:Father). Note that the created father and family are connected with a FamilyToPerson correspondence. In contrast, r_3 creates a Father that is not responsible for any children and requires, therefore, an adult who corresponds to the family as context.

The remaining rules of the TGG for the running example are:

r_4: *FamilyToMotherRule*, which is identical to r_2 but creates a Mother instead of a Father in the target model and connects the created Member via the mother reference instead of father.

r_5: *MemberToMotherRule*, identical to r_3 in an analogous manner as r_4 to r_2.

$r_{6/7}$: *MemberToSonRule* and MemberToDaughterRule, which are both identical to r_3 but connect the created Member to the Family via the son/daughter reference instead of the father reference in the source model. Furthermore, the rules create a Child instead of a Father in the target model, connecting the Child to the responsible adult via the wards reference.

Looking closer at the rules r_2 and r_3, one can observe that r_3 is a copy of r_2 with an additional element in the target domain and a few changes (some elements are required as context instead of being created and the attribute assignment is adjusted). Similar to code duplication in programs, such *pattern duplication* in the rules of a TGG has an averse effect on productivity and maintainability. For our running example, pattern duplication increases for the remaining rules $r_4 - r_7$ turning the rule specification process into an error-prone copy-and-paste task. Changing the transformations now implies multiple changes in different rules resulting in a maintenance nightmare, which gets worse with time as the relationships between rules is not explicit, i.e., new developers cannot know what must be adjusted. To avoid pattern duplication, a means of *reusing*

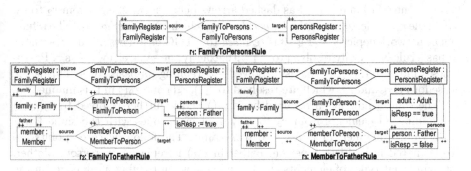

Fig. 2. TGG rules for handling fathers without rule refinements

common patterns in multiple rules is required. In addition, the reuse mechanism must be flexible enough to handle cases where the common pattern is not exactly the same but is only slightly changed. Our concept of rule refinements addresses this challenge by providing a concise pattern language with which higher-order transformations (using rule patterns to transform rule patterns) can be specified.

Figure 3 depicts the complete TGG for the running example using *rule refinements*. The TGG is now represented as an acyclic network of rules, with a

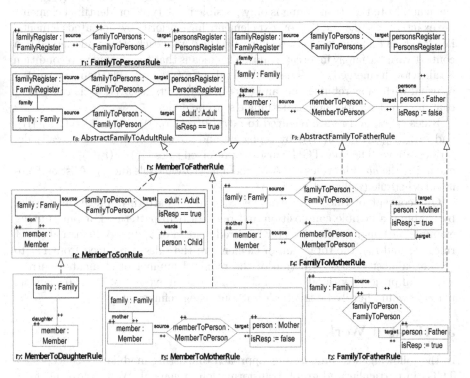

Fig. 3. Refinement network for complete TGG from running example

refinement relation depicted as dashed arrows between rules, e.g., from r_2 to r_9. The rule r_9 is referred to as the *basis rule* of r_2, which in turn *refines* r_9. The refinement network depicted in Fig. 3 is *resolved* to a TGG as follows. A rule r without a basis rule is trivially resolved to $r()$ with exactly the same elements as r. Parentheses indicate that the rule is "resolved" by refining its basis rules. This is the case for r_1, r_8 and r_9, which are resolved to $r_1()$, $r_8()$ and $r_9()$ in this manner.

The rule r_2 now has a resolved basis $r_9()$ and is further resolved to $r_2(r_9())$ by adding all elements from r_2 to $r_9()$, replacing nodes with the same label. In a similar manner, r_4 is resolved to $r_4(r_9())$. The following three points are to be noted here: Firstly, person: Father in $r_9()$ is replaced by person: Mother, showing that types of elements can be changed when refining, if all edges in the resolved basis rule can be reconnected to the new element. Secondly, the father edge between family and member in $r_9()$ is deleted as it is not in r_4. Finally, a mother edge between family and member is created as it is in r_4 but not in $r_9()$.

Resolving r_3 involves *multiple refinement* as it refines both r_8 and r_9. This is accomplished by *merging* all resolved basis rules to a single basis rule, which is then refined as usual. In this case, $\oplus(r_8(), r_9())$ is constructed by merging elements with the same label together, e.g., familyRegister from $r_8()$ is merged with familyRegister in $r_9()$ to form the same element in $\oplus(r_8(), r_9())$. Note that infix notation is not used here as the merge operator is n-ary. Elements such as adult and person that cannot be identified with a counterpart are added directly to $\oplus(r_8(), r_9())$ as new elements. Note that (i) merging is only possible if the types of identified elements are exactly the same and (ii) context elements have priority over created elements, i.e., family in $r_8()$ and family in $r_9()$ are identified with each other and merged to a context variable family in $\oplus(r_8(), r_9())$. This means that the stronger precondition is taken for the merged rule. The resolved rule $r_3(\oplus(r_8(), r_9()))$ is then constructed as usual with r_3 as refining rule and $\oplus(r_8(), r_9())$ as its resolved basis rule. As r_3 contains no elements, there is nothing else to be done.

Rules r_5, r_6, and r_7 are resolved to $r_5(r_3(\oplus(r_8(), r_9())))$, $r_6(r_3(\oplus(r_8(), r_9())))$, and $r_7(r_6(r_3(\oplus(r_8(), r_9()))))$ by replacing and creating elements as already described above. The final TGG consists of resolved rules $r_1()$, $r_2(r_9())$, ..., $r_7(...)$, excluding the *abstract* rules r_8 : AbstractFamilyToAdultRule and r_9 : AbstractFamilyToFatherRule (italicized in Fig. 3).

Our concept of rule refinement helps to avoid pattern duplication in rules by enabling a flexible composition and reuse of (sub)patterns. For our running example, although 9 rules are now required instead of 7, due to 2 extra abstract rules (r_8 and r_9), the total sum of elements in the rules is reduced from 117 to 65, i.e., almost a 50% reduction of the required number of elements. Current industrial projects with $50 - 100$ TGG rules and an average of $15 - 20$ elements per rule would hardly be tractable without using refinements.

3   Related Work

In the following, we compare our approach to existing modularity concepts for TGGs in particular and graph transformation in general. We refer to [11] for a broad survey of modularity concepts for model transformation languages.

Modularity Concepts for TGGs: Klar et al. [7] introduce a reuse mechanism for TGGs, which avoids pattern duplication by allowing rules to *refine* a basis rule. Greenyer et al. [5] extend this idea by introducing *reusable nodes*, i.e., nodes in TGG rules that can be created or parsed as context as required. As this can be simulated with our rule refinement concept, our approach can be viewed as a generalization of [7,5] with the following extensions:

1. We support and formalize *multiple* basis rules, i.e., multiple refinement, which is crucial for a flexible composition of modular TGG rules.
2. In the approach of [7], every rule can only create a single distinct correspondence type. This leads to a confusing mix of two different and orthogonal concepts: (i) Support for inheritance and abstract types in the metamodels (especially the correspondence metamodel) according to [4], and (ii) Refinement of TGG rules. In our approach, this restriction is removed completely; both reuse concepts are clearly separated and can be combined freely.
3. Rather strong restrictions are posed in [7,5] to guarantee the property that a basis TGG rule is always applicable when its refining rules are. We have decided to lift these restrictions as: (i) TGGs are usually *operationalized* to derive, e.g., forward and backward transformations. The mentioned property does *not* apply to these operational scenarios in general and is thus of questionable use in practice. (ii) The approach in [7] is formulated for MOF2 which supports advanced modularity concepts such as inheritance on *edge types*. The *de facto* standard EMF/Ecore is simpler in this respect and, as a consequence, requires a more flexible modularity concept for rules.
4. Both approaches use some form of rule priorities to resolve ambiguities caused by conflicts between basis and refining rules. As neither approach employs backtracking due to efficiency reasons, this can either lead to wrong decisions [5], or requires the user to constantly adjust priorities as rules are added and changed [7]. To resolve such conflicts, we utilize instead a *look-ahead* [8] as a form of application condition, which simulates rule application to detect obvious dead-ends in the transformation. We are thus able to handle a well-defined class of TGGs without backtracking or user intervention.

Modularity Concepts for Graph Transformations: There are numerous modularity concepts in the mature field of graph transformation. The concept of *variable nodes* in rules [6], which can be expanded to instantiate concrete rules, leads to "template" rules and requires separate, explicit expansion rules. Compared to our approach, this increases flexibility but also complexity. A related approach is amalgamation [2], where fragments of a rule can be denoted as being allowed to be matched arbitrarily many times. In this manner, a single rule can be also expanded at runtime by matching such fragments as *often as necessary*.

4   Formalization of Rule Refinements

The basic idea is to establish a suitable and compact language for describing *rule refinements*, i.e., the changes required to produce a new rule from a set of basic rules. We first of all define the syntax of the language, which is chosen to fit to the existing TGG syntax for rules, and specify how a *rule refinement* is decomposed into a set of *primitive transformation steps*. The semantics of rule refinement is then given by executing these primitive (atomic) transformations in a certain sequence to yield the corresponding higher-order (refinement can be seen as rewriting of triple rules) model transformation. Furthermore, refinements can be composed into complex *networks* with support for multiple refinement and abstract rules. For presentation purposes and due to space limitations, we focus in the following discussion on formal details necessary for rule refinement for TGGs, omitting details concerning, e.g., attribute manipulation, inheritance, and negative application conditions. We refer to [1,4,8] for further details.

4.1   Preliminaries: Models, Metamodels and Model Transformation

Models and metamodels are formalized as graphs, with a *conforms to* relationship between a model and its metamodel represented by a structure preserving map, i.e., a graph morphism *type* from a *typed graph* to its *type graph*.

Definition 1 (Typed Graph and Typed Graph Morphism)
A graph $G = (V, E, s, t)$ consists of a finite set V of nodes and a finite set E of edges, and two functions $s, t : E \to V$ that assign to each edge source and target nodes, respectively.

A graph morphism $f : G \to G'$, with $G' = (V', E', s', t')$, is defined as a pair of functions $f := (f_V, f_E)$ where $f_V : V \to V'$, $f_E : E \to E'$ and
$\forall e \in E : f_V(s(e)) = s'(f_E(e)) \,\wedge\, f_V(t(e)) = t'(f_E(e))$.

A type graph is a distinguished graph $TG = (V_{TG}, E_{TG}, s_{TG}, t_{TG})$.
A typed graph is a pair $(G, type)$ of a graph G and a graph morphism
type: $G \to TG$.

Given $(G, type)$ and $(G', type')$, $f : G \to G'$ is a typed graph morphism *iff $type = type' \circ f$.[2] The set of all graphs of type TG is denoted as $\mathcal{L}(TG)$.*

The following definition provides a rule-based, declarative formalization for model transformation. Changes to a model are represented as a *rule*, i.e., a pair of graphs representing the state of the model before and after the transformation.

Definition 2 (Monotonic Creating Rule, Graph Grammar). *Given a type graph TG, a* monotonic creating rule *$r = (L, R)$ consists of a pair of typed graphs $L, R \in \mathcal{L}(TG)$, with $L \subseteq R$.[3] A* graph grammar *$GG := (TG, \mathcal{R})$ consists of a type graph TG and a set $\mathcal{R}$ of monotonic creating rules.*

As TGG rules describe the simultaneous evolution of *triples of typed graphs*, all concepts are generalized accordingly. In the following, plain letters such as G denote *typed triple graphs*, whereas letters with a subscript such as G_S denote single *typed graphs*.

---

[2] $f \circ g$ denotes the morphism obtained by composing f and g and reads "f after g".
[3] $L \subseteq R$ denotes $L \xrightarrow{r} R$, where r is an *injective* typed graph morphism.

Definition 3 (Typed Triple Graph, Typed Triple Graph Morphism)
A triple graph $G := G_S \xleftarrow{\gamma_S} G_C \xrightarrow{\gamma_T} G_T$ *consists of typed graphs* $G_X \in \mathcal{L}(TG_X)$,
$X \in \{S, C, T\}$, *and morphisms* $\gamma_S : G_C \to G_S$ *and* $\gamma_T : G_C \to G_T$.

Given a triple graph $H = H_S \xleftarrow{\gamma'_S} H_C \xrightarrow{\gamma'_T} H_T$, *a triple morphism*
$f := (f_S, f_C, f_T) : G \to H$, *is a triple of typed morphisms* $f_X : G_X \to H_X$,
$X \in \{S, C, T\}$, *s.t.* $f_S \circ \gamma_S = \gamma'_S \circ f_C$ *and* $f_T \circ \gamma_T = \gamma'_T \circ f_C$.

A type triple graph is a triple graph $TG = TG_S \xleftarrow{\Gamma_S} TG_C \xrightarrow{\Gamma_T} TG_T$.

A typed triple graph is a pair $(G, type)$ *of a triple graph* G *and triple morphism*
$type : G \to TG$.

Given $(G, type)$ *and* $(G', type')$, $f : G \to G'$ *is a typed triple graph morphism*
iff $type = type' \circ f$. $\mathcal{L}(TG)$ *denotes the set of all triple graphs of type* TG.

Definition 4 (Triple Rules, Triple Graph Grammar (TGG))
Given a type triple graph TG, *a triple rule* $r = (L, R)$ *is a monotonic creating*
rule, where $L, R \in \mathcal{L}(TG)$, *and* $L \subseteq R$.

A triple graph grammar $TGG := (TG, \mathcal{R})$ *is a pair consisting of a type triple*
graph TG *and a finite set* $\mathcal{R}$ *of triple rules.*

Example 1. The TGG schema for our running example depicted in Fig. 1 is,
according to our formalization, a type triple graph. The TGG rule r_2 depicted
in Fig. 2 is a triple rule, i.e., a pair of typed triple graphs (L_{r_2}, R_{r_2}) where L_{r_2}
consists of all black elements and R_{r_2} of all black *and* green ("++") elements.

Although TGGs can be used directly to generate triples of consistent models,
e.g., for test generation, TGGs are often *operationalized* in practice to derive
a pair of unidirectional forward and backward transformations for bidirectional
model transformation. As our concept of rule refinement is completely resolved at
compile time, details of TGG operationalization are not necessary to understand
our formalization and are omitted. We refer to [8] for further details.

4.2 Syntax of Refinements

We now formalize the syntactic structure of a *refinement*, which consists of two
triple rules connected in such a manner that it is clear which elements are to be
deleted, replaced, or newly created. We take a compositional approach and define
a series of refinement *primitives*, representing executable atomic modifications to
the basis rule. Complex refinements are composed by combining these primitives.

Definition 5 (Refinement). *A refinement* $\Delta(r^*, r)$ *con-*
sists of two triple rules $r^* = (L^*, R^*)$ *and* $r = (L, R)$, *con-*
nected by triple morphisms $\delta_L, \delta_{L^*}, \delta_R, \delta_{R^*}$ *and typed triple*
graphs Δ_L, Δ_R, *with* $\Delta_L \subseteq \Delta_R$, *such that the diagram de-*
picted on the right commutes. The rule r^* *refines its* basis
rule r. *Note that* $\delta_L, \delta_{L^*}, \delta_R, \delta_{R^*}$ *are not necessarily typed.*

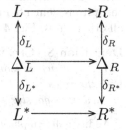

Definition 6 (Refinement Network). *A Refinement Network is an acyclic graph* $\mathcal{N}(V, E, s, t)$ *where each node* $n \in V$ *in the network is a triple rule and each edge* $e \in E$ *indicates that* $s(e)$ *refines* $t(e)$ *in the sense of Def. 5.*

Definition 7 (DeleteEdge). *A DeleteEdge source refinement is a refinement* $\Delta(r^*, r)$, *which is isomorphic to one of the five diagrams depicted in Fig. 4 below. DeleteEdge target refinements are defined analogously, i.e., with non-trivial components only in the target components of* $L, R, \Delta_L, \Delta_R, L^*,$ *and* R^*.

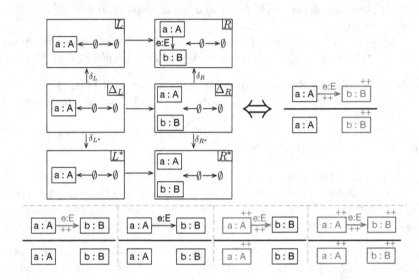

Fig. 4. DeleteEdge source refinements

The first *DeleteEdge* diagram is depicted in both a detailed syntax to the left, and an equivalent compact syntax to the right. In the detailed syntax, elements in the typed graphs are denoted by label:type giving a label for the element and its type. The graph morphisms $\delta_{L_S}, \delta_{L_S^*}, \delta_{R_S}, \delta_{R_S^*}$, depicted as arrows, are given by requiring all element labels to be unique in each graph and mapping equally labelled nodes (not necessarily of the same type) to each other, and equally labelled edges *of the same type* to each other. In the compact syntax, only non-trivial graphs are shown (in this case only the source components). The basis rule is placed above the black horizontal line, while the refining rule is placed below. Elements in $R_S \setminus L_S$ are annotated with a "++" markup[4] to differentiate them from elements in L_S. This allows for a compact notation, which is used for all other cases. Fig. 4 depicts in sum five different diagrams for *DeleteEdge*.

Definition 8 (CreateEdge). *A CreateEdge source refinement is a refinement* $\Delta(r^*, r)$, *which is isomorphic to one of the five diagrams depicted in Fig. 4 but with the roles of* L/L^* *and* R/R^* *exchanged. CreateEdge target refinements are defined analogously.*

---

[4] Additionally emphasized by depicting them in green instead of black.

Example 2. Consider the refinement $\Delta(r_4, r_9())$ in Fig. 3. In this case, the edge *father* in r_9 is removed via a *DeleteEdge* primitive, while the edge *mother* in r_4 is added via a *CreateEdge*. We denote this in the following as *DeleteEdge(father)* and *CreateEdge(mother)*, respectively.

Definition 9 (ReplaceNode)

A ReplaceNode source refinement is a refinement $\Delta(r^*, r)$, *which is isomorphic to one of the four diagrams depicted to the right.* ReplaceNode *target refinements are defined analogously.*

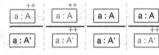

Note that the type of the replaced node can be changed in general, i.e., the graph morphisms $\delta_{L_S}, \delta_{L_S^*}, \delta_{R_S}, \delta_{R_S^*}$ are not necessarily type preserving (cf. Def. 5).

Definition 10 (CreateNode).

A CreateNode source refinement is a refinement $\Delta(r^*, r)$, *which is isomorphic to one of the two diagrams depicted to the right.* CreateNode *target refinements are defined analogously.*

Definition 11 (DeleteCorr).

A DeleteCorr refinement is a refinement $\Delta(r^*, r)$, *which is isomorphic to one of the five diagrams in Fig. 5.*

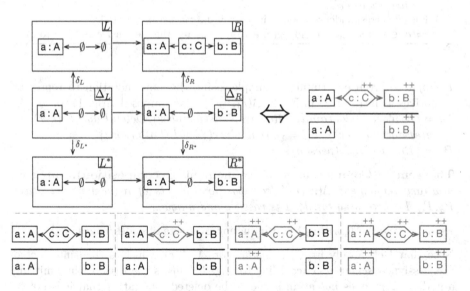

Fig. 5. DeleteCorr refinements

Note that, analogously to Fig. 4, the first *DeleteCorr* refinement is depicted in a detailed formal syntax to the left and a compact syntax to the right. Due to space limitations, the latter is used for the rest of the refinements.

Definition 12 (CreateCorr)
A CreateCorr *refinement is a refinement* $\Delta(r^*, r)$, *which is isomorphic to one of the five diagrams in Fig. 5 but with the role of* L/L^* *and* R/R^* *exchanged.*

Definition 13 (Refinement Primitive)
A refinement primitive *is a* DeleteEdge, ReplaceNode, CreateNode, CreateEdge, CreateCorr *or* DeleteCorr *refinement.*

4.3   Semantics of Refinement

To formalize the semantics of our rule refinement concept, we start by defining how a given refinement can be decomposed into primitives:

Algorithm 1. Refinement Decomposition

A refinement $\Delta(r^* = (L^*, R^*), r = (L, R))$ can be decomposed into sets P_S, P_C, P_T of refinement primitives as follows:

(i) For all nodes n in $V_{R_S^*}$, if $n \notin range(\delta_{R_S^*, V})$ then add a corresponding *CreateNode* to P_S, else add a *ReplaceNode* to P_S.

(ii) For all edges e^* in $E_{R_S^*}$, if $e^* \notin range(\delta_{R_S^*, E})$ then add a *CreateEdge* to P_S.

(iii) For all edges e in E_{R_S}, if $e \notin range(\delta_{R_S, E})$ and $s(e) \in range(\delta_{R_S, V})$ and $t(e) \in range(\delta_{R_S, V})$, then add a *DeleteEdge* to P_S.

(iv) Perform steps (i) - (iii) for target components $V_{R_T^*}$, $E_{R_T^*}$, E_{R_T}, and P_T.

(v) For all correspondence nodes c^* in $V_{R_C^*}$, if $c^* \notin range(\delta_{R_C^*, V})$, then add a *CreateCorr* to P_C.

(vi) For all correspondence nodes c in V_{R_C}, if $c \notin range(\delta_{R_C, V})$ and $\gamma_S(c) \in range(\delta_{R_S, V})$ and $\gamma_T(c) \in range(\delta_{R_T, V})$, then add a *DeleteCorr* to P_C.

Example 3. From our running example, using the same notation to represent primitives as introduced in Ex. 2, $\Delta(r_4, r_9())$ is decomposed (Alg. 1) to:
$P_S = \{ReplaceNode(family), ReplaceNode(member), DeleteEdge(father),$
$CreateEdge(mother)\}$, $P_C = \{CreateCorr(familyToPerson)\}$,
$P_T = \{ReplaceNode(person)\}$.

Theorem 1 (Completeness of Refinement Decomposition). *Given an arbitrary refinement* $\Delta(r^*, r)$, *decomposition in sets of refinement primitives* P_S, P_C, P_T *according to Alg. 1 is possible and unique.*

Proof. (Sketch) Algorithm 1 and induction over sets of nodes/edges in $\Delta(r^*, r)$.

Note that Def. 5 only fixes the *syntax* for $\Delta(r^*, r)$, which is then interpreted (i.e., assigned *semantics*) according to Alg. 1. This is the reason why omitting a node n in r^* does *not* mean it should be deleted, but rather that it is not to be refined in any way and does not induce any refinement primitive.

Algorithm 2 specifies the executable, atomic higher-order transformation each primitive represents. Based on this, we are now able to define the transformation a refinement represents via decomposition in primitives and execution of the primitives in a fixed order (given by the dependencies between primitives).

Algorithm 2. Refinement Primitive Resolution

Given a triple rule $r = (L, R)$, a refinement primitive $\Delta(r^*, r)$ is *resolved* to yield a new rule $r^*(r)$ from r by executing the corresponding higher-order model transformation given in pseudo code as follows (target primitives are handled analogously):

DeleteEdge(e): Remove e from E_{R_S} and, if $e \in E_{L_S^*}$, from E_{L_S}. Adjust source and target functions appropriately by removing entries for e.

CreateEdge(e): Add e to E_{R_S} and, if $e \in E_{L_S^*}$, also to E_{L_S}. Adjust source and target functions appropriately by adding entries for e.

ReplaceNode(n, m): If all incident edges to n can be transferred to m whilst retaining type conformity, remove n from and add m to V_{R_S} (repeat for V_{L_S} if $m \in V_{L_S^*}$). Transfer all incident edges. If this violates type conformity abort (primitive can not be resolved).

DeleteCorr(c): Remove c from V_{R_C} and, if $c \in V_{L_C^*}$, from V_{L_C}. Adjust graph morphisms between source/target and correspondence components appropriately by removing entries for c.

CreateCorr(c): Add c to V_{R_C} and, if $c \in V_{L_C^*}$, also to V_{L_C}. Adjust graph morphisms between source/target and correspondence components appropriately by adding entries for c.

Definition 14 (Refinement Resolution). *A refinement $\Delta(r^*, r)$ is resolved to yield a new rule $r^*(r)$ by decomposing it into sets of primitives P_S, P_C, P_T according to Alg. 1 and resolving the primitives (Alg. 2) in the following order: (i) All DeleteCorrs in P_C, (ii) all DeleteEdges in P_S and P_T, (iii) all ReplaceNodes in P_S and P_T, (iv) all CreateNodes in P_S and P_T, (v) all CreateEdges in P_S and P_T, and finally, (vi) all CreateCorrs in P_C.*

The next step on the way to formalizing a network of refinements is to specify how multiple refinement is handled via a merge operator defined on rules.

Definition 15 (Merge Operator ⊕)
Given a finite set $\{r_1, r_2, \ldots, r_n\}$ of rules $r_i = (L_i, R_i)$, $r = (L, R) = \oplus(r_1, r_2, \ldots, r_n)$ can be constructed as de- picted in the diagram to the right. $\{L_{1,2,\ldots,n}, \rho_{l_1}, \rho_{l_2}, \ldots, \rho_{l_n}\}$ and $\{R_{1,2,\ldots,n}, \rho_{r_1}, \rho_{r_2}, \ldots, \rho_{r_n}\}$ are constructed as the co-products of $L_1, L_2, \ldots, L_n$ and $R_1, R_2, \ldots, R_n$, respectively. The typed triple morphism $\mu_R : R_{1,2,\ldots,n} \to R$ must be provided (e.g., via a labelling function) and represents the decision which elements are to be regarded as equal and, therefore, merged in R. L, μ_{L_e} and μ_{L_m} are uniquely fixed by the choice of μ_R.

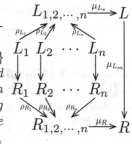

Example 4. From our running example, $\oplus(r_8(), r_9())$ is constructed by building the co-product (disjoint union of edges and nodes) of the left-hand sides of the rules (the black elements). This means $L_{8,9}$ consists of all elements in $r_8()$ (of interest is the node *family*!) and all black elements from $r_9()$. $R_{8,9}$ is constructed analogously and consists of all elements in both rules. The merging morphism μ_R (and thus L, μ_{L_e} and μ_{L_m}) is given implicitly by merging all elements with

the same label together. Note that both family nodes are glued together to a single family node, i.e., family is now a node in L as well as R and is, therefore, a context node in the merged rule.

Theorem 2 (Merge Operator is Sound). *The merge operator is commutative w.r.t. its arguments and uniquely defined for a given* μ_R *(Def. 15).*

Proof. (Sketch) The co-product construction is basically a disjoint union defined for graphs and is commutative. As $L_i \subseteq R_i$ for all rules r_i, it is also easy to show that the choice of μ_R fixes L, μ_{L_e} and μ_{L_m} with standard arguments.

Using the merge operator and refinement resolution, we can now provide an algorithm for resolving a refinement network to a TGG (without refinements):

Algorithm 3. Refinement Network Resolution

A refinement network $\mathcal{N}(V, E, s, t)$ is resolved as follows:

1. Every node r without outgoing edges is regarded as a *resolved* triple rule $r()$.
2. Every node r^* with a single outgoing edge e to a resolved rule $r()$ is regarded as a refinement: $\Delta(s(e), t(e))$.
3. Every node r^* with multiple outgoing edges $e_1, e_2, \ldots, e_k$ to resolved rules $r_1(), r_2(), \ldots, r_k()$ respectively, is regarded as a refinement over the result of merging all rules: $\Delta(r^*, r = \oplus(r_1, r_2, \ldots, r_k))$.
4. Every refinement $\Delta(r^*, r(\ldots))$ is resolved according to Def. 14, transforming the refinement network $\mathcal{N}$ in $\mathcal{N}'$ by removing all from r^* outgoing edges $e_1, e_2, \ldots, e_k$, and replacing r^* with the resolved rule $r^*(r(\ldots))$ in the network.
5. As $\mathcal{N}$ is acyclic, there exists a partial order $k_0, k_1, \ldots, k_l$ in which the network can be transformed with steps (1) – (4) until there are no edges left, i.e., $\mathcal{N} \overset{k_1}{\Rightarrow} \mathcal{N}_1 \overset{k_2}{\Rightarrow} \ldots \overset{k_l}{\Rightarrow} \mathcal{N}_l = (V_{\mathcal{N}_l}, \emptyset)$.
6. A refinement network without any edges is *resolved* and consists only of TGG rules. The final TGG is constructed from a resolved refinement network by excluding all rules that are tagged by the user as being *abstract*.

Theorem 3 (Completeness of Refinement). *A refinement network* $\mathcal{N}(V, E, s, t)$ *can be resolved to a TGG if all induced* ReplaceNode *primitives are restricted to using type preserving morphisms. If the refinement network can be resolved, the resulting TGG is unique up to isomorphism.*

Proof. The refinement network is acyclic so there exists at least one linearization in which the network can be resolved according to Alg. 3 (decomposition is always possible by Thm. 1). Demanding that all *ReplaceNode* primitives are restricted to using type preserving morphisms ensures that all refinement primitives can be resolved. There might be multiple sortings of the network but the resolution process for a rule r only depends on its transitive dependencies, which are *before* r in any valid sorting. The merge operator is commutative (Thm. 2), so the resulting TGG is independent of the order in which basis rules are resolved.

Example 5. A valid sorting for the refinement network of our running example is: $r_1, r_8, r_9, r_2, r_4, r_3, r_5, r_6, r_7$. The rules r_1, r_8 and r_9 can be resolved to $r_1(), r_8(), r_9()$ with Alg. 3.1. Resulting refinements are $\Delta(r_2, r_9())$, and $\Delta(r_4, r_9())$ according to Alg. 3.2, and $\Delta(r_3, \oplus(r_8(), r_9()))$ according to Alg. 3.3. With Alg. 3.4, these four refinements can be resolved to yield the new nodes $r_2(r_9())$, $r_4(r_9())$, and $r_3(\oplus(r_8(), r_9()))$ removing all outgoing edges from r_2, r_4 and r_3 and replacing r_2, r_4 and r_3 with their resolved versions (Alg. 3.4). The remaining network r_3, r_5, r_6, r_7 is resolved analogously.

4.4   Design Choices vs. Simplifications

In practice, correspondence graphs are often constructed as simple sets of correspondence nodes without any edges. To simplify the discussion in this paper, this common simplification is assumed, i.e., there are no *CreateCorrEdge* primitives. *DeleteNode* and *ReplaceEdge* primitives, however, are omitted on purpose as one could construct confusing refinement networks by introducing and removing nodes arbitrarily in the refinement network via *CreateNode* and *DeleteNode*.

The merge operator requires a typed triple morphism μ_R that decides which elements in the basis rules are to be merged together to result in a single element in the resulting rule. There are different ways to specify this morphism in practice. A user could provide the mapping explicitly by choosing the elements to be merged (in a dialogue or with a textual specification), or the mapping can be indicated implicitly by using equal labels for elements to be merged.

The readability of refinement networks has a considerable effect on usability. Although tool support can provide a "preview" of the complete rules, experience indicates that users actually appreciate the focus on a small section of the rule that is changed with respect to the basis rule. Concerning debugging of refinements, the resulting TGG can already be pretty printed in our textual concrete syntax and an import in our visual modelling environment is in development.

According to the classification of modularization concepts according to [11], our rule refinement is *flattened*, i.e., resolved at compile time. This means that the dynamic semantics of TGGs with respect to the resulting TGG is neither changed nor affected by using refinements. At first sight this might seem inefficient, why not use the information concerning rule similarities to control the choice of rules and possibly reduce unnecessary pattern matching? A similar challenge is also relevant in the context of incremental pattern matching and has already been analyzed in detail. We plan to employ the algorithm of [10] to detect rule similarities and enable efficient pattern matching even in cases where the extra information from refinements is not available or is insufficient (e.g., for weakly typed metamodels).

5   Conclusion and Future Work

In this paper we have introduced and formalized *rule refinement* as a pragmatic modularization concept for TGGs. Our approach generalizes existing work providing support for multiple refinement and increased flexibility as required for

EMF/Ecore. Although we focus in this paper on TGGs, our approach can be transferred to (transformation) languages with rules consisting of graph patterns.

An implementation of rule refinement as proposed in this paper is integrated in the current version of our metamodelling and model transformation tool eMoflon.[5] As future work we plan to improve readability by providing a visualization of the flattened TGG, which can be produced on demand. We plan to analyze our existing collection of TGGs to develop a catalogue of *bad smells*, and a set of systematic *refactorings*, which can be used to introduce refinement and reduce pattern duplication in existing TGG rules. A further important extension is to generalize our concept to refinement between complete TGGs, i.e., with primitives such as *AddRule* or *ReplaceRule*.

References

1. Anjorin, A., Varró, G., Schürr, A.: Complex Attribute Manipulation in TGGs with Constraint-Based Programming Techniques. In: Hermann, F., Voigtländer, J. (eds.) BX 2012. ECEASST, vol. 49. EASST (2012)
2. Biermann, E., Ehrig, H., Ermel, C., Golas, U., Taentzer, G.: Parallel Independence of Amalgamated Graph Transformations Applied to Model Transformation. In: Engels, G., Lewerentz, C., Schäfer, W., Schürr, A., Westfechtel, B. (eds.) Nagl Festschrift. LNCS, vol. 5765, pp. 121–140. Springer, Heidelberg (2010)
3. Czarnecki, K., Foster, J.N., Hu, Z., Lämmel, R., Schürr, A., Terwilliger, J.: Bidirectional Transformations: A Cross-Discipline Perspective. In: Paige, R.F. (ed.) ICMT 2009. LNCS, vol. 5563, pp. 260–283. Springer, Heidelberg (2009)
4. Ehrig, H., Ehrig, K., Prange, U., Taentzer, G.: Fundamentals of Algebraic Graph Transformation. Springer (2006)
5. Greenyer, J., Rieke, J.: Applying Advanced TGG Concepts for a Complex Transformation of Sequence Diagram Specifications to Timed Game Automata. In: Schürr, A., Varró, D., Varró, G. (eds.) AGTIVE 2011. LNCS, vol. 7233, pp. 222–237. Springer, Heidelberg (2012)
6. Hoffmann, B., Janssens, D., Van Eetvelde, N.: Cloning and Expanding Graph Transformation Rules for Refactoring. In: ENTCS, vol. 152, pp. 53–67 (2006)
7. Klar, F., Königs, A., Schürr, A.: Model Transformation in the Large. In: Crnkovic, I., Bertolino, A. (eds.) FSE 2007, pp. 285–294, No. 594074. ACM (2007)
8. Klar, F., Lauder, M., Königs, A., Schürr, A.: Extended Triple Graph Grammars with Efficient and Compatible Graph Translators. In: Engels, G., Lewerentz, C., Schäfer, W., Schürr, A., Westfechtel, B. (eds.) Nagl Festschrift. LNCS, vol. 5765, pp. 141–174. Springer, Heidelberg (2010)
9. Schürr, A.: Specification of Graph Translators with Triple Graph Grammars. In: Mayr, E.W., Schmidt, G., Tinhofer, G. (eds.) WG 1994. LNCS, vol. 903, pp. 151–163. Springer, Heidelberg (1995)
10. Varró, G., Deckwerth, F.: A Rete Network Construction Algorithm for Incremental Pattern Matching. In: Duddy, K., Kappel, G. (eds.) ICMT 2013. LNCS, vol. 7909, pp. 125–140. Springer, Heidelberg (2013)
11. Wimmer, M., et al.: A Comparison of Rule Inheritance in Model-to-Model Transformation Languages. In: Cabot, J., Visser, E. (eds.) ICMT 2011. LNCS, vol. 6707, pp. 31–46. Springer, Heidelberg (2011)

---

[5] www.emoflon.org

Polymorphic Single-Pushout Graph Transformation

Michael Löwe, Harald König, and Christoph Schulz

FHDW Hannover, Freundallee 15, 30173 Hannover

Abstract. The paper extends single-pushout graph transformation by polymorphism, a key concept in object-oriented design. The notions *subrule* and *remainder*, well-known in single-pushout rewriting, are applied in order to model dynamic rule extension and type dependent rule application. This extension mechanism qualifies graph transformation as a modelling technique for extendable frameworks. Therefore, it contributes to the applicability of graph transformation in software engineering.

1 Introduction

Algebraic graph transformation has been extended by many object-oriented modelling concepts, for example types and attributes, compare [2]. However, the central structure of object-orientation, namely inheritance with polymorphism, has not been completely integrated yet. We propose a concept for polymorphism in the single pushout approach [13].

Object-oriented polymorphism is a concept that allows several methods for the same operation. The late-binding mechanism of the corresponding runtime system selects the "best" method dependent on the types of the involved objects. Typically the most special of all fitting methods is selected and executed. We transfer this concept to typed algebraic graph transformation systems without attributes. Here, transformation rules play the role of methods. In order to mimic the late binding mechanism of object-orientation, we need a specialisation hierarchy on types *and* on methods, i. e. on transformation rules.

In contrast to [2], we model the specialisation hierarchy on types by a partial order in the type graph and do not allow cycles in the specialisation relation. Again in contrast to [2], we do not get rid of the specialisation relation by a flattening process. Instead, we use it to design a category $\mathbb{G}^T$ of ordinary directed graphs typed in the type graph T where morphisms are allowed to map *up to specialisation*: A morphism can map a vertex v to any vertex the type of which is a specialisation of the type of v, compare Section 3 and [16].

The hierarchy on transformation rules is modelled by subrule relations, i. e. a rule t is more special than t', if t' is a subrule of t. The subrule concept is borrowed from the theory of single-pushout rewriting, compare Section 2. It perfectly models polymorphism, since general results guarantee that the behaviour of t extends the behaviour of t', if t' is a subrule of t, in the following sense:

S. Gnesi and A. Rensink (Eds.): FASE 2014, LNCS 8411, pp. 355–369, 2014.

Every transformation with t can be decomposed into a transformation with t' followed by a transformation with a uniquely determined remainder $t - t'$.

The paper is organised as follows. Section 2 recapitulates the theory of single-pushout graph transformation [9,11,13,14], especially the concepts sub-rule, remainder, and amalgamated rule. Section 3 summarises the results of [16]. It introduces the basic category $\mathbb{G}^T$ of graphs typed in a type graph T with inheritance hierarchy. In Section 4, Theorem 25 shows the sufficient conditions for $\mathbb{G}^T$ to admit single-pushout rewriting presented in Section 2. Section 4 also introduces the new concept of a polymorphic graph transformation system. It allows type dependent rule selection and application. The increase in the expressive power is demonstrated by some examples. Section 6 discusses topics of future research. We assume that the reader has basic knowledge of category theory.

2 Single-Pushout Transformation Framework

Single-pushout graph transformation simplifies the classical double-pushout approach [2,3] with the help of a category that represents double-pushout rules $(L \xleftarrow{l} K \xrightarrow{r} R)$ as partial morphisms.

A *span base* $(\mathcal{C}, \mathcal{M})$ consists of a category $\mathcal{C}$ and a subclass $\mathcal{M}$ of the morphisms of $\mathcal{C}$ such that:

1. $\mathcal{M}$ contains all isomorphisms of $\mathcal{C}$.
2. $\mathcal{M}$ is closed under composition.
3. $\mathcal{M}$ is prefix-closed: $q \circ p \in \mathcal{M}$ and $q \in \mathcal{M} \implies p \in \mathcal{M}$.
4. $\mathcal{C}$ has all pullbacks for all pairs of morphisms (p, q) with $p \in \mathcal{M}$.
5. Pullbacks in $\mathcal{C}$ are $\mathcal{M}$-closed: (p^*, q^*) pullback of (p, q), $p \in \mathcal{M} \implies p^* \in \mathcal{M}$.

Given an object $A \in \mathcal{C}$, $\mathcal{C} \downarrow_{\mathcal{M}} A$ denotes the restriction of the comma category $\mathcal{C} \downarrow A$ to $\mathcal{M}$-morphisms.[1] The conditions 1, 2, and 3 guarantee that $\mathcal{C} \downarrow_{\mathcal{M}} A$ is a category. The conditions 4 and 5 provide a pullback functor $h^* : \mathcal{C} \downarrow_{\mathcal{M}} B \to \mathcal{C} \downarrow_{\mathcal{M}} A$ for every morphism $h : A \to B$ in $\mathcal{C}$.

A *concrete $\mathcal{M}$-span* is a pair of $\mathcal{C}$-morphisms (p, q) such that $p \in \mathcal{M}$ and $\mathrm{domain}(p) = \mathrm{domain}(q)$. Two $\mathcal{M}$-spans (p_1, q_1) and (p_2, q_2) are equivalent and denote the same *abstract span* if there is an isomorphism i such that $p_1 \circ i = p_2$ and $q_1 \circ i = q_2$; in this case we write $(p_1, q_1) \equiv (p_2, q_2)$ and $[(p, q)]_\equiv$ for the class of spans that are equivalent to (p, q). The *category of abstract $\mathcal{M}$-spans* $\mathcal{M}(\mathcal{C})$ over $\mathcal{C}$ has the same objects as $\mathcal{C}$ and equivalence classes of spans wrt. $\equiv$ as arrows. The identities are defined by $\mathrm{id}_A^{\mathcal{M}(\mathcal{C})} = [(\mathrm{id}_A, \mathrm{id}_A)]_\equiv$ and composition of two spans $[(p, q)]_\equiv$ and $[(r, s)]_\equiv$ such that $\mathrm{codomain}(q) = \mathrm{codomain}(r)$ is given by $[(r, s)]_\equiv \circ_{\mathcal{M}(\mathcal{C})} [(p, q)]_\equiv = [(p \circ r', s \circ q')]_\equiv$ where (r', q') is a pullback of (q, r).

---

[1] The $\mathcal{M}$-morphisms are the objects of $\mathcal{C} \downarrow_{\mathcal{M}} A$ and, due to condition 3, each $\mathcal{C} \downarrow_{\mathcal{M}}$ A-morphism is an $\mathcal{M}$-morphism.

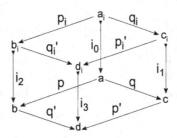

Fig. 1. Pushout/pullback cube

Note that there is the natural embedding faithful functor $\iota : \mathcal{C} \to \mathcal{M}(\mathcal{C})$ defined by identity on objects and $(f : A \to B) \mapsto [A \overset{id_A}{\leftarrow} A \overset{f}{\to} B]_\equiv$ on morphisms. By a slight abuse of notation, we write $[A \overset{d}{\leftarrow} A' \overset{f}{\to} B]_\equiv \in \mathcal{C}$ if d is an isomorphism. From now on, we write $A \overset{f}{\leftarrow} B \overset{g}{\to} C$ for the abstract span $\left[A \overset{f}{\leftarrow} B \overset{g}{\to} C\right]_\equiv$.

$\mathcal{M}(\mathcal{C})$ is called a category of *partial morphisms* over $\mathcal{C}$, if $\mathcal{M}$ is a subclass of all monomorphisms of $\mathcal{C}$. The following property guarantees that pushouts in $\mathcal{C}$ are pushouts in a category of partial morphisms $\mathcal{M}(\mathcal{C})$.

Definition 1. *($\mathcal{M}$-Hereditary Pushout[2]) A pushout (q', p') of (p, q) in $\mathcal{C}$ is $\mathcal{M}$-hereditary if for each commutative cube as in Figure 1, which has pullbacks (p_i, i_0) and (q_i, i_0) of (i_2, p) resp. (i_1, q) as back faces such that i_1 and i_2 are in $\mathcal{M}$, in the top square (q'_i, p'_i) is pushout of (p_i, q_i), if and only if in the front faces (p'_i, i_1) and (q'_i, i_2) are pullbacks of (i_3, p') resp. (i_3, q') and i_3 is in $\mathcal{M}$.*

The following fact reformulates the sufficient criterion of [14] for a category of partial morphisms to possess not only hereditary but all pushouts.

Fact 2. *(Pushout of Partial Morphisms) A category of partial morphisms $\mathcal{M}(\mathcal{C})$ has all pushouts, if (i) $\mathcal{C}$ has all pushouts and all small limits, (ii) pushouts in $\mathcal{C}$ are $\mathcal{M}$-hereditary, (iii) for every $h : A \to B$ in $\mathcal{C}$, the pullback functor $h^* : \mathcal{C} \downarrow_\mathcal{M} B \to \mathcal{C} \downarrow_\mathcal{M} A$ has a right adjoint $h_* : \mathcal{C} \downarrow_\mathcal{M} A \to \mathcal{C} \downarrow_\mathcal{M} B$.*

The theory of single-pushout transformation is built on a category $\mathcal{C}$ and a class $\mathcal{M}$ of monomorphisms such that $\mathcal{M}(\mathcal{C})$ has all pushouts. An example is the category $\mathcal{M}(\mathbb{G})$ of graphs where $\mathcal{M}$ is the class of all monomorphisms:

Definition 3. *(Category of Graphs $\mathbb{G}$) A graph $G = (V, E, src : E \to V, tgt : E \to V)$ consists of a set of vertices V, a set of edges E, and two mappings $src, tgt : E \to V$, which provide a source resp. target vertex for each edge. A graph morphism $f : G_1 \to G_2$ from a graph $G_1 = (V_1, E_1, src_1, tgt_1)$ to a graph $G_2 = (V_2, E_2, src_2, tgt_2)$ is a pair $(f_V : V_1 \to V_2, f_E : E_1 \to E_2)$ of mappings such that $f_V \circ src_1 = src_2 \circ f_E$ and $f_V \circ tgt_1 = tgt_2 \circ f_E$.*

---

[2] For details on hereditary pushouts see [9,11].

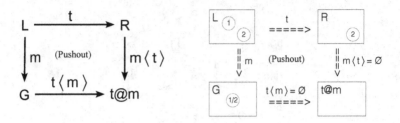

Fig. 2. Substitution and Partial Co-Match

Further examples are hyper-graphs or graph structures as in [13] where $\mathcal{M}$ is again the class of all monomorphisms.

Definition 4. *(Rule, Pre-Match, and Substitution) A rule $t : L \to R$ is a morphism in $\mathcal{M}(\mathcal{C})$. A pre-match for t in a host graph G is a morphism $m : L \to G \in \mathcal{C}$. A substitution $t@m$ of a rule t along a pre-match m is given by the $\mathcal{M}(\mathcal{C})$-pushout $(t\langle m \rangle : G \to t@m, m\langle t \rangle : R \to t@m)$ of (t, m). The object $t@m$ is the* substitution result. *The partial morphism $t\langle m \rangle$ is called the* trace, *the partial morphism $m\langle t \rangle$ the* co-match, *compare left part of Figure 2.*

Note that the co-match need not be total, i. e. need not be in $\mathcal{C}$. An example in $\mathcal{M}(\mathbb{G})$ is depicted in the right part of Figure 2. It shows the substitution of a rule $t : L \to R$ at a pre-match $m : L \to G$. The left-hand side L of t consists of two vertices, namely ① and ②. The rule deletes ① and preserves ②. The pre-match maps both vertices in L to the same and only vertex in the host graph G.

Definition 5. *(Conflict- and Confusion-Free Pre-Match) A pre-match m for rule t is* conflict-free,[3] *if its co-match is in $\mathcal{C}$. It is* confusion-free, *if it is conflict-free for every prefix of t, i. e. $m\langle p \rangle \in \mathcal{C}$ for each $p \in \mathcal{M}(\mathcal{C})$ such that $x \circ p = t$.*

In [13], conflict- and confusion-freeness have been characterised for $\mathcal{M}(\mathbb{G})$.

Fact 6. *(Conflict and Confusion in $\mathcal{M}(\mathbb{G})$) A pre-match m for a rule $t : L \to R$, which is a span $t = L \xleftarrow{t^l} D^t \xrightarrow{t^r} R$, in $\mathcal{M}(\mathbb{G})$ is (i) conflict-free, if and only if*

$$\forall x, y \in L : m(x) = m(y) \implies x, y \in t^l(D^t) \vee x, y \notin t^l(D^t),$$

and it is (ii) confusion-free, if and only if

$$\forall x, y \in L : m(x) = m(y) \implies x, y \in t^l(D^t) \vee x = y.$$

Confusion-free pre-matches induce decompositions of substitutions for each rule decomposition:

---

[3] Single-pushout derivations at conflict-free matches coincide with sesqui-pushout rewritings [1] with monic left-hand sides in rules.

Fact 7. *(Substitution at Confusion-Free Pre-Match) If $t@m$ is a substitution of rule t at confusion-free pre-match m and $t = t_2 \circ_{\mathcal{M}(C)} t_1$ is an arbitrary decomposition of the rule, then $t \langle m \rangle = t_2 \langle m \langle t_1 \rangle \rangle \circ t_1 \langle m \rangle$ and $m \langle t \rangle = m \langle t_1 \rangle \langle t_2 \rangle$.*

Fact 7 shows that every transformation at a confusion-free pre-match can be decomposed in elementary actions, namely (i) the addition of a single object (vertex or edge), the deletion of a single object, and the identification of two objects. Due to these positive properties, it is reasonable to allow only confusion-free pre-matches in direct derivations:

Definition 8. *(Match and Direct Derivation) The* matches *for a rule are its confusion-free pre-matches.* Direct derivations *are substitutions along matches.*

The compact notion of direct derivation allows for a straightforward and simple theory of single-pushout rewriting.[4] We repeat some results of [13] which are used below when we add inheritance.

Definition 9. *(Parallel Independence) Direct derivations $t_1@m_1$ and $t_2@m_2$ starting from the same host graph are* parallel independent *if $t_2 \langle m_2 \rangle \circ m_1$ is a match for t_1 and $t_1 \langle m_1 \rangle \circ m_2$ is a match for t_2.*

Derivations at independent matches lead to the same trace in any application order:

Fact 10. *(Parallel Independence) If direct derivations $t_1@m_1$ and $t_2@m_2$ are parallel independent, then $t_2 \langle t_1 \langle m_1 \rangle \circ m_2 \rangle \circ t_1 \langle m_1 \rangle = t_1 \langle t_2 \langle m_2 \rangle \circ m_1 \rangle \circ t_2 \langle m_2 \rangle$.*

Definition 11. *(Sub-rule and Remainder) A rule $t : L \to R$ is an (i,j)-sub-rule of another rule $t' : L' \to R'$, written $t \subseteq_{i,j} t'$, if $i : L \to L', j : R \to R'$ are two total* morphisms *(i. e. $i, j \in C$) such that (i) $j \circ t = t' \circ i$ and (ii) i is a match[5] for t. The (i,j)-remainder of t' wrt. t is the universal morphism $t' -_{i,j} t : t@i \to R'$ that satisfies (a) $(t' -_{i,j} t) \circ t \langle i \rangle = t'$ and (b) $(t' -_{i,j} t) \circ i \langle t \rangle = j$.*

Fact 12. *(Composition of Matches) If $t : L \to R \subseteq_{i,j} t' : L' \to R'$ and $m : L' \to G$ is match for t', then $m \circ i$ is match for t.*

This fact together with property (a) of Definition 11 immediately provides:

Corollary 13. *(Sub-Rule) Direct derivations with sub-rule-structured rules can be decomposed into a derivation with the sub-rule followed by a derivation with the remainder, i. e. if $t : L \to R \subseteq_{i,j} t' : L' \to R'$ and $m : L' \to G$ is a match for t', then $t' \langle m \rangle = t' -_{i,j} t \langle m \langle t \langle i \rangle \rangle \rangle \circ t \langle m \circ i \rangle$ and $m \langle t' \rangle = m \langle t \langle i \rangle \rangle \langle t' -_{i,j} t \rangle$.*

Definition 14. *(Amalgamation) If $t_0 : L_0 \to R_0$ is a (i_1, j_1)-sub-rule of $t_1 : L_1 \to R_1$ as well as a (i_2, j_2)-sub-rule of $t_2 : L_2 \to R_2$, the amalgamation of t_1*

---

[4] All necessary proofs can be performed just by using well-known general composition and decomposition results for pushouts.

[5] Remember, that, due to Definition 8, all matches are confusion-free!

and t_2 along[6] t_0 is the universal morphism $t_3 : L_3 \to R_3$ from the pushout ($i_1^* :$ $L_2 \to L_3, i_2^* : L_1 \to L_3$) of (i_1, i_2) to the pushout ($j_1^* : R_2 \to R_3, j_2^* : R_1 \to R_3$) of (j_1, j_2) that satisfies $t_3 \circ i_1^* = j_1^* \circ t_2$ and $t_3 \circ i_2^* = j_2^* \circ t_1$.

Fact 15. *(Induced Matches) The morphisms i_1^* and i_2^* constructed in Definition 14 are matches[7] for t_2 and t_1 resp.*

Lemma 16. *If m is match for rule t, then it is match for $j \circ t$, if $j \in C$.*

The derivation with an amalgamated rule results in the same trace as applying the common sub-rule followed by the two remainders in any order.[8] This is an immediate consequence of the following fact:

Proposition 17. *(Amalgamation) Let $t_1 +_{t_0} t_2$ be the amalgamation of t_1 and t_2 along t_0, where t_0 is a (i_1, j_1)-subrule of t_1 and a (i_2, j_2)-subrule of t_2. Let $i_0 = i_1^* \circ i_2 = i_2^* \circ i_1$, $m_1^R = i_2^* \langle t_0 \langle i_1 \rangle \rangle$, $t_1^R = (t_1 - t_0) \langle m_1^R \rangle$, $m_2^R = i_1^* \langle t_0 \langle i_2 \rangle \rangle$, and $t_2^R = (t_2 - t_0) \langle m_2^R \rangle$, then we obtain the following two properties:*

$$t_1 +_{t_0} t_2 = (t_2 - t_0) \langle t_1^R \circ m_2^R \rangle \circ (t_1 - t_0) \langle m_1^R \rangle \circ t_0 \langle i_0 \rangle$$
$$t_1 +_{t_0} t_2 = (t_1 - t_0) \langle t_2^R \circ m_1^R \rangle \circ (t_2 - t_0) \langle m_2^R \rangle \circ t_0 \langle i_0 \rangle .$$

Proof. Direct consequence of Facts 12 and 15, Lemma 16, and the observation that all quadrangles in Figure 3 are pushouts due to general pushout properties.

3   The Category of Typed Graphs with Inheritance

In this section, we recapitulate definitions and results from [16].

Definition 18. *(Type Graph) A type graph $T = (G_T, \leq)$ consists of a graph $G_T = (V, E, src, tgt)$ and a partial order $\leq \subseteq V \times V$, which has least upper bounds $\bigvee S$ and greatest lower bounds $\bigwedge S$ for every subset $S \subseteq V$.* □

The interpretation of *type graphs* from a software engineering perspective is the following: Vertices stand for *types* and edges model *associations* between types. The partial order $\leq$ on types represents the *inheritance* relation, i.e. $x \leq y$ means that x is a *sub-type* of y.

Note that the vertex set of a type graph cannot be empty, since *the least element* $\bigvee \emptyset$ and *the greatest element* $\bigwedge \emptyset$ must be vertices. Therefore, the simplest type graph consists of a single type vertex and no edges.

From a practical point of view, the existence of all greatest lower bounds and all least upper bounds seems to be a very strong and restrictive requirement. But it can easily be satisfied:

---

[6] More precisely, along (i_1, j_1) and (i_2, j_2).

[7] Confusion-free.

[8] I. e. the remainders are parallel independent.

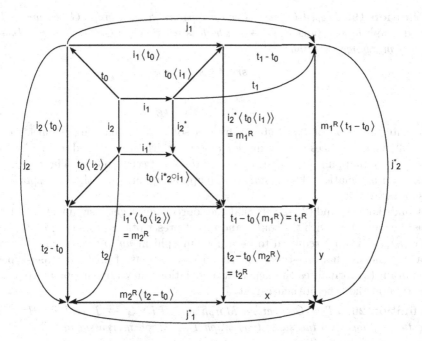

Fig. 3. Decomposition of Amalgamated Rule

For example any graph without inheritance relation can be turned into a type graph by adding the diagonal (reflexive vertex pairs), the greatest type $\bigwedge \emptyset$, an abstraction of all types, and the least type $\bigvee \emptyset$, a type that specialises all types, with the induced ordering. Any single-inheritance type hierarchy H can be turned into a type graph in our sense the same way: Add $\bigwedge \emptyset \cong$ Anything if H has more than one root and add $\bigvee \emptyset \cong$ Everything as a type for *objects of every shape*.

For an arbitrary type hierarchy H, there is the Dedekind/MacNeille-completion [17], which provides the smallest partial order closed under least upper and greatest lower bounds containing the original H. In the completion, any added element is a missing bound. In the finite case, the bounds in the completion coincide with the original bounds if they already existed in H.

If we are given an arbitrary type hierarchy H, which does not satisfy the type graph requirements of Definition 18, we calculate the type graph $T(H)$ by the Dedekind/MacNeille-completion. If, in any rewriting computation, added types, i. e. types in $T(H) - H$, occur, they can be interpreted as follows: Everything almost always indicates an error and all other added types indicate "uncertainty" in the sense that the concrete type in H cannot be computed on the basis of the given information.

Definition 19. *(Typed Graph) Given a type graph T, a graph G becomes a T-typed graph by a typing $i : G \to T$ which is a pair $(i_V : G_V \to T_V, i_E : G_E \to T_E)$ of mappings such that[9]*

$$i_V \circ src_G \leq src_T \circ i_E \tag{1}$$

$$i_V \circ tgt_G \leq tgt_T \circ i_E \tag{2}$$

The interpretation of *typed graphs* from a software engineering perspective is the following: Vertices of G stand for *objects*, which are assigned a type by the *instance-of* mapping i_V. Edges og G are *links* between objects. The type of a link is an association: The *instance-of* mapping i_E provides the corresponding assignment.

Conditions (1) and (2) specify that the source and target assignments of a link must be consistent with the source and target prescriptions of its type $i_E(l)$: The pair (i_V, i_E) is only required to be a homomorphism *up to inheritance*. Condition (1) means that sub-types inherit all associations of all their super-types. Condition (2) formalises the fact that associations may appear polymorphic at run-time in the type of their target.

Definition 20. *(Type-Compatible Morphism) If $i : G \to T$ and $j : H \to T$ are two typings into the same type graph T, a graph morphism $m : G \to H$ is type-compatible, written $m : i \to j$, if*

$$j_V \circ m_V \leq i_V \tag{3}$$

$$j_E \circ m_E = i_E \tag{4}$$

A morphism is called strong, *if $\leq$ in (3) can be replaced by $=$, i. e. $j_V \circ m_V = i_V$.*

The typings in T together with the type-compatible graph morphisms between them constitute the category of T-typed graphs $\mathbb{G}^T$.

There is a functor $\tau : \mathbb{G}^T \to \mathbb{G}$ which forgets the typing, i. e. maps a $\mathbb{G}^T$-morphism $m : (i : G \to T) \to (j : H \to T)$ to the $\mathbb{G}$-morphism $m : G \to H$.

A type-compatible morphism can map an object of type c to an object the type of which is a sub-type of c. *Strong* morphisms do not use this flexibility.

Fact 21. *(Strong Morphisms) (a) Isomorphisms are strong. (b) The composition of two strong morphisms is strong. (c) Strongness is prefix-closed, i. e. if $f \circ g$ is strong, then g is strong.*

Proposition 22. *(Limits and Co-Limits) For every small diagram $\delta : D \to \mathbb{G}^T$, there is a limit $(l_o : \mathbf{L} \to \delta(o))_{o \in D}$ and co-limit $(c_o : \delta(o) \to \mathbf{C})_{o \in D}$, such that $\tau(l_o)_{o \in D}$ and $\tau(c_o)_{o \in D}$ are the limit and co-limit of the diagram $\tau \circ \delta : D \to \mathbb{G}$ resp. The typings $l : \tau(\mathbf{L}) \to T$ and $c : \tau(\mathbf{C}) \to T$ map $x \in \tau(\mathbf{L})_V$ to $\bigvee\{\delta(o)(y) : y = l_o(x), o \in D\}$ and $x \in \tau(\mathbf{C})_V$ to $\bigwedge\{\delta(o)(y) : x = c_o(y), o \in D\}$ resp.[10]*

---

[9] If $f, g : X \to G$ are two mappings into a partially ordered set $G = (G, \leq)$, we write $f \leq g$ if $f(x) \leq g(x)$ for all $x \in X$.

[10] The notation $o \in D$ stands here for $o \in Object_D$.

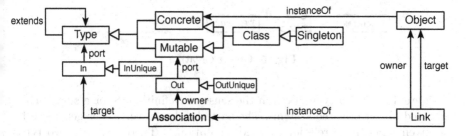

Fig. 4. Type Graph for Typed Object-Oriented Systems

Proof. Direct consequence of the results in [16] and the fact that all least upper bounds and greatest lower bounds exist in T.

To apply the single pushout transformation framework of Section 4, strong monomorphisms are of special interest:

Fact 23. *Pushouts and pullbacks preserve strong morphisms in $\mathbb{G}^T$, i.e. if (p^*, q^*) is pushout or pullback of (p, q) and p is strong, then p^* is strong.*

4 Single Pushout Transformation with Polymorphism

In this section, we instantiate the single-pushout framework of Section 2 for the category $\mathbb{G}^T$ of typed graphs presented in the last section. The span base category is $(\mathbb{G}^T, \mathcal{S})$ where $\mathcal{S}$ is the class of all strong monomorphisms. Thus, $\mathcal{S}(\mathbb{G}^T)$ is a category of (strong) partial morphisms. $(\mathbb{G}^T, \mathcal{S})$ satisfies the requirements (1) – (5) on page 356 of a span base, compare section 3.

Since $\mathbb{G}^T$ has all small limits and co-limits,[11] it remains to show the requirements (ii) and (iii) of Fact 2 for $\mathcal{S}(\mathbb{G}^T)$ to be a suitable category for single-pushout rewriting.[12]

Proposition 24. *(Pushout Conditions)* (a) *Pushouts in $\mathbb{G}^T$ are $\mathcal{S}$-hereditary.* (b) *Given a morphism $b : (h : H \to T) \to (k : K \to T)$ in $\mathbb{G}^T$, the pullback functor $b^* : \mathbb{G}^T \downarrow_{\mathcal{S}} k \to \mathbb{G}^T \downarrow_{\mathcal{S}} h$ has a right-adjoint.*

Theorem 25. $\mathcal{S}(\mathbb{G}^T)$ *has all pushouts.*

Proof. Direct consequence of Propositions 22 and 24 and Fact 2.

These results provide the fundament on which a concept of inheritance for single-pushout graph transformation can be built. We are already able to write *generic* rules. This is illustrated by the example depicted in Figures 4, 5, and 6.

---

[11] Compare Proposition 22.

[12] A detailed proof for the following proposition can be found in [15].

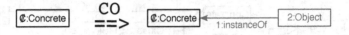

Fig. 5. Object Creation

Figure 4 depicts a type graph in the sense of Definition 18 for a small model for typed object-oriented systems. The partial order on vertices is generated by the given inheritance relations in UML notation.[13] There are only two types missing for the vertex order to possess all limits, namely $\bigvee \emptyset$ (Everything) and $\bigwedge \emptyset$ (Anything). We assume that these types are always implicitly added. The type graph specifies a type level and an instance level connected by the instanceOf-edges.

The most prominent type on the type level is Type. Types are orthogonally classified two times, namely in *concrete* versus not concrete (i. e. abstract) types on the one hand and in *mutable* versus immutable types on the other hand. Type-objects represent abstract *and* immutable types. Concrete-objects stand for *concrete* (i. e. not abstract) and immutable types, i. e. these objects can be target of instanceOf-edges. Mutable-objects model *mutable* and abstract types, i. e. these objects can be target of port-edges from Out-Objects. The type Class is derived from Concrete *and* Mutable. Therefore classes *inherit* the properties of *both* direct super-classes, i. e. objects of type Class (or more special) can be target of instanceOf-edges *and* can be owner of Associations. Singleton-types [4] are modelled as a specialisation of Class. The edges of type extends model specialisation. We assume that the set of these edges represents a hierarchy, i. e. includes edges for all paths (reflexive and transitive), and does not contain cyclic paths of length greater than zero (anti-symmetric). Association-objects connect Out- with In-ports. The specialisations of these port classes, i. e. OutUnique and InUnique, will be used later to model multiplicity specifications for associations.

The instance level is very simple. There are Object-objects which obtain a type (Concrete-object) on the type level by an instanceOf-edge. And there are Link-objects representing instances of Association-objects. Link-objects can connect Object-objects the instanceOf-target of which has type[14] Class (owner)[15] with Object-objects the instanceOf-target of which has type Concrete (target).[16]

Figure 5 depicts the method CO for the operation createObject(¢:Concrete). [17] The method is generic because it can be applied to objects of all sub-types of Concrete, namely Concrete, Class, and Singleton.

---

[13] http://www.uml.org/

[14] A t'-object is of type t, if t' is equal to a direct or indirect sub-type of t.

[15] Note that the owner of a link must be concrete *and* mutable.

[16] The **owner-** and **target**-relations on the instance level must be consistent with the corresponding relations on the model level. We model this constraint by the link creation rule, compare Figure 6.

[17] We use the UML notation for object diagrams.

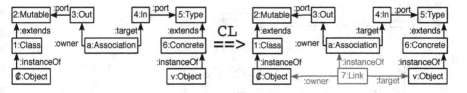

Fig. 6. Link Creation

The operation `createLink(¢ : Object, a : Association, v : Object)` is implemented by the method `CL` which is depicted in Figure 6. It allows the creation of a link only if the types of the receiver (¢) and the given value (v) are specialisations of the `owner`- and `target`-type of the given association parameter (a) resp. This method is also generic, since the object `1:Class` for example can be matched with `Class`- or `Singleton`-objects and there are 5 type choices for the object `5:Type`. Without specialisation, we would have to write 90 concrete rules for the type variations of the objects 1, 2, 5, and 6.

But *generic methods* are not the end of the game. Now, we introduce a mechanism that allows to extend rules. This is equivalent to method redefinition or polymorphism in object-oriented programming. A good example is the object creation rule `CO` in Figure 5. It does not always work right: The rule can create several instances for a `Singleton`-object.

Figure 7 shows the redefinition of `createObject(¢:Concrete)` in Figure 5 by a more special method CO_S, namely `createObject(¢:Singleton)`. The redefinition does not create an `Object`, if there is already one instance for the `Singleton`-class.[18] Note that CO has been made a sub-rule of CO_S by the morphism pair (i, j).

Figure 7 also shows the application $CO@i$ which provides the remainder $CO_S - CO$, compare Definition 11. Note, that every direct derivation $CO_s@m$ with the redefinition coincides with the derivation sequence that applies the sub-rule CO at the match $m \circ i$ followed by the remainder application $(CO_S - CO) @m \langle CO \langle i \rangle \rangle$, compare Corollary 13. Thus, the application of a sub-rule-structured rule corresponds to a **super**-call in object-oriented programming. We can think of the sub-rule as "shared code" that is always executed, in the example "adding an instance", and the remainder as the set of *additional* actions specified by the redefinition, in the example "identification of the new and the old instance".

Before we look at more complex examples, we formalise the presented feature of rule-extension and "application of the most specific rule".

Definition 26. *(Polymorphic Graph Transformation System) A polymorphic graph transformation system* $(T, P, \leq_P, M_P)$ *consists of a type graph* T, *a finite set of partial morphisms* $P \subseteq \mathbb{G}^T$, *representing the rules, a partial rule order* $\leq_P \subseteq P \times P$, *representing the specialisation relation on rules, and a family* M_P

---

[18] Note that the redefinition is the identity morphism.

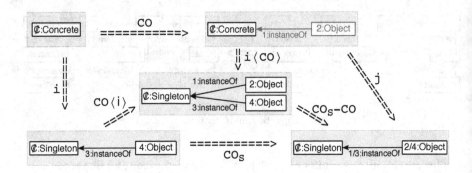

Fig. 7. Singleton Creation

of sub-rule specifications[19] $(l_{t,t'} : L \to L', r_{t,t'} : R \to R')$ for every pair $t' : L' \to R' \leq_P t : L \to R$ satisfying:

(a) Every rule has a unique most general rule, i. e.

$$t_3 \leq_P t_1 \wedge t_3 \leq_P t_2 \implies \exists t : t_1 \leq_P t \wedge t_2 \leq_P t \tag{5}$$

(b) The sub-rule specifications are consistent with the sub-rule order, i. e.

$$(l_{t,t}, r_{t,t}) = (\mathrm{id}_L, \mathrm{id}_R) \text{ for each } t : L \to R \in P \tag{6}$$

$$(l_{t,t''}, r_{t,t''}) = (l_{t',t''} \circ l_{t,t'}, r_{t',t''} \circ r_{t,t'}) \text{ for each triple } t'' \leq_P t' \leq_P t \tag{7}$$

Note that t' is a sub-rule of t, if t is a specialisation of t', since specialisation on rules means extension.[20] The analogy to Condition (a) in object-orientated programming is the fact that each method implements a unique operation.

From object orientation, we inherit the idea that the most specific method has to be chosen, if several methods for the same operation are applicable. This concept translates to our approach as follows:

Definition 27. *(Match and Derivation in Polymorphic System) A match m for a rule t in a system $PGT = (T, P, \leq_P, M_P)$ is a most specific match, if for all rules $t', \hat{t} \in P$ with $t' \leq_P \hat{t}$, $t \leq_P \hat{t}$ and all matches m' for t' we have: $m' \circ l_{\hat{t},t'} = m \circ l_{\hat{t},t} \implies t \leq_P t' \wedge m \circ l_{t't} = m'$. A direct derivation in PGT is a direct derivation at a most specific match.[21]*

The specialisation `OutUnique` of `Out`-ports stands for the multiplicity $0 \ldots 1$. Figure 8 depicts an extension CL_0 of the rule CL in Figure 6 which guarantees the

---

[19] Compare Definition 11.

[20] Thus, the partial orders on types and rules are consistent: "less than" means "more special".

[21] Note that rule redefinition formulates a negative application condition in the sense of [8]: A rule is *not* applicable if a more special rule is.

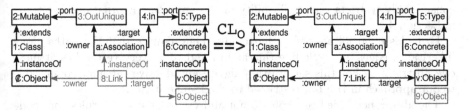

Fig. 8. Extension of Link Creation

corresponding uniqueness property for outgoing edges. The rule CL is redrawn in Figure 8 in black, the additional parts of CL_0 − CL are drawn in grey: CL_0 removes an existing link, when a new link is added.

Symmetrically, we can extend CL by a rule CL_I that removes an existing In-link of an object o, when a new In-link of the same association with a InUnique-port is added to o. Now, we have the situation $CL_0 \leq CL \geq CL_I$ which makes it possible that there is no most specific match, namely if a link shall be added the Association of which is unique at the In- and the Out-end between two objects that both possess such a link on the owner resp. target side. We need a special rule for this situation. It can be automatically generated, namely by the computation of the amalgamated rule $CL_0 +_{CL} CL_I$, compare Definition 14. Due to Proposition 17, it provides the correct effect. Thus, the automatic addition of all amalgamated rule extensions can help to solve the "method selection problem" in multiple redefinition situations.

The example demonstrates a maximum of code sharing: CL_0 and CL_I reuse CL and $CL_0 +_{CL} CL_I$ reuses CL_0 and CL_I and, indirectly, also CL. Every extension adds behaviour and *does not change* behaviour of the more general rules. These properties are guaranteed by Corollary 13 and Proposition 17. Therefore, we obtain a predictable system behaviour although we admit specialisation of rules.

5   Related Work

Most related theoretical research lines do not admit polymorphism. H. Ehrig et al. [2] introduce inheritance as an additional set of inheritance edges between vertices in the type graph. It is not required that this structure is hierarchical. Cycle-freeness is not necessary, since they do not work with the original type graph. Instead they use a canonically flattened type structure, in which inheritance edges are removed and some of the other edges are copied to the "more special" vertices. By this reduction, they get rid of inheritance and are able to reestablish their theoretical results. E. Guerra and J. de Lara [7] extend this approach to inheritance between vertices and edges.

F. Hermann et al. [10] avoid this flattening and define a weak adhesive category based on the original type graph with inheritance structure. The rule morphisms are required to reflect the sub-type structure: If an image of a morphism possesses sub-types, all these sub-types have pre-images under the morphism. This feature considerably restricts the applicability of the approach in situations like those in Section 4.

U. Golas et al. [6] also avoid flattening. They require that the paths along inheritance edges are cycle-free (hierarchy) and that every vertex has at most one abstraction. For this set-up, they devise an adhesive category comparable to our approach in [16] but restricted to single-inheritance.

The above mentioned concepts do not address redefinition of rules and "code sharing" by using rule specialisation and polymorphism. One approach in this direction is the model of object-oriented programming by A. P. Lüdtke Ferreira and L. Ribeiro [5], which is based on single-pushout rewriting. They allow vertex and edge specialisations in the type graph and show that suitably restricted situations admit pushouts of partial morphisms. Their framework is shown to be adequate as a model for object-oriented systems. They do not address further categorical properties. The work in [5] aims at modelling object-oriented concepts like inheritance and polymorphism by single-pushout graph grammars. It does not equip general single-pushout rewriting with polymorphism.

There are some practical approaches that allow rule extension. One example is [12] which is based on triple graph grammars. The operational effects are comparable to ours, but the devised mechanisms are described informally only.

6   Conclusions and Future Research

In this paper, we extended single-pushout graph transformation by inheritance and polymorphism. The introduced polymorphism is controlled, since it allows to add behaviour by rule extension but forbids changes of behaviour. This extension mechanism qualifies graph transformation as a modelling technique for extendable frameworks. Since non-monic rules are possible, effects of negative application conditions [8] can be modelled, compare for example Figure 7.

There are two directions for future theoretical research. After having handled inheritance for the double- and the single-pushout approach in [16] resp. in this paper, the concepts have to be generalised to the sesqui-pushout approach [1]. And theoretical results of the algebraic approach, e. g. the critical pair analysis, have to be generalised to polymorphic systems.

From the practical point of view, future research has to investigate the gained increase in expressiveness. Besides addition, deletion and identification of objects, the application of a single-pushout rule $L \leftarrow_l D \rightarrow_r R$ with inheritance at match m can also specialise the types of objects, namely for those $x \in D$ for which (i) r is not strong, i. e. $R(r(x)) \nleqq D(x)$, or (ii) which are identified by r with an item $y \neq x$ such that the types of $m(l(x))$ and $m(l(y))$ are different.

Another interesting practical issue is the invention of a methodology for the development of *message-based* object-oriented systems, for example in the sense of [5], starting from arbitrary polymorphic graph transformation systems.

References

1. Corradini, A., Heindel, T., Hermann, F., König, B.: Sesqui-pushout rewriting. In: Corradini, A., Ehrig, H., Montanari, U., Ribeiro, L., Rozenberg, G. (eds.) ICGT 2006. LNCS, vol. 4178, pp. 30–45. Springer, Heidelberg (2006)
2. Ehrig, H., Ehrig, K., Prange, U., Taentzer, G.: Fundamentals of Algebraic Graph Transformation. Springer (2006)
3. Ehrig, H., Pfender, M., Schneider, H.J.: Graph-grammars: An algebraic approach. In: FOCS, pp. 167–180. IEEE (1973)
4. Gamma, E., et al.: Design Patterns: Elements of Reusable Object-Oriented Software. Addison-Wesley (1994)
5. Lüdtke Ferreira, A.P., Ribeiro, L.: Derivations in object-oriented graph grammars. In: Ehrig, H., Engels, G., Parisi-Presicce, F., Rozenberg, G. (eds.) ICGT 2004. LNCS, vol. 3256, pp. 416–430. Springer, Heidelberg (2004)
6. Golas, U., Lambers, L., Ehrig, H., Orejas, F.: Attributed graph transformation with inheritance: Efficient conflict detection and local confluence analysis using abstract critical pairs. Theor. Comput. Sci. 424, 46–68 (2012)
7. Guerra, E., de Lara, J.: Attributed typed triple graph transformation with inheritance in the double pushout approach. Technical Report UC3M-TR-CS-06-01. Technical Report Universidad Carlos III de Madrid (2006)
8. Habel, A., Heckel, R., Taentzer, G.: Graph grammars with negative application conditions. Fundam. Inform. 26(3/4), 287–313 (1996)
9. Heindel, T.: Hereditary pushouts reconsidered. In: Ehrig, H., Rensink, A., Rozenberg, G., Schürr, A. (eds.) ICGT 2010. LNCS, vol. 6372, pp. 250–265. Springer, Heidelberg (2010)
10. Hermann, F., Ehrig, H., Ermel, C.: Transformation of type graphs with inheritance for ensuring security in e-government networks. In: Chechik, M., Wirsing, M. (eds.) FASE 2009. LNCS, vol. 5503, pp. 325–339. Springer, Heidelberg (2009)
11. Kennaway, R.: Graph rewriting in some categories of partial morphisms. In: Ehrig, H., Kreowski, H.-J., Rozenberg, G. (eds.) Graph Grammars 1990. LNCS, vol. 532, pp. 490–504. Springer, Heidelberg (1991)
12. Klar, F., Königs, A., Schürr, A.: Model transformation in the large. In: Crnkovic, I., Bertolino, A. (eds.) ESEC/SIGSOFT FSE, pp. 285–294. ACM (2007)
13. Löwe, M.: Algebraic approach to single-pushout graph transformation. Theor. Comput. Sci. 109(1&2), 181–224 (1993)
14. Löwe, M.: A unifying framework for algebraic graph transformation. Technical Report 2012/03, FHDW-Hannover (2012)
15. Löwe, M., König, H., Schulz, C.: Polymorphic single-pushout graph transformation. Technical Report 2013/04, FHDW-Hannover (2013)
16. Löwe, M., König, H., Schulz, C., Schultchen, M.: Algebraic graph transformations with inheritance. In: Iyoda, J., de Moura, L. (eds.) SBMF 2013. LNCS, vol. 8195, pp. 211–226. Springer, Heidelberg (2013)
17. MacNeille, H.M.: Partially ordered sets. Trans. Amer. Math. Soc. 42(3), 416–460 (1937)

Causal-Consistent Reversible Debugging*

Elena Giachino[1], Ivan Lanese[1], and Claudio Antares Mezzina[2]

[1] Focus Team, University of Bologna/INRIA, Italy
[2] SOA Unit, FBK Trento, Italy
{giachino,lanese}@cs.unibo.it, mezzina@fbk.eu

Abstract. Reversible debugging provides developers with a way to execute their applications both forward and backward, seeking the cause of an unexpected or undesired event. In a concurrent setting, reversing actions in the exact reverse order in which they have been executed may lead to undo many actions that were not related to the bug under analysis. On the other hand, undoing actions in some order that violates causal dependencies may lead to states that could not be reached in a forward execution. We propose an approach based on causal-consistent reversibility: each action can be reversed if all its consequences have already been reversed. The main feature of the approach is that it allows the programmer to easily individuate and undo exactly the actions that caused a given misbehavior till the corresponding bug is reached. This paper major contribution is the individuation of the appropriate primitives for causal-consistent reversible debugging and their prototype implementation in the CAREDEB tool. We also show how to apply CAREDEB to individuate common real-world concurrent bugs.

1 Introduction

Reversible debugging has been known for the last 40 years [8,22], and gets all its interest and motivation from assisting the programmer in the search of possible bugs by exploring the computation both forward and backward. Retracing back the steps is very useful when investigating a misbehavior. In a sequential setting it is also very natural: steps are simply undone in the reverse order of execution.

In a concurrent world, where multiple threads execute concurrently, there may not be a unique "last" action. Thus, the concept of reversibility has been interpreted and implemented in different ways, depending on the answer to the following question: When a misbehavior is encountered, how can one proceed in order to retrace the steps towards the bug?

We will describe the different approaches on a simple scenario. Train passengers are taking their seats on a train. Some of them have reserved a seat, some others have not. Those without reservation pick randomly a free seat. Those with reservation take their assigned seat unless they find it has been occupied by someone else, in which case they pick a free one. What should not happen is

---

* This work has been partially supported by the French National Research Agency (ANR), project REVER n. ANR 11 INSE 007.

S. Gnesi and A. Rensink (Eds.): FASE 2014, LNCS 8411, pp. 370–384, 2014.

that some passenger X with a reservation finds himself standing without a seat. If this happens, how do we find the problem and fix it? Following the approaches in the literature, we could:

Non-deterministic replay debugging [20,1,19]: send everyone out of the train and start again the sitting algorithm. But this time passengers may choose seats in different orders, thus the problem may not occur, or a different passenger may be left without the seat he is entitled to.

Deterministic replay/reverse-execute debugging [9,4]: start asking people to stand up in the exact reverse order they occupied the seats. Then we risk making many innocent people leave their seats before finding the one who is occupying the seat of passenger X.

What one would like to do is to undo the sitting of the "causal predecessor" of passenger X: the one who took his seat. If, in turn, he had another reservation, then one would undo the sitting of his causal predecessor and so on. In this way, one can possibly find a place for the passenger with reservation by undoing a limited number of seat actions.

This form of reversibility, called *causal-consistent*, is quite natural in practice as the example above shows, but has never been applied to debugging as far as we know. The term causal-consistent highlights that actions are reversed by respecting causes: only actions that have caused no successive actions can be undone. In other words, concurrent actions can be reversed in any order, while dependent actions are reversed starting from the consequences. Causal-consistent reversibility has been studied mainly in the field of process calculi [6,17,12,5]. The key contribution of this paper is to individuate the primitives allowing to apply the abstract theory of causal-consistent reversibility to help programmers to debug concurrent applications. In general, one finds a misbehavior in a concurrent program and has to find the instruction in the code that caused it. This instruction may be in any of possibly many threads, and far back in the code. We provide new primitives allowing the programmer to go back in the computation following the causes of the misbehavior till the bug is reached. For instance, if the fault is a wrong value of a variable, we provide a primitive to find and undo the (last) assignment to this variable. We show how this and similar primitives can be applied to various categories of common bugs found in real-world concurrent applications. We also present CAREDEB, a prototype implementation of our approach.

In principle, causal-consistent reversibility can be applied to debugging for any concurrent language, and the primitives needed to implement this idea do not change much from one language to the other. However, their actual implementation relies on the definition of a causal-consistent reversible semantics for the language. As far as we know, the only programming language equipped with a causal-consistent reversible semantics is μOz [15]. Thus, we have chosen μOz for our studies.

$S ::=$		Statements
	skip	Empty statement
	$\mid S_1 \ S_2$	Sequential composition
	$\mid$ **let** $x = v$ **in** S **end**	Variable declaration
	$\mid$ **if** x **then** S_1 **else** S_2 **end**	Conditional statement
	$\mid$ **thread** S **end**	Thread creation
	$\mid$ **let** $x = c$ **in** S **end**	Procedure declaration
	$\mid$ { $x \ x_1 \ldots x_n$ }	Procedure call
	$\mid$ **let** $x = $ NewPort **in** S **end**	Port creation
	$\mid$ { Send $x \ y$ }	Send on a port
	$\mid$ **let** $x = $ { Receive y } **in** S **end**	Receive from a port
$v ::=$ **true** $\mid$ **false** $\mid$ 0 $\mid$ 1 $\ldots$		Simple values
$c ::=$ **proc** { $x_1 \ldots x_n$ } S **end**		Procedure

Fig. 1. μOz Syntax

2   The μOz Language

In this section we informally present μOz, a fragment of the Oz language, whose complete theoretical treatment can be found in [15]. Some details relevant for debugging are summarized in Section 6. μOz is a higher-order language featuring thread-based concurrency and asynchronous communication via ports.

The syntax of μOz is in Figure 1. Values in μOz are booleans, natural numbers, (communication) ports and procedures. Variables are immutable, i.e. read-only variables that are initialized at the time of their declaration. Communication is asynchronous and is realized by means of send and receive actions on a port, to which a FIFO queue is associated. Variable declaration, procedure declaration, port creation and reception are binders. Specifically, x is bound in S in **let** $x = v$ **in** S **end**, **let** $x = c$ **in** S **end**, **let** $x = $ NewPort **in** S **end**, and **let** $x = $ { Receive y } **in** S **end**.

3   Causal-Consistent Debugging

In this section we describe the commands enabling causal-consistent reversible debugging, which are also implemented in our causal-consistent reversible debugger prototype CAREDEB [2]. Clearly, some of the available commands are standard for (reversible) debuggers, while others are peculiar of our causal-consistent approach. We give more emphasis to the last ones. For simplicity, we also distinguish commands for controlling the execution (labeled with "control" in Table 1) from those for exploring the configuration of the program under debugging (labeled with "explore" in Table 1). Most of the commands can be abbreviated: abbreviations are in parenthesis after the command name in Table 1.

Table 1. CAREDEB main commands

control	forth (f) t	(forward execution of one step of thread t)
	run	(runs the program)
	rollvariable (rv) id	(causal-consistent undo of the creation of variable id)
	rollsend (rs) id n	(causal-consistent undo of last n send to port id)
	rollreceive (rr) id n	(causal-consistent undo of last n receive from port id)
	rollthread (rt) t	(causal-consistent undo of the creation of thread t)
	roll (r) t n	(causal-consistent undo of n steps of thread t)
	back (b) t	(backward execution of one step of thread t (if possible))
explore	list (l)	(displays all the available threads)
	store (s)	(displays all the ids contained in the store)
	print (p) id	(shows the state of a thread, channel, or variable)
	history (h) id	(shows thread/channel computational history)

Commands for forward execution are standard: command **forth t** executes a single step in a given thread **t**, while command **run** executes the program under a round-robin scheduler (breakpoints may be used to stop the execution).

Commands for backward execution are more peculiar. The main feature of our debugger is a suite of commands that undo the last action that produced some unexpected behavior (visible by analyzing the state of the application). We present these commands by listing the possible visible bad behaviors:

Wrong value in a variable: if a variable **id** has an unexpected value, command **rollvariable id** allows the programmer to go to the state just before the creation of variable **id**;

Wrong value in a queue element: if an element of the queue associated to port **id** has an unexpected value, command **rollsend id n** allows the programmer to undo the last **n** sends to this port. If **n** is unspecified, the last send is undone;

Thread blocked on a receive: if a thread is blocked on a receive on an empty queue, it may be the case that the desired message has been read by another thread. This can be checked by looking at the history of the queue, which contains the messages that were in the queue in the past. In this case, command **rollreceive id n** allows the programmer to undo the last **n** receives on the port **id**. If **n** is unspecified, the last receive is undone;

Unexpected thread: if an unexpected thread **t** is found, command **rollthread t** allows the programmer to undo the creation of the thread.

All these commands are causal-consistent, i.e. they undo all the actions that depend on the target action, while not undoing concurrent actions. For instance, undoing the send of a value requires to undo the receive of the same value, if performed and not yet undone. Similarly, undoing the creation of a thread requires to undo all the actions performed by the created thread. This is fundamental to ensure causal consistency: on one side this ensures we go back to a past state that could have been reached by a forward execution, on the other side we undo the minimal number of actions needed to reach this aim. These commands also print information on which actions have been undone, and in which order.

While these commands are the ones more in line with our philosophy of going back following the causes of misbehavior, other commands can be used by the programmer to go back following his intuition. In particular, we provide command **roll t n** which undoes (in a causal-consistent way) the last **n** steps done by thread **t**. Command **back t** is the symmetric of **forth t**, and undoes a single step of thread **t**. Notably, this command is enabled only if all the consequences of the step (if any) have already been undone.

Commands for exploring the configuration can be divided in two categories: commands for exploring the standard information (state, code, ports), and commands for exploring the history of the computation and of ports. Note that variables have no associated history information, since their values never change.

Standard commands include the command **list**, to display the list of threads (including whether they are active or terminated), and the command **store** to display the identifiers in the store. The content of a given identifier **id** can be printed by command **print id**. According to what **id** is, it may print the value of a variable (possibly a procedure), the queue associated to a port, or the code still to be executed by a thread. History information is displayed by command **history id**. Here **id** may refer to a thread, and in this case the history is the list of the past actions executed by the thread, or to a queue, and in this case the history is the list of messages that were in the queue and have been read.

4   Assessment: Real-World Concurrency Bugs

In this section we evaluate our debugging techniques against real world concurrency bugs as described in [16]. Amazingly, all real world concurrency bugs reported have a simple pattern, involving a small number of variables, threads, and resources. They are however small snippets immersed in thousands of lines of code of huge applications such as Mozilla, Apache, MySQL and OpenOffice. This tells us that it is not necessary to find complex bug examples in order to reason about real world.

According to [16], real world concurrency bugs are mainly of three kinds: *order violation*, *atomicity violation*, or *deadlock*. We show below an example for each class of bug, and apply our debugging primitives to isolate them. The bugs were originally in C/C++ programs, but we recast them here in μOz.

An order violation bug occurs when the programmer assumes a given order among two actions, but those actions may actually occur also in a different order. A simple example of order violation bug in μOz follows:

```
let one = 1 in
let two = 2 in
let k = port in
thread {send k one} end; // t_1
thread {send k two} end; // t_2
thread let x = {receive k} in skip end end //t_3
end end end
```

Here the programmer assumed that value one would be sent before value two, but did not enforce this property. In fact, even if thread t_2 is created after thread t_1, it may run faster and execute its sending of value two before the sending of value one from thread t_1. When this happens, the programmer may note two possible misbehaviors: (i) variable x is 2, while 1 was expected, or (ii) the port k contains value 1, while 2 was expected.

In the first case, the most natural thing to do is to execute **rollvariable x**. This would put back the variable in the queue. Notice that one can do this without knowing where, in a possibly huge code, the receive was. One can see by inspecting the queue that the two values are not in the expected order. Using the command **rollsend k** twice one can put back the two messages, thus finding the send which caused the misbehavior. Also, the fact that, when undoing the send of one, the send of two is not undone by the causal-consistent mechanism confirms that the expected dependency was not enforced.

In the second case one can inspect the history of port k using command **history k** and see that value two was indeed put in the queue by t_2, but has been already read by t_3. Using command **rollreceive k** the value is put back in the queue. From here the same technique used above can be applied.

We stress here the fact that it may seem easy to catch this kind of bugs in this simple example, but actually these threads may not be so much distinguishable when immersed in the whole program, and our debugging techniques can be applied in the exact same way, since they require only to know the misbehavior, not of being aware of the involved instructions: these are highlighted by the debugging commands.

An atomicity violation bug occurs when the programmer assumes that two actions are executed in an atomic way, but does not enforce this atomicity constraint. A simple example of atomicity violation bug in μOz follows:

```
let t = true in
let f = false in
let k = port in
thread {send k t};let x = {receive k} in skip end end; // t_4
thread {send k f};let y = {receive k} in skip end end  // t_5
end end end
```

Here the programmer assumed the pairs of send and receive on channel k in threads t_4 and t_5 to be atomic, but did not enforce this property. In fact, it is possible that thread t_5 receives the value intended for thread t_4 and vice versa. One can see as misbehavior the fact that x and y have not the expected value. Without knowing where this value has been assigned, one can use commands **rollvariable x** and **rollvariable y** to undo the corresponding assignments. From the output of the debugger one immediately discovers which thread is responsible of the assignment. When the two values are back in the queue of port k one can use command **rollsend k** and immediately discover that the send has not been performed by the expected thread, thus finding the bug.

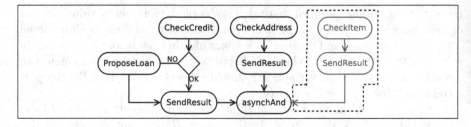

Fig. 2. The purchase workflow

A simple example of *deadlock* in μOz is the following:

```
let t = true in
let k = port in
thread {send k t} end;  // t_7
thread let x = {receive k} in {send k t} end end;  // t_8
thread let y = {receive k} in skip end end// t_9
end end end
```

Here, if the send from thread t_7 is received by thread t_9 instead of t_8, then the execution of thread t_8 blocks indefinitely because its receive precedes its send. By looking at the list of threads using command **list**, one can see that thread t_8 has not terminated its computation. One can look at the code of the thread using command **print** t_8 and see that it is waiting on a receive on port k. The first thing that one can do is to look into the history of the port in order to see if some message was ever put into the queue. By executing command **history k** one finds that a message was actually inside the queue in the past, and was picked up by another thread. Then, by means of command **rollreceive k**, one can undo the receive of the message. One can see from the output of the debugger that this requires to undo actions of thread t_9. This highlights the fact that thread t_9 is also involved in the deadlock. Even more, one has discovered exactly which are the two receive actions and the unique send action critical for the deadlock to occur, and has all the needed information to fix the bug.

An interesting fact reported in [16] is that most of the bugs (101 out of the 105 reported) involve no more than 2 threads. This highlights the importance of the fact that the techniques above allow the programmer to immediately find the involved threads starting from the unexpected behaviors, and to avoid to undo all the actions of the many unrelated threads.

5   Debugging a Concurrent Application

In this section we describe a use case for CAREDEB [2], more complex than the paradigmatic examples discussed in the previous section. Differently from those bugs, the bug considered here is not concurrent per se. Nevertheless, the concurrent nature of the application makes it more difficult to individuate.

Our sample program (inspired by [18]) implements a procedure for handling purchase orders. Figure 2 (without the dashed part) depicts its intended behavior. Before an order is placed, two conditions must be verified: the availability of the customer's credit, and the completeness of the delivery details. The two independent checks CheckCredit and CheckAddress are performed concurrently. If the credit is insufficient, CheckCredit invokes the procedure ProposeLoan that offers to the client a loan of 20% of his credit for the purchase. A positive answer is sent as a result if the updated credit is enough to match the price, a negative response otherwise. The results of the checks are sent to the asynchAnd procedure as soon as they are available. The asynchAnd procedure performs a short-circuit evaluation of n-ary AND: if it receives the value _false_, then it immediately produces _false_ as a result, otherwise it waits for another value. If no more values are expected, then it sends the value _true_ as a result.

The definition of the procedure asynchAnd is as follows, where n, inp and out are the formal parameters corresponding to the number of expected operands, the input and the output ports, respectively.

Listing 1.1. The asynchronous AND procedure

```
let asynchAnd = proc {n inp out}
                if (n>0) then let k={receive inp} in
                              let v={receive k} in
                              let m = n-1 in
                              if v then {asynchAnd m inp out}
                              else {send out false} end
                              end end end
                else {send out true} end
                end in ...
```

Since the operands are computed independently, they are sent to different ports. The statement k={receive inp} receives the id of the port k on which to wait for the operand v. If v is true, then the procedure is recursively called waiting for the n-1 values left. Otherwise, the conjunction fails and _false_ is sent over the result port out. When all the expected values have been gathered (n=0) the item can be delivered (i.e., _true_ is sent over out).

The program defines three concurrent threads:

```
thread {asynchAnd 2 input result} end;  //t_1
thread {send input outCr};{checkCredit outCr inCr} end; //t_2
thread {send input outAdd};{checkAddress outAdd} end;  //t_3
```

The first thread invokes the asynchronous AND on two values expected on ports whose names are sent over port input. The result is sent on port result. The other two threads send on input the ports outCr and outAdd, respectively, on which the value will be communicated, and then invoke the corresponding check procedure.

Assume we perform perfective maintenance on this software: to avoid that clients wait for long periods of time, we make sure that the item is actually in stock before concluding the purchase. Thus, a new procedure checkItem implementing such a check is incorporated in the system (as shown in the dashed part of Figure 2). A new port outIt and a new parallel thread are created:

```
thread {send input outIt}; {checkItem outIt} end //t_4
```

Hence we have three concurrent sends over port input. The order in which asynchAnd is going to process the results of the checks depends on the scheduling order of those sends.

Before putting the upgraded version of the program to work (the code is available on CAREDEB web site [2]), we want to test its behavior. We consider a test case where the price of the item is 15 euros and the credit amount is 10 euros. We also assume that the item is in stock and that the delivery details are fine. We execute the test using the **run** command of CAREDEB, which executes the program till the end. We know that, in this test case, the purchase should be rejected. Instead, within our test run, the procedure asynchAnd returns true. A bug is somewhere in our program and we need to find it. The problem may lie either in a wrong assessment of the credit, or in a wrong assessment of the loan, or in a bug within the asynchronous AND. Even in this simple example we cannot say a priori where the bug can be found.

Since something is clearly wrong with the value received on port result, we jump back just before that value was sent, by performing **rollsend result**. This points us back to thread *t_1* executing the else branch in the body of asynchAnd. Unfortunately, in this case, we do not get much insight on the source of the bug, because it happens to roll back of one step only thread *t_1*. Anyway, we are now sure that the problem was not related to conflicting sends to port result.

At this point, following the intuition that something wrong may be within the control of the credit performed by the procedures in thread *t_2*, we execute **roll t_2 1** and we cause the reversing of the last action within procedure proposeLoan, namely the sending of the result to asynchAnd. Somehow surprisingly, this does not cause the undo of other actions. The fact that no receive inside the asynchAnd procedure needed to be undone means that the result of proposeLoan has not been considered by asynchAnd. By looking at the send just undone we also notice that the sent value is correct. Therefore we can exclude that the problem is in the check of the credit availability, which is performed properly.

Notably, if we would have undone the execution of thread *t_4*, managing the checking of the item availability, we would have seen a very different behavior. This could have been done, for instance, by using command **rollthread t_4**. As a result, also part of the computation of thread *t_1* performing the asynchAnd would have been undone, showing an actual dependency between the two threads.

Let us go back to our debugging strategy. Since we now think that the problem is due to the asynchAnd procedure, we can undo its execution step by step looking for the bug, using command **back t_1**. When we reach the beginning of the thread we notice that asynchAnd was invoked with 2 as number of operands, while we would have expected 3 operands. This is the bug we were looking for. This was due to the fact that the invocation was not updated after the check of the item had been introduced.

The commands **roll** and **back** allowed us to check the guesses about the location of the bug, independently from the possible interleavings of thread execution. With the non-deterministic replay debugging one could have experienced a different scheduling of the threads at every attempt of action reversing, thus the bug could have showed or hidden itself in an unpredictable way. With the deterministic replay/reverse-execute debugging, instead, one would have needed to reverse the actions following a strict chronological order, possibly needing to reverse many unrelated actions before finding the bug.

6 Underlying Theory

We summarize here a few theoretical notions, mainly adapted from [15], which ensure the soundness of our debugging strategy.

6.1 Causality Relation

Causal consistency is defined for μOz relying on the notion of causality below.

Definition 1 (Dependent actions). *We define below when two (forward) actions are causally dependent:*

1. *an action of a thread depends on the previous actions of the same thread;*
2. *all the actions of a thread depend on the thread creation;*
3. *all the uses of a variable depend on its creation;*
4. *a receive of an element from a queue depends on the send of this element;*
5. *a send on a queue depends on the previous sends to the same queue;*
6. *a receive from a queue depends on the previous receives from the same queue.*

Remark 1. The conditions $1 - 4$ above correspond to the conditions defining the well-known Lamport's *happens-before* relation [11]. Conditions 5 and 6 above instead have no correspondence in the happens-before, and formalize the fact that queues are order preserving. Thus our causality model is stricter than Lamport's.

6.2 μOz Semantics

The debugger relies on the definition of a causal-consistent semantics for μOz, whose main features are described below.

The operational semantics of μOz is defined in [15] by a simple stack-based abstract machine. It exploits an extended syntax featuring also tasks and threads (used for statement execution), port queues (for communication), and the store. Tasks are a parallel composition of threads. Threads are stacks of statements. The store is a conjunction of bindings, procedures, and ports (essentially implemented as named FIFO queues). The standard μOz semantics is defined as a reduction relation, denoted $\to$, between configurations of the form (U, σ), where U is a task and σ is a store (0 is the empty store).

Let us comment a few sample reduction rules. Rule R:npt creates a new port x', by putting a new binding $x' = \xi$ in the store. Also, x' is substituted for x in the scope S to avoid variable capture. A queue is associated to ξ and initialized to $\bot$ (the empty queue). Task T is the continuation of task S.

$$[\text{R:npt}](\langle \textbf{let } x = \texttt{NewPort in } S \textbf{ end } T \rangle, \, 0) \to (\langle S\{^{x'}\!/_x\} \, T \rangle, \, x' = \xi \parallel \xi : \bot),$$

with x', ξ fresh.

Rule R:snd performs a send, by enqueuing variable y in the queue of port x.

$$[\text{R:snd}](\langle\{ \text{ Send } x \ y \ \} \ T\rangle, \ x = \xi \parallel \xi : Q) \to (T, \ x = \xi \parallel \xi : y; Q)$$

Rule R:rcv performs a receive, dequeuing the corresponding element z and fetching its value w. The value w is assigned to the fresh variable x' that substitutes the formal variable x.

$$[\text{R:rcv}](\langle\text{let } x = \{ \text{ Receive } y \ \} \text{ in } S \text{ end } T\rangle, \ y = \xi \parallel \xi : Q; z \parallel z = w)$$
$$\to (\langle S\{^{x'}/_x\} \ T\rangle, \ y = \xi \parallel \xi : Q \parallel z = w \parallel x' = w)$$

with x' fresh. The reduction relation $\to$ is closed under evaluation contexts (and structural congruence). We refer to [15] for further details.

Debug-mode semantics. The debugger relies on a causal-consistent reversible semantics, which keeps track of history and causality information. This semantics is proved to be a conservative extension of μOz semantics, i.e. forward computations during debugging are indeed a decorated version of the μOz reductions [15].

In the reversible semantics, threads have a name t (which is unique) and a history H, and execute an extended statement stack C. The history stores information about executed statements. Sent variables are stored in the queue, not in the history. Also, for an if statement just the discarded branch has to be stored, since the other one is available in the thread code. History is needed also inside ports, to remember the order of communications.

The semantics is defined by means of two reduction relations, a forward relation $\twoheadrightarrow$ and a backward relation $\rightsquigarrow$. Let us see, as an example, how the instrumented forward reduction rules for communication and the corresponding backward rules are defined. Rule R:fw:npt stores $*x'$ in the history, meaning that x' has been used as fresh port, and uses the scope delimiter **esc** to recall the scope of the binding. The created queue comes with an empty history $\perp$.

$$[\text{R:fw:npt}] \ (t[H]\langle\text{let } x = \text{NewPort in } S \text{ end } C\rangle, \ 0)$$
$$\twoheadrightarrow (t[H * x']\langle S\{^{x'}/_x\} \ \langle\textbf{esc } C\rangle\rangle, \ x' = \xi \parallel \xi : \perp|\perp) \qquad x', \xi \text{ fresh}$$

Rule R:fw:snd stores $\uparrow x$ in the history, to record the sending on port x. Also, the name t of the thread sending the value is stored in the queue together with the variable y, to avoid that a different thread takes the value when rolling back.

$$[\text{R:fw:snd}] \ (t[H]\langle\{ \text{ Send } x \ y \ \} \ C\rangle, \ x = \xi \parallel \xi : K|K_h)$$
$$\twoheadrightarrow (t[H \ \uparrow x]C, \ x = \xi \parallel \xi : t{:}y; K|K_h)$$

Rule R:fw:rcv stores $\downarrow x(y')$ in the history, to record that y' has been received from port x. The read value is also kept in the queue history, with information on which thread read it.

$$[\text{R:fw:rcv}] \ (t[H]\langle\text{let } y = \{ \text{ Receive } x \ \} \text{ in } S \text{ end } C\rangle, \ \theta \parallel \xi : K; t'{:}z|K_h)$$
$$\twoheadrightarrow (t[H \ \downarrow x(y')]\langle S\{^{y'}/_y\} \ \langle\textbf{esc } C\rangle\rangle, \ \theta \parallel \xi : K|t'{:}z, t; K_h \parallel y' = w)$$
$$\text{if} \quad y' \text{ fresh} \wedge \theta \triangleq x = \xi \parallel z = w$$

The backward rules are in one to one correspondence with the forward ones, and use the stored information to get back to the original state. Notably, rules R:bk:npt and R:bk:rcv below go back to a term which is not the starting one, but which is equivalent up to α-conversion. Also, they exploit the scope delimiter **esc** to identify the scope of the statement to be reversed. The occurrence of **esc** in the rule is always matched by the nearest occurrence in the term. In rule R:bk:npt the $\perp$ in the history ensures that the actions on the port are rolled back before its creation is rolled back.

$$[\text{R:bk:npt}] \ (t[H \ * x]\langle S \ \langle \textbf{esc} \ C \rangle\rangle, \ x = \xi \parallel \xi : \perp|\perp)$$
$$\rightsquigarrow (t[H]\langle \textbf{let} \ x = \texttt{NewPort in} \ S \ \textbf{end} \ C\rangle, \ 0)$$

$$[\text{R:bk:rcv}] \ (t[H \ \downarrow x(z)]\langle S \ \langle \textbf{esc} \ C \rangle\rangle, \ z = w \parallel x = \xi \parallel \xi : K|t':y,t;K_h)$$
$$\rightsquigarrow (t[H]\langle \textbf{let} \ z = \{ \ \texttt{Receive} \ x \ \} \ \textbf{in} \ S \ \textbf{end} \ C\rangle, \ x = \xi \parallel \xi : K;t':y|K_h)$$

6.3   Properties of Debugging

The soundness of our debugging follows from two results from the theory of causal-consistent reversibility [6]. Without going into the technical details, we just want to emphasize their relation with the debugging.

Proposition 1 (Debugging Soundness)

1. *Every reduction step can be reversed.*
2. *Every state reached during debugging could have been reached by a forward-only execution from the initial state.*

The first item ensures that the debugger can undo every forward step, and, viceversa, it can re-execute every step previously undone. This property is known as Loop Lemma [6, Lemma 6], and has been proved for μOz in [15, Lemma 3]. The second item ensures that any sequence of forward and backward debugging commands can only reach states which are part of normal forward-only computations. This property is known as Parabolic Lemma [6, Lemma 10], and its proof for μOz is analogous to the one in [6].

7   Implementation Aspects

We have implemented in JAVA a prototype of our causal-consistent debugger, CAREDEB [2], to test it in practice. It provides all the primitives presented in Section 3. The most interesting aspects of the implementation lie in the treatment of the **roll** command, and its variants **rollvariable**, **rollsend**, **rollreceive**, and **rollthread**. In fact, the step-by-step backward command **back** follows strictly the semantics presented in Section 6, and it is guaranteed to be correct by Proposition 1.

The command **roll** undoes actions in the target thread following the semantics in Section 6, and thus the correctness result holds also for it. However, if one such action has dependencies, these dependencies must be retrieved and rolled back beforehand, including their own dependencies. This requires to find both the dependent thread and the dependent action inside it. One could in principle find these actions by inspecting the histories of the threads in the system, but for efficiency reasons we explicitly annotate the action having the dependency with a pair (thread_id, n), where n is a natural number pointing to a specific action of thread thread_id. Note that only communication actions and thread creation actions may have dependencies.

When reversing a thread creation action, if the child thread memory is not empty, then a ChildMissingException is thrown containing the name of the child thread: this thread will be fully reversed before continuing.

When a send operation on some port k is reversed, the corresponding message must be removed from the queue of k. However, this can be done immediately only if the message has not been read yet, and it is the last one sent on port k. If the first condition fails also the receive of the message must be reversed. If the second condition fails, the send of successive messages to the same queue have to be reversed to maintain causal consistency. In both the cases a WrongElementChannel exception is raised with a list of pairs (thread_id, n) pointing to the instructions of the receiving and/or sending threads to be reversed as argument.

The same approach is used for receive actions, to ensure that successive receives from the same port are undone beforehand.

One may think that also port creation should check for dependencies, but this is not the case. In fact, assume that some other thread interacted on the port. Then, it must know the name of the port, either by receiving it via communication from the port creator, or by being its child. In both the cases, these actions are undone before the port creation can be undone, thus undoing all the communications on the port.

A last issue is to find the target of commands **rollvariable**, **rollsend**, **rollreceive**, and **rollthread**. For **rollsend** and **rollreceive** this is done using the same pointers above. For **rollvariable** and **rollthread** this is done by associating a similar pointer to each variable and each thread, respectively.

8   Related Work and Conclusion

We presented a debugging technique allowing the programmer to look for bugs in a concurrent program by following backward causal dependencies from the misbehavior to the bug. We also presented CAReDeb [2], a prototype debugger for μOz, a fragment of the Oz language, enabling such an approach. The approach relies on storing history and causality information, and is based on the solid theory of causal-consistent reversibility.

Reversibility for debugging of sequential programs has been quite extensively explored [14,7,10,3]. The interplay between reversibility and concurrency makes things more complex: concurrent reversible debugging is a less explored world. All the approaches to concurrent reversible debugging we are aware of fall in the two categories below:

Non-deterministic replay debugging [20,1,19]: in order to go back to a previous step, the execution is replayed non-deterministically from the start (or from a previous checkpoint) until that step.

Deterministic replay/reverse-execute debugging [9,4]: a log is kept while executing, and when going back thread activities are either undone in the exact reverse order they were executed, or the execution is replayed from a previous checkpoint following the particular interleaving in the log.

Both approaches present drawbacks. In the first case, actions could get scheduled in a different order at every replay, and the error may not get reproduced. Even if it does, one may not get any insight on the causes of the error. Following the second approach, if the error was due to one among a million of independent parallel threads, and that one was the first one to execute, one needs to undo all the program execution before finding the bug. Even more, one does not understand which threads are related to a given misbehavior, since there is no information on the relations among them.

Causality in the context of non-reversible concurrent debugging has been addressed in different works [13,23,21], which mainly rely on the Lamport's *happens-before* causality relation [11] (we sketched a comparison between our causality notion and Lamport's in Section 6.1). In all these works causality is used to support determinism in replaying techniques and to define efficient dynamic slicing. In contrast, we use causality as a support for rollback primitives allowing the programmer to find the causes of a misbehavior.

As far as we know, the only work that addresses reversibility and causality together is about Causeway [18]. However, Causeway is not a full-fledged debugger, but just a post-mortem traces analyzer. It exploits a causality notion, based on the Lamport's *happens-before*, more liberal than ours.

Up to now, we mainly focused on the design of the right primitives to support our causal-consistent reversible debugging strategy. We are aware that causality can be exploited also for efficiency reasons [23]. As future work, we plan to exploit the causality information we have also for improving the efficiency, possibly integrating our techniques with others from the literature.

The debugger CAREDEB we presented is just a prototype. The interaction with it is console-based, but we are in the process of upgrading it to an Eclipse plugin. Moreover, it targets the toy language μOz. Our long term goal is to develop a causal-consistent reversible semantics and a causal-consistent debugger for a mainstream language, such as Java, Erlang or C++.

We also plan to test in practice the impact of causal-consistent primitives on the efficiency of the debugging process.

References

1. Arya, K., Denniston, T., Visan, A.M., Cooperman, G.: Fred: Automated debugging via binary search through a process lifetime. CoRR, abs/1212.5204 (2012)
2. CAREDEB 0.5.0, a causal-consistent reversible debugger (2013), http://www.cs.unibo.it/caredeb

3. Chen, S.-K., Fuchs, W.K., Chung, J.-Y.: Reversible debugging using program instrumentation. IEEE Trans. Software Eng. 27(8), 715–727 (2001)
4. Chronon Systems. Commercial reversible debugger, http://chrononsystems.com/
5. Cristescu, I., Krivine, J., Varacca, D.: A compositional semantics for the reversible pi-calculus. In: LICS, pp. 388–397. IEEE Computer Society (2013)
6. Danos, V., Krivine, J.: Reversible communicating systems. In: Gardner, P., Yoshida, N. (eds.) CONCUR 2004. LNCS, vol. 3170, pp. 292–307. Springer, Heidelberg (2004)
7. Feldman, S.I., Brown, C.B.: Igor: A system for program debugging via reversible execution. In: Workshop on Parallel and Distributed Debugging, pp. 112–123 (1988)
8. Grishman, R.: The debugging system AIDS. In: AFIPS 1970 (Spring), pp. 59–64. ACM (1970)
9. King, S.T., Dunlap, G.W., Chen, P.M.: Debugging operating systems with time-traveling virtual machines. In: USENIX Annual Technical Conference, General Track, pp. 1–15 (2005)
10. Koju, T., Takada, S., Doi, N.: An efficient and generic reversible debugger using the virtual machine based approach. In: VEE, pp. 79–88. ACM (2005)
11. Lamport, L.: Time, clocks, and the ordering of events in a distributed system. Commun. ACM 21(7), 558–565 (1978)
12. Lanese, I., Mezzina, C.A., Stefani, J.-B.: Reversing higher-order pi. In: Gastin, P., Laroussinie, F. (eds.) CONCUR 2010. LNCS, vol. 6269, pp. 478–493. Springer, Heidelberg (2010)
13. LeBlanc, T.J., Mellor-Crummey, J.M.: Debugging parallel programs with instant replay. IEEE Trans. Comput. 36(4), 471–482 (1987)
14. Lewis, B.: Debugging backwards in time. CoRR, cs.SE/0310016 (2003)
15. Lienhardt, M., Lanese, I., Mezzina, C.A., Stefani, J.-B.: A reversible abstract machine and its space overhead. In: Giese, H., Rosu, G. (eds.) FORTE 2012/FMOODS 2012. LNCS, vol. 7273, pp. 1–17. Springer, Heidelberg (2012)
16. Lu, S., Park, S., Seo, E., Zhou, Y.: Learning from mistakes: a comprehensive study on real world concurrency bug characteristics. In: ASPLOS, pp. 329–339. ACM (2008)
17. Phillips, I., Ulidowski, I.: Reversing algebraic process calculi. J. Log. Algebr. Program. 73(1-2) (2007)
18. Stanley, T., Close, T., Miller, M.S.: Causeway: a message-oriented distributed debugger. Technical report, HPL-2009-78 (2009), http://www.hpl.hp.com/techreports/2009/HPL-2009-78.html
19. Undo Software. Commercial reversible debugger, http://undo-software.com/
20. Visan, A.M., et al.: Temporal debugging using urdb. CoRR, abs/0910.5046 (2009)
21. Xu, G., Rountev, A., Tang, Y., Qin, F.: Efficient checkpointing of java software using context-sensitive capture and replay. In: ESEC/SIGSOFT FSE 2007, pp. 85–94. ACM (2007)
22. Zelkowitz, M.V.: Reversible execution. Commun. ACM 16(9), 566 (1973)
23. Zhang, X., Tallam, S., Gupta, R.: Dynamic slicing long running programs through execution fast forwarding. In: SIGSOFT FSE, pp. 81–91. ACM (2006)

An Expressive Semantics of Mocking

Josef Svenningsson[1], Hans Svensson[2], Nicholas Smallbone[1],
Thomas Arts[2], Ulf Norell[1,2], and John Hughes[1,2]

[1] Chalmers University of Technology, Gothenburg, Sweden
[2] Quviq, Gothenburg, Sweden

Abstract. We present a semantics of mocking, based on a process calculus-like formalism, and an associated mocking framework. We can build expressive mocking specifications from a small, orthogonal set of operators. Our framework detects and rejects ambiguous specifications as a validation measure. We report our experience testing software components for the car industry, which needed the full power of our framework.

1 Introduction

Software components rarely exist in isolation; most components not only provide an API, but depend on the APIs of other components. When a component is tested in isolation, then these other APIs must be replaced by a suitable simulation. Nowadays "mocks" are often used for this purpose, which not only simulate the other components, but also help to check that they are used correctly.

There are many mocking frameworks available to support mocking, such as Google Mock [9] for C++, or jMock [11] or Mockito [12] for Java. Yet we developed a new framework of our own—why?

We recently designed conformance tests for parts of the AUTOSAR automotive software standard [3]. The goal was to test different vendors' implementations of AUTOSAR components for compliance with the standard. We needed mocks in order to test each component in isolation. We had three main requirements which ruled out existing mocking frameworks.

Expressive. AUTOSAR does not completely specify how a compliant component must behave, and different vendors interpret the standard differently. Therefore, the system under test might invoke the mocks in a variety of very different ways. As we cannot tailor our tests to the vendor's implementation, our mocks must handle this diversity instead. To allow diverse behaviour without making the mocks too permissive, we need an expressive mocking framework.

Orthogonal. Many mocking frameworks have a non-orthogonal feature set. For example, mocking frameworks support optional calls, which the system under test may call or ignore, but it is often *not* possible to mark a sequence of calls as optional, so that either the whole sequence must be called or none at all.

In the AUTOSAR project we used QuickCheck [6,2] to model the software components. From the model we can generate test cases and corresponding

S. Gnesi and A. Rensink (Eds.): FASE 2014, LNCS 8411, pp. 385–399, 2014.

mocks; generating the mocks is extremely painful if the mocking framework imposes arbitrary restrictions on what we can write. We want the freedom to combine the features of the mocking framework however we like.

Clear and unambiguous specifications. In most mocking frameworks, the meaning of a specification can be quite subtle, a point we illustrate in Section 2. For example, these frameworks have rules for resolving ambiguity, and the user can exploit these rules in writing specifications. This is convenient but makes it hard to say what a given specification means.

Our AUTOSAR mocking specifications are, by necessity, sometimes long and complex. They are tricky to get right. The last thing we want from our framework is a subtle semantics! We want each mocking specification to have a simple, declarative meaning. Likewise, we want the mocking framework to reject ambiguous specifications, rather than make arbitrary choices: this reduces the number of potential pitfalls.

One might expect that we could use an ambiguous specification to mock a *nondeterministic* component, if the framework resolves ambiguity randomly. We believe this is the wrong approach, because it makes tests unrepeatable. Instead, the test suite itself should choose a particular deterministic interpretation.

This paper presents a new mocking framework which is expressive, is built from a small core of orthogonal features, has a simple, compositional semantics where every specification has a clear meaning, and which avoids making arbitrary choices during test execution by rejecting ambiguous specifications. Although our requirements came from the AUTOSAR testing project, we believe these features are compelling in their own right, and are especially important when testing large components. The contributions of the paper are as follows:

- We present a new framework for mocking (Sections 3–4). The framework is given two semantics, a simple, compositional denotational semantics and a small-step operational semantics. The two semantics have been proved equivalent (see the accompanying technical report [13]).
- We avoid making arbitrary choices during test execution by ruling out ambiguous mocking specifications. Specifically, we provide a procedure to validate specifications (Section 5) which rules out specifications which are ambiguous. The validation is sound with respect to the semantics. Perhaps surprisingly, it is also complete, which means that if we reject a specification, it must be ambiguous, and we can moreover find a trace that demonstrates the ambiguity. The soundness proof, a sketch of the completeness proof, and a link to the full formalization are found in the tech. report [13]
- We extend our basic framework to make it practical and describe how to implement it in a memory-efficient way (Section 6).
- We report on our experience using an earlier version of this framework in a large industrial case study writing specifications for, and then testing implementations of, automotive software (Section 7).

2   Why a Mocking Semantics?

Before going into the details of our new mocking framework, we will explain why we are dissatisfied with the non-compositional semantics of conventional mocking frameworks. We use Google Mock [9] (and Google Test [10]) purely as a representative for existing mocking frameworks.

Consider a small test for a Dashboard component. The dashboard is connected to a speed sensor and a display, and is supposed to read the speed and update the display appropriately. In this example, the dashboard has a correct C implementation which we want to test. In order to test it, we mock the sensor and display component.

```
TEST(Dashboard, Test1) {
 MockSensor mSensor;
 MockDisplay mDisplay;
 EXPECT_CALL(mSensor, readSpeed()).WillOnce(Return(10));
 EXPECT_CALL(mDisplay, updateDisplay(Display::SPEED, _));

 Dashboard dashboard(&mSensor, &mDisplay);
 dashboard.main(); // Actual test
}
```

The test creates a mock sensor and a mock display, and a concrete Dashboard object containing the mock objects. Thereafter, the mock objects are prepared to expect a call of readSpeed() (returning 10) and updateDisplay(Display::SPEED, _) respectively (where _ matches any argument). The test finally calls the main function of Dashboard. When a mocked object is destroyed, the framework checks that all and only the expected calls have been made. This test will pass provided that dashboard.main() calls the mocked functions exactly as specified.

Let us enrich the example test by adding two more calls of dashboard.main() and having the mocked function readSpeed return a different value each time. We tell updateDisplay that it will be called three times (by adding Times(3) to the specification), and call the main function three times:

```
MockSensor mSensor;
MockDisplay mDisplay;
EXPECT_CALL(mSensor, readSpeed())
  .WillOnce(Return(10))
  .WillOnce(Return(6.7))
  .WillOnce(Return(12.5));

EXPECT_CALL(mDisplay, updateDisplay(Display::SPEED, _)).Times(3);

Dashboard dashboard(&mSensor, &mDisplay);
dashboard.main();
dashboard.main();
dashboard.main(); // main x3
```

This test will pass for correct implementations of the dashboard. Next, suppose we want to be a little bit more precise. It so happens that the `Dashboard` should convert the sensor speed, given in m/s, to km/h; i.e. if `readSpeed` returns 10, `updateDisplay` should be called with 36 as its second argument. We change the expected calls to:

```
EXPECT_CALL(mDisplay, updateDisplay(Display::SPEED, 36)).Times(1);
EXPECT_CALL(mDisplay, updateDisplay(Display::SPEED, _)) .Times(2);
```

Surprisingly, this test fails even if the implementation does the correct thing. It turns out that expectations are put on a stack, so are tested in the reverse order that they are defined. Thus, the correct way to specify this would be

```
EXPECT_CALL(mDisplay, updateDisplay(Display::SPEED, _)) .Times(2);
EXPECT_CALL(mDisplay, updateDisplay(Display::SPEED, 36)).Times(1);
```

even though the call returning 36 happens first. And indeed, this test passes.

Now suppose that we change the specification so that the final call to `readSpeed` returns 10 instead of 12.5:

```
EXPECT_CALL(mSensor, readSpeed())
  .WillOnce(Return(10))
  .WillOnce(Return(6.7))
  .WillOnce(Return(10));

EXPECT_CALL(mDisplay, updateDisplay(Display::SPEED, _)) .Times(2);
EXPECT_CALL(mDisplay, updateDisplay(Display::SPEED, 36)).Times(1);
```

We might expect this test to pass, but it does not! The reason is that (by default) expectations are not removed from the stack once they are fulfilled. Thus as soon as the function `updateDisplay` is called with argument 36 it remains on the stack as being called once. The second time it is called it increases the call count of the `updateDisplay` with argument 36 instead of increasing the call count of `updateDisplay` with arbitrary argument.

The above mocking specification looks ambiguous, since a second call with argument 36 can be handled in two ways: it can be accepted by the first clause or rejected by the second. The mocking framework has arbitrarily chosen the second way.

The way to fix this test in Google Mock is either to expect 36 twice, or to tell the second expectation to retire once it is fulfilled with the feature `RetiresOnSaturation()`. We choose the second option and the test now passes:

```
EXPECT_CALL(mDisplay, updateDisplay(Display::SPEED, _)) .Times(2);
EXPECT_CALL(mDisplay, updateDisplay(Display::SPEED, 36)).Times(1)
  .RetiresOnSaturation();
```

While conventional mocking frameworks have a precise semantics, it is quite complicated. There are subtle interactions between features because the semantics is not compositional and ambiguous specifications are given an arbitrary, though documented, semantics.

In this case, the test failed and therefore we found out that the mocking specification was ambiguous. More worrying is that, by resolving an ambiguity the wrong way, the framework might allow a test to pass that should fail. We would like to be alerted to such problems.

A complex semantics also places a mental burden on the user. We believe that this burden becomes worse as the mocking specifications become bigger. We will now present our approach to mocking, which brings a simple, surprise-free semantics, and ambiguity checking to avoid having to make arbitrary choices.

3   Introduction to the Mocking Language

Our running example will be a dashboard similar to that of Section 2. The dashboard executes a main loop 25 times per second. Each time round, it reads a number of signals, such as the speed, battery status, outside temperature, etc., and updates a display accordingly. The display is a different software component and is mocked by an **update_display** function.

We start with a simple main loop that only reads the speed and then updates the display. It will first call the mocked function **read_speed**, which returns a value in m/s; let's say that it should return 5.833 m/s. The mocking specification $read\_speed \mapsto 5.833$ says that the software under test must call **read_speed**, and the mocked function will return 5.833. We refer to a single call and return as an *event*; by combining events we can build more complex mocking specifications.

Next, the dashboard must make the display show 21 km/h. It does this by calling **update_display(speed,21)**; as before, we model this call with an event $update\_display(speed, 21) \mapsto ()$.[1] To say that the dashboard must call **read_speed** and **update_display** in that order, we combine the two events with the sequential composition operator "·". The resulting specification is:

$$read\_speed \mapsto 5.833 \cdot update\_display(speed, 21) \mapsto ()$$

Now we turn to the battery level. This display only needs to be updated once a second, though it may be updated more often. Since our mocking specification only captures 1/25 of a second, we cannot check this directly; instead, we allow the dashboard *optionally* to update the display, and will check in the test suite itself that the display is updated often enough by counting the calls to **update_display**. To express optional behaviour we add two new constructs to the mocking language. The + operator allows the software under test to behave according to either of two specifications, while the empty specification ε forbids any calls. We may then express an optional behaviour by giving the software under test the option of having that behaviour or not doing anything:

$$(read\_battery \mapsto 234 \cdot update\_display(battery, 70) \mapsto ()) + \varepsilon$$

Another feature of the dashboard is that when driving in bright sunlight, the display may light up. Not all cars have this feature. Moreover, some dashboards

---

[1] If a function's return type is **void**, we use () for the return value.

read the light sensor each time they update a part of the display, while others
only read it once per loop. But whenever the dashboard reads the light sensor,
it must then update the display brightness. The dashboard may read the light
sensor any number of times per loop, which we can model using the $*$ operator:

$$(read\_light \mapsto 6 \cdot light\_display \mapsto ())^*$$

The three specifications above capture three aspects of the dashboard. To
mock the dashboard as a whole, we combine the three specifications with the
parallel composition operator "$||$". This says that the dashboard may interleave
the execution of the three specifications, but must respect the order of events
within each single specification. For example, the dashboard may read the speed,
then the light sensor, then set the display brightness, then update the display:

$$(read\_speed \mapsto 5.833 \cdot update\_display(speed, 21) \mapsto ())$$
$$|| (read\_light \mapsto 6 \cdot light\_display \mapsto ())^*$$
$$|| ((read\_battery \mapsto 234 \cdot update\_display(battery, 70) \mapsto ()) + \varepsilon)$$

From this specification we can automatically generate mocks. Our mocks check
that the calls made by the dashboard precisely match the calls in the specification: no extra calls, no missing calls, and all calls in the right order.

4   A Process Calculus for Mocking

We have now seen all of the features of our mocking language, and begin a formal
treatment of its semantics. Mocking specifications resemble terms in a process
calculus, and their syntax is summarised below. An event $a \mapsto z$ denotes calling
the function a to get result z. For now we treat a and z abstractly; in Section 6
we will breathe life into the calculus by allowing events to be real function calls.

$$p \quad ::= \quad \varepsilon \mid a \mapsto z \mid p \cdot q \mid p \, || \, q \mid p + q \mid p^*$$

We want to assign meaning to mocking specifications. We therefore define a
denotational semantics in terms of traces; a trace is a sequence of events. The
language $\mathcal{L}(p)$ of a process is the set of traces that the process accepts, i.e. that
satisfy the mocking specification, and is defined as follows:

$$\mathcal{L}(p \cdot q) = \{st \mid s \in \mathcal{L}(p) \wedge t \in \mathcal{L}(q)\}$$
$$\mathcal{L}(p + q) = \mathcal{L}(p) \cup \mathcal{L}(q)$$
$$\mathcal{L}(p \, || \, q) = \{u \mid s \in \mathcal{L}(p) \wedge t \in \mathcal{L}(q) \wedge u \text{ is an interleaving of } s \text{ and } t\}$$
$$\mathcal{L}(p^*) = \{s_1 s_2 \cdots s_n \mid n \in \mathbb{N} \text{ and for all } i, s_i \in \mathcal{L}(p)\}$$
$$\mathcal{L}(a \mapsto z) = \{a \mapsto z\}$$
$$\mathcal{L}(\varepsilon) = \{\varepsilon\}$$

This semantics is compact and easy to understand, and ideal for understanding
the behaviour of a mocking specification. However, it is of little use for implementing the mocking framework. It accepts or rejects whole execution traces,

but during test execution we are given a single call at a time and have to return a single result. Therefore, we also provide a small-step semantics. The small-step semantics is more complicated than the denotational one. In order to make sure that we have not made a mistake, we have proved that both semantics are equivalent: see the accompanying tech. report [13].

The small-step semantics is based on two judgements: reduction $p \rightarrow_{a,z} q$ means that on a call to a, the process p will return z and behave as q thereafter, while "p is accepting" means that p accepts the empty trace: the test case may finish without calling any mocked functions. We design both judgements so that they coincide with the denotational semantics.

A process p should be accepting if $\varepsilon \in \mathcal{L}(p)$. Looking at the denotational semantics, we get the following rules: $p \cdot q$ is accepting if both p and q are accepting (likewise $p \parallel q$), $p + q$ is accepting if either p or q are accepting, p^* is accepting, ε is accepting and $a \mapsto z$ isn't.

The most interesting case for reduction is sequential composition. To reduce $p \cdot q$, we can either reduce p or, if p is accepting, remove it and reduce q. This gives the following rules:

$$\frac{p \rightarrow_{a,z} q}{p \cdot r \rightarrow_{a,z} q \cdot r} \; (\textsc{ThenL}) \qquad \frac{p \text{ is accepting} \qquad q \rightarrow_{a,z} r}{p \cdot q \rightarrow_{a,z} r} \; (\textsc{ThenR})$$

We can also derive these rules from the denotational semantics. Suppose we have a trace $st \in \mathcal{L}(p \cdot q)$, where $s \in \mathcal{L}(p)$ and $t \in \mathcal{L}(q)$. ThenL: If s is non-empty, the first event in st is from $\mathcal{L}(p)$, hence we should reduce p to, say, p'. The remainder of st is a trace from $p' \cdot q$, so we should reduce to that. ThenR: If s is empty, which can only occur if $\varepsilon \in \mathcal{L}(p)$, the trace is simply $t \in \mathcal{L}(q)$, hence we should reduce q to, say, q'. The remainder of st is a trace from q', so we should reduce to that.

Reasoning either informally or from the denotational semantics, we find the other reduction rules. To reduce a parallel composition $p \parallel q$, reduce either p or q; to reduce a choice $p + q$, remove one of the choices and reduce the one that's left. To reduce p^*, expand it to $p \cdot p^*$ and then reduce p; finally, an event $a \mapsto z$ reduces to ε. This is captured in the rules below.

$$\frac{p \rightarrow_{a,z} q}{p \parallel r \rightarrow_{a,z} q \parallel r} \; (\parallel L) \qquad \frac{q \rightarrow_{a,z} r}{p \parallel q \rightarrow_{a,z} p \parallel r} \; (\parallel R) \qquad \frac{p \rightarrow_{a,z} q}{p^* \rightarrow_{a,z} q \cdot p^*} \; (*)$$

$$\frac{p \rightarrow_{a,z} q}{p + r \rightarrow_{a,z} q} \; (+L) \qquad \frac{q \rightarrow_{a,z} r}{p + q \rightarrow_{a,z} r} \; (+R) \qquad \frac{}{a \mapsto z \rightarrow_{a,z} \varepsilon} \; (\textsc{Event})$$

If we are not interested in the result of the call, we write $p \rightarrow_a q$, and say that p a-reduces (or just reduces) to q; if we are not interested in the resulting process q either, we just write $p \rightarrow_a$, and say that p can consume a. We lift the terminology from single events to whole traces in the natural way.

5   Ambiguity Detection

As argued in the Introduction and Section 2, we want to forbid ambiguous specifications, because they lead to complex semantics, or to unrepeatable tests if resolved at random. An example of an ambiguous specification in our language is $a \mapsto z_1 + a \mapsto z_2$: if the program calls a, we do not know whether to return z_1 or z_2. We will see in Section 6.1 that the user does not decide what value an event will return until that event is called, so we must also reject $a \mapsto z + a \mapsto z$—we have no way of knowing that both events will always return the same value.

This suggests the following definition of ambiguity: p is ambiguous if for some call a, there are two applicable reduction rules for $p \rightarrow_a$. A process is also ambiguous if it reduces to an ambiguous process. Our process $a \mapsto z + a \mapsto z$ is ambiguous because, for the call a, the rules +L and +R both apply.

Here are some examples of ambiguous processes:

- $a \mapsto z_1 + a \mapsto z_2$ is ambiguous, as above. In general, if $p \rightarrow_a$ and $q \rightarrow_a$, then $p + q$ is ambiguous.
- $(a \mapsto z_1 \cdot b \mapsto z_2) \parallel b \mapsto z_3$ is ambiguous: after a call to a, it reduces to $b \mapsto z_2 \parallel b \mapsto z_3$, in which there are two b-reductions. In general, if p and q have overlapping alphabets, then $p \parallel q$ is ambiguous.
- $(a \mapsto z_1 + \varepsilon) \cdot a \mapsto z_2$ is ambiguous: calling a, we could return either z_1 or z_2.
- Along the same lines, $a \mapsto z_1 \cdot (a \mapsto z_2 + \varepsilon) \cdot a \mapsto z_3$ is ambiguous: after a call to a, we are left with $(a \mapsto z_2 + \varepsilon) \cdot a \mapsto z_3$, essentially the previous example.

The examples above tell us how to detect ambiguity. We will start with $+$ and $\parallel$. Note that the two constructs need different rules: the second example is ambiguous, but replacing $\parallel$ by $+$ it becomes unambiguous. With $+$, the first call needs to tell us which alternative to choose, but with $\parallel$ every call needs to have this property.

- If $p \rightarrow_a$ and $q \rightarrow_a$, then $p + q$ is ambiguous because rules +L and +R both apply.
- If $a \in \text{alphabet}(p) \cap \text{alphabet}(q)$ then $p \parallel q$ is ambiguous because we can reach a process $p' \parallel q'$ where $p' \rightarrow_a$ and $q' \rightarrow_a$; rules $\parallel$L and $\parallel$R then both apply. (The alphabet of a process is simply the set of events that appear syntactically in it.)

We will define a function $p \checkmark$ that checks that p is unambiguous. For now we only define the easy cases:

$$p + q \checkmark = p \checkmark \wedge q \checkmark \wedge \neg \exists a\, (p \rightarrow_a \wedge q \rightarrow_a)$$
$$p \parallel q \checkmark = p \checkmark \wedge q \checkmark \wedge \text{alphabet}(p) \cap \text{alphabet}(q) = \emptyset$$
$$a \mapsto z \checkmark = \text{true}$$
$$\varepsilon \checkmark = \text{true}$$

Sequential composition is trickier. Looking at $(a \mapsto z_1 + \varepsilon) \cdot a \mapsto z_2$, we see that the reduction rules THENL and THENR both apply, the first because $a \mapsto z_1 + \varepsilon$ can consume a and the second because $a \mapsto z_1 + \varepsilon$ is accepting and $a \mapsto z_2$ can consume a. Generalising to an arbitrary sequential composition $p \cdot q$:

- If $p \to_a$, then rule THENL applies.
- If p is accepting and $q \to_a$, then rule THENR applies.

If both conditions are true, $p \cdot q$ is ambiguous. The final example above, $a \mapsto z_1 \cdot (a \mapsto z_2 + \varepsilon) \cdot a \mapsto z_3$, does not satisfy the above conditions, but is still ambiguous because it a-reduces to a process that does. Let us say that a overlaps p, or $p\,?\,a$, if there is a trace under which p reduces to a process p', such that $p' \to_a$ and p' is accepting. Then we may generalise our remarks above: if $p\,?\,a$ and $q \to_a$, then by our argument above, $p' \cdot q$ is ambiguous; hence $p \cdot q$ is too.

$$ p \cdot q \,\checkmark = p \,\checkmark \wedge q \,\checkmark \wedge \neg \exists a \, (p\,?\,a \wedge q \to_a) $$

Finally, we take replication p^*. Informally, p^* is a sequence $p \cdot p \cdot \,\cdots\, \cdot p$ of ps, so it should be enough to check that $p \cdot p$ is unambiguous. This, though, is slightly too restrictive: the process $(a \mapsto z + \varepsilon)^*$ is unambiguous (only rule $*$ can ever apply) but we would reject it. The first reduction of p^* must be rule $*$, so it cannot be ambiguous unless p is ambiguous. Therefore, we find all one-step reductions $q \cdot p^*$ of p^*, and check that for all of *those*, $q \cdot p$ is unambiguous:

$$ p^* \,\checkmark = p \,\checkmark \wedge \neg \exists a \exists b \exists q \, (p \to_a q \wedge q\,?\,b \wedge p \to_b) $$

We must also be able to say whether a overlaps p, according to the definition of overlapping that we gave earlier. We have a number of simple structural rules:

$$ \frac{p\,?\,a}{p \parallel q \,?\, a} \;(\parallel\text{L}) \qquad \frac{q\,?\,a}{p \parallel q \,?\, a} \;(\parallel\text{R}) \qquad \frac{p\,?\,a}{p^* \,?\, a} \;(*\text{-INNER}) $$

$$ \frac{p\,?\,a}{p + q \,?\, a} \;(+\text{L}) \qquad \frac{q\,?\,a}{p + q \,?\, a} \;(+\text{R}) \qquad \frac{q\,?\,a}{p \cdot q \,?\, a} \;(\text{THENR}) $$

We also have a couple of "nearly" structural rules. Since p^* is always accepting, if $p \to_a$ then $p^* \,?\, a$. And if q is accepting, then $\mathcal{L}(p) \subseteq L(p \cdot q)$, so if $p\,?\,a$ then $p \cdot q \,?\, a$:

$$ \frac{p\,?\,a \quad q \text{ is accepting}}{p \cdot q \,?\, a} \;(\text{THENL}) \qquad \frac{p \to_a}{p^* \,?\, a} \;(*\text{-OUTER}) $$

Finally, $p + q$ can introduce an overlap, if p is accepting and $q \to_a$ or vice versa:

$$ \frac{p \to_a \quad q \text{ is accepting}}{p + q \,?\, a} \;(+\text{LR}) \qquad \frac{p \text{ is accepting} \quad q \to_a}{p + q \,?\, a} \;(+\text{RL}) $$

Our ambiguity detection is both sound and complete. Because of soundness, we never accept an ambiguous specification; because of completeness, when we reject a specification we can give a trace showing that it is ambiguous. The proof of soundness and a sketch of completeness are found in the tech. report [13].

6   From Process Calculus to Mocking Framework

The goal of this section is to turn the process calculus into a fully-fledged mocking framework. A basic implementation is simple. We first check that the mocking specification p is unambiguous. To execute p, we wait for the system under test to make a call a. We check if $p \to_{a,z} q$ for some q; if not, the call is erroneous. Otherwise, we return the result z to the caller, and continue by executing q. Finally, when the test finishes, we check that the final process is accepting.

6.1   Matching

In our examples so far, an event specifies a single concrete call such as $update\_display(speed, 21)$ and a concrete result like 5.833. In reality, we do not always know the function arguments so precisely, and need a richer event language. In our framework, an event specifies a *pattern* of function calls. For example, we may write $update\_display(speed, \_)$, where the "$\_$" is a wildcard; this matches any call to $update\_display$ where the first argument is $speed$. A pattern simply stands for any of the concrete calls which it matches.

We also allow the event's return value to depend on the call arguments. The user can associate an *evaluation function* with each event, which is given the call's concrete arguments and computes the return value.[2] Note that each occurrence of an event in the mocking specification can have a different evaluation function: the same call need not always return the same result. An event that returns a constant result is a degenerate case where the evaluation function ignores its arguments.

We need to be careful that we can still execute mocking specifications that use pattern matching, and check them for ambiguity. Executing the specification is not a problem: we only need to be able to check if a concrete call matches a particular event. Given a process p and a call c, we check if there is an event that p can consume and which matches c. Finally, we use the evaluation function associated with the event to calculate the return value, and reduce p.

We can also check the specification for ambiguity, as long as we can tell whether any two events intersect. (Two events intersect if there is a single concrete call that matches both of them.) It will help to write out the existing rules, using equality explicitly whenever we compare the events of two processes:

$$p + q \checkmark = p \checkmark \land q \checkmark \land \neg \exists a \exists b \, (p \to_a \land q \to_b \land a = b)$$

$$p \parallel q \checkmark = p \checkmark \land q \checkmark \land \neg \exists a \exists b \, (a \in \text{alphabet}(p) \land b \in \text{alphabet}(q) \land a = b)$$

$$a \mapsto z \checkmark = \text{true}$$

$$\varepsilon \checkmark = \text{true}$$

$$p \cdot q \checkmark = p \checkmark \land q \checkmark \land \neg \exists a \exists b \, (p \, ? \, a \land q \to_b \land a = b)$$

$$p^* \checkmark = p \checkmark \land \neg \exists a \exists b \exists c \exists q \, (p \to_a q \land q \, ? \, b \land p \to_c \land b = c)$$

---

[2] This is why we could not tell if two events have the same return value in Section 5.

Now, instead of checking if two events are equal, we need to check if they intersect. All we have to do is replace each occurrence of "$a = b$" above with "a and b intersect"! This gives a sound and complete ambiguity detection algorithm for our mocking language with patterns. We will, for example, consider $update\_display(speed, 36) \mapsto () + update\_display(speed, \_) \mapsto ()$ to be ambiguous.

For now we have only implemented quite basic matching. In particular, we can match each argument against either a constant or the wildcard "$\_$"; these were all that we needed for the AUTOSAR testing. However, it is easy to add more powerful patterns, provided they meet the two requirements above. For example, we could easily add value ranges ("x must be between 0 and 200").

6.2   Efficient Implementation

For our AUTOSAR testing we implemented the mocking framework in C. We could simply have implemented the reduction rules of the process algebra, but then reduction would need to allocate memory. We wanted to allocate all memory before running the test, and to avoid heavy term manipulation while testing.

An obvious choice is to translate the mocking specification to a finite-state automaton. Unfortunately, the $\|$ operator suffers from exponential blowup: an automaton that implements $p \parallel q$ needs to remember "how far" it has got in both p and q, so the number of states it needs is the *product* of the number of states in p's automaton and q's automaton.

Instead, we keep the terms of the process calculus but *augment* them with flags that record how far execution has got. During test execution we need only update the flags and not modify the structure of the terms.

For example, we annotate the sequential composition $p \cdot q$ with the flag "left". This indicates that we are reducing p. When we apply rule THENR to start reducing q, we change the flag to "right", and from then on we ignore p and treat the composition as if it were just q. This gives us the following rules for the augmented "$\cdot$" operator:

$$\frac{p \to_{a,z} q}{(p \cdot r)_{\text{left}} \to_{a,z} (q \cdot r)_{\text{left}}} \text{ (THENL)} \qquad \frac{p \text{ is accepting} \qquad q \to_{a,z} r}{(p \cdot q)_{\text{left}} \to_{a,z} (p \cdot r)_{\text{right}}} \text{ (THENR)}$$

$$\frac{q \to_{a,z} r}{(p \cdot q)_{\text{right}} \to_{a,z} (p \cdot r)_{\text{right}}} \text{ (THENR2)}$$

Notice that we no longer change the structure of the term, we only change the flag. The first two rules correspond exactly to the rules we had before; the third one is an extra structural rule that arises because we can no longer get rid of p once we have finished reducing it.

Here is how we augment the other constructs:

- For alternation, $p + q$, we add a flag that records which alternative, p or q, we have chosen. It is initially "neither". If we make a p-transition it becomes "left", and we ignore q from then on, and vice versa.

- We do not need to augment $p \parallel q$, though p and q themselves are augmented. The reduction rules are the same as before.
- We augment a single event, $a \mapsto z$, with a flag that indicates whether we have performed the event. If the flag shows that we have already performed the event, we may no longer perform it.

Replication is the trickiest case, because in executing p^* we may execute p an unlimited number of times. To handle this we need to be able to *reset* a term, which sets its flags back to their initial state. Whenever p in p^* does not accept an event $a \mapsto z$, but does accept the empty trace, we reset p and feed $a \mapsto z$ to it; this corresponds to unrolling p^* in the original semantics. We also augment p^* with a flag that records whether we have performed any reductions on it; this flag is set after the very first reduction, and allows us to model the fact that p^* always accepts the empty trace.

6.3   Extensions

The mocking language we have presented so far is quite minimal. When writing mocking specifications in practice we use a larger repertoire of constructs. Constructs we've found useful include permutations, optional behaviours and finite repetition. The permutation construct operates on a list of behaviours and is similar to parallel composition but doesn't allow interleaving of behaviours: the behaviours must execute one after another, but in an arbitrary order.

Constructs like these are definable in the language we've already presented. For example, an optional p is simply $p + \varepsilon$. However, in our implementation we've added them as primitives for reasons of efficiency. It is particularly important to have permutations be a primitive in the implementation since its encoding into our calculus causes an exponential blow-up in the size of the process.

As an example of using permutations consider the example with parallel composition from Section 3:

$$(read\_speed \mapsto 5.833 \cdot update\_display(speed, 21) \mapsto ())$$
$$\parallel (read\_light \mapsto 6 \cdot light\_display \mapsto ())^*$$
$$\parallel ((read\_battery \mapsto 234 \cdot update\_display(battery, 70) \mapsto ()) + \varepsilon)$$

This specification allows all values to be read before any updates are performed. This might be exactly the freedom one wishes to express. However, suppose that we wish to ensure that the calls to *read_speed* and *update_display* should happen in immediate sequence without being interrupted by any of the other calls, and likewise with the calls to *read_battery* and *update_display*. We can achieve this by using permutations instead of parallel composition, writing the permutation of p, q and r as $perm[p, q, r]$, as follows:

$$perm[read\_speed \mapsto 5.833 \cdot update\_display(speed, 21) \mapsto (),$$
$$(read\_light \mapsto 6 \cdot light\_display \mapsto ())^*,$$
$$(read\_battery \mapsto 234 \cdot update\_display(battery, 70) \mapsto ()) + \varepsilon]$$

The components we are testing are currently single-threaded, but provided our implementation of mocking is thread-safe then there is no reason not to use it with multi-threaded code—we would synchronise on each mocked call, thus establishing a sequential order of calls. It is likely that multi-threaded code would require mocking specifications to use the || operator to handle the inevitable non-determinism in the order of mocked calls, but our framework supports this.

7 Mocking in the AUTOSAR Testing Project

Our mocking semantics arose out of a recent project testing AUTOSAR Basic Software components [3] for Volvo Cars [14]. We modelled around twenty AUTOSAR components using an earlier version of the mocking framework. These included the layers of protocol stacks for CAN, LIN, and FlexRay, a router and some diagnostic components. Each component corresponded to an approximately 150-page written specification. Our testsuite has been used to check a handful of implementations from Volvo Cars' subcontractors.

We modelled the AUTOSAR software components in QuickCheck [2], a model-based testing tool that can automatically create random test cases from state machine specifications written in a domain-specific functional language. During the project we developed our mocking framework and integrated it with QuickCheck so that for each generated test case appropriate mocks were also generated. The complexity of the mocking generators varied wildly: from a single line of code to several hundred for the most complicated function we tested. To be able to write these complex mocking generators it was absolutely essential to have a compositional mocking framework where specifications can easily be combined. The simple and clear semantics is also crucial to be able to understand complex mocking generators.

One of the particular challenges with modelling AUTOSAR is that it does not always completely specify the behaviour of the software. Not only may the mocked functions behave in a number of ways, components also have some freedom in which mocked functions to call and how often they are called. And sure enough, whenever the specification allowed for some leeway we found that implementations typically differed in behaviour. The expressiveness of our mocking framework proved invaluable for developing mocking specifications which could handle all legal behaviours mandated by the standard.

8 Related Work

It would be natural to compare our work to existing C mocking frameworks. However, there does not seem to be very many, and the few that exist (like *CMock* [7] and *Cgreen* [5]) have very limited functionality. Instead, we compare to *Google Mock*. Google Mock provides mocking functionality for C++ and is feature-wise close to *jMock* [11] and *EasyMock* [8] for Java. Thus it should, to the best of our knowledge, be representative of modern mocking frameworks.

Since C has no objects, we will simply compare the expressiveness of the two approaches.

The main difference is that Google Mock provides lots of default behaviour: expectations are put in parallel by default, there are default return values, etc. The language we define has no default behaviour—everything is explicit. Both approaches have their merits, but hidden defaults require a well-educated user. In terms of expressiveness, we have observed three key differences:

- Google Mock has state, i.e. one action may set a variable that can be read by a later action. This is not included in our language since we have not had the need for it. It would be possible to extend our language with state, but the more interesting question is why we haven't had the need for it. We believe the reason is the compositionality and expressiveness of our mocking language. Compare to writing a regular expression and implementing an equivalent state machine. Regular expressions provide a declarative and compositional interface without the need for state which is much simpler to use than having to maintain the state of the state machine explicitly.
- Google Mock only does *replication* of single events; it is not possible to repeat, for example, a sequence of calls. In our particular use case, L^* is a central ingredient, thus not having it would have presented a problem to us.
- Finally, there does not seem to be a way to express $p + q$ in Google Mock. One could say atMost(1) for both p and q, but that would not catch the case when neither or both are called. Again this is central to our use case, but perhaps one often manages without it in ordinary unit testing.

An area closely related to mocking is runtime monitoring. In particular, Jass [4] allows monitoring of "trace assertions" expressed in a CSP-like language; if the monitored code performs an event in the alphabet of the process that is not part of any trace, then an exception is raised. The trace assertion language is described by example and formal properties are not stated or proven. In general, run-time monitors can allow non-determinism in the monitor, because this cannot lead to non-determinism in the test outcome. Because mocking supplies return values to the code under test, then non-deterministic mocking will lead to non-deterministic test outcomes. Similarly, model checkers can allow non-deterministic environments since they can explore branching executions, collect constraints, and use solvers to find interesting cases: since each test execution can follow only one branch then we do not enjoy the same freedom.

Our mocking language shares many similarities with the language PSL [1], used by the hardware community for specifying and verifying circuits. PSL is divided into several layers and one of these layers is a modelling layer, used for specifying parts of the design which are not yet implemented. Although similar in spirit to our language, PSL's mocking language naturally differs on many details as it targets hardware, not software.

9   Conclusions

This paper provides a fresh look at mocking and presents a new expressive and compositional semantics. It is the first such semantics we are aware of; other mocking frameworks have a precise semantics, but only defined by their implementation. The expressiveness is inspired by a large use case of mocking in a model-based testing project in the automotive software domain, but the solution is generally applicable in other domains as well.

Since we have a formal semantics for mocking, we can check mocking specifications for ambiguity. We prove that this verification is sound and complete. Thus, whenever we accept a user-defined mocking specification, the result is unambiguous and if the specification is unambiguous, we accept it. Unambiguous specifications are important because a mocking framework must either make arbitrary choices or random choices in the face of ambiguity; the first leads to surprising behaviour and the second to unrepeatable tests. The formal semantics also makes it clear that our feature set is orthogonal.

Acknowledgements. This research was sponsored by EU FP7 Collaborative project *PROWESS*, grant number 317820.

References

1. Property specification language. IEEE Standard 1850 (2005)
2. Arts, T., Hughes, J., Johansson, J., Wiger, U.: Testing telecoms software with Quviq QuickCheck. In: Proceedings of the ACM SIGPLAN Workshop on Erlang. ACM Press, New York (2006)
3. AUTOSAR consortium. AUTomotive Open System ARchitecture specifications, http://www.autosar.org
4. Bartetzko, D., Fischer, C., Möller, M., Wehrheim, H.: Jass – java with assertions. Electronic Notes in Theoretical Computer Science 55(2), 103–117 (2001)
5. Cgreen, http://www.lastcraft.com/cgreen.php
6. Claessen, K., Hughes, J.: QuickCheck: a lightweight tool for random testing of haskell programs. In: Proceedings of ACM SIGPLAN International Conference on Functional Programming, pp. 268–279 (2000)
7. CMock, https://github.com/ThrowTheSwitch/CMock
8. EasyMock, http://www.easymock.org
9. Google C++ mocking framework, http://code.google.com/p/googlemock
10. Google C++ testing framework, http://code.google.com/p/googletest
11. jMock, http://jmock.org/index.html
12. Mockito - simpler & better mocking, http://code.google.com/p/mockito
13. Svenningsson, J., Svensson, H., Smallbone, N., Arts, T., Norell, U., Hughes, J.: An expressive semantics of mocking. Technical Report 2014:01, Computer Science and Engineering, Chalmers University of Technology (2014) ISSN 1652-926X
14. Svenningsson, R., Johansson, R., Arts, T., Norell, U., Svenningsson, J., Svensson, H.: Testing AUTOSAR software components with QuickCheck. In: Proceedings of IXe Conf. on AMCTM. SP, Sweden (2011)

Integration Testing in the Test Template Framework

Maximiliano Cristiá[1], Joaquín Mesuro[1], and Claudia Frydman[2]

[1] CIFASIS and UNR, Rosario, Argentina
cristia@cifasis-conicet.gov.ar, joaquin.mesuro@gmail.com
[2] LSIS-CIFASIS, Marseille, France
claudia.frydman@lsis.org

Abstract. The Test Template Framework (TTF) is a model-based testing method for the Z notation, originally proposed for unit testing. In this paper we analyze how the TTF can be extended to integration testing. Since integration testing is related to software design, we decided to investigate the relation between the TTF and the *uses* relation, a key element in David Parnas' design theory. We propose how a Z specification should be structured for the TTF to be able to generate integration tests by following the *uses* relation. The problem of stub generation and the kinds of errors that these integration tests can discover are also discussed.

1   Introduction

The Test Template Framework (TTF) is a model-based testing (MBT) method proposed for the Z notation [25]. In the TTF each Z operation schema is analyzed to generate (abstract) test cases. Each operation schema in a Z model is the specification of a piece of code in the implementation that sometimes corresponds to a unit of implementation. This is why we say that the TTF generates unit tests. Recently the TTF was automated roughly to the same degree of other MBT methods by a tool called Fastest [8]. This makes the TTF and Fastest appealing options for unit testing within the Z community.

According to the accepted practice of Software Engineering, after each unit of implementation has been tested in isolation, they should be incrementally integrated and tested [14,24]. This phase or level of testing is known as integration testing. On the other hand, software design is defined as the decomposition of a system into software elements, the description of what each element is intended to do (i.e. its specification) and the relations among these elements [14]. Therefore, integration testing is influenced by the software design of the system under test. Furthermore, the design and the structure of the (functional) specification influence a MBT method when is applied during integration testing because test cases are derived from the specification and executed on the elements of the design. On the other hand, if software elements are related to each other, then errors in one of them may cause errors in the others. The accepted solution is to build so-called stubs units which mimic the behavior of the real units but

S. Gnesi and A. Rensink (Eds.): FASE 2014, LNCS 8411, pp. 400–414, 2014.

only for a few inputs. Manually crafting such stubs is a source of costs and errors. Building the minimum number of stubs avoiding as much manual work as possible can be considered as the *stub generation problem*. Stubs are necessary because, in general, units are tested correct (and not proven correct), so these units cannot be used while other units are tested (because the formers can induce errors in the latter).

The contributions of this paper are the following: a) a set of guidelines for writing Z specifications that will simplify (TTF-based) test case generation during integration testing; b) an integration strategy based on Parnas' *uses* relation that reduces the number of manually crafted stubs; c) a set of conditions that guarantee that a unit can be used as stub of itself without inducing errors (in other units) during integration testing; and d) an analysis of the types of (integration) errors this method can discover.

An example motivating the issues discussed in this paper is given in Sect. 2. After introducing the TTF in Sect. 3, three main problems are addressed: a) how a Z specification should be structured and linked with the design to best serve for integration testing, in Sect. 4; b) what is the best strategy in the TTF to incrementally integrate units so integration testing can benefit from unit testing, in Sect. 5; and c) the stub generation problem, in Sect. 6. The kinds of errors that the extended TTF can find are analyzed in Sect. 7. Section 8 discusses all the results obtained in this paper. A comparison with similar approaches can be found in Sect. 9 and our conclusions in Sect. 10.

In this paper "unit" means "subroutine" which in turn includes "function", "procedure" and "method". Our work aims at integrating units for which the source code is available. All the units that are integrated belong to the same executable but can belong to different modules. This work does assumes any particular implementation technology. A general theory of software design and first-order logic over a set theory (i.e. Z) are the fundamentals.

This paper is a summary of an unpublished paper available on-line [10]. We assume the reader is familiar with the Z notation.

2   Motivating Example

In this section we show some of the issues that MBT faces when integration testing is considered. We will do it by means of a simple example. Assume we need to implement the following functionality: receive an integer number, check whether it belongs to a list and, if it does not, then add it to the list and sort the list. A possible Z specification for this requirements is as follows.

$$S \mathrel{\widehat{=}} [list : \mathrm{seq}\,\mathbb{Z}]$$
$$InList \mathrel{\widehat{=}} [\Xi S;\ x? : \mathbb{Z} \mid x? \in \mathrm{ran}\,list]$$

$$InsertOk \mathrel{\widehat{=}}$$
$$[\Delta S;\ x? : \mathbb{Z} \mid x? \notin \mathrm{ran}\,list \wedge \mathrm{ran}\,list' = \mathrm{ran}\,list \cup \{x?\}$$
$$\wedge\ (\forall\, i,j : \mathrm{dom}\,list' \bullet i < j \Rightarrow list'\,i < list'\,j)]$$
$$InsertAndSort \mathrel{\widehat{=}} InsertOk \vee InList$$

Clearly, a first design could be to implement *InsertAndSort* with a single subroutine. However, since *InsertAndSort* includes the specification of a sorting algorithm, it is reasonable to decompose (i.e. design) its implementation into two subroutines, insert and sort, with the following functionality: insert reads the element to be inserted, checks whether it belongs to the list and, if not, calls sort, which inserts the element in the list and sorts it[1]. Then, a possible Z specification reflecting this design is as follows.

$$
\begin{array}{l}
\underline{Sort_1} \\[2pt]
\Delta S \\
x? : \mathbb{Z} \\
\hline
\#list' = \#list + 1 \\
list' \upharpoonright \{x?\} = (list \upharpoonright \{x?\}) \frown \langle x? \rangle \\
\forall\, y : (\mathrm{ran}\, list) \setminus \{x?\} \bullet list \upharpoonright \{y\} = list' \upharpoonright \{y\} \\
\forall\, i, j : \mathrm{dom}\, list' \bullet i < j \Rightarrow list'\, i \le list'\, j
\end{array}
$$

$$Input_1 \cong [\Delta S;\ x? : \mathbb{Z} \mid x? \notin \mathrm{ran}\, list]$$
$$InsertAndSort_1 \cong (Input_1 \wedge Sort_1) \vee InList$$

where S and *InList* are the same as above. In this case, sort implements $Sort_1$ whereas insert implements $InsertAndSort_1$ replacing $Sort_1$ by a call to sort. $Sort_1$ is more complex than *InsertOk* because it can sort lists with or without duplicates. In other words, $Sort_1$ is more general than *InsertOK*, although in this example it is called only when a new element is to be inserted.

In summary, we have two designs with different subroutines for the same requirements. Given that the specification of each unit is different in each design, test cases generated by a MBT method should be different when applied to each design. Furthermore, the specification is saying that the correctness of insert depends upon the correctness of sort because $Sort_1$ is part of $InsertAndSort_1$. This dependency should impose an order for testing these units that should be taken into account by the MBT method. If, on the contrary, insert is tested before sort has passed all of its test, errors in insert may be difficult to track down because they may come from itself or from sort. However, even if sort has passed all of its test, an error found while insert is tested cannot be blamed just to itself because sort has not been proven correct, it was just tested. Then, we either build a (correct) stub of sort for testing insert, or we prove that test cases run on insert always call sort as it was called when it was tested—and since it passed all its test then errors found while insert is tested can be blamed just to itself. Finally, if, for instance, insert calls an error reporting routine, say err, when $x? \in \mathrm{ran}\, list$, should err be tested before insert? We believe it should not necessarily be the case because err is not part of insert's specification (i.e. $InsertAndSort_1$). In other words, the correctness of insert does not depend on

---

[1] In this paper, we use *math* text to represent the specification of subroutines written in sans serif. For example, $InsertAndSort_1$ is the specification of insert.

err. This implies, in turn, that any stub of err will do during insert's testing. In summary, a convenient adaptation of a MBT method can help in many ways during integration testing as we will show in the rest of this paper.

3   Introduction to the TTF and Fastest

In this section we present just the main concepts of the TTF and Fastest; for deeper presentations consult [25,8,9]. Fastest generates test cases for each operation schema selected by the user in a Z model. If A is an operation schema then its valid input space (*VIS*) is defined as the following Z schema:

$$A^{VIS} \cong [x_1 : X_1; \; \ldots; \; x_n : X_n \mid \text{pre } A]$$

where $x_1 : X_1; \; \ldots; \; x_n : X_n$ are all the input and state variables declared in A after full schema expansion, and pre A is the precondition of A.

The goal of the TTF is to partition A^{VIS} by applying so-called testing tactics. A testing tactic is a systematic way of dividing the *VIS* of a Z operation. Some tactics are: disjunctive normal form (DNF), standard partitions (SP), free types (FT), etc. [8,9]. After a testing tactic is applied to A^{VIS} a family of test conditions[2] is obtained. These test conditions usually form a partition of the *VIS*. In Fastest they are formalized as Z schemas as follows:

$$A_1^{T_1} \cong [A^{VIS} \mid P_1^{T_1}(x_1,\ldots,x_n)] \quad \ldots \quad A_{m_1}^{T_1} \cong [A^{VIS} \mid P_{m_1}^{T_1}(x_1,\ldots,x_n)]$$

where T_1 is the name of the tactic and $P_i^{T_1}(x_1,\ldots,x_n)$ for $i \in 1 \mathinner{.\,.} m_1$ are predicates generated by T_1. These predicates are called characteristic predicates of the test conditions. $P_i^{T_1}$ defines the conditions for a test case. In other words, a test condition is a set of test cases satisfying a given condition or predicate.

Perhaps the most important feature of the TTF is that it proposes to apply other tactics to one or more of the test conditions already generated, thereby getting progressively more detailed test conditions. For example, if testing tactic T_2 is applied to $A_1^{T_1}$ the following test conditions are generated:

$$A_1^{T_2} \cong [A_1^{T_1} \mid P_1^{T_2}(x_1,\ldots,x_n)] \quad \ldots \quad A_{m_2}^{T_2} \cong [A_1^{T_1} \mid P_{m_2}^{T_2}(x_1,\ldots,x_n)]$$

Observe how schema inclusion is used to link test conditions between them and with the *VIS*. Note, also, that schema inclusion adds more predicates to a test condition. In effect, if $A_1^{T_1}$ is expanded, for instance, inside $A_2^{T_2}$ we have:

$$A_2^{T_2} \cong [A^{VIS} \mid P_1^{T_1}(x_1,\ldots,x_n) \wedge P_2^{T_2}(x_1,\ldots,x_n)]$$

Schema inclusion organizes test conditions in a so-called *testing tree* which has the *VIS* in the root, the first test conditions in the first level, and so forth.

In the TTF a test case is a Z schema where each variable declared in the *VIS* is equal to a constant value such that the corresponding test condition is satisfied. For example, a test case for $A_2^{T_1}$ is:

$$A_2^{TC} \cong [A_2^{T_1} \mid x_1 = c_1 \wedge \ldots \wedge x_n = c_n]$$

---

[2] Also called test templates, test specifications, test classes, etc.

4   Structuring a Z Specification for Integration Testing

As we have said in the introduction, integration testing is strongly related to software design. The approach to integration testing based on a MBT method proposed in this paper is based on what David L. Parnas calls "uses relation" or "uses structure" [22], a key concept of his seminal work on software design. The *uses* relation is a binary relation between subroutines. If P and Q are two subroutines, then P *uses* Q if "there exist situations in which the correct functioning of P depends upon the availability of a correct implementation of Q" [22]. Note that the *uses* relation differs from the *calls* (or *invokes*) relation[3] because: (a) if P's specification requires only that P *calls* Q then it is enough for P to call Q when its specification says so, from P's perspective Q can be correct or not; and (b) P may use Q by sharing some data structures although P never calls Q. According to Parnas, "the design of the *uses* hierarchy should be one of the major milestones in a design effort".

The *uses* relation is relevant to MBT methods since it is based on the specification of a subroutine. In effect, P *uses* Q means that the *specification* of P says that it needs a correct version of Q. From a functional perspective P and Q could be implemented in a single unit whose specification is, roughly, the conjunction of P's and Q's specifications. However, from a design perspective it is better to split this unit into two in such a way that one uses the other. We have shown an example of this situation in Sect. 2. Given that the TTF uses Z specifications, it is worth to study how to write them so it is easy to find the *uses* relation.

We propose the following guidelines for writing Z specifications that will be used during integration testing.

- Each subroutine is specified by a schema. More precisely, for each subroutine P there must be a named schema A which is its specification.
- Users must generate test cases only for those schemas that are the specifications of subroutines. For example, users must generate test cases for $InsertAndSort_1$ and $Sort_1$ but not for $Input_1$ and $InList$. In fact, test cases covering the functionality specified in $Input_1$ and $InList$ will be generated as part of the test cases generated from $InsertAndSort_1$ [8].
- Let A and B be Z schemas describing the specification of subroutines P and Q, respectively—we will use this naming convention across the paper. If P *uses* Q and P *calls* Q, then A must be written as follows:

$$A \mathrel{\hat{=}} \mathcal{SE}(B, A_1, \ldots, A_n) \tag{†}$$

where $\mathcal{SE}$ is some schema expression depending on schemas B and $A_1, \ldots, A_n$. That is, Q's specification is part of P's which is completed by the A_i schemas. An example of (†) is $InsertAndSort_1$ given in Sect. 2. If P uses other subroutines besides Q, then their corresponding Z schemas will also participate in (†) like B. For the remaining of this paper we will use (†) but all the results can be extended to the more complex case where P uses more than one subroutine.

---

[3] P *calls* Q includes the case where P calls Q indirectly by a chain of calls through some intermediate subroutines. *uses* is also a transitive relation.

– If P *calls* Q but P *uses* Q, then B must not be part of A because P *uses* Q means that P's specification says that it does not depend on Q. So including B in A would be an error because this would indicate a functional dependency of P on Q. An example of this second scenario is when insert calls err, also discussed in Sect. 2.

– If P *uses* Q but P *calls* Q, then B must not be part of A, at least concerning integration testing. This case is further discussed in *Global errors* in Sect. 7.

Since the case P *uses* Q $\wedge$ P *calls* Q is analyzed several times in this paper, we will write P $\overline{uses}$ Q as a shorthand for it. Furthermore, we will write $\overline{uses}$ as a synonym of "use and call".

Capturing the differences between the *uses* and *calls* relations in the specification has important consequences for integration testing. Assume that P *calls* Q. Then, a stub of Q will be necessary when P is unit-tested. In general, this stub should verify B (i.e. Q's specification) because otherwise P might look erroneous when, actually, the errors may come from Q's stub. Now, also assume that P *uses* Q. Then, Q's stub can be anything complying with Q's signature (even Q itself) because P's correctness does not depend on Q's. Therefore, if P *calls* Q but P *uses* Q we can conclude that when P is tested: (a) Q's stub can be automatically generated or Q can be used if it is available; and (b) if integration testing shows errors in P they cannot be due to the presence of an incorrect Q.

5   Integration Testing within the TTF

Guiding integration testing by the *uses* relation has a number of benefits. If P *uses* Q the very nature of testing impedes to restrict the search for the cause of an error exposed during the testing of P just to itself because it depends at least on Q which, at best, was already tested, but not proven correct. This is one of the greatest difficulties during integration testing as testing of subroutines who use dozens of others tend to exacerbate that problem. If integration testing is guided by the *uses* relation this problem is minimized, as we will show below.

Parnas restricts the *uses* relation to a hierarchy because otherwise "one may end up with a system in which nothing works until everything works" [22]. If *uses* is a hierarchy, there is a set of subroutines, $\mathfrak{U}_0$, which do not use other subroutines. These should be the first to be tested because the cause of an error in one of them should be located only in itself. Then, there is another set of subroutines, $\mathfrak{U}_1$, whose members only $\overline{uses}$ subroutines in $\mathfrak{U}_0$. These should be the second to be tested, right after those in $\mathfrak{U}_0$ have passed all of their tests. Moreover, in general, there will be a family of sets $\mathfrak{U}_1^0(i) \subseteq \mathfrak{U}_1$, for $i \in 1 .. \#\mathfrak{U}_0$, whose subroutines use exactly i subroutines (of $\mathfrak{U}_0$)[4]. Then, it would be better to test the subroutines of $\mathfrak{U}_1$ according to the following order: $\mathfrak{U}_1^0(1), \ldots, \mathfrak{U}_1^0(\#\mathfrak{U}_0)$. In this way subroutines using less subroutines are tested before those using more, which is helpful when searching for the cause of an error.

---

[4] In general, some of the $\mathfrak{U}_1^0(i)$ will be empty.

Clearly, a family of sets $\mathfrak{U}_i$, with $i \in 2 .. n$ for some n, whose subroutines $\overline{uses}$ one or more subroutines in $\mathfrak{U}_0 \cup \cdots \cup \mathfrak{U}_{i-1}$ should be defined to organize integration testing as was just explained for $\mathfrak{U}_0$ and $\mathfrak{U}_1$. This is what we call integration testing guided by the *uses* relation. Note that all these sets can be computed automatically from the Z specification if our guidelines are followed (cf. Sect. 4). See [10] for more details, examples and formal definitions of sets $\mathfrak{U}_k$ and $\mathfrak{U}_k^j(i)$.

Test Case Generation during Integration Testing. If P and Q are going to be tested using a MBT method then their specifications, A and B, must be analyzed in order to generate their abstract test cases. The question is whether the relation P $\overline{uses}$ Q, and thus the fact that A includes B, would change the standard way in which the MBT method is applied. If the MBT method analyses the inner details of formulas A and B then some adaptation is required because otherwise it will expand B inside A meaning that test cases generated for P will be influenced by Q as well. However, Q was already tested as a unit and has passed all of its tests, so, in principle, there is no point in considering it again. Moreover, if the transitive closure of $\overline{uses}$ includes a long chain of subroutines starting from P, then fully expanding A will result in a huge formula which will be hard to analyze by any implementation of the MBT method. This is in line with the idea that during integration testing units already tested should be treated as black boxes. On the other hand, if B is not expanded inside A it might be the case that Q is not tested as thoroughly as it would if the expansion had been performed. This point will be discussed in Sect. 7.

Adapting the TTF to Integration Testing. The TTF is applied to elements belonging to $\mathfrak{U}_0$ as it is [8]. If P $\in \mathfrak{U}_1$, then its specification is $A \,\widehat{=}\, \mathcal{SE}(B, A_1, \ldots, A_n)$ for some B such that it is the specification of some Q $\in \mathfrak{U}_0$. In this case, when the TTF is applied to A, B is not fully expanded, contradicting the original presentation of both the TTF and Fastest. Only variables declared in B and referenced by some A_i are exported from B to A, for consistency reasons. This implies that test cases for A are generated solely by analyzing P's own functionality, i.e. the structure of $\mathcal{SE}$ and the predicates in $A_1, \ldots, A_n$. In other words, B influences A's test case generation only as a whole and by its place in $\mathcal{SE}$. This means that the TTF will generate, at least, test cases that are going to make P to call Q from different places and with different parameters. For example, if the DNF tactic [8] is applied to $InsertAndSort_1$ there will be test cases that are going to test insert with an element belonging to the list and with one that does not. That is, these test cases will test whether or not insert correctly implements $x? \in \mathrm{ran}\, list$ and if it calls sort when it should. In a sense, this is all that it is worth to be tested of insert given that the correctness of the sorting algorithm implemented by sort was already tested. Indeed, for example, if tactics SP [8] and UQ [9] are applied to $InsertSort_1$, then sort will be tested with empty and non-empty lists of several lengths and where $x?$ belongs and does not belong to them.

6   Subroutines as Stubs of Themselves

The distinction between the *uses* and *calls* relations reduces the need for manually crafted stubs (cf. last paragraph in Sect. 4). However, a stub of Q is still needed when P $\overline{uses}$ Q. One way to avoid building a stub of Q would be to use Q itself, but it cannot be done because Q is not proven correct, it was just tested. Nevertheless, if Q has passed some tests then we can be sure that it is correct for those inputs. Now, if P is tested in such a way that Q is always called as when it was tested, then Q itself can be used as stub. Furthermore, the cause of an error found during P's testing can only be blamed to P since Q has been tested correct for those inputs. We have made an attempt to formalize these ideas, thus yielding the basis for the mechanization of the search of those subroutines that can be stubs of themselves.

We have proved a theorem that gives conditions for a subroutine to be used as stub. Before stating the theorem 1 we need a little bit of notation. Consider schemas $A, A_1, \ldots, A_n$ and B like in (†). According to Sect. 5 only $A_1, \ldots, A_n$ are unfolded in A. Let $vars(A)$ be the set of the variables declared in schema A^{VIS} that are declared in at least one A_i. That is, $vars(A)$ does not include variables declared only in B. If a is a test case derived from schema A and B is another schema, then $B^A(a)$ means the substitution of variables in $vars(B) \cap vars(A)$ by the values of the same variables in a (recall, from Sect. 3, that a test case in the TTF is a conjunction of equalities between variables in the *VIS* and constant values). We will note $A^A(a)$ simply as $A(a)$.

Theorem 1 assumes that A performs only one state change. This is the case, for instance, of *InsertAndSort*$_1$ in Sect. 2. See [10] for a theorem dealing with two state changes (one for P and one for Q). This theorem relies on the uniformity hypothesis as stated in [16, page 17].

Theorem 1. Let P and Q be two subroutines such that P $\overline{uses}$ Q and let A and B be their Z specifications, which in turn comply with (†). Assume there is just one state change in A. Let $B_1, \ldots, B_n$ be the leaves of the testing tree generated by applying the TTF to B. Assume Q has passed all the tests derived from all these test specifications. Let a be a test case for P derived from A. If there is a B_j such that $B_j^A(a) \neq \emptyset$, then Q can be used as a stub when P is tested on a.

Proof. If there is one state change in A then Q executes with the same values than P for variables in $vars(A) \cap vars(B)$. If $B_j^A(a) \neq \emptyset$, then there is $b \in B_j$ such that a and b are equal on variables in $vars(A) \cap vars(B)$. Since Q has passed all its tests then it has passed a test from B_j. By the uniformity hypothesis Q is also correct on $b \in B_j$. Therefore, when P is executed on a, Q will be executed on b, thereby returning a correct answer to P. So Q can be used as a stub when P is tested on a.   □

This theorem will be further discussed in Sect. 8.

7 Errors Detected during Integration Testing

Leung and White give a classification of errors that can be detected during integration testing [19,20]. They try to make a distinction between those errors that could have been detected during unit testing and those that are specific to integration testing. Below we briefly explain each of these errors and show that the TTF extended to integration testing can detect them.

Interpretation errors. There are three subclasses of these errors.

- Wrong function errors (WFE). Q does not provide the functionality indicated by its specification and P does not know that.

  Given that the TTF (and other MBT methods) generates test cases for Q from its specification, then WFEs will be detected when Q is tested as a unit. In other words, if a test case for Q, generated by the TTF, finds an error in Q this is an indication that it does not provide the functionality indicated by its specification
- Extra function errors (EFE). Q provides more functionality than P needs. P's developers know this but they wrongly implement P making it to call these extra functions.

  The TTF will generate at least one test case for each of the functionalities in the specification of Q. For instance, testing tactics such as DNF and FT will be very useful [8]. If P is tested in such a way that Q is called as to exercise all these functionalities, then P's problems will surface (because these extra functions will be called). In other words, it is necessary to apply the TTF to A in such a way that it generates enough test cases for P which will make it call Q in such a way that executes all its functionalities. In turn, this will be achieved if test cases derived from A verify the following theorem (the proof is omitted for brevity).

  Theorem 2. Let $a_1, \ldots, a_m$ be the test cases for P; and $B_1, \ldots, B_n$ be the leaves of the testing tree of Q. Assume these leaves represent all the functionalities provided by Q. The TTF will detect all EFE in P if for each $j \in 1 .. n$ there exists $i \in 1 .. m$ such that $B_j^A(a_i) \neq \emptyset$.

- Missing function errors (MFE). Inputs used by P to call Q are outside the domain of Q making it to behave unexpectedly.

  If B is total then P cannot make Q behave unexpectedly because there is a specified behavior for each input expected by Q. If B is partial then P should call Q with $b \notin B^{VIS}$ to execute it outside its input domain. But from b the input for P, a, must be found. It is easier to calculate a if A performs only one state change. For this case, we define a new testing tactic, called MF, that should be applied to operations whose corresponding subroutines are in the domain of the $\overline{uses}$ relation. The test specifications generated by MF are: $A_1^{MF} \cong [A^{VIS} \mid \exists x_1, \ldots, x_n \bullet \text{pre } B]$ and $A_2^{MF} \cong [A^{VIS} \mid \exists x_1, \ldots, x_n \bullet \neg \text{pre } B]$, where $x_1, \ldots, x_n$ are the variables declared in B but not in A. Note that MF is applied to A, not to B but B is part of A as in (†). The TTF then encourages to further partition these test specifications by applying more testing tactics. Certainly MF will help to discover MFE because it will force P to call Q outside its domain due to A_2^{MF}.

Miscoded Call errors. P calls Q from wrong places. There are three subclasses.

- Extra call instruction (ECI). The calling instruction is placed on a path that should not contain such invocation.
- Wrong call instruction placement (WCI). The call is located on the right path, but in a wrong place.
- Missing instruction (MIC). Missing call on a path that should contain it.

Detecting these errors is one of the reasons for defining A as in (†). If A specifies exactly all the calls that P should make to Q, then the TTF will help to discover all of these errors. In effect, DNF applied to $\mathcal{SE}(B, A_1, \ldots, A_n)$ will generate test specifications for all the situations where Q is called and those where it is not; other tactics, such as FT and UQ, will generate more detailed conditions under which Q is called. For example, when DNF is applied to $InsertAndSort_1$ it will generate a test specification characterized by the precondition under which $Sort_1$ is called and another characterized by its negation. Then, if insert does not call sort in the first case (MIC) the result will be $list' = list$ when it should be $\#list' = \#list + 1$; if it calls sort in the second case (ECI), the result will be $\#list' = \#list + 1$, when it should be $list' = list$.

Global errors (GER). These are errors related to the wrong use of global variables [19]. If P *uses* Q but P *calls* Q, it means that they interact through a shared resource that can be thought of as a global variable, g. In this case Q defines a value for g that is later used by P. If this value is not what P expects, then P may fail. There are two causes that can make P to find an unexpected value in g: (a) Q does not verify B; or (b) Q does verify B but P assumes Q implements a different specification, say $\widehat{B}$.

In analyzing how the TTF can detect GER we will assume that P *uses* Q but P *calls* Q, because when also P *calls* Q, all the previous results apply. If (a) causes the error, then it reduces to WFE because it means to see whether Q verifies its specification. Therefore, the true problem of integration testing regarding global variables is given under the following conditions: P *uses* Q but P *calls* Q and Q verifies B but P assumes Q implements a different specification, $\widehat{B}$. One possible way of detecting these errors is by executing Q before P while testing P. This way, however, complicates P's testing because now it is necessary to run other units before it, and they must be run in such a way as to make P fail.

Hence, we propose a different approach based on specification verification rather than on testing. In effect, the problem is a mismatch at the specification level, causing errors at the implementation level. That is, A assumes $\widehat{B}$ rather than B, so the problem is to find out this wrong assumption. If the involved operations are proven to verify some properties (state invariants, for instance) then these wrong assumptions will be detected. In this way, B will be changed for $\widehat{B}$ and it will become Q's specification. Therefore, $\widehat{B}$ cannot be wrong with respect to A, because the proven properties act as a common consistency ground for them. Then, if Q verifies $\widehat{B}$ it cannot set a wrong value for g from P's perspective. From here, all reduces to ensure that P and Q implement their specifications which means performing a thorough unit testing of each of them in isolation from each other. This is why in Sect. 4 we proposed not to include B in A when P *uses* Q but P *calls* Q.

8   Discussion

Although we are interested in extending the TTF to integration testing, our results use only some of its details. Therefore, they can be used in other specification languages and MBT methods. Most of the results are based on fundamental concepts of Software Engineering like the *uses* relation, first-order logic and MBT in general.

Describing operations as in (†) is not a severe restriction on the use of the language and it has a non negligible impact on the application of the TTF to integration testing. The form of (†) makes it possible to automatically calculate all the ordered pairs belonging to $\overline{uses}$. In turn, organizing integration testing around the *uses* relation provides several places for optimizing this process. The first one is given by the definition of the family of sets $\mathfrak{U}_i$. If integration is based on these sets then many errors can be caught with as less units already integrated as possible. The definition of the families of sets $\mathfrak{U}_i^k(j)$ provides a finer level for guiding integration testing. All this aims at making the search for the cause of an error as simple as possible, discarding errors as earlier as possible.

The fact that *uses* would have an important impact on reducing the costs of testing and that it can be automatically computed from a Z specification, might turn Z and *uses* more cost-effective. In this way they will be used not only as essential documents but they will be reused during testing as well.

Testing a unit in isolation is a rather ambiguous statement. In effect, if P $\overline{uses}$ Q, what it means testing P in isolation? If it means not using Q but a stub of it, then unit testing is faced with the problem of building stubs. Manually-crafted stubs are not only error prone but costly [15,4,18]. The approach presented here also aims at reducing the costs of stub generation and at making them reliable enough as not introducing errors. If integration follows the *uses* relation and each unit is certified at least for the inputs used during its testing, then they can be used as stubs for themselves, provided they are always called as when they were tested. Furthermore, those stubs implied by the *calls* relation can be automatically built, as was discussed in Sect. 4. Theorem 1 gives rather simple conditions under which a subroutine can be used as a stub for itself— although they are probabilistic given that the proofs depend upon the uniformity hypothesis. In this way, we are trading the cost and risk of building stubs for the cost of describing the *uses* relation and applying Theorem 1, which is almost automatic in many cases—see below. Finally, if this theorem cannot be proved for a given test case of P, i.e. this test case satisfies no leaf used to test Q, it is an indication that Q was poorly tested because one of its callers will call it in a functional situation not covered during its testing.

The use of subroutines as stubs for themselves somewhat blurs the distinction between unit and integration testing. However, integration testing may find new errors that are difficult or impossible to find during unit testing, as was shown in Sect. 7. In fact, the TTF extended to integration testing can cope with almost all the errors classified by Leung and White. Z and the TTF enable a formal analysis of some of these classes of errors. Theorem 2 and testing tactic MF show that the TTF can be further extended to deal with particular issues of integration testing.

A case study applying all these results can be found in [10].

More Detailed Issues. In Theorem 1, proving that $B_j^A(x) \neq \emptyset$ involves either the evaluation of a constant Z predicate or solving a satisfiability problem. In effect, if $vars(B) \subseteq vars(A)$ then all the free variables in B_j will be replaced by constant values when $B_j^A(x)$ is calculated; otherwise, there will be free variables in $B_j^A(x)$. In the first case $B_j^A(x) \neq \emptyset$ can always be automatically solved; in the second case it is necessary to decided whether $B_j^A(x)$ is satisfiable or not. This problem is undecidable because $B_j^A(x)$ can be a first-order predicate over the set theory. However, Fastest uses advanced Constraint Logic Programming techniques (the $\{log\}$ tool) for solving these predicates with very good results for real specifications [11,8]. Then, even when $B_j^A(x)$ has free variables Theorem 1 can be automatically applied in many situations.

9   Related Work

There is a lot of research on integration testing, from a MBT perspective [1,23,5,3,13,15] or not [12,2,6,21,18,17,20], but we could not find articles analyzing in detail how Parnas's *uses* relation and the Z notation can be used for integration testing. Clements and others [7, pages 68–71] pay attention to the *uses* relation and remark its importance in integration testing. In particular they say it can be used to narrow the search for the cause of an error found during integration testing but they do not go any deeper.

Leung and White [19,20] study integration testing in the context of regression testing. Although they use the *calls* relation, they define sets of test cases to test subroutines during integration testing that have some similarities to those presented here. Apparently they are not interested in the stub generation problem, but in reducing the number of tests during regression.

Benz [5] acknowledges the fact that critical relationships for integration testing are not explicitly modeled and that MBT methods applied to integration testing may yield large state spaces. In his work Benz uses task models for specifying the interaction between components. Ali et al. [3] use UML collaboration diagrams to model interactions among classes and Statecharts for specifying their behavior. They propose a list of mutation operators that can be used to assess the effectiveness of integration testing methods. Since this list is aimed at object-oriented programs we preferred the taxonomy of errors proposed by Leung and White, also used by Orso [21]. Class State Machines (CSTM) are used by Gallagher, Offutt and Cincotta as the specification method for classes of object-oriented programs. These CSM are then combined into a component flow graph which is used to derive integration tests.

Testing components that can only be accessed through a system interface is the goal of the work by Schätz and Pfaller [23]. They use transition systems to model the behavior of components and hierarchical transition systems to model component interactions. The authors define the notion of Satisfied Integrated Test Case which plays a similar role as Theorem 1 in the present work. Another work that focuses on a specific problem, carving and replay based integration testing, is that of Elbaum and his colleagues [12]. However, the four steps of unit testing they use are the same used in Fastest: identify a program state, set it, execute the unit from it and evaluate the results.

Hartmann, Imoberdorf and Meisinger [15] use a method based on category partition to generate test cases from UML Statecharts specifying the behavior of components whose interactions are described be means of concepts borrowed from CSP. Category partition is essentially what the TTF does with the *VIS* of a Z operation. The authors aim at the stub generation problem but is not clear to us how their method reduces the number of manually-crafted stubs.

Labiche et al. [18] define an integration strategy based on class diagrams with the goal of minimizing the stub generation problem. Essentially they test a class after the classes it depends on. Labiche's integration order is an extension of Kung's [17] when dynamic dependencies and abstract classes are present. However, class or similar diagrams seldom include the functional specification of classes. In fact, these methods make a syntactic analysis of these diagrams resulting in a larger number of dependencies because they include not only "used" classes but also "called" classes.

10   Conclusions and Future Work

The TTF has been extended to integration testing providing, in principle, a good coverage during this level of testing because it covers almost all the errors in Leung and White's classification. Organizing integration testing around the *uses* relation shows several advantages that should be further investigated. The favorable impact that *uses* has on testing may make developers to describe it thereby reusing a key design document. Moreover, if a logical specification is cleverly structured, *uses* can be computed automatically. The extension minimizes the need for manually-crafted stubs by giving simple conditions that say when a stub can be automatically generated or when a subroutine can be used as a stub of itself.

However, it should be investigated what testing tactics should be applied to two subroutines belonging to the *uses* relation to prove Theorem 1 for all test cases, while still providing good unit coverage for both of them. Another issue that should be studied is the relation of Z's θ operator and operation promotion with integration testing.

Acknowledgments. Ana Cavalcanti made a number of corrections and suggestions to an early version of this paper. We thank her a lot for that.

References

1. Aiguier, M., Boulanger, F., Kanso, B.: A formal abstract framework for modelling and testing complex software systems. Theor. Comput. Sci. 455, 66–97 (2012), http://dx.doi.org/10.1016/j.tcs.2011.12.072
2. Alexander, R.T., Offutt, A.J.: Criteria for testing polymorphic relationships. In: Proceedings of the 11th International Symposium on Software Reliability Engineering, ISSRE 2000. IEEE Computer Society, Washington, DC (2000), http://dl.acm.org/citation.cfm?id=851024.856208
3. Ali, S., Briand, L.C., Rehman, M.J.U., Asghar, H., Iqbal, M.Z.Z., Nadeem, A.: A state-based approach to integration testing on UML models. Inf. Softw. Technol. 49(11-12), 1087–1106 (2007), http://dx.doi.org/10.1016/j.infsof.2006.11.002
4. Baresi, L., Pezzè, M.: An introduction to software testing. Electron. Notes Theor. Comput. Sci. 148(1), 89–111 (2006), http://dx.doi.org/10.1016/j.entcs.2005.12.014
5. Benz, S.: Combining test case generation for component and integration testing. In: Proceedings of the 3rd International Workshop on Advances in Model-Based Testing, A-MOST 2007, pp. 23–33. ACM, New York (2007), http://doi.acm.org/10.1145/1291535.1291538
6. Buy, U., Orso, A., Pezze, M.: Automated testing of classes. In: Proceedings of the 2000 ACM SIGSOFT International Symposium on Software Testing and Analysis, ISSTA 2000, pp. 39–48. ACM, New York (2000), http://doi.acm.org/10.1145/347324.348870
7. Clements, P., Garlan, D., Bass, L., Stafford, J., Nord, R., Ivers, J., Little, R.: Documenting Software Architectures: Views and Beyond. Pearson Education (2002)
8. Cristiá, M., Albertengo, P., Frydman, C., Plüss, B., Monetti, P.R.: Tool support for the Test Template Framework. Software Testing, Verification and Reliability 24(1), 3–37 (2014), http://dx.doi.org/10.1002/stvr.1477
9. Cristiá, M., Frydman, C.: Extending the Test Template Framework to Deal with Axiomatic Descriptions, Quantifiers and Set Comprehensions. In: Derrick, J., Fitzgerald, J., Gnesi, S., Khurshid, S., Leuschel, M., Reeves, S., Riccobene, E. (eds.) ABZ 2012. LNCS, vol. 7316, pp. 280–293. Springer, Heidelberg (2012)
10. Cristiá, M., Mesuro, J., Frydman, C.: Extending the Test Template Framework to integration testing, https://www.dropbox.com/s/8dlyu2mctmzw57m/ttf-integration-testing.pdf
11. Cristiá, M., Rossi, G., Frydman, C.: {log} as a test case generator for the Test Template Framework. In: Hierons, R.M., Merayo, M.G., Bravetti, M. (eds.) SEFM 2013. LNCS, vol. 8137, pp. 229–243. Springer, Heidelberg (2013)
12. Elbaum, S., Chin, H.N., Dwyer, M.B., Dokulil, J.: Carving differential unit test cases from system test cases. In: Proceedings of the 14th ACM SIGSOFT International Symposium on Foundations of Software Engineering, SIGSOFT 2006/FSE-14, pp. 253–264. ACM, New York (2006), http://doi.acm.org/10.1145/1181775.1181806

13. Gallagher, L., Offutt, J., Cincotta, A.: Integration testing of object-oriented components using finite state machines: Research articles. Softw. Test. Verif. Reliab. 16(4), 215–266 (2006), http://dx.doi.org/10.1002/stvr.v16:4
14. Ghezzi, C., Jazayeri, M., Mandrioli, D.: Fundamentals of software engineering, 2nd edn. Prentice Hall (2003)
15. Hartmann, J., Imoberdorf, C., Meisinger, M.: UML-based integration testing. In: Proceedings of the 2000 ACM SIGSOFT International Symposium on Software Testing and Analysis, ISSTA 2000, pp. 60–70. ACM, New York (2000), http://doi.acm.org/10.1145/347324.348872
16. Hierons, R.M., Bogdanov, K., Bowen, J.P., Cleaveland, R., Derrick, J., Dick, J., Gheorghe, M., Harman, M., Kapoor, K., Krause, P., Lüttgen, G., Simons, A.J.H., Vilkomir, S., Woodward, M.R., Zedan, H.: Using formal specifications to support testing. ACM Comput. Surv. 41(2), 1–76 (2009)
17. Kung, D.C., Gao, J., Hsia, P., Lin, J., Toyoshima, Y.: Class firewall, test order, and regression testing of object-oriented programs. JOOP 8(2), 51–65 (1995)
18. Labiche, Y., Thévenod-Fosse, P., Waeselynck, H., Durand, M.H.: Testing levels for object-oriented software. In: Proceedings of the 22nd International Conference on Software Engineering, ICSE 2000, pp. 136–145. ACM, New York (2000), http://doi.acm.org/10.1145/337180.337197
19. Leung, H.K.N., White, L.: Insights into testing and regression testing global variables. Journal of Software Maintenance 2(4), 209–222 (1990)
20. Leung, H.K.N., White, L.: A study of integration testing and software regression at the integration level. In: Conference on Software Maintenance 1990, San Diego, CA, pp. 290–301 (1990)
21. Orso, A.: Integration Testing of Object-Oriented Software. Ph.D. thesis, Politecnico di Milano, Milan, Italy (February 1999)
22. Parnas, D.L.: Designing software for ease of extension and contraction. In: ICSE 1978: Proceedings of the 3rd International Conference on Software Engineering, pp. 264–277. IEEE Press, Piscataway (1978)
23. Schätz, B., Pfaller, C.: Integrating component tests to system tests. Electron. Notes Theor. Comput. Sci. 260, 225–241 (2010), http://dx.doi.org/10.1016/j.entcs.2009.12.040
24. Sommerville, I.: Software Engineering, 9th edn. Addison-Wesley, Harlow (2010)
25. Stocks, P., Carrington, D.: A Framework for Specification-Based Testing. IEEE Transactions on Software Engineering 22(11), 777–793 (1996)

Data Flow Coverage for *Circus*-Based Testing

Ana Cavalcanti[1] and Marie-Claude Gaudel[2]

[1] University of York, Department of Computer Science, York YO10 5GH, UK
[2] LRI, Université de Paris-Sud and CNRS, Orsay 91405, France

Abstract. *Circus* is a state-rich process algebra based on Z and CSP
that can be used for testing. In this paper, we consider data-flow coverage. In adapting the classical results on coverage of programs to *Circus*
models, we define a notion of specification traces, consider models with
data-flow anomalies, and cater for the internal nature of state. Our results are a framework for data-flow coverage of such abstract models,
a novel data-flow criterion suited to state-rich process models, and the
conversion of specification traces into symbolic traces.

1 Introduction

The use of formal models, especially those underlying process algebra, as a basis
for testing is now widely studied. *Circus* [5] is a very expressive and feature-rich
algebra; it belongs to the important family of notations that combine the advantages of operational calculi like CSP [14] with specification languages like Z [17],
thus comprising abstract data types at their core. For testing from such notations, it is appealing and natural to guide selection of test data from symbolically
derived test traces using data-oriented criteria [13] that have been demonstrated
to be good at detecting faults on data dependencies.

In previous work, we have defined a testing theory for *Circus* [2]. Following
its operational semantics, this theory uses constrained symbolic traces: pairs
formed by a symbolic trace and a constraint over the symbolic variables in the
trace. Tests are built from such traces, enriched by observations (that is, refusals
or acceptance) and verdict events; test sets that are exhaustive with respect to
refinement in *Circus* have been defined. The constrained symbolic traces, however, capture the constraints raised by data operations and guards, but not
their structure. We have, therefore, so far defined test-selection criteria based on
notions like coverage of bounded symbolic traces or synchronisation coverage;
information is missing to address data-flow coverage.

Here, we introduce specification traces, which include, besides communication
events, internal data operations and guards. Based on these traces, we formalise
notions of definitions, uses, and definition-clear paths for *Circus*. We define the
conventional data-flow coverage criteria, and formalise a novel criteria inspired
by [15] to cater for internal data flows. Finally, we consider how to construct constrained symbolic traces, and thus, symbolic tests from the specification traces,
providing the link to the operational semantics. This result is relevant for all
selection criteria based on specification traces (and not only data-flow criteria).

S. Gnesi and A. Rensink (Eds.): FASE 2014, LNCS 8411, pp. 415–429, 2014.

In summary, we present here the first collection of coverage criteria for *Circus* based on the structure of models. It is the first technique that takes advantage of the data model itself, rather than its semantics, in selecting tests. We prove unbias of the selected tests. This means that they cannot reject correct systems.

Data-flow coverage in the context of *Circus* requires adjustments. Firstly, data-flow anomalies must be accepted, because repeated definitions and definitions without use are routinely used in *Circus* abstract models. Second, due to the rich predicative data language of *Circus*, a concrete flow graph is likely much too big to be explicitly considered. Thus, tests are not based on paths of a flow graph, but on specification traces. Finally, the state of a *Circus* process is hidden, and so not all definitions and uses, and, therefore, not all data flows, are visible.

In the next section, we give an overview of the notations and definitions used in our work. Section 3 presents our framework, and Section 4, our new criterion. Section 5 addresses the general issue of constructing tests from selected specification traces. Finally, we consider related works in Section 6 and conclude in Section 7, where we also indicate lines for further work.

2   Background Material

This section describes *Circus*, its operational semantics, and data-flow coverage.

2.1   *Circus* Notation

A *Circus* model defines channels and processes like in CSP. Figure 1 presents an extract from the model of a cash machine. It uses a given set *CARD* of valid cards, a set *Note* of the kinds of notes available (10, 20, and 50), and a set *Cash* == bag *Note* to represent cash. The definitions of these sets are omitted.

The first paragraph in Figure 1 declares four channels: *inc* is used to request the withdrawal using a card of some cash, *outc* to return a card, *cash* to provide cash, and *refill* to refill the note bank in the machine. The second paragraph is an explicit definition for a process called *CashMachine*.

The first paragraph of the *CashMachine* definition is a Z schema *CMState* marked as the **state** definition. *Circus* processes have a private state, and interact with each other and their environment using channels. The state of *CashMachine* includes just one component: *nBank*, which is a function that records the available number of notes of each type: at most *cap*.

State operations can be defined by Z schemas. For instance, *DispenseNotes* specifies an operation that takes an amount $a?$ of money as input, and outputs a bag *notes!* of *Notes*, if there are enough available to make up the required amount. *DispenseNotes* includes the schema $\Delta CMState$ to bring into scope the names of the state components defined in *CMState* and their dashed counterparts to represent the state after the execution of *DispenseNotes*. To specify *notes!*, we require that the sum of its elements (Σ *notes!*) is $a?$, and that, for each kind n of *Note*, the number of notes in *notes!* is available in the bank. *DispenseNotes* also updates *nBank*, by decreasing its number of notes accordingly.

channel $inc : CARD \times \mathbb{N}_1$; $outc : CARD$; $cash : Cash$; $refill$

process $CashMachine \,\hat{=}\,$ **begin**

state $CMState == [\, nBank : Note \rightarrow 0 \mathbin{..} cap \,]$

$\underline{\quad DispenseNotes \quad\rule{5cm}{0pt}}$
$\Delta CMState$
$a? : \mathbb{N}_1$; $notes! : Cash$
$\rule{11cm}{0.4pt}$
$\Sigma\, notes! = a?$
$\forall\, n : Note \bullet (notes! \mathbin{\natural} n) \leq nBank\, n \wedge nBank'\, n = (nBank\, n) - (notes! \mathbin{\natural} n)$

$\underline{\quad DispenseError \quad\rule{5cm}{0pt}}$
$\Xi CMState$
$a? : \mathbb{N}_1$; $notes! : Cash$
$\rule{11cm}{0.4pt}$
$\neg\; \exists\, ns : Cash \bullet \Sigma\, ns = a? \wedge \forall\, n : Note \bullet (ns \mathbin{\natural} n) \leq nBank\, n$
$notes! = [\![\ ]\!]$

$Dispense == DispenseNotes \vee DispenseError$

$$
\bullet \left(\mu\, X \bullet \left(\begin{array}{l} inc?c?a\rightarrow \\ \quad X \\ \sqcap\; outc!c \rightarrow X \\ \sqcap \left(\begin{array}{l} \textbf{var}\ \ notes : Cash \bullet \\ Dispense; \\ \left(\begin{array}{l}(notes \neq [\![\ ]\!])\ \&\ cash!notes \rightarrow \textbf{Skip} \\ \square \\ (notes = [\![\ ]\!])\ \&\ \textbf{Skip} \end{array}\right) \end{array}\right) ; outc!c \rightarrow X \\ \square \\ refill \rightarrow (nBank := \{\, 10 \mapsto cap, 20 \mapsto cap, 50 \mapsto cap \,\}\, ;\ X \end{array}\right)\right)
$$
end

Fig. 1. Cash machine model

Another schema *DispenseError* defines the behaviour of the operation when there are not enough notes in the bank to provide the requested amount $a?$; the result is the empty bag $[\![\ ]\!]$. The Z schema calculus is used to define the total operation *Dispense* as the disjunction of *DispenseNotes* and *DispenseError*.

State operations are called actions in *Circus*, and can also be defined using Morgan's specification statements [11] or guarded commands from Dijkstra's language. CSP constructs can also be used to specify actions.

For instance, the behaviour of the process *CashMachine* is defined by a recursive action at the end after the '•'. A recursion $\mu\, X \bullet F(X)$ has a body given by $F(X)$, where occurrences of X are recursive calls. In our example, the recursion first offers a choice between an input $inc?c?a$, which accepts a card c and a request to withdraw the amount a, and a synchronisation on *refill*, which is a request to fill the *nBank*. The actions that offer these communications are combined in an external choice (□) to be exercised by the environment.

If *refill* is chosen, an assignment changes the value of *nBank* to record a number *cap* of notes of all kinds. If *inc?c?a* is chosen, then we have an internal (nondeterministic) choice of possible follow-on actions: recursing immediately (without returning the card or producing the money), returning the card via an output *outc!c* before recursing, or considering the dispensation of cash before returning the card and recursing. In the dispensation, a local variable *notes* is declared, the operation *Dispense* is called, and then an external choice of two guarded actions is offered. If there is some cash available (*notes* ≠ ⟦ ⟧), then it can dispensed via *cash!notes*. Otherwise the action terminates (**Skip**). Here, nondeterminism comes from the fact that the specification does not go into details of bank management (stolen cards, bank accounts, and so on).

This example shows how Z and CSP constructs can be intermixed freely. A full account of *Circus* and its semantics is given in [12]. The *Circus* operational semantics is briefly discussed and illustrated in the next section.

2.2   *Circus* Operational Semantics and Tests

The *Circus* operational semantics [2] is distinctive in its symbolic account of state updates. As usual, it is based on a transition relation that associates configurations and a label. For processes, the configurations are processes themselves; for actions A, they are triples of the form $(c \mid s \models A)$.

The first component c of those triples is a constraint over symbolic variables used to define labels and the state. These are texts that denote *Circus* predicates (over symbolic variables). We use typewriter font for pieces of text. The second component s is a total assignment $x := w$ of symbolic variables w to all state components x in scope. State assignments can also include declarations and undeclarations of variables using the constructs $var\ x := e$ and $end\ x$. The state assignments define a specific value (represented by a symbolic variable) for all variables in scope. The last component of a configuration is an action A.

The labels are either empty, represented by ϵ, or symbolic communications of the form $c?w$ or $c!w$, where c is a channel name and w is a symbolic variable that represents an input (?) or an output (!) value.

We define traces in the usual way. Due to the symbolic nature of configurations and labels, we obtain constrained symbolic traces, or *cstraces*, for short.

Example 1. Some of the cstraces of the process *CashMachine* are as follows.

$(\langle \rangle, \mathtt{True})$ and $(\langle\, \mathtt{refill}, \mathtt{inc}.\alpha_0.\alpha_1, \mathtt{outc}.\alpha_2 \rangle, \alpha_0 \in \mathtt{CARD} \land \alpha_1 \in \mathbb{N}_1 \land \alpha_2 = \alpha_0)$

The first is the empty cstrace (empty symbolic trace with no constraint). The second records a sequence of interactions where a request for a *refill* is followed by a request for a withdraw of an amount α_1 using card α_0, followed by the return of a card α_2. The constraint captures those arising from the declaration of *inc*, namely, α_0 is a *CARD* and α_1, a positive number. It also captures the fact that the returned card is exactly that input ($\alpha_2 = \alpha_0$).   □

As usual for process-algebra, tests of the *Circus* theory are constructed from traces. A cstrace defines a set of traces: those that can be obtained by instantiating the symbolic variables so as to satisfy the constraint. Accordingly, we have symbolic tests constructed from cstraces, and a notion of instantiation to construct concrete tests involving specific data. This approach is driven by the operational semantics of the language and led to the definition of symbolic exhaustive test sets and to proofs of their exhaustivity.

We observe that cstraces capture the constraints raised by data operations and guards, but not their structure.

Example 2. The following is a cstrace of *CashMachine* that captures a withdraw request followed by cash dispensation.

$$(\langle inc.\alpha_0.\alpha_1, cash.\alpha_2 \rangle,$$
$$\alpha_0 \in \mathsf{CARD} \wedge \alpha_1 \in \mathbb{N}_1 \wedge \Sigma \alpha_2 = \alpha_1 \wedge \forall \mathsf{n} : \mathsf{Note} \bullet (\alpha_2 \,\sharp\, \mathsf{n}) \leq \mathsf{cap})$$

The constraint defines the essential properties of the cash α_2 dispensed, but not the fact that these properties are established by a variable declaration followed by a schema action call, and a guarded action. ☐

So, while cstraces are useful for trace-selection based on constraints, they do not support selection based on the structure of the *Circus* model. To this end, in [1] we have presented a collection of transition systems whose labels are pieces of the model: guards (predicates), communications, or simple *Circus* actions. The operational semantics for *Circus* defined by these transition systems is entirely compatible with the *Circus* original operational and denotational semantics, although it records information about the text of the model.

Thus, we use the transition relation $\Longrightarrow_{RP}$ from [1], written $\Longrightarrow$ here, to define a notion of specification traces, used to consider data-flow coverage criteria.

2.3   Data-Flow Coverage

Normally, the application of data-flow coverage criteria requires the absence of anomalies in the data-flow graph; this is not required or adequate here.

Data-flow coverage criteria were originally developed for sequential imperative languages based on the notion of definition-use associations [13]. They are traditionally defined in terms of a data-flow graph as triples (d, u, v), where d is a node in which the variable v is defined, that is, some value is assigned to it, u is a node in which the value of v is used, and there is a definition-clear path with respect to v from d to u. The strongest data-flow criterion, *all definition-use paths*, requires that, for each variable, every definition-clear path (with at most one iteration by loop) is executed. In order to reduce the number of tests required, weaker strategies such as *all-definitions* and *all-uses* have been defined.

When using these criteria, it is often assumed that there is no data-flow anomaly: on every path there is no use of a variable v not preceded by some node with a definition of v, and that after such a node, there is always some other node with a use of v [6]. These restrictions require preliminary checks and facilitate the comparison of the criteria; they also ensure that there is always some test set satisfying the criteria. In *Circus*, anomalies lead to empty test sets.

Data-flow based testing in the case of abstract specifications with concurrency and communications requires adjustments (see, for instance [15] and Section 6) even if the notion of data-flow and the motivation are the same: to check dynamically data-flow dependencies via the execution of selected tests.

3   Data-Flow Coverage in *Circus*

Here, we define specification traces resulting from the transition relation $\Longrightarrow$, state the notions of definition and use of *Circus* variables, discuss anomalies, and present the definition of one of the classical coverage criteria.

3.1   Specification Traces

The main distinctive feature of the specification transition system in [1] is its labels. They record not only events, like in the operational semantics, but also guards and state changes. Moreover, they are expressed in terms of terms of the model, rather than symbolic variables. For example, for the *CashMachine*, we have labels inc?c?a, var notes, and Dispense. Finally, the specification-oriented system has no silent transitions, since they correspond to evolutions that are not guarded, and do not entail any communication or state change. These transitions do not capture observable behaviour, and so are not interesting for testing.

Like in the operational semantics, we have a transition relation $\Longrightarrow$ between texts of process. It is defined in terms of the corresponding relation for actions. For actions, a transition $(c_1 \mid s_1 \models A_1) \xrightarrow{g} (c_2 \mid s_2 \models A_2)$ establishes that in the state characterised by $(c_1 \mid s_1)$, if the guard g holds, then the next step in the execution of A_1 is the execution of A_2 in the state $(c_2 \mid s_2)$. Similarly, a transition $(c_1 \mid s_1 \models A_1) \xrightarrow{e} (c_2 \mid s_2 \models A_2)$ establishes that in the execution of A_1 the event e takes place and then again the next step is the execution of A_2 in $(c_2 \mid s_2)$. Finally, $(c_1 \mid s_1 \models A_1) \xrightarrow{A} (c_2 \mid s_2 \models A_2)$ establishes that the first step is the action A, followed by A_2 in $(c_2 \mid s_2)$ and the remaining action to execute is A_2.

It is simple to define sequences of specification labels based on $\Longrightarrow$ and its associated transition relation $\Longrightarrow\!\!\!\!\rightarrow$ annotated with traces and defined as usual [3].

Example 3. For *CashMachine*, for instance, the following traces of specification labels, as well as their prefixes, are reachable according to $\Longrightarrow\!\!\!\!\rightarrow$.

⟨inc?c?a, outc!c, inc?c?a, var notes⟩
⟨inc?c?a, var notes, Dispense, notes ≠ ⟦ ⟧ , cash!notes, outc!c⟩   □

We need, however, to consider enriched labels that include a tag to distinguish their various occurrences in the specification.

Example 4. In the traces in Example 3, the two occurrences of outc!c correspond to different occurrences of this piece of syntax in the model. Since we cannot consider repeated occurrences of labels to correspond to a single definition or use of a variable, we use tags to distinguish them.   □

The tag can, for instance, be is related to the position of the labels in the model. We need a simple generalisation of the definition of $\Longrightarrow$, where a label is a pair containing a label (in the sense of Section 2.2) and a tag. We take the type *Tag* of tags as a given set, and do not specify a particular representation of tags.

For a process P, we define the set $sptraces(P)$ of sptraces of P: specification traces whose last label is observable, that is, a non-silent communication. This excludes traces that do not lead to new tests with respect to their prefixes.

Definition 1. *If we define* $obs(1, t) \Leftrightarrow 1 \in Comm \wedge 1 \neq \epsilon$, *then we have*

$$sptraces(\text{begin state}[x : T] \bullet A \text{ end}) = sptraces(w_0 \in T, x := w_0, A)$$

$$sptraces(c_1, s_1, A_1) = \{ spt, c_2, s_2, A_2 \mid$$
$$(c_1 \mid s_1 \models A_1) \stackrel{spt}{\Longrightarrow} (c_2 \mid s_2 \models A_2) \wedge spt \neq \langle \rangle \wedge obs(\text{last } spt) \bullet \text{spt} \}$$

Without loss of generality, we consider a process begin state$[x : T] \bullet A$ end, with state components x of type T and a main action A. Its sptraces are those of A, when considered in the state in which x has some value identified by the symbolic variable w_0, which is constrained to satisfy $w_0 \in T$. For actions A_1, the set $sptraces(c_1, s_1, A_1)$ of its sptraces from the state characterised by the assignment s_1 and constraint c_1 is defined as those that can be constructed using $\Longrightarrow$ from the configuration $(c_1 \mid s_1 \models A_1)$ and whose last label is observable.

Example 5. Some sptraces of *CashMachine* are as follows. (In examples, we omit tags when they are not needed, and below we distinguish the two occurrences of outc!c by the tags tag1 and tag2.)

$\langle \text{inc?c?a}, (\text{outc!c}, \text{tag1}) \rangle$ $\langle \text{inc?c?a}, (\text{outc!c}, \text{tag1}), \text{inc?c?a} \rangle$
$\langle \text{inc?c?a}, \text{var notes}, \text{Dispense}, \text{notes} \neq [\![\ ]\!], \text{cash!notes} \rangle$
$\langle \text{inc?c?a}, \text{var notes}, \text{Dispense}, \text{notes} \neq [\![\ ]\!], \text{cash!notes}, (\text{outc!c}, \text{tag2}) \rangle$

We note that the first specification trace in Example 3 is not an sptrace.   □

3.2   Definitions and Uses

In an sptrace, a definition is a tagged label, where the label is a communication or an action that may assign a new value to a *Circus* variable, that is, an input communication, a specification statement, a Z schema where some variables are written, an assignment, or a **var** declaration, which, in *Circus* causes an initialisation. The set defs(x, P) of definitions of a variable x in a process P is defined in terms of the set defs(x, spt) of definitions of x in a particular sptrace spt.

Definition 2. $\text{defs}(x, P) = \bigcup \{ \text{spt} : sptraces(P) \bullet \text{defs}(x, \text{spt}) \}$

The set defs(x, spt) can be specified inductively as follows.

Definition 3. $\text{defs}(x, \langle \rangle) = \varnothing$
$$\text{defs}(x, \text{tl} \frown \text{spt}) = (\{\text{tl}\} \cap \text{defs}(x)) \cup \text{defs}(x, \text{spt})$$

The empty trace has no definitions. If the trace is a sequence formed by a tagged label tl followed by the trace spt, we include tl if it is a definition of x as characterised by defs(x). The definitions of spt are themselves given by defs(x, spt).

The tagged labels in which x is written (defined) can be specified as follows.

Definition 4. defs(x) = { tl : $TLabel$ | $x \in$ defV(tl) }

The set defV(tl) of such variables for a label tl is specified inductively; g stands for a guard, d for a channel, e an expression. The tags play no role here, and we ignore them in the definition below.

Definition 5

$$defV(g) = defV(\epsilon) = defV(d) = defV(d!e) = defV(end\,y) = \varnothing$$
$$defV(d?x) = defV(d?x : c) = \{\,x\,\} \qquad defV(f : [pre, post]) = \{\,f\,\}$$
$$defV(Op) = wrt V(Op) \qquad\qquad defV(x := e) = \{\,x\,\}$$
$$defV(var\,x : T) = \{\,x\,\} \qquad\qquad defV(var\,x := e) = \{\,x\,\}$$

A Morgan specification statement $f : [pre, post]$ is a pre-post specification that can only modify the variables explicitly listed in the frame f.

The set $wrt V(Op)$ of written variables of a schema Op is defined in [5, page 161] as those that are potentially modified by Op, and their identification is not a purely syntactic issue. This set includes the state components v of Op that are not constrained by an equality $v' = v$. Following the usual over-approximation in data-flow analysis, we can take the pessimistic, but conservative, view that Op potentially writes to all variables in scope and avoid theorem proving.

We note that we are interested in variables, not channels. In an input $d?x$, the variable x is defined, but the particular channel d is not of interest. This reflects the fact that we are interested in the data flow, not the interaction specification.

Example 6. Coming back to the *CashMachine* (and ignoring tags) we have:

$$defs(c, CashMachine) = \{inc?c?a\}$$
$$defs(a, CashMachine) = \{inc?c?a\}$$
$$defs(notes, CashMachine) = \{var\,notes : Cash, Dispense\}$$
$$defs(nBank, CashMachine) = \{\,Dispense,$$
$$nBank := \{\,10 \mapsto cap, 20 \mapsto cap, 50 \mapsto cap\,\}\,\}$$

□

The notion of (externally visible) use is simpler: a tagged label with an output communication. Formally, the set e-uses(x, P) of uses of a variable x in a process P can be identified from its set of sptraces.

Definition 6. e-uses(x, P) = $\bigcup$\{ spt : $sptraces$(P) • e-uses(x, spt) }

The set e-uses(x, spt) of uses of x in a trace spt can be specified as follows.

Definition 7. e-uses(x, $\langle\,\rangle$) = $\varnothing$
$$\text{e-uses}(x, tl \frown spt) = (\{tl\} \cap \text{e-uses}(x)) \cup \text{e-uses}(x, spt)$$

Finally, uses of a variable x are labels $(d!e, t)$ where x occurs free in the expression e. $FV(e)$ denotes the set of free variables of an expression e.

Definition 8. $\text{e-uses}(x) = \{d : CName; \ e : Exp; \ t : Tag \mid x \in FV(e) \bullet (d!e, t)\}$

At this point, we consider e-uses, but not the classical notion of p-uses, which relates to uses in predicates and, in the context of *Circus*, are not observable. We introduce a notion of internal uses (i-uses) later on in Section 4.1.

Example 7. We have $\text{e-uses}(c, \text{CashMachine}) = \{(\text{outc!c}, \text{tag1}), (\text{outc!c}, \text{tag2})\}$ and $\text{e-uses}(\text{notes}, \text{CashMachine}) = \{\text{cash!notes}\}$. There are no other externally visible uses in *CashMachine*. □

We observe that a label cannot be both a definition and a use of a variable, because a use is an output communication, which does not define any variable. Besides, a label can be neither a definition nor a use (this is the case for **refill**) and then not considered for data-flow coverage.

The property clear-path$(\text{spt}, \text{df}, \text{u}, \text{x})$ characterises the fact that the trace **spt** has a subsequence that starts with the label **df**, finishes with the label **u**, and has no definition of the variable x. (We consider subsequences of a trace, but, for consistency with classical terminology, we use the term path anyway.)

Definition 9

$$\text{clear-path}(\text{spt}, \text{df}, \text{u}, \text{x}) \Leftrightarrow \exists i : 1 \mathinner{\ldotp\ldotp} \# \, spt \bullet spt \, i = \text{df} \, \wedge$$
$$\exists j : (i + 1) \mathinner{\ldotp\ldotp} \# \, spt \bullet spt \, j = \text{u} \, \wedge$$
$$\forall k : (i + 1) \mathinner{\ldotp\ldotp} (j - 1) \bullet spt \, k \notin \text{defs}(\text{x}, \text{P})$$

A e-use **u** of a variable x is said to be reachable by a definition **df** of x if there is a trace **spt** such that clear-path$(\text{spt}, \text{df}, \text{u}, \text{x})$.

3.3 Data-Flow Anomalies and *Circus*

Three data-flow anomalies are usually identified: (1) a use of a variable without a previous definition; (2) two definitions without an intermediate use; and (3) a definition without use. While these all raise concerns in a program, it is not the case in a *Circus* model. Because a variable declaration is a variable definition that assigns an arbitrary value to a variable, it is common to follow it up with a second definition that restricts that value.

In addition, it is not rare to use a communication **d?x** to define just that the value x to be input via the channel **d** is not restricted (and also later not used). In an abstract specification, a process involving such a communication might, for example, be combined in parallel with another process that captures another requirement concerned with restricting these values x, while the requirement captured by the process that defines **d?x** is not concerned with such values.

For the data-coverage criteria that we consider, when a definition involved in any of the above anomalies is considered, it imposes no restriction on the set of tests under consideration for coverage. In practical terms, no tests are required.

3.4   All-Defs

The data-coverage criterion that we present here, all-defs, requires that all definitions are covered, and followed by one (reachable) use, via any (clear) path. We formalise coverage criterion by identifying the sets of sptraces $SSPT$ that satisfy that criterion. For all-defs, the formal definition is as follows.

Definition 10. *For every variable name x and process P, a set $SSPT$ of sptraces of P provides all-defs coverage if, and only if,*

$$\forall \, df : \mathrm{defs}(x, P) \bullet$$
$$(\exists \, spt : sptraces(P); \; u : \text{e-uses}(x, P) \bullet \text{clear-path}(spt, df, u, x)) \Rightarrow$$
$$(\exists \, spt : SSPT; \; u : \text{e-uses}(x, P) \bullet \text{clear-path}(spt, df, u, x))$$

If there is an sptrace that can contribute to coverage, then at least one is included.

Example 8. As previously explained, in *CashMachine*, inc?c?a is the only definition of c, and its two uses are (outc!c, tag1) and (outc!c, tag2). Examples of sets of sptraces that provide all-defs coverage are the three singletons below.

$$\{\langle \mathrm{inc?c?a}, (\mathrm{outc!c}, \mathrm{tag1})\rangle\,\}$$
$$\{\langle \mathrm{inc?c?a}, \mathrm{var\ notes}, \mathrm{Dispense}, \mathrm{notes} = [\![\,]\!]\,, (\mathrm{outc!c}, \mathrm{tag2})\rangle\}$$
$$\{\langle \mathrm{inc?c?a}, \mathrm{var\ notes}, \mathrm{Dispense}, \mathrm{notes} \neq [\![\,]\!]\,, \mathrm{cash!notes}, (\mathrm{outc!c}, \mathrm{tag2})\rangle\}$$

Other sets that provide all-defs coverage are the supersets of the above sets, and the sets that include any of the extensions of the sptraces above.   □

In [3] we define the classical all-uses and all-du-paths criteria.

The *CashMachine* variables $nBank$ and a are used internally only. There is no clear path from their definition to an external use, and so every set of sptraces provides coverage (according to all-defs and the other classical criteria) with respect to these variables. They contribute, however, to our next criterion.

4   sel-var-df-chain-Trace

This criterion is based on the notion of a var-df-chain. The idea is to identify sptraces that include chains of definition and associated internal uses of variables, such that each variable affects the next one in the chain. Given the characteristics of *Circus*, it is very likely that most specifications contain a number of such chains.

4.1   var-df-chain

A suffix of an sptrace spt starting at position i (that is, $(i \mathinner{\ldotp\ldotp} \# \, spt) \upharpoonright spt$) is in the set var-df-chain(x, P) of var-df-chains of P for x if it starts with a label $spt\, i$ that defines x and subsequently has a clear path to a label $spt\, j$. This label must either be a use of x, and in this case it must be the last label of spt, or affect the definition of another variable y, and in this case spt must continue with a var-df-chain for y. The continuation is $(j \mathinner{\ldotp\ldotp} \# \, spt) \upharpoonright spt$, the suffix of spt from j.

Definition 11

var-df-chain$(x, P) =$
{ spt : $sptraces(P)$; $i : 1 .. \# spt$; $j : (i + 1) .. \# spt$ |

$$\left(\begin{array}{l} spt\, i \in \mathrm{defs}(x, P) \wedge (\forall k : (i + 1) .. (j - 1) \bullet spt\, k \notin \mathrm{defs}(x, P)) \wedge \\ \left(\begin{array}{l} (spt\, j \in \mathrm{e\text{-}uses}(x, P) \wedge j = \# spt) \vee \\ (\exists y \bullet \mathrm{affects}(x, y, spt\, j) \wedge (j .. \# spt) \upharpoonright spt \in \mathrm{var\text{-}df\text{-}chain}(y, P)) \end{array} \right) \end{array} \right)$$

$\bullet (i .. \# spt) \upharpoonright spt$
}

A variable x affects the definition of another variable y in a tagged label **tl** if it is an internal use of x and a definition of y.

Definition 12. affects$(x, y, \mathtt{tl}) = x \in \mathrm{i\text{-}useV}(\mathtt{tl}) \wedge y \in \mathrm{defs}(\mathtt{tl})$

The set i-useV(**tl**) of variables used internally in **tl** is defined as follows.

Definition 13

$$\begin{array}{ll} \mathrm{i\text{-}useV}(g) = FV(g) & \mathrm{i\text{-}useV}(\epsilon) = \mathrm{i\text{-}useV}(d) = \varnothing \\ \mathrm{i\text{-}useV}(d!e) = \mathrm{i\text{-}useV}(d?x) = \varnothing & \mathrm{i\text{-}useV}(d?x : c) = FV(c) \setminus \{x\} \\ \mathrm{i\text{-}useV}(f : [\mathbf{pre}, \mathbf{pos}]) = FV(\mathbf{pre}) \cup FV(\mathbf{pos}) & \\ \mathrm{i\text{-}useV}(\mathtt{Op}) = FV(\mathtt{Op}) & \mathrm{i\text{-}useV}(x := e) = FV(e) \\ \mathrm{i\text{-}useV}(\mathbf{var}\, x : T) = \varnothing & \mathrm{i\text{-}useV}(\mathbf{var}\, x := e) = FV(e) \\ \mathrm{i\text{-}useV}(\mathbf{end}\, y) = \varnothing & \end{array}$$

This notion of internal use subsumes the classical notion of p-uses.

4.2   The Criterion

We observe that var-df-chains are not sptraces, but suffixes of sptraces. So, coverage is provided by sptraces that have such suffixes, rather than by the var-df-chains themselves. In particular, sel-var-df-chain-trace coverage requires that every chain in a model is covered by at least one sptrace.

Definition 14. *For every variable name x and process P, a set SSPT of sptraces of P provides sel-var-df-chain-trace coverage if, and only if,*

$\forall \mathbf{spt}_1 : \mathrm{var\text{-}df\text{-}chain}(x, P) \bullet$
$\quad \exists \mathbf{spt}_2 : SSPT; \mathbf{spt}_3 : \mathrm{seq}\, TLabel \bullet spt_2 = spt_3 \frown spt_1$

The specification trace $\mathbf{spt}_3$ is an initialisation trace that leads to the chain.

This criterion is the most demanding of the data-flow criteria defined in [3] where a formal proof of this result is available.

Example 9. The very basic var-df-chains, where the same variable is considered as the starting definition and the final use, with a clear path with respect to this variable in between, are covered by the classical all-du-paths criterion.

Table 1. Operational semantics of sptraces; w_0 stand for fresh symbolic variables

$$\frac{c \wedge (s;\ g)}{(c \mid s \models \langle g \rangle \frown spt) \overset{\epsilon}{\longrightarrow}_{ST} (c \wedge (s;\ g) \mid s \models spt)}$$

$$\frac{c \wedge T \neq \varnothing}{(c \mid s \models \langle d?x : T \rangle \frown spt) \overset{d?w_0}{\longrightarrow}_{ST} (c \wedge w_0 \in T \mid s;\ var\ x := w_0 \models spt)}$$

$$\frac{c}{(c \mid s \models \langle d!e \rangle \frown spt) \overset{d!w_0}{\longrightarrow}_{ST} (c \wedge (s;\ w_0 = e) \mid s \models spt)}$$

$$\frac{(c_1 \mid s_1 \models A_1) \overset{\epsilon}{\longrightarrow} (c_2 \mid s_2 \models \texttt{Skip})}{(c_1 \mid s_1 \models \langle A_1 \rangle \frown spt) \overset{\epsilon}{\longrightarrow}_{ST} (c_2 \mid s_2 \models spt)}$$

The label $\texttt{nBank} := \{\, 10 \mapsto \texttt{cap}, 20 \mapsto \texttt{cap}, 50 \mapsto \texttt{cap} \,\}$ is such a definition, and *nBank* is used in $\texttt{Dispense}$. Moreover, *notes* is externally used in the label $\texttt{cash!notes}$. This leads to the following var-df-chain.

$\langle \texttt{nBank} := \{\, 10 \mapsto \texttt{cap}, 20 \mapsto \texttt{cap}, 50 \mapsto \texttt{cap} \,\},$
$\quad \texttt{inc?c?a}, \texttt{var notes}, \texttt{Dispense}, \texttt{notes} \neq [\![\ ]\!], \texttt{cash!notes} \rangle$

Its coverage leads to coverage of the effect of a *refill*, after which the value of *nBank* is updated. An initialisation trace for the above var-df-chain is $\langle \textit{refill} \rangle$.

5   Conversion of Specification Traces to Symbolic Traces

Converting an sptrace to a symbolic trace requires an operational semantics for sptraces, which we provide in Table 1. It defines a transition relation $\longrightarrow_{ST}$ using four rules: one for when the first label is a guard, two for when it is either an input or an output, and one for an action label A. In this last case, the rules of the operational semantics transition rule $\longrightarrow$ define the new transition relation.

Like in the operational semantics, the configuration is a triple, but here, we have an sptrace associated with a constraint and a state assignment. From a configuration $(c \mid s \models \langle l \rangle \frown spt)$ we have a transition to a configuration with spt. The new constraint and state depend on the label l.

For a guard, a transition requires that c is satisfiable and g holds in the current state $(s;\ g)$. In this case, the transition is silent: it has label ϵ.

Input and output communications give rise to non-silent transitions with labels that are symbolic inputs and outputs. Inputs $d?x : T$ are annotated with the type T of channel d. The new constraint records that the input value represented by the fresh symbolic variable w_0 has type T and the state is enriched with a declaration of x whose initial value is set to w_0.

Finally, we have a transition relation $\overset{st}{\longrightarrow}$ that defines a symbolic trace st that captures the interactions corresponding to an sptrace. It is defined from $\longrightarrow_{ST}$

in the usual way [3], and used below to define the function $\text{cstrace}_{\text{SPT}}{}^{\text{a}}(P)$ that characterises the set of cstraces of P in terms of $sptraces(P)$. The parameter a is an alphabet: a sequence of fresh symbolic variables. The cstraces defined by $\text{cstrace}_{\text{SPT}}{}^{\text{a}}(P)$ use these variables in the order determined by a.

Definition 15

$$\text{cstrace}_{\text{SPT}}{}^{\text{a}}(\text{begin state}[x : T] \bullet A \text{ end}) =$$
$$\text{convSPT}^{\text{a}}(w_0 \in T, x := w_0) \, (\!| \, sptraces(\text{begin state}[x : T] \bullet A \text{ end}) \, |\!)$$

As before, we consider a process begin state$[x : T] \bullet A$ end and define its cstraces by applying a conversion function $\text{convSPT}^{\text{a}}(c, s)$ to each of its sptraces.

Definition 16. *For every alphabet* a, *constraint* c, *state assignment* s *and sptrace* spt, *we have that* $\text{convSPT}^{\text{a}}(c, s)\,\text{spt} = (\text{st}, \exists(\alpha c \setminus \alpha \text{st}) \bullet c_1)$ *where* st *and* c_1 *are characterised by* $\alpha \text{st} \leq \text{a} \wedge \exists s_1 \bullet (c \mid s \models \text{spt}) \xrightarrow{\text{st}} (c_1 \mid s_1 \models \langle \rangle)$.

Each sptrace gives rise to exactly one cstrace, since any nondeterminism in the actions is captured by the constraint on the symbolic variables. The alphabet αst of the symbolic trace st is a prefix of a: $\alpha \text{st} \leq \text{a}$. We note that convSPT is a linear translation and can be implemented with a good computational complexity compared to the test cases generation itself.

Example 10. The following cstraces correspond to the sptraces in Example 8.

$$(\langle \text{inc}?\alpha_0?\alpha_1, \text{outc}!\alpha_2 \rangle, \alpha_0 \in \text{CARD} \wedge \alpha_1 \in \mathbb{N}_1 \wedge \alpha_2 = \alpha_0)$$
$$(\langle \text{inc}?\alpha_0?\alpha_1, \text{cash}!\alpha_2, \text{outc}!\alpha_3 \rangle, \alpha_0 \in \text{CARD} \wedge \alpha_1 \in \mathbb{N}_1 \wedge$$
$$\Sigma\alpha_2 = \alpha_1 \wedge (\exists w_0 : \text{Note} \to \mathbb{N} \bullet (\forall n : \text{Note} \bullet \alpha_2 \, \sharp \, n) \leq w_0 \, n)) \wedge \alpha_3 = \alpha_0)$$

We take the alphabet to be $\langle \alpha_0, \alpha_1, \ldots \rangle$. The first cstrace comes from both the first and the second sptrace. The second cstrace comes from the last sptrace. The symbolic variable w_0 denotes the internal value of $nBank$, which is not observable in the trace, but contributes to the specification of the observable value α_2.

Two sptraces give rise to the same cstrace because after a withdraw request, the card may be returned immediately for one of two reasons: a problem with the card account (like insufficient funds) or no money in the cash machine. Since the model abstracts away the existence of accounts, they cannot be distinguished by tests from this model. This is reflected in the fact that the two sptraces have different tags associated with $outc!c$. This indicates that they correspond to two different occurrences in the model.   □

Contrary to the cstraces defined by the operational semantics, which capture just observable labels, sptraces are defined specifically to capture the structure of the model, and thus guards and data operations that may not be visible in the interface of the SUT. So, it is not surprising that there are sptraces that lead to the same cstrace. They come from paths in the model that are not distinguishable by observing the SUT. Requiring their absence in programs is reasonable, but abstract specifications may lead to such situations. It is not an issue for test generation, but it may be a problem for understanding or observing the SUT when running the tests. A test generation tool might, for example, warn that a distinction may need to be introduced, or instrumented, in the SUT.

The next theorem establishes that tests identified by sptraces are unbiased with respect to the operational semantics because they specify valid cstraces of the process. Construction of unbiased tests from cstraces was addressed in [2].

Theorem 1. $\text{cstrace}_{\text{SPT}}{}^{\text{a}}(P) \subseteq \text{cstraces}^{\text{a}}(P)$

We do not have equality: there is no empty sptrace, for instance. A proof is in [3]. The main lemma is proved by induction on the specification traces of P.

6   Related Works

Data-flow based testing for state-based specification languages has been applied to Lotos [15], to SDL and Estelle (that is, EFSM) [16], and extended with control dependencies in [8]. Our sel-var-df-chain-trace selection criterion is inspired from [15], but different, due to the notion of internal state in *Circus* and to the forms of symbolic tests considered in the *Circus* testing theory (see [3] for details). These differences, however, should not prevent its extension to control dependencies, possibly by some slight enrichment of our tagged labels.

In another context, Tse et al. have adapted data-flow testing to service orchestrations specified in WS-BPEL in [9], and to service choreographies in [10]. From the specifications, they build an XPath Rewriting Graph, which captures the specificities of the underlying process algebra, which is very different from *Circus*, with loose coupling between processes, XML messages, and XPath queries.

Testing tools based on symbolic input-output transition systems, and a symbolic version of the *ioco* conformance relation have been presented by Clarke et al. in [4] and by Frantzen et al. [7]. The models and relations are different from ours, since there is a semantic distinction between inputs and outputs, no data structures, and no hidden state. In both [4] and [7], test selection is based on test purposes. In [7], there is a similar notion of symbolic traces, with a formula constraining the interaction variables of the trace, and another constraint on the update of the state variables. Data-flow coverage, however, was not addressed and is less relevant than for *Circus* given the limited operations on data.

7   Conclusions

We have presented a framework for test selection from *Circus* models based on data-flow coverage criteria for specification traces, which record sequences of guards, communications and actions of a model. Using these definitions, we have formalised some coverage criteria, including a new criterion that takes into account internal definitions and uses. Proof of unbias of the selected tests is possible due to formal nature of our setting. We have formalised also the construction of cstraces (used to construct tests) from specification traces.

The specification traces defined in this paper can be used for other selection criteria, data-flow based and other ones as well, since most features of the models are kept. On these bases, it is our plan to consider a number of selection criteria for *Circus* tests, and to explore criteria that consider a variety of *Circus* constructs in an integrated way, to include, for instance, notions of Z schema coverage, case splitting in the pre and postcondition of specification statements, control dependencies and test purposes expressed in *Circus*. We plan also to address in a formal framework the problem of monitoring such tests.

Acknowledgments. We warmly thank Frédéric Voisin and referees for several pertinent comments. We are grateful to the Royal Society and the CNRS for funding our collaboration.

References

1. Cavalcanti, A., Gaudel, M.-C.: Specification Coverage for Testing in *Circus*. In: Qin, S. (ed.) UTP 2010. LNCS, vol. 6445, pp. 1–45. Springer, Heidelberg (2010)
2. Cavalcanti, A.L.C., Gaudel, M.-C.: Testing for Refinement in *Circus*. Acta Informatica 48(2), 97–147 (2011)
3. Cavalcanti, A.L.C., Gaudel, M.-C.: Data Flow Coverage of *Circus* Specifications - extended version. RR 1567, LRI, Univ. Paris-Sud XI (December 2013), https://www.lri.fr/ bibli/Rapports-internes/2013/RR1567.pdf
4. Clarke, D., Jéron, T., Rusu, V., Zinovieva, E.: STG: A Symbolic Test Generation Tool. In: Katoen, J.-P., Stevens, P. (eds.) TACAS 2002. LNCS, vol. 2280, pp. 470–475. Springer, Heidelberg (2002)
5. Cavalcanti, A.L.C., Sampaio, A.C.A., Woodcock, J.C.P.: A Refinement Strategy for *Circus*. FACJ 15(2-3), 146–181 (2003)
6. Clarke, L.A., Podgurski, A., Richardson, D.J., Zeil, S.J.: A Comparison of Data Flow Path Selection Criteria. In: ICSE, pp. 244–251 (1985)
7. Frantzen, L., Tretmans, J., Willemse, T.A.C.: A Symbolic Framework for Model-Based Testing. In: Havelund, K., Núñez, M., Roşu, G., Wolff, B. (eds.) FATES 2006/RV 2006. LNCS, vol. 4262, pp. 40–54. Springer, Heidelberg (2006)
8. Hong, H.S., Ural, H.: Dependence testing: Extending data flow testing with control dependence. In: Khendek, F., Dssouli, R. (eds.) TestCom 2005. LNCS, vol. 3502, pp. 23–39. Springer, Heidelberg (2005)
9. Mei, L., Chan, W.K., Tse, T.H.: Data flow testing of service-oriented workflow applications. In: ICSE, pp. 371–380 (2008)
10. Mei, L., Chan, W.K., Tse, T.H.: Data flow testing of service choreography. In: ESEC/FSE, pp. 151–160 (2009)
11. Morgan, C.C.: Programming from Specifications, 2nd edn. Prentice-Hall (1994)
12. Oliveira, M.V.M., Cavalcanti, A.L.C., Woodcock, J.C.P.: A UTP Semantics for *Circus*. FACJ 21(1-2), 3–32 (2009)
13. Rapps, S., Weyuker, E.J.: Selecting software test data using data flow information. IEEE TSE 11(4), 367–375 (1985)
14. Roscoe, A.W.: Understanding Concurrent Systems. Springer (2011)
15. Schoot, H.V.D., Ural, H.: Data flow analysis of system specifications in LOTOS. Int. Journal of Software Engineering and Knowledge Engineering 7, 43–68 (1997)
16. Ural, H., Saleh, K., Williams, A.W.: Test generation based on control and data dependencies. Computer Communications 23(7), 609–627 (2000)
17. Woodcock, J.C.P., Davies, J.: Using Z—Specification, Refinement, and Proof. Prentice-Hall (1996)

Author Index